HUMANITY AND SOCIETY
A World History

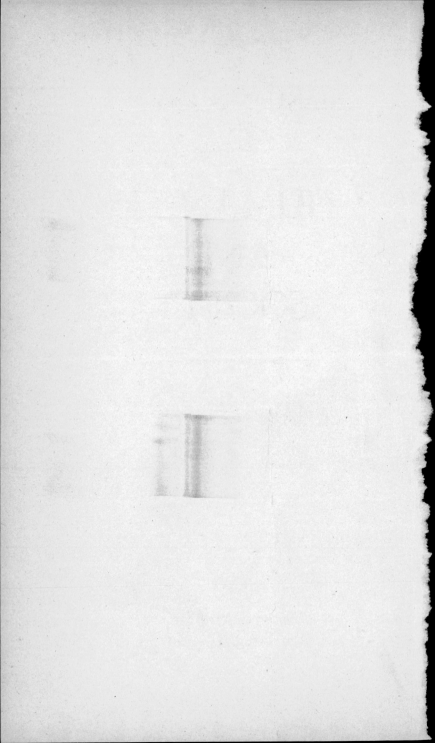

Kenneth Neill Cameron

HUMANITY AND SOCIETY

A World History

Monthly Review Press
New York and London

Copyright © 1973 by Kenneth Neill Cameron
All rights reserved

Library of Congress Cataloging in Publication Data
Cameron, Kenneth Neill.
  Humanity and society.
  Bibliography: p. 437
  Includes index.
  1. Civilization—History. 1. Title.
CB69.C35   1977   909   76-55618
ISBN 0-85345-408-6

First paperback edition 1977

Monthly Review Press
62 West 14th Street, New York, N.Y. 10011
21 Theobalds Road, London WC1X 8SL

Manufactured in the United States of America

To my daughter,

KATHLEEN,

teacher and artist,

weaver of patterns in the present

Contents

Preface

THIS BOOK WAS MOSTLY WRITTEN while I was editing the four volumes of *Shelley and his Circle*,* and it formed a welcome antidote to specialization. During the day I did manuscript editing and research, in the evenings and on weekends I wrote about world history. The book could not have been written at all, of course, if it had not been for the work of other specialists—in everything from the Tierra del Fuego Indians to the Renaissance. My procedure was simply to take what seemed to me the best general books on each period or subject, put their findings together, and see what patterns emerged. The list of References at the end—many of them paperbacks—may be taken as a kind of do-it-yourself-kit for world history.

One of the most recent and informative of such histories is titled *The Rise of the West* and is subtitled *A History of the Human Community*. The title contradicts the subtitle. The "West" is not the "Human Community" but only a part of it. Many "world histories" are, in fact, European-United States histories with but peripheral reference to the rest of the world. I have tried to redress the balance—in regard to Asia, Africa, Polynesia, South and Middle America. I differ from some other world historians also in that I am not interested in a survey—of kings, parliaments, wars, and such—but in finding main-line developments and the integrations between social and

---

* Harvard University Press; Oxford University Press; Volumes I–II, 1961. Volumes III–IV, 1970.

ix

cultural movements. In discussing the societies of the past I place the emphasis upon larger social matters—the conditions of labor (slavery, serfdom), the social status of women, war, economic history, political structures, and so on. In discussing cultural movements, especially in the arts, I try to convey an essence by specific examples.

I stop at the threshold of the present. The present, with its industrial civilizations and mass revolutions, although rooted in the past, is clearly a new era and requires special analysis.

During most of the time that I was working on this book I was not connected with a university but with a rare book and manuscript library. Consequently I had little opportunity to talk matters over with academic colleagues. And the book has no doubt suffered as a result. But my wife, Mary Bess Owen Cameron, has not only watched this work grow over the years with fortitude and forbearance but, as a sociologist, has made some valuable contributions toward its growth. Dr. George Howard of the United Nations, an anthropologist with experience in Africa and South America, very kindly read my chapter on Africa.

A great many people have typed parts of the manuscript, some of whose names I may, alas, have now forgotten, but I do remember the following and extend my heartfelt thanks to them for battling valiantly with cancellations, interlineations, passages on the backs of pages or insert sheets: Miss Rose Clinton, Mrs. Rose Horowitz of the English Department secretarial staff at New York University, Mrs. Doucet Fischer and Miss Jerry Fifer of The Carl H. Pforzheimer Library, Miss Pamelia Coe, once temporarily employed at The Carl H. Pforzheimer Library, and a student of Indian anthropology, who annotated learnedly while she typed.

KENNETH NEILL CAMERON
New York University

HUMANITY AND SOCIETY
A World History

I

The Roots of Humanity

EVEN THE MOST advanced intellects of the eighteenth or early nineteenth century could not account for "Man." The French materialists, taunted by their religious antagonists, suggested rather desperately that, like matter, he had always existed, a view which was soon shown to be untenable by the geologists, who found no human fossils in rock strata. Today we are so used to thinking in evolutionary terms that it seems incredible that someone did not think of "Man" as having evolved, but, although we find the general theory of life rising from lower to higher forms in the late eighteenth century and there was some speculation about that gifted creature, the orangutan, who was claimed to be something of a musician and a philosopher, it was not until the mid-nineteenth century that scientists seriously began to think of the human race as having evolved. With the theory of evolution new depth was given to the human perspective.

Man is part of life, from its lowest to its highest forms. His blood bears the salt of the sea; his spermatozoa and ova are essentially the same as those of the starfish or the frog; he is born, matures, and dies like the crab or the swallow. He shares with the amoeba and the ant the quality of restless, driving activity. But he is not an ant or a frog, but a mammal, and he has the specific characteristics of the mammal: warm blood, lungs and limbs, and residual fur, not cold blood or gills or fins or scales or shells. He propagates by the live-bearing of young, young that, like those of the bear or the cat, need rearing or they will perish. He evolved—as the horse evolved, an illuminating parallel, for we have specimens of the horse in all or most of its stages of evolution, as we do not for Man. The key to the development of the horse was apparently its change of habitat from the forest to the plain. Some 50 million years ago, the horse was a small, soft-pawed creature not unlike a dog in appearance and with meat-biting teeth. Another fossil of the horse, some 15 million years later, shows the central toe growing and hardening, and the crowns of the teeth lengthening to make a grinding surface. The horse has become about the size of a sheep. Presumably it was moving from jungle to hard plain, from meat to grass. Some 10 million years later the central toe dominates the whole foot and the other nails have shrivelled to form a hoof, all the teeth have become full grinders, and the horse has become about as large as a small pony.

Everything, of course, did not in the actual process happen so neatly as this. These are the main-stem highlights only. "The feet . . . ," writes George Simpson,[1] "hardly evolved at all in the Eocene [about 55 to 35 million years ago, according to the latest reckonings], then evolved rapidly to a basic three-toed Oligocine type [about 35 to 25 million years ago] which remained nearly static in later times, in others evolved gradually to different three-toed types mechanically sounder for larger animals, and in one line only finally evolved rapidly in one phase to a one-toed type." Evolution apparently worked in a series of trials and errors and moved at an uneven pace.

The facts of evolution, then, indicate a connection between environmental and biological change. But the genetic process involved — to note one of the larger skeletons in the evolutionist's closet — is unknown. There is, for instance, no recorded case of environmental conditions producing evolutionary change, and no known biological mechanism which could enable them to do so. A brown bear can live in snow all its life and it will not become white. And if it did bleach out by some miracle its offspring would be brown. If — as Bernard Shaw used to delight in telling us — we cut off the tails of mice for twenty generations we would not produce a race of tailless mice. "Acquired characteristics" do not seem to be inheritable. But, on the other hand, it has been shown that germ cells can be changed by radiation and that these changes can be transmitted. If we bombard a fruitfly with X-rays and hit, say, the gene that produces wings, its offspring might have red wings, and this, once established, becomes part of the general inheritance of the strain. Faced with the "acquired characteristics" problem, biologists have turned to natural radiation as a possible explanation for evolutionary change. If in a race of brown bears in the arctic the hair color gene was hit by cosmic rays, a race of white bears could arise; and they would soon become dominant as they would have a better chance for survival. But although this theory seems to work well enough for a comparatively simple change, such as fur color, it would not explain a complex one, such as, say, the acquiring of an upright stance by an apelike creature, for such a change involves millions of changes in bones, blood vessels, muscles, nerves throughout the body, all related to each other in a complex pattern, and it does not seem conceivable that they could come about by chance radiation even over a long period of time. The explanation may be that in some way not now known acquired characters *can* be transmissible. The most profitable direction for research would appear to be in the nucleic acids, which have both volatility and stability. They are not, as one would sometimes gather, unrestrainedly volatile. For instance, genetic change is not capable of producing a winged horse or a monkey with antlers. It has to act within a general animal form already established at various stages and to proceed from lesser to greater changes little by little. There is clearly some system of checks and balances present, some perhaps within the nucleic acids, some resulting from their interaction with the amino acids of the body cells. But on these matters we can at present only guess.

Man is not only a mammal. He is also a primate. And the simplest way to grasp the meaning of this is to think first of a gorilla and then of a dog. It is conceivable that people evolved fairly directly from something akin to a gorilla but not from something akin to a dog.

The remote ancestor alike of people and the gorilla appears from the fossil record so far known to have been a small tree creature of some 45 millions of years ago not unlike the modern lemur. This creature doubtless evolved, like the horse, in various directions (some of them dead ends), one of which appears to have been that of increase in size. At least we find evidence of primitive apes some 10 million years later. This change also appears to be correlated with environmental conditions, this time those not of plain but tree life, for a larger creature in trees would require the characteristics which we find among apes, namely a grasping hand with an opposable thumb (to seize a branch), long fore-limbs, vision in depth (to see through the web of trees), and considerable agility, characteristics which would require the greater brain size (relative to other animals) of the ape.

When we move forward another 10 million years we find the remains of an apelike creature (proconsul) that lived in East Africa. His skull was about as large as that of a modern gibbon. The most interesting thing about him, however, was that—as his skeleton indicates—he was coming close to an erect posture. This suggests that he had left the trees and was living on the ground either part or all of the time.

The next significant fossil remains—also in Africa—are of about

1.7 million years ago, those of what has been called by its discoverer, Dr. Louis Leakey, *homo habilis*. These creatures, as the name (roughly "handyman") indicates, were more manlike than apelike. They were of pygmy size, three to four feet tall, their brain capacity was between 600 and 700 cubic centimeters (that of a chimpanzee is about 400); their teeth, hands, and the shape of their skulls were essentially human. They walked upright, apparently built rough windbreaks or shelters, and used crude tools and weapons.

These creatures were believed by Dr. Leakey to have been unique, perhaps in the direct line of human descent, and to have died out about one million years ago. It has been argued, however, that they were, in fact, related to another pre-human species, one not in the direct line of human descent and which continued to exist until 250,000 years ago—the Australopithecines. Certainly, the two seem to have been of the same general nature.

The Australopithecines ranged from almost human size to about four feet high; they walked upright (their large toes had lost the thumblike position of the apes' and was directed forward); their skulls were almost balanced on the tips of their spines; their brain capacity was about the same as that of *homo habilis*—mid-way between human and ape; their jaws were large and ape-like, but their teeth were closer to the human than to the ape; their fingers were too slender to have been used regularly in locomotion; they were meat-eaters, as the opened braincases of baboons frequently found with their bones indicate; they made crude tools, including clubs, axes, and hammers out of the bones and teeth of hyenas and other animals which they hunted.

The general pattern, then, seems similar to that of the horse, of biological changes arising in some unknown manner from environmental changes, some of which went off into dead-end lines.

A next major stage toward the human (the famed *pithecanthropus erectus*) used to be represented by but one skull top and a few bone fragments, but a remarkable discovery in China in 1939 uncovered parts of skeletons of some forty individuals of a similar race that lived about 500,000 years ago and is known as Pekin Man.

Bison, beasts of the musk-ox family, gazelle, horse, wild boar, leopard, tiger, hyena, bear, rhinoceros, and elephant, all fell victims to this early hominid hunter. The absence of anything that might be construed as a missile weapon suggests that traps must have played a large part in securing the quarry. While there is no sign that Sinanthropus made elaborate tools from the bones, antlers, and horns yielded by his rich hunting bag, there is plenty of evidence that he utilized them in a variety of ways, breaking them in such a manner as to be easily handled. The meat he probably roasted over an open fire, evidence for which in the shape of bands of carbonaceous ash, associated with signs of burning on bones and antlers, was widespread. . . . The commonest tools were crude choppers formed by striking a few flakes from a pebble or small boulder, but naturally fractured pebbles and a few flakes struck artificially from parent nodules were also utilized.[2]

Although the remains of these Pekin sub-people were found in caves, it is possible that they constructed houses, for remains of houses have recently been found near Nice which are thought to be 300,000 years old. If so, both fire and houses may go back some half a million years, much earlier than used to be thought.

What was the community life of these sub-peoples? Did they live in families? What were their social relations with one another? How did they behave? What was their level of intelligence? Certain limited deductions can be made on these matters from the existing physical evidence. For instance, it is clear that the Pekin sub-people must have hunted in groups and used traps; and such hunting requires a coordination that implies some language. But we can go beyond the existing physical evidence into something of an outline reconstruction by combining two other sets of evidence, one preceding and one following this kind of society: that from ape society and that from observed early-form food-gathering societies (for example the Bushmen).

The ape which appears to be closest to Man is the gorilla. Until recent years little was known about the gorilla in its native habitat, but in 1959–60 a young scientist, George B. Schaller, observed the mountain gorillas of East Africa; he virtually lived with them, quite unarmed, for many months. He found that these gorillas lived in groups varying from 5 to 27 members. They were not tree animals but lived on the ground 80 to 90 percent of the time and normally walked on all fours, seldom going upright for more than five feet but occasionally for as many as sixty feet. The different groups sometimes met but did not mingle (except for "juveniles and infants"), although apparently some gorillas occasionally transferred allegiance from one group to another. They lived by food-gathering (mostly wild celery), ate no meat, constructed crude nests, usually on the ground, but no shelters. Schaller did not observe them using tools. Each group had a leader, an older male, who determined when and where they would travel and when and where they would bed down for the night. Within the group there was a social hierarchy, with the old males at the top, then the younger males, then the mature females, then the juveniles, and lastly the infants. Their sexual life was promiscuous; the leader male did not object or objected ineffectively to the other males copulating with the females. The care of the young was mainly the function of the mothers but the males played with the infants and juveniles. Schaller noted that the psychological tone for the group was largely set by the leader, who could vary from "irascible" to "shy." The gorillas mostly communicated by gesture and stance but they had a rudimentary language. Schaller counted 21 "more or less distinct vocalizations," of which eight were frequently used. They also had a store of knowledge—of plants, of the food-gathering area, of nest-building—and memory. Schaller cites an instance in which the gorillas had discovered and later recalled an obscure natural bridge.

Of the other apes, chimpanzees also live in groups but these are apparently less stable than those of the gorillas. Dr. R. C. Carpenter, who observed gibbons in Siam, saw[3] "mated or friendly gibbons showing positive affection and pleasure in each other's company, and greeting one another, after having been foraging separately for a brief time, by what can only be described as smiles and hugs." The use of tools has been observed among chimpanzees in the wild: rocks to break open nuts, twigs to extract honey, sticks to trap termites.

One cannot, of course, draw direct analogies between ape and even the most primitive human societies. At first, as Schaller notes, the gorillas "gave the superficial impression of being slightly retarded persons with rather short legs, wrapped in fur coats," but he soon began to see that there was a great psychological gulf between apes and humans. Nevertheless, the gorilla's anatomy, physiology, and instinctive and emotional behavior patterns are so close to the human that both creatures must have evolved from the same species (perhaps, it has been suggested, 15 or 20 million years ago). The gorillas frown when annoyed, bite their lips when uncertain, smile when happy. As a trip to the zoo will show, many of our human gestures and postures are found in apes. If we have doubts that these are remnants from the remote, pre-human past we must remember that, after all, the chain of evolution is unbroken and that all things have a history. We are simply not used to thinking specifically in evolutionary terms, even when we intellectually accept evolution as a theory. An observer of a sub-human community—anywhere from 1.7 million to 250,000 years ago—would certainly have seen behavior which resembled that of the gorillas and other apes. He would have found youngsters playing follow-the-leader and king-of-the-castle, the grown-ups resting in the sun with hands behind their heads and legs crossed, mothers tending to their young and mingling with each other in a female community, the older males running the community (as in "primitive" human societies), the returning men being greeted with "smiles and hugs." But he would have found differences also. He would have found meat-eaters and hunters as well as food-collectors, husband, wife, and children, plus some promiscuity (as among observed food-gathering peoples), language, shelters, tools, weapons, and, above all, dawning consciousness.

It has long been argued by philosophers that consciousness (or "mind") is a unique phenomenon unconnected with "matter." And if we look at mind in its highest form, in a Shakespeare or a Beethoven, it does so appear. The real question, however, is not, is mind a function of matter, but how did consciousness develop out of sensation? The prior links we already know even though we do not yet fully understand them: sensation developed out of "irritability" and "irritability" is an attribute of living tissue; sensation has the virtually infinite chain reactive quality of the conditioned reflex. One cannot omit these links and place the question as though one had to explain how a human mind developed out of atoms.

To see the difference between sensation and consciousness we have only to observe a dog and a child. We tend to read our own thought processes into the dog, and the analogy roughly fits, but a little testing shows us that dog's mind is essentially a mechanism reacting to stimuli. Although it can love, fear, hate, exhibit devotion or pride, and although it has some powers of reason, it works mainly on reflex action in a colorless world of sound-smell-sight, set by instinct and built by nonconscious experience. It does not know that it exists or what existence is or nonexistence. But the child soon begins to understand that he is a child. He still has sensation but his life is not dominated by it. He is not trapped, as is the dog, within the biological cage of uncontrollable response. In short, he can think.

When in the brains of sub-people several hundreds of thousands of years ago the first dim lights of consciousness spread and they began to be aware of themselves and the world around them, this was a unique event. In the hundreds of millions of years before this, life had been an unconscious process, one, at the lowest level, of the irritation of simple tissue, at the highest, of sensation, a process dominated by mechanical interactions. And before the development of life, the earth has been simply a large chemical test tube gravitationally aligned in space.

The child and the dog are operating at different levels of existence. Nevertheless we can see that, for all their differences, the one level — the conscious — could grow out of the other — the reflex. It is not a rise in one step but in many. All the intermediary steps we do not know and some may have vanished irrevocably. But some of them are still with us.

The step about which we know most is the ape, and this step has been documented in a series of revealing experiments by Köhler,

Pavlov, Yerkes, and others. Chimpanzees can not only learn and retain their learning to a much higher degree than the dog but they can pass on their learning. For instance, at the Yerkes Laboratories,[4] "the pioneer chimpanzees were shown how to work the drinking fountain, and through the years, ape has aped ape, and no further instruction of new generations has been necessary."

Even more extraordinary is the chimpanzee's capacity to reason. In one of Köhler's classic experiments,[5] fruit was hung from a wall, a box was placed between three and four meters away; the ape could reach the fruit only by moving the box and standing on it.

He first jumped straight upwards several times toward the objective, then took his rope in his hand, and tried to lasso the prize with a loop of it, could not reach so far, and then turned away from the wall. . . . After some time, on turning away from the wall, his eye fell on the box: he approached it, looked straight towards the objective, and gave the box a slight push, which did not, however, move it; his movements had grown much slower; he left the box, took a few paces away from it, but at once returned, and pushed it again and again with his eyes on the objective, but quite gently. . . . The box had now been moved ten centimetres in the direction of the fruit. The objective was rendered more tempting by the addition of a piece of orange . . . , and in a few seconds Koke was once more at the box, seized it, dragged it in one movement up to a point almost directly beneath the objective (that is, he moved it a distance of at least three metres), mounted it, and tore down the fruit. A bare quarter of an hour had elapsed since the beginning of the test.

The ape, then, certainly reasons; yet the ape, no more than the dog, has consciousness. We know this not only from psychological experiment but from the nature of its brain. The human brain consists of four parts, the medulla, the cerebellum, the mid-brain, the cerebrum. The medulla is a small knob-like extension of the spinal cord, which controls the mechanical functions of the body—the beating of the heart, breathing, and so on. It is to be found in the lowest forms of animal life and far down on the evolutionary scale. The cerebellum, which sits above and around the medulla, controls equilibrium. The mid-brain, above the cerebellum, controls reflex actions connected with the senses, touch, seeing, and hearing. Finally, comes the cerebrum, convoluted, with great frontal lobes; here is the center for consciousness, the conscious remembrance of the past, awareness of the present, conscious reason and imagination, and planning of future actions. The ape brain has almost no cerebrum and no frontal lobes.

The reasoning of the ape, then, is a nonconscious reasoning, a kind of computer-like reasoning based on the formation of complex reflex patterns in response to stimuli, external and internal. It is for this reason that it cannot acquire a true language; and this lack of language provides a barrier against which all its endeavors soon grind to a halt.

What of the sub-humans? To judge from their skulls and skeletons, their tools, habitations, and hunting abilities, one might conclude that the Australopithecines had developed, say, quarter-consciousness and the Pekin sub-people half- or three-quarter consciousness. Some of the behavior patterns of sub-humans would doubtless have seemed to an observer to be apelike but the differences would, in fact, have been basic. For instance, the feeling of a mother ape for her child is purely instinctual and reflex, but a Pekin sub-people mother would have known, even though dimly, that the baby was a baby and that it was hers. Similarly, mating among the apes is essentially biological, but among the Pekin sub-people it had perhaps begun to develop conscious psychological overtones. Other forms of sub-people's behavior had no parallel even in appearance to that of the apes. The apes could not construct traps for game but Pekin hunters could.

Consciousness, then, came by degrees. And something of the nature of the degrees can be seen in comparative brain sizes (resulting in the main from cerebrum development). Chimpanzees have an average brain capacity of 400 cubic centimeters, gorillas (a much larger beast), 550; *homo habilis* and the Australopithecines, both tiny people, 600–700; *pithecanthropus erectus,* 860; the Pekin sub-people, 1,075; human, 1,350. In time, as actual sequential links are discovered, more exact figures will doubtless be substituted for these, but even these tell, as it were, in skeletal form, the story of the birth of that consciousness that makes humanity unique.

II

The First Societies

IF WE MOVE FORWARD from a period in the order of 500,000 years ago to one of about 20,000 years ago, we find ourselves in the presence of people like ourselves, acting and thinking much as we do—courtship, marriage, family life, work groups, daily conversation, dancing, painting, story telling.

With this development a new entity was born on our planet, and, perhaps, in the universe, namely human society or, more simply, *society*. There was, of course, no one century, or even one millennium, in which this development took place. Human society evolved out of sub-human society (like that of the Pekin sub-people) just as sub-human society had evolved out of apelike society. The beginning of the change can be seen in the relics of roughly 100,000 years ago. In this period, for instance, flaked stone axes begin to assume symmetry. This makes them no better as axes but it shows pride in workmanship and a sense of balance—both indications of growing consciousness. And for the next 70,000 to 80,000 years the process continued until—as the European cave paintings suffice to show—society was born.

The anthropologists define these early societies by the way in which they provided for their basic material needs, namely by hunting, by fishing, and by food collecting (plants, tubers, berries, grains, nuts, fruits, sea food), the totality known as "food-gathering." By about 12,000 years ago and perhaps earlier, some of these societies had supplementary farming (plants and animals), but, so far as we now know, none of them had become actual farming communities. In this predominantly food-gathering world there must have been a population of several million, perhaps 10 million or more, and the point requires emphasis for one often gets the impression in textbooks that it was much smaller. The food-gathering native population of Australia when "discovered" has been calculated at 250,000, that of the mainly food-gathering population of the North American Indians at one million. As the food-gathering techniques of 12,000 years ago were about the same as in observed food-gathering societies (the bow and arrow, for instance, had been invented), we can assume that these populations were about the same also. And to them we have to add the food-gathering societies of Asia, Africa, Europe, and South America.

To what degree the sections of this worldwide society on the different continents were in contact with each other is not known, but the indications now are that it was much greater than had been previously thought. Stone tools over the immense area of West Asia, Europe, and Africa show similarities in construction; so, too, do those in East Asia and those in North America (for example the thin, leaf-shaped blade known as the "Folsom" point). All of them, however, are stone tools and they are all generally the same kind of tool (axes, scrapers, and so on). As we shall see, there is also evidence of extensive trade routes within these areas, and of parallels in customs, beliefs, and art both within and between them. That some of these things could have grown up independently is true, but the evidence is accumulating that all of them could not. It is conceivable that people in Europe and China could have independently invented a stone tip for a spear but it is inconceivable that they could independently have arrived at the notion that one could predict the future by examining the internal organs of animals. However slow and inconstant the contacts may have been between widely separated areas, they unquestionably existed, and the evidence indicates that many of them were made by water, some perhaps by ocean travel.

In this society of 12,000 years ago all the main races of today were in existence, no matter whether we consider them, with some anthropologists, to be three in number (Mongoloid, Caucasoid, and Negroid), or with others, to be five or six (adding, for instance, as separate main races, the Australian natives and the American Indians). Siberian statuettes of perhaps 20,000 or more years ago show Mongoloid, Caucasoid, and Negroid types; some remains of "early man" in America more than 10,000 years ago indicate Indian characteristics. Moreover the main races were geographically distributed about as they have been throughout most of recorded history: Caucasoid in West Asia, Europe, and northern Africa; Mongoloid in East Asia; Indian in America; Australoids in Australia; Negroid in Africa and some Asian areas (although the populating of southern Africa by Negroid peoples seems to have come somewhat later). Despite all the great migrations and such interracial areas as Central Asia the main racial areas seem to have been generally stable (until the recent Caucasoid invasions of America, southern Africa, Australia, and so on).

In this society there must have been many languages, perhaps several hundred, for language, as we have seen, had probably begun in some form 500,000 years ago, and languages spread and change rapidly with migrations. There are at present in the world some 3,000 languages related to some 50 language stocks (for example, the Indo-European, which includes the Celtic, Germanic, Slavic, Persian, and Indic). Several hundred languages have passed out of existence within the past few centuries. Whether it will be possible to determine some of the characteristics of the languages of these early times remains to be seen. But some of them—as the social and cultural level indicates—must have been quite highly developed.

By at least 12,000 years ago, then, there was a world population of several million people of several races speaking many languages. Out of this world-society all that followed arose.

THE NATURE OF SOCIETY

What is society? What are the general functions, divisions and units of the social body? Ape society, as we saw, had three functions, to gather food, to propagate and rear young, and to "manage" the affairs of the group (where and when to bed down or to seek food), the first two being part of what anthropologists call respectively, "self-maintenance" and "self-perpetuation." Blended with these three functions are various physical, mental, and emotional activities: fighting, copulation and birth, teaching and learning, solving problems, play, "hugging and kissing," dancing.

The sub-human societies, to judge by the remains of *homo habilis,* the Australopithecines, and the Pekin sub-people, must have had the same functions but in a more highly developed form. Food-gathering was aided by tools, traps, and weapons; another aspect of "self-maintenance" had come into being in the use of caves and perhaps the building of crude shelters. "Self-perpetuation" had doubtless begun to assume family form. The management of a community must also have required a more complex apparatus than among the ape bands with their "leaders." For one thing, hunting large game requires social organization. Hunting also requires a large storehouse of knowledge;

with the development of language and partial consciousness, this and other knowledge could be transmitted to the young.

As early human society emerged we would expect to find the same basic functions continuing, and, by putting together various types of evidence, this is what we do find. Food gathering continues but has become organized and specialized; and added to it as part of "self-maintenance" are house-building, clothes-making, manufacturing of tools and weapons, transportation, trade. The propagation and the rearing of the young has definitely assumed family form and has ramified out into other areas of society (courtship, clubs, ceremonials). Management has divided into total community management and group-affairs (clubs, families). The development of conscious memory has made possible the retaining of learning in a social continuum; the solving of problems has become primarily conscious and not reflex in nature; general ideas, religious and otherwise, have arisen; play continues; there are plastic and graphic arts, dancing, singing, instrument playing, buffoonery, story telling.

The evolution of society from apelike to sub-human to human, however, was not simply a matter of the old functions remaining and being performed consciously. Language and consciousness in conjunction with various social processes transformed society into a new entity whose functions and divisions have roots in those of apelike and sub-human societies but do not simply continue them. Work, for instance, grew out of apelike food-gathering; but work is not just conscious food-gathering. It also embraces tool making, house building, and transportation; and this complex constitutes the *economic life* of a society.

Similarly, the social patterns which had their roots in the propagation of the species have spread beyond mating, mother-care of the young, and loose group-life forms and have joined with the family and community management to form a separate sphere, that of *social life.* Then, in the more advanced food-gathering societies, one aspect of community management split off to form a separate functional area, that of *political life,* embracing tribal government and law. Finally, the body of knowledge and the arts of sub-human society have developed to a conscious level and blended with its store of general ideas (for instance, religious ideas), to form a fourth functional division of society, namely its *cultural life.*

The functions of the first three divisions are obvious — to supply food and shelter, to continue the species, and to manage the community. Without them there would be no society. But what are those of cultural activity? One is clear enough; without bodies of knowledge or ideas there could be no economy, social life, or government. But what of the arts? Are they necessary to the existence of society? That they are is indicated by the fact that there has never been a society without them and that they are basically connected with the other aspects of life. There cannot be pottery without design or building without architecture or weaving without color. Music and song and dance and story are often intimately a part of social life and work. So that the arts, too, seem to have a sustaining function for the other aspects of society.

But culture serves more than a sustaining function. It seems to fulfill needs of people which cannot otherwise be fulfilled, a need for investigation and a need for creation. The mind loves to pursue, arrange, and solve. The scientist and scholar feel mental exhilaration in their work. In art, too, investigation and discovery are present, but they are subordinate to creation—really a re-creation of the patterns of life. Both needs appear to have biological roots, the first in the hunting instinct, the second in the mating instinct (as manifested in the mating dance of birds).

Although the cultural life of society is mixed in with its economic, social, and political life, it is also, it seems to me, an area of its own. Moreover, it is an area of a different general nature from these others. The first three are all in the broad sense of the word "social," and, as such, have basic aspects in common, but the cultural area has its own essence. A poem or a symphony differs from the actions of work or family life or government in a more fundamental way than they do from each other.

I have spoken of "bodies of knowledge or ideas." The distinction between the two is obviously often slim, but, in general—and without getting into metaphysical hairsplitting—we can perhaps consider knowledge as embodying concepts which have been shown to correspond to some area of reality and ideas as embodying concepts which may or may not so correspond. At least this is the distinction which I shall use in this work as a rough rule of thumb for examining the culture of various societies.

Society presents a picture of processes and units of various kinds acting and reacting upon each other in and between what I have designated as its four main functional divisions. As in biological life, the processes and units are indissolubly connected, but they are not the same.

What are the units of society, its cells and molecules? There are, it seems to me, three kinds—individuals, groups, and organizations.

The main difference between a group and an organization seems to be one of degree of structure. Political parties, armies, churches, banks, tribes, villages, city states, nations, empires, I consider to be organizations; families, classes, and racial minorities to be groups. Sometimes it may not be possible to determine whether a specific social entity is a group or an organization, but in spite of border areas they are distinct social entities and they function differently.

Although groups and organizations consist of individuals their processes are not simply the same as those of individuals reacting to each other (although some historians continue to write as though they were). The behavior of a class or a political party, even when an individual leader exerts great influence, usually represents group or organizational objectives. Furthermore, these objectives often arise from a chain of previous actions over which neither the individual nor the group or organization has had control.

Cutting across the units and functions of human as of animal society are the two biologically based entities of the life cycle and sex. As a result of the life cycle — birth, growth, maturation, decline, and death — society consists of children, young people, middle-aged people, and old people. Those within these age divisions tend to associate with each other, so that we have groups and organizations of each, but in other groups (notably the family) and in organizations (churches, political parties) they mingle. Society could not, in fact, function without this mingling, the young bringing energy, the middle-aged and old bringing experience, both essential elements for social and cultural life.

The social phenomena resulting from sexual division are obvious and extensive, affecting all the functional divisions of society. In the economic division we have, in all societies, men's work and women's work (with some overlap). In social life, men and women play different roles; in some aspects of social life the woman's role is the more important. Political life, on the other hand, is usually male dominated. Some of the divisions in cultural life reflect the difference between men's work and women's work; men, for instance, dominate in science or such arts as architecture. In the arts in which men and women both participate — dancing, singing, literature — the nature of their performance differs in some respects. As a result of the nature of men's work and their dominance of the political division, what is usually called history — reigns, wars, revolutions, the rise and fall of empires and so on — is essentially a male phenomenon.

To what degree are these differences the result of social and to what of biological factors? To this question few definitive answers can be given in our present stage state of knowledge. There are, however, obviously psychological differences and some of them seem to accord with physical differences. For instance, men are more highly muscled and women are softer and more graceful. These characteristics appear to carry with them some psychological differences; for instance, men (on the record) are more aggressive and brutal than women. Biopsychological matters, however, should not be exaggerated; there is no simple biological determinism at work. The visibly operative factors in keeping women out of economic and political power are clearly not biological but social. In general it appears that biological factors form a base on which social factors operate—to what degree depends on the nature of the society.

THE EVIDENCE OF THE PAST

In order to reconstruct some of the general characteristics of society as it appeared some 12,000 years ago we have to coordinate two kinds of evidence: (a) the physical remains—mainly bone and stone—of the societies themselves; (b) similar societies which have continued into modern times.

It might seem at first that the second kind of evidence is not very reliable. Such societies, one would think, must have changed in fundamental ways in 12,000 years; especially must they have taken things over from civilized societies. But change does not take place automatically (the platypus is still a platypus after 200 million years); societies can persist virtually unchanged for many thousands of years—each generation living as the previous one had done—unless there are special factors making for change. In some food-gathering societies there have been no such factors. This is especially true of the isolated ones, those of the "fringe" peoples. Of these the anthropologists stress two in particular, that of the Australian natives and that of the Ona Indians of Tierra del Fuego (and note also the Bushmen of Africa, some Eskimos, and the Andaman Islanders). These societies were observed before any serious influence from civilized societies had touched them. Furthermore, anthropologists are usually able to tell which patterns of life are native and which are derived from civilized society. Those recently derived are usually obvious overlays; the old, native ones are deeper and, moreover, are found in other observed food-gathering societies. The general principle involved is that similar determinative factors produce similar social and cultural patterns no matter how remote they may be in time or place.

The original Australians apparently arrived in Australia about 19,000 years ago. At this time there may have been almost continuous land passage between Southeast Asia and Australia, but even so the migration must have involved boats or rafts. As for the inhabitants of Tierra del Fuego, a cave near the Strait of Magellan has been discovered, the upper layers of which contain modern Ona arrow points, the lowest spear points alongside of the bones of now extinct animals.

The indication is that the area has been inhabited for at least 10,000 years. Both regions reflect in their general patterns of life world food-gathering society as it was in the period before farming communities arose.

The evidence from physical remains of the nature of early food-gathering societies mainly spans a period from 30,000 to 10,000 years ago. It indicates considerable variety in the standard of living and ways of life of such societies but the general social and cultural patterns remain very much the same. Hence, one can use evidence from various periods — wherever it is most revealing — in order to perceive these general patterns.

From ash and other remains in caves we can tell that fire was used (and perhaps had been continuously for some 500,000 years). Apparently crude oil lamps had been invented, for in the dark recesses of caves there have been found stone artifacts which could have contained oil (from animal fats). In addition to the caves there are remains of houses, some quite large, some in settlements. The houses contained hearths and holes for cooking food. Early food-gathering people — popular notions to the contrary — did not normally live in caves but used them mainly for religious and other ceremonies. They lived in houses, sometimes large communal ones. The fact that caves remain (with their relics) whereas houses usually vanish without trace has created the myth of the "cave man."

The range of the stone and bone tools is extraordinary. We find among these relics in stone the ancestral forms of many basic tools: the axe, the knife (flint), the chisel ("burin"), the spoke shave, the drill or awl, the plane, the hammer (the back of the axe). And in bone there were knives and needles. If we ask ourselves what most of these tools were used for, the answer is clearly for work in wood; stone, that is to say, provided the machine tools of food-gathering society, but most weapons, tools, and houses must have been made of wood. Other tools were used for working bones, antlers, and leather — scraping tools to scrape it, needles to sew it. These people must have worn leather clothing, and perhaps used hides on the floors and walls of their houses. If so, they were in advance of the modern Ona Indians and the Tasmanians, both of whom had but wind shelters and no sewn clothing (covering themselves with thick grease in cold weather and wrapping hides around their bodies). That this should be so is not surprising (once we get over the idea that time produces change of itself), for whereas the Ona and Tasmanians had poor hunting resources, some of these early European peoples had an extensive and prosperous hunting economy. Their camp sites were widely spread throughout Europe. At one of them, in what is now the U.S.S.R., the remains of some 2,400 large wild oxen have been uncovered, at another, in what is now Czechoslovakia, the remains of more than 1,000 mammoths. "There was," as V. Gordon Childe comments on this latter find, "food enough for a vigorous population."[1] And other deductions are possible also. "But the meat could only be obtained by the effective cooperation of a substantial number of individuals and by detailed knowledge of the habits of the herds; the clever location of the camp sites proves the application of such knowledge." The bones of horses and other large animals at the foot of cliffs reveal the continuation of certain hunting techniques for many thousands of years; modern hunting peoples have been seen to herd animals *en masse* over cliffs or into corrals.

Along with bone and stone, shells also tend to survive. In the caves in Central France we find shells from the Mediterranean. "Presumably," Professor Childe comments, "they were brought hither by some rudimentary form of trade." Certainly they indicate an extensive movement of peoples (around shores and along rivers); so the individual communities were not isolated from each other, and inventions, such as the bow and arrow, could spread quite rapidly.

Sometimes the art work is socially revealing. There are pictures of houses, and, in cave drawings, of the hunt. A Russian statuette carved from a mammoth tusk shows a fur hood similar to those worn by Eskimos today. A European cave drawing depicts a man wearing a deer head and hide; we find among modern hunting peoples—from the Plains Indians in North America to the Bushmen of South Africa—the hunter disguising himself as the animal he is stalking. A rock carving of perhaps 20,000 years ago shows a woman holding a bison horn in her hand; because of the similarity between it and later depictions of mother-goddesses with cornucopias, it has been suggested that it indicates early mother-goddess worship.

From the days of the early emergence of humanity no evidence of formal burial of the dead exists. Such burial first appeared apparently about 50,000 years ago. In the period which we are considering burial had become a ceremonial. The relics of tools, weapons, animal bones, body ornaments, and traces of red ochre in recognizable grave sites along with human skeletons show that meat, tools, and weapons were buried with the dead, and that they were decorated with red ochre (perhaps to simulate blood) and adorned with ornaments (belts, bangles, head-dresses of perforated shells, and animal's teeth). Again by noting parallels with later societies, we can presume from this a belief in an "afterlife" in which the "spirit" was conceived of as requiring tools, weapons, and ornaments.

The most extraordinary relics of all are those of the graphic and sculpturing arts. Drawings and paintings on the walls of caves are often in brilliant color and powerful line. Such paintings—some of them 20 to 30,000 years old—reveal that people had by this period all the potential which was later expressed in civilized societies. But if the people of this period had these abilities in the graphic arts they must have had similar abilities in other arts (say story-telling). Nor can these abilities have been limited to art alone. They must indicate general intellectual capacity. Along with the "mute, inglorious" Michelangelos who lived and perished in these remote times were Einsteins and Goethes also.

The Economy

That the picture of the economic life of early food-gathering societies as derived from their stone and bone relics is narrowly deceptive becomes dramatically apparent if we visit a natural history museum and move from its "Old Stone Age" section into its "modern primitives" section. For instance, in the American Museum of Natural History in New York, if we go from the cases of early stone and bone tools through the next room into that displaying the life of the Australian and other Pacific native peoples we begin to see what is missing; and if we then take the elevator down to the first floor to the American Pacific Coast Indians we can fill out the picture. In the Australian cases we note that the so-called "hand axes"—which look very like some in the early society cases—are attached to wooden handles by hardened mud and gum. There is a case showing an Australian native making fire by twirling a stick into another stick on the ground, a practice which may go back for many thousands of years. In the North American Pacific Coast Indians exhibit we see first a large display in which a woman is shown weaving what looks like cedar bark shreds into clothing of a fine texture which she and the others are wearing. In a nearby case are spinning sticks to spin hair into continuous strands; then comes an exhibition of magnificent basket work. That such weaving goes back into early food-gathering society is indicated by weaving designs on the first pottery.

Further down the room is a case showing a model of a wooden house, built partly underground—as were those of some early societies also. Of all the tools which must have existed and exist no more, the most important is the "digging stick"—which is universally used by primitive peoples to dig up edible roots—for it was the digging stick that pointed the way to agriculture.

"Food-gathering" seems to conjure up for some a picture of a few women and children gathering berries. Actually the range of the total economic activities of a food-gathering society is considerable; so, too, is the ingenuity with which they are pursued. The food-gathering instruments and processes used by the American Indians, for instance, included the following: for hunting — spears, spear-throwers, clubs, bows and arrows, slings, bolas (bola-like rocks are found in the relics of early hunting societies), nets (for birds and game), pitfalls, snares, spring traps, weighted traps, and hunting dogs; for fishing — weirs, nets with floats and sinkers, fish-hooks and lines, harpoons (with bladders), basket traps, poisons or stupefacients; for food collecting — digging sticks, seed-beaters and basket trays (to beat seed-bearing plants and catch the seeds), mortars and "metates" (in which acorns, etc., were pounded). Meats and some vegetables were cooked; meats and fish were dried, salted, or smoked to preserve them; poisonous substances were removed by complex processes from manioc (tapioca) and acorns. For the early food-gathering societies the spear points remain, but the digging sticks, traps, nets, baskets, cradles, and preserving processes have vanished.

Transportation was perhaps more extensively carried on by water than has been thought. The shipbuilding skills of early civilizations must have had a long history behind them, and it seems probable that by 10 to 12,000 years ago some peoples had boats comparable in size to, say, the long canoes of the Maoris or the North American Pacific Coast Indians. At least rafts, such as those common to the Tierra del Fuego Indians and the Tasmanians, must, as we have seen, have existed 20,000 years or so ago for the Australians to have got to Australia. For land transport there may have been sleds or "travois" (two converging poles tied to a dog's back), such as were later used by the North American Indians.

From modern food-gathering societies we can perceive something of the organizational structure of these early economies, their property and productive relationships, their divisions of labor. The universal pattern among modern primitive peoples is that of the individual ownership of weapons and tools (for example, the woman owning the household pots, the man the spears) plus the community ownership of hunting, fishing and wild food-plant areas. The hunting territory of each community is the exclusive right of that community — solemnized by the "totem" — and its products are the common right of all members. These patterns must have existed also in early food-gathering societies.

The only major division of labor in observed food-gathering societies is that between men on the one hand and women, children, and old people on the other. The men hunt, the others collect. Some of the reasons for this sex and age division of labor in a food-gathering society are not difficult to perceive. Women bear, suckle, and care for children, and therefore have some physical limitations. Although women have the endurance they do not have the muscular capacity needed for strenuous hunting; and boys and old men have neither sufficient strength nor endurance.

In observed food-gathering societies we find also a minor division of labor between the mass of the tribe on the one hand and the chief and shaman (both "witch doctor" and embryonic priest) on the other. Most do some physical labor but they are partly excused in order to perform their governmental and religious-medical functions.

When surplus is produced, it is traded. In Australia trade fairs were held in which all kinds of goods were exchanged: spears, mats, baskets, eggs, red ochre, pearl shells, and so on. Each territory seemed to have its own specialties, and there were crisscrossing trade routes everywhere. The indication is that parts of Europe, Asia, Africa, and America of 10 to 12,000 years ago were similarly crisscrossed.

SOCIAL LIFE

For those not acquainted with anthropological matters one of the main blocks in attempting to understand food-gathering societies is the framework of ideas into which we fit, often unconsciously, the facts that we acquire, framework ideas reflected in such words as "primitive," "barbarian," and "savage," with their connotations of stupidity and brutality. True, "primitive" people can at times be "savage" (although less so than "civilized" people), but they have the same kind of family life as in civilized societies, the same kind of daily talk, play, friendship, sport, love, and so on. So, too, the people who created the cave art of Europe. In conceiving of early food-gathering societies, we should substitute a framework concept of varied community life for that of the grunting "cave man" with his club and "mate."

Groups

It used to be argued that in its beginnings society was a "primitive horde" in which men and women lived in sexual promiscuity. There never was any evidence to support this theory and the present evidence indicates that human society from its beginnings has been divided into families. In all probability family patterns were inherited from sub-human society, for, as we have seen, there are rudimentary family patterns among the apes. And there are families in all observed food-gathering societies, including even those on the lowest economic level such as the Tasmanians or the Ona Indians. It used to be argued, also, that following the "primitive horde" there came various curious forms of marriage ("group marriage," polygamy, polyandry) and that these evolved into monogamy with the coming of "private property" (and, hence, the necessity of willing such property). But, although in the more wealthy food-gathering societies the chief often has several wives, the basic marriage form in these societies as observed everywhere is monogamy; and the probability is that monogamy was the marriage form from the first societies on. This monogamy, however, is not "pure." Some marriages last for life; others last but a short time, and there is usually some allowance for divorce. There can be successive mates, and periodic infidelities (sometimes orgiastic). In short the pattern is generally the same as in civilized societies.

So, too, with the family. Although there are variations in the family structure as a result of the marriage of girls at puberty, the expansion of the family living unit by the peripheral accumulation of relatives, the care of the younger children by the older ones, and so on, the general patterns of family living are everywhere the same. Anthropologists often comment on the "deep love" felt by "primitive" parents for their children. For instance among the Australians:[2] "People try to teach him [the baby] to talk. They laugh and play with him, petting and teasing him, saying the same words over and over again until he repeats them." "Romantic attachments" are seen among Australian husbands and wives. And so, too, among other food-gathering peoples.

All this, of course, means still further reframing of our popular ideas about "savages"—especially those which "our own" nation has been exploiting. For instance, in American popular media almost the only Indians depicted are males on the warpath. We seldom see or read about the tender love of an Indian husband and wife for each other or for their children. The Indian, in fact, has been dehumanized. And this kind of dehumanization has been extended into our concepts of early food-gathering societies.

In addition to groups revolving around family life or the social life of men or women—bachelor's clubs or secret societies—there is a series of groups with special functions, functions which are largely cultural, namely, religious, medical, and educational groups. In civilized societies these groups have become well defined and have evolved into organizations, but in food-gathering societies they are often embryonic and undifferentiated. Religious and medical functions are, as we have seen, combined in the shamans, and education is divided among other groups—the family, men's clubs, and so on. Shamans were believed to "possess unusual powers; among other things, they are said to call forth or suppress storms and banish or summon game animals. Their most important function, however, is to cure disease, which is thought to result from the loss of the soul. Soul loss is serious, for if the patient does not recover his soul, he will eventually die."[3] During the "curing rite" the shaman "gradually works himself into a frenzy by singing spirit songs, beating on a drum" and so on; he then "calls upon his familiar spirit, and urges him to recover the soul of the patient." The main function of the shamans everywhere is to struggle against death. It is in this struggle that medical and religious actions combine.

One can see how a church and priesthood could grow out of food-gathering society rites and ceremonials by noting those among observed food-gathering or early-farming peoples, for instance the puberty rites for girls among the Apaches:

> On the morning of the first day, the shaman in charge directs the construction of the ceremonial structure, a large tipi, built especially for the occasion. Materials are brought together, holes are dug to receive the four main poles, and tall spruce trees selected to form this sub-structure. The shaman recites a prayer and, to the accompaniment of a rattle, sings the sacred songs which must accompany the building. It is a solemn ritual, to produce a ceremonial home, linked symbolically to White Painted Woman, an important Chiricahua divinity. . . .[4]

It might at first seem that such rites among the Apaches have little bearing on the rise of a church, and, of course, in certain specifics there is no connection, but the universality of such ceremonies among food-gathering peoples shows that similar ones must have existed among the tribal ancestors of the Sumerians and Egyptians and other early civilized peoples. Indeed, that such ceremonies went back for many thousands of years is shown also, as we have noted, in the cave drawings and other art of early food-gathering societies in Europe and elsewhere.

Individuals

The relationships of individuals in food-gathering societies are conducted essentially on a basis of equality. In more wealthy food-gathering societies, for instance those of the Pacific Coast Indians of North America, considerable inequalities in wealth between families do, it is true, arise, but this is exceptional. In most food-gathering societies all families are on about the same level, and this must have been so in most early food-gathering societies. The remains of dwellings show them as either communal or of about the same family unit size. And this general economic equality must in all ages and all places have resulted in general social equality, so that the relationships of men with men or women with women were just that and nothing more. There were no masters and no servants. The only exceptions were those of the distinctions between an ordinary tribe member and a chief or a shaman; but these were not sufficiently numerous to change the general pattern.

In view of a tendency to lump all "primitives" into simple stereotypes, we might note that in observed food-gathering societies individual psychological characteristics exist to the same degree as in civilized societies. Every individual differs from every other individual; for example, among the Australians, the Berndts mention "women who take loving care of their husbands and children, and women whose domestic efforts are reluctant and sketchy. There are quiet men devoted to their wives, and men who believe in using their weapons to keep peace in the family."[5] There are differences also in ability and in kinds of talent. "Then there is Guningbal of western Arnhem Land, a young man still but a famous composer of 'gossip' songs. Or white haired Midjaumidjau of Oenpelli, a skilful artist whose ochred lines on a stringybark canvas are a constant delight to the eye."

Similar individual variation must have existed in early food-gathering societies and, indeed, in apelike and sub-human societies because it is true of animals in general. Pavlov began his pioneering conditioning experiments with dogs on the assumption of hereditary sameness but soon perceived that there were inherited individual differences in temperament and intelligence. And Köhler noted similar differences among apes.

One other fact that emerges from a study of food-gathering society is that although all individuals are different, these differences fall into certain general types, again both in temperament and in ability. Some people are naturally of a quieter disposition than others; some are vigorous and assertive. Some take naturally to the song or to art work; some turn to religious ceremonial, others to social leadership. Curiously little attention seems to have been given to this question of types but observation alone shows us that all societies contain them and that much of the character of society results from them. They, too, must come from a combination of genetic with social factors.

Men and Women

It has perhaps been noted that in this work I have used the term "man" to refer only to the biological species; otherwise I used "humanity," "people," and so on. The restriction is deliberate. For although the argument is that "man" in social studies is a generic term, it is, in fact, often used to denote the male sex only; for instance:[6]

"Perhaps fifteen to twenty thousand years ago man first trod American soil, crossing from Siberia to Alaska via the Bering Strait." Such a use of "man" or "men" should be avoided because it obscures the role of women in social development and suggests an oversimplified framework picture of society. The author of the above sentence, for instance, does not seem to be envisaging an interactive community of men, women, and children, but an isolated male grouping. There is, in fact, a tendency not only to dehumanize early food-gathering society but to "dewomanize" it. In the process the fact that there were personal relationships between men and women in these early societies has been lost sight of. In trying to seek these out we have, once again, to turn to observed food-gathering societies, for instance, Malinowski's observations on courtship:[7]

> Gossip about other people's business, and especially about their love affairs, is also a common subject of conversation between two lovers; and so on many occasions much of it ultimately came my way, in that a boy would repeat what he had heard from his sweetheart. For the rest, they talk of what they are doing at the moment, the beauties of nature, and of the things they like or do not like. Sometimes, too, a boy will vaunt his exploits in those pursuits in which women do not usually participate, such as *Kula* expeditions, fishing, bird-snaring, or hunting.

All this, of course, sounds familiar, and once more we have the feeling of a pattern of behavior which must go back into the first human societies.

In addition to love relations between men and women there is also antagonism. These, too, are observed among modern food-gathering peoples, finding direct sexual expression in rape (including mass rape), virtual rape (in which the woman submits but is used as a sexual instrument), wife-beating, and—on the other side—occasional orgiastic attacks by bands of women upon solitary men.

POLITICAL LIFE

Among such peoples as the Polar Eskimos of Northern Greenland political life is still a subdivision of social life. The village families conduct community affairs in an informal way. Occasionally, in times of danger to the community, a shaman may act as a temporary leader, but there is no chief and no governing council. This situation we may presume to have been that of the earliest food-gathering societies. But in the wealthier food-gathering societies of the past, such as those that piled up the great heaps of bison bones in Europe, the situation must have been closer to that found among the Australians, where the family communities have been amalgamated into tribes which are normally run by a chief and a council. Chiefs and other leaders, however, we should note, owe their position not to superior wealth (for there is none) but to their personal qualities, and they retain their positions only so long as they retain the confidence of the community.

According to most anthropological accounts, both local and tribal government is male dominated. Women can be shamans but not chiefs. Among the Australians, the older men are the rulers. Among other food-gathering people the leaders include younger as well as older men, but not women. This may not, it is true, have been so in the earliest food-gathering societies in which political life was not clearly differentiated from social life, but there is no adequate evidence to support the theory of a general "matriarchate stage" of female domination through which society passed.

In addition to a political system, observed food-gathering societies have an elementary legal system. There are, it is true, no written laws and no judges but past community decisions are codified orally, and political rulers can enforce them.

Culture

Knowledge

Knowledge, as some of us—particularly academics—tend to forget, arises not primarily from thought but from activity.

The economic activity of food-gathering people produced a vast storehouse of knowledge. From their work they learned the characteristics of such natural materials as stone and wood in all their variety. They learned in their work how to use these materials—the drill, the needle, the digging stick. From hunting and food-collecting they acquired knowledge of animals and plant life. The Australians of northern Queensland, for instance, knew and used some 240 plants. The Ona Indians of Tierra del Fuego "note every peculiarity of shape and coloring on an animal, and have taught their normally yelping dogs to move in absolute silence on the hunt. Butchering a guanaco, with the discarding of the undesired spleen and entrails, amounts to a laboratory course in anatomy."[8]

Most of the knowledge of plants must have come from women, for it was women who did the plant-collecting. Out of women's work, too, must have developed the knowledge and techniques of reed weaving, clothes making and other basic household processes, all of which branched off later into other fields.

Social life also made its specific contributions, for instance, in knowledge of society itself, its groups and functionings, of people, their biological and psychological nature, of child rearing, of medicine. This latter is surprisingly extensive among observed food-gathering peoples:[9]

> The Havasupai cut boils and squeeze out the pus; bathe a bleeding nose in cold water; set a fractured arm, bandage it and bind it between thin splints tied close to the body. . . . The Lesu cure inflammation and swellings by heating ginger leaves and then pressing them on the affected parts. This serves the purpose of a counter-irritant like our mustard plasters. Melanesians and Peruvians skilfully cut out broken bones of the skull to relieve pressure on the brain.

And to this list we have to add knowledge of pregnancy and childbirth. A large fund of knowledge on childbirth must have been handed on through a kind of world community of women for many thousands of years.

Another basic source of knowledge must have been political life, particularly when it exploded into fighting. In later societies, war has been one of the great spurs to knowledge; and doubtless in food-gathering societies community and tribal combats furnished much of the motive for the improvement and invention of weapons. The bow and arrow may have arisen primarily not for killing animals but men. Political life also created knowledge of governmental and legal techniques.

Ideas

As Locke contended and as modern psychology has demonstrated, the contents of the mind are derived through the senses and reflect areas of reality. True, some ideas seem so far removed from reality that it seems difficult to believe that they are a reflection of it. However, as Locke also perceived, if we examine even the most fantastic idea, we shall find that all its component parts exist in reality. No one has seen a flying horse, but he has seen a horse and he has seen a bird.

Among observed food-gathering peoples, some views are based on knowledge, but others are rooted in ignorance. The hunter learns the habits of the animals he must hunt; and this is knowledge. But say he can find no animals in the forest? He may then draw a picture of an animal and hurl a spear at it in the hope that this may cause the animals to appear. As Sir James Fraser and others have pointed out, he controls that which he can control by knowledge; he tries to control that over which he has no control by magic. Associated with magic, we find among observed food-gathering peoples a series of general views on the relationships between people and nature. The Ona Indians of Tierra del Fuego believe that the "world" was "created" by a supreme god whom they call Temaukel:[10]

> The most powerful of beings, he is pictured as living wifeless and child-less in the sky where the souls of ordinary mortals join him; and he punishes with death those who flout his laws. As for creation, he originated the sky when it was yet without stars and the first amorphous earth. Virtually everything else was left to his deputy, Kenos, ultimately a star, who raised the sky, transformed the world, created human beings and taught them Temaukel's code.

Along with the creator god exists a multitude of spirits and ghosts of ancestors. Essentially the same kind of belief is found among the Australians and other food-gathering peoples. Sometimes the creator god has other gods associated with him. Among the Chirachuahua Apaches, along with the creator god, Life Giver, we find a child god and a goddess. And these Apaches also believe in spirits (Mountain Spirits, Water Beings) and ghosts of the dead. The workings of these various spiritual creatures cause such phenomena as pregnancy, disease, death, good hunting or bad hunting, and so on. Among the Tierra del Fuego Indians, the Australians, and the African Bushmen, we find the sucking of the flesh in treatment of disease to suck out the evil spirit. And food-gathering peoples everywhere have fertility rites.

Behind magic and other ceremonials there lies a belief in invisible spirits; and it is in this belief that the essence of the general religious views of observed food-gathering peoples is to be found. There are spirits everywhere. The human body has a spirit; animals have spirits; the wind and trees have spirits; there is a supreme spirit. Alongside the material world exists an invisible spirit world.

As with other aspects of society, these views cannot have developed rapidly; they must have roots. The only question is, how far back do the roots go? It may at first seem incredible that these roots extend back 10,000 or 20,000 years; but the indications again are that they do. The possession of similar beliefs and ceremonials in so many widely scattered places—Australia, Tierra del Fuego, Africa—suggests a long history. Furthermore, as we have noted, the artifacts of early food-gathering societies indicate similar beliefs: burial tools, weapons, and meat with the dead; the coloring of the dead body with ochre; cave paintings of animals associated with magic ceremonials designed to bring about good hunting; probable fertility-rite and mother-goddess carvings. When we consider the situation of early food-gathering peoples a belief in spirits appears inevitable. Everything must have seemed magical to them. They did not know what caused day or night or the seasons or the weather. Day was accompanied by a flaming ball in the sky which seemed but a few miles off; night was accompanied by a circling ball of silver and innumerable points of light. They saw the movement of animals and of grass in the wind, but they had no idea what caused these movements. Thunder storms or dreams must have had great importance in their lives. In dreams one could perceive a reality which had no substance — it must be a spirit reality. The movement of people, animals, or plants must be caused by similar spirits — there must be invisible spirits everywhere.

The role of fear in human society seems to have been little studied, and it may be more important than is realized. Certainly it is always present to one or another degree, and sometimes dominates social behavior, seizing individuals and groups with terror. In food-gathering societies with their utter dependence for life on the chances of nature it must have been particularly potent, and the power of the shaman, believed to be able to control the uncontrollable, and using fear as a weapon, must have been immense. In early food-gathering societies fear of death must have been particularly potent, giving sharp edge to the uncertainties created by the lack of social controls. The death rate must have been very high. Human fertility is apparently a constant, yet population increase in food-gathering societies is generally slight. Particularly this must be so in regard to infant mortality, for, although I know of no specific statistics in regard to observed food-gathering people, the trend must be similar to that in "underdeveloped" countries; in these countries more than 25 percent of all deaths take place before five years of age (in "highly developed countries" less than 4 percent). In early food-gathering society, then, death must have ravaged daily through family after family. The grief and terror which it produces is only too evident in modern food-gathering societies. In Australia at a death:[11] "Kinsfolk and campfellows wail and sob, gashing themselves with spears and knives, axes and sharp stones, until the blood flows. . . . Soon the whole camp moves away from the scene of the death: the dead man's name becomes tabu, at least for a year or so, and all his possessions may be ritually destroyed." The dark fear that produces lacerations, tabus even on uttering a name, the moving of a whole camp away from the scene of a death, prolonged and frenzied rites with each death, could obviously help to lay a basis not only for concepts of an uncontrollable spirit world, everywhere existing like shadows or the wind, but of human spirits also.

When a person is dead the body remains but it cannot move. Hence, movement was not caused by the body. To people having no concept of the interconnections of body and brain, it must have seemed that some special spirit substance (ghost) was responsible for bodily move-ment, emotions and thought—the same spirit substance that manifested itself in dreams. And it was not difficult to believe that this spirit con-tinued to exist after death. There was, however, no universal concept of its permanent existence. It was often thought of by modern food-gathering peoples as a ghost that haunted the vicinity for a time and then somehow vanished.

From the concept of a spirit-ghost world to that of one god-spirit was not a great step. In fact, it may not have been a step at all, for, as we have noted, modern food-gathering peoples believe in both a god and spirits, and this was doubtless true of early food-gathering people also. The two beliefs may have grown together. Nature to early food-gathering peoples did not signify a planet or a universe but a small area of apparently flat land with a bowl of sky over it. That this area plus its sky and its inhabitants, human and animal, should have been "made," as a man makes a spear, would seem reasonable, and as no maker was visible he, too, must have been a spirit—a super-chief spirit.

Crude though these views may appear, they represented an im-portant advance, for they meant that people had moved beyond specific thinking about specific processes—such as shaping a stone axe—to general thinking, forming ideological frameworks to which individual ideas and events could be related. They show also that in the begin-nings of religion we find some of the basic beliefs of later religions. The concept of the Creator God plus spirits (angels, saints) and sometimes other gods (Vishnu, Christ) is to be found in Hinduism, Christianity, Judaism, Mohammedanism, and Zoroastrianism; that of ghosts of the dead is to be found in the ancestor worship of China and India and other parts of the world (including Roman Italy). All these beliefs must have come out of the great reservoir of ancient food-gathering society.

Art

The only art of early food-gathering societies that has remained is plastic or graphic, and of these only that which was made of or on stone, tooth, bone, or shell: paintings and drawings on the walls of caves, stone carvings, etchings on bone, shell jewelry, and so on. Of the art work done in these materials almost all has been lost. Of the similar work with wood, reeds (baskets), or feathers we have nothing but some indication of designs which were later used in pottery. We have, that is to say, only scattered and fragmentary remains of what must have been an enormously fruitful plastic and graphic art of many peoples over many thousands of years. Even this, however, is but a small part of the story. There cannot have existed a plastic and graphic art without other arts also: music and song, dance, stories and poetry, dramatic representation.

Once again we must turn to observed food-gathering societies to fill in the picture. If, for instance, we had nothing of the Bushman or Australian societies except stone, bone, and shell remains, these would roughly parallel the art remains of the ancient food-gathering societies of Europe and elsewhere. The cave paintings of the Australians equal or surpass those of ancient Europe, and those of the Bushmen are not far behind. But these cave paintings form but a segment of the total. Tools, weapons utensils, dwellings, clothing—all are designed and ornamented to make them beautiful: the great war canoes of the Pacific coast Indians, the Australian houses, the decorated needle cases of the Eskimo, the magnificent feather cloaks of the South American Indians, the basketry of the southwest North American Indians—to give but a few random examples of a universal cultural phenomenon. The plastic and graphic arts are blended with craftsmanship in all food-gathering societies.

The arts of music, song, and the dance are found everywhere. The instruments possessed by ancient food-gathering societies have vanished, but drums, sticks for beating rhythms, "bull roarers," and some wind instruments are found in so many modern food-gathering societies that they must have a long history. Music, song, and dance are all closely connected and at times go over into dramatic representation. The Tierra del Fuego Indians in their dances impersonate their gods and spirits. The Australians have a play on the story of Lumaluma, a man who became a whale. Buffoonery (comedy) is found also. The roots of drama go back not to "the Greeks" but to food-gathering societies.

Folk tales are found among all modern food-gathering peoples and hence must also be of ancient origin. Some of the actual tales still told may, in fact, have a continuous history—with changes of locale and characters—of many thousands of years, for we find them in widely scattered places in variant forms. Some of these tales are masterpieces of narrative and beauty. We find in many of them (in all continents) a curious similarity of pattern, that of rhythmic repetition which leads to a climax (often in a series of three—as in the Irish folk and fairy tales).

In addition to folk tales and drama, three other literary forms are found among all modern food-gathering peoples, namely poetry (linked with song), riddles, and jokes. The poetry matches, in its sensitive beauty, the narrative skill of the folk tale; for instance, the following fragment from the Dulngulg cycle of the Mudbara tribe in Australia:[12]

> The day breaks—the first rays of the rising Sun, stretching her arms.
> Daylight breaking, as the Sun rises to her feet.
> Sun rising, scattering the darkness; lighting up the land . . .
> With disc shining, bringing daylight, as the birds whistle and call . . .
> People are moving about, talking, feeling the warmth.
> Burning through the Gorge, she rises, walking westwards,
> Wearing her waist-band of human hair.
> She shines on the blossoming coolibah tree, with its sprawling roots,
> Its shady branches spreading. . . .

Here, however embryonically, we have the true craft of the poet, the skilful repetition (on the theme of the brightness of the sun, for example), the imaginative use of simile (the sun stretching her arms and rising to her feet), the use of varied imagery to build a mood of sensuous beauty—in the original language all, doubtless, coordinated with the rhythm. And, once again, this cannot have been a newly learned art but one with deep roots in the past. The people who created the cave paintings of Europe must have had a poetry like this—perhaps 20,000 years before Homer.

III

Farming Societies

FOOD-GATHERING SOCIETY, in spite of its advances, was a dead-end society for it left humanity dependent for its food and raw materials upon what the planet naturally provided. The bow and arrow could enable one to kill more animals than the spear but it could not increase the total number of animals; nor could the digging stick increase the number of tubers. Further advance had to depend upon the creation of food (grains, animal breeding) and raw materials (hides, wool, cotton) and not merely a more skilful exploitation of what already existed.

The best way for a layman to grasp what happened is, once more, to visit a museum. If, in New York, for instance, we leave the early food-gathering ("stone age") cases in the American Museum of Natural History and walk across Central Park to the First Egyptian Room in the Metropolitan Museum, the transition is dramatically demonstrated on the shelf of one case. This shelf contains the following items found at the village site of Merimde: (1) Two rather crude clay pots. (2) Toothed flints probably from a sickle blade. (A nearby case, of a slightly later period, contains flint sickle blades.) (3) Flint arrowheads. (4) Two stones that form "upper and nether grindstones." (5) A handful of dark grains—"sample of scorched wheat." (6) Two small, round stones with a hole through the center of each—"spindle whorls." (7) A stone axehead.

These few sample items represent a new way of life. The grindstone and the wheat—a handful from how many fields in how many generations?—show the beginnings of farming. The clay pots reveal the transition from basket and skin containers to pots. The stone whorls are all that is left of the spindles and looms which made the first cloth. Both pottery and cloth-making represent not a single invention but a series of inventions, each step of which requires the application of considerable knowledge and techniques; and they represent also the beginnings of manufacturing. These remains also show us that what we are dealing with is not, as often stated, the "invention" of "agriculture." "Agriculture" could not have developed—it never was "invented"—if other things had not developed also; for instance, pot-making and cloth-making. "Agriculture" developed as part of an economic complex, each part of which was dependent upon each other part. Furthermore, this economic complex could not have developed without certain social, political, and cultural advances, as is clear from our brief survey of food-gathering society. What we are dealing with is not agriculture alone, nor even agriculture plus other economic advances, but a total societal entity—farming society.

Origins and Development

That farming developed not in one but in many places is shown, for one thing, by the various regions in which we can trace the ancestral forms of farming plants and animals. There appear to have been at least four centers: Southeast Asia, Southwest Asia; West Africa (in the Niger area), Middle America. Of these the most significant from the historical point of view was Southwest Asia, for it seems to have been both the earliest and the one from which civilized societies first arose. The European (and possibly the West African) farming centers grew out of it.

A recent radiocarbon dated find may indicate that the Southeast Asian center arose at about the same time as the Southwest Asian center. The most important crop was rice (which, when irrigated, produced twenty times as much grain per acre as wheat). The West African center, in the Niger area, apparently arose some two thousand or more years later than the Southwest Asian center. Cotton perhaps originated there, and certain grains and the yam have been traced to it. Apparently the Negro civilizations of West Africa had their roots in this center. The Middle American center produced a great variety of domesticated plants including maize (Indian corn), various beans, tomatoes, cacao, and some species of cotton. The American Indian civilizations (Aztec, Inca, Maya, and so on) were based on this center.

The Southwest Asian center was mainly concentrated in the area now covered by Turkey, Syria, Israel, Iraq, and Iran. That it was one of the great originating centers of farming is indicated by various points of evidence. (1) The wild ancestors of wheat and rye are found there. (2) The wild ancestor of the goat, sheep, and one variety of pig existed in this area (the other main variety of pig apparently originated in East Asia). (3) The terrain is in places particularly adapted to the origin of farming. (4) The earliest farming villages and cave remains indicating farming have been discovered in this area.

If we consider the evidence from this one area alone, it is apparent that the farming of farming societies did not originate in any one region within it and that it embraced manifold forms, including both plants and animals and several kinds of each. It must, then, have been the production of many people in many places, each making different kinds of contribution to the total.

When did these developments take place? The evidence on dating is beginning to accumulate, some of it coming from caves—which tend to preserve materials—and some from village sites. One of the oldest caves is that at Shanidar (radiocarbon dated at about 8700 B.C.), located near where modern Turkey, Iran, and Iraq join. There is some indication of village sites as early as Shanidar but the most dramatic find so far has been that on the site of Jericho uncovering a well-developed farming village of about 7000 B.C. It may have contained as many as two thousand people; it was surrounded by a ditch cut in rock 27 feet wide and 8 feet deep in which was erected a stone wall which contained a tower 35 feet in diameter and 25 feet high. The houses were made of stone and furnished with wooden furniture.

A second important village site (date estimated as about 6750 B.C.) was discovered at Jarmo in Turkey; in it were found indications of grain, sickles, hoes, grain-grinding stones, mortars, dome-shaped clay baking ovens, sheep, goats, cattle, pigs, stone containers. The houses (about 25 in number) were made of mud brick; some grains have survived and show signs of domestication. Other village sites, mostly of a later date—some of them two thousand years later—stretch from Sialk in Iran to Merimde in Egypt (from which the display in the Metropolitan Museum was taken), and include all that was found at Jarmo plus pottery and silos or bins for storing grain, and spindle whorls. At the two extremes beyond this general area early farming sites have been discovered, in Yugoslavia (perhaps 7000 B.C.), Cyprus, and in the region of the Indus River (both of somewhat later date). If we put the evidence of the caves and villages together, the indication is that farming communities had come into existence in West Asia by about

8500 B.C. and slowly spread over the area for the next three or four thousand years, improving their techniques (for instance pottery making and weaving) as they spread.

The beginning of farming communities, however, was clearly not the beginning of farming techniques. Farming society cannot have arisen suddenly from "pure" food-gathering society but (as some cave remains indicate) must have come out of a mixed form of a food-gathering society with supplementary farming. We would not, it seems to me, be too far off the mark if we conceived of the situation in early West Asia as roughly similar to that of the North American Indians at the time of the European invasion.

The grains found at Jarmo and other early village sites, when subjected to botanical analysis, indicate a long period of previous cultivation and breeding. A similar history is indicated for such domesticated animals as pigs, goats, sheep, and oxen. It must, for instance, have taken many generations of careful cross-breeding to turn the wild sheep — which had little wool — into a wool-producing animal. Women must many times in many places have learned to plant tubers and yams, slivers (e.g., for bananas), and seeds (for wheat, rye, barley, and rice) in their plant-gathering terrains. They must have learned also the necessity and techniques of weeding and watering. Hunters must — again, many times and in many places — have attempted to domesticate animals, for it was obviously an advantage to breed them and have them at hand for eating rather than to rely on the uncertainties of the hunt. Modern food-gathering people have been observed to bring home the young of animals and rear them.

What were the forces which finally pulled these processes together into full-time farming? One of the most prominent and argued-about theories is that glacial recession between 12,000 and 7000 B.C. dried out the area to the south and east of the Mediterranean with the exception of the river valleys, and forced people to concentrate in these valleys and develop their farming potential. This theory has received some support from recent indications of aridity in early farming sites. And it certainly seems to suggest that farming communities began to develop during a period of what must have been great climatic change. But the acceptance or rejection of the view will have to await further research and evidence. On the basis of the existing evidence, however, it seems unlikely that such climatic change actually created farming as a form of life (although it could certainly have speeded it up). For one thing, farming also developed in Southeast Asia, which was not "dried out." Furthermore, the evidence indicates that food-gathering society had developed to the threshold of full-time farming by 10 to 12,000 years ago and that its own internal sociological processes would in some places have driven it over the line, climatic change or no climatic change. In envisaging such a transition we have to think not only of the planting of seed or the tending of animals but of a total socio-cultural complex.

Let us consider, for instance, the implications of food-gathering society's advances in tools, weapons, and techniques. With the supplanting of the chipped flint axe by the ground stone axe and other tools, people were for the first time able to cut and shape timber, to clear the forest, and to make plows, boats, and wheels. The bow and arrow, the hunting dog, the fish hook, and the net combined to increase the food supply.

As part of this development there were certain tools and productive methods which could have led directly to the raising of plants and the domestication of animals. The digging stick is a stick with a cut-off branch projecting near the bottom, on the back of which the foot can be placed for leverage in uprooting plants. Used as a chopping tool it becomes a rudimentary hoe. If it is pulled along the ground, it becomes a small plow. And that such an evolution did sometimes occur is indicated by an early Egyptian illustration.

The elements of the art of weaving are present in basketry. As to spinning, some food-gathering peoples who have not advanced to cloth-making spin hairs into continuous plaits, and this must have been true in early food-gathering societies also. The transition to spinning and then weaving in wool, flax, and cotton is not so great as it at first appears even though the loom itself is a complex machine (the different forms of which may indicate separate inventions). Pottery, as a developed art, is also complex. But before there were fired clay pots people must long have handled and experimented with clay until they were able to construct a kiln that would provide an 1,100 degree temperature, just as they hand wove before they learned to make a loom.

The evidence of remains from early food-gathering societies, then, indicates that by about, say, 11,000 or 12,000 years ago in Southwest Asia many of the economic prerequisites for farming society had come into being, and the evidence of observed food-gathering societies suggests that in some of these societies some cultivation of plants and domestication of animals had taken place. To these factors one other is clearly necessary for full-time farming to develop, namely a geographically stable community. One of the general characteristics of early food-gathering societies is their mobility. The main food supply normally came from hunting and the community had to follow the migrations of the animals hunted. Such mobile societies could perhaps have had supplementary agricultural practices for many thousands of years without becoming farming communities. Obviously some communities did become stable, and one might guess that these were primarily fishing rather than hunting ones, for fishing communities would tend to be stable and some of them would have fresh water available for crops and animals.

Another important fact must have been contact between communities whereby techniques could be exchanged. That there was such contact is shown by the evidence of wide trading during the later stages of food-gathering society. In some areas physical conditions — the great river valleys, rich in seas, lakes, and rivers along and around which to trade — facilitated communications and trade.

One great spur to change must, as always, have been competition. Observed food-gathering and semi-farming communities (in Africa, for instance) exist in competition and often in armed conflicts with each other wherever the population of a territory exceeds the food supply. Communities with more farming would have a considerable advantage, both economically and militarily, over those which had less or none. Their greater food supply, their remaining in a small, encloseable area, and their greater material wealth all would contribute to this.

Nor would economic and military competition and conflict cease with the development of actual farming communities. On the contrary, as we know from observed farming societies, competition and conflict between farming peoples are more extensive and ferocious than between food-gathering peoples for the simple reason that with farming the population increases to a greater degree in a smaller area. In these early centuries in West Asia it has been calculated that the population of the area increased 16 times between 8000 and 4000 B.C. This must mean that the struggle became unprecedentedly intense.

We have also to keep in mind the probable size of the process, for archaeology tends to shrink social reality. Some of the later farming societies raided by the Egyptians in the centuries around 3000 B.C. seem to have been large and prosperous, for instance, Libya and Nubia. The Sumerian cities were early attacked by powerful peoples, some of whom must have been from advanced farming societies. It may be, then, that the population of West Asia in the centuries of the later establishment of farming societies was several million.

One more general point should perhaps be emphasized. No matter what economic or other techniques were developed, the tide of advance could only reach so far. The combined abilities of the society were trapped within its bounds just as were those of food-gathering society before it. The advance could not, for instance, encompass the setting up of cities, for there was not the concentrated economic capacity to support or supply a city population. In short, it could not — in the centuries from, say, 8000 to 4000 B.C. — have gone further than it did.

The advance was clearly also not the result of planning, either individual or collective, for it covered too vast an area and assumed too many forms over too long a span of time. No person or group of persons perceived that the solution to their economic problems lay in establishing farming and then went ahead to establish it. They were forced in the struggle for existence to put the pieces of a vast puzzle together without knowing that it was a puzzle or what it would look like when completed. They built like a colony of ants, except that they solved each tiny part of the puzzle consciously, by reason and practice, not by instinct.

ECONOMIC, SOCIAL, AND POLITICAL CHANGES

The main economic changes inherent in the new form of society may be summarized as follows: (1) new material means of production (the ground stone axe, the hoe, the sickle, and, later, the plow); (2) new kinds of work (plant cultivation, animal tending and breeding, pottery and cloth-making); (3) a new division of labor with, probably, the men as hunting decreased taking the heavier work (plowing and herding) and women the lighter work (sowing, weeding, milking); (4) increased specialization of labor as some people or groups in each community became unusually skilled in the new kinds of work. As a result of these changes there must have been a great increase in production (of food, clothing, houses, weapons, tools, boats) and, consequently, of trade.

Other changes were more complex and far-reaching. They included the extension of private property, increasing inequalities in property, increasing social inequalities, and slavery. These developments, too, may be seen among observed early-type farming peoples. They did not, however, develop all at once or without a struggle. For instance, popular counter forces in some areas seem to have held up the development of private property in land. Even as late as the Mycenaean period the (Homeric) chieftains had no private property in land although they did in cattle. In the most undeveloped of observed farming communities land is still held in common. This was true of the Germans when Caesar (I.2) observed them: "the magistrates and tribal chiefs annually assign a holding [of land] to clans and groups of kinsmen . . . and the following year make them move on somewhere else." In many observed farming societies land is allocated to each family by the chief, which is apparently an attempt by the tribal members to prevent land-grabs by the more powerful families. The custom in early Greece was that of equal division of land between families distributed by lot with special holdings for the chief and the church respectively. So, too, among the Aztecs and other peoples.

In the first farming societies the archaeological evidence indicates that what chiefs there were did not possess exceptional wealth. "Of chieftainship," writes V. Gordon Childe,[1] "there is no definite evidence in early neolithic cemeteries or villages. There are, that is to say, no outstandingly wealthy graves, evidently belonging to a person of rank, and no dwellings that could pass for palaces."

We may presume, therefore, that early farming societies were essentially equalitarian but that private property was increasing, and along with it social inequality and slavery. Some slavery may, in fact, have existed in high level food-gathering societies, as it did later among the North American Pacific Coast Indians, the slaves (apparently mostly war-captives) being at first not personal but community property. Slavery, however, cannot have been of great economic importance in this early period for these societies were not wealthy enough to support a large slave population.

The increase in wealth, the new kinds of work and divisions of labor, the struggle for property must have necessitated new forms of government. At first, doubtless, these changes were slight. But soon there would have been valuable land plots and animal herds at stake. Conflicts between families and tribes for their possession must have arisen and have followed a similar pattern to that in observed early-type farming communities. The usual political reaction was probably to strengthen the authority of the chief and establish a ruling council, both moves apparently intended to restrain economic inequalities. The common people retained a basic power into at least the early stages of farming society. Tacitus[2] also commented on the Germans:

> On matters of minor importance only the chiefs debate, on major affairs the whole community; but, even where the commons have the decision, the case is carefully considered in advance by the chiefs. . . . When the mass so decide, they take their seats fully armed. Silence is then demanded by the priests, who on that occasion have also power to enforce obedience. Then such hearing is given to the king or chief as age, rank, military distinction or eloquence can secure; but it is rather their prestige as counsellors than their authority that tells. If a proposal displeases them, the people roar out their dissent; if they approve, they clash their spears.

Let us move over the centuries to Samoa, an example of a society frozen in an early-farming state.

The village is a locally autonomous political unit, and owns, as a corporation, a certain bounded territory (on which its members build their houses and grow their crops), communal fishing grounds, and a large community house for meetings, ceremonies, and the entertainment of visitors. It is governed by a village chief chosen by the group, who is aided by a council or *fono* composed of titled men or so-called nobles. The village chief and council both legislate and judge for the village as a whole, and, as well, direct and control all community enterprises. . . . Though the Samoan village is locally autonomous, it is usually associated with other villages in a larger political entity called a district. This is governed much in the same way as the village, that is, by a district chief and a district council.[3]

Clearly we are dealing with a general social process. The increased economic and social affairs of a farming community would everywhere and in every period of time require a more highly organized government than a food-gathering one. A community political structure with a chief and representative council tends to become set and these structures amalgamate to form larger ones—tribal and inter-tribal—as land-grabbing spreads.

When we move into a later stage of farming society—farming society on the verge of civilization—we find that these phenomena have developed further. And here again we can best envisage the process by another frozen "fringe" society, that of the Canary Islands.

In each kingdom two social classes existed: commoners and nobles. The commoners, who wore short hair, tilled the fields and herded the animals, milked them, and made the cheese. The nobles were not permitted to perform any economically useful task; their business was administrative and military. . . . It should be noted that the division of labor in this Neolithic community was not primarily between men and women, as with the garden-tillers of Melanesia and aboriginals of North America, but between nobles of both sexes and commoners of both sexes. Not all the men were warriors, only noble men. The king himself stood at the head of the noble group, their leader in war and peace, but he could take action only after full consultation with his council of nobles, who convened for this purpose in a special place. . . .[4]

That similar general changes were taking place in farming societies just prior to the emergence of civilization in West Asia and North Africa is indicated by the archaeological record. For instance in Mesopotamia:[5] "the Al Ubaid period [about 4000 B.C.] has left us some remains which suggest that certain centres began to be of outstanding importance and that a change in the rural character of the settlements was taking place. At Abu Shahrein in the south, and at Tepe Gawra in the north, temples were erected." Or in Iran (Sialk) at about the same time:[6] "The village quarters, intersected by narrow, winding alleys, marked off the boundaries of the estates . . . ; the external walls of houses were decorated with buttresses and recesses." In the graves were found "large goblets" and "elegant chalices."

The economic changes indicated by such archaeological discoveries must have produced similar social and political changes to those in the observed, frozen farming societies. The most important of these were the emergence of social classes and the shift of the main political control to one of them, namely the "nobles." Both the anthropological and the archaeological evidence indicate the establishment of a church with its priests to take the place of the shamanism of the food-gathering and early farming societies.

There is evidence also of one other major social change accompanying the advances of later farming societies, namely, the beginning of the lowering of the social status of women. The anthropological evidence suggests that in earlier farming society there was a raising of this status, as women turned from plant-collecting to simple farming and so became economically more important. But in later farming societies the decline begins. In West Asia it had declined in the first civilization (by 3000 B.C.) and in other early civilizations; and the decline is unlikely to have been sudden. Certain factors which would produce it are apparent. (1) The introduction of the ox-drawn plow to replace the hoe must have removed much of farming from women's to men's work (as in observed farming societies). (2) The introduction of the potter's wheel and the loom brought about the rise of the craftsman who earned his keep by his work (also as in observed farming societies). (3) Wherever animal herds arose, their tending and ownership were in the hands of men (inherited from the days of hunting). Men were thus able to acquire private property and wealth whereas women were not. The tradition of the common ownership of agricultural land perhaps also worked against women making similar accumulations. (4) The coming of war gave added power and prestige to men. These changes doubtless did not take place automatically but only after a prolonged and bitter social struggle such as we find women making later in Chinese and other societies.

CULTURE

That these economic, social, and political upheavals brought about and were coordinated with a cultural revolution goes without saying. Particularly affected was the realm of knowledge. Early farmers had to know about plants, soil, harvesting, animal tending and breeding, carpentry, well-digging, and how to make cloth, tools, and equipment. The knowledge required for pottery making is considerable. And the complexities of spinning and weaving are such that no adequate verbal description can convey them.

In some popular accounts one gets the impression of early farming society consisting of a few farms in a limited area raising wheat. In reality, there must have been many thousands of farms over a large area producing a great variety of crops. Each of these crops required special knowledge. All of them presented problems of storage and preservation. The farmer — unlike the hunter — has at all steps to measure and plan, measure his field, plan the nature and size of his crop, the amount of seed that must be preserved, and so on. He has to count his cattle or sheep. He must learn to know the seasons and calculate their approach; to do this he must have knowledge of the ways of the sun and the stars beyond that needed by the hunter. Planning and measuring were required also in the new carpentry made possible by the grinding of stone into axes and chisels and used in constructing the larger houses and villages.

With the increase in knowledge there were also changes in old ideas (we find added to the hunting weapons and tools left in graves little statues of cattle) and the rise of new ones. A new department of magic with its accompanying rituals and beliefs — in fertility and rainmaking — came into being. Rain, of but secondary interest to the hunter, was a matter of life and death to the farmer. The old hierarchy of gods and spirits was supplemented or supplanted by a new one, those of the grain, cattle, the sun, sky, the wind, rain, and fertility. These we perceive among the first civilizations, the Sumerian and the Egyptian, which grew directly out of the early farming societies, and among observed farming peoples. For instance, the Hawaiians have Longo, the god of agriculture, the Dahomeans (an African farming people) have Sagbata, whose function is to inspire abundant crops. Obviously such gods could not have been conceived of until farming existed.

CHANGE AND CONTINUITY

The change from food-gathering to farming society was the first great change in human history, and as we consider it we can see in it something of the nature of historical change in general. It was not planned but arose out of undirected community activities, particularly economic ones. We can see also that great though the change was it was not absolute. The old society was not completely destroyed when the new took its place. Society did not cease to be society. For instance, those aspects of society which depended upon such biological matters as birth, maturity, aging, death, and sexual differences continued: the family, puberty rites, mourning, courtship, marriage. There were doubtless differences in some of the forms of these phenomena but the phenomena themselves must have remained essentially as they had been in food-gathering society.

Not even economic changes were absolute. The forms of work changed but work as such remained. New divisions of labor arose but the old one between men and women also continued. The economy had given some new controls over nature but it had given no fundamental control. Famine could arise still, not from a lack of game but from drought or storm or flood. Disease still ravaged, the death rate was still high. The new political controls gave no control over war. As a consequence, certain basic patterns of thought continued. New gods arose but superstition remained. The new priest was but the old shaman writ large.

Pottery and weaving gave rise to new forms of plastic and graphic art but the basic techniques were the same. In general it seems that the basic realm of change was economic and the basic realm of continuity was social. The life patterns which had evolved out of the biological-social aspects of people did not change fundamentally.

Just as the various spheres of society acted and reacted one upon the other in food-gathering society, so did they as it began its evolution to farming society and then as farming society itself progressed. Economic advance brought about social classes and some concentration of wealth, both of which then produced further economic advances which made possible greater accumulations of wealth. Farming produced war and war aided farming (by eliminating food-gathering peoples and forcing technical advances). Economic concentration produced political concentration and the latter, in turn, aided the former. The large became larger, the small, smaller.

If change is not absolute, however, neither is continuity. Changes in the parts of society — as with the human body — in time bring about change in the whole. For instance, the family remained, but with the declining status of women certain general changes in time took place in it, and in courtship and other personal relationships of men and women also. What these were we can tell better when we see them in more fully developed form in the first civilized societies.

In essence what we witness is a tremendous advance, indeed, the most significant advance humanity has yet made — for on it all the rest depended — but an advance that carried along with it some of the fundamental aspects of the past.

IV

The First Civilized Societies

IF WE NOW TAKE another leap forward in time (but a much shorter one) and move from about 4500 B.C. to about 3000 B.C. we find that, in at least three areas of the world, a new step in social evolution has taken place. It used to be thought that this step was confined to the Nile valley and delta, but then it was found that it had taken place also in the Tigris and Euphrates river lands, and, several centuries later, in the Indus valley, this latter being the most extensive of all, covering twice the area of Egypt and more than four times that of Sumer. And it may have taken place in other nearby areas also by 3000 B.C. or shortly thereafter (for instance in the eastern Mediterranean). But it did not take place anywhere else so far as we now know—for instance in Europe or China—until much later.

THE ORIGINS OF CIVILIZATION

The more we look at this new society the more we get the feeling of looking in a mirror, for many of the main characteristics of what is familiarly known as "Western civilization" are present: cities and city life, an integrated farming-manufacturing economy, extensive and organized trade, "upper" and "lower" classes, town and country, government, organized religion, schools, writing and written literature, businessmen, farmers, workers, intellectuals, poets, generals, armies, and wars. The past, formerly so remote, seems suddenly to have become the present. Looked at thus, the change seems miraculous. But if we consider the total society and not its urban aspect only, the miracle begins to fade, for the total society is still mainly a farming society. The city manufacturing shops used the produce of the farms for raw materials. The main trade in the city markets was in agricultural produce or the goods made from them. The rulers of the cities were the owners of the farms. The real question, then, is how did cities arise? For once we have cities the rest follows. And the answer to this question is to be found in certain developments in advanced farming society.

As acreage increased some farmers discovered that the plow could be pulled by oxen, and thereby they increased both their areas of cultivation and the time which they had for pot-making and weaving and other activities. Increased production meant increased trade, and trade goods have to be transported. Donkey-power was added to ox-power. As ships grew larger they also grew more difficult to handle by oars. Sails came into general use in Egypt and Mesopotamia, on the Mediterranean, the Red Sea, and the Persian Gulf. Wind power was added to animal power.

In discussing these matters we have to beware of the word "invention," for the essential process must, as in other similar situations, have been economic and social. The word "invented" gives the impression of an individual inventing something which from that point on became adopted (on the analogy of modern patents). Sails, for instance, may have been "invented" many times and discarded—perhaps they had been used by children on toy boats. Children, being less tied by custom than adults, tend to innovate and may be responsible for more inventions than is realized. Society as a whole had to have reached a point at which the "invention" had economic value before it would actually be used.

Archaeologists are, in fact, discovering that there are few isolated inventions. Most are part of a developing continuum, each part of which had a social and economic motivation. The much-touted "principle" of the wheel, for instance, is inherent in a rolling log and was used in the rotating shaft of the drill or spindle in food-gathering societies. In fact, the first wheel was perhaps the humble spindle whorl, and the second the potter's wheel. (The first representation of cart wheels comes in Sumerian tombs and seals of about 3000 B.C.)

So, too, with the generally recognized second great invention of the period (4500 to 3000 B.C.), namely the smelting of copper. Smelting of ore is the final stage of a process which embodied a series of inventions and discoveries including beer brewing, bread baking, and pot making. Unleavened bread could be baked over an open fire (and still is in parts of Asia); but once yeast (used in beer brewing since at least 4000 B.C.) was added, an enclosed oven was needed as the bread required even heat all around. Such an oven with forced draft would produce the temperature needed for pot making. This temperature (600° C., 1,100° F.) also melts copper. Without bread, no pots; without pots, no copper.

Copper was the first metal used because it sometimes occurs in visible, handleable lumps in surface rocks, unlike iron, which is always in ore form (peppered into rocks). Spectroscopic analysis has shown that the first copper implements were simply made by heating and hammering natural lumps into the required shape (as was done later by the North American Indians). Copper was known and used before the potter's oven made its smelting possible. Unlike stone or wood, copper could be turned into weapons and implements *in any shape;* it gave people new powers over other materials, for instance, wood and leather. When tin was added to it to produce the hard alloy, bronze, these powers were increased.

One further process related to what we might call the "fire-oven complex" was brick-making, in which clay mixed with straw is placed in a mold and heated. This process, simple though it was, made possible the rapid building of better dwellings and laid the architectural basis for cities.

To these manufacturing processes we must add one agricultural one, namely irrigation. Irrigation is perhaps as old as farming society itself. Jericho (7000 B.C.), was situated by a natural spring, and it has been plausibly conjectured that this was used for irrigation. With general social and technological advances, irrigation systems would become better engineered and cover increasing areas.

As we look back, it becomes apparent that this total complex, sociological and technological, if concentrated anywhere within a limited area, could have resulted in the creation of cities (i.e., of civilization). Let us now consider the specific regions in which the first cities of which we have record arose, and see how they arose.

Although there are three such regions, we do not yet have sufficient information about one of them, the Indus Valley, to come to conclusions on its origins. As presently excavated (there are no written records) it consists of two cities, Mohenjo-Daro and Harappa, some 400 miles apart, with village and town remains in between. The cities are laid out systematically, and so were probably built by people who had occupied cities previously, but, if so, we do not know where they were. Radiocarbon analysis and other evidence point to about 2300 B.C. as the time of early occupancy of Mohenjo-Daro and Harappa, and to about 1700 B.C. as that of their destruction, but the possibility seems still open that the origins of the Indus Valley civilization go back to

3000 B.C. or earlier. Who these people were or what language they spoke we do not know. There is some suggestion that they were Negroid or partly Negroid. Passages in the *Rig-Veda* apparently referring to them indicate that they had black skins and flat noses; and there are Negroid characteristics in some present day Indian peoples. Of the only two statuettes found in these cities, one, a dancing girl, shows distinct Negroid features, and another, a man's bust, may also have Negroid characteristics, including what look like the evenly spaced scarring lines on the face characteristic of some African societies. On the other hand, however, the pottery remains do not look African but rather Iranian (Persian), and there is some indication that earlier Indian farming society was influenced from Iran.

Although there is evidence of farming villages in the hills and rivers of nearby Iran and northern Mesopotamia by 7000 B.C. or earlier, it was not in these higher regions but in the south, in the marshy lower reaches of the Tigris and Euphrates, that the cities grew up. That in this region there were farming villages and towns is shown particularly by the remains of temples, and that the towns increased in size is indicated by an increase in the size of the temples. One of the later ones, the White Temple, at Erech, was a towering structure, 240 feet high.

The dating is uncertain. Sumerian dating has been largely dependent on reckoning backward from the reign of Hammurabi, and this reign, on recent evidence, has been moved forward from 2000 B.C. to about 1700 B.C. It now appears that the famous Royal Tombs at Ur are of about 2300 B.C., and the first Sumerian kings about 2800 B.C. That there was a considerable period between the earliest temples and the later ones is shown by the fifty feet of debris layers between them but just how long a period this represents is unknown. (For some reason there seems to be little radiocarbon dating of Sumerian or pre-Sumerian remains.) The Sumerians, however, probably did not originate in Mesopotamia, for their language is as different from the other (for example, Semitic) languages of the area as Chinese is from English. They themselves had a tradition that they came from the south, and as their art bears a resemblance to earlier Persian art, it is now thought likely that they came from Iran, where there were farming settlements by 8500 B.C. or earlier. There was also in the centuries around 3000 B.C. a small but apparently civilized Persian state, Elam, with its capital at Susa.

When we turn to Egypt, we find the opposite problem to that of Sumer. Here we have comparatively firm dating for the beginnings of civilization—partly because the Egyptians built in stone and the dry climate of Egypt is a remarkable preservative—but the previous sequencing is unclear. From radiocarbon dating, from archaeological evidence, from later historical records – which fit in well with the other evidence – and from other sources, it is possible to place the beginnings of Egyptian civilization between 3500 and 3100 B.C. The difficulty is, however, that it seems to arise all at once. We have evidence of early-type farming society – going back, as we have seen, to about 5000 B.C. at Merimde – some indication of what seems to have been a briefly flourishing advanced-farming society, and then, almost immediately it would seem, a civilized state with great stone tombs and a written language. To account for this apparent suddenness, two theories have been put forward: either the civilization was transplanted from else-where – the transplanters being known as the "dynastic race" – or much of the evidence for a succession from early farming society to advanced farming society to civilization has been washed away by the flooding of the Nile, especially in the delta region (where we would expect extensive trading and farming). In the present state of things the second view seems the more likely. Although there is indication of Sumerian influence on early Egyptian art and architecture, Egyptian society and culture are clearly not derivative from Sumerian in any important way. No site in Asia has been found which shows evidence of the imprint of the hypothetical "dynastic race."

Were Egypt and Sumer alone in the world in 3000 B.C., or were there other civilized states? The indication is that they were not alone but there was nothing elsewhere comparable to them in size. The Egyptian records show that Egypt very early traded with communities on the east Mediterranean shore – Sinai, Lebanon, Syria – and fought against its neighbors, Libya to the west and Nubia to the south. The Sumerian records show early contact with "Kish" to the north and Elam to the east, across the Persian Gulf, and there is some evidence of a civilized state having existed on the island of Bahrain in the Persian Gulf. New archaeological material on these states (for instance, Nubia and Syria) has been gathered in recent years, and it appears that some of them must have been quite highly developed. Egypt apparently had no easy task in subduing Libya, and Elam, although smaller than Sumer, seems to have been rather similar in nature.

The picture, then, in the centuries preceding 3000 B.C., seems to be that of two large civilized centers plus a number of wealthy farming and trading societies in the West Asia-North Africa area, some of them on the verge of being civilized societies, some of them perhaps being small civilized states. The essential difference between these societies and Egypt, Sumer, and, later, the Indus Valley cities was irrigation on a scale that these smaller societies could not have approached. It was this that produced the surplus of farm produce which made it possible for Egypt, Sumer, and the Indus Valley to become large trading and manufacturing centers, concentrate population within cities, and fight off hostile peoples.

Why could farming not develop to this extent at this time without irrigation? The answer is to be found in the state of farming technology. Land in West Asia, away from a few river valleys and deltas, was similar to that of the usual European or Northern American countryside. Until a plow with a sharp and deep cutting edge, to be pulled by animals, was developed and knowledge of land renewal acquired, it was not possible to get a high and steady yield over a large area. But, in a river valley such as the Nile, the river itself each year brought down a fresh supply of nutrient soil (silt), soft and easy to work. As at the same time the river flooded over its banks into the flat surrounding plain, all that was needed were dikes with sluice gates to retain water when the flood subsided and then release it little by little.

The indication is that extensive irrigation systems arose independently in Sumer and Egypt, for the two systems were different in principle. Whereas the Nile is a comparatively slow river with long, gentle floods, the Tigris and Euphrates are swift and turbulent. A simple system of dikes and sluices was impossible for the Sumerians, who had to build and maintain an elaborate gridwork of canals. This does not, of course, mean that there could not have been influences back and forth between Sumer and Egypt and other developing communities; but in regard to "influences" in general one has to distinguish between those which affect the social foundations of a society and those which affect only its superstructure. The latter appear to be much more frequent. Nor must one regard "influence" naïvely. Influence is not a simple matter of a member of one community perceiving a process in another and returning home to spread the happy news to a receptive populace. On the contrary, influence is usually a matter of survival and comes from war or trade.

One further general question is involved: would civilization* not

---

* It would perhaps be well to insert a note on nomenclature. I use the word "civilization" for the general state of society which succeeded advanced farming society but "civilized society" or "civilized state" for a specific community. The use of civilization in conjunction with specific communities—"Egyptian civilization," "Roman civilization"—connotes an essentially cultural entity and dims the social reality. I find also that the word "civilization" is used loosely, even by anthropologists, to denote farming societies or even food-gathering societies with a farming component. There can be, however, as the word itself implies, no civilization without cities (at least there have been none so far). Such terms as "stone age," "neolithic," "bronze age," "iron age" may have some meaning for the archaeologist or anthropologist who is attempting to organize scattered and difficult data, but in a historical study they obscure the social process by exclusive emphasis upon raw materials or technology. Sometimes both kinds of error are combined, as in "the northward spread of Neolithic civilization" (Clarke, *World Prehistory*, p. 132), in reference to farming societies—which were neither neo-

have come into being at all if it had not been for the presence of irrigational rivers? Some historians seem not only to argue this but to con-
tend that civilization would not have arisen without the specific presence of the Nile, Tigris, and Euphrates, the argument being that such
later civilized states as Crete, Phoenicia, Greece, Carthage, Rome,
even India and China, could not have come into being if Sumer and
Egypt had not sent out trading offshoots which began a chain of development toward "civilizations." There is certainly some truth to this.
Sumer and Egypt did early enrich the area under consideration and
their trade doubtless had a catalytic effect in some regions. But the
large Indus Valley civilization was certainly no offshoot of Sumer or
Egypt, and the evidence, as we shall see, suggests independent developments for the Grecian, Italian, and other non-irrigational states
from advanced farming societies. Irrigation likely did not create civilization but enabled civilized states to arise some centuries earlier than
would otherwise have been possible.

THE NEW ECONOMY

The economy of food-gathering and farming societies we could
consider as a unit, but in Sumer and Egypt (the economy of both was
essentially the same) production has split into two basic and different
sections, farming and industry, and the whole has become an integrated
complex.

There had, of course, always been some division between food production and non-food-goods production; in food-gathering society
between hunting, fishing, and food-collecting on the one hand and the
making of tools, weapons, houses, household implements, and clothing
on the other; in farming society between farming and home manufacturing: spinning, weaving, pot-making, carpentry. In the new society there was, in addition to home manufacturing, professional
manufacturing—on large farms and in city shops. And in addition to
manufacturing there was what we might call extractive industry, the
production of raw materials in quarries, mines and forests. Manufacturing rose to entirely new levels and combined with industry in large
building and engineering projects. The great pyramid of Cheops, for
instance, built in about 2700 B.C., used 2.5 million blocks (6 million
tons) of stone, which took ten years to quarry. A few centuries later

---

lithic (new stone age) in any meaningful sense nor civilization. A few pages later we
come across "Neolithic peasants." Obviously there could not be "peasants" until there
was an exploitive social structure, and the farmers of advanced farming societies—which
is what is meant—had little to do with stones (*lithos*), everything to do with farming, and
were not exploited because there was no ruling class to exploit them.

an Egyptian king built a fleet of sixty ships each 167 feet long. New trades came into being (quarrying, stone cutting, brick-making, masonry, mining, smelting, blacksmithing) and old ones assumed new complexities (pot-making, carpentry, butchering, baking, brewing, weaving). Manufacturing went on in city workshops and country estates. The workshops varied in size from the large linen factories of the Pharaohs to the small smithy visited by the Sumerian hero Gilgamesh.

Early farming economy consisted of self-sufficient units, farms and villages which produced their food in the fields and their material goods by home industry. And this self-sufficing character was continued to a large degree in the rural areas of the new society. The large estates had their own workshops, and home industry continued among the peasantry on their farms and in the villages. The city-dweller, however, purchased products from a variety of sources, bread from bakeries, pots from potteries, cloth from a weaving shop, and so on. Each of these activities was dependent upon the other, and all were dependent on producing sources, the farm, the quarry, the mine, the sea.

The river Nile was alive with boats and barges (shown on the tomb walls) bearing goods for the royal treasury (taxation), for the markets of the towns, for foreign trade. Sumerian merchants travelled from the Indus Valley to Syria exchanging grain, dates, carpets, textiles, weapons and jewelry for raw materials lacking in Sumer—copper, lead, wood, and so on. It used to be generally assumed that most of this trade was by land; and archaeologists had for years attempted in vain to find the trade route between Sumer and the Indus Valley cities until it was discovered that it was not by land but by sea—from the mouth of the Tigris and Euphrates, down the Persian Gulf, with a stop at the island of Bahrain, and, then along the shore of the Arabian Sea to the mouth of the Indus. Trading houses, with branch offices and foreign connections arose. For simple and local transactions barley was the standard medium of exchange. For big business and foreign trade money was developed—the silver shekel or gold (at the rate of one to eight against silver). Credit was recognized, and merchants could go out with tablets authorizing specific accounts to be drawn. They could also borrow at interest, up to a ceiling of 33.3 percent per annum for barley, and 20 percent for silver.

OWNERSHIP OF LAND

The basic question of ownership involved land, and on this there has been some confusion, even some misrepresentation. But, although some details are obscure, the general pattern can be discerned. Legally, in Egypt, the king "owned" the land. But legal and actual ownership were not the same.

According to Flinders Petrie, the Church owned one-third of the land, the army one-third, and "husbandmen" one-third. Half of the best land in the Nile delta belonged to the Church. The army land, Petrie believed, was mainly border land which the army used for attack or defense and it was probably cultivated by the soldiers. According to this account not only did the king not own all the land, he did not own any. Furthermore, the "husbandmen" did not really own any land either, for, as Petrie informs us[1] in another passage, the "lower class" was "servile" (serfs) and "without property." And the "lower class" and the "husbandmen" must be about the same because all authorities agree that there was no substantial middle group of land owners.

"Hereditary offices and property," writes Henri Frankfort,[2] "turned the officials into landed proprietors who were no longer entirely dependent upon their function at court, although, as long as the central power remained strong, Pharaoh could cancel all rights to land or to office at any time." If Petrie is right, the land of the "husbandmen" and these hereditary landowners must overlap, for there is no other land left, the other two-thirds belonging respectively to the Church and the army. Hence, the "husbandmen's" land contained not only the land worked by small farmers but large private estates also. These estate owners clearly possessed real power, for when it came to a showdown and revolt had to be suppressed they did the suppressing.

Frankfort[3] quotes a passage from an Old Kingdom will which gives us another clue to the situation. "Him were given 50 aruras of land, from his mother's estate, when she made out a will for her children. It was handed over to him by royal decree." The mother was an "estate" owner; she could will the land of this estate to her children; but approval had to be had from the head of the State, and it was this approval which constituted royal "ownership." "The great man of a village," we learn from Petrie,[4] "could own anything from 100 to 1,000 acres;" and we read in Frankfort of a state official who owned 1,000 head of cattle, 760 asses, 2,200 goats and nearly 1,000 sheep.

The key to the problem apparently is that there were two forms of land ownership, private and State,* and each form contained elements of the other. The great estate owners really owned land; they had serf labor to work it; they could enlarge it; they could rent it out; they could will it. But they were subject to certain restrictions. The land was always nominally in the possession of the State. The State, however—

---

* State, capitalized, as I shall use it, refers to the totality of ruling institutions, as distinguished from state in the sense of "nation."

as we shall see — was simply a corporation of the great estate owners, of whom the king was one. But this was not all. These great estate owners, the "officials" of the royal government, were also high priests and generals, and, hence, they got their share also of the produce of the Church and army land. In short, they reaped profit, in one way or another, from all the land of the realm. Of the two sources of profit, however, that from the joint landowning was greater than that from the private estates, as is shown by the "immense hordes" of government officials needed to collect the peasants' taxes and from observing similar systems in modern societies (in India, for example). The Egyptian system was not an individual feudal system like the later European, in which private estates dominated the economy, but a system of State feudalism and joint landowning. (This latter system is sometimes called "landholding" rather than land owning. The term, however, implies acceptance of the legal fiction that these great landowners simply "held" the land in the name of the State.)

No thorough examination of landowning practices in Sumer seems to exist, but it is clear that in each city state the Church owned considerable land and "rented" some of it out. The king or governor (*ishakku*) owned land also, some of it presumably State land, some certainly private. The *ishakku* had extensive lands, which appear to have been worked by peasants taxed in kind. Some of these may have been his private property but most of them probably were not. For instance, when Gilgamesh, king of Erech, wished to make war he convened an "assembly of the elders of his city" to obtain their assent. Obviously these elders had power, and power must have rested largely upon land. That this land was not held mainly as private estates but owned by the government and Church as in Egypt is made likely by the fact that it was irrigated land, which normally requires collective agreements. The Church land was doubtless also worked by peasants taxed in kind (which means that they were serfs). What proportion of the land was owned by the Church and what by secular landowners we do not know. At Lagash the picture seems to have been one of secular dominance, although the Church apparently had more independence than in Egypt.

By 3000 B.C., then, in Egypt and Sumer, and by 2300 B.C. in the Indus Valley (where we find the remains of palaces and temples along with small, cramped workmen's quarters), the real power over the land had passed from the community into the hands of a small group of large landowners. The great mass of the people in these areas had, in effect, been dispossessed.

A similar situation existed also in the manufacturing section of the economy. In early farming society — as the anthropological evidence indicates—the spindles, looms, ovens, tools, and so on were operated on a family basis. Generally speaking, all farming families possessed them, and their products were family property. But the men and women who worked in the new estate workshops owned neither the shops nor the tools nor the products. Except for some small city workshops all was owned by the same small group that owned the land, occasionally as individuals but usually as the State (the "royal workshops" of Egypt, the Church workshops in Sumer). And so, too, the mines and quarries.

Thus the economy of the new societies, both agricultural and industrial, was in the hands of a group of great property owners, primarily landowners. And wherever the same kind of society arose the same general ownership pattern accompanied it—from China to Europe, from Middle America to Africa. How did the pattern arise? The patient accumulation of anthropological evidence has begun to provide the answer. Let us look, for instance, at the process as it took place among two widely separated people, the Greeks and the Aztecs. George Thomson depicts the situation in early Greek society as follows:[5]

> In early Greece this principle [of economic equality] had already been limited by the custom of reserving portions of land for the special benefit of priests, chiefs, and kings. In the plantation of Lesbos a tithe of the holdings was "set aside" for the gods. The settlers at Brea were granted the whole of the land with the exception of certain estates "set aside" for the priesthood. Similar estates were "set aside" at Kyrene for the king.

G. C. Vaillant's picture of the Aztecs[6] shows a similar general pattern:

> The tribal council divided the land among the clans, and the leaders of each, in turn, apportioned its share among the heads of families justly and equitably. Sections were also reserved for the maintenance of the chief and the temple staff, for war supplies and the payment of tribute; these were worked communally, with some amount, no doubt, of slave labour. At the death of a tenant the land passed to his sons. If he died without issue the holding reverted to the clan for re-division, as was also the case if a tenant failed to cultivate his plot for a period of two years. Such a system could work equitably and profitably for all concerned so long as a society was relatively static and plenty of arable land was at hand. However, in the Valley of Mexico inequalities developed in the system. . . . The chiefs and priests who lived off the public lands would be far better off than the ordinary citizen whose holding, generation by generation, tended to diminish.

The struggle for land, as farming society advanced, must have been a bitter one. Family and tribal units within each community must have tried to grab all that they could, and, in the interest of the whole, chiefs were given power to regulate the process. But as well as regulating general land distribution—as noted by Caesar—the community made special grants of land for government, war, and Church purposes. In time, despite the watchfulness of the primitive democracy of the community, these lands would inevitably increase in size and those of the rest of the population decline until the transition took place from mainly an economically equalitarian society to an unequal and class-divided one. By the time of the first civilized societies these processes have been distorted out of all proportion and we have a small group of government, army, and Church men owning all the land and the mass of the population dispossessed.

If we ask why farming communities began to make special grants of land the answer is that it was in their interest to do so. As farming society developed the only way to acquire more land was by war; hence, the granting of land for the maintenance of an armed force was of the utmost importance, both for defense and offense. The granting of land to the chief (government) was doubtless in good part also connected with war but, as a community expanded, government functions would also expand and land was needed to maintain their functionaries. And land was given to the Church because, as we shall see, the Church rendered a number of services to the community and its secular rulers. This concentration of land in the hands of government (king), army, and Church seems to have existed in all emerging civilized states. That Sumer and Egypt went through the same general process is clear from the end-result. Just how or by what stages they went through it we do not know, but in them the process must have been affected by irrigation and the nature of the terrain. In irrigated land the interests of one landowner are the interests of all. If one landowner up-river fails to maintain his irrigation system, all below him suffer. If part of the irrigation system is captured in war the whole can be affected. (In the Sumerian wars we find that such capture was, in fact, used to subdue a rival state.) A flat river valley terrain is open to attack as a whole; one lord cannot (as in Persia or Japan) hold out in a mountain fastness; all fight together or perish together. Finally, a river brings all parts of a territory within easier reach of a central authority. Hence, the development in Egypt and Sumer of the pattern of primarily State rather than private landownership. With landownership went industrial ownership —of the forests, quarries, and mines. This tended also, from the beginning, to give a great landowner cast to manufacturing and trade, although small manufacturers and merchants also came into being— doubtless springing from the craftsmen and traders of farming society villages.

SOCIAL LIFE

The best way to get a general concept of early civilized societies is, again, to visit a good museum. As we enter the Metropolitan Museum's Egyptian section we are faced by the reconstruction of the chambers of a tomb of an Egyptian official of about 2500 B.C. From a small scale model of the whole we can tell that it was a large and magnificent structure. On the walls are paintings showing long lines of servants carrying food and other offerings to the master. Another painting shows (below) men preparing a banquet and (above) servants waiting on guests, for whom other servants play dinner music. In a second room the eye is caught by two statues, one of a "foreign captive" with his arms bound behind his back, the other of a "Granary overseer." A frieze on the wall depicts two companies of soldiers marching into battle. Another frieze depicts the privately owned cattle of King Cheops (for whom the Great Pyramid was built). In a third room is the model of a boat taken from a tomb. It is rowed by eighteen oarsmen while in the bow, "smelling a lotus flower and listening to a singer," the owner reclines. Further down the room is a case containing a model of a slaughter house. Seven men are at work (butchering an ox); two men are supervising, each with a kind of short spear in his hand. One of them is holding the point of the spear behind the neck of one of the workers.

In order to appreciate the significance of what has happened, we should go back to the First Egyptian Room and look again at the humble tools of the early farmers of Merimde. We have moved in two thousand years from subsistence farming to a wealthy farming-manufacturing economy, from village life to estate and city life, from general economic equality to inequality, from a society without social classes into one whose life is dominated by them.

Sumer and Egypt, in spite of the rise of trade and cities, still had mainly agricultural economies; and the great bulk of their work was farm work. This farm work was performed by peasant labor taxed "in kind" (a portion of the peasants' produce was seized by the government or the church). A second major form of labor was "forced labor," used for building, construction, upkeep of the irrigation system, and so on (the peasants had to work for specified periods as slaves on projects assigned to them by the government, the church, or the army). The Cheops pyramid, it has been estimated, employed a labor force of 100,000 men for twenty years, working three months a year.

Although most of the labor in these civilizations was peasant labor or forced labor there were also slaves. "Slaves," according to Margaret

Murray,[7] "were common to all periods." Petrie[8] notes that a first dynasty pharaoh captured 120,000 men in a war against Libya and that a twentieth dynasty pharaoh gave 113,433 men slaves to the temples. In Sumer, prisoners of war were kept as slaves, and the temple employed a large number of women slaves. In contrast to this mass of State-owned slaves there seem in the centuries around 3000 B.C. to have been comparatively few privately owned slaves; but later, as wealth increased, we find some households with twenty or more slaves and rich fathers willing three, four, or five slaves to their daughters as part of their dowry. In the Royal Tombs of Ur (about 2300 B.C.) the bodies of slaves of the royal estate were found slaughtered in sacrifice to their dead masters; one grave alone contained the bones of fifty-nine slaves. How many of the slaves were war captives we do not know, but it must have been a large proportion, for the Sumerian ideograph for a man slave was "male of a foreign land," and that for a woman slave was "woman from the mountains" (Sumer was on the plains).

In Egypt there was no mass enslavement of the men of the native people by its own ruling class; rather the great majority of the male slaves seem to have been foreign captives. Women slaves seem to have been household servants, and although some of these were certainly foreign, there seem to have been too many of them for this to have been more than a minor proportion. The pattern of mainly native women but mainly foreign men slaves we find later in Asia, the Mediterranean area, and elsewhere.

In addition to peasant labor, forced labor, and slave labor, there was also the paid labor of craftsmen. In a later period these craftsmen — carpenters, tanners, masons, furriers, jewelers, weavers, potters, and so on — sometimes had slaves to work with them and this may have been true in this earlier period also. (We read of paid linen weavers who had slave assistants in the third century B.C.) The status of craftsmen was rigidly set; they were, in effect, frozen into trade castes with no hope of rising above them (as was true also in later feudal societies in Asia).

If we now put these strands of evidence together the following picture emerges: (a) the peasants' farm labor on a tax-in-kind basis provided the food supply for the society; (b) the peasants' "forced labor" maintained the irrigation system, constructed State buildings and did some quarrying, mining, and manufacturing; (c) the slave labor of women maintained the estate households, that of men was used in the estate workshops and some city workshops and probably in mines, forests, quarries, and in transportation; (d) the only paid labor was apparently that of skilled artisans and was a very small proportion of the total labor of the society. In the Egyptian economy, then, almost all labor was unpaid and the proportion of slaves was small compared to the number of peasants. It was neither primarily a slave society nor an individual-estate feudal society but was based on centralized exploitation of the peasantry as taxed peasants on the land and as forced laborers.

The most appropriate name for such a system that I have encountered is one inherent in a comment by Margaret Murray,[9] that the peasant was "merely a serf under the state." The system could appropriately be called "State feudalism." Its main social classes were slaves, peasants, merchants and craftsmen, great landowners. There was probably not by this time – as there was to be later – a separate class of professionals. The large landowners included, as we have seen, the heads of the government, of the Church and of the army, most of whom were also private landowners, "great men of the village" with their own estates. Some merchants apparently had small workshops but the main business incentive came from trade profits and not manufacturing profits; moreover, extensive or foreign trade was under the dominance of the government or the Church. The professionals must have been mainly government, army, and Church officials (generals, priests, tax gatherers, judges, lower rank army officers) and were also landowners, although in Sumer, as we shall see, some of them seem to have been connected with the merchants.

Although each of these classes had a central core of identity each also obviously overlapped to some degree with others. Thus, in general social terms, the great landholders and the wealthy merchants formed the "upper classes"; the peasants, slaves, and craftsmen formed the "lower classes"; and there was even a small "middle class" of some poorer merchants and professionals and possibly a few small, independent farmers. Society in Egypt and Sumer had been split essentially into two worlds.

Along with the new, much of the old, of course, continued. Society still consisted of men and women, of families, of individuals and the relationships between them. But the new cut across the old, cracking and distorting its patterns. The social status of women, for instance, was now basically class-determined. Whether a woman was a peasant or a princess was more important in determining her life style than whether she was a woman. In both Sumer and Egypt the laws which were the special concern of the husband-wife relationship generally favored the husband, but women were not without rights. For instance, in Egypt[10] "the husband could dismiss his wife without compensation if he detected her in adultery," but "if he divorced her for other reasons he was required to turn over to her a substantial share of the family property." The only professions open to women were those of priestess and (at least in Egypt) doctor, both of them perhaps outgrowths of the woman shaman, who had both religious and healing functions.

Peasant women, like peasant men, had no property. Men and women worked together in the fields (as we can see in Egyptian paintings), much as they must have done in early farming society, with this difference, that they were now working in the fields of the landowning class and not in community-owned fields. Both were exploited economically. However, as we have seen, native women of the lower classes were enslaved while men were not. What is often glossed over is that these women slaves were automatically the sexual instruments of their masters; a new social phenomenon, namely sexual exploitation, enters the human story with the establishment of civilized society. Women were traded like cattle. We hear of an Egyptian king receiving a gift of three hundred women. Prostitution arose and soon flourished, especially in the Church (the "temple prostitute").

Although on the whole these phenomena resulted in a deterioration of the status of women, they resulted also, for the first time, in the social and cultural elevation of a small group of women above the majority of men: the women of the upper classes above the men of the lower classes. Furthermore male dominance in general did not assume the extreme forms in early Egypt and perhaps in Sumer that it later did. Women were not secluded in Egypt as they were later in Asian and other civilizations. As Durant notes:[11] "The monuments picture them eating and drinking in public, going about their affairs in the street unattended, and freely engaging in industry and trade [in small shops or the marketplace]. Greek travelers were later amazed at the liberties allowed to women in Egypt."

The new society, for all its oppression and servility, marked a big step forward. "The division [of society into classes]," Childe writes,[12] "is typified for the archaeologist by the contrast between the overpowering magnificence of royal tombs and the simplicity of private graves in Egypt or by that between the luxurious houses of merchants and the hovels of artisans in an Indus city. As compared to these the graves in a pre-dynastic cemetery or the huts in a neolithic village reveal equality, albeit equality in squalor." The economic changes which brought about class divisions gave a degree of wealth, dignity, power, and vigor for the few that none had previously experienced.

When we consider these two divergent aspects, exploitation, degradation, and oppression on the one hand, and the advance in upper class life on the other, it is easy to see how by placing the emphasis one way or the other one can give a one-sided impression. Particularly does this seem to be done in regard to Sumer, whose champions seem curiously protective, usually giving a glowing picture of a happy, bustling "democratic" society and (except for some muted undertones) conveniently forgetting the situation of the mass of the population.

POLITICAL LIFE

The word political, as I have indicated, I use in its broad sense — to denote the overall direction and rule of society. In the first civilized societies this embraces not only the government but also the army, the Church, and the legal system (including the police), a totality of ruling institutions generally known as the State. The State cannot, as Will Durant[13] and others seem to think, have arisen from deliberate decision: "Men decided that it was better to pay taxes than to fight among themselves; better to pay tribute to one magnificent robber than to bribe them all." Like social phenomena in general, the State must have developed as part of an integrated sociocultural process. Its regulatory functions grew with the growth of farming surplus and trade, its oppressive functions — physical and ideological — with the development of classes, its military functions with economic expansion and competition between communities. Deliberate decisions were certainly made, and some of them were perhaps crucial for certain local developments, but the whole was governed by forces beyond social control.

The political divisions of Egypt followed its economic divisions into irrigation districts. There were about twenty such districts averaging 230 square miles apiece with a population up to 100,000 each and ruled by a provincial governor and officials appointed by the king (pharaoh). The central government consisted of two main departments, Agriculture and the Exchequer (headed by the royal Treasurer). The government, acting through the Ministry of Agriculture, exercised a dictatorial central control over every detail of agricultural production. The farmer was told what to grow and how much to grow, and at least one-fifth of his produce was taken from him as tax. Everything was taxed — crops, animals, wool, trees, canals, textiles, leatherwork, oil — and the government had the right to buy the remaining four-fifths of a farmer's produce at its own fixed price. The taxes were sometimes collected by force, as a contemporary account tells us:[14]

And now the scribe lands on the river bank and is about to register the harvest tax. The janitors carry staves and the Nubians (policemen) rods of palm, and they say, "Hand over the corn," though there is none. The cultivator is beaten all over, he is bound and thrown into the well, soused, and dipped head downwards. His wife has been bound in his presence, his children are in fetters. His neighbors abandon him and are fled.

Whether the taxes of a particular individual were collected by force or not, the threat of such force was constantly present. Tomb wall paintings of peasants coming to pay their rent or taxes show an overseer with a whip. To collect these taxes the government employed "immense hordes" of officials.[15]

What were the taxes used for? Some of them were used for the upkeep and development of the irrigation system. If, however, they had been used mainly for that or allied purposes, there would have been little need for police coercion. Most of them went into the upkeep of the estates and palaces with their innumerable retinues, into royal and aristocratic tombs, into the army, into the coffers of provincial governors, into the maws of the official "hordes." The pyramids form a material monument to the system, for the workers who built them were fed during their three months of annual forced labor from the produce (taxes in kind) which had come from their labor as peasants in the other nine months.

When the interests of the great landowners happened to coincide with those of other classes, the government worked in their interests also, but in a secondary and peripheral way. Its basic function was to seize part of the peasant's produce, but it also kept the merchants in check and maintained a government control over trade. The nature of government, that is to say, had changed. It no longer represented the community interest, as it did in food-gathering and early-type farming societies, but one section of the community only; and this change must have begun in advanced farming society with the development of economic inequalities and social classes. Finally, as anyone familiar with Asian history will recognize, this form of government, established in Egypt in the centuries preceding 3000 B.C., became general in Asian and other feudal societies.

Associated with the government in Egypt (and elsewhere) were the two other great landholding forces, the church and the army. The army was immense. The first available figure, of about 1300 B.C., indicates an army of 650,000 men out of a total population of 12 million. Doubtless, as in later such states also, this huge armed force was for domestic as well as foreign use.

In early Sumer there was no single central government but a number of city states strung up and down the Tigris and Euphrates, each having a population of ten to twenty thousand and subdivided into communities of about a thousand, each one to some degree economically regulated by a temple. In addition to the temples each state also had its palaces with a hereditary governor or king.

There seems, at least in some states, to have been a struggle for power between the governor and the church. In Lagash the governor at one time seized the church lands. "The oxen of the gods [i.e., of the church]," a Sumerian church historian lamented,[16] "plowed the *ishakku*'s onion patches," which "were located in the god's best fields." In this Lagash struggle, the merchants apparently supported the church, for when the governor oppressed the church he seems to have oppressed the merchants as well. The upshot seems to have been that the merchants and the church joined forces to overthrow the old regime and establish a ruler of their own in his place. This ruler, we hear, brought about reforms, for instance (in the words of a Sumerian historian):

> The house of the lowly man was next to the house of a "big man," and the "big man" said to him, "I want to buy it from you." If, when he (the "big man") was about to buy it from him, the lowly man said, "pay me as much as I think fair," and then he ("the big man") did not buy it, that "big man" must not "take it out" on the lowly man.

The "lowly man" was not, we might note, a peasant or slave, but a merchant or a moderately wealthy landowner. In fact "the poor man" in Sumerian and other texts always means a middle class man. The real poor, slaves and peasants, were assumed to be outside the pale of humanity.

Whether a parliament or congress existed in all Sumerian states we do not know. We hear of no parliament during these disputes at Lagash. But there was a parliament of some kind at Erech. When, as we have seen, Gilgamesh wished to make war against Kish, he first put the proposal before "the convened assembly of the elders of his city" and when the elders turned him down he went before "the convened assembly of the fighting men," where his proposal was accepted.

These differences in political structure between Sumer and Egypt may derive ultimately from the fact that Egypt had raw materials, stone, metals, wood, and so on, either within or near its boundaries, but Sumer lacked them. Hence, while in Egypt the great landowners dominated everything, in Sumer there seems to have been a strong and independent merchant class. Some of these merchants may also have been farmers and rented land and farm animals from the temples.

In both Egypt and Sumer there were regular law courts, both local courts and higher courts. And, at least in Sumer, there was a written code, of which only fragments have so far been discovered, but the later famed Babylonian code of Hammurabi (about 1700 B.C.) embodies earlier law and doubtless reflects similar codes in Sumer. In fact, its similarity to still later codes of similar societies in India and elsewhere—which also must have early roots—indicates a general phenomenon for this type of society. Hammurabi's code had, in effect, three different sections, one to apply to the upper classes, one to the middle, and one to the lower. The usual penalty for upper class crimes was a fine, for the middle class, fines or (for debt) servitude, for the lower class death or torture. Death was the penalty for stealing, for buying or selling stolen goods, and for assisting fugitive slaves. Corporal punishment, including mutilation, was common and reserved mainly for the lower classes; a slave who struck a freeman had an ear cut off; a man who attacked a social superior was whipped (sixty strokes of an ox-hide whip). In Egypt penalties were similarly severe. For the great mass of the population—peasants and slaves—the legal system was not and was not intended to be for the redress of grievances but for terroristic punishment. As for the middle class, an early Egyptian document put the matter succinctly:[17] "The poor man [i.e., as usual, the man of middle income] has no strength to save himself from him that is stronger than he."

The army was used to wage war and put down rebellion. Rebellions were of two kinds, those of upper class groups and those of the peasantry, the first aiming at a reshuffling of power within the State, the second at the destruction of the State. War has not, as we sometimes hear, "always" existed. In fact it is—if we consider the total history of humanity—a comparatively recent phenomenon. In early food-gathering society, to judge by later such societies, there was doubtless feuding and fighting but nothing one could call warfare. War begins in farming society with large-scale fighting over land and animal herds. Lands and herds were seized and prisoners enslaved. The earliest war of which we have actual record was a war for land (i.e., for peasant labor), that between Upper and Lower (Delta) Egypt, the war which unified the kingdom. It is recorded on King Narmer's votive macehead and a slate palette (of about 3000 B.C.). The palette depicts, on one side, the Pharaoh killing the king of north Egypt, and tells us that he has captured 120,000 prisoners; on the other side, it depicts a series of bound and headless captives. The second recorded war—the beginning of a long tradition—was fought over the copper mines of Sinai. A sculptured rock in Sinai shows the Egyptian king "smiting a Bedawy chief, signifying that the military escort had to fight for the possession of the mines."[18] How savage were the Sumerian wars we can see in an early poem on the destruction of Ur (quoted below on page 79). One early war was waged (by Akkad against Elam) to get control of silver mines.

What, finally, of the church? It seems strange at first glance that the church should be associated with the government, the army, and the legal system in political functioning, but in food-gathering society a similar relative position existed between the chief and the shaman, the chief who was the social ancestor of the king and the shaman of the head priest. Even in early farming society, the anthropological evidence indicates, the shaman had developed into the priest; in later farming society a church organization supporting a large group of priests emerged (as shown by the early Sumerian temple remains of about 4000 B.C.). Even then the church, as in observed advanced farming societies, was doubtless closely associated with the government. Wherein lay the political power of the church?

Although Sumer and Egypt had constructed magnificent cities, set up governments, armies, and law, their peasantry and slaves had no more control over natural or social forces than did food-gathering peoples. Farm land and irrigation systems could be destroyed by drought, storm or flood:[19]

> The rampant flood which no man can oppose,
> Which shakes the heavens and causes earth to tremble,
> In an appalling blanket folds mother and child,
> Beats down the canebrake's full luxuriant greenery,
> And drowns the harvest in its time of ripeness.

The people were still ravaged by periodic plagues and famines. Poverty, disease, and death were the peasants' constant companions, their intestines riddled with debilitating worms and bacteria, their skin and hair plagued by lice (as in similar societies today). To these evils were added those of exploitation, oppression, and war, social evils they had no more control over than natural ones. And although, as also with peasants in later similar societies, they doubtless faced these evils with courage and resisted as they could, they must, nevertheless, have lived on the black edge of terror. It is easy to speak condescendingly of the "superstition" of the peasantry. But they could hardly not be superstitious. And superstition became an element for rule, the particular element of the church in the State.

CULTURE AND SOCIETY

As I have indicated, I find the catchall use of "culture" to signify the whole of the sociocultural process of society incorrect and confusing. The general social process I consider to embrace the economic, social, and political aspects of society, and of the two I consider the general social process as primary and the cultural as secondary. This is the attitude also of most standard anthropological studies of food-gathering and farming societies. Hunting rituals arise from the hunt, grain gods from farming, and so on. But when we come to the historians of Sumer and Egypt we begin to find some ambiguity (and in the historians of later society even more).

As a simple example of a sociocultural process let us consider the development of metallurgy. The technological basis for metallurgy was, as we have seen, laid by previous processes, those of baking and pottery in particular. The basic drive to metallurgy was also social (essentially economic)—to make better tools and weapons. But the metallurgist's furnace—using charcoal and a forced draft—could not have arisen out of this drive if the potter's oven had not already been in existence. Thus the metallurgist's furnace arose out of three factors, a socioeconomic drive, a material basis, and technological knowledge. But all three were not of equal generative importance: the knowledge was dependent upon the economic drive to bring it into existence, and the material basis set the limits to its development; the material basis itself grew from a previous social need. Knowledge, although creative, is socially derivative and limited in its scope.

It may be argued that while this derivative and limited creativity holds for knowledge it does not hold for ideas, but ideas clearly arise in the same way as knowledge does, namely, *via* the senses and through activity and thought in a given society. We could no more have had Darwin's theory in ancient Sumer than airplanes.

Art is also based upon experience. Its content derives from both the specific factors of a particular society (portraits of Dutch burghers) and the general factors of any society (family life). Its form derives from the aesthetic sense, which is as much a part of the human mind as was the potter's capacity for knowledge, but even the most imaginative soarings of the "mind in creation" are syntheses of experience in a specific society. Sumer gave us *Gilgamesh* but it could not have given us *Hamlet*.

KNOWLEDGE: WRITING, MATHEMATICS, SCHOOLS

One of the great advances of knowledge in the first civilized societies was the development of a written language. The prime river of language through the ages, existing for tens of thousands of years before writing, has been that of spoken language. Written language is a secondary and derivative phenomenon, a method of recording spoken language, its rules of grammar being essentially a codification of spoken forms. In food-gathering and early farming societies the speech of each community must (as in such societies today) have been common to the community. But in all class-divided societies upper class speech differs from lower class speech in vocabulary, grammar, and pronunciation, and becomes a major mark of class distinction. Little by little a standard, upper class speech, the speech of the great landholders, must have risen to dominance in Egypt and Sumer (as it did in Rome).

Writing is found on jars and other objects in the earliest Egyptian tombs; and this writing has already developed somewhat beyond the simple pictographic stage. In Sumer we can trace in more detail the development of writing from pictures to symbols, some of which are sound (phonetic) and not sight (graphic) representations. But, once again, we are less sure of the Sumerian than of the Egyptian dates. It may be that similar development took place independently in both areas and perhaps in others also (as it apparently did later among the Chinese or the Mayas) for it would seem natural for the first writing to be pictographic and then to be changed step by step into formalized signs as more demands were made upon it. These demands were, at first, primarily economic. In Egypt, for instance, painted texts on pots in first dynasty tombs give the contents of the pot and the name of the owner. In Sumer, according to Frankfort, "The earliest tablets, found in the temple at Erech, were memoranda — aids for the running of the temple as the production centre warehouse, and workshop of the community."[20]

Writing, then, was not a "spiritual" creation but grew out of the social needs of the new society. Commodities had to be labelled; increased production necessitated stock lists; business required accountancy and legal arrangements. These matters had become too complex to be trusted to memory or transacted on the basis of oral agreements. And they must have become so before civilized states arose in Egypt and Sumer. It was only after it was first developed for these practical purposes that writing became an instrument for literary, religious, or scholarly expression.

Mathematics, unlike language, cannot develop without being graphically recorded. Early efforts at such recording have only recently been recognized in the discovery that certain markings on bone of some food-gathering peoples of perhaps 30,000 years ago represent a crude attempt at a calendar. In early farming society, as we have seen, the necessities of life must have demanded a great increase in mathematical knowledge. In later farming society, problems must have arisen requiring mathematics of quite a high order: for instance the mathematics required in the construction of the early Sumerian village temples. There does not, however, seem to be any record of written mathematics until civilization came into being. The Sumerian tablets indicate that it grew up with written language and for similar reasons: mathematics was required in the new manufacturing and industrial processes, such as mining, quarrying, building, ship-building. The pyramids required intricate and exact calculations. The Egyptians not only measured the area of squares and circles but the cubic content of cylinders and spheres. With the development of trade, farmers and merchants had to use the same weights and measures; temple builders and stone quarriers had to employ the same linear and cubic measurements. More accurate measurements of time became necessary, especially for agricultural purposes. A calendar dividing the year into ten months of thirty-six days plus five "intercalary" days had been developed in Egypt before 3000 B.C.

Another large area of knowledge was that associated with the new social and political developments, for instance, the knowledge required by the estate overseer, provincial governor, priest, general, or judge. There was some advance also in the knowledge of the human body and medicine, particularly in Egypt, in part as a result of embalming. It was recognized—just how early is not clear—that the brain controlled the lower limbs and that the heart was the center of the circulatory system, but the actual circulatory mechanism was unknown. Surgery—practiced in crude form in food-gathering societies—developed; stones were removed from the urinary bladder and amputations performed. Along with these advances, however, magic continued (lizard's blood and incantations). The necessities of agriculture, trade, and navigation led to systematic observations of the stars. The calendar was based on the "heliacal rising" of the star Sirius. Particular knowledge began to crystallize into general knowledge—for the few but not for the many. In early Egypt we hear only of "palace schools," and these were restricted to the sons of the great landowners. A study made in 1946[21] established that school graduates in Sumer were the sons of "governors, 'city fathers,' ambassadors, temple administrators," and other high officials. No women's names appear in the student lists, but it seems probable that some upper class women—as later in similar societies—acquired some education at home. The mass of the population, however, was shut off from the new knowledge. A slave could pull an oar but he could not build a ship; a soldier could hurl a spear but he could not plan a battle.

IDEAS: COSMOLOGY, SOCIAL VIEWS

With the coming of the first civilized societies we have for the first time written records of the ideas of people, and it is no longer neces-

sary to rely only on reconstruction by coordinating ancient archaeological remains with modern anthropological observations. This latter
method, however, cannot be entirely discarded. Because these records are written they were not the work of the (nonliterate) peasants
and slaves, and if we wish to find something of the outlook of the majority of the population we still have to examine later societies of a
similar nature.

The ideas in the Sumerian records on the basic philosophical problem of the earth and its origins may conveniently be gathered from two
early poems. The first, part of the Gilgamesh material, runs as follows:[22]

> After heaven had been moved away from earth,
> After earth had been separated from heaven,
> After the name of man had been fixed,
> After An carried off the heaven,
> After Enlil carried off the earth. . . .

The second is similar:[23]

When a sky above had not (yet even) been mentioned
(And) the name of firm ground below had not (yet even) been thought of;
(When) only primeval Apsu, their begetter,
And Mummu and Ti amat — she who gave birth to them all —
Were mingling their waters in one;
When no bog had formed (and) no island could be found;
Had been named by name, had been determined as to (his) lot,
Then were gods formed within them.

In spite of the reference to the gods the explanation in both fragments is essentially rational and materialistic; before there were any
gods there was a primeval sea or chaos from which both earth and sky
arose. As Thorkild Jacobsen has pointed out, the second poem appears to reflect the kind of clearing of alluvial land for the extensive
irrigation which was necessary in the river delta of Sumer — where
river and sea mingled "their waters in one." But whatever the origin
of the concept, it seems apparent that we have in Sumer the beginnings of philosophy (as distinct from theology).

No one of the gods or goddesses had absolute power. The Sumerians, like the Greeks, had an assembly of great gods, with An as
chairman (really a kind of elder statesman). The executive secretary
of the gods was named Enki, who like Enlil was a "son" of An. Enki
had charge — among other matters — of irrigation projects. In general

Enlil decreed and Enki executed. In addition to these and the other gods and goddesses of the Assembly there were several lesser gods — city gods, temple gods, personal and household gods (as in feudal China or Roman Italy). Both the "great gods" and the personal gods were besought for divine intervention in their various spheres of activity, for rain, for a good harvest, for the safety of the city, for personal success. Along with prayer went magic. Images of an individual were destroyed to injure him (again a concept going back into food-gathering society).

In Egypt also we find both philosophy and theology. Let us take a passage from the *Book of the Dead* on Re-Atum the creator god:

> I am Atum when I was alone in Nun (the primordial waters); I am Rē in his (first) appearances, when he began to rule that which he had made. What does that mean? This "Rē when he began to rule that which he had made" means that Rē began to appear as a king, as one who existed before (the air-god) Shū had (even) lifted (heaven from earth), when he (Rē) was on the primeval hillock which was in Hermopolis.

Behind this, one might assume, was essentially the same concept as the Sumerian of the earth arising from chaos, a mingling of land, water, and sky. But the emphasis is more religious and less rationalistic than the Sumerian. The creator god, himself, the text goes on to explain, was self-created and then created the other gods.

According to another Egyptian school of thought the creator was not Atum but Ptah. The concept of Ptah (the worship of whom goes back to the earliest days of Egyptian civilized society) includes the essence of later idealistic philosophy including that of Hinduism and Platonism — the concept of matter arising from a cosmic creative mind-force which is also diffused through all things.

Egyptian theology was basically the same as the Sumerian. There was a god of the sky (Horus), of the sun (Ra), of the earth and agriculture (Osiris), of the wind (Shu), and several hundred lesser gods. Although the Egyptian and Sumerian gods and their functions were essentially the same, there was one significant difference between them — the Egyptian gods existed in a celestial bureaucracy similar to that of the Egyptian state, without an assembly. We also find in Egypt a prototype of later religious wars, a struggle between the worshippers of Horus and of Set. When the Horus people were in command, Set became the devil; when the Set people won, Set displaced Horus as the royal deity. In the end the Horus people triumphed and Horus reigned secure.

In considering these various beliefs we have to remember how limited the intellectual horizons of humanity were at the time. The

Sumerian and Egyptian records speak of the origin of the earth and sky. But even the educated knew no more of the earth than their immediate river valleys and the seas and mountains beyond, little more, that is to say, than food-gathering peoples in North America at the same time knew. They conceived of this small section of the earth as a kind of shallow bowl; and above this bowl was the "inverted bowl" of the sky, with its traveling bright light by day and its lesser lights by night. They traced the paths of the stars but they did not know what the stars were; they worked with matter but they had no understanding of the nature of matter; they walked the earth but they did not know the earth was a planet; they charted time but they did not know what caused the seasons.

The views of the early Egyptian upper classes on the nature and functions of society do not seem to have been recorded, and in Sumer we find no extended expression of them but there are some revealing fragments in the form of satiric fables and proverbs, for instance:[24]

> The lion had caught a "bush"-pig and proceeded to bite him, saying: "Up until now, your flesh has not filled my mouth, but your squeals have created a din in my ears!"

> The pork butcher slaughters the pig, saying: "Must you squeal? This is the road which your sire and your grandsire traveled, and now you are going on it too! (And yet) you are squealing!"

> > You go and carry off the enemy's land;
> > The enemy comes and carries off your land.

> > The poor man is better dead than live;
> > If he has bread, he has not salt,
> > If he has salt, he has no bread,
> > If he has meat, he has no lamb,
> > If he has a lamb, he has no meat.

> > Not all the households of the poor are equally
> > submissive.

This last, as Kramer remarks, indicates "a certain degree of class consciousness."

Brief and fragmented though the record is, it is suggestive. If for Renaissance Italy we had but one picture by Leonardo, one piece of sculpture by Michelangelo, and one bronze by Cellini, we could not avoid perceiving that they must be representatives of a culture of a high level. So, too, with these Sumerian fragments. Those who devised and laughed over these fables, with their compact wit, would have been at home in the intellectual circles of Athens or Florence or New York. The intellect which created the pig and butcher story could in another age have written *Candide*. In brief, a new phenomenon has arisen in human history, the formation of a group of intellectuals. Some of them were doubtless allied with the landowners but others were clearly close to those merchants and professionals who suffered oppression at the hands of the wealthy and often viewed their situation with cynical helplessness but sometimes revolted (as at Lagash). The situation in some Sumerian cities was apparently similar to that of Athens 2,500 years later, in which political conflict between well-matched opposing classes churned up society and provided both freedom and inspiration.

Art

As one stands in the main Egyptian hall of New York's Metropolitan Museum the massiveness of its statuary gives a sense of the greatness of ancient Egypt beyond that conveyed by historical narrative. But this massiveness is, in a way, misleading, for if we also examine the nearby wall paintings, we find that Egyptian art could handle color and design as delicately as could the Chinese (some 1,500 years later). In fact some of it is rather reminiscent of the Chinese. Sumerian art has a beauty of its own, at once delicate and bizarre — in the intricate gold jewelry of the "Gold Bull's Head" or the brightly colored "Ram Caught in the Thicket" from the Ur tombs, and in the strange and somehow mobile figures on the cylinder seals. There had never been art of this quality — both Egyptian and Sumerian — so far as we know, in the world before. Even the best art of food-gathering or farming societies, fine though they were — the cave paintings of France or early Iranian pottery — cannot compare with this in depth and scope and beauty. It is as though we had come out into a new kind of country, from soft hills to great mountains.

When we turn to literature, however, the difference between the Egyptian and the Sumerian is considerable. Whereas early Egyptian literature is largely either religious dogma, as in the *Book of the Dead*, or light, romantic narrative, the Sumerian is a literature of ideas, imaginative and free in scope. Early Egyptian art, in fact, avoids ideas, especially critical ones.

The roots of these differences must lie in the economic, social, and political differences between the two societies which we have already surveyed, the commercialism and political conflict of the Sumerian cities, the centralized Egyptian great landowners' State, differences which were reflected also in the theological concepts of the Egyptian divine oligarchy and the Sumerian "Assembly" of the gods.

Gilgamesh

The most important literary work of these early societies is the epic *Gilgamesh,* the first written masterpiece of world literature.

The historical figure Gilgamesh was, as we have seen, a Sumerian king of the city of Erech (Uruk). Several poems were written about his feats in Sumerian times, but the epic as we now possess it, on twelve tablets, is Babylonian and was apparently put together about 2000 B.C., partly from earlier sources (some of which have survived) and partly from later ones. Comparing the two with each other and with other Sumerian poems we can see that the basic elements of style and content were Sumerian. Even in its later recension, we might note, it comes at least a thousand years before Homer or Solomon and several centuries before the *Rig-Vedas.* (I use the translation by my old teacher, William Ellery Leonard, who was himself a poet.)

The poem opens with the complaint of the people of Uruk against Gilgamesh. He is working them too hard to build the walls of the city. In order to exert some control over him the god An (chairman of the Assembly of the gods) calls Aruru, who made Gilgamesh, and tells her to create another man of equal strength to keep him in check. Aruru creates Engidu, a wild man, his body shaggy with hair, who lives in the desert with the beasts, drinking with them at their drinking holes: "he knew naught of land and people." Gilgamesh, at Uruk, instead of going to fight with Engidu, decides to have him tamed by a priestess of the temple. The priestess and a hunter go to a watering hole and find Engidu:

> "There he is, woman!
> loosen thy buckle,
> unveil thy delight,
> that he may take his fill of thee!
> hang not back, take up his lust!
> when he sees thee he will draw near.
> open thy robe that he may rest upon thee!
> arouse in him rapture, the work of woman.
> then will he become a stranger to his wild beasts,
> who on the steppes grew up with him.
> his bosom will press against thee."

> then the priestess loosened her buckle,
> unveiled her delight,
> for him to take his fill of her.
> she hung not back, she took up his lust,
> she opened her robe that he rest upon her.
> she aroused in him rapture the work of woman.
> his bosom pressed against her.
> Engidu forgot where he was born.
> for six days and seven nights
> was Engidu given over to love with the priestess.
> when he had sated himself with the fill of her,
> he raised up his face to his wild ones,
> at the sight of Engidu, the gazelles flee away,
> the wild of the field shrink back before him.
> then Engidu marvelled,
> his body stood as in a spell,
> his knees quivered, because his wild ran off . . .
> the speed of his onset is not what it was.
> he harkens and opens his ear:
> he turns about and sits at the feet of the priestess.
> he looks the priestess in the face,
> and to what the priestess now speaks
> his ears give heed.
>
> the priestess says to him, to Engidu:
> "Engidu, how beautiful thou art, how like a god!
> why must thou rush with animals over the steppes?
> come, I will lead thee into ramparted Uruk,
> to a pure house, the dwelling of Anu and Ishtar,
> where Gilgamesh lives, matchless in mind. . . ."

(There is perhaps meaning in these passages beyond what appears on the surface, possibly that city dwellers should blend their qualities with those of the people of the plains. Perhaps it contains traces of an early myth of the civilizing of man by woman.)

The priestess takes Engidu to Gilgamesh. They fight, but soon become friends. Gilgamesh asks Engidu to go with him to slay Khumbaba, a monster living in a cedar forest beyond the mountains.

> "My friend, let us call the workers;
> in our sight shall they cast us hatchets."

> they went and called the workers.
> there sit the masters, setting the time:
> they cast hatchets,
> they cast heavy axes,
> they cast great daggers.

The two warriors travel far to the forest. After a long struggle the heroes are victorious. They then fight with and kill a ferocious bull set upon them by the goddess of war, Inanna. After this fight, Engidu, apparently for his part in destroying this "heavenly" bull, is doomed by the gods. With the death of Engidu the second part of the poem opens, one rather different in mood and tempo, its theme the mystery and inevitability of death. Gilgamesh, who previously had thought of death only in a general way, now sees it as a personal tragedy:

> "what kind of sleep is this
> that hath now seized upon thee?
> dark is thy look,
> and thine ears take not my voice!"
> Gilgamesh touched him on the heart,
> but the heart beats no more.
> then he covered up his friend like a bride.

Gilgamesh, frightened, goes to Siduri, cup-bearer to the gods:

> "my friend, whom I love,
> hath turned into earth.
> must not I too, as he,
> lay me down
> and rise not up again
> for ever and for ever?" . . .

> the cup bearer, she says to Gilgamesh:
> "Gilgamesh, whether runnest thou?
> life, which thou seekest, thou wilt not find.
> When the gods created mankind,
> they allotted to mankind Death,
> but life they withheld in their own hands.
> So, Gilgamesh, fill thy body,
> make merry day and night,
> keep each day a feast of rejoicing!
> day and night leap and have thy delight!
> put on clean raiment,

> wash thy head and bathe thee in water,
> look cheerily at the child who holdest thy hand,
> and may thy wife have joy in thy arms!"

Uncomforted, Gilgamesh goes on a search for eternal life. He receives a plant which will give him such life but he is careless and it is devoured by a snake (elements of the Garden of Eden story of some two thousand years later clearly blend in here). He hears the story of the Flood (anticipating Noah) and sees the shade of Engidu. But eternal life he does not achieve. The poem ends on a note of philosophical pessimism:

> what was left over in the pot,
> what was thrown in the street,
> that is thy fare.

The more one reads *Gilgamesh* the more does it become apparent that it is no "primitive" tale but a polished, sophisticated, and original work of art. It is, in fact, great poetry with a style of its own. If this style at first seems over-direct, in time we come to realize that it is deliberately so and that it has, in fact, considerable range, from the tragic tenderness of "he covered up his friend like a bride" to the stark bitterness of the final lines. Nowhere else do we find such a sense of restless, goaded searching as that which dominates the latter half of the poem, and few works of literature in the succeeding forty-five centuries have conveyed so vividly the tormented shock of the individual on first confronting death.

We have to recognize also, however, that the poem is written within a limited social and moral framework. The hero is a king, not a peasant or a slave; the poet (or poets) accepts slavery—it is right and "natural" for the metal workers to make Gilgamesh's sword; he accepts prostitution—the priestess is a sexual instrument. The death theme is limited: the tragedy of death to the great individual, the prince, not to people in general. The poet would not, one gathers, worry overmuch about the death of a slave.

There are cultural limitations also. At the time of *Gilgamesh* some of the major literary forms had not yet grown up. The poet had no conception of the range and richness of the Homeric or Indian epics, or of the possibilities of the dramatic method for the exhibiting of character or thought; and the novel was four thousand years away. Other limitations arise from the low general level of knowledge and ideas, as compared to that of, say, the fifth century B.C. Greeks or Chinese.

The limitations of the Gilgamesh poet are the general limitations of a very early, State-feudal society. But within them he enjoyed considerable freedom. Gilgamesh is shown as a man with human faults and fears. He is granted no immortal life as a god but shares with all the oblivion of death. The poet is not hampered by super-naturalism. The gods are present, it is true, but they are strangely separate from man and his interests. And the emotional and intellectual emphasis in the poetry itself is really such as to deny immortality. The mind is—certainly by implication—part of the body; it will die with the body.

The poet has an unusual freedom, too, in his treatment of sexual love. Here, again, his attitude reflects that earthy materialism also found in other Sumerian poems. Love is physical, of the body. It is not degrading but joyous, an overwhelming rapture in which a man's senses are carried beyond consciousness. Its effects are mainly good: Engidu is turned from his savage state toward civilization. Such certainly is the main emphasis even though moral condemnation is apparently implied in Engidu's wild beasts running away from him after he makes love to the priestess.

The Sumerian Lyric

The original writers of the Gilgamesh story were part of a school of Sumerian poets, fragments of whose work have survived. Some of these I have already used to illustrate various aspects of Sumerian life. One of the most powerful of them is a poem on the destruction of Ur by the Elamites, which might aptly be entitled "The Storm." It ends as follows:[25]

The storm ordered by Enlil in hate, the storm which wears away the country,
covered Ur like a cloth, enveloped it like a linen sheet.

On that day did the storm leave the city;
    that city was a ruin.
O father Nanna, that town was left a ruin.
    The people mourn.
On that day did the storm leave the country.
    The people mourn.

(Dead) men not potsherds
Covered the approaches.
The walls were gaping,
The high gates, the roads,
Were piled with dead.
In the wide streets, where feasting crowds would gather,
Scattered they lay.

In all the streets and roadways bodies lay.
In open fields that used to fill with dancers,
They lay in heaps.
The country's blood now filled its holes, like metal in a mould;
Bodies dissolved—like fat left in the sun.

Here, 4,500 or more years ago, is a poet of almost tempestuous power and high technical development, who must have had a tradition behind him and a school around him. Like all great poets he gives us an insight into the essence of his age. The destruction of Ur is not just a battle with opposing armies but a social storm, let loose by Enlil, god of the sky. The poet was so overwhelmed with the horror of the event that as he struggled to give expression to it the parallel with a storm must have arisen naturally out of the maelstrom of his emotions. And it is in so envisaging the destruction as a storm that he gives us insights that the historian could not. This basic creative concept dominates the poem, but within it come others: the emotional intensity, the imagery, the language—all integrated in the total creative response. It is also a poem of a period in which humanity has little control over natural and almost none over social forces, and has no vision of achieving such control. The only hope is Enlil and Enlil works as he wishes.

When we read such poems as these, especially *Gilgamesh,* we may feel that all at once literature has leapt into existence. But both the city states of Sumer and their literature had long antecedents. The written, upper class literature of Sumer had a vast reservoir behind it of twenty thousand and more years of oral literature, a literature in which many of the basic techniques of structure and style had been developed. Furthermore, this reservoir still existed, both in the rest of the world and among the peasantry of Sumer (and Egypt), in folk tales and songs and folk art.

FROM APE TO SUMER

As we look back over the course of natural and social evolution from our remote apelike ancestors to the first civilized societies, some basic questions arise: Was there a purpose behind this development? Was it inevitable? These are, as Candide once remarked, "great questions." Furthermore they are questions on which there are no specialists and many answers; to which the following may, for what it is worth, be added.

When we, as humans, speculate from the human point of view there does indeed appear to be purpose and inevitability. How else are we to explain so intricate a dove-tailing of events without which the end result — people — would not have emerged? But, as Rupert Brooke has suggested, if we were fish we would feel the same way and speculate about "a Purpose in Liquidity." If, on the other hand, we were dinosaurs, we would have considerable doubt about purposefulness. The answer is perhaps simply that once evolution started, something had to develop. The development of each particular part of this something necessitated a complex of events, which in each case seems purposeful, but which, viewed in terms of the whole, appears to have resulted solely from the interaction of natural forces, sometimes creating, sometimes destroying.

There was, for instance, nothing inevitable about the evolution of people. If there had not been mammals, primates, trees, etc., almost *ad infinitum,* there would not have been people. But there would have been something. The problem seems similar in a general way to that of the existence of an individual. The chance of you or me having come into existence is virtually infinity to one — the probability of any one individual existing is infinitely small. But this is only the beginning; for the probability of those parents having existed is likewise infinite; and those parents' parents, and so on *ad infinitum.* And yet you came into existence and I came into existence. The problem may be put thus: some individual has to be born, but that it should be any specific individual is infinitely improbable. And this perhaps holds for any one species considered in relation to the totality of life as for individuals considered in relation to their species. Yet we cannot argue on the basis of genetic evidence that there was any purposeful selection of individuals. Nor can we make a similar argument in regard to any one species.

Just as there was nothing inevitable about the evolution of people, so there was nothing inevitable about the evolution of the plants and animals that are useful to people. If there had not been these there would have been others and they, too, would have been useful because people are a part of life and each part of life lives on other parts. On the other hand if we view the complexity of the factors which led to the evolution of the human species it would appear to be infinitely improbable that this species exists elsewhere in the universe.

Although there is no general inevitability, there may be what we might call a limited inevitability: when a certain stage in an evolutionary process (natural or social) is reached, certain other immediate stages have to follow. Whether next stages are inevitable or not would seem to depend on the complexity of the factors involved. If there are many such factors, then several lines of development may take place; but if there are comparatively few only one may be possible. We may have an example of this in certain apparently parallel developments which took place in Old World and New World monkeys.

Such a process of limited inevitability seems to pertain to the early development of society, which is a comparatively non-complex process. Once people evolved and society developed, this society had to be a food-gathering society, for it arose out of a sub-human food-gathering society, and there was nothing else that it could be. And once such a society arose it would be driven into higher forms of productivity by competition between communities toward farming — as is again perhaps indicated by a parallel between the Old and New World, not an evolutionary, biological parallel but a social parallel: farming society apparently developed independently out of food-gathering society in Asia and in America. Furthermore, in America and in various parts of Asia, as we shall see, farming society began to develop into the same kind of society as in Sumer, Egypt, and the Indus Valley (with, however, certain limitations to further growth in America). And, although there were doubtless outside "influences" on some, perhaps on all these shifts to civilization, influences cannot, as we shall see, have been the main factor at work. Rich farming centers would tend to form cities for trading and administrative centers; and when we have cities we have the foundation for civilized society.

V

Civilization in Asia

THE TWO THOUSAND YEARS between about 4500 and 2500 B.C. witnessed the birth of civilization in three centers in the same general area, namely West Asia-North Africa; the next two thousand years witnessed the further spread of civilization in these areas and its development in Europe and East Asia (1500 B.C.). Still later it began to develop in Oceania, Africa, and Middle America.

In the next three chapters I shall discuss civilization's course in Asia, Oceania, and Africa; and after that in Europe and America. In doing so, I shall ask the same elementary questions that I have asked about Sumer and Egypt. What was the economy? Who owned the land? Who did the work? What kinds of lives did people lead? What was the status of women (of, that is to say, half of humanity)? Who ran the government? How was it run? How did people think? What knowledge did they have? What of their artistic creation?

This task is much less complex than it first appears. For one thing, these civilizations fall into groups, and for these groups the answers, in each individual case, are essentially the same. For another, movement in history does not necessarily mean development. In the history of Asia during the 4500 years from 3000 B.C. to 1500 A.D., the movement is immense — empires and dynasties rising and falling, invasions, migrations, and wars — but most of this movement was the result of a struggle for land (or, more accurately, for control of labor power) and it usually ended where it had begun, namely with a new division of land of the same kind as the old. By the historians of these countries all these facts have to be sorted and recorded; but from the point of view of the total evolution of society only a few of them are important.

Asia, like Gaul, falls into three parts: West Asia, East Asia, and Northern Asia (usually called Central Asia). In West Asia there have been two main areas of civilization, namely India itself and the lands above India to the Mediterranean (Iran, Mesopotamia, Arabia, Turkey). In East Asia there have been three main areas, namely China and Japan, of which the former is older and more influential, and, between India and China, the great Indo-China peninsula (Burma, Thailand, Vietnam), and down into the long thin arm of the Malay peninsula. Northern Asia is an enormous territory extending east to west roughly from Mongolia and the Great Siberian plains through Russia to the Black Sea. Of the history of this territory we know comparatively little. Its peoples, variously known as Huns, Turks, Scythians, Tartars, or Mongols are generally, and incorrectly, considered of historical importance only when they invade the rest of Asia or Europe (Attila, Tamerlane, Genghis Khan).

I: WEST ASIA

India

The civilization of the Indus Valley, with its great cities, Mohenjo-Daro and Harappa, lasted for more than six hundred years (a period about the same as that from Chaucer to the present day). About 1700 B.C. Mohenjo-Daro and Harappa were destroyed by Indo-European speaking invaders (apparently from upper West Asia) after a long struggle which is perhaps recounted in some of the conquerors' *Rig-Veda* poems.

Of the new civilized societies which arose, apparently largely seeded by the old, we have to wait until about 300 B.C. for our first detailed account. By that time India was divided into 118 kingdoms of which the greatest was that ruled by the emperor Chandragupta Maurya, stretching over the great plains of the Indus and the Ganges. We have a special knowledge of that state because of the presence in Maurya's domains of a Syrian ambassador, Megasthenes, a Greek, who wrote a book on his stay there. Megasthenes, as a foreigner, observed everything that seemed strange and new.

ECONOMY

That the economy of India, and of similar Asiatic countries, was mainly agricultural is generally known, but the degree of the preponderance of agriculture over industry and commerce is not. In the early part of the seventeenth century, when there was proportionally more industry than in Maurya's time, the revenue of the major port of Surat[1] (according to the *Cambridge History of India*) ran to but half a million rupees, whereas the revenue from land taxes was 220 million rupees.

As in Egypt three thousand years previously, the land was legally owned by the king, but as in Egypt also, this legal, royal ownership was, in fact, limited. There was a class of joint landowners, including the churchmen (Brahmans), some of whose private estates ran to a thousand acres. They could be willed. Figures on the expenditure of revenues in the ancient Asian states are hard to find, but we have some for India and they are very revealing. They show, for instance, that only one-twelfth of the national revenue from taxation was for the king's use. One-sixth went to the court ministers and officials, and the ministers and high officials were the joint landowners. In addition to this and their own estates, they could also be assigned the total revenue from a village or town. All accounts, however, make it clear that only a small proportion of the land was privately owned. Almost all of it was divided into small peasant "holdings," from which the great bulk of the revenue came. Over these "holdings" the peasants had no control. The king could "evict" them if they "defaulted" in the payment of taxes. The Egyptian pattern, in short, is duplicated even to the details; a great landowning class lives off the peasantry and has a king as its nominal head. And although we have only archaeological evidence for the Indus Valley civilization, the indications are that its social structure was like the Egyptian. We probably have, that is to say, a continuity in northern India of the same kind of society from at least 2300 B.C. to 300 B.C. (and beyond).

Although the economy was predominantly agricultural, there was also considerable industry and commerce. Megasthenes commented on "extensive mines of gold and silver,"[2] and there must also have been mines of copper and other minerals. We hear of large forests, the lumber from which was used for shipbuilding and other construction work; and the architectural remains point to a large quarrying industry. There was considerable manufacturing (of cloth, pottery, leather goods, weapons, jewelry), and trade was extensive. There were trade routes all over India, both in the north and in the peninsula, some by land and some by water. There were even rest houses for the merchants and regular ferry services. Contact had apparently been made with Burma, Indonesia, and Malaya but the main sea-borne trade appears to have been coastal. (In later times it extended to the Roman Empire, to Africa, and to China.) Extensive though this trade was, however, it was mainly trade in luxury goods, a pattern we shall find many times repeated — jewelry, spices, silks.

Some of the manufacturing (as in Sumer) was done by small crafts-men, some in State workshops. The basic economic control was kept in the hands of the State, that is, of the great landowners who appointed superintendents of forests and forest products, of graneries, of trade, of tolls and customs, of mines, of workshops, and of shipping. Mer-chants were not allowed to own ships but rented them from the State. One-tenth of the prices of all articles sold was appropriated in taxes. There were road taxes to be paid by merchants using the trade routes, and there were tolls at all city gates. As in Egypt the great landholders extended their power, based on the exploitation of peasant labor, to control the non-agricultural economy.

SOCIAL LIFE

The Indian upper classes themselves recognized that their society was divided into social classes, which they determined by occupation: the Brahmans (priests), the Kshatriya (the generals and high officials of the state), the Vaisya (the merchants), and the Sudra (farm and industry workers — peasants, slaves, and hired workers).

Between one-quarter and one-third of the peasant's crop was taken by the State in a "land tax." He was also taxed for his cattle and use of water. When he was not working on the land, he was working at forced labor for the State. How extensive slavery was in Mauryan India we do not know but it must have been small by the standard of Mediterranean countries because Megasthenes declared that there were no slaves at all. This, we know, was not true, but the comment certainly means that there was no massed slave labor readily in evidence in town or country. Nevertheless, there must have been (absolutely) a large number of slaves. There was a kind of continuation of class among slaves. "Slaves of the upper classes [captured in war] cannot be forced to perform defiling duties,"[3] a pattern we shall find also in Greece. Some slaves of this category apparently held important tech-nical positions in agriculture or mining. "All craftsmen," we learn, "were expected to devote one or two days' work per month to the king" and "there was also liability to forced labor (visti)." No one, Megas-thenes informs us, was allowed to "exchange one profession or trade for another."[4] Hence, craftsmen were frozen into castes from which there was no escape for either a man or his heirs (as in Egypt).

In addition to these classes there was one other, an amorphous professional class, which consisted largely of minor state officials, tax gatherers, spies, minor administrators, magistrates, police, architects, physicians, sculptors, tutors, and so on.

The social status of women depended primarily upon their class.

Women of the working classes led impoverished, hard lives. In addition to economic exploitation they also suffered sexual exploitation. Prostitution was rife, some of it supervised by the government, some by the Church. "The Superintendent of Prostitution looked after public women, controlled their charges and expenditures, appropriated their earnings for two days of each month, and kept two of them in the royal palace for entertainment and intelligence services."[5]

Women of the upper classes were allowed to own and will property, but a husband could, in an emergency, sell his wife's property; she was also limited in the amount of money that she could possess. Some upper class women were educated; one of the earliest Indian philosophers, in fact, was a woman (Gargi). But in general such education was frowned upon. And in this connection Megasthenes makes a revealing comment: "the Brahmans keep their wives—and they have many wives—ignorant of all philosophy; for if women learned to look upon pleasure and pain, life and death, philosophically, they would become depraved, or else no longer remain in subjection."[6] Here surely, is the nub of the matter. The unspoken thought is that which Megasthenes brings out into the open, namely that one of the functions of society is to keep women in subjection. and one of the means of doing this is to deprive them of knowledge. Why, however, do they have to be kept in subjection? To this Megasthenes gives no answer but implies that it is understood; it is, presumably, that if women were not kept in subjection—and Megasthenes is speaking of upper class women—they would want political and economic rights. On the other hand, there was no general "seclusion" of women as in later, Moslem times. In Mauryan India women "appeared freely at feasts and dances, and joined with men in religious sacrifice."[7] And—if we can trust the later but still pre-Moslem *Kamasutra*—sex was regarded neither as sin nor sadism but as a source of mutual pleasure.

POLITICAL LIFE

Within the hierarchy of officials and superintendents in control of the various functions of the government was a small ruling group, the most important members of which were the chief counsellor, the court chaplain, the treasurer, the chief judge. The members of this council were both public and private landowners, their estates continuing generation after generation in the same families. The king was the greatest landowner, possessing extensive private estates, and, as in Egypt, was represented as divine. Nevertheless, his power was circumscribed by the council, which could, when necessary, exert control over the State funds.

Under the central government came city, provincial, and local governments. In the country, each village was organized under a "head man" with a small council consisting of local property owners. The headman and council collected the taxes. Every five to ten villages were under an official called a "gopa"; and each province was under a governor. One of the main functions of the city government was the control of manufacturing and trade. There were city "gopas" who each had charge of forty households and checked the income and expenditure of each. The overall picture is that of a well-organized dictatorship with a firm line of controls from top to bottom of the social pyramid.

This, however, applies only to what we might call the realm proper of the king and his council. Outside of that realm were two further circles, one beyond the other. The first circle consisted of a group of smaller kingdoms ruled by vassal kings, who were supposed to render annual tribute to the emperor and assist him in war. Beyond the realms of the vassal kings was a ring of "tribal states," which were unified communities of farming peoples exercising the same kind of democratic controls which Caesar noted among the Germans.

Megasthenes gives the size of Maurya's army as 600,000 foot and 30,000 cavalry. The leaders of the Mauryan State fought their way to supremacy through a series of bloody battles extending over many years. And when they had achieved it they had to fight to keep it. Vassal kings, provincial governors, peripheral farming societies, and peasant rebellions kept up constant conflicts—sometimes with armies of 150,000 men.

The army was, as we should expect, class divided. The officers came from the upper classes, the soldiers from the lower classes and were forced into army service. The officers (warriors) had horses or elephants, protective metal armor and metal weapons, the soldiers fought on foot with spears and had no metal armor.

The army was not, of course, any more than it had been in Egypt, the main suppressive force used against the peasants or other exploited classes. For these purposes, to back up the hordes of tax gatherers, there was a police force, law, and spies. Megasthenes was especially impressed by the spy system. The country was, he found, "riddled from top to bottom with secret agents." "The spies might be recruited from any walk of life, and might be of either sex. . . . A special class of spy was the *satr*, an orphan trained from childhood for the work, and usually masquerading as a holy-man or a fortune-teller. . . . One of the spy's chief duties was protecting the king's power."[8] The spies handed suspects over to the police and the police "relied chiefly on the use of torture."[9]

The legal system was also class-determined. In general the upper classes were fined, the lower imprisoned, executed, tortured to death, or sent to the mines. The death penalty was imposed for theft or house-breaking, that is, for the crimes committed by the lower classes. Execution was usually by impalement.

The Church was, as I have already indicated, closely connected with the government and integrated with the administration of public affairs at all levels. It was a great landowning institution with independent sources of income. As in Sumer the temple was one of the two main centers of each town:[10]

> The city had two foci, the palace and the temple. . . . The temple, especially if it was a great and famous temple in one of the sacred cities, was itself a city in miniature in the medieval period. It was enormously wealthy, and a source of wealth to the town from the many pilgrims who visited it. Such a temple was a great landowner, with many employees. . . .

If we put all these facts together we can reconstruct in remarkable detail the life of Mauryan India. One thing that is difficult to resurrect, however, is the general atmosphere of such a society. But we can feel something of what it must have been in the observations of a modern observer of a similar society, Jawaharlal Nehru, on an Indian princedom: "One feels hedged, circumscribed, bound down in mind and body. And one sees the utter backwardness and misery of the people, contrasting vividly with the glaring ostentation of the prince's palace. How much of the wealth of the State flows into that palace for the personal needs and the luxuries of the prince, how little goes back to the people in the form of any service. . . ."[11]

State Feudalism

I have noted some of the parallels between the societies of Egypt and Sumer of 3000 B.C. and this in India some 2,700 years later, and others must have been obvious. In brief the civilizations were virtually identical economically, socially, politically, with but one major exception, namely, that Sumer consisted of a series of city states within which were governmental assemblies with some participation by merchants.

The indication is, as we have noted, that the same form of society existed in northern India in 300 B.C. as in 2300 B.C. Had there been in the intervening centuries any progress within that form? Curiously little attention has been given to this question. But some relevant information is apparent even in the standard histories, and investigation would doubtless reveal others. For instance, we have evidence of the size of cities. The ruins of Harappa (destroyed about 1700 B.C.) reveal its walled area to have measured half a mile on each side. Megasthenes informs us that Maurya's capital city, Pataliputra— surrounded by wooden walls—measured nine miles in length and two in breadth. Such an increase implies an increase in total wealth, and this indication is supported by archaeological and other evidence of the size and number of buildings, the nature and number of jewels and objects in precious metals; by the apparently great increase in trade in the Mauryan empire; and, finally, by the greater area of that empire and the extent of its subject peoples. Slow though it may have been, there seems to have been considerable economic expansion during these centuries. There does not seem, however, to have been concomitant social or political advance. Whatever increase in wealth took place was still restricted to a narrow top group, and, although there may have been more and wealthier merchants, the condition of the great mass of the population remained unchanged. The State was still firmly in the hands of a small clique of great landowners.

Let us now move our historical camera forward another eighteen hundred years and look briefly at the realm of another great Indian ruler, Akbar, founder of the Moghul empire, who reigned in the sixteenth century A.D. The following notes gathered from *The Cambridge History of India* and other general sources reveal the nature of this society. Akbar, we learn, introduced "reforms." The first of these "reforms" was to increase the land tax on the peasant from one-quarter to one-third (either in money or kind); that this was the main source of revenue is clear from the figures previously noted on the comparative revenues from the land and the leading port. (Peasants who failed to pay were flogged.) In addition there was "a bewildering variety of petty taxes and duties, . . . most of all on transport." The salt mines were "administered by the state," and presumably the other mines were also. Akbar had had trouble with his vassals and had to conquer his territory all over again. Among other "reforms" he converted "the whole of the imperial territory into crown lands." He was, that is to say, faced with a situation similar to that which history notes as having once occurred in Egypt. The vassal lords had grown so powerful on their own great estates that they had carved out kingdoms for themselves; a new combination of great landowners had formed around the king and had reconquered the territory for the central State. Akbar then put his own great landowners in charge (the realm was to be "administered by his own revenue officers"). And he paid the army from the central treasury.

In the eighteen hundred years between Maurya and Akbar, India had witnessed titanic and terrible events. In the fifth century came the invasion of White Huns, who "converted India into a Hun province." In the eighth century the Arab conquest began; by 1200 A.D. "the entire northern plain . . . lay under the Mohammedan yoke." In the fourteenth century came the invasion of Tamerlane, in the sixteenth century the Moghul conquest. Dynasties and empires rose and fell. But the same society continued. Akbar and his associates lived on the backs of the peasants, held the controls over raw materials, regulated manufacturing and commerce just as had Maurya and his associates. What had all these invasions, wars, and rebellions of vassals been about? Essentially, as I have indicated, they were struggles for the control of peasant labor. The masters changed but the peasant continued; sometimes the peasant paid a quarter, sometimes a third, sometimes even a half, but always he paid, and the ruling class lived on him whether it was Indian, Hun, Arab, or Moghul. Megasthenes tells us that the peasants in the days of Maurya continued their work in the fields during war, letting the battles rage around them. And so, too, throughout the long centuries.

The society remained and the political system with it. Once again, however, there is indication of economic progress. The empire of Akbar, according to the *Cambridge History of India,* was "richer probably than any other in the world"; and this when Elizabethan England was beginning its rise and the Spanish Conquistadores had already begun their looting of the New World. The empire had a "huge population, fertile soil, numerous manufactures and vast commerce, both internal and sea borne." This certainly seems to be wealth on a greater scale than Maurya's.

This economic development, however, impressive though it was, was still within the feudal framework. The basic wealth was agricultural and remained in the hands of the landowning class, and although the merchants and manufacturers must have been making important gains they were in no position to challenge the landholding oligarchy, nor would they have been for many centuries. Whatever the course of development might have been, however, it was distorted by the impact of an external social force, namely British imperialism.

Upper West Asia

If we move west by northwest from India we come first to the great plateau of Iran (Persia), then to the fertile lands of the Tigris and Euphrates (Mesopotamia-Iraq) — below which hangs the squat boot of the Arabian Peninsula — and, finally to the area between the eastern

Mediterranean and the Black Sea (mainly occupied today by Syria and Turkey). These four areas comprise Upper West Asia. The main lines of the early history of this region run briefly as follows.

(1) Babylonia. The beginnings, in Sumer, we have already seen. In about 2500 B.C. the fertile lands of the lower Euphrates and Tigris were united to form the kingdom of Babylonia, which grew to be an empire holding sway over much of Upper West Asia, and, after various ups-and-downs, was overthrown by the Persians in about 500 B.C.

(2) The Hittites. The scene next shifts to the north, to the area now occupied by Turkey and Syria. There, about 1500 B.C. arose the kingdom of the Hittites—hidden from us until comparatively recent years. In 1269 B.C. the rulers of Hatti (the land of the Hittites), Babylonia, and Egypt signed treaties of nonaggression and mutual assistance (against both foreign aggression and domestic uprisings), and virtually the whole of Upper West Asia-North Africa was under their joint dominion.

(3) Assyria. This situation was upset by the rise of another Mesopotamian people (north of the Tigris and Euphrates valleys), the Assyrians, about 1100 B.C., with their capital city at Nineveh. They did, indeed, "come down like a wolf on the fold." "Their war-chariots, their cavalry, and their archers spread terror whenever they appeared. They burned villages. They decapitated, impaled, flayed or walled up alive their prisoners. They disemboweled the women, and systematically enslaved and deported the inhabitants of whole tracts of country."[12] Sedillot's vivid thumbnail sketch reminds us of the savagery and sadism that accompanied all these wars—as they do all war.

(4) The Persian Empire. During the centuries from 3000 to 800 B.C., civilization had been growing in the area between the scene of these various events and India, namely Iran. By about 500 B.C. this development had reached a point at which Iran was able to conquer Egypt, Babylonia, and Assyria, and the great Persian Empire began its ascendency. This empire, divided into thirty-one provinces, with roads linking the capitals, was on a much vaster scale than Babylonia, Hatti, Egypt, or Assyria. It extended over the whole of the area of West Asia down into northern India and reached into Africa to embrace both Egypt and Ethiopia. With the "overthrow" of this empire by Alexander of Macedon in 329 B.C. we move into a period of mixed west Asiatic and European history which can better be discussed later. One word of caution might be introduced here. When historians speak of Persia "overthrowing" Assyria, or Macedonia "overthrowing" Persia, this does not mean an absolute overthrow. Babylonia and Assyria, for instance, "overthrew" one another periodically. All it meant was that one ruling class subjugated, usually temporarily,

another ruling class. The people continued, and often the great estates continued—although sometimes under new management. In fact, the people inhabiting West Asia today are presumably the descendents of the Babylonians, Assyrians, Hittites, Persians, and so on, who were given other names in later historical periods, for example "Moslems."

What is usually known as the history of this area, then, is an account of the dominant States, their dynasties, kings, wars, and conquests. Formerly there was in the histories only passing reference to the kinds of societies involved, their economy, social structure, government, and so on. But in recent years historians have been paying more attention to these matters. For instance, O. R. Gurney's *The Hittites* gives a good deal of such information.

The Hittite king, we learn,[13] had private estates of "vast extent"; the Church was one of "the largest landholders." Some of the temples formed "small states within the State" and let out land to tenant farmers. There was also[14] a class of "nobles" who were "the possessors of large estates, held as fiefs conferred by the king." These estates were entailed, i.e., they were passed on by law from father to son; other lands could be bought and sold.

The "majority" of the people were "peasants working on the land," but there were some slaves—apparently mainly servants—and paid workmen. There were merchants and craftsmen, but the main sources of raw materials—for example, the mines—were owned by the State. The king is represented as a god; under him came a number of vassal kings who paid tribute. The government "assembly" consisted of nobles and "dignitaries." There were local village and town councils but they were not represented in the central government.

In marriage the wife was regarded as the property of the husband:[15] "the bridegroom 'takes' his wife and thereafter 'possesses' her; if she is taken in adultery, he has the right to decide her fate." On the other hand[16] the queen had a "strongly independent position" and signed all documents of state with "her own official seal." And possibly the wives of the great "nobles" had similar rights.

All of this is familiar; some of it reads like a duplication of Sumerian society. But there may have also been an important socioeconomic difference between Hittite and Sumerian (or Egyptian and Indian) society. As Gurney points out,[17] much remains to be known about the problems of land tenure in the Hittite empire, yet one gets the impression of a society shading more toward individual-ownership feudalism of the European type than the State feudalism of Egypt or India.

Let us look at one more West Asian civilization before moving on to East Asia, that of Iran (Persia), which provides an example of a long continuous history in one area, and take as one end of the line, the

Persian empire of Darius and Xerxes (about 500 B.C.), and as the other, the last empire of the Sassanian kings — Iranian society as it was just before the Arab conquest in the seventh century A.D.

R. Ghirshman, in his informative study, *Iran,* writes as follows of the early empire society:[18] "The prince lived with the vassal lords of his retinue and ruled over the peasantry. He drew his revenues from his estates and levied dues on hunting, fishing, and stockbreeding. He owned private lands worked by slave labour, and his peasants owed him service in all kinds of courvées and also for public works such as roads, canals, bridges, and fortifications." The "great lords" also had estates whose households "seem to have consisted of male and female servants, slaves, and all kinds of artisans." The merchants were "protected" by the prince for the "increasing of his revenues." The main tax was the land tax, which varied between one-third and one-sixth of the yield. The nobles, priests, and royal officials were exempt from taxation. Once again we have the same basic patterns: a ruling class of great landholders living — *via* the State — off the peasantry, owning also private estates, controlling the sources of raw material, trading in luxury goods, keeping the merchant in his place.

Of the Iranian society a thousand years later, Ghirshman gives the following pictures. The "greater part" of the land[19] was "divided between State lands and great estates." The peasants "formed the great mass of the population, and, though free *de jure,* were *de facto* reduced to the condition of serfs attached to the soil and sold along with the land and villages."[20] The "director of taxes" controlled "an army of accountants, tax-collectors, and agents. This was a post of great responsibility, since on it depended the existence and functioning of the State." As with India there was economic progress — to judge by the trade — but the basic social pattern remained unchanged.

What, however, is the specific form of the pattern? Once again the shading seems to be toward individual rather than State feudalism. There does not seem, for instance, to be, as in India, a central area of absolute State control with vassal lords on the periphery. The vassal lords seem to be everywhere, exploiting their own peasants and turning over only part of the loot to the State; and sometimes they seem not vassals but equals, with revolts against the central authority more frequent than in Egypt or India.

There occurs also in Iran a phenomenon which does not appear to have occurred in India, namely massive peasant wars against the great landowners, wars which aimed at the establishment of a kind of primitive communist social system to take the place of the existing system (the theories of Mazdak and his followers). Ghirshman notes several such wars, some of them led by dissident landowners, for instance:[21]

At the beginning of the eighth century the Mazdakite theories seem to have inspired the rising of Khurzad, brother of the Shah of Chorasmia. Having seized power, he meted out harsh treatment to the local nobility, confiscating their possessions, flocks, wives, and daughters, and distributing them among the poor. The King was forced to enlist the help of the Arabs, who under the leadership of Quteiba restored him to power and put an end to the activity of the Khurzad.

FEUDAL FORMS AND ORIGINS

If we consider all these phenomena together there is certainly an indication of two forms of feudal states in West Asia: State feudalism and individual estate or private property feudalism. Neither, of course, was an absolute, for each shaded off into the other. The great land-holders of Egypt and India revolted periodically and set up individual domains; in both the Hittite empire and Iran, the king was the legal owner of the land and the central government had to fight continually to enforce its power. Yet as we shall see later, there could be important differences in social evolution following from the two systems, at least in their extreme forms.

In searching for an explanation for this divergence of feudal patterns one finds the most obvious factor to be that of terrain. The two civilizations which we have noted particularly as following the State feudal pattern, Egypt and northern India, were mainly river valley civilizations with large, flat, open areas cultivated by irrigation and policed along the rivers. The two which appear to follow the individual estate pattern have no such open, flat, river-valley centers and are not primarily irrigational. Both Anatolia and Iran are mountainous. Within their separate valleys individual feudal domains could grow and flourish. There would, of course, be a trend toward a central government for mutual protection but the centripetal forces of open country and central irrigation (which demanded unity at the cost of existence) were not present and the natural centrifugal forces of individual land grabbing would receive fuller play. Once these basic differences were present, others would arise. For instance, there would be more warfare between the individual feudal lords. And there would be more and bigger peasant revolts because the presence of individual competing feudal lords gave the peasants more power. They could desert an over-harsh master and go to another. They could revolt against individual masters more easily than against a centralized State. Individual lords would attempt to harness this revolutionary power for their own ends. And once revolts got underway they would be more difficult to control.

In spite of these differences, however, the fact remains that in the

West Asia-North Africa area the societies which followed later farming societies were essentially the same. They were all feudal. Why? The answer is that no other society could develop from farming society. The first civilized societies had to be based upon the land, and the form they took was determined by the way in which that land was divided. Once the landowners were in control the struggle for land and other forms of wealth did not cease but continued even more extensively and savagely. Out of the scramble to increase wealth to the hilt arose wars between states, rebellions within states, and an attempt to drive taxation to the furthest possible limits. The general form of the State had already been determined by the fight for land in later farming society; the same general form served for the feudal struggle also, but it became wider in its operations.

The bifurcation of society into social classes affected almost all aspects of rule. A class-divided legal system and army were the best forms for maintaining great landowning dominance. So, too, was a government run by a council of great landowners. For the collection of taxation a pyramid of power reaching into each community was needed; hence, provincial and village rulers.

The general situation was that of a population of many millions living in later farming societies in the large West Asia–North Africa area concentrating property and wealth in the social struggle for existence and developing their towns into cities. The same factors would in each area have produced the same results, sometimes earlier, as at Sumer, sometimes later, as in Assyria, but the same result nevertheless. In considering this development we have, of course, as in considering the rise of later farming society itself, to take influences back and forth into account. These could have been of many kinds; trading posts from Sumer could have assisted in the economic development of the eastern Mediterranean; but they could not have assisted it if the society had not already been ripe for development. Important external help could have come from technological processes or inventions. Late farming society rulers, in competition with other communities, would soon see the advantage of metal weapons and chariots, and, if they had had the necessary wealth, would soon have begun to make them. But influence cannot explain development, for influence is, after all, an exchange of what already exists.

II: EAST ASIA

In discussing the beginnings of civilization in East Asia the first factor that we have to take into account is simply ignorance. Compared to, say, Egypt or Mesopotamia, little archaeological excavation has been done in the whole vast area embracing Southeast Asia, China, Korea, and Japan. We know, of course, that here, as everywhere, people lived for tens of thousands of years in food-gathering societies and then in farming societies, but some of the specifics of development are only beginning to emerge.

Southeast Asia

Although some anthropological and botanical evidence has been gathered on the farming center of Southeast Asia, the gaps between it and the early civilizations in the area have not yet been bridged. We do not know when and where civilizations first arose in the large territory stretching across from Burma to south China, down the thick body of the Indo-China peninsula to the thin arm of Malaya and beyond to Indonesia with its great islands of Sumatra, Java, and Borneo. When presently known historical and archaeological records begin to become meaningful (roughly about 1000 A.D.), the civilizations in the area fall into two main types, feudal and commercial-feudal, with the feudal dominating and the various states caught between the giants of India and China and fighting with each other. (Siam invaded and defeated Cambodia in the fifteenth century, and so on.) Burma, Cambodia and Siam (Thailand) were predominately feudal and probably the feudal rulers as usual in such situations controlled what commercial centers existed, but on the island of Sumatra a primarily commercial-feudal state was flourishing in 1180 A.D. and had established control over Malaya and western Java. And for many centuries before that Indonesian ships had plied the Indian Ocean (establishing an outpost in Madagascar) and the China Seas (with settlements in the Philippines perhaps as early as 1700 B.C.). There is even some indication that by about 1500 B.C. Malayan tin was being shipped up the China coast to the Yellow River area, and excavations in 1944 produced evidence of trade (perhaps indirect) with the Roman Empire. By the time of the historical records, the dominant culture of the area had been strongly influenced from India (Buddhism, the architecture of Angkor Wat), but elements of the indigenous culture remain (in the music, in the Javanese "puppet shadow theatre," in batik).

China

As we have seen, part of China was inhabited by the Pekin sub-people some 500,000 years ago; and the assumption is that it has been continuously inhabited ever since. There is, however, little archaeological evidence of such inhabitation between 500,000 and about 25,000 years ago.

The Chinese society of 25,000 years ago was a food-gathering society with stone tools, a society similar to that in Europe (with its cave-artists) of about the same period. Whether these people were Mongoloid does not appear to be known; but the population of the same kind of society of about 10,000 years ago was definitely Mongoloid. Just when this food-gathering society began to move into farming is not known — again the archaeological evidence is sparse — but that grain farming was well underway by 2500 B.C. is shown by remains of pottery and grinding mills (curiously similar to the Middle American Indian *metates*), a trade in jade covering a 2,000 mile route into Chinese Turkestan, and evidence of a great increase in population. By 2000 B.C. there is evidence of large farming villages protected by ramparts.

Civilized societies first arose in China in the Yellow River valley about 1500 B.C., the central city being known as "the Great City Shang." As this is some 1,500 years later than the rise of civilized societies in West Asia, and as there is evidence that very early in this society there were both chariots and intricate bronze work, it seems likely that there was technological influence from West Asia. In spite of the great distance of China from the early West Asian civilized societies, such influence is possible. There were passes through the mountains, later traversed by silk trade merchants. The Huns crossed the great plains of North Asia from China to Europe. And a sea route — with intermediate stopping places — between, say, the Ganges and the Yellow River is not impossible. A clearly flourishing farming society prior to the rise of the Shang state seems to indicate external technological influence speeding up a development already underway.

ECONOMY

The "Great City Shang" was situated close to the river and was surrounded by rich land. The main crop was millet (a wheatlike grain). Rice, later the great staple of the Chinese city population, did not become important until "dry" rice was supplanted by "wet" (irrigated) rice some fifteen hundred years later. Early China, then, like West Asia, had a mainly wheat-type agriculture. The fields were ploughed, as they were in the beginnings in West Asia also, by crude hand-pulled wooden ploughs and perhaps also dug by spade. The ox-pulled plough did not come into use until the sixth century B.C. or even later. Among the domestic animals were pigs (native to Southeast Asia), cattle, sheep, and chickens. The indication is that irrigation was known but was not widely used.

In regard to land ownership, Creel[22] writes as follows (other specialists give a similar picture):

> In theory all land belonged to the king, who gave it to his vassals in return for service. They gave lands to still lesser vassals, who might parcel it out still further. The king had the right to take back any land from any of his vassals and give it to another, . . . but just as in medieval Europe, the powerful vassals soon ceased to look upon their title to lands as provisional. . . . In practice the vassal looked upon his territory as his by inherited right, and it was necessary to wage war to displace him. As lesser vassals grew in power, and possessed private armies, the same situation grew up all along the line, so that if land changed hands it ordinarily did so either as a result of sale or exchange, or with the accompaniment of violence.
>
> Each individual who held land as a fief from a superior was commonly expected to turn over to that superior a portion of the revenue which he received from it as tribute.

If there was some question as to the divergence of the Hittite empire and Iran from the Mesopotamian-Egyptian-Indian pattern, clearly there is none about China. What developed in early China was not State-feudalism but individual ownership feudalism similar to that in Europe. Although the king theoretically owned the land the real ownership lay with the feudal lords. Even during the century of Mongol domination (when Marco Polo visited China) the central authority was comparatively weak. There was no area of absolute centralized control with vassals on the periphery; the vassal system was the only system; and some of the vassals were almost as powerful as the king—the system which later developed into "war-lord" rule.

One question which Creel does not discuss is what proportion of the land was owned by the Church. In the Great City Shang there were found the remains of what was apparently a temple and of two early poems on the building of a city, one describes the erection of a temple, the other of a palace, but there does not appear to have been a vast, semi-independent church power similar to that in India.

Although the chief form of wealth lay in land, as in all feudal societies, there was considerable manufacturing and trade. Various metal objects have been uncovered, at first copper or bronze, and later iron. The trade Creel describes as follows:[23] "The goods which the merchants carried must have been chiefly luxuries, such as articles of

clothing and food, which could not be procured everywhere with e-
qual ease. Salt, fish (dried, undoubtedly), furs, cloth of various
kinds, and silks are named as articles of trade."

In reading national histories it is surprising to note how seldom the
authors draw attention to parallels between countries. Basham discusses India as a unique phenomenon; and so, too, Gurney on the
Hittites and Ghirshman on Iran. The same applies also to Childe,
Frankfort, Petrie, Murray, and other writers on the beginnings of civilization in Egypt and Mesopotamia. From time to time, it is true, a close
and specific parallel will be mentioned, but the basic fact that all these
civilizations have certain essentials in common is either not known or
not discussed. We find the same implications of uniqueness in regard
to China, and the same lack of explanation for phenomena.

SOCIAL LIFE

On the general question of how large a population this Shang society encompassed we have no accurate figures. The census of A.D. 2,
however, gives the population of China (mainly the great plains between the Yellow and the Yangtze rivers) as 60 million. Even if we
assume that the introduction of wet rice culture in south China made
for a considerable increase in the population (the staple in North China
remained millet or wheat), nevertheless, the same basic economy existed in about 1000 B.C. (the end of the Shang period) as in 2 A.D.,
even though in a smaller area, and the probability is that Shang China
had a population of several millions. Archaeological remains tend not
only to hide the size but also the variety and richness of a society's
life. From the Shang remains of palaces, temples, and bronzes we tend
to envisage a kind of tableau of kings and priests rather than a bustling,
toiling society of millions.

Of these millions the vast majority were peasants; a small percentage owned the land. There is no more indication in China than in
Egypt or India of a class of middle landowners. Although the essential
class status of the peasant was the same as that in West Asia, it differed in that he was a serf, not of the State but of the individual landowner. There was no set portion of his produce to be yielded. Each
landowner took as much as he could get, and apparently there was a
considerable range. The peasants were subject, as ever, to forced
labor—to build roads, city walls and palaces—and to unpaid army
service. They lived in small one-room houses and worked from dawn to
dark—"The sun is rising: we must get up!—He is setting: we will
rest!"—massed in ranks in the fields: "The bamboo hats are moving!
—All the hoes are turning up the soil."[24]

In addition to the peasants there were slaves. L. Carrington Goodrich asserts[25] that "male slaves never constituted more than 1 percent of the Chinese population." Even if we assume that the figure is too low—Creel implies a larger number—the evidence points to a comparatively small fraction of the industrial labor force being slaves. The only massed slave labor noted in the general histories was in river transport. Most of the slaves, again as in West Asia, were women, probably mostly household workers. And so it remained even into the present century. When slavery was finally illegalized in China in 1910 the vast majority of the slaves were women.

The paid workers must have ranged from the master craftsmen—who made the magnificent Shang bronzes—to the lowly helper who perhaps worked for his keep and little beside. The archaeological evidence indicates that as in the Indus Valley they lived mostly in cities. And, as in Egypt and India, they were apparently forbidden to change their trade.

There was a considerable class of merchants, some of whom "became very rich." They had to pay "taxes and tariffs," but how considerable these were does not seem to be recorded, and they are said to have "carried on their trade with little restriction."[26] Some of them invested their money in land—the sale of land was legalized in about 350 B.C.—but as a class they were subordinate to the great landowners. They could not, in this period, hold titles and were not allowed to wear the clothes of the aristocracy.

Finally there was a professional class, consisting not mainly, as in West Asia, of central State officials but local feudal officials, plus doctors, scholars, judges, and so on.

The status of women differed, as in all early civilizations, in accordance with class. Upper class women were kept out of government and "were not ordinarily present at public ceremonies," although some were educated. They "lived in a considerable degree of seclusion in the women's part of the household."[27] Some upper class women were educated—as in India—and the *Book of Poetry* contains a protest by one woman (675 B.C.) against her exclusion from public affairs:

> I would have gone to my lord in his need,
>> Have galloped there all the way,
> But this is a matter concerns the State,
>> And I, being a woman, must stay.

Among the peasantry women had certain rights within defined spheres: "The peasant house was (and in fact has remained) a feminine matter. The man scarcely entered it: the furniture was part of the woman's dowry. In primitive times the village itself belonged to the women; the divinity which protected it was called the 'Mother of the hamlet.'"[28] Apparently in China, exploited though they were, women were able to put up stronger resistance to male dominance than in West Asia, retaining more of the rights they had had in farming society.

Nevertheless a large number of peasant women were, as we have noted, forced into slavery. The female slave was, as usual, also sexually exploited. Out of this situation developed the widespread Chinese institution of concubinage. Some women slaves worked in the household and others were "put to work at labour of various sorts" around the estate. They could be executed on the orders of the mistress of the household. How widespread prostitution was in this early period we do not know, but according to Marco Polo, it was practically a State industry in Mongol times:

> The number of public women who prostitute themselves for money, reckoning those in the new city as well as those in the suburbs of the old, is twenty-five thousand. To each hundred and to each thousand of these there are superintending officers appointed, who are under the orders of a captain-general. The motive for placing them under such command is this: when ambassadors arrive charged with any business in which the interests of the Great Khan are concerned, it is customary to maintain them at his Majesty's expense, and in order that they may be treated in the most honourable manner, the captain is ordered to furnish nightly to each individual of the embassy one of these courtezans, who is likewise to be changed every night. As this service is considered in the light of a tribute they owe to the sovereign, they do not receive any remuneration.[29]

Marriage, as in most societies, was mainly monogamous, but we find the usual pattern of kings and great lords owning harems and lesser officials possessing several wives. As in India, wives could be sacrificed on their husbands' death. When the First Emperor of Ch'in died in 210 B.C. his entire harem was immolated with him. Within the upper class family the father held actual power of life and death over his children.

POLITICAL LIFE

The head of the central government, the king or emperor, was—as in Sumer, Egypt, India—represented as divine and holding his authority by the Decree of Heaven. But, in actual fact, he was simply a kind of committee chairman of the top group of great landowners. If he failed to work satisfactorily in their interests he was discarded and a new landowner put in his place. Each great landowner had his own army, his own police and his own law—in short, his own little State.

Warfare between these great landowners was practically continuous and sometimes accompanied by mass terroristic executions. (We read of 400,000 decapitations after one battle.) Marco Polo describes one battle as follows:

> This signal, by the orders of the Great Khan, was first given to the right and left wings, and the great drums of Kublai Khan began to sound. Then a fierce and bloody conflict began. The air was instantly filled with a cloud of arrows that poured down on every side, and vast numbers of men and horses were seen to fall to the ground. . . . So large were the heaps of the carcasses of men, and more especially of horses, on the field, that it became impossible for the one party to advance upon the other.[30]

With the coming of the explosive projectile to dominate war we have forgotten about arrow wounds. But as we contemplate Kublai Khan's showers of arrows we might bring them into human terms by considering some comments summarized from an English twelfth century surgeon: "In cases of wounds in which the arrow is lodged in the thorax, Gilbert recommends that the surgeon first trephine the thorax wall and extract the shaft and then withdraw the arrowhead through this opening. In the event that the head of the arrow is lodged just within the ribs, its removal, he states, will be much more difficult. The ribs may then be spread apart by a wedge, after which the removal of the arrowhead will be greatly facilitated."[31] All this, of course, in the days before anesthetics.

The Chinese legal system, like those of West Asia, was classdivided. "The fine in lieu of cutting off the feet," we read in a legal document, "extends to five hundred cases, that in lieu of castration to three hundred, that in lieu of death to two hundred."[32] As a peasant, slave, or workman had no money to pay fines, the system in China was apparently the same as in West Asia: the poor were punished bodily or executed; the rich were fined (except in occasional extremes, such as treason). Within his realms the great landowner had absolute, arbitrary power over his peasants. They could be beaten or killed at will—up to the point, of course, of inciting mass rebellion. There were, in fact, many such rebellions, for instance, the peasant war of 18 to 25 A.D., the so-called revolt of the "Red Eyebrows."[33] The peasants, men and women together, marched upon the capital city of Peking, captured it, fought against and defeated the armies of the king and the aristocrats in extensive campaigns for some six years. The casualty lists ran into millions. Clearly this was full-scale civil war. One reason for the outbreak of such wars, according to Marcel Granet,[34] was "the development of the large domains." Presumably as the larger land-owners gobbled up the smaller ones they increased the exploitation of the peasants. Revolts, however, could not have developed into civil wars (as India shows us) if there had been centralized State feudalism (Maurya with his 600,000 troops). The peasants could fight against individual landowners and even get some landowners to join them (as happened in Iran also) in the hope of eliminating rivals. Even in normal times, a peasant mistreated on one estate could escape and go to another, so that "the territories of very oppressive landlords were almost depopulated."[35] The peasants had more scope both for day-by-day resistance and for rebellion against a partially fragmented State than against a unified State. We have to note also that the soldiers in the feudal lords' armies were mostly peasants and frequently deserted or fraternized.

As in West Asia the great landowners struck out against the merchants and manufacturers. All merchandise, raw materials, transport wagons, and boats were taxed. Prices were regulated throughout China. In 115 B.C. the State took charge of all transport. By a law of 10 A.D., one-tenth of all profits were to be handed over to the State. But in spite of these measures, manufacturing and commerce developed. Even in Shang society there were rich merchants. In time the landowners, in spite of all their efforts at suppression, had to make concessions. During one period the merchants were even integrated into some feudal governments and became administrative officials. Merchants, in short, were able to make gains in a society of individual feudal estates in which land could be bought and sold.

One particular characteristic of Chinese political life began to develop in the Chou period (which followed the Shang) and is often presented as of major importance in determining Chinese social and historical patterns, namely the existence of professional civil servants, some of them scholars — of whom Confucius is the best known. This group, continuing generation after generation, established a "merit system" in government and developed a philosophy of "justice." But their main function seems to have been to preserve the status quo by placing before each ruler the total great landowning interest, which might be injured by his individual actions, especially by indicating how far he could go in regard to exploiting his peasants without risking rebellion.

Finally, what of "development"? Some indication exists that there was development and it had been generally continuous, although necessarily with minor ups and downs. For instance, the great canal connecting the Yellow and Yangtze rivers was built in the early seventh century A.D. and was traversed by ships of 500 to 800 tons, far beyond anything in European shipbuilding until quite recent times. (The May-flower was 180 tons.) In the tenth century, Chinese ships were trading with Arabia. In 1279 the emperor ordered the construction of six hundred ships within two years (for an attack on Japan) and in the same period, as the descriptions of Marco Polo testify, there was a great and rich internal trade. (One matter we might note in passing. The great trade expeditions of the Chinese—vast fleets with more than 25,000 men sailing around Malaya and India to Arabia—are never mentioned in accounts of what the popular histories call the Age of Discoveries—the voyages of Columbus, Vasco da Gama, and others —nor are the voyages of the Arabs or Indians across the Indian Ocean from Southern Africa to Indonesia.)

There is evidence in China of social as well as economic progress. Centuries of peasant revolts, increasing in scope in the eighteenth and nineteenth centuries, wiped out the great feudal estates, so that China in the nineteenth century was ruled by innumerable landlords with comparatively small holdings. They were able to stay in power only by amalgamations in which they pooled their armed forces, and they were less effective in stifling commerce and manufacturing. They were, however, still powerful enough to prevent China from moving into the industrial revolution,[36] "not only [by] the prevention of pro-duction on an increased scale and [by] the imposition of enormous taxes (official and private), but also [by] interference with transport and so with marketing."

By the opening of the present century large sea-coast and river areas in China were strongly mercantile, and if events had continued on the course they had followed in the preceding centuries, the mer-cantile interests would in time have been able to establish political controls, either over China as a whole or in independent states, and would have advanced from mercantile to industrial capital. But, as in India, the course of events was changed by external—imperialist—forces, and these forces combined with those of the "gentry" to drive matters to a revolutionary—communist—solution.

Japan

The ancestors of the present Japanese people came to Japan from Korea and to Korea from eastern Siberia. There they must have been living in a later farming society because they had metal weapons when they arrived in Japan. And they must have been associated with the Mongols because the two languages belong to the same (Ural-Altaic) group, which is as far removed from Chinese as it is from English. When the Japanese came to Japan they found the islands occupied by a food-gathering Caucasoid people (Ainus). They made war on them and drove them into the northern mountains, where they seem to have held out for many centuries. (Some of them, in fact, still exist.) The early Japanese annals are full of stories of expeditions against the inferior, "hairy" white "savages." Chinese traders visiting Japan about 200 A.D. "found the country divided into scores of small clan states, each ruled by a high priestess or a high priest."[37] It was mainly an agricultural economy using irrigation. Classes existed.[38] "They have distinctions of rank. Some are vassals to others." Slaves were buried with their masters but later (as in Egypt) images were substituted, presumably after rebellions. A man could sell his children into slavery or prostitution (there were 15,000 licensed prostitutes in Tokyo). A husband could divorce his wife at will.

The land, although nominally the king's, early had passed into the hands of individual great landowners.[39]

> The local gentry needed protection for their holdings from the tax collectors of the central government. On the other hand, powerful court families and great monasteries were acquiring large tax-free estates, and needed local men to represent their interests on these lands. From these reciprocal needs a pattern of land-holding gradually developed in which the provincial manors and estates were controlled and operated by local aristocrats but were owned, at least in theory, by influential court families or monasteries.

An early poem reveals the same situation of forced taxation that we saw in early Egypt: "Then would come the village head-man rod in hand calling for taxes or service in loud and angry tones."[40] Another modern authority speaks of "serfs" and "forced labor."

Political results accompanied and flowed from these economic and social changes:

> The net result of all this was that centralized government ceased to exist for most parts of Japan. Each estate, freed from encroachment by tax collectors and other state agents, became a small autonomous domain, a semi-independent economic and political unit. . . . The imperial family . . . became in fact simply one among these central economic and political units.[41]

The picture is again clearly that of individual (and not State) feudalism, an individual feudalism more advanced than that of China. And, as in China, it led to incessant and bloody wars between rival landowners. A by-product of such conflict were the famed "Samurai," who provided a method for warfare between rival landowners without resort to mass armies, which, in individual feudal systems, are fraught with revolutionary dangers.

The reason for this dominance of individual landowning in Japan — as in China or Iran — is doubtless ultimately to be found in the topography. A range of mountains extends like a spine down the middle of Japan; from it project ribs on each side to the sea. There are no wide river valleys or plains, like the Nile or the Indus. Within the smaller valleys between the ribs of mountain there was, it is true, some irrigation, but this was a segmented irrigation, not the centralized irrigation of Sumer or Egypt. And not all the crops were irrigated. In modern Japan irrigated rice paddies occupy the bottom of the valleys; on the hills are nonirrigated crops.

By the tenth century Japan was a feudal kingdom similar to twelfth century Italy or England. And within two hundred years it began to take the same course of development as these countries in another respect also, namely commercialism. In the twelfth century we find large, organized trading companies with government representatives and share-holding members. The town of Osaka became a "free city" like London or Genoa, run by the merchants and beyond feudal power. Great merchants, in fact, became bankers for the large estates, as in the Italy of the Medici. Late in the seventeenth century ten corporations had been established in Tokyo and 24 in Osaka; jointly they set up their own marine transport company. The size of the trade is indicated by the fact that 1,500 ships sailed into Tokyo each year. By the middle of the eighteenth century, Osaka had a banking system with bills of exchange and promissory notes.

These developments, no doubt, were due ultimately to the fact that Japan had a small land area, less than one-fifth of which was arable, and an immense seacoast — a ratio of one mile of coast to every 9.5 miles of area. Furthermore, the comparatively calm and sloping Japan Sea coast had fine harbors. Thus a relatively small and non-united landowning class confronted a relatively large manufacturing-merchant class. And, although the landowners feared this class, they also made money out of it. Some intermixture of the two classes took place (as in China), although the two main cores remained distinct. Hence the feudal class found itself opposed by a formidable antagonist — even ruling in one or more cities — which it attempted to suppress only in extremities. And it was able to do so, as when the feudal lords invaded and captured the "free city" of Osaka in 1615. Time, nevertheless, was on the merchants' side. Following the defeat at Osaka, they rallied and in the next two centuries made big strides. The surplus wealth that can be obtained from the soil under feudalism is limited; and in Japan, as in India or China, the limit had been reached. No major increases were possible. But the wealth obtained from commerce and manufacturing did not have such limits and was increasing. By the seventeenth or

eighteenth century, Japan had not a simple feudal but a commercial-
feudal civilization (a phenomenon we shall discuss later in considering
Europe). By the nineteenth century it was ripe for the industrial revolution. European and American influences simply speeded up a process
already prepared for by centuries of commercial development.

III: NORTHERN ASIA

Scythians and Huns

Comparatively little is known of the early history of the vast plains
that stretch from the Baltic Sea to the Pacific Ocean, for the peoples
of this area were nonliterate and did not erect stone buildings, so there
are no remains of cities for archaeologists to investigate and no native
historical records. We have to rely on other sources: more intensive
archaeological research (for weapons, town sites, tombs); anthropological investigations of the people still inhabiting the area (oral traditions, continuity of customs); the records of literate peoples bordering
the area (mainly Greek, Roman, and Chinese).

In about 400 B.C., the Greek historian, Herodotus, described a
people who inhabited the area roughly above and between the Black
Sea and the Caspian Sea, the Scythians, whose way of life he found
strange. The Scythians did not practice agriculture but lived off great
herds of cattle and horses; they constantly roamed with their herds
from territory to territory in search of pasture; the men travelled on
horseback, the women and children in covered wagons with felt tops;
the men wore trousers and boots, the trousers tucked into the boots;
their weapons were bows, spears, short swords, and axes; they wore
gold jewelry (how intricate and how beautiful may be seen in the Treasury of the Hermitage in Leningrad). From Greek vase depictions and
other evidence, we learn that the Scythians were Caucasoid and not
Mongoloid. Archaeological evidence shows that they had been in the
area from at least about 700 B.C., that they buried implements, and
sometimes slaves, with their dead leaders. One grave yielded fifty
slave skeletons.

A similar society was that of the "Huns."

Just how long the Huns had been in the area is not known. There is,
however, evidence of a food-gathering society having existed for tens
of thousands of years in northern Asia and of farming in south Turkestan from about 4000 B.C. The evidence indicates that these early Huns
were Caucasoid (later sometimes mixed with Mongoloid). Their lan-

guage was akin to Turkish and they themselves were originally perhaps a Turkish people.

That they were a powerful people is clear from the Chinese records of wars against them. In 214 B.C. the Chinese drove them out of Outer Mongolia; but a few years later they were back and consolidating a vast empire (a confederation of tribal territories) under the emperor Maodun, an empire extending from Manchuria almost to the Urals. In a battle in 121 B.C., the Chinese record capturing or killing 40,000 Huns, two years later, 70,000; but within twenty years the Huns returned with an army of 80,000 warriors on horseback and defeated the Chinese. Only after a long and savage struggle were the Huns finally defeated; and even then they were not conquered but remained free and in their own territories.

Some five hundred years after the Huns were defeated in China they had moved 4,000 miles across Asia and were virtually under the walls of Rome. Their great leader Attila set up a capital in Hungary, perhaps near the site of modern Budapest. "The so-called palace of Attila . . . seems to have consisted of a vast circular enclosure, a wooden palisade, within which there were a number of separate . . . log or block houses. . . . The whole capital boasted of but a single stone edifice, and this was a bath house." A Roman observer, Ammianus Marcellinus, made comments similar to those Herodotus had made of the Scythians some eight hundred years before:[42]

> None of the Huns plows or even touches a plow handle. For they have no settled home, but are alike homeless and lawless, continually wandering with their wagons, which are indeed their homes. . . . On horseback they buy and sell; they eat and drink, bowed on the narrow neck of their steeds, they even sleep and dream. On horseback too they discuss and deliberate.

In these same years, the vast armies of a people called the Ephtalites were invading Iran. By 500 A.D. they had conquered and ruled over not only Iran but all north and central India. Little seems to be known of them. A Roman observer, however, informs us that they "are of the Hunnish race and bear the Hunnish name, but they are completely different from the Huns whom we know. They alone among the Hunnish peoples have white skins and regular features."[43]

If we take these pictures of the Scythians, Huns, and Ephthalites together, it is apparent that the vast territories of northern Asia from at least 500 B.C. and probably much earlier were occupied by various peoples living in a society economically dependent on domesticated animal herds. The people ate these animals, drank their milk, made clothing of their hides and dwellings from felt made from their wool, used them for transportation and for war. Their social lives were determined by this method of securing their food, clothing, and shelter. They could not live mainly in settled communities because of the great size of their herds and the constant need to move to new pasture lands. Even the very form of their dress—trousers and boots in contrast to the robes and sandals prevalent elsewhere from Rome to China—was determined by the necessities of horseback riding; and their form of warfare—fighting from horseback—was determined by this also.

The society of these peoples is usually called "nomadic," but the term is unfortunate, for it gives the impression of restless wandering by a small group. The essence of the society, moreover, was not its movement but its animal tending; and the society was often, as with the Huns, immense and well-organized. The word "nomadic" also tends to obscure the fact that these peoples must have had a considerable industry. In order to equip their huge armies (which must over the centuries have totalled many millions) with metal weapons and armor, they must have had mining and metallurgical centers. And they must have had considerable leather, wood, and felt manufacturing also, to produce their clothing, leather armor and shields (which they used along with metal), their multitudes of carts and yurts. How much of this was home industry and how much centralized we do not know. But in all these regards we have to remember that the accounts we have of the Huns and others came from hostile peoples. The Greek, Roman, Chinese, and Indian observers all tend to play down their achievements and depict them as "brutal barbarians." Roman and, later, Christian Church anti-Hun propaganda, in fact, still pervades our histories (the "barbarian invasion of Rome," Attila, the "scourge of God," and so on. It would be interesting to know what Attila said of the Romans.)

The different parts of the Hunnish territory were ruled over by various tribes. Within each tribe there were leaders and these leaders had certain special privileges (more than one wife, some slaves), but this, as we have seen, is true of all later farming societies. There was no established Church or hereditary priesthood; there were shamans, and the chief and subordinate chiefs conducted religious ceremonies (sacrifices and prayers to the earth and heaven and ancestors). As among the Germanic farming tribes, the rulers must have been responsible to the total adult male population of the tribe. If we put all these facts together, it appears that this society is a variation of farming society, and not a basically new type of society. It did not, however, make the next step in social evolution and become a civilized society. The reason for this is presumably that animal herding does not allow sufficient wealth to concentrate in one spot for extensive manufacturing or trade centers to develop. This particular farming society, in fact, seems to have been as much a dead-end society as was food-gathering society. In times of stress it could break out of its native territories and make conquests in the surrounding fertile plains-and-valley civilized states — in China, West Asia, and Europe — because of its horsepower and metallurgy, but after conquest it could not maintain a regime against the inherently superior economic and social forces of these civilizations. As the Huns failed in China so did the Mongols a thousand years later; the empire of Attila collapsed in the fourth century, that of Tamerlane in the fifteenth. The two great exceptions were the Moghuls in India and the Turks in Turkey; but both succeeded in conquering and holding not because of their own native social evolution but because they were able to adopt the way of life of the peoples they had conquered.

IV: THE CULTURE OF ASIA

The Chinese have been more facile in making inventions than in using them. . . . Despite the contribution of the compass and gunpowder, of paper and silk, of printing and porcelain, we cannot speak of the Chinese as an industrially inventive people. They were inventive in art, developing their own forms, and reaching a degree of sensitive perfection not surpassed in any other place or time; but before 1912 they were content with ancient economic ways, and had a perhaps prophetic scorn of labor-saving devices that hectically accelerate the pace of human toil and throw half the population out of work in order to enrich the rest.

So Will Durant in *Our Oriental Heritage*.[44] If we read the passage — typical in approach of many historians — superficially, the measured language gives the impression of a man presenting an explanation. Yet the plain fact is that he explains nothing. That the "Chinese" are "inventive in art" but not "industrially inventive" means only that the Chinese had art but not industry. They were "content with ancient economic ways" until "1912" when their national character inexplicably changed. They had Oriental powers of divination which revealed that capitalism would go through economic crises and so should be avoided; hence, we have capitalism in Europe and feudalism in China — and we are in a kind of Mad Hatter's Historical Universe in which anything can happen. Insofar as any explanation at all is involved in such an approach it is presumably genetic. The Chinese apparently lacked the gene for "industrial development" but possessed that for inventiveness "in art."

Pre-Science in India and China

Although the significant advance of knowledge between 3000 B.C. and 1000 A.D. was small compared to that of the preceding two thousand years (when some societies advanced from farming to civilization), the total knowledge amassed was considerable. And this was as true for Asia as for Europe. Asia, in fact, requires special emphasis, for there is in Western accounts often both an ignorance of Asian contributions to knowledge and a tendency to underplay Asian origins. The problem, it is true, is complicated by the fact that place of origin is often difficult to pinpoint because knowledge seems to have spread much more rapidly and widely than had previously been believed, and some inventions could have arisen independently in societies with similar needs. The diffusion of specific inventions, however, seems more and more certain as our knowledge of the extensiveness of trade between and within Asia and Europe increases, both by land and—especially—by sea. A Greek merchant's guidebook of about 60 A.D., the *Periplus of the Erythraean Sea* (the Red Sea, Persian Gulf, and Indian Ocean), describes voyages between Africa and Arabia, Africa and India, Arabia and India, around India from the mouth of the Indus to that of the Ganges, voyages some of which had apparently been made for many centuries. Between the Ganges and the Indus, the *Periplus* lists sixteen trading ports. Beyond the Ganges lay China, which the *Periplus* author knew of but had not visited.

In view of the high development of Chinese shipbuilding, it may well turn out that there was as extensive a trade across the Bay of Bengal and up the China Seas as in the Indian Ocean area. Even though there may have been little direct contact between Europe and China, there was certainly indirect contact, with India as the great way-station. The probability is, then, that when we can establish priority, we can say that an invention was copied from its point of origin.

And in some instances priority can now be established. For example, the following inventions and processes were known in China substantially before they were known in West Asia or Europe: the wheelbarrow, the horse collar, the drawloom, the cross-bow, the technique of deep drilling, casting of iron, the segmental arch bridge, the iron-chain suspension bridge, canal lock-gates, the stern-post rudder, gunpowder, the magnetic compass, porcelain, paper, printing and movable-type printing, the piston-bellows. (On the other hand, the Chinese did not have the screw — used, for example, for wine presses — the force-pump, or the crankshaft.)

Let us now turn to that other great giant of Asia, India, and note something of Will Durant's compact account of Indian knowledge:[45]

> The greatest of Hindu astronomers and mathematicians, Aryabhata, discussed in verse such poetic subjects as quadratic equations, sines, and the value of pi; he explained eclipses, solstices and equinoxes, announced the sphericity of the earth and its diurnal revolution on its axis. . . . The Hindus developed a system of mathematics superior, in everything except geometry, to that of the Greeks. Among the most vital parts of our Oriental heritage are the "Arabic" numerals and the decimal system, both of which came to us, through the Arabs, from India. . . . By the sixth century the Hindus were far ahead of Europe in industrial chemistry. . . . Sushruta described many surgical operations — cataract, hernia, lithotomy, Caesarian section, etc. — and 121 surgical instruments.

If we place this account alongside the list of Chinese inventions just given, the scope of the Asian contribution to knowledge during these centuries begins to appear. And the "Western" bias appears also. If, for instance, in textbooks or histories, any predecessors for Copernicus are given, they are Greek and not Indian. If we look up astronomy, medicine, mathematics, architecture, sculpture in most encyclopedias, we find that by astronomy is meant European-U.S. astronomy, by architecture European-U.S. architecture, and so on. In the *Encyclopedia Britannica* (fourteenth edition) article on sculpture, for instance, we find that the examples given are all either European or from civilizations that are supposed to have led to the European. Wherever, in most accounts, there are references to "contributions" from Asia they are usually either those from the early Near East which "contributed" to the formation of "our heritage," or are included as freakish curiosities outside the mainstream of (European-U.S.) culture.

There also appears to be a tendency to date Asian discoveries later rather than earlier. Many Indian discoveries clearly antedate the existing treatises on them by many centuries, but they are often loosely dated by the treatises alone. The decimal system, we are informed, was known in the fifth century B.C. But there is evidence of its having been known in the Indus Valley civilization by 2000 B.C. or earlier. And the decimal system cannot have existed in isolation; if it was known other mathematical facts must have been known also; and mathematical facts do not grow out of nothing; they arise from the necessities of farming, construction (of buildings, ships, bridges), manufacturing and commerce, and from the astronomical data needed by farming and commerce.

Indian civilization has a continuous history from at least 1700 B.C. when the Indus valley civilization was overthrown, and if it was integrated with that of its conquerors — as seems likely — this has to be extended back to 2300 B.C. It is to be expected, therefore, that some of the "discoveries" of Greece (the great century of Athens was from 500 to 400 B.C.) were taken over from India.

A second fact to emerge from an account such as Durant's is that we cannot simply list discoveries as though they were self-generating phenomena, but must relate them to the general culture of which they were part. For instance, to speak of "industrial chemistry" in ancient India gives the impression that chemistry could grow up in any place and at any time that someone happened to think of it. But there cannot be "industrial chemistry" without industry. Not only was there no "industrial chemistry" in India, there was no true science, but only elements of science and a groping toward a scientific method. What "science" there was in these societies mainly fulfilled the needs of commercial development (the demands of feudal agriculture for knowledge are limited and are soon met), and commercialism could not and did not advance to industrialism in feudal-dominated India.

What is true of India is true of all West and East Asian civilized societies. Because these societies were of the same general type as those of Egypt, Sumer, and the Indus Valley, their knowledge could not rise to a significantly higher level. They all either inherited this knowledge or arrived at it independently out of the same social situations; and the additions which they made were within the same overall framework. They further plotted the stars but they had neither the telescope nor the prism. Their "industrial chemistry" took pottery a step further into glazing and porcelain making, but it could not result in the development of new materials (aluminum) or processes (vulcanizing). Nor could it lead to an understanding of matter (the molecular theory or the periodic table). Their medicine had no microscope, organic chemistry, biology, or physiology upon which to build. There seems, to judge by the number of significant inventions in China, to have been greater advance in China with its individual feudalism and greater commercial independence than in India. But even in China the advance was limited. "Throughout this province," wrote Marco Polo with amazement, "there is a sort of black stone, which they dig out of the mountains, where it runs in veins. When lighted it burns like charcoal, and retains the fire much better than wood." Coal had, in fact, been known in China for some fourteen hundred years before Marco Polo observed it. But the discovery of coal did not and could not of itself produce industry.

What, finally, of the vast tracts of Northern Asia? The only major original contribution of Northern Asia to human knowledge, so far as is now known, was that of the horse, both as a fighting and a working animal. But this, too, was a discovery whose full use had to await the socioeconomic advance that resulted in the horseshoe and harness. In general the level of knowledge of northern Asia was lower than that of East and West Asia to the same degree that its social development was lower.

New Religions and Philosophies

The history of Asian culture during these centuries is marked by advances in human thought that laid foundations for much that was to follow, and by the rise of the major religions of the world: Hinduism, Jainism, and Buddhism in India, Zoroastrianism, Judaism, Christianity, and Mohammedanism in upper West Asia, Confucianism and Taoism in China, Shintoism in Japan. Christianity (and, to some extent, Judaism) we shall discuss later when we discuss the Christian Church, Mohammedanism when we discuss the Arab Empire. Shintoism, formed more than a thousand years later then Buddhism, Confucianism, or Taoism, appears to be largely a codification of earlier animistic and polytheistic beliefs.

THE *Rig-Veda*

The beginnings of West Asian religious and philosophical ideas about nature and humanity we have already seen in considering Sumer and Egypt. We were not able to discuss those of India because there are no written records of the Indus Valley civilization. The earliest record of Indian thought that we possess is in the poems of the *Rig-Veda,* which, it is now believed, extends back to 1500 B.C. and was perhaps first shaped before its authors came to India. Its great god, Indra, was a typical late farming society deity (with parallels from Ireland to Middle America), "the apotheosis of the Aryan battle-leader."[46] Some of the poems, however, reflect a rather sophisticated skepticism:

> Who verily knows and who can here declare it, whence it
>   was born and whence comes this creation?
> The gods are later than this world's production. Who
>   knows, then, whence it first came into being?

Some are wittily anticlerical (in rather Voltairean style). The *Rig-Veda* poems contain, except for the Egyptian and Sumerian fragments, the first written philosophy. Their skeptical note may, however, go back for several centuries, for *Gilgamesh*, as we saw, had skeptical philosophical overtones.

Jainism

The first recorded materialist philosophy is also Indian, that of the Jains, which was formulated in the sixth century B.C. by Mahavira but apparently had still earlier roots. According to Mahavira and his followers, there was no Creator: "matter is eternal." The Jains rejected the theory of the four elements (earth, air, fire, and water) on the nature of matter and advanced an atomic theory (a hundred years before Democritus). "The changes of the physical universe are traced to atomic aggregation and disintegration. The atoms are not constant in their nature but are subject to change or development (parinama). . . . Homogeneous atoms produce different elements by varying combinations."[47] The Jains believed matter and the soul were alike eternal (a dualism anticipating Leibniz). On most questions they were skeptical. "Every proposition gives us only a perhaps, a may be, or *bhàngī*. We cannot affirm or deny anything absolutely. . . ."

How can we explain the development of a skeptical materialism in sixth century B.C. India? The answer must be that, as with Greek materialism, it was connected technically with the sciences and socially with the artisans and merchants. Today, Jainism (in diluted form) is said to be largely the religion of merchants, manufacturers, and professionals. Perhaps it has always been so, changing its views as its adherents changed. Certainly its early atomic materialism suggests the influence of people working with matter (metallurgy or pottery). And its atheistical tendencies suggest the views of a nonruling (but educated) class, for a ruling class normally favors providential concepts as an aid to rule.

Hinduism

The State religion in these centuries in India was Hinduism, as expressed, for instance, in the *Upanishads*. Its philosophical essence and sociopolitical function may be seen, in brief form, in the famous *Bhagavad-Gita* which was originally part of the epic *Mahabharata*. In this epic, when the warrior Arjuna refuses to fight in battle against his own kinsmen, the god Krishna tries to persuade him to change his mind. The four classes of Indian society (the great landholder, the priest, the merchant, and the peasant), Krishna explains, were "created by Me," and, hence, are unchangeable. As to war, Arjuna should have no hesitation. In the first place, the people who will be killed will eventually die anyway: "I am eternal, world-destroying Time, manifested here for the destruction of these people. Even without Thee, none of these warriors, arrayed here in the hostile armies, shall live." In the second place their souls are immortal; Arjuna will be destroying their bodies only: "These bodies are perishable but the dwellers in these bodies are eternal, indestructible and impenetrable. Therefore fight, O descendant of Bharata!" These souls will go through a series of rebirths (reincarnations) and eventually achieve immortality in God: "The great-souled ones, having reached Me, do not come to re-birth, the ever-changing abode of misery, for they have attained the highest perfection." Spiritually strengthened, Arjuna goes forth to battle—the Church and the Army hand in hand.

The doctrine of Hinduism may be summarized as follows: The world was created by a God (Krishna) who is himself unchangeable, indivisibly One, immortal and living in an unchangeable and immortal (invisible) realm. The world itself, on the contrary, is ever-changing and filled with "many" ever-changing, ever-dying phenomena, including the human body. The human soul, however, has some of the attributes of God; it is immortal, unchangeable, and One (indivisible). The human soul can approach the eternal realm of Krishna by transmigrations. Seen in the glorious light of the immortality of the spiritual realm, this changing world, including the human body, is of little consequence.

Here, we may remark, we have the essence of Platonism two centuries or more before Plato.

BUDDHISM

Although many of the doctrines of Hinduism and Buddhism later mingled, this was not always so. The founder of Buddhism, Siddhartha Gautama, the Buddha (the "enlightened" one), was not, strictly speaking, a religious leader at all but, like Confucius, an ethical teacher. Little actually is known of the life of Gautama. His father is said to have been a provincial governor, and his views seem to indicate that he was of middle class, perhaps small landowner, origin. He consistently refused to state whether there was a creative God, a soul, or immortality. His doctrine was, in fact, a repudiation of Hinduism. Whereas Hinduism placed the emphasis on a creative deity, a mystical spiritual world beyond the senses, and immortality, Gautama scoffed at all three and asserted life in this world as the only reality. He attacked the Brahmanical clergy directly: "Neither abstinence from flesh nor fish . . . will cleanse a man." He attacked their wealthy

patrons, the "worldly-minded" with their self-indulgence. He opposed
the Brahmanical sanction for war and capital punishment; he attacked
the established church; he repudiated the church-supported caste
system.

Gautama, however, was no Mazdak advocating peasant revolts
and a peasant communistic state. He specifically urged his followers to
"have restraint under the law"; his method taught personal reformation
and the example of good works. In fact, the general tenor of his doctrine is against social reform, for the underlying note is one of despair.
How deep this note goes does not always seem to be appreciated.

The Buddhist goal is to achieve by renunciation a state of calm
contemplation. The Buddhist must renounce all passions, all ambitions,
all hope of immortality, even all "cogitation"; first, in so doing, he
will come to a state of "joy and ease"; but, in the end, joy, too, will
depart, he will feel neither happiness nor melancholy, but be, as it
were, without feeling or thought, in the state known as Nirvana (liter-
ally the act of extinguishing a lamp). Life, Gautama is saying, is over-
whelmingly pain and at the end is only death. Death is the supreme
evil; it is everywhere and from it there is no escape; facing death, life
seems insignificant; all one can do is to achieve a numbed state of
mind in which its horror is lessened, eventually, perhaps abolished.

What emotions in particular have to be "renounced"? Although
Buddha does not specifically say so, apparently those having to do with
sex — always the main enemy in ascetic doctrine; and the attack on sex
invariably contains a kernel of anti-feminism. This, too, we find in
Gautama, even though he admitted women followers.

> "How are we to conduct ourselves, Lord, with regards to womankind?"
> "As not seeing them, Ananda."
> "But if we should see them, what are we to do?"
> "No talking, Ananda."
> "But if they should speak to us, Lord, what are we to do?"
> "Keep wide awake, Ananda."[48]

In the centuries following Gautama's death his philosophy of
skeptical asceticism was turned into one of mystical asceticism. Nirvana became synonymous with immortality and the doctrine of reincarnation was incorporated. The object of ascetic living was to achieve
not quiescent contemplation but spiritual immortality; and this is the
view which we find later in the Christian Church. (Some of the parallels
between Gautama and Jesus — 500 years later — are extraordinary,
parallels both in doctrine and in career.)

ZOROASTRIANISM

Apparently somewhat before Hinduism and Buddhism were growing up in sixth century India, a new religion was founded in Iran—
Zoroastrianism. In histories of religions it is more fashionable to stress
differences than similarities, but even a brief examination of the main
tenets of Zoroastrianism will suffice to show that it is the germinal
religion from which Judaism (which seems to have taken shape after
the Jews left Babylonia in 538 B.C.), Christianity, and Mohammedanism arose.

There is one supreme god, Ormazd or Ahura Mazda, who created
and rules the world and humanity. Under this god are a group of "min-
istering angels." The god and angels dwell in paradise. Opposed to the
god is an evil spirit, Ahriman (Satan). Under the evil spirits are subordinate evil spirits, or devils, who live in hell. Man possesses not only
body and mind but also "soul," and each soul is immortal. Ormazd
and Ahriman (God or Allah and Satan) wrestle for the souls of people.

After death the good deeds of the soul are weighed before the "ac-
countant's bridge" and if its possessor's good deeds outweigh his evil
deeds the soul is sent for eternity to paradise, but if the evil outweighs
the good it is sent for eternity to hell.

In Paradise one finds "all comfort, pleasure, joy, happiness, and
welfare, more and better even than the greatest and supremest welfare
and pleasure in the world." (The Koran is more specific: "On couches
ranged in rows shall they recline; and to the damsels with large dark
eyes will we wed them.") Hell "is sunken deep, and, descending, most
dark, most stinking, and most terrible, most supplied with wretched
existences, and most bad, the place and cave of the demons and fiends."
At the end there will be a resurrection of the bodies of all the dead, a
last judgment, and the establishment of paradise on earth.

The word of Ormazd is revealed by a great prophet, Zoroaster or
Zarathustra (Moses, Christ, Mohammed), who was born of a virgin
birth. This word is written down in a sacred book, the *Avesta* (Bible,
Torah, Koran).

Several of the above points are clearly but modifications of the
religious beliefs of world food-gathering society: the visible world and
the invisible world; the one supreme god and the subordinate spirits;
evil spirits and good spirits; the body and the soul (or ghost)—beliefs
which were carried into farming society and thence to civilization. It
was apparently in the first civilized societies that the doctrine of the
immortality of the soul became firm and central. In Zoroastrianism, a
series of doctrines developed around immortality: the specific nature
of paradise and hell; the resurrection of the body; the last judgment;

paradise on earth. There is little in it of the serious wrestling with philosophical problems of Hinduism, Jainism, or Buddhism.

CONFUCIANISM

When we turn to China we find a situation similar to that in India: two seriously philosophical religions arising, Confucianism and Taoism, the first of which was, in its origins, like Buddhism, essentially ethical and later was given a supernatural slant.

Confucius, like Gautama, refused to discuss God, the creation of the world, the soul, or immortality. "Chi Lu asked about serving the spirits of the dead. The Master said, 'While you are not able to serve men, how can you serve their spirits?' Chi Lu added, 'I venture to ask about death.' He was answered, 'While you do not know life, how can you know about death?'"[49] (In reading both West and East Asian philosophers a European or American reader is apt to miss their humor —usually a refined irony. Confucius certainly had it, and so, too, did Gautama: "Keep wide awake, Ananda.")

Like Gautama also, Confucius emphasized conduct, without, however, Gautama's asceticism or pessimism, and not so much individual conduct as political conduct. " 'The relation between superiors and inferiors is like that between the wind and the grass. The grass must bend, when the wind blows across it.' "

Knowledge to Confucius was not knowledge of metaphysical abstractions but of people, knowledge that could be helpful in securing better government. His political philosophy was that of the Chinese scholar-officials, who, as we have seen, were sometimes in disagreement with individual feudal rulers, opposing, as did Confucius, war and excessive oppression and urging a policy of benevolent despotism. They did not, however, advocate any basic changes.

TAOISM

The philosophy of Confucius appears to have arisen partly in reaction to that of Lao Tze and the Taoists. In its original form Taoism seems to have been a naturalistic doctrine reminding one somewhat of Aristotle (with his Prime Mover and immanent essences):

> There is a thing inherent and natural,
> Which existed before heaven and earth.
> Motionless and fathomless,
> It stands alone and never changes;

> If I am forced to give it a name,
> I call it Tao, and I name it as supreme.
>
> . . .
>
> Man follows the laws of earth;
> Earth follows the laws of heaven;
> Heaven follows the laws of Tao;
> Tao follows the laws of its intrinsic nature.[50]

The "Tao" (the word simply means "the way" — both in nature and society) is, like Aeschylean Fate, above "heaven" (i.e., above God) and, like Godwinian Necessity, penetrates all matter. There is, however, also a curious, subjective, mystical element in the Taoist philosophy: "Confucius and you are both dreams; and I who say you are dreams, — I am but a dream myself." Paralleling the naturalistic philosophical strain of Taoism goes that of realism and radicalism in regard to society (this time reminding us of Rousseau):

> The people have certain natural instincts; — to weave and clothe themselves, to till and feed themselves. These are common to all humanity, and all are agreed thereon. Such instincts are called "Heaven-sent."
>
> And so in the days when natural instincts prevailed, men moved quietly and gazed steadily. . . . There were no distinctions of good and bad men. Being all equally without knowledge, their virtue could not go astray. Being all equally without evil desires, they were in a state of natural integrity, the perfection of human existence.
>
> But when sages appeared, tripping people over charity and fettering with duty to one's neighbour, doubt found its way into the world.[51]

What we seem to be dealing with here is a kind of peasant communist outlook with ascetic overtones. The "sages" (apparently court scholars such as the Confucians) "fettered" the people to false ideas; social conflicts arose; "the empire became divided against itself." And along with a harking back to a prefeudal egalitarian "golden age" is the concept of human nature as fundamentally good but distorted into evil patterns by social injustice. The Taoist opposition to feudal evils was often direct: "Here is one who steals a buckle (for his girdle) — he is put to death for it. Here is another who steals a State — he becomes its prince."[52]

Taoism, as Joseph Needham has pointed out, had a strong feminist element. This perhaps stemmed from old farming society feminist patterns, which, as we saw, were kept alive among the Chinese peasant women. The Taoists had "noted" women preachers, were opposed to male dominance, and extolled the feminine way to wisdom.[53] For the "masculine, managing, hard, dominating" method of the Confucians, the Taoists opposed the "feminine, tolerant, yielding" way of seeking truth, receiving truth from the universe as the valley receives rain.

One distinguishing characteristic of Taoism was its association with magic, and we find alongside the Taoist priest "the Taoist magician" with his "liturgical rites for the control of dragon-spirits."[54] If at first this sounds like a repudiation of the naturalistic elements in Taoism, we must remember that originally magic was a kind of prescience, an attempt, in fact, to control nature. The use of magic is also perhaps a further indication of the peasant connections of Taoism, possibly reflecting the ancient magic of food-gathering and farming society continued by the peasants. In time, however, the magic and the mystical elements both became stronger. Like Confucianism, Taoism adopted ancestor worship and became a popular religion. (Early in the present century it had 50 million followers.)

THE STATE RELIGIONS AND THE RISE OF PHILOSOPHY

If we put these various facts together it becomes apparent that beginning in the seventh or sixth century B.C. and continuing into the fifth, there was an extraordinary period of religious and philosophical creativity in both West and East Asia. In searching for the forces which gave birth to and sustained this movement we find that at least two of the religions—Zoroastrianism and Hinduism—supplanted earlier, farming-society ones. The "Aryan" gods, such as Indra and Agni, were supplanted by new gods, such as Siva and Vishnu in India and Ormadz in Iran, and the old magic-type beliefs by theological doctrines. In no case, however, was the supplanting complete; various forms of the old continued beside the new. Even today one finds in Asiatic (and other) countries that the mass of the population still adheres to some aspects of ancient forms of religion that go back into farming and even food-gathering societies. With these have been mixed views from the dominant religion in simplified and personified forms.

The actual process of transition is one area interestingly demonstrated from Hittite records:[55]

> The local shrines remained, their cults unimpaired. The policy of the kings seems to have been to enhance rather than to diminish their importance, while at the same time assuming in their own person the office of the supreme high priest of the realm. . . . High acts of State must be placed under the solemn guarantee of all the gods and goddesses of the realm; and so the Hittite scribes compiled lists of all the local deities for invocation in the treaties and royal decrees.

Farming peoples had their gods, some of them going back into food-gathering times; as civilized societies developed they retained them. But such gods, especially those of local origin, were a potential threat to the growing State church. A compromise was reached whereby the peasants were allowed to retain their own gods but admit their subservience to the State gods, just as they were allowed to keep their own village governments if they obeyed the State government.

If we now put these various facts together, two characteristics of Hinduism and Zoroastrianism emerge: they are State religions and are mainly directed toward the peasantry. And the two phenomena are obviously connected. As the new States of civilization spread out to take in more and more farming communities they had to ensure the loyalty of the peasantry and consolidate their political structure. The retention of the same old religious forms (Brahma, magic, ancestor worship) was clearly a concession to the peasantry and its local priests. And it was a concession which the ruling classes could well afford, for, after all, who cared whether some of the old gods and ceremonies were retained so long as they were subordinated to the State pantheon? Both these religions and the philosophies — Jainism, Buddhism, Taoism, and Confucianism — probably go back ultimately to the same basic phenomenon, namely, the slow but steady increase in wealth. It was this increase that provided the arms and men that enabled the State to spread and consolidate. It was this increase, also, that strengthened the middle classes, both agricultural and urban, and perhaps rendered more restless a greatly larger peasant mass, the first developing philosophy, the second religion. There is evidence that this increase was under way by at least the sixth century, B.C.

Within this general picture we find specific characteristics that are sometimes difficult to account for. Why, for instance, did the doctrine of immortality take the form of transmigration in India, paradise in Iran, and ancestor survival in China? Nor is it clear why philosophies such as Buddhism and Confucianism became State religions. One might presume that they spread to such a degree that the ruling classes in time found it more expedient to adopt and change than to fight them (as later with the views of Jesus and Christian theology). One other question that naturally arises is whether we can detect any notable difference between the religions of West Asia with its predominantly State feudalism and East Asia with its predominantly private property feudalism? One difference has been noted, namely that (State) religion seems more pervasive in India than in China or Japan. And this is as one could expect, for a wealthy centralized State church would clearly wield more influence than individual churches corresponding to each feudal regime.

If we now separate the philosophical and ethical ideas from the religious ones (reincarnation, magic) and compare them with what we know of Sumerian and early Egyptian views, it becomes evident that there was considerable advance in human thought during these centuries. This advance had not, of course, taken place overnight. There were some one thousand five hundred years between Sumer and the *Rig-Veda* poems. The *Rig-Vedas,* however, do not rise above a skeptical agnosticism, and while this may be the beginning of wisdom it is far from its end. Of the four main schools of philosophy, skepticism is but one. There are also materialism, dualism, and idealism, materialism arguing the eternity of matter and explaining all phenomena in terms of natural processes, dualism positing mind and matter as independent entities, idealism (idea-lism and not ideal-ism) positing all phenomena as created by and being the projection of divine Mind (God). Skepticism offers no solutions but contents itself with questioning and with the implication that the basic problems of philosophy are insoluble. That skepticism in some form probably goes back to 3000 or so B.C. we have already noted; and there is an embryonic idealism in the Egyptian text: "Ptah, the Great One; he is the heart and tongue of the Ennead of gods . . . who begot the gods. . . . There came into being in the heart, and there came into being on the tongue (something) in the form of Atum [the Creator]."[56] Nevertheless, there is no evidence of dualism, materialism, a developed idealism or skepticism until about 600 B.C.

If it seems strange at first to think that such philosophies grew up in certain specific places and times, we have to remember that they have not always existed. There is no indication of them in the creation myths and rain gods of farming society. Materialism could hardly have arisen before science began to form, and a broader philosophical view in general must have depended upon a concept of the size of the earth (which depended upon an extensive foreign trade). At any rate, at least by the sixth century B.C., the old belief in an invisible world of local spirits supplemented by agriculturally inspired creation myths had begun to be supplanted on a growing scale by various philosophical views.

The Diffusion of Ideas

If we put together the philosophical concepts which had developed by the sixth century B.C., we find that they anticipate in varying degrees almost all later philosophies. Hinduism and Jainism respectively anticipate Platonic idealism and the atomic materialism of Democritus (and Lucretius). The more solipsistic elements in Taoism and the more mystical in Hinduism anticipate the subjective idealism of Berkeley. And so on.

Without making a detailed examination we might suggest some of the reasons for this anticipation. By the sixth century many of the basic economic and social patterns of civilization had been formed, the patterns, that is to say, which mold general ideas; and the level of knowledge (the immediate source for ideas) was not to make any spectacular advances until the capitalist revolution in Europe was on the threshold of industrialism. Thus, for instance, though the Greece of Plato and the England of Berkeley differed both from each other and from the China of Confucius, all shared the general characteristics of a nonindustrial, commerical-agricultural economy with city life and country life, farm labor and commercial-manufacturing labor, and these general social forms dictated not only certain general patterns of thought but set limits to the level of knowledge. Finally, certain basic concepts in regard to the relationship of people to nature are, after all, limited, and once they have been said they have been said.

On the other hand we must not exaggerate. Only certain concepts arose in these centuries in Asia, not the whole of philosophy. Both Plato's and Berkeley's idealism are more reasoned and less directly religious than Hinduism. The skepticism of Hume, although based on the same premises as that of Gautama or of Confucius, is a fully worked out philosophical system, whereas to them skepticism is little more than an acknowledged fact mainly useful for directing one to other problems. The materialism of the Jains, as we have seen, is mixed with dualism and the necessitarianism of the Taoists with mysticism, whereas Diderot was free from both. Both Plato's Greece and Diderot's Europe, that is to say, although having certain general characteristics in common with feudal Asia, also had special characteristics of their own (for instance, later European commercialism and science which provided new stimuli and materials for philosophy).

The religious and philosophical movements of the sixth and fifth centuries B.C. seem also to have produced a considerable advance in social thought, for instance, that of the Taoists with their universal ethics (including women and the peasantry within the pale), and their concept of human nature as molded by society instead of being a set entity of good and evil at the disposition of supernatural forces. The Confucian ethic, narrow and class-bound though it appeared to the Taoists, was, nevertheless, an antidote to superstition; and so, too, with some of the teaching of Gautama.

In social thought, too, these centuries anticipate later concepts, anticipations which are seldom taken into account. The Taoists antici-pate Rousseau, and the Confucian "middle way" anticipates Aristotle's "golden mean." Just as one cannot speak absolutely of the "contribu-tions" to philosophy as such of Plato or Berkeley, so one cannot speak of the "contribution" of Aristotle or Rousseau without taking the

Taoists or Confucians into account. Were these and other ideas simply a matter of anticipation or could there have been an influence from early Asian thought upon European? It seems likely that there was such influence. The parallels in Plato, Aristotle and Democritus with Indian thought seem too great to be coincidental, and, in view of what we now know of East-West trade, influence from China is possible also. The Greeks, in turn, influenced the Romans (for instance Democritus influenced Lucretius), and Roman thought early penetrated European thought. Indian and other philosophies influenced the Arabs and the Arabs influenced European thinkers. There is perhaps more complex intertwining of human thought up the cultural rope of the centuries than is generally believed. Not, of course, that later thinkers simply took over the ideas of earlier ones but they adapted and developed certain concepts which particularly fitted the needs of their societies, much as happened with inventions; and, also as with inventions, so long as the need persisted so did the ideas.

Art

The first room of the Metropolitan Museum's "Near Eastern and Far Eastern Galleries" contains a series of Persian rugs hung from ceiling to floor, rugs in brilliant colors and intricate designs. In the next room is a picture of the Indian Emperor Shah Jehan; he sits straight and stiff on his horse, a lance in his hand, and on the caparisons of the horse we see the same elaborate designs as on the rugs, and the same richness of color throughout. The rugs are Persian, the picture Indian, but the spirit and technique are the same. In other cases are bronze coffee urns and other vessels with most intricate patterns etched upon them; and in still others glassware with brightly colored designs. But if we move next to the room containing Chinese porcelains we find they have a simple, swanlike grace and are in plain colors. In the first Chinese painting room we see "Landscape with Birds." The landscape is in browns and blacks of the most delicate and blending shadings; the only other patches of color allowed are on the birds and most of these are simply white and black; a few only have brief touches of red. Some of the pictures are on silk or paper scrolls and only a part is visible in the curtained cases.

The same simplicity of line is seen in the jade room, with its small jars, dishes, and jewels. In the Japanese room, we find a six panel screen painting, "Mountain Landscape," in a style similar to the Chinese, with a blending of blacks and whites rather than blacks and browns, but with the same delicacy of touch, the suggestion of the looming mountains, the black hairline bridge, the touch of mist, the quiet, curving stream. An eight panel screen, "Scenes from the Tale of Genji," has more color and more movement than the Chinese but the general technique is the same.

The difference in architecture is even more striking. In India and West Asia in general we find towering stone temples and palaces (the cave temples at Ajanta carved from the solid rock, the Taj Mahal). Not only are these edifices massive, they are worked in the most intricate detail with bas reliefs, friezes, and statues. We have only to place beside them a photograph of the Summer Palace at Peking or a Japanese temple to see the difference. The Chinese and Japanese buildings are not in stone but in wood, not towering massively in the air but built on one floor only, with sloping roofs delicately upcurved at the ends, like wings. The emphasis is not on massiveness and detail but lightness of line and delicacy.

Similar differences are to be found in literature, as is obvious if we put the massive Indian and Persian epics (*Mahabharata* or *Shahnamak*) side by side with the slight *hokkus* of Japan or the almost equally brief poems of the Chinese classical tradition. The Indian-Persian emphasis is once again upon the vast and splendid, the Chinese-Japanese upon the elegant and slight, the Indian-Persian upon intricacy of design or plot, the Chinese-Japanese upon simplicity of form. And so, too, with the interminable Indian dramas (in eight or more acts) and the brief Nō plays of Japan.

The fundamental explanation for the difference must surely somehow lie in the fact that in West Asia there were in most times and places powerful centralized governments, military establishments, and churches, in China and Japan individual regimes with a less pervasive religious influence. In regard to architecture, for instance, it is clear that the expense of massive stone temples is more easily borne by a centralized State than by individual landowners, and a centralized State could more easily concentrate a large block of labor power.

These factors, however, cannot have been the only ones, for expense and labor power do not determine the length of poems or the design of pottery. What we are dealing with is an all-pervasive cultural atmosphere which must have roots in the deeper structures and conflicts of the society (of which expense and labor power are but manifestations). It is not difficult, for instance, to perceive that the psychological atmosphere of the ruling landowning class in an unstable private property feudal society would differ from that of one in the relative security of State feudalism. Elegance, as opposed to ostentatious magnificence, might well seem "the way." There is, of course, magnificence in East Asia, particularly in Indo-China; whenever a landowner can safely display magnificence he does so. And one will find elegance in West Asia. There are elaborate Chinese porcelains and simple designs in Indian art. These things are not absolutes. But there is a basic trend in one direction in West and another in East Asia.

There are, however, also, it must be emphasized, basic points in common, for, however much the two kinds of feudalism differed from each other, they were both feudalism. We might note, for instance, in the art of both the same characteristics that we saw in early Egyptian art also: the static quality, the stylized uniformity of conventional patterns, the emphasis on form rather than on content, and, finally, the narrow scope of the art. The great stream of life, the life of the peasants, or the great upheavals of society—wars and revolts with their massive violence and suffering—are almost untouched in a plethora of depictions of royal personages, landscapes or animals. These are also, we might note, the characteristics of European feudal art: the motionless, stylized figures in illustrated manuscripts or tapestries; the patterned friezes and pillars of the great cathedrals.

There was also, as always, "folk" art which originated in food-gathering societies and continued as lower class (primarily peasant) art; and there grew up an art of the commercial city centers. Furthermore, there must have been reciprocal influences between all three kinds of art, aristocratic, commercial and lower class. As in Sumer or Egypt the craftsmen who built the temples or smelted the bronzes were of the lower classes and brought folk motifs into their work; and homecraft art must have been influenced by the dominant modes.

Literature

West Asia

The only works of Asian literature which have become part of the general European or American cultural stream are *The Arabian Nights* (*The Thousand and One Nights*) and Omar Khayyam's *Rubaiyat*, the first a collection of tales from Persia, India, and other West Asian countries put together in Arabic in the fifteenth century, the second a series of poems expressing the antireligious skepticism of an eleventh century Persian mathematician (rather similar to that of the Jains):

> Some for the Glories of this World; and some
> Sigh for the Prophet's Paradise to come;
> Ah, take the Cash, and let the Credit go,
> Nor heed the rumble of a distant Drum!

The vast bulk of Asian literature has not even been translated into English; hence the English-speaking critic labors under a severe handicap.

The *Rig-Veda*, with its 1,028 poems, is not only a religious or philosophical work. Even in translation and in brief samples one can sense the presence of true poetry:

> The horse likes a light-laden cart,
>   gay hosts attract the laugh and jest:
> Man longs for woman, natural as
>   the parched frogs longing for the rains.

The two classic Indian (Sanskrit) epics, the *Mahabharata* and the *Ramayana*, were apparently originally composed about 500 B.C. — a thousand years after the *Rig-Veda* — and added to in the succeeding centuries. The *Mahabharata* is about eight times the combined length of the *Iliad* and *Odyssey* (which precede it by some 300 years). The *Ramayana* is considerably smaller but still contains 24,000 couplets in seven books. The *Bhagavad-Gita*, as we noted, is incorporated in the *Mahabharata*, which deals largely with war, a war said to be based on an actual struggle for the fertile farm land of the Ganges valley in about 1000 B.C. Interspersed with the action are moral digressions, religious homilies, prayers and romantic episodes, apparently added later by various priests who used the popular story (the beautiful princess Draupadi is the heroine) as a vehicle for religious propaganda. The *Mahabharata*, in its original form, seems to have been an epic of the same general nature as the *Iliad*, a story of romance and heroic war. Both the *Mahabharata* and the *Ramayana* (the story of Prince Rama and his wife Sita) are very different in style from the direct *Rig-Veda* poems and display that romantic sense of wonder and magnificence which one finds also in the Homeric epic. Whether there was an actual influence from Homer on these epics does not seem to be known, but whether there was or not — both might have roots in a common folk epic tradition — it is clear that both the Indian and Grecian societies had certain common ideas and interests.

As a sample of the drama let us consider Kalidasa's *Shakuntala* (written about 500 A.D.). In the opening scene the king Dushyanta, hunting in the forest, enters the grounds of a hermitage, and there sees Shakuntala, the foster-child of the chief of the hermits, and two girl companions.

King (listening): Hark! I hear voices to the right of yonder grove of trees. I will walk in that direction. (Walking and looking about.)
    Ah! here are the maidens of the hermitage coming this way to water the

shrubs, carrying watering-pots proportioned to their strength. (Gazing at them.) How graceful they look! In palaces such charms are rarely ours; The woodland plants outshine the garden flowers. I will conceal myself in this shade and watch them.

                                       (Stands gazing at them)

(Enter Sakoontala, with her two female companions, employed in the manner described.)

Sakoontala: This way, my dear companions; this way.

Anasuya: Dear Sakoontala, one would think that Father Kanwa had more affection for the shrubs of the hermitage even than for you, seeing he assigns to you who are yourself as delicate as the fresh-blown jasmine, the task of filling with water the trenches which encircle their roots. . . .

King: This youthful form, whose bosom's swelling charms

By the bark's knotted tissue are concealed,

Like some fair bud close folded in its sheath,

Gives not to view the blooming of its beauty.

    But what am I saying? In real truth, this bark-dress, though ill-suited to her figure, sets it off like an ornament.

From this first scene it is apparent that we are not being shown real characters in real settings but ideal figures in colorful pictures, reminiscent of Indian (or Persian) paintings of graceful, motionless figures in flowered landscapes, but if we will indulge that "willing suspension of disbelief" that Coleridge called for we can be enchanted by a quiet, sensuous charm and beauty that comes through the poetry even in translation. The romantic, magical, and melodramatic elements of the play remind one of the European medieval "romances" of lovers separated by evil spells and finally reunited, or the plays of Peele or Lyly. Kalidasa can also, like the Elizabethans, alternate his serious scenes with comedy.

In spite of its beauties, however, we have to recognize that *Shakuntala* (written, we might note, at a time when the English people were still living in farming society), is essentially a feudal product. It has the charm and prettiness of such "medieval" romances as *Aucassin and Nicolette* and suffers from the same limitations. Its life-range is narrow. Only the feudal aristocracy is seriously depicted; lower class characters are treated with comical condescension. The lives of the peasantry or even the middle classes are as absent as they are, say, in Malory's *Morte d'Arthur*. And even the aristocratic characters are unreal—godlike figures displaying conventional emotional patterns like so many tableaux, their speech not that of life but the dead language of the classics. The wonder is, however, how much Kalidasa is able to achieve within these bounds.

If we consider no more than these three works, it is clear that literature made considerable strides in Asiatic civilization following Sumer and ancient Egypt. The drama has developed. The Indian epics are more extensive and varied than was *Gilgamesh*. Development in literature, or any other art, however, is not the same kind of thing as development in knowledge. Development in knowledge is essentially quantitative; in general, the more knowledge the more control and understanding. But in literature neither range nor variety necessarily imply superiority. *Gilgamesh* lacks the range and variety of the *Ramayana* but it has greater depth of thought (into agnosticism), superior unity of form, and sharper intensity of mood and style. On the other hand, the new scope in epic form contained possibilities for development that the narrower form of *Gilgamesh* did not.

East Asia

The earliest of the upper class literary arts in East Asia was poetry. The *Shih Ching* or *Book of Odes* goes back beyond the sixth century B.C. In reading some of its poems and other Chinese poetry in the brief collections of Arthur Waley and others we fail to grasp how vast is the body of Chinese poetry and how small the sample that we are getting. For instance, the "Complete Collection of the Poetry of the T'ang Dynasty," published in 1707, contains 48,900 poems in 900 volumes.

The poems which are usually given in translations are also almost exclusively upper class poems, although they are presented simply as "Chinese," or "Japanese." For instance, the evocative fragility of a Japanese *Haiku:*

> The summer grasses grow.
>   Of mighty warriors' splendid dreams
>   the afterglow—

or the brittle irony of Po Chu-I, poet and politician:

> Sent as a present from Annam—
> A red Cockatoo.
> Colored like the peach-tree blossom,
> Speaking with the speech of men.
>
> And they did to it what is always done
> To the learned and eloquent

> They took a cage with stout bars
> And shut it up inside.

Whatever the range, the dominant East Asian feudal tradition must be adhered to, namely subtlety and understatement. Just as the artist or the architect must achieve his effect with a minimum of line, so the poet must achieve his with a minimum of words.

The aristocratic tradition, however, is not the only tradition in Chinese or Japanese poetry. One of the favorite Chinese poets, and one of the world's great poets, Tu Fu (712–770 A.D.), was a man who, like Dante, knew poverty, exile, and suffering. It is startling to place beside a body of aristocratic verse his direct and powerful denunciation of war:[57]

Last night a government order came
To enlist boys who had reached eighteen.
They must help defend the capital. . . .
O Mother! O Children, do not weep so!
Shedding such tears will injure you.
When tears stop flowing then bones come through,
Nor Heaven nor Earth has compassion then. . . .

Boys are only born to be buried beneath tall grass.
Still the bones of the war-dead of long ago are beside the Blue Sea when
   you pass.
They are wildly white and they lie exposed on the sand,
Both the little young ghosts and the old ghosts gather to cry in a band,
When the rains sweep down, and the autumn, and winds that chill,
Their voices are loud, so loud that I learn how grief can kill. . . .

The poem is a Chinese poem, marked as such not only by its language but by the delicate picturesqueness of the imagery, even amid the central storm of the verse. But in its violence of emotional and intellectual commitment it flies in the face of the dominant mode, almost, it would seem, deliberately. One wonders how many other such poems and other works there are which do not find their way into the standard translations.

Poetry was the old "classic" form of Chinese aristocratic literature. The novel came many centuries later and is said to have been introduced by the Mongols from West Asian models, but no West Asian novel earlier than the earliest Chinese novel (apparently about the thirteenth century A.D.) seems to be recorded in general literary histories. Nor were there European models. The first real novel on record comes not from West Asia or Europe, but Japan, Lady Murasaki's *The Tale of Genji* written about 1000 A.D.

The novel when it did appear in China was a middle class literary form reflecting the hurly-burly everyday life of the cities (and not "spiritual" concepts of the aristocracy). It was, in consequence, looked down upon as vulgar. One scene from Chin P'ing Mei may serve as a sample. Hsi Men and his mistress, Gold Lotus, have murdered Gold Lotus' husband, One hundred days later the mourning ends with an official ceremony in which Gold Lotus has participated as chief mourner.

During the midday pause [the priests (bonzes)] went back to the cloister for a frugal meal. When the recess was over, it happened that one of them returned to the house of mourning before the others. By chance the room wherein the priests had discharged their liturgical duties was divided from the bedroom of the young widow only by a flimsy wooden partition. The bonze stepped over to wash his hands in a bucket of water that stood beneath the bedroom window when he suddenly became aware of a suspicious whispering and panting, of sighs and moans, of grunts and stifled outcries — in short, of all the unmistakable sounds that betray the act of love. Pretending still to be washing his hands, he stood on the spot and listened. And now there came to his ears, quite clearly, broken phrases, uttered in a woman's voice.

"Darling! — Take care, you're hurting me! — Oh, they'll be back directly, and they'll hear us. — Let me go! Go away, quick! — "

And then in masculine tones:

"Don't be afraid! Now the stove door is open, I must just burn another quickly. . . ."

It is difficult to conceive of anything less "Chinese" (or a greater contrast to *Shakuntala*) than this — in accordance with the usual equating of "Chinese" with subtlety, serenity, and half-tones. Full of the same rollicking, sardonic lustiness as the masters of European fictional comedy (who also derived from the commercial as opposed to the feudal strata of society) its author, too, takes aim at feudal values. This is apparent not only in its anticlericalism but in its unrestrained depiction of the joys of sensuous living and its emphasis on middle class life.

In Japan the novel apparently began as an aristocratic medium. The social conditions that nurtured the atmosphere of cultural freedom which produced *The Tale of Genji* (written by a woman, Murasaki Shikibu) are indicated in the novel itself. They are those of the commercialized nature of Japanese feudalism and the almost continuous warfare between the (comparatively small) feudal estates. *Genji* gives us a picture of an imperial court in which the Emperor has no absolute authority but has to juggle rival feudal domains in order to maintain a balance of power. In such a situation each faction would need certain freedoms which would be discouraged in a State feudal order or within the larger domains of the Chinese aristocracy. In the novel Genji first encounters Murasaki (the heroine) as a child, and, after the death of her grandmother, adopts her:

> Gradually he persuaded her to get up and look about her. In her shabby dress made of some dark grey material she looked so charming, now that she was laughing and playing, with all her woes forgotten, that Genji too laughed with pleasure as he watched her. When at last he retired to the eastern wing, she went out of doors to look at the garden. As she picked her way among the trees and along the side of the lake, and gazed with delight upon the frosty flower-beds that glittered gay as a picture, while a many-coloured throng of unknown people passed constantly in and out of the house, she began to think that this was a very nice place indeed. Then she looked at the wonderful pictures that were painted on all the panels and screens and quite lost her heart to them. . . .

Some years later Genji marries Murasaki; after many years of happy married life she dies:

> Certain priests had, it was found, stayed behind to watch the body, and sending for them Yugiri now instructed them in their duties. It was many years since his thoughts about Murasaki had been other than he could publish to all the world. But since he caught sight of her on the morning of the typhoon, he had often wondered whether they would ever again be brought together. Her voice he now knew he would never hear; but there was still a chance to see her once again, and while scolding one of the maids for the loudness of sobbing, as though absent-mindedly, he pulled up a corner of the curtain. The daylight was still feeble, and he could see very little. But at that moment Genji himself held up the great lamp, bringing it so close to the couch that Yugiri suddenly saw her in all her loveliness. "And why should he not see her?" thought Genji, who knew that Yugiri was peeping. But in a moment he covered his eyes with his sleeve. "It is almost worse to see her now, while she is still unchanged," he said, "One thinks that she will speak, move. . . ." Yugiri brushed away the tears that kept on dimming his eyes. Her hair lay spread across the pillows, loose, but not tangled or disorderly, in a great mass, against which in the strong lamplight her face shone with a dazzling whiteness. Never, thought Genji, had her beauty seemed so flawless as now, when the eye could rest upon it undistracted by any ripple of sound or motion.

Although her world is circumscribed by the imperial court, its intrigues (of love and politics) and its personages, Lady Murasaki depicts it with a quiet humanity, at times (as in the death scene of Murasaki) with poignant power and with a psychological penetration beyond anything in previous literature.

There is, of course, no possibility of ascertaining personal details about individuals in early nonliterate societies; and in Egyptian and Asian civilizations literature was not, with few exceptions, biographical or autobiographical. Insofar as it dealt with individuals it dealt with them as historical figures, recording acts and facts, as in the Chinese historical annals, or it consisted of anecdotes about religious leaders. One exception is the diary of Murasaki Shikibu. Her diary focuses a light on the life of the individual in the tenth and eleventh centuries, giving, as it were, one close-up in the annihilating sweep of life. It is not, of course, representative of the lives of the majority; but of the lower classes, of the peasants, in their hundreds of millions, no such record exists, and we have to make do with what we have.

Lady Murasaki tells the following anecdote about her childhood, and we may let it stand as representative of many childhoods:

When my brother Nobunori (the one who is now in the Board of Rites) was a boy my father was very anxious to make a good Chinese scholar of him, and often came himself to hear Nobunori read his lessons. On these occasions I was always present, and so quick was I at picking up the language that I was soon able to prompt my brother whenever he got stuck. At this my father used to sigh and say to me: "If only you were a boy how proud and happy I should be." But it was not long before I repented of having thus distinguished myself; for person after person assured me that even boys generally become very unpopular if it is discovered that they are fond of their books. For a girl, of course, it would be even worse; and after this I was careful to conceal the fact that I could write a single Chinese character. This meant that I got very little practice; with the result that to this day I am shockingly clumsy with my brush.

In the winter of 1008 she returned home for a visit:

Two days after I arrived, the snow did indeed begin to fall. But here, where everything is so sordid, it gives me little pleasure. As, seated once more at the familiar window, I watch it settling on the copses in front of the house, how vividly I recall those years of misery and perplexity! Then I used to sit hour after hour at this same window, and each day was like the last, save that since yesterday some flower had opened or fallen, some fresh song-bird arrived or flown away. So I watched the springs and autumns in their procession, saw the skies change, the moon rise; saw those same branches white with frost or laden with snow. And all the while I was asking myself over and over again: "What has the future in store for me? How will this end?"

The diary ends in 1010 and we know no more of the life or thoughts of the Lady Murasaki.

In the sixteenth century, as we have seen, the commercial port city of Osaka became a virtually independent State under merchant-manufacturer control similar to the "free" cities of Italy. The leading novelist of Osaka was Ihara Saikaku, born in 1642. His story called *The Barrelmaker Brimfull of Love* concerns the love of a barrelmaker for a peasant girl who has come to the city to work as a servant; and a former abortionist, now making her living by grinding flour, as a go-between. We are now out of the palace and into the city with a vengeance, and not the upper but the lower strata of city life. Saikaku does not, it is true, absolutely identify with these characters; his attitude conveys, even in the opening, a certain element of ironical condescension; but mixed with this there is also genuine interest; they are not perhaps, he seems to be saying to his readers, quite "our class," but they are "ordinary people" like us and their story is of interest. In his defiance of the aristocratic mode he goes further than Boccaccio or Chaucer (writers of the European "free" cities), using at times a certain deliberate roughness of style.

Such phenomena are never, of course, confined to one art. As in Italy, so in Japan, we find a transformation in painting. By the time of Kiyonaga (1752–1815) and Hokusai (1760–1849) both of Tokyo, the old style of muted color and fine line in filmy landscapes has been supplanted by vivid color and firm line in a wide variety of subjects. In Kiyonaga and Hokusai we have no leisured court artists but men caught in the rush of commercial life. Kiyonaga painted theatrical playbills, Hokusai pictures for greeting cards; both specialized on prints; the output of both was enormous; in his top year (1783) Kiyonaga published 144 works. He concentrated on colorful and sensuous pictures of Tokyo courtesans; Hokusai applied the new techniques to nature (in his famous "wave" pictures or his "Mount Fuji on a Clear Day"), but also—in his "Life in the Eastern Capital"—produced a series of realistic sketches of everyday city life that rival the best of Hogarth.

With Kiyonaga and Hokusai we stand on the edge of modern industrial Japan; and with this a new story opens.

VI

Oceania

OCEANIA (using the word in its broadest sense) embraces, first, the islands off the coast of East Asia, Sumatra, Borneo, Java, the Philippines, New Guinea, then the semicontinent of Australia, and finally the smaller islands beyond these greater ones extending out in the Pacific to the vast triangle of Polynesia—with Hawaii at the north apex, New Zealand at the southwest, and Easter Island at the southeast. Sumatra, Borneo, and Java (now, with their smaller islands, known as Indonesia) were socially and historically part of the Asian mainland, and most of the other islands, as we shall see, were originally projections of Asian farming society out into the Pacific. The most notable exception was Australia, which was inhabited by food-gathering people, who apparently moved over from the mainland about 20,000 years ago. But most of the islands were without human habitation during the long millenia of food-gathering society and were first occupied by farming people within the past four thousand years. Present evidence indicates a steady movement outward into the Pacific from Asia and then long movements north and south into Polynesia. There is evidence of migration to the Philippines by 1700 B.C., of occupation (by radiocarbon dating) of the Marianas, directly east of the Philippines, by 1500 B.C., of Samoa by 1 A.D., of Tahiti by 200 B.C. Tahiti apparently became a taking off point: north to Hawaii (290 A.D.), and south to New Zealand (1100 A.D.).

Was this far-flung colonization done by one people, or by many? The evidence is conclusive that most of it was done by one people, and that they came from East Asia, for everywhere in Polynesia and its outlying islands we find the same kind of tools, craftsmanship, boats, traditions, language, physical characteristics, and imported plants (for instance, the sweet potato) and animals (pigs and hens), and all these have East Asian parallels. A good test of language similarity is that of numerals (those of Indo-European languages far and long removed from each other still show the same roots). In Hawaii, the number one is "kahi," in Tahiti (some 2,000 miles away), "tahi," in New Zealand (some 4,000 miles from Hawaii) "tahi," and so on. The Polynesian languages as a group are connected with those of the Philippines and Malaya; and the Malaya-Polynesian languages are affiliated with the Thai-Kadai group, spoken in Thailand and parts of Taiwan.

It is thought that the migration from the mainland began between 2000 and 1600 B.C. and that it then moved out in successive waves across the Pacific. What began the migration is not known, but perhaps it was connected with the rise of the realm of the Shang in North China. The tide of empire moving south may have threatened to engulf farming peoples and some of them in the coastal areas took to the sea.

When we hear that the Polynesians used "canoes" we tend to discount their capacity for long voyages, but when we perceive the size and nature of these canoes, the picture changes. They were dugout canoes, sometimes 6 feet wide by 60 to 100 feet long; two of them were placed well apart and a deck with sails was constructed between them. Such craft, as modern experience has shown, could certainly navigate the Pacific and survive everything but the worst of storms. Drawings and pictures show that they could carry a large number of people and supplies and we know that they made voyages of 2,000 miles, for although these people had no compass, they had considerable knowledge of the stars, particularly of the constellations, and made star-navigation charts of large areas.

As examples of the kinds of society which these Asian migrants established when they got to their Pacific islands, I shall take New Zealand and Hawaii, both of which are far enough away from Asia to illustrate maximum independent development and large enough to have integrated and varied social structures. They also differ considerably from each other.

NEW ZEALAND

The earliest record of habitation of New Zealand comes from a radiocarbon dating of 1125 A.D., although this seems remarkably late when we consider that New Caledonia was inhabited by 800 B.C., but unless further research gives other results we have no choice but to accept the dating. The people who inhabited it, unlike those on other islands, appear to have been food-gatherers (who lived in part by hunting a large bird called the moa). Whether they were the ancestors of the later farming inhabitants (the Maoris) is not clear; nor is it known whether this food-gathering society developed into a farming society or whether the farming society was begun by a large expedition which is said to have come from Tahiti in about 1350 A.D. (about the time of the birth of Chaucer). When Captain Cook arrived at the islands in 1769 the population is thought to have been at least 200,000 and was divided into some twenty tribes, living mainly on the (warmer) North Island.

Although the Maoris, like the other Polynesians, were primarily a farming people — and it is well to stress this, as one gets the impression from some popular accounts that they were primarily fishers and hunters — they had few crops and no domesticated animals. Their main crops were the usual Polynesian root plants: the sweet potato, the yam (a kind of large non-sweet sweet potato), and *taro* (from which the Hawaiian *poi* was made), and they had flax but no cotton. They had no pigs or hens, no draft animals (oxen, donkeys, or horses), no metals, and no pottery. If we add to these natural and social lacks the fact that the Maoris were isolated from other people and hence unable to trade except among themselves, it is clear that they could acquire no great surplus of wealth and, hence, could have no advanced economic or social structure. The remarkable thing is how far they got with what they had. In addition to farming they manufactured a variety of things. They had looms and "plaited and wove flax into baskets, cloaks and skirts. . . . They made adzes and axes of stone, fishhooks and needles of bone."[1] They made great war canoes and out-rigger boats, magnificently crafted and carved, and large meeting houses, some of them 20 feet high.

The Maoris are rare among food-gathering or farming peoples in that one of their number became a world-famous anthropologist and wrote a book about them — Te Rangi Hiroa (Sir Peter Buck), *The Coming of the Maori* — in which he unites a wide knowledge of Polynesia with his own reminiscences as a child in a Maori village. He describes the kind of communal activity that characterized food-gathering and early farming societies as they did later ones: "when one family had completed their work they helped their neighbours." "Only the skilled craftsmen, such as builders, carvers or tatooers received recompense in food and material goods for their labour. The general tasks requiring a number of people were accomplished by community cooperation without thought of pay."[2]

The reason for this community cooperation was that the bulk of the land was owned by the tribe. Families had rights to its use but could not own it. In addition there were also communal storehouses (root plants store comparatively well). Not all the land, however, was thus communally owned. Te Rangi Hiroa also informs us[3] that chiefs sometimes seized "desirable portions of land" for themselves. The chiefs, then, had land of their own and presumably in larger portion then the average; that this was also true — as in other such societies — of subordinate chiefs, warriors and priests is indicated in the social structure.

The Maoris recognized three social classes, the "rangatira" (nobles), "ware" (commoners), and slaves; and to these we should add craftsmen. The slaves were war prisoners or the descendants of war prisoners and apparently few in number. The great mass of the population must have consisted of the commoners — the village families each with its own plot of the common land. The result was a mixed social structure in which a ruling class began to form. But even as it formed it came into collision with tribal democracy. The picture in Sinclair's *History of New Zealand*[4] reminds us again of the Germans as observed by Caesar and Tacitus:

> Chieftanship, with its prerogatives of leadership and power, was hereditary, but a weak chief would find himself superseded. . . . The person of the chief was to some extent *tapu* (sacred); high chiefs were regarded with considerable awe and even dread. . . .
>
> The early Polynesian inhabitants do not seem to have been a warlike people, but they apparently began to fight one another as the population increased and the tribes began to compete for the best land. . . . The fortified hill-top village . . . [and] the intricate combinations of buildings, terraces and scarps, the stockades of tree trunks . . . made the *pa* extremely difficult to storm. These fortifications the Maoris found useful when their islands were invaded by the British.

In culture the Maoris also exhibited the characteristics of farming society peoples. Their knowledge comprised the usual storehouse inherited from universal food-gathering society plus the technical and other knowledge required by farming. Their material and social lacks, however, produced large gaps in their knowledge, for instance, of animal tending, pottery, and metal work. As a result they did not develop a written script or mathematics. Their general ideas on the relation of people to nature seem to have been closer to those of food-gathering than farming society peoples. They do not seem to have had a god of agriculture but had the usual collection of sky-gods and lesser spirits, with a rather wispy belief in an afterlife. Their creation and other myths seem to suggest roots in the ancestral home on the Asian mainland.[5] "Maori religious tradition had its Flood. As in the Mesopotamian theogony, there was the Maori legend of the separation of the earth and sky."

The Maoris shared with other Polynesian people the concepts of *mana* and *taboo*. "The nearest equivalent for *mana* would be 'power for accomplishment.' Thus any object or person who was capable of more than ordinary performance, whether the subject was a hook that caught more than the usual number of fish or a chief who was more than usually good in diplomatic maneuvering, showed in this way that it had *mana*."[6] These ideas are not—as one would sometimes gather— mysterious or unique. The general concept, as Linton also points out, is not restricted to the Polynesians but is found among many food-gathering and farming societies. In such societies, as we saw, invisible spirits, large and small, were thought to be everywhere. Obviously in some things or persons they could be regarded as stronger than in others. Those with stronger spirits—or a bigger slice of a larger spirit —had *mana*. And *mana* was sometimes tied up with *taboo*. For instance to people with lesser spirit-content, people or things with more were *taboo*.

Although the Maoris had no written literature they had a considerable oral one, passed down by word of mouth through the generations and gathering volume as it went. Their poetry is generally similar to that of the Australians or of the North American Indians, and doubtless, like both, reflects an oral literary tradition going back for many thousands of years. In art, like other peoples, they developed their own individual style which utilized[7] "the spiral and scroll as dominant motifs. Woodcarving was very advanced, and everyday articles were often elaborately carved. House posts and walls, canoe prows, food funnels, bird snares, and other such objects were highly decorated." To get the feel of the beauty and originality of this Maori art, one must visit a museum or look at such representations of it as those in Margaret Mead's informative little booklet, *The Maoris and Their Art*. Particularly interesting was their work in jade, for jadework, as we have noted, was typically East Asian, and like their religious myths may go far back in an ancestral tradition.

HAWAII

According to the present evidence the Hawaiian Islands were first occupied about 120 A.D. (a radiocarbon dating—plus or minus 120 years) by an expedition from Tahiti. As Tahiti is more than 2,000

miles south of Hawaii one can presume that the voyage took place
through the numerous islands which lie between the two and that there
had been previous exploratory voyages. The voyagers brought with
them the inevitable sweet potato, yam, and taro; and the Hawaiians
were more fortunate than the New Zealanders in bringing also the
pig and the hen. But like the New Zealanders they had neither cows,
horses, goats, sheep, grains, cotton, pottery, nor metals. And, also like
the New Zealanders, they were isolated from major manufacturing
or trading centers.

Archaeological and other evidence indicates that the first settlers
lived in a farming society similar to that in New Zealand but perhaps
on a somewhat lower level.

By 1500 A.D., however (i.e., about the time of Columbus' voyages),
this society had undergone considerable evolution, perhaps assisted
by Tahitian contacts. By this time "many houses were built on platforms and terraces averaging about 18 feet in width by 25 to 30 feet
in length."[8] The temples now often "consisted of one or more stone-
paved platforms or terraces enclosed by stone walls."[9] Some of them
had stone towers, and all of them formed a center for a "ceremonial
complex" around which were "numerous houses"[10] for the priests and
idols. These artifacts were the expression of a society in a later farming stage of development (rather like that on the Canary Islands):

> The Hawaiian paramount chiefs and their close relatives of nearly equal
> high rank ruled entire islands or large territorial divisions. The land of each
> paramount chief was subdivided into smaller districts, each of which was
> ruled by a sub-chief (*konohiki*) who traced his ancestry to some collateral
> branch of the royal line. . . . The majority of the Hawaiian population were
> commoners (*makaainana*), of course. They were dispersed over the land in
> hamlets, some of which were growing to fairly large size by the time of
> white contact in Hawaii. The commoners worked the taro and sweet po-
> tato patches. . . . Specialists were numerous and varied in Hawaiian cul-
> ture, foremost among them being the priesthood, which possessed a great
> deal of power in profane affairs.[11]

One explanation for these developments is to be found in Roger
Suggs:[12] "Great power would accrue to the chief whose responsibility
it was to control this productive potential and administer such a surplus; at the same time, the separation of the chiefly classes from the
lower classes would be correspondingly wider with every increase in
the economic power of the aristocracy." Social development continued
until by the late eighteenth century an incipient feudal system had become a full-fledged feudalism, with a king at the top: "In theory, a
new king owned all the land of his realm, and after setting aside what

he wanted for himself, he parcelled out the remainder to his loyal followers, who became governors, regional chiefs, or owners of estates."[13] Taxes were, as usual, mainly in goods and produce, but some were in labor also. And, again as usual, there was forced labor, for the king, the chief, or the church.[14] The situation was summed up as follows by a native Hawaiian historian:[15] "The condition of the common people was that of subjection to the chiefs, compelled to do their heavy tasks, burdened and oppressed, some even to death."

As usual in feudal states there was no elected government. Although tribal democracy perhaps—as in India and elsewhere—held sway in the village, in the realm as a whole the king ruled by the aid of a chief counselor and the chief priest. The ancient beliefs in *mana* and *taboo* (*kapu* in Hawaiian), which were relatively harmless superstitions in New Zealand, were used for rule. The upper class was presumed to have a virtual monopoly on *mana* (somewhat like the "elect" of Calvinism). As for *taboo:* "successive rulers and a well-organized priesthood imposed more and more taboos until the commoners were reduced to poverty and desperation."[16]

The real feudal power rested with the major landowners, of whom the king (or chief) was but one. The king had to keep in line with the chiefs, and the chiefs with the sub-chiefs. "The *konohiki* were quick to sense an affront and could effectively overthrow the high chief without so much as a sideward glance at the vaunted supernatural powers of the chiefly line."[17] At least once a mass rebellion similar to the Asian peasant wars erupted but on a smaller scale:[18] "The commoners arose, overthrew the priests and destroyed the temples, so that Hawaii was without an official religion when the first missionaries arrived." As in all later-stage farming or feudal societies there were frequent wars for the land and the labor that went with it.

Hawaiian culture, like that of the Maoris, was generally similar to that of Polynesia as a whole. Its level of knowledge suffered from the Polynesian deficiencies in plants and animals, from its remoteness, and from its lack of pottery and metals. Its more complex economic, social, and political life, however, must have raised this level above that of the Maoris; and its religion is closer to that of a later farming society. Although it had the usual array of greater and lesser gods and spirits, one of its main gods was Longe, the god of agriculture, and another was Ku, the god of war.

Like the Maoris the Hawaiians had a great storehouse of oral literature, particularly of poetry. "The poetry of ancient Hawaii," writes one modern authority, "evinces a deep and genuine love of nature, and a minute, affectionate, and untiring observation of her moods, which it would be hard to find surpassed in any literature."[19] Hawaiian art was similar to that of the Maoris — with variations in level one way or the other. Maori woodcarving seems to be generally regarded as finer than the Hawaiian; the Hawaiians developed the art of the dance (the Hula).

In societies so isolated as these, separated from the mainland and from each other by thousands of miles of ocean, the question of native development versus outside influence assumes particular interest. In general the pattern seems to have been that of the transplanting of a simple farming society from East Asia with development beyond it primarily the result of native sociological evolution. Such development certainly took place in Hawaii, and there is indication of some development in New Zealand also. There seems, then, every reason to assume that the developmental process in Polynesia was the same as that which we have witnessed many times both in West and East Asia. Once a struggle for land begins, certain social, economic, and political patterns must follow. The society is polarized into peasants and landowners, a State arises, consisting of political, military, and religious sections, the king is nominally — as was the chief before him — owner of the land but the real ownership lies with a group of great landowners. But it also seems apparent that Hawaiian society, and perhaps that in New Zealand also, had reached its limit. In a society so limited in natural, social, and technological assets, further progress could only have come through links with other societies. As it happened, both in New Zealand and Hawaii, these influences were imperialistic, British in one case, American in the other.

VII

Africa

THERE ARE SEVERAL DIFFICULTIES in the way of attempting a sketch of early African historical development. In the first place, it is only within recent years that sufficient information for such a sketch has been gathered and put together in general studies, and large parts of the story are still only known in bits and patches. Furthermore, what information on Africa is available is known to comparatively few people. Elementary textbooks, for instance, still point out that all Africa below the Sahara is not "jungle," and that African Negroes until the present century were not all "savages." Even those who are aware of the recently independent African states know little of the African past. "Civilizations" such as Egypt or Carthage, often are considered simply not African.

In this brief sketch I shall consider Africa as a whole, working from West Africa, where the continent bulges out into the Atlantic, into the Mediterranean area, and down the Red Sea and Indian Ocean coast into East Africa.

In the period just preceding the development of farming societies some 10,000 years ago, Africa like the other continents was inhabited by food-gathering peoples. A Caucasoid people lived in the north, along the Mediterranean and Red Sea coast areas, a Negroid people inhabited the territory around the Niger river; the Pygmies inhabited the Congo rain-forest area, and the rest of the vast south was the territory of the Bushmen (with the related Hottentots). How long these various peoples had inhabited Africa is unknown. The fact that some of the earliest sub-human remains have been found in Africa (*homo habilis* of about 1 million years ago) does not mean that man "evolved in Africa" and has been there ever since.

WEST AFRICA

Farming and Trade

Let us begin our survey with the area known as the West Sudan, which is a wide belt of grassland (with trees) stretching out below the Sahara Desert from the Atlantic Ocean eastward to Lake Chad and beyond. It was apparently in the West Sudan that farming societies first began to develop natively in Africa:[1]

> Ancient Egypt acquired agriculture and domestic animals from adjacent Southwest Asia. . . .
>
> It has hitherto escaped attention, however, that agriculture was independently developed at about the same time by the Negroes of West Africa. This was, moreover, a genuine invention, not a borrowing from another people. Furthermore, the assemblage of cultivated plants ennobled from wild forms in Negro Africa ranks as one of the four major agricultural complexes evolved in the entire course of human history.

Some modification of Murdock's remarks needs to be made in the light of recent radiocarbon datings. Farming in West Asia, as we have seen, had developed by 8000 B.C. There is evidence of farming in Morocco by 4200 B.C. and in Libya by 4400 B.C. As the earliest date near the Niger center (some 500 miles to the northeast) so far discovered, is about 3000 B.C., it seems probable that this center was initially influenced directly by more northern African and indirectly by Asian centers. Nevertheless, it appears to have been a genuine agricultural center because of the variety of crops that originated there — cotton, sorghum, okra, watermelons, the bottle gourd, sesame, the oil palm, and the Guinea yam, and possibly rice. The specific area in which these crops developed was that around the headwaters of the Niger, stretching down (for the yam) into the delta region of the lower Niger.

It is doubtless significant that it was in this farming area that civilized states later developed, the states of Ghana, Mali, Songhai, and in lower Nigeria, Ife and Benin. In West Africa the first traces of civilization are just beginning to be put together. Let us take the archaeological evidence first. The discovery of a "tall Negroid skeleton" of "Paleolithic times"[2] indicates that Negro people have inhabited the region for at least 10,000 years and perhaps much longer. Art-work

found in the Sahara indicates that "peoples of Negro type were painting men and women with a beautiful and sensitive realism before
3000 B.C."[3] "Pottery heads and figures of central Nigeria" have been
dated by radiocarbon techniques as early as 900 B.C.

The second set of evidence comes from trade. The Sahara is not,
contrary to popular concept, a vast, impassable stretch of sand. It
contains mountains, hills, oases, and, in large areas, sufficient vegeta-
tion to support people and animals. Moreover, for many centuries it
has been crisscrossed by caravan trails. Extensive trade used these
trails. By 1400 A.D. annual caravans across the Sahara through the
Hoggar Mountains contained 12,000 camels. And there were at least
six other major routes through the desert. In recent years caravans of
25,000 camels have been observed. It was across these trails that the
Romans traded with the Sudan: "Ivory, precious stones, gold-dust,
ostrich feathers, slaves, . . . animals for the amphitheatres of Rome
and elsewhere."[4] Before the Romans the Carthaginians used these
caravan trails—apparently horse-drawn chariots or pack-donkeys
or bullock teams were used before the advent of the camel (around
300 A.D.). Rock carvings indicate that chariots were crossing the
Sahara into the Sudan by 500 B.C. Murdock flatly declares that the
Carthaginians "built their power and wealth on the basis of the trans-
Saharan trade with Negro Africa. . . ."[5] (Carthage flourished from
about 600 B.C. to 142 B.C.) And apparently before the Carthaginians
there were the Berbers, and before animal convoys there were human
convoys. "This traffic doubtless dates from early in the Neolithic
period, for along stretches where some of the principal trails pass over
rocky hammada the bedrock has been polished smooth by the bare
feet of countless thousands of human porters before animal transport
came into general use."[6] It is possible, too, that there was trade by sea;
a Carthaginian voyager, apparently with a large fleet, sailed around the
coast and beyond the mouth of the Niger, perhaps as early as 500 B.C.

GHANA, MALI, AND SONGHAI

The first accounts of the actual states with which this trade was
conducted come from educated observers following Arab trade into
the Sudan. In 800 A.D. an Arab mentioned the state of Ghana, which
was located roughly in the territory between the upper Niger and the
Sahara, stretching westward to the Atlantic. But it was not until 1067
that the first account of the state appeared, written by El Bekri, who
based his account on contemporary records and first-hand reports. The
state was said to have had 22 kings before the Hegira (622 A.D.), which
would take its founding back to about 300 A.D. What states had existed

before it are not recorded, but the trading and archaeological records indicate that there may have been many, perhaps stretching back for a thousand or more years.

El Bekri informs us that in his day the Arab Empire merchants had a separate city of their own near the Negro capital. The Negro king's court he describes as follows: "When he gives audience to his people, to listen to their complaints and set them to rights, he sits in a pavilion around which stand his horses caparisoned in cloth of gold; behind him stand ten pages. . . . The governor of the city is seated on the ground in front of the king, and all around him are his vizirs in the same position."[7] He tells us something of the economy, also: "All nuggets of gold that are found in the mines of this empire belong to the king; but he leaves to his people the gold dust that everyone knows." The king "exacts the right of one dinar of gold on each donkey-load of salt that enters the country, and two dinars of gold on each load of salt that goes out." There was a similar tax on copper and other taxes on merchandise in general.

Of the capital city itself—the exact site of which is unknown—El Bekri apparently says little. The king's residence he describes as consisting of "a fortress and several huts with rounded roofs, all being enclosed by a wall." The city, although obviously quite large and bustling with trade, was not a capital of the wealth or magnificence of those of Maurya or Ghengis Khan.

The Arab Empire traders, one would gather, were primarily interested in gold (and this is thought to have been the Carthaginians' main interest in the region, also). But there was also copper and, as we have seen, a great amount of miscellaneous merchandise. It is clear, however, both from El Bekri's comments and from those of later observers, that although there was smelting of copper, gold and iron, there was comparatively little manufacturing and that the main trade was in the export of raw materials to the richer cities of the Mediterranean and other distant areas. Murdock sums up as follows:

> The products shipped southward from the Mediterranean region throughout the historical period have consisted chiefly of grain to the Sahara and of arms, glass, other manufactured goods, and luxury items to both the Sahara and the Sudan. The Sudan has supplied the Sahara with grain, dried fish, kola nuts, and cotton goods, and the Mediterranean region with a constant flow of ivory, gold, ebony, ostrich feathers, and slaves. A substantial proportion of the gold and ivory held by the peoples of Europe and the Near East prior to the Discoveries Period seems to have been derived ultimately from Negro Africa through the trans-Saharan trade.[8]

The early observers from the Mediterranean world were naturally most interested in trade, and it is this that they emphasize, but trade cannot have been the basis of the economy. As in similar societies elsewhere, this basis must have been farming. Murdock writes of the region's present economy:

> The Nuclear Mande subsists primarily by agriculture, which they occasionally conduct with the aid of irrigation but mainly by shifting hoe cultivation. . . . Animal husbandry holds a significant, though subsidiary, place in the economy."⁹

The plow was not used; and the surplus yield from hoe agriculture convertible into other wealth is very limited. The fact that some grain was exported must indicate a large cultivated area. In fact, the thing that stands out in general is the massiveness of the economy. There must have been extensive mining operations, both of gold and copper. Hunting, especially for elephants, must have been organized on a large scale. And there was clearly some manufacturing if "cotton goods" were exported, but whether this was done in royal workshops or by home industry does not seem to be known.

But before speculating further on the nature of these early civilizations as represented by Ghana, let us look at some later observations. In the eleventh century the state of Mali began to arise and by 1240 had conquered Ghana; in the fifteenth century Mali was overthrown by Songhai; and in 1591 Songhai was conquered by Moroccan armies sweeping down from the Sahara. Both Mali and Songhai were centered in the same region of the West Sudan, namely along the upper Niger, their main cities being Timbuktu, Jenne, and Gao.

On these cities we have considerable information, in part because an Arabic scholar from Fez, known as Leo Africanus, visited the region about the year 1500 and wrote down his impressions. As one used to Moorish cities he found the physical appearance of Timbuktu unimpressive, its houses mere "cottages built of chalk and covered with thatch,"¹⁰ but he found evidence also of great wealth and power— "the rich king of Timbuktu hath many plates and sceptres of gold. . . . He hath always three thousand horsemen, and a great number of footmen . . ."—and of a rich agriculture: "Corn, cattle, milk and butter this region yieldeth in great abundance."

Jenne, he observed, abounded in barley, rice, cattle, fish, and cotton. "Their cotton they sell unto the merchants of Barbary, for cloth of Europe, for brazen vessels, for armour, and other such commodities." Of Gao he wrote:

The houses thereof are but mean, except those wherein the king and his courtiers remain. Here are exceeding rich merchants: and hither continually resort great store of negroes which buy cloth here brought out of Barbary and Europe. . . . Here is likewise a certain place where slaves are to be sold. . . . It is a wonder to see what plenty of merchandise is daily brought hither, and how costly and sumptuous all things be.[11]

If we put all this information together it becomes clear that what we are dealing with is a feudal state somewhat but not greatly above the level of higher farming society. The land, like the gold, was doubtless held theoretically to be the king's, but the real ownership, as everywhere, must have resided with a group of landowners, the wealthy group around the court — in contrast to the usual dismal poverty of the mass of the population. Labor was presumably mainly peasant labor with some forced labor and some slavery. Many of the slaves seem to have been for export. The king and other landowners lived on the taxation of the peasants (a proportion of the crop) and from trade profits and taxation of merchants. The government appears to have been the usual feudal council of top landowners, but doubtless within the villages tribal communal patterns remained strong as they did in similar societies elsewhere. As with Asian and other feudal societies, the various states were in conflict with one another — for land, gold, labor power, booty, and so on.

In Ghana, as we have seen, there were two capitals, one for the foreign merchants and one for the Ghanaian landowners. None of the Ghanaians seem to have been merchants; and in Mali and Songhai also the merchants all appear to be Arabs, Moors, or Berbers. At first this might seem to mean that the Arab and other traders would not permit the Ghanaians to become merchants; but Ghana, Mali, and Songhai were independent states which imposed taxes and other restrictions on the outside merchants and had large armed forces of both cavalry and foot soldiers. The prohibition, therefore, must have been enforced primarily by the native ruling class. The great landowners, that is to say, prevented their countrymen from becoming merchants or manufacturers, at least on any large scale, keeping what manufacturing and trading there was within their own control — the natural tendency of a landowning class.

In spite of these retarding feudal factors, however, were these states progressing economically? This is a question for further research, but the impression one gets from general sources is that they were getting larger and wealthier right up until Songhai was invaded by the Arab Empire. Indeed, it may be that the Arabs decided upon this invasion because they feared developments in the West Sudanese states.

BENIN

When we move south from the West Sudan a little way into southern Nigeria, from the upper waters of the Niger towards its delta, we come to the city States of Ife and Benin. There do not appear to be any Arabic accounts of these states, but when the Portuguese ships arrived at Benin about the year 1500 they found a city about three miles long—"from gate to gate"—and "surrounded by a large moat, very wide and deep, which sufficeth for its defence."[12] The houses of the city were "made of mud walls [a form of stucco?] covered with palm leaves." From the city the king ruled an area about 240 miles long and 120 miles wide and was "usually at war" with neighboring states. The Portuguese purchased slaves for "twelve or fifteen brass bracelets each." The king of Benin sent an ambassador to Portugal— "a man of good speech and natural wisdom"—because "he desired to learn more about these lands, the arrival of people from them in his country being regarded as an unusual novelty."

The political system of Benin is described by Murdock as follows:

> The Edo king maintains a court and a large harem at the capital city of Benin. Here he concerns himself primarily with state rituals, cult activities, and judicial cases. A Queen-Mother and a Queen-Consort hold positions of great influence and prestige, as does the heir apparent, the ruler's eldest son. A hierarchical administrative organization assures the support of the state apparatus by levying *corvée* labor and collecting tribute semiannually in palm oil, livestock, and agricultural produce. These sources of revenue are augmented by court fines, trade monopolies, fees received from prospective titleholders, and the booty obtained in war. Routine decisions are made by a supreme council of seven ranking ministers; . . . for decisions of greater moment they are joined by eighteen town chiefs and twenty-nine palace chiefs to form a grand council.[13]

The states of the lower Niger, then, were essentially the same as those of the upper, feudal states whose rulers lived on peasant taxes, forced labor and slavery, with State control extending down to the village level, although some communal democracy apparently continued in the towns and villages, the "town chiefs" perhaps (as in India or Hawaii) to some degree representing this. We might note, too, in the power of the Queen-Mother a remnant of the higher status of women in food-gathering and early farming society (as found also among the Hittites and in China), but along with this went the degradation of the harem.

Culture — Negro and Arab

Of the culture of these various states much has yet to be learned, but at least the picture is no longer, as it was until quite recently, virtually a blank. We know of no major contribution to knowledge in the area following the initial development of agriculture and it is unlikely that there was any because the societies did not rise above an early feudal level. But there seems to have been considerable interest in knowledge and ideas.

"In Timbuktu," wrote Leo Africanus, "there are numerous judges, doctors and clerics, all receiving good salaries from the king. He pays great respect to men of learning. There is a big demand for books in manuscript, imported from Barbary. More profit is made from the book trade than from any other line of business."[14] The reference to Barbary brings up another problem in investigating the culture of the region, namely, the degree of Arabic influence, for books from Barbary were Arabic books, and these states, following penetrations from the Arab Empire, were subject to Moslem religious and other beliefs and customs. This influence is sometimes misleading because when one reads of a "Moslem" ruler of a Sudanese state, one immediately thinks of an Arab or Moor or Berber, but the basic population and its rulers remained Negro. They were Negro Moslems. And so, too, with the culture. The basic culture remained Negro, the Arabic influence was mainly superficial. To see this we need only visit a museum with an exhibit of West Sudanese and Nigerian art or examine reproductions in books.

In the West Sudanese cases in the Museum of Natural History in New York one can begin to detect the Moorish influence — for instance, in a curiously curved long-stemmed coffee urn. But it is apparent also that this influence is secondary and the primary quality is African: in the beautiful cotton robes in white and blue, the figured carvings on elephant tusks, the decorated gourds, the gracefully designed and elaborately decorated drums and swords, and the distinctive bronzes.

The same uniqueness of character is present also in West African music:[15]

The world's highest development of [rhythm] occurred in Africa. Nobody knows why. The "tempered" scale was never adopted there and no system of notation grew up, so harmony remained comparatively undeveloped.

Although there is some harmony and a lot of melody in West African music, the great emphasis is upon complex rhythms or polyrhythms. "The syncope [off-beat], an African commonplace," says the late Professor Hornbostel, "is a European achievement."

In comparing and contrasting the music of the world, Professor Herskovits describes African music:

> Music styles are found where polyrhythms are the counterpart of the polyphony of Euroamerican music, where drums are more important than singers; where voice quality is of little significance, but alertness to rhythmic details paramount; where the drummer, not the singer, is recognized as the virtuoso musician.

NORTHERN AFRICA

On the Mediterranean coast of Africa the Egyptians and the Berbers were apparently both living in farming society villages by about 4500 B.C. How long the Egyptians had been in Africa, whether or not they came from Asia, and, if so, when, are, as we have seen, matters still in dispute, but, although we can see obvious similarities between the art of Babylonia, Assyria, Persia, and so on, that of Egypt is unique. Whatever its roots Egypt was an African not an Asian state. The length of time during which it maintained its power is unusual, namely from about 3000 B.C. to 1000 B.C. Apparently what happened was that the commercial component of its feudal economy — always subordinate to the agricultural interests — collapsed in the face of the superior economy of the rising commercial civilizations in Crete and elsewhere. When Alexander of Macedon conquered Egypt in 332 B.C., there was little resistance, and Roman conquest followed almost as a matter of course.

The Berbers

The Berbers seem to have inhabited an immense stretch of coast, from the Egyptian borders into what is now the Atlantic shore of Morocco, even establishing themselves on the Canary Islands. What their society was like we can tell by the "pockets" of it which have been left behind, on the Canary Islands and in the Sahara interior regions. The mainland Berbers advanced from hoe to plow cultivation; both had developed social classes, but tribal democratic patterns were still strong. Murdock's comments on the mainland pockets seem to indicate less class polarization than existed in the Canary Islands:

Government at the community level is notably democratic. All authority is vested in an assembly (jemaa) composed of all adult males. . . . The heads of lineages and extended families usually exert a major influence and are often assigned special seats, but younger men may always attend and express their opinions. . . .

The district is governed by a council, usually also called a jemaa, composed normally of representatives of each of the sibs or major lineages of the component communities. Since these groups tend to appoint their older, wealthier, and more influential men, the district council has a somewhat oligarchical character in contrast to the democratic local assembly.[16]

As with the Canary Island society, this is a higher farming society on the verge of civilization. That it never arrived at it was presumably due in the Canary Islands to isolation, and in Africa to subjugation by more highly developed societies. The Egyptians raided Libya as early as 2475 B.C. (which incidentally showed how rich Berber agriculture was, for one raid netted 100,000 head of cattle), and after the Egyptians came the Phoenicians, Greeks, Romans, and Arabs.

Carthage

Early civilization on the Mediterranean coast of Africa was focused in Egypt and Carthage; Carthage (near modern Tunis) was a commercial state. It was founded by Phoenicians (Semites) in 814 B.C., and although by 600 B.C. it had broken its ties with Phoenicia, the descendants of the Phoenicians apparently continued to be its ruling class, since Carthage had retained the Phoenician religion — including Moloch and Astarte. Carthage, nevertheless, like Egypt, was an African state. Apparently its working population was largely Berber. The Berber crops were still raised, and it has been recently argued that its political constitution was partly taken over from the Berbers. Some of these matters are obscure for the simple reason that when Rome finally destroyed Carthage in 146 B.C., it destroyed its historical records also. We owe our knowledge of Carthage almost entirely to Greek and Roman sources.

In the flood of Roman hatred, which has continued to influence some historians, the greatness and magnificence of Carthage — a city of 600,000 with houses six stories high — seem to have been forgotten. In order to redress the balance, let us look at James Henry Breasted's vivid thumbnail sketch:

In matters of household equipment and city building the Carthaginians were quite the equals of the Greeks. The city of Carthage itself was large and splendid. It was in area three times as large as Rome. Behind wide docks and extensive piers of masonry, teeming with ships and merchandise, the city spread far inland, with spacious markets and busy manufacturing quarters humming with industry. Beyond the dwellings of the poorer crafts-men and artisans rose the stately houses of the wealthy merchants, with rich and sumptuous tropical gardens. Around the whole swept imposing walls and massive fortifications, inclosing the entire city and making its capture almost an impossibility. Behind the great city, outside the walls, stretched a wide expanse of waving palm groves and tropical plantations, dotted with the luxurious country houses of the splendid commercial lords of Carthage who were to lead the coming struggle with Rome.[17]

This magnificence was maintained not, as was the Egyptian, primarily by farming, but by industry, manufacture, and trade, not by peasant but by slave labor.

Carthaginian caravans moved across the Sahara to the Sudanese civilizations of the Niger and elsewhere, and one of its leaders explored the African coast by sea. Its ships sailed to Britain to obtain the tin of Cornwall; some even sailed to the Azores. The Carthaginians had colonies in Corsica and Sardinia and ports in the Balearic Islands. They colonized southern Spain with its rich silver mines. In exchange for tin, copper, silver and other merchandise they traded their produce up and down the Mediterranean: grain, timber, wine, olive oil, pottery, glass-ware, linen, and metal tools and weapons.

As one might expect from a predominantly commercial economy, the Carthaginian political system was based on a balance between wealthy capitalists who dominated one legislative assembly and the small businessmen and craftsmen who dominated the other, a situation similar to but more advanced than that in some Sumerian states:

> A senate of 300 exercised executive as well as legislative authority. This body, or usually an executive committee composed of thirty of its more in-fluential members, decided on matters of war and peace, sent and received embassies, levied troops, imposed taxes, and determined over-all military strategy. The senators were chosen exclusively from the aristocratic mer-chant families or lineages, inferentially as their formal representatives. The lower house was a popular assembly, which every free male Carthaginian was privileged to attend and where he could express his opinions with complete freedom. The assembly elected the presidents by popular vote and probably appointed a treasurer and finance minister. Its legislative and executive powers, however, were limited to issues brought before it at the instigation of the senate.[18]

Nubia and Ethiopia

The archaeological evidence indicates that 10,000 and more years ago the area to the south of Egypt was inhabited by a Negroid food-gathering people. By about 3900 B.C. the people of the area, still Negroid, were turning to farming. By about 3400 (radiocarbon dating) farming was in full force. This farming, however, was apparently not derived from nearby Egypt but, as the crops indicate, from West Africa (1,800 miles away). The next development apparently was the joining of this agriculture by domestic animals from Egypt, apparently about 3000 B.C., and with this the story of Egyptian contact and conquest begins. By about 2560 B.C. the Egyptians were trading with the area (called, alternately, Nubia or Kush) and about 2200 B.C. they conquered it. The Egyptian control continued for about a thousand years before the Nubians were able to achieve independence. What kind of state Nubia was during these years is not known, but presumably it was a rich farming and trading territory with various towns. By 725 B.C. Nubia must have been a powerful state, for its armies invaded and conquered Egypt.

"Ruling from the Mediterranean to the borders of modern Ethiopia and, for all we know, Uganda too, these kings gave Egypt its twenty-fifth or 'Ethiopian' dynasty, and made Kush briefly into a world power."[19] We know from the archaeological evidence that Nubia in these days had at least three cities: Napapa just below the third cataract of the Nile, and Meroe and Naga further south. Unfortunately we know little more, for, although the Nubians were literate, their script cannot yet be understood, and comparatively little archaeological work has been done in the area. We do know, however, that in 530 B.C., Meroe became the capital and sometime later developed into a center for an extensive iron industry, with smelting works producing tools and weapons. The story seems to end rather abruptly about 350 A.D. when Nubia was conquered by Ethiopia. Today only the ruins remain.

These ruins lie about a hundred miles down the Nile from modern Khartoum, a little way beyond the riverside town of Shendi. Royal pyramids mark it from the distance. Between these and the Nile across a gravel plain some two miles broad, the surface of the ground is curved by long low mounds which show where Meroe once flourished. To the left, close by the river, are the partly cleared ruins of that Temple of the Sun of which Herodotus heard faint news. Nearby, the railway running northward goes straight through two thirty-foot mounds of pebblelike material that is glittering and black—the lavalike slag and "bloom" of smelters' ovens long since cold.[20]

The agriculture which penetrated from the West Sudan into the Sudan about 3400 B.C. did not stop there, but penetrated into the plateaus of adjoining Ethiopia. There the Negroid people bearing it encountered a food-gathering Caucasoid people known to anthropology as "Cushites" (from the Cushite language, which is part of the Semitic-Hamitic group). The Negroes and Cushites apparently intermarried, for their descendants, the modern Ethiopians, are mixed Caucasoid and Negroid, and the Cushites adopted "agriculture and a sedentary mode of life from the culturally more advanced Negroes," including, in time, domesticated animals from Egypt via Nubia.[21] As a result Ethiopia became an important independent agricultural center, from which emerged coffee and several varieties of cereal and oil plants.

Commerce also developed early. By at least 2500 B.C. the Egyptians were trading with Ethiopia (Eritrea) by the sea. In about 1500 B.C., Queen Hatshepsut of Egypt—"the first great woman of history,"[22] writes Breasted—sent five ships down the Red Sea to the "land of Punt" (perhaps about where the French Dijoubti is today) and had an account of it carved into her temple at Thebes. Rich though the trade was, the inscription does not give the impression that the Egyptians considered Ethiopia, or at least coastal Ethiopia, as a civilized state similar to their own. The probability is that, like Nubia, it was at this time a farming society with a developing trade.

The next great impetus apparently came from Arabia, in the form of an invasion (about 700 B.C.) across the narrows between the Red Sea and the Gulf of Aden from Yemen. These invaders (the Sabaeans) presumably followed the usual pattern of establishing themselves as a ruling class over the Ethiopians. At any rate, they set up a state with a capital city at Axum (Aksum), inland from the Eritrean coast. This state became so powerful—with a rich agriculture as well as trade—that by the sixth century B.C. it, in turn, invaded Yemen and for a time seized the rich Yemenite trade with India. In the fourth century it not only reconquered Yemen, but was at war with Nubia. Later, "in alliance with Rome, it became an entrepôt of African and Eastern trade, particularly as a focus for African ivory, and received a miscellany of imports, which included gold and silver plate for the king and iron and muslin from India."[23] This trade between Africa, Asia, and Europe continued for many centuries, apparently reaching a high point between about 300 and 700 A.D. when, for some unexplained reason, the Red Sea maritime commerce failed and Ethiopia economically fell into the shadows until the sixteenth century.

These civilizations in Nubia and Ethiopia seem to have been on a higher level than those of the West Sudan and Nigeria. Certainly they seem to have had greater economic wealth, the inhabitants were literate and they built in stone. Few details on their form of society seem to be available but presumably they were feudal civilizations with strong commercial components. As they do not appear to have had sufficient wealth to have been based primarily on slave labor, they must have followed the usual pattern of great landowners and a taxed peasantry. The trade of Nubia was presumably largely up and down the Nile—at least its main cities were strung out along the Nile—and then overland, to Ethiopia on the east and perhaps as far as the Niger on the west. We know that caravans later regularly made the immense trek from the Niger to the Indian Ocean and they could have done so earlier. The basic trade of Ethiopia, on the other hand, was by sea, reaching as far as India and later China. And it was perhaps for this reason that Ethiopia became more powerful than Nubia and has had such a long-continuing history.

East Africa

If we consider the outline of Africa as a large human head, we began our journey at the elongated back of the head, the great bulge out into the Atlantic, with what we might call the Niger Civilizations, then made our way up along the top of the head, where we encountered the Berbers, Carthage, and Egypt, and finally we have made our way down the forehead and along the nose to Nubia and Ethiopia. Now we must swing around the nose (the Horn of Africa) where the Gulf of Aden meets the Indian Ocean and down the long line of the jaw (the Indian Ocean coast from the Horn to the Cape of Good Hope). We shall not, however, go quite as far as the Cape, but, beginning with Somaliland, move down through Kenya and Tanzania (Tanganyika) to Mozambique.

The Coastal Cities

As with so much of African history, so, too, with that of the East Coast, the Indian Ocean coast, one can begin with "it is not generally known." What is "not generally known" about the East African coast is that by at least 60 A.D. a great Indian Ocean trade was flourishing there—and continued to flourish until it was driven under by the Portuguese in the sixteenth century. We know that this trade existed in 60 A.D. because it is described in that ocean guide book for mariners, the *Periplus of the Erythraean Sea* (the Indian Ocean and adjoining waterways), but it had apparently begun much earlier.

Roman and Egyptian coins of the third century B.C. have been discovered on the coast, and a Persian inscription of 293 B.C. apparently refers to this African trade. It is known also that a Greek navigator sailed from the Red Sea to India along the coast in 326–327 B.C. It has recently been demonstrated that the Monsoon route directly across the Indian Ocean was "in full and undisguised use at the end of the reign of Augustus,"[24] who died in 14 A.D., and it may have been used secretly for many decades before that by Arab and Indian navigators. Merchants naturally tried to keep their trade routes secret.

The author of the *Periplus* called at ports from the Gulf of Aden to somewhere beyond Zanzibar, some of them towns, others only anchorages. The trade which he describes was with the Roman Empire, Arabia, and India. Unfortunately, he tells us little about the inhabitants of these East Coast African ports. He describes them as "savages" and "men of piratical habits, very great in stature," who caught turtles and fished from dugout canoes and plank boats. "This country is not subject to a king," he noted, "but each market town is ruled by a separate chief."

It has often been assumed that these African people — known at the time as "Azanians" — were Negroid, but, according to Murdock, "the archaeological evidence demonstrates indisputably the complete absence of Negroes in this part of Africa for centuries to come."[25] Murdock is of the opinion that they were a mainly Caucasoid Ethiopian people who began to fan out southward from Ethiopia about 1000 B.C., settled in Kenya, and then moved down the coast. That they were Caucasoids (although doubtless dark Caucasoids) is indicated also by the failure of the *Periplus* author to note that they were Negro. Whoever they were, they do not seem to have advanced to a civilized society. Their exports and imports show that they had little manufacturing. They had no centralized state, no ships of their own (dugout canoes and plank boats only), apparently no cities (at least none observed by the *Periplus* author), and were regarded as "savages." They were probably a farming society people with an unusually large trading component because of their situation on the sea coast.

For our next account of the East African coast, we have to wait some 900 years. About the year 947 A.D. an Arab observer, El Mas'udi, recorded his impressions. By this time the coastal ports had been extended much farther south, to Sofala (opposite southern Madagascar). The inhabitants of the coast were now known as "the Zanj," and they occupied the whole of it, 2,500 miles from the Horn to Mozambique. This vast territory was apparently one sovereign state, the king of which could command 300,000 troops. The land around Sofala "produces gold in abundance," for the Zanj were great metal workers. They were also a farming people, raising sorghum and cattle. Furthermore, the Zanj were jet-black and had "hanging lips."[26] The Zanj, therefore, were clearly Negroid. They traded, farmed, and worked in metals, had a unified state but not a State religion and maintained a strong element of tribal democracy.

Trade had now become much more extensive. It reached, in fact, to China. Elephant tusks, Mas'udi informs us, "ordinarily go to Oman where they are sent on to China and India. That is the way they go, and if it were not so, ivory would be plentiful in Muslim countries. In China the kings and civil and military notables use chairs of ivory."[27] Some of the famed Chinese ivory, then, came from East Africa. To this we have to add the evidence of African and Indo-China and Malay connections (of uncertain date):

> Botanically the cultivars introduced to East Africa compare more closely with those of south-east Asia than of India and ethnology points in the same direction: the outrigger boats of the east coast and the xylophones of wide distribution can both be derived more plausibly from south-east Asia; and the Malagache language of Madagascar has Malayo-Polynesian affinities.[28]

Two hundred years after El Mas'udi came another Arab, Edrisi (in about 1154). Edrisi is not so much interested in gold as in iron: "Hither come the people of the islands of Zanedj [variously rendered, and possibly the Maldives and Laccadives off the southern coast of India] to buy iron and transport it to the mainland and the islands of India, where they sell it for a good price; for it is the object of a big trade there, and is in big demand."[29] This iron, according to Edrisi, was made into steel for swords in India and Damascus. The famed "Damascus steel," that is to say, came in part at least from African iron. "A great number of iron mines," Edrisi noted, "are found in the mountains of Sofala." He had heard that there were coastal settlements as far south as the mouth of the Limpopo River which processed and exported iron. He also informs us that the Zanj "have no ships of their own; but they use the ships of Oman and of other countries." In these ships were borne to India not only iron and other metals, but farm produce also, and these apparently made an important impact on Indian agriculture:

> The seventeen major crops of India, whose distribution Janaki Ammal (1956) has mapped for that subcontinent, include five of African origin, namely, castor, cotton, pearl millet, sesame, and sorghum. All five, significantly, reveal similar distributions in western India, in the very region to which the monsoon winds would carry vessels coming from East Africa, whereas all twelve non-African crops are concentrated in quite different areas.[30]

A third Arab traveller, Ibn Battuta, in 1331, described one of the coastal ports, Kilwa, as "one of the most beautiful and best constructed towns, all elegantly built."[31] Kilwa, in fact, is known to have stretched for a mile along the coast and to have extended half a mile inland. Another port city, Mombasa, was estimated to have had 20,000 inhabitants. Of Kilwa, Ibn Battuta commented that most of the inhabitants, the Zanj, were jet-black with tattoo marks on their faces. The "minority" were presumably mainly Arabs, for the present population of the coast—the Swahili—are mixed Arab and Negro. The earlier inhabitants of the region, with their dugout canoes and simpler trade, were presumably overwhelmed by the agricultural and cattle-rearing Negroes, who, as we shall see, began to enter the area about 500–700 A.D.

In the centuries between the *Periplus* comments and the Arab observers, the region had advanced into a civilized state apparently based very largely upon trade and manufacturing. In these East African states, however, as with those of the West Sudan and Nigeria, one gets the feeling of a strong parasitic and foreign element in the trade. Manufacturing, for instance, did not rise to the production of ships—surely a basic prerequisite for the economic independence and advancement of a coastal people. Whether this defect would in time have been remedied, we shall never know, for the whole fabric was torn down by the Portuguese in the early sixteenth century. In 1497, Vasco da Gama rounded the Cape of Good Hope into the Indian Ocean. Within a few years each of these East African coastal towns was destroyed, one after the other, including Zanzibar, Kilwa, and Mombasa.

The Arabs came to these coastal cities primarily, it would appear, for gold and iron. Where did the gold and iron come from? Who were the Negroes who took over from the first settlers? Let us see what answers we can find in the territory behind the coast—from Kenya to Rhodesia.

The Interior—Zimbabwe and the Bantu

Until quite recently it was not known that there was any history to the interior of East Africa. Now archaeology has shown us that there was such a history, and, putting the archaeological and anthropological evidence together, we can see a few of its outlines.

Let us begin in the north, in Kenya, Uganda, and Tanzania, and move south. As with the rest of Africa, the whole area bears evidence of early habitation by food-gathering peoples. One digging, for instance, to the south of Lake Tanganyika, gave evidence of such occupation about 53,000 years ago. Perhaps about 1500 B.C. a food-gathering people evidently on the verge of agriculture—they made stone bowls, pestles, and pottery—lived in southern Kenya and northern Tanzania, roughly 200–300 miles from the coast. In the same area and in others have been found a remarkable set of stone works, roads, terraces, and wells. In Kenya and Tanzania have been found ancient roads, "as a rule about ten or twelve feet wide," which may have stretched 600 miles north and south. "Irrigation works include canals, terraces and walls."[32] The date of these roads and other works is unknown, but one deposit, containing the remains of cattle and sheep, has been estimated at 850 B.C. Whoever these people were or whenever they lived they obviously had highly developed farming and trade. Furthermore, the road directions seem to indicate that much of this trade was inland, possibly stretching from what is now Zambia to Ethiopia. One theory, indeed, is that the whole area was inhabited by farming society migrants from Ethiopia who began fanning out from their homeland about 1000 B.C., perhaps the same people who inhabited the coastal areas. It is probable, too, that at least part of the trade was in iron. Evidence of iron smelting by at least 1000 A.D. has been found at the southern end of Lake Tanganyika. And this, too, seems to point to northern influence, ultimately from Nubia.

In 1868 a hunter roaming in the deserted, hilly "King Solomon's Mines" country in southern Rhodesia came across a massive set of stone ruins, later to be known as Zimbabwe. On a hilltop towered a granite fort with walls and terraces and stone steps leading upward; below was a walled enclosure, the outer walls of which were 20 feet wide and 30 feet high and which covered in all an area 300 by 200 feet, with an inner wall and two conical towers.[33] All are made of granite cut into flat brick-like sections and built without cement. Yet the builders achieved not only massiveness, but fine workmanship of detail. "The whole complex of buildings," Davidson found, "whether in the valley or perched on the bouldered *kopje* overhead, has a dignity and strength of purpose in this lonely place that is irresistibly impressive." As early as 1905 a prominent Egyptologist declared that in their architecture there was "not a trace of Oriental or European style of any period whatever." Their "character" he found to be "typically African."

Discovered among the ruins were art objects—"soapstone birds, bowls and smaller carvings, monoliths, iron gongs, and copper and bronze ornaments and objects"—and imported trade goods—for example, "beads, china and glass." The walls, too, are often decorated "with chevrons, chequer, dog-tooth, and herring-bone patterns, and with courses of black coloured dolerite."[34]

At first, Zimbabwe was thought to stand alone, but in recent years more than three hundred other stone ruins have been found, stretching over the whole of Rhodesia (150,000 square miles). Most of these are small, but some are apparently quite impressive and in the mass they must represent an immense settlement — now long vanished. One of the largest is that known as Mapungubwe, in the valley of the Limpopo River, south of Zimbabwe (which is itself just south of the modern town of Salisbury).

What was the meaning of these settlements? When were they used? Who were the people who built them and lived there? Some of the answers seem clear enough. The settlements were connected with mining, smelting, and metalworking — gold, silver, iron, copper, and tin. These, then, were clearly the hinterland settlements from which came the gold, iron, and other metals that flowed out from Sofala and Kilwa across the seas to Arabia and India. Zimbabwe lies directly behind Sofala, and the land of Sofala, Edrisi noted, produced gold "in abundance."

In what "abundance" may be seen from the fact that these workings yielded between 15 and 75 million pounds sterling, a sum sufficient, comments Murdock,[35] to "account in considerable measure for the fabulous wealth of medieval Indian rulers." Edrisi noted also that Sofala was famed for its iron and that these iron workings were on the Limpopo — and Mapungubwe was on the Limpopo. Here was also the ultimate source for that iron that went to India to turn up in the famed swords of Damascus; and although no estimate appears to have been made either for iron or copper (silver was of minor importance), the size and nature of some of the workings as well as their immense number indicate that the amount must have been enormous. No mines were found at Zimbabwe, but evidence of smelting was found. Zimbabwe was perhaps a smelting and dispersal point.

The dating of these ruins and mining sites is based on two types of evidence, the comments of Arab, Portuguese, and other observers and archaeological estimates. Some of these comments we have already noted. The *Periplus* writer (60 A.D.) made no mention of metal exports and, indeed, noted that metal was being imported, so probably mining had not begun in the area by that time. By about the year 950, however, there was "gold in abundance"; iron is noted about 1150 and also seems to be abundant; at least its working seems to extend from Sofala to the Limpopo. Next come various Portuguese references to Great Zimbabwe or some similar place in the early sixteenth century. And, finally, a record by the Portuguese taking control of the area in 1629. Some workings were continued into the nineteenth century, when various European powers seized the whole territory and its minerals with it.

The earliest archaeological dating comes from Zimbabwe, a radio-carbon dating of 471–794 A.D. from a wooden beam; then gold orna-ments of 600–1100 A.D. But other evidence indicates that the main building in stone took place much later than this, beginning perhaps in 1300. The earliest radiocarbon dating from Mapungubwe is 1050 A.D., and Chinese porcelain found there is of about 1200 A.D.

The datings indicate that the people who occupied these settlements and worked the mines and smelted were Negroid, for, as we have seen, the coastal cities were populated by Negroes as early as 947, and if the coastal cities which exported the metals were in Negro hands, the hinterland which produced them must also have been in Negro hands. That this was so is indicated by other evidence. "Be-yond this country towards the interior," wrote a Portuguese observer in 1517, "lies the great kingdom of Benametapa pertaining to the heathen whom the Moors call Kaffirs; they are black men and go naked save from the waist down."[36] Who were these "Kaffirs" ruled over by the king of Benametapa? Where did they come from? The archaeological evidence, as we have seen, indicates that there were no Negroes in East Africa when the author of the *Periplus* made his ob-servations. Although Negroid peoples had long inhabited a vast and scattered area from the Pacific through the Indian Ocean into Africa, the Negroes proper were for many centuries a comparatively small racial group centered in the Niger region of upper west Africa. They appear to have moved out from this homeland in two waves, the first from about 4000 to 3000 B.C., when they migrated directly east as far as Nubia and Ethiopia. The second wave was even more extensive.

If we draw a line across Africa from southern Nigeria to Ethiopia, the whole vast territory below it was, as we have noted, mainly in-habited by the Pygmies, Bushmen, and Hottentots, all food-gathering peoples. Then in about the first century A.D. a farming people, the Bantu, having both crops and cattle, began to spread out from their homeland, mainly in the Cameroon highlands (to the south of Nigeria), and migrated into the vast territories below in a great fan-shaped move-ment east and south.

By about the year 700, the Bantu had reached the east coast, where one group forked north into Tanzania and another south to-ward the Cape. As they moved, they left settlements and tribal states behind. If we look at one of these, that in the Congo region (we find the same situation in Rhodesia), we can get a general picture of what the kingdom of Benametapa was like.

As an example of the states in this region we may select the great em-pire of Mwata Yamwo, founded among the Lunda by a Luba dynasty around 1625. It expanded through conquest after 1675 to within 300 miles of the Atlantic coast, dominating all the Central Bantu peoples of this vast territory until near the close of the nineteenth century. The ruler possessed the attributes of divinity, and no one might observe him eat or drink, on pain of death. He appointed provincial governors and lesser district chiefs, who supplied troops for his army and levied tribute in ivory, salt, copper, slaves, and produce. They resided at the capital town, where they exercised additional functions. The four highest among them formed an advisory council called the Kannapumba. Ranking even above them, however, was the Lukokesha, or Queen-Mother. Always the daughter of a former king, she remained unmarried, possessed independent tributary territories for her support, maintained her own court, and shared supreme authority with the monarch. When a king died, the Queen-Mother and the Kannapumba constituted an electoral college to choose his successor from among his own sons or those of former rulers.[37]

To this let us add the archaeological evidence and the deductions to be made from it.

Recent excavation at Khami Ruins, an extensive system of stone structures some thirteen miles west of Bulawayo in Southern Rhodesia, and dating probably from the Ba-Rozwi hegemony after about A.D. 1600, . . . [indicates the] social stratification. "Only a small portion of the population," notes Robinson, "lived on the stone-walled platforms; many more dwelt in huts, mainly west of the Hill Ruin, where walling was absent or very slight." But "the material culture associated with these huts is identical with that of the main ruins."

Yet the people living on the stone-walled platforms had lived better than those in the huts. Imported china, ornamental gold, and ceremonial pottery were found in the walled ruins, but not elsewhere. "In short, the Hill Ruin probably represents the residence of a powerful chief, and the buildings in its vicinity may have been occupied by members of his family, or by various functionaries attached to his court: while the common people lived outside the walls."[38]

The society, then, of the people who inhabited the area of Rhodesia and built Zimbabwe and other centers was a later stage of farming society with strong remnants of tribal democracy. How much of the economic wealth of the society came from metalworking, and how much from farming we do not know, but the metalworking, no matter how extensive, did not serve to build what is usually called an "iron age" civilization (e.g., that of the Greeks or Romans), and we can once again see the fallacy of considering such matters as primary instead of taking them in their total sociological context. Iron does not create a civilization any more than "inventions" do (or the Chinese, with coal and gunpowder, would have early dominated the world).

Zimbabwe is sometimes referred to as having been the site of a "civilization," but the evidence does not support such a view. Zimbabwe was not a city but a fortified center, presumably for smelting, trading, and religious purposes, and surrounded by a large village-type area with huts and kraals. The impression one gets is of a society straining on the verge of civilization but having been undermined before reaching it. That it was undermined so easily was doubtless due to the fact that, like the coastal cities, it was economically parasitic. These interior settlements did not use their mineral wealth to develop their economy further but allowed it to be drained off in foreign trade. The primary power doubtless remained, as in the Congo, in the hands of the landowners who kept the mines and smelting sites as their own taxable monopoly and suppressed the rise of an independent class of manufacturer-owners. If the trade failed, the economy would fail with it. And whoever had control of the trade had control of the society.

VIII

The Slave–Commercial

Civilizations

IT IS GENERALLY AGREED that there have been two main streams of world history, Asian and European, and the differences between the two have often been stressed. But few observers have attempted a serious examination of the reasons for the differences. One who has is the eminent anthropologist, Carleton Coon.[1]

What then gave the Europeans an initial advantage over Indians, Chinese, and Japanese which was to lead to the later cultural Westernization of the world, comparable to the physical spread of Western man in late Pleistocene times? The answer lies in the field of energy. The Asiatic peoples based their economies on the intensive cultivation of cereals and legumes that gave a high yield per acre and could support dense populations. The cultivation of these plants, particularly rice, required intensive manual labor with a minimum of animal power and little use of machinery powered by air or water. There was no particular need of that animal which in Europe provided overland transport and heavy farm traction: the horse. In Asia shipping was developed largely for use in inland waterways, while in Europe trade followed the open sea. The Asiatic lands each included a variety of climates, ranging from tropical or sub-tropical to temperate and cold, and contained a great variety of natural resources. International trade was not as vital to them as to Europeans, nor did warfare hold out as many promises. These peoples had reached a state of cultural equilibrium as stable as that of the hunting tribes of Australia. Once they had filled their ecological space to the limit possible under the natural restrictions of their

Iron Age material culture, the accent had turned to a refinement of human relations through elaborate ritual and politeness, calculated to cause a minimum of friction. Exploration, trade, and conquest interested them little.

Coon is not, of course, tackling the whole problem (his remarks, in fact, are slipped in at the end of a chapter called "Gunpowder"), but only one aspect of it, namely, why did later European civilization forge ahead of Asian. His answer seems to boil down to the following points: (1) The Asians raised cereals, "particularly rice"; (2) the Europeans made more use of the horse; (3) the Europeans traded on the open seas, the Asians on "inland waterways"; (4) there was more trade in Europe because there were fewer "natural resources" and a less varied climate; (5) the Europeans made more use of warfare; (6) the "Iron Age material culture" of the Asian peoples placed "restrictions" upon their possibilities for development. As a result of all these factors they "reached a state of cultural equilibrium" and spent their energies upon the "refinement of human relations through elaborate ritual and politeness" (instead of trying to get somewhere). And one final summarizing point: Europeans are absorbed in exploration, trade and conquest; Asians are but "little interested."

To these points we might reply as follows: (1) With the exception of rice, the cereals raised in Europe from the beginnings of farming to the present day are about the same as those of Asia. Hence, the difference must lie not "particularly" but solely in rice. Rice, however, is not raised everywhere in Asia. For instance, as we have noted, millet has been the staple of northern China, rice of southern China. But northern China did not conform to the European pattern. (2) Some Asian peoples, for instance, the Huns, made very considerable use of the horse. So did the Chinese, Arabs, Japanese, Persians, and so on. The Chinese had the horse-collar before Europeans did. (3) The Europeans (the Greeks and Romans, for example) traded for many centuries mainly in inland waterways and yet had during this period a society different from those of Asia. As we have seen, Asian trade began to move out into the open sea before the European (the Arab and Indian trade across the Indian Ocean; Chinese fleets sailing to Arabia). (4) There are proportionately about the same "natural resources" in Europe as in Asia and almost the same range of climate (partly as a result of the Gulf Stream, which makes for greater variation in a smaller area). (5) There seems to have been proportionately as much warfare in Asia as in Europe. (6) Europeans also had what is known as an "Iron Age material culture." Why was it "restrictive" in Asia but not in Europe? As to "ritual" and "politeness" there was probably as much or almost as much in European as in Asian feudalism. (7) It is not true that the Asian "peoples" were little interested in "exploration, trade and conquest." They did a great deal of exploring; they traded on a vast scale; their history is a history of conquests. In any case the assertion that a people is "little interested" in something is no explanation. The question is, why?

As an addendum we might notice "the physical spread of Western man in late Pleistocene times" and the "later cultural Westernization of the world." "In both Europe and North Africa," Coon informs us in an earlier passage to which he presumably refers here, "the very earliest Upper Paleolithic skeletons were slender, and had narrower heads and faces than those that followed them." Traces of these slender "men" can be found in Asia and southern Africa (the Watusi). "Along all of these Neolithic routes we can find traces of this gracile [fine-boned and slender] branch of the white race today." How it was determined that these "gracile" skeletons found in Europe and Africa were "white" and "Western" is not clear; and the implication that whatever "cultural" progress has been made depended on them is left hanging (there were more of them in Europe). As for the later "cultural Westernization of the world," this is true, of course, only in a very superficial sense. The basic cultural patterns of Asia and Africa have remained and have developed in their own way.

Coon, although writing of civilized societies, writes like an anthropologist discussing homogeneous food-gathering or early farming society. He speaks of "peoples" as such. He parallels the "cultural Westernization" of the world with tribal movements in early food-gathering society.

One final general objection can be levelled at Coon's comments—and they are not his alone but typical of a general approach—namely his assertion that Asian society reached a "state of cultural equilibrium," that is to say, of social stagnation. But as we have seen, the evidence indicates that Asian States did progress, even though slowly, and that by about 1500 A.D. were roughly at the same level as the European. The problem, then, is not that of accounting for a kind of ingrown Asian "equilibrium" but of different rates of development in recent centuries. What enabled Europe, so far behind Asia in 1000 A.D., to overtake and then surpass it within a half dozen centuries? In seeking answers we must remember that the general socioevolutionary forces of European civilized societies have to be the same as those of Asia for the simple reason that they are both civilized societies. We cannot be dealing with fundamentally different phenomena, one "Western," and the other "Oriental," but with variations of the same phenomenon.

I: THE ATHENIAN EMPIRE

Athens of the fifth century B.C. was a bustling, brawling port city, one of the main centers of Mediterranean manufacturing. It was a city of immense wealth obtained through the exploitation of slave labor and the subject peoples of its empire. But when we have said this, we also have to say that thought and art rose to heights in Athens that surpassed the best that had gone before it and were not again to be scaled for some two thousand years. We have, that is to say, once again, the phenomenon of an aggressive, energetic, and creative upper class living on the toil of others. And we can emphasize the exploitation or the creativity in isolation and get two very different pictures. The problem is to see both and to see also how they are related.

Athens, as has often been stated, is not Greece. We are beginning to perceive continuities in Greek civilized societies from the Greek-Aegean to the Macedonian empire of Alexander (from about 1500 to about 300 B.C.) and beyond. But Athens, especially in the fifth century B.C., represents that society's height and its essence.

Let us first note a few framework facts. Athens was the city of Attica, a peninsula of about 1,000 square miles (about one-sixteenth the size of Denmark) but the word Athens usually includes both the town and country—the city state. The population of Athens in the fifth century B.C. was about 315,000, of whom 43,000 (all male) were citizens. Athens was also the center of an empire which included five provinces and a population of some 2 million. Athenian trade spread over an area with a population of more than 20 million, an area containing Egypt, Carthage, Sicily, Phoenicia, and the societies of the Black Sea.

Athens is often referred to as "old" and its citizens as "the ancients." But in terms of civilization Athens was a newcomer, in fact, something of an aggressive upstart. Egypt had had a continuous history of 2,500 years and China 800 years before the great days of Athens began; Sumer had lain in the dust for 2,000 years; Crete had reached its apex some 1,200 years before. The "ancients," too, had their "ancients," and Athens had many roots.

The Economy

In Athens the Asian economic picture is reversed. Agriculture is subordinate to manufacturing and trade; it is, in fact, molded by them. The type of agriculture depends on the type of manufacturing and commerce. The pattern of the production of the food supply within the home boundaries is broken; subsistence agriculture is supplanted by specialized agriculture. Athens depends upon trade not for its luxuries alone but for its necessities.

Hence, so far as Athens is concerned, some of the questions which were basic in regard to the Egyptian and Asian civilizations are of secondary importance, for instance, land ownership and agricultural labor. The indication is that the farming pattern was mainly feudal. We hear of "tenant-farmers" in the sixth century who paid one-sixth of their produce to the "great landowners."[2] In Sparta the "helots" (serfs) paid half of their produce to the landowners.

The raw materials for Athenian manufacture and trade came in part from farming — particularly olives and grapes, made into olive oil and wine, which required pots for their storage and transport — and in part from the mines, quarries, clay pits, and forests. Athens owned the great silver mines at Laurion, which were so rich that their annual income alone was enough to pay for all the buildings and statuary of Athens. A particularly good vein provided sufficient silver to finance the construction of a fleet of 200 ships. One hardly ever hears of the mines of Laurion; but it is clear that without them there would have been no Athens. From the marble quarries at Mount Pentelicus came the stones for the buildings and statuary; and there was in Attica a "wonderful clay" for pottery.

Unlike the Asian feudal pattern, manufacturing seems to have been done entirely in privately owned workshops with considerable specialization. Demosthenes' father owned a sword factory, but bought the hilts "ready-made from other firms."[3] We hear of a shield factory and a bedstead factory, and there were at least 150 potteries. A shipbuilding industry supplied a merchant marine of several hundred vessels, some of them 300 and more tons. (The *Mayflower* was 180 tons.)

The basic labor in industry and manufacturing was slave labor. When the Spartans invaded Attica, 20,000 fugitive slaves, mostly from the mines, ran up to join them. It was once proposed that the state take over the mining concessions (rented to private businessmen) and hire slaves up to ten thousand. Massed slave labor was employed in the quarries, in the building industry, road-making, and in the transport business with its great trains of wagons and oxen and its ships. In manufacturing, as the units themselves were usually small, the number of slaves per establishment was small. Demosthenes' father employed 33 slaves in his sword factory. The picture is that of massed slave labor in the raw material industries and in transport and a large number of slaves in small units in manufacturing, mixed with some paid labor.

This vast labor power, both slave and paid, made use of only the most elementary machines: the wheel and axle, the lever, the pulley, the wedge, and the screw. Of these most important not known to the early Egyptians or the Sumerians was the screw, which was used in olive and wine presses. The Greeks also invented the rotary millstone which could be operated by animal power.

The most important technological advance of which the Greeks made use but which had been developed much earlier was the smelting and working of iron. The surprising thing, however, is not how much but how little iron was used. The few machines that existed were made mostly of wood with some iron and leather parts. Iron appears for many centuries to have been largely converted (laboriously) into steel for weapons and armaments. If we ask ourselves why iron was so little used and metal machinery was not developed, the answer is slave labor. Slave labor was cheap, plentiful, and highly profitable. In mining there was an "annual profit of 33%" from slave labor, in manufacturing "between 23% and 31%."[4] Hence there was little incentive to develop machinery. The steam engine, although invented by the Greeks, was no more harnessed to iron than was coal by the Chinese, but remained a toy for entertaining guests and children.

For so small a state, Athenian trade was extraordinarily extensive —from the Black Sea to the Marne valley in northern France. Like Asian trade it was still largely—but not entirely—directed toward the upper classes, both of civilized and later farming societies: olive oil, wine, gold, silver, ivory, costly metalwork, valuable vases, woven cloths, ornaments and slaves.

This trade was almost entirely carried on by sea. The significance of this for the economy is apparent from the following figures. "The carting of a block of marble from the port of Epidauros up to the temple [i.e., by land] cost 42% of the purchase price," but to transport tiles by sea from Corinth to the port of Athens cost only 5 percent of the purchase price, and wood from Eleusis only 7 percent of the purchase price.[5] With wagon trains, even over comparatively good roads and with slave labor, the cost of land transportation was prohibitive, but sea transportation was comparatively cheap, even though it took two to two and a half days to sail from Athens to Crete, and 8 to 9 days from Athens to Egypt.

The manufacturing and commercial activities of Athens were assisted by a highly developed banking system. One banking house had accounts in thirteen cities. Banks made loans and issued letters of credit; banking capital merged with manufacturing capital; bankers owned factories and ships.

As the above facts indicate, factories, shops, ships, commercial companies, and banks were privately owned. Government contracts were let out to business firms with their own working force of slaves.

Wages and working hours were not set by law but were subject to bargaining between the paid workers and the employers. The usual government duty on goods was only 2 percent.

Social Life

In the country around Athens, although the nature of the work differed from that in some Asian countries—olive, grape, and fruit-tree farming instead of grain farming—the social relationship of peasant and landowner was not changed. Nor does there appear to have been a class of small independent farmers.

In the cities, the manufacturers, merchants, and bankers have an independence, size, and coherence which we do not find in earlier Asian countries. They form a unified class of capitalists, although not, it is true, a capitalist class of the modern industrial type. They have no machine-factories, and they employ slave labor; but they have capital, they are in business for profit, they manufacture and trade freely, they have a financial system.

There appears also to have been a class intermediary between the capitalists and the paid workers which we might call that of small businessmen-craftsmen. These were distinct from the ordinary paid workers, many of whom apparently lived at a mere subsistence level.

SLAVES

In various accounts we get divergent pictures of the conditions of slaves in Athens. It has always been difficult for those who extol the intellectual life of Athens to admit that this life depended on slavery. Recent years, however, have brought some realistic accounts. Let us take the following, for instance, from Gustave Glotz.[6] The vast majority of slaves, he points out, came (as in Asia also) from war. Very few of them were Greeks. They were Syrians, Scythians, Persians, Arabs, Egyptians, Carians, Illyrians, and Libyans. To dispose of the slaves "a monthly fair was held in the Agora [marketplace] of Athens. Part of the cargoes was sent to Sunion for the mines. The surplus of imports were re-embarked for Sicily." Prices of slaves varied greatly. Field workers sold at 125 to 150 drachmas, mine workers 154 to 184. Skilled workers came higher. There was a great horde of household slaves of both sexes: "chamber-maids, wet-nurses, dry-nurses, housekeepers, lady's maids, valets, footmen, coachmen, grooms." There were also professional slaves. A captured teacher could become a household tutor. Slaves were captured and traded but not bred. "The breeding of human live-stock was not a good speculation. Most of the new born infants were killed or exposed." Most slaves had no family life. When one died a new one was purchased.

The same pattern existed in Greece as prevailed in Asian feudal states. Slave labor was universally employed in industry and transportation, in workshops, and in households. The difference was that in Athens industry and manufacturing constituted so much larger a proportion of the economy that the proportion of slaves to the total population was much greater.

By concentrating on the servants, craftsmen, and professionals, writers have maintained the illusion of the comparative benignity of Athenian slavery. To redress the balance let us look at the picture given by Diodorus Siculus of the slaves in the mines.

> There they throng, all in chains, all kept to work continuously day and night. There is no relaxation, no means of escape; for, since they speak a variety of languages, their guards cannot be corrupted by friendly conversation or casual acts of kindness. Where the gold-bearing rock is very hard, it is first burned with fire, and, when it has been softened sufficiently to yield to their efforts, thousands upon thousands of these unfortunate wretches are set to work on it with iron stonecutters. . . . Young children descend the shafts into the bowels of the earth, laboriously gathering the stones as they are thrown down, and carrying them into the open air at the shafthead, where they are taken from them by men over thirty years, each receiving a prescribed amount, which they break on stone mortars with iron pestles into pieces as small as a fetch. They they are handed on to women and older men, who lay them on rows of grindstones, and standing in groups of two and three they pound them to powder as fine as the best wheaten flour.[7]

Although Athens differed from Egypt and the dominant civilizations of Asia in so many respects, it did not differ from them in this basic social one: the great majority were brutally exploited and oppressed. In one case the majority were peasants, in the other slaves. Of the two the situation of the slaves was the worse, for the peasants at least lived with their families.

Women

One other basic social pattern was also similar, namely, the situation of women. The majority of women shared the poverty, exploitation and oppression of their class. Upper class women were largely deprived of property rights, were excluded from the professions, and were secluded in the household and oppressed: "All that was per-

mitted to the wife was housework in the company of slaves and fidelity
to a husband who spent most of his time away from home and was free
to associate with other women. The result was the rapid growth of
concubinage, prostitution and also male homosexuality."⁸ It had not
always been so. In the earlier days of Athens, women had had the vote
and some had apparently owned considerable property in land. The
situation seems to have steadily worsened as Athenian (male controlled) industry and commerce expanded and land became less important. In spite of these special restrictions on women, however,
domestic life in Athens was apparently not too different from that in
other class-divided and male-dominant societies—as we can gather
from Theocritus' chatty dialogue in *The Syracusan Ladies,* which,
although of a somewhat later period, doubtless also reflects the earlier
situation. It is also one of the first pieces of naturalistic (if somewhat
satiric) reporting in history and adds the dimension of everyday reality
to an otherwise over-abstract picture.

> Gorgo. Oh, what a thing spirit is! I have scarcely got to you alive,
> Praxinoe! What a huge crowd, what hosts of four-in-hands! Everywhere
> cavalry boots, everywhere men in uniform! And the road is endless: yes,
> you really live *too* far away!
> Praxinoe. It is all the fault of that madman of mine. Here he came to
> the ends of the earth and took—a hole, not a house, and all that we might
> not be neighbors. . . .
> Gorgo. Praxinoe, that full body becomes you wonderfully. Tell me
> how much did the stuff cost you just off the loom?
> Praxinoe. Don't speak of it, Gorgo! More than eight pounds in good
> silver money,—and the work on it! I nearly slaved my soul out over it!
> Gorgo. Well, it is *most* successful; all you could wish.
> Praxinoe. Thanks for the pretty speech! Bring my shawl, and set my
> hat on my head, the fashionable way. No child, I don't mean to bite. Boo!
> Bogies! There's a horse that bites! Cry as much as you please, but I cannot
> have you lamed. Let us be moving. Phrygia, take the child, and keep him
> amused, call in the dog, and shut the street door.

The scene could be Sumer or Detroit, Athens or London. It is not,
however, "universal." It could not have occurred in an early farming
or food-gathering society, for it is a scene from a society with private
property, cities, rulers, and servants.

The Power Structure

The political institutions of fifth century Athens began with the
famed reforms of Solon in the early sixth century. Solon was placed

in charge in 594 B.C., when the ruling class of great landowners were threatened by twin revolts, one from the peasants and another from the capitalists (the mines were just opening, manufacturing and trade were beginning to flourish). Solon, himself a landowner who was also engaged in trade, arrived at a compromise. He divided the population into four groups in accordance with their wealth. He then established or reestablished two political bodies: the Assembly and the Council. Although all four economic groups were members of the Assembly, only members of the wealthiest group were allowed to hold the highest offices (chief magistrates and treasurer). Only those belonging to the three wealthiest groups were eligible for membership in the Council.

Solon then, set up a quasi-democracy which excluded peasants, paid workers, slaves, and women, and allowed the capitalists to share some political power with the landowners. What happened in the succeeding two centuries was that the balance of this power passed more and more to the capitalists, as industry, manufacturing, trade, and empire expanded at a faster rate than the wealth from landed property. And there developed a greater overlap between the two classes as specialized agriculture in olives, grapes, figs, and so on developed ties with commerce and manufacturing (especially pottery) and more capitalists bought land.

Although the ultimate political power of the state theoretically rested in the (large and unwieldy) Assembly (in the fifth century it had 43,000 eligible members), the actual power lay in the Council and its special committees. The Council determined taxation, awarded contracts for public works and the concessions for the mines. It controlled the cavalry and the navy. It directed foreign affairs, had police powers, and sometimes acted as a court of justice. During a war crisis we learn that the main burden of the war was borne by the 1,200 wealthiest citizens. This core of 1,200 (out of 43,000), we can assume, passed membership around among themselves, and—as is the way in "democracies"—controlled the leading committees, known as the Commissions. One Commission (of ten members), for instance, controlled all naval construction.

A core of wealthy citizens also controlled the military committee, a top political body elected by the Assembly. Nomination to this committee was open only to those who owned land in Attica, that is to say, the old landed families and those capitalists who had bought land. In wartime—and Athens was frequently at war—it assumed wide dictatorial powers.

When Solon introduced his reforms the most powerful political body in Athens was the Council of the Areopagus, which (like the British House of Lords) consisted of great landowners holding life membership. With the rise of the capitalists it lost its power, but it remained as a potential threat and after Sparta's defeat of Athens seized political control.

The Athenian government, then, in the fifth century B.C. was essentially a government of capitalists subjected to some checks from the "left" (via the Assembly in particular) by small businessmen-craftsmen and professionals, and considerable checks from the "right" by the landowners, especially, it would seem, in the military committee. It was, in short, a democracy for the capitalists and great landowners, a pseudo-democracy for the middle class, and a dictatorship over the majority.

These characteristics of the Athenian government extended also into the other departments of the State—the army, the legal system, the police, and the church. The church seems to have had little independent power. There were many religious ceremonies, the Assembly was opened with a religious service, and so on. But the property of the church was under the control of the Council.

The Athenian legal system excluded from its protection most of the inhabitants of the State. Slaves were responsible to their masters and women (as in India and elsewhere) to their husbands, fathers, or other male relatives. Slaves were legally pieces of disposable property. They could be sold or destroyed. They could not marry, and if a woman slave had a child it became the property of her master, who as we have seen, customarily killed it, as it did not pay to raise slaves. A slave could not lodge an accusation in law except through his master. As in Asia so in Athens the upper classes were fined, the lower beaten (fifty lashes with a whip was standard punishment for a slave) or executed. Ironically, the police themselves were mainly slaves. It is these limitations to the legal system—which did give some service to middle class citizens—that are often forgotten. Even in so advanced a study as Gustave Glotz's *The Greek City and Its Institutions*[9] we find comments such as the following: "The whole penal code of Athens was dominated by the desire to assure full and complete freedom of person." Whose person?

The Athenian political scene was not, as one would sometimes gather, one of happily balanced harmony. Quite the contrary. "From the seventh century to the time of the Roman conquest," writes Glotz, "Greek history is full of revolutions and counter-revolutions, of massacres, banishments and confiscations."[10] Of the reasons for these struggles the Greeks themselves were well aware. "The poor and the rich," Aristotle comments, "quarrel with one another, and whichever side gets the better, instead of establishing a just or popular government, regards political supremacy as the prize of victory, and the one party sets up a democracy and the other an oligarchy."[11] Oligarchies assume "various forms according to the kind of superiority possessed by the oligarchs." Aristotle himself favors democracy. "Democracies are safer and more permanent than oligarchies, because they have a middle class which is more numerous and has a greater share in the government."

In the quarrel between the poor and the rich, capitalists and landowners stood side by side against the common foe—the "artisans and labouring class," who were sometimes aided by the peasantry and sometimes by the slaves as noted by Thucydides in his description of a revolution in the Corinthian colony of Corcyra (427 B.C.):

> When night descended, the proletariat took refuge in the citadel and the highlying parts of the town and concentrated their forces upon establishing themselves in that position. . . . They sent emissaries round the countryside inviting the slaves to join them and promising them their liberty. The proletariat were joined by the majority of the slaves, while the other party were reinforced by 800 mercenaries from the Continent. Their women also gave them courageous support by pelting the enemy with tiles from the houses and facing the uproar and commotion with a steadfastness unusual in their sex.

Expansion and Collapse

Following the defeat of Persia the Athenian empire began to expand, leaving the other Greek states—Sparta, Corinth, Thebes—far behind, for these other states were feudal-agricultural and too small in area to build up major farming wealth. Athens had a great fleet, both naval and merchant marine, and the commercial manufacturing organization to back it up. In time the empire became the major source of Athenian wealth and the mainstay of the economy.

One hears so little of the Athenian empire that many are not even aware that Athens had an empire; and when it is mentioned in general historical accounts the impression is conveyed that it was of a mild and beneficient nature unlike "real" empires such as the Persian or the Roman. Here Thucydides provides an antidote: when Lesbos rebelled against Athenian domination the leaders of the rebellion were executed and the inhabitants turned into plantation serfs. Some twelve years later (416 B.C.) the Athenians goaded the inhabitants of the free island of Melos into rebellion and then descended upon them with 38 warships and 2,700 infantry. Before beginning the attack they sent ambassadors to the Melians to pursuade them to submit without fighting. The following revealing debate ensued.

> Athenian: We propose now to demonstrate, first, that we have come here in the interests of our Empire and, secondly, that the arguments which we shall expound are conducive to the salvation of your country. We wish to avoid trouble in imposing our Empire upon you and to consult our mutual interests by saving you from destruction.
>
> Melian: It may be in your interest to impose your Empire, but how can it be in ours to submit to slavery?
>
> Athenian: Because you would gain the advantage of submitting before suffering the *ultima ratio,* while we should profit by not having destroyed you. . . . The stakes are not honor but salvation, and the problem is to avoid resistance to an adversary who utterly outmatches you.[12]

The Melians chose to fight, with the following outcome: "The Athenians used their discretion to put to death all Melian prisoners of military age and to sell the women and children into slavery. They afterward colonized the place themselves with five hundred Athenian settlers."[13]

The Athenian empire was acquired with as much violence and preserved with as much brutality as any other empire. Its subject peoples were forced to pay tribute both on their farm produce and on their trade and manufacturing. It differed from the Assyrian, Persian, and other empires, however, in one basic respect: they were agricultural, it was commercial. And this difference led to others. Asian colonies were ruled over by the small dictatorial groups of great landowners extracting wealth directly from the peasant labor of the subject peoples just as they did at "home." The Athenian colonies were mostly ruled by native, quasi-democratic, capitalist governments which taxed their fellow capitalists—whose wealth was extracted largely from slave labor. The reason for the quasi-democracy was not magnanimity but the fact (noted by Aristotle) that such a regime was more stable in a commercial state than a dictatorial one. One could impose a direct dictatorship over a scattered peasant mass but it was more difficult to do so over a city-concentrated group of small businessmen-craftsmen and paid workers; it was best to let their "own" capitalists handle it.

In time, however, the Athenian empire, like all empires, fell. The turning point came with an attempt to subjugate the large and comparatively distant island of Sicily, an attempt which ended in the almost complete destruction of the Athenian army and fleet. In the same decades, the landowning state of Sparta, whose rulers feared the growing commercial power of Athens, formed a league of similar states and the Peloponnesian War began. In this war the Athenian landowners' hatred of their mercantile compatriots surpassed their loyalty to the State. They worked against their own government. Through their long-established power within the top military and naval committees they were able to bring about two disastrous naval defeats. The second of these defeats (at Aegospotami) proved to be the end. The flower of the Athenian youth, three to four thousand men, were captured and executed. Xenophon has left an unforgettable picture of the reception of the news at Athens — "On that night no man slept" — as the Athenians realized that "they must now, in their turn, suffer what they had themselves inflicted upon others."

The Athenian empire fell, then, because Athens had neither the wealth nor the manpower, and yet tried to expand beyond a certain limit. Why did it go beyond that limit? Was it simply an error of judgment? The answer is that Athens had no choice. The empire had to be preserved, for the life of Athens had begun to depend on it. A constant demand for imperial expansion must have come from rival commercial and banking firms, each striving to forge ahead of the other, from generals, from slave-dealers, from plantation owners. Other commercial empires were rising, for instance, the Carthaginian and the Etruscan; greater economic power was needed to stave off the threat of Sparta and the other landowning states (who were to some degree also commercial rivals). A policy of limited development might have delayed the end, but there was no attempt at modification. Competition, internal and external, was irresistible; the same forces that led to the creation of Athens led to its destruction.

The general historical development of Athens, in short, was no more under the conscious control of its successive sets of rulers than was that of India or China or Japan. Only occasionally was its fate in the hands of governmental rulers, and then only when it was threatened by an outside force. If the Persians had won at Marathon the Greek empire would, it is true, have crashed a hundred years earlier and commercial development in the Mediterranean area might have been retarded. Still, the resurgent capacities of commercialism in such an area could no more have been held back than could Chinese or Japanese commercialism in the China Sea. The defeat of Greece at Marathon or Salamis would not have hindered, perhaps not even delayed, the rise of Rome.

The Roots — Crete and the Aegean

How did this new form of society arise in Athens? What were its roots? They go back, so far as is now known, to the island of Crete about 2100 B.C. and had begun to emerge on the mainland within a century or two of the rise of Sumer.

As little Cretan writing has survived and the deciphering of what there is is still being worked on, we have to depend largely upon archaeological evidence. This evidence, however (as presented in Gustave Glotz's *The Aegean Civilization*), is sufficient to show the nature of the economy. Among the ruins of the Cretan cities have been found many presses and tanks used for refining olive oil, which along with numerous storage jars and other artifacts indicate that Cretan agriculture was specialized like that of Athens (olives and grapes) and was subordinated to manufacturing. In the towns, especially in the manufacturing town of Gurnia, the remains show that "shops and workshops jostled one another, particularly round the big square."[14] Evidence includes fragments of a considerable bronze "industry" and from Knossos the remains of a "factory for spinning and weaving."[15] The products of specialized agriculture and manufacturing were traded widely in a great fleet of ships, of between 70 and 100 feet in length. (Columbus's *Nina* was about 70 feet.) Exports included oil, wine, pottery (some of it as containers for the oil and wine), dyed cloths, "weapons and utensils of bronze, jewels, precious cups"—again, as with Athens, primarily a luxury trade.

To what degree slave labor was used does not seem to be known. Archaeological evidence gives but a general indication. There exist the remains of a working class district—as in Egypt and the Indus Valley cities—in which "humble workers" were "housed in mean quarters."[16] That all or most of them were slaves is indicated by the general pattern throughout both Asia and the Mediterranean area of craftsmen with slave helpers. Cretan society, then, was a class-divided society, with the slaves at one extreme and the inhabitants of the royal palace at the other. In between, there presumably came small manufacturers, traders, master craftsmen, and professionals.

The archaeological and other evidence shows also that the women of the upper classes had a higher social status than in Athens or most Asian civilizations. They are depicted in art works as appearing in public—in contrast to the Athenian "seclusion" pattern. Women were employed as charioteers, acrobats, and potters. Perhaps the reason for this comparative superiority in the social status of women is that the social roots of Cretan civilization went back more directly to farming society than the Athenian, and Cretan capitalist influence was not so pervasive.

Of the Cretan political system little seems to be known. We do know, however, that the head of state was a priest-king—a general phenomenon in beginning civilizations, from Sumer to China, emerging directly from later farming society. This priest, however, was not a landowner but a merchant. The old form had been modified to suit the new economy.

In time Crete acquired a commercial empire, with colonies on the Greek mainland (Thebes, Mycenae), in the Aegean (the Cyclades), perhaps even as far as Sicily. And it was this empire which apparently led to its undoing. Between 1450 and 1400 B.C. the Cretan civilization was overthrown, apparently by its own erstwhile (Greek) colonial subjects, who had become something of empire builders themselves.

If we now ask the question, not about Athens, but, as we should first, about Crete, how did this type of civilized society come into being, the primary answer is that Crete was an island, and, moreover, an island with comparatively little arable land. If a civilized society was to survive there it could do so only by manufacturing and trade. How did Crete arise?

The situation, in brief, seems to have been somewhat as follows. By 4000 B.C. a large part of upper west Asia and north Africa was covered by farming communities which first developed into civilized societies in the rich river valleys. These civilizations were, economically and socially, mainly farming river-valley societies, so rich that they had both agricultural and manufactured goods to trade. They traded with each other and with the surrounding farming societies. As sea trade was so much cheaper than land trade, seacoast trading centers sprang up (in Syria and Turkey) along the eastern Mediterranean which formed a kind of extension of the great agricultural civilizations, and then Crete formed a kind of extension from them. Crete, moreover, being an island, could not easily be dominated by a great landowning class from Asia or Africa.

The commercial states that conquered and succeeded Crete were apparently those based on Greece and the islands of the Aegean. They began to rise to power about 1700 B.C.; by 1400 they dominated the eastern Mediterranean; then about 800 B.C. they began to give way to the new power based on the Greek mainland alone, the central state of which later became Athens.

We know a great deal more about this Aegean civilization than we do about Crete, in part because it is the civilization reflected (in idealized fashion) in the Homeric poems. From Homer we get the picture of a sea-society led by warrior-princes who held land and owned ships. Homeric leaders at Troy are nostalgic about their "wide ploughlands," but their real pride is in their "dark prowed ships" plunging over the "wine-dark sea." (A very different picture from that in the land-centered Indian epics.) We learn from Homer, too, that along with the priest-king there was also the popular assembly, which was, like the Sumerian, clearly a holdover from farming society.

It is difficult to gather from Homer how prevalent slave labor was, and his depiction of slaves is misleading because he speaks mainly of household slaves, who were comparatively privileged (for instance, the servants of the princess Nausicaa). We learn, however, that when Odysseus wished to make himself look like a slave he did so by "flogging his own body till it showed all the marks of ill-usage." And the custom of the Homeric warriors of taking all the women into slavery force.

The society which Homer depicts is a wealthy society. The Aegean area had an abundance of raw materials—stone, copper, tin, silver, gold, wood, and potter's clay—and its cities manufactured goods from all of them as well as from such farming products as hides and wool. Trade was carried on with Thrace, southern and western Asia Minor, Phoenicia, Syria, Palestine, Egypt, Sicily, and southern Italy. Colonies were established on Cyprus and on the nearby Asian coast. The rival trading center at Troy—strategically situated so as to control entrance to the rich Black Sea area—was invaded and conquered.

II: THE ROMAN EMPIRE

Two general questions on Rome seem to fascinate historians, namely, "our heritage" from Rome and the reasons for the decline of the empire. One history discusses the heritage (typically) as follows:

> With the final failure of popular government and the establishment of the Empire, the Roman genius for order and organization again showed itself in the combination of local self-government and centralized control. In the field of law Rome's contribution to the modern world is even clearer. . . . She also preserved and transmitted to us the culture of Greece, which, in almost every sphere of thought and action, is the very foundation of our life today.[17]

Rome, then, "transmitted" the ideas of Greece to "us" and these now form the "foundation of our life." Apparently if the Eskimos had been fortunate enough to tune in on this "transmission" their "lives" would have had similar foundations. And, once more, we encounter the "national genes" theory: the Roman empire was the result of the "Roman genius for order and organization."

The question of the fall of the Roman Empire has long intrigued historians, especially British historians (who perhaps have felt that if they could but understand why the Roman Empire collapsed they might be able to bestow immortality upon their own). For instance, in *The Cambridge Medieval History* we learn that "the two greatest problems in history" are "how to account for the rise of Rome, and how to account for her fall."[18] ("In history," one might note in passing, covers quite an area.)

The Beginnings

There is evidence of the existence of a farming people in the Italian peninsula at least as early as 4000 B.C.; by 1000 B.C. pottery, bronze, and iron remains indicate advanced farming communities; by 800 B.C. some of these communities are developing into city states and are inhabited by peoples speaking an Indo-European language, Italic. One of these city states was established on the banks of the only really navigable river in the peninsula, the Tiber.

Into this evolving farming society there came three commercial invaders. The Etruscans conquered the upper third of the peninsula, the Greeks seized the "boot" and eastern Sicily, the Carthaginians took western Sicily, Sardinia, and Corsica. Of the three the most influential in determining the future course of Italian history were the Etruscans, who apparently arrived much earlier than the others and advanced first to civilized society. They smelted metals from the iron and copper mines of Etruria, established a series of commercial city-states across northern Italy, and set out to dominate the western Mediterranean as Greece did the eastern. Their great navies enabled them to seize Sardinia and Corsica and hold their own for many centuries against both the Greeks and the Carthaginians, but in the end they were defeated (in the sea battle of Cumae, in 474 B.C.), and their erstwhile Italic subjects began a struggle on land that resulted in Italic domination of the peninsula—fanning out from the flourishing commercial center established by the Etruscans themselves. As later historians, including the Romans themselves, fail to emphasize, Rome was ruled by the Etruscans for 250 years; and the Rome the Etruscans left was very different from the Rome they had entered. Italic Rome was rooted in Etruscan Rome and grew in the struggle for both Italy and empire.

With the decline of Athens the commercial balance of power in the Mediterranean moved from east to west, and the Roman Empire arose out of the struggle for the western Mediterranean just as had the Greek from that for the eastern. There were, however, important differences between their situations. The Italian peninsula is larger and has more arable land than the Greek. There was extensive farming in the early Italian states and, hence, a solid agricultural basis for wealth upon which the commercial economy could build. Rome was able to conquer Italy but Athens was not able to conquer Greece. This was partly due to differences of terrain, but it must have been related also to the fact that Rome lay on the only navigable river in a fertile area and was able to build great farming as well as commercial wealth from an early period.

From some historical accounts of the Mediterranean empires one gets the impression of a series of sterile Spenglerian cycles: Crete, the Greek-Aegean, Phoenicia, Greece, Carthage, Rome, all simply repeating a pattern and passing out of existence. Such was not the case. We are dealing not with cycles but an expanding spiral. This can most simply be seen by a comparison of the size of cities:

Troy II	2 acres
Gurnia (Crete)	6½ acres
Mycenae	11 acres
Pompeii	160 acres
Roman Naples	250 acres
New Carthage	1,200 acres
Rome (ca. 200 A.D.)	3,060 acres

Athens was a city of about 300,000 inhabitants, Rome of between 2 and 4 million; the Athenian Empire had a population of 2 million, the Roman Empire of 54 million. We must not allow ourselves to be deceived by the comparative slowness of the evolutionary process— between Gurnia and Rome lie some 1,500 years—into denying that it was evolutionary. And slow though the pace may seem compared to modern developments, it was more rapid than that of the agricultural empires of Asia. Yet in one respect there is something to be said for the cycle theory. There was no major qualitative development; the change is almost entirely quantitative. The Roman Empire, like the Athenian, was based on slave labor; like the Athenian it was commercial and not industrial (in the modern sense of the word). The tools and machines of production were the same; there were simply more of them.

The Economy

AGRICULTURE AND INDUSTRY

Agriculture, as in Greece, was specialized, and produced the raw materials for much of the trade and manufacturing. Olives and grapes were again major crops, but now there were also grain, cattle, and sheep, plus an enormous variety of secondary products, partly raised in Italy, partly in the colonies: honey, figs, cheese, nuts, and melons (from Egypt), cotton, beets, apricots, citron, geese, buffalo, and barn-yard fowl (from Greece). This vast and varied produce was raised by the most skillful farming technology so far developed: crop rotation, fertilization, seed selection, greenhouses, experiments in cross fertilization. The cherry was grafted upon the elm, the walnut upon the arbutus.

For many centuries there had been a large class of small farmers in Italy, but little by little the great estates devoured the small farms. (Pliny, for instance, tells of one that had 7,000 oxen and 257,000 other farm animals.) These great estates were able to grow so rapidly be-cause the control of the land was essentially private, for land which was nominally state property was actually controlled — really, in effect, owned — by individual great landowners. Nor was all this land in Italy. As the Romans conquered in Gaul and elsewhere vast tracts were turned over to Italian great landowners.

These landowners, largely engaged in specialized agriculture and intertwined with commercial interests, were able to concentrate wealth on a scale far beyond that of feudal economies or Athens, and this enabled them to make a basic socioeconomic innovation — instead of peasant labor they used slave labor. (The estate mentioned by Pliny, for instance, had 4,117 slaves.) The reason for this use of slave labor — once it became economically possible — was twofold: there was a large and steady supply of slaves from foreign conquest, and slave labor was cheaper than peasant labor. Cato in his estate records in-forms us that it cost about 78 denarii to keep a slave for one year and 250 to 300 denarii to keep a peasant and his wife (slaves did not have wives). As a peacock (considered a table delicacy) cost about 50 denarii, Cato could keep a slave for one year for less than it cost him to buy two peacocks. In addition to these estate-owned slaves there were also slave gangs owned and rented to farmers by contractors. The Roman upper classes, in short, extended slave labor, long established in Asia and Greece for work in the mines, forests, and quarries, to agriculture.

There were, of course, still mines, quarries, and forests. As every-where these were State property, but as in Athens mining rights were leased out to individual capitalists. Presumably this held also for lum-bering and quarrying. Public works were let out to private contractors. There were iron and lead mines in Noricum (south Austria), silver and lead mines in Gaul and Spain, lead and tin mines in Spain and Britain, copper mines in Cyprus and Portugal, iron mines in Gaul, Dalmatia, and on the island of Elba, sulphur mines in Sicily; there were marble quarries at Luna, Hymettus, and Paros, porphyry in Egypt. The

Roman armies on the Rhine were supplied with weapons by the "Gallic mines," those on the Danube by the Dalmatian mines. Metalworking centers grew up at Puteoli (now Pozzuoli, near Naples) where the iron ore from Elba was smelted, at Capua (copper and bronze), at Minturnae, Aquileia, and Como.

Large though this metallurgical enterprise was in comparison to that of other states, it was no more a modern metal industry than was the Greek (or Chinese). Metal was not used for building or for machines except in a secondary capacity (hinges, bolts, bands along with wood, stone, rope, and leather). It was still used mainly for weapons on the one hand and luxury objects on the other (bronze vases, gold jewelry). Although several forges and smelters were combined into large workshops in the main metal centers of the empire, the standard method of production was still, as in Greece or India or China, the individual forge worked by the blacksmith and a few helpers. And the methods of iron smelting and shaping were as crude and as cumbersome as ever. The Roman fuels were still wood and charcoal. Coal, which could have produced the requisite temperatures for easier smelting and refining, was still not used. And petroleum was used to make flaming torches for war missiles.

SLAVE LABOR

The basic labor everywhere was slave labor. The Roman legions were supplied with their armaments by slave labor (in the "Gallic" and other mines). The famed "Roman roads" over which these legions marched were built by slaves. The architectural wonders cf Rome, the Colosseum, the Forum, the Baths of Caracalla, on whose ruins tourists gaze today, were constructed by slave gangs owned by building contractors. The great aqueducts were built and maintained by slaves; the sewers of Rome were built by slaves and cleaned by slaves. Slave labor predominated in manufacturing. In the potteries of Arretium, 123 out of 132 workers were slaves. The 9 workers who were not slaves were craftsmen, some of whom signed their wares. And this, in general, was the relationship of slave labor to paid labor: the paid worker was the skilled worker, the slave the laborer. The paid craftsmen were both numerous and highly specialized, as we can tell from a mere listing of crafts: stonemasons, joiners, cement mixers, marble-floor-pavers, plasterers and whitewashers (separate crafts), arch-builders, bricklayers, goldsmiths, silversmiths, ring-makers, wreath-makers, rope-makers, fullers, dyers, glass blowers. All of these paid workers had slaves working for them.

The total produce of farming, industry, and manufacturing in the empire resulted in trade of a variety and scope never before seen. The movement away from the exclusive dominance of luxury trade, which began with the cheap pottery of the Greek-Aegean cities and continued in Athens (which imported its wheat), had in Rome developed to a new degree. There is clearly a considerable trade in necessities — wheat, hides, wool, linen — along with the luxury trade in jewelry, silks, ivory, and spices. And from everywhere came slaves. The main slave market at Delos handled as many as ten thousand slaves a day.

Much of the trade going into Italy was tribute (both in money and goods) forced from the colonies — Britain, Gaul, Spain, North Africa, Egypt, central Europe, Greece, Syria, Palestine, Mesopotamia — a tribute of unprecedented vastness, derived ultimately from the labor of millions of slaves and peasants.

To accommodate this trade a vast transportation system was needed. The Empire's 51,000 miles of paved highways were traversed by great ox-cart and pack-mule trains manned by slave labor. Ships ran up to 200 and 300 tons. An elaborate system of lighthouses dotted the Mediterranean; ports were improved by the use of hydraulic cement and pile driving in deep water.

The whole economic process, farming, industry, manufacturing, trade, and transportation, was serviced by an elaborate financial and banking system replete with checking accounts, interest-bearing deposits, travellers' checks, bills of exchange, stock investments, and interest rates. There were great banking firms — Balbus and Ollius, Maximus and Vibo, the Pettius Brothers — not only at Rome but at Lyons, Carthage, Corinth, Byzantium. And the State treasury acted as a banker, making loans to farmers and businessmen.

Social Life

CLASS STRUCTURE

No state before Roman Italy and none for a thousand years after has left so much information about its social life. We know more about the Rome of Augustus than about the England of Alfred or the France of Charlemagne. And what we know shows that in Rome, as elsewhere, the nature of the social life was basically determined by the class structure. The social life of a great landowner was one thing, that of a slave was another.

The class structure of Rome differed from that of Athens primarily in that the landowning class was larger and more powerful, both absolutely and in relation to the capitalist class. Socially, politically, and culturally it was, in fact, the dominant class. Why, then, did Rome not become a feudal state like China or Sparta but a slave-commercial state like Athens? The answer is that the Mediterranean area was a commerical rather than an agricultural area, and whatever powers rose to dominance had to be (and were) commercial. And in spite of the great landowning power Roman commercialism was so extensive that it penetrated deeply into the social scene.

The Roman capitalists possessed wealth far beyond that of the Greeks. Let us take Marcus Licinius Crassus as an example. Crassus, like many capitalists, had some base in land. The money from his farms he used to buy up tenements at Rome and rent them at high rentals. With the money from his (several hundred) tenements he bought up State mines which had been put on the open market. Within a few years he ran his fortune from 7 million sesterces to 170 million — about equal to the total yearly revenue of the State treasury. Capitalists like Crassus lived in magnificent mansions in Rome with as many as 400 household slaves, mansions with marble floors and onyx columns, walls decorated with rare stones, ceilings coffered in gold, tables of citrus wood standing on legs of ivory, beds of bronze, and bathrooms with silver taps.

Below the capitalists came, as in Athens, a large class of small tradesmen and craftsmen. But there was also a distinct class of paid workers, working in factories or for contractors, at an average wage of 4 sesterces (about 40 cents) a day. In *The Golden Ass* Apuleius tells us of a man who "depended for his livelihood on his small earnings as a jobbing smith;" coming home unexpectedly one day he explains to his wife: "What fault of mine is it if the contractor has to spend the day in court and lays us off until tomorrow?"[19] The man was a paid worker, economically little above the level of the slave and below that of the master craftsman. His "contractor" was a capitalist who hired his labor. In Rome these workers lived in crowded tenements on streets but a few feet wide. They ate grain and vegetables. Meat, as from China to Egypt, was the food of the rich.

The range of income and of living conditions within the professional class seems to have been considerable. There are, at one extreme, schoolteachers depending somewhat precariously for their salary upon the number of their pupils and, at the other, millionaire lawyers like Cicero or wealthy actors like Roscus. But on the whole the professional class seems to have lived at a level about midway between the wealthy and the poor, for instance, like the professor for whom Pliny tried to secure a country house:

In this little plot of ground, if the price is right, there is much that appeals to the taste of my Tranquillus: its nearness to the city, its access to the highway, the moderate size of the house, the small amount of ground, enough for diversion without making it a burden. Teachers, such as he is, want only enough ground to rest their head, refresh their eyes, saunter along its borders, wearing a single path, know the history of every vine in the little vineyard, and the number of its trees.[20]

Slavery

No estimate seems to have been made of the total number of slaves in the Roman Empire. The figure previously cited of 54 million population was based on the Roman census, which did not include slaves. It has been calculated, however, that in Italy alone in the reign of Claudius there were some 21 million slaves. As we have noted, the slave market at Delos could handle 10,000 slaves a day. We have to note also the massive captures of slaves in the Roman wars of conquest, for example:

201 B.C.	35,000 Carthaginians
197 B.C.	80,000 Sardinians
177 B.C.	150,000 Macedonians
147 B.C.	55,000 Carthaginians

And these captures took place in the period of the Republic before the real expansion of slavery under the Emperors. Caesar's armies alone are estimated to have enslaved one million Gauls.

The great mass of the slaves — of which we hear the least — worked on the estates, in mines and quarries, building, manufacturing, and transportation. They were branded on the forehead and limbs and wore chains both in the fields during the day and in their barracks at night. Cato's maxim, which he followed on his estate, was that a slave should "work or sleep."[21] In the mines, they worked in chains under the lash. Plautus refers to the quarries as a "hell" filled with "the torments of the damned."[22] Apuleius gives us a picture of slaves at a flour mill: "Their skins were seamed all over with the marks of old floggings, as you could easily see through the holes in their ragged shirts that shaded rather than covered their scarred backs; but some wore only loin-cloths. They had letters branded on their foreheads, and half-shaved heads and irons on their legs."[23] The difference between the lives of these slaves and the "professional" slaves — who are sometimes given as representative of Roman slavery — is shown in the difference in price. A farm slave cost 330 sesterces, "Daphnis the grammarian" cost 700,000.[24]

Nearly all Roman slaves had originally been free citizens of some other country, often coming from civilizations culturally on a level with Rome. Furthermore, Roman slaves could not — as could the later

American Negro slaves—be readily distinguished on sight from the Romans themselves. Many of them were racially akin to the Italians. When a bill was introduced into the Roman Senate to decree a distinguishing dress for slaves, it was defeated on the ground that it would reveal to the slaves how great was their number (and this did not include the great mass of slaves, who were never seen on the streets).

What were the relative proportions of the various classes to each other? We do not know exactly or for each period, but we may use the time of Cicero (which was prior to the main expansion of the empire and the great increase in slavery) as an example. The census figures show 10,000 large and middle capitalists and 900,000 total citizens (all male). There were said on good contemporary authority to be 2,000 large landowners. We do not know how many large capitalists there were, but it seems unlikely that there were more than the landowners. For the same period the number of slaves has been calculated at 4.5 million (including women).

What is usually meant by such generalities as "the Roman way of life" is the way of life of the wealthier classes. Slaves are not considered either as Romans or as human (which is simply a reflection of the attitude of the Roman ruling classes themselves). If we wonder how sensitive and compassionate people like Ovid or Catullus could live amid such a sea of human misery without being constantly revolted, the answer is that, although they had some sympathies with the sufferings of individual slaves, they automatically excluded the slave mass from the human world. Horace could even comment humorously on the crucifixion of a slave.

As in Greece, Egypt, and Asia, Roman education meant education for the children of wealthier classes only. Cicero's son was educated at the university of Athens—more exclusive than the Italian universities—but the children of the "plebes" received no education at all. Literacy was a sign of upper class membership.

The famed Roman "sports" and "baths" were class diversions. Rome's 856 "public" baths were built, maintained, and serviced by slaves for the pleasure of the upper classes. Chariot races and other sports were indulged in only by the wealthy or by professionals. The only "sports" in which slaves took part were those of the arena where they were torn to pieces by wild beasts, castrated, burned to death or slaughtered in mass gladitorial combats.

WOMEN

The situation of women varied, as ever, with their class. Women slaves were mainly household slaves. A woman slave was sexually at the disposal of her master and had no redress if raped. Girl slaves were bought by rich young men; a woman slave for sexual purposes cost about one-twentieth the price of a town house. There were also, as in Egypt and other countries, a large number of women slaves in manufacturing, especially, it would seem, in textiles. In addition to slave women used for sexual purposes, there were vast numbers of prostitutes. Brothels were legal, prostitutes were registered and were required to wear the man's *toga* (instead of the usual woman's dress of the *stola*). Every inn on the highway of the 51,000 miles of paved Roman roads seems to have had its quota of prostitutes. In the Roman Empire as in China (as noted by Marco Polo) or India we find mass economic and sexual exploitation of women.

Roman women of the upper classes had higher status than did Athenian women. They were not secluded. "Ladies rode through the street in sedan chairs 'exposing themselves on every side to the view'; they conversed with men in porticoes, parks, gardens, and temple courts; they accompanied them to private or public banquets, to the amphitheatre and the theatre, where 'their shoulders,' said Ovid, 'give you something charming to contemplate.'"[25] Girls as well as boys went to school. There were women lawyers and doctors. Women in various towns and localities were united in clubs and assemblies. Unable to vote, they wrote the names of their favorite candidates on the walls.

In 195 B.C. the Roman women marched into the Forum and demanded (and secured) the repeal of a law which forbade women to wear gold ornaments or varicolored dresses or to use chariots. It was on this occasion that Cato, the Tory of all Roman Tories, delivered an alarmed speech (to be repeated endlessly through the centuries):

"If we had, each of us, upheld the rights, and authority of the husband in our own households, we should not today have this trouble with our women. As things are now, our liberty of action, which has been annulled by female despotism at home, is crushed and trampled on here in the Forum. . . . Call to mind all of the regulations respecting women by which our ancestors curbed their license and made them obedient to their husbands; and yet with all those restrictions you can scarcely hold them in. If now you permit them to remove these restraints . . . and to put themselves on an equality with their husbands, do you imagine that you will be able to bear them? From the moment that they become your equals they will become your masters."[26]

As we consider this Roman and other situations it once more becomes apparent that antifeminism is a powerful force in society. The more one reads in history the more it appears that women have continuously struggled for property and other rights, while men have tried to keep them from such rights. Sometimes women advanced in this struggle (as the peasant women did in early China), sometimes they suffered severe defeats (as in the Arab Empire), but unless one perceives the fact of the struggle itself, its fluctuations have little meaning.

Political Life

The main differences between the political structure of the Roman State (that in the Republic and that in the Empire periods were essentially the same) and the Athenian resulted from the relatively greater power of the landowning class in Roman Italy. The capitalists were never able, as in Athens, to secure political control. They were, however, powerful enough to exert important (sometimes even decisive) influence upon the landowners.

The great bastion of landowning power was the Senate. The members of the Senate were traditionally aristocrats. That control should not pass into the hands of businessmen who bought land, a decree was passed that no senator could engage in trade. The powers of the Senate included control over the Treasury, all State property and finances, including the colonization and allotment of conquered land, and the army budget. It controlled also the leasing of contracts for the mines, quarries, and salt works. As it appointed ambassadors and received foreign representatives it had virtual control of foreign affairs also.

The political center for big-business power was the Centurial Assembly, which consisted of all male Roman citizens of military age arranged in divisions ("centuries") according to their wealth. The nonpropertied citizens were essentially disfranchised, and the voting power of the smaller businessmen was cut down. Women and slaves had no vote.

The Assembly, although subordinate to the Senate, had considerable powers. It elected the Consuls, Censors, and other major governmental and judicial officers. It could give final judgment in political trials. It had the power of deciding upon a war of aggression.

We have an interesting example of day-to-day Roman politics in an electioneering manual for Cicero's election campaign for Consul (chief magistrate) in 63 B.C. The manual begins by warning Cicero that he must never forget that he is a "new man," not having come from an old landowning family. He could, he was told, count on "all the business men, nearly the whole of the equestrian order," and "many municipal towns." The "rising generation" was for him also. The problem was the landowning aristocracy. "All these men must be canvassed with care. Agents must be sent to them and they must be convinced that we have been at one politically with the optimates [i.e. the aristocrats] and that we have never been demagogues."[27] The aristocrats had to be convinced that Cicero had never played the capitalist's pressure-politics game of rousing the lower orders of the Assembly against the Senators. Cicero himself, when in the Senate, considered his objective the establishment of the "harmony of the classes."[28] The manual ends with a point of practical advice which shows that the processes of electioneering once established did not much change: "See if possible that some new scandal is started against our competitors for crime or looseness of life or corruption, such as is in harmony with their characters."

The other parts of the Roman State, the legal system and police, the church, and the army did not differ markedly from those in Athens. The famed "Roman law," of which we hear so much as a model, excluded the majority of the population from legal protection. As in Athens or India a woman was legally responsible not to the law but to her father (or nearest male relation) or husband. Roman women, however, won the right to administer their own dowries and to divorce their husbands. And some laws disadvantageous to women were ignored in practice.

A slave was not considered under the legal category of *persona* (person) but of *res* (thing). He could not be examined as a witness except by torture; if he was injured or killed under the torture his owner was compensated. Slaves could not marry; if a union of a man and woman slave took place it was legally a cohabitation (*contubernium*) and could be terminated at will by the master.

Penalty, as usual, was determined by class. A master could legally kill a slave as he could an animal; but if a slave killed a master all the slaves in the household could be executed.

With the Church at Rome so at Athens. There were many and magnificent temples and a large body of clergy, but there was no separate caste or order for the clergy; within each family (as in Sumer or China) the father conducted the religious ceremony. The revenues and property of the Church were controlled by the Senate. The head of the Church, the *pontifex maximus,* was elected by the Centurian Assembly. If we may judge by Polybius (writing in about 150 B.C.) the Church was frankly regarded by some Roman rulers as a political tranquilizer: "The masses in every State are unstable, full of lawless desires, irrational anger and violent passion. All that can be done is to hold them in check by fears of the unseen and similar shams. It was not for nothing but of deliberate design that the men of yore introduced to the masses notions about God and views on the afterlife."[29]

Some historians give the impression of Roman military power as an unpredictable force dwelling above the sociopolitical structure. But, although like other armies, it was sometimes used against one segment of the upper classes by another (the army group under the control of Mark Antony, for example, slaughtered 300 Senators and 2,000 businessmen), it was part of the State and generally controlled by the upper classes. The leading Roman officers were members of the landowning or business class. Out of 200 Consuls between 233 and 133 B.C., 159 belonged to 26 great landed families. The army pursued an erratic course only in times of shifting power such as that which marked the transition from the Republic to the Empire. Normally, it was under the control of the Senate, sometimes of the great landowning group around the Emperor.

The Roman State, like all States, had the dual function of ruling internally and externally. Internally, it reacted to and adjusted the struggle between and within the propertied classes and kept the non-propertied classes, especially the slaves, in subjugation. Externally, it conquered and administered the empire, and regulated relations between the empire and other countries.

The internal political conflicts of ancient Rome arose, as Cicero's campaign showed, from the division between the capitalists and the landowners (the "equestrians" and the "patricians"). Leon Homo, for instance, in his *Roman Political Institutions* speaks of "the growing tension" between these two classes as "the main characteristic of their relations from the end of the third century" B.C.[30] F. R. Cowell describes the early days of the conflict as follows:

> A new force, the men of the business, trading and moneyed interest, the *equites*, were making themselves felt in Roman politics [about 175 B.C.]. . . . Aided by the *equites* and by the small farmers and city mob [i.e., the small businessmen-craftsmen] Gaius Gracchus [d. 121 B.C.] was able to get sufficient support to out-vote the great landowning class from whom the Senators were mainly chosen.[31]

Sometimes, of course, landowners and capitalists worked together against other classes. For instance, the bankers assisted the great landowners to rob the small farmer of his land by keeping interest rates on loans high. Their joint opposition to the small businessmen-craftsmen caused these men to form guilds (*collegia*) for their protection. Almost every trade seemed to have its guild and in some of them slaves were admitted. Landowners and capitalists alike attacked them, but they survived, just as the illegal early trade unions did in England. Landowners and capitalists were united also in maintaining slavery and putting down slave revolts.

SLAVE REVOLTS

It is interesting that popular historians of Roman and American history alike present a picture of the slave as docilely accepting his lot and the slave-master ruling undisturbed. The record, however, shows otherwise. There were slave revolts in 419, 198, 196, 185, 139, 132, 104, and 73 B.C. in various parts of the Roman Empire.

Of these revolts, that of Spartacus in 73 B.C. was the most threatening. Spartacus, a gladiator slave from Thrace, formed an army of slaves 120,000 strong, and for two years a full-fledged war raged up and down the Italian peninsula from the "boot" to the Alps. The equipment, the discipline, and the organization of Spartacus' forces can be judged by the fact that they defeated three Roman armies before finally being beaten. The leader of the fourth army was the capitalist Crassus (assisted by Pompey) who made his money from tenements and mines. The slave armies fought to the end, spurning surrender. In one engagement more than 12,000 of them were killed. Six thousand who were captured were crucified on crosses lined up for miles along the famed Appian Way between Rome and Capua where their dying torments could be watched by the wealthy Romans driving along the Way to their country villas.

Slave revolts, as Rostovtzeff comments, "were probably more frequent than the meagre evidence would lead us to believe."[32] The evidence is "meagre" for the simple reason that the Roman historians suppressed it. They devoted tomes to the war with Carthage, but made only brief and scattered references to Spartacus.

The only slave war of which we have a detailed account is one which raged in Sicily for eight years (139–131 B.C.). The story, as told by Diodorus of Agyrium, is a classic of its kind.[33] The revolt began on the estate of Damophilus of Enna, "a particularly arrogant multi-millionaire." The slaves, led by a Syrian slave called Eunus, seized and executed Damophilus and his wife. They were then joined by "a number of town slaves." Eunus was "elected" as leader and "proceeded to call a public meeting," which set up a "council," and Eunus began to equip an army with makeshift and captured weapons. As this army advanced over the countryside, "immense numbers of slaves flocked to him." His army grew from ten thousand to twenty thousand; "before long two hundred thousand had gathered to their standards, and they conducted a succession of campaigns against the Romans in which they acquitted themselves with credit and established a superiority. As the news spread, slave revolts flared up everywhere. . . . Towns were captured with their entire population and one army after another was cut to pieces by the insurgents, until the Roman commander Rupilius recovered Tauromenium for his government." The Roman forces also captured Enna and the back of the revolt was broken. Within thirty years, however, another large slave revolt began in Sicily.

It is clear from Diodorus' picture that we are dealing with a mass revolt, which, along with that of Spartacus, was of a scope not to be witnessed again in Europe until the peasant revolts. It was, like the peasant revolts, well-organized, disciplined, and democratic. Eunus was "elected"; once elected, he did not assume dictatorial powers but called a general assembly and had other elected leaders work with him in a "council." Eunus could, in fact, have acted in no other way. He had no power over his fellow slaves beyond his own abilities as a leader. The slaves set up a kind of rudimentary communistic government, but it was one which could not develop further because the economic and social foundations were insufficient to permit such development. It was simply a matter of time before it was destroyed.

If we consider all these revolts together, they reveal the existence of a ceaseless, bitter and brutal struggle between the slaves and their masters in Roman Italy, a struggle of which they are but the peaks, and which — as in other slave societies — must have taken many forms — strikes, minor revolts, slowdowns, sabotage, only from time to time flaring out into full-scale war. It is a picture similar to that of the Chinese peasant revolts, with, however, this difference: the Chinese peasant revolts slowly gathered power over the centuries, until they merged with other revolutionary forces in the 1940's, whereas the last of the great slave wars in the Roman Empire was in 71 B.C. Apparently the Roman rulers learned how to prevent revolt from breaking out into civil war, perhaps simply by keeping the mass of the slaves chained day and night. But the Chinese feudal lords, faced with peasants, had a more formidable opponent, for peasants have powers for resistance and freedom of movement that slaves do not. Furthermore, unlike China, Rome for many centuries had been a centralized State with a centralized army.

SUBJECT PEOPLES

The Roman Empire was acquired by the absorption of older empires (the Macedonian, the Egyptian) and later farming societies (the Gauls, the Britons, the Germans). The savagery of the struggle involved in this imperial conquest does not seem to be generally appreciated. We hear much of the Punic Wars with Carthage, but how many know that at the final destruction of Carthage more than 450,000 men, women, and children were butchered, and at Jerusalem (70 A.D.),

600,000? The impression is sometimes given that this empire was acquired with triumphant ease; actually, people everywhere fought heroically for their freedom. The Roman armies, Tacitus complains, had fought against the Germans for 210 years and still had not completed the conquest. Into the mouth of one of the British leaders he puts a speech which must many times have been made in the bloody centuries of conquest:

> We, the last men on earth, the last of the free, have been shielded till today by the very remoteness and the seclusion for which we are famed. . . . [But], brigands of the world [the Romans] have exhausted the land by their indiscriminate plunder, and now they ransack the sea. The wealth of an enemy excites their cupidity, his poverty their lust of power. East and West have failed to glut their maw. They are unique in being as violently tempted to attack the poor as the wealthy. Robbery, butchery, rapine, the liars call Empire; they create a desolation and call it peace.[34]

The Roman rulers knew well enough what they were fighting for. Quite early in the game of empire Cicero spelled it out. "The whole system of credit and finance which is carried on here at Rome is inextricably bound up with the revenues of the Asiatic provinces. If these revenues are destroyed, our system of credit will crash. . . . Prosecute with all your energies the war against Mithridates, by which the glory of the Roman name, the safety of our allies, our most valuable revenues, and the fortunes of innumerable citizens will be effectively preserved."[35] More than a hundred years later Tacitus remarked, almost casually, "Britain yields gold, silver and other metals, to make it worth conquering."[36]

Decline and Fall

For more than three hundred years, from the beginnings of the invasion of Greece in 200 B.C., the wars of conquest continued. The landowners acquired more land, the capitalists more profits; the stream of slaves and booty was endless and ever-swelling.

In time, however, the swell stopped. In the second century A.D., "No new lands were acquired." In 301 the Emperor Diocletian issued an edict to regulate wages and prices. The wages of farm laborers were frozen; the expansion of cities ceased, and contraction began. "After A.D. 275 Autun had shrunk from nearly five hundred to less than twenty-five acres."[37] Other cities fell into ruins and were not repaired. The great estates became more and more self-sufficient units relying on their own workshops and cutting off city trade. Peasant labor began to take the place of slave labor. Economic crises struck. Banks failed, one after the other. The State (i.e., the great landowners) took over the mines, quarries, and salt deposits, seized factories, and bound the workers to their jobs like serfs.

What failed was business rather than agriculture. As business failed, the capitalists declined and as the capitalists declined the landowners advanced to the attack. Roman Italy, in short, began to revert to the feudal pattern, with industry and trade subordinate in a State run by a landowning oligarchy, and without the wealth to support slave labor on the land.

Why did Roman manufacturing and trade cease to expand? The answer is simply that they had reached the limits of their market. Within Italy and the Empire in general purchasing power was relatively low. The great mass of slaves had virtually none, the hired workers and peasants almost none, the small-businessmen-craftsmen little; only the landowners and capitalists had much, which meant, in essence, that they were selling to each other. Expansion, therefore, had to be external, mostly by conquest. But in time the economy reached its limits for sustaining conquest. The Roman capitalists could, it is true, have expanded further had they (hypothetically) been able to develop a modern industrial capitalism, but they were blocked from this possibility also by their system with its slave labor center. With profits so high from slave labor, there was not only no incentive toward technological development but opposition to it.

The decline, in any case, would have come sooner or later. When it did come it was helped by the fact that Rome, like Athens, had overexpanded, seized territories and markets which it had not the military (ultimately the economic) power to hold. In time these territories became important economic centers (Gaul, Spain, Portugal) and, as Rome declined, they broke away and hastened the decline. Why did Rome overexpand? The answer is the same as for Athens: the total competitive drive for slaves, profits, loot, and tribute was not to be curbed.

The decline, however, was relatively slow (in contrast to that of the Athenian Empire). Expansion ceased about 100 A.D., but Rome did not fall until almost 500. Why was it so slow? The answer is that Roman capitalism (unlike Athenian) was integrated with a powerful agricultural economy which assisted its rise, gave it stability, and cushioned its decline. When this decline reached a certain point the cushioning became envelopment. Even so, Rome could have continued as a mainly agricultural but partly capitalist State for many years if there had been no power strong enough to push it over. Such a power did not arise until the fifth century (in the combined forces of the Germanic peoples and the Huns).

The Roman upper classes had no more control over their destiny than did the Athenian. They had built, as the unplanned result of their total competitive activity, an intricate mechanism, each part of which integrated with each other part; although each part was run by separate capitalists no group or organization ran, or could run, the whole.

If we look back over the history of the Mediterranean area we can see a developing monopoly of commercial empire, from the Cretan to the Greek Aegean, from the Phoenician to the Carthaginian, from the Greek Aegean to the Athenian, from the Athenian to the Macedonian, and then finally the devouring of the whole by the Roman. With this development the commercial-slave civilization of the Mediterranean rested upon but one foundation; when that went, all went. Thus the fall of Rome marked more than the fall of the Roman Empire; it marked the end of slave-commercial civilization. The ever-increasing spiral of empires reached a certain point and then exploded like a giant pinwheel.

III: GREEK AND ROMAN CULTURE

In discussions of Greek and Roman culture it is, as usual, on general questions — those that fall between specialties — that we find some scholars writing with a confident sweep that evades the basic questions. Why, for instance, did Greek culture rise to unprecedented heights? Why did the Roman differ from it in so many ways? Only occasionally is a direct answer attempted, for instance, by Sir William Dampier:

> In the ancient world scientific thought was almost entirely confined to the Greeks. It would naturally seem probable that the composition of the population of Italy must have been similar in character to that of Greece. But the inhabitants of the two countries showed considerable differences in development and achievement, thus suggesting differences in race. The Romans, with their exaltation of the State, and their exceptional aptitude as soldiers, administrators and framers of law, had little creative intellectual force, though the numerous compilations that came into being seem to indicate a considerable curiosity about natural objects.[38]

"Scientific thought" was not, as we have seen, "almost entirely confined to the Greeks." Or is Asia, perhaps, excluded by definition from the "ancient world"? As to "race" — the Greeks and Romans were part of the same race, and, in any case, no genes for "exaltation of the State" have so far been discovered.

Or let us consider the following in Mason's *Main Currents of Scientific Thought:*

The Romans and the Hebrews came to civilization during the iron age, but they were primarily agriculturalists, not seafarers, and they did not make notable contributions in the field of science.

The Greeks alone were a people who came to iron-age civilization directly from barbarism and who took to sea-going commerce from the start. The Greeks had the traveller's feel for space, the sense of geometry which was lacking in the settled agricultural communities of pre-Greek times and later ones, such as the civilization of China, which were cut off from Greek thought.[39]

Mason's approach is so typical of much recent historical writing that it deserves particular notice, not only for what it says but for its method. It appears to make causal statements without actually making them. The Romans and Hebrews, it is implied, had little science because (a) they came to civilization during the "iron age" and (b) they were primarily agriculturalists. But Mason does not actually say this. He simply links his clauses by the noncommittal conjunction "and." He implies that the Greek "feel for space" arises from the "sea-going commerce" and that the "sense of geometry" in turn arises from the "feel for space"; but again he does not say this but hides behind a simple sequencing of statements and a balanced construction: "the traveller's feel for space, the sense of geometry." The overall implication is that there is no causality but simply a Humean meaningless sequence of events. The door is always left open for retreat: the sequence could be the other way around; perhaps there is really no sequence. Perhaps "Greek thought" could have turned "China" to geometry—and commerce.

Elements of Science—Archimedes and Others

Although, as we have seen, there had been considerable advances in India toward science and scientific method, the Greeks surpassed these earlier efforts. And this is what we would expect. Both the demands for science and the possibilities for its free development are greater in a commercial civilization than in a predominantly feudal one. The Greeks, in fact—contrary to the notion that the experimental method began with the Renaissance—did many scientific experiments and began to grasp that experiment was essential to the scientific method. For instance, let us take an experiment by Strabo (who succeeded Aristotle and Theophrastus at the Lyceum) described in his own words:

. . . vessels which are generally believed to be empty are not really empty but are full of air. Now air, in the opinion of the natural philosophers, consists of minute particles of matter for the most part invisible to us. Accordingly if one pours water into an apparently empty vessel, a volume of air comes out equal to the volume of water poured in. To prove this make the following experiment. Take a seemingly empty vessel. Turn it vertical, and plunge it into a dish of water. Even if you depress it until it is completely covered no water will enter. This proves that air is a material thing which prevents the water entering the vessel because it has previously occupied all the available space. Now bore a hole in the bottom of the vessel. The water will then enter at the mouth while the air escapes by the hole.[40]

The experiment is certainly elementary but it and similar experiments represent milestones in the advance of human knowledge. A commercial society is beginning to seek new answers on the nature of matter; the old answers — of religion or philosophy, based on "revelation" or a priori generalizations — no longer satisfy; the path to truth through testing and experimentation is being charted. The words may be Strabo's but the method is that of Galileo or Boyle.

In food-gathering and farming societies, people had no concept of the earth as a planet. The earth was hunting land or cultivated fields. Even the Sumerians did not advance much beyond this. With the coming of long-range commerce, however, speculation on the total nature of the earth, its shape, and its size, began. Here again the Greeks made a notable advance, and here, again, it was made by the experimental method.

The first estimate of the earth's circumference was made by Eratosthenes (c. 250 B.C.). As librarian of Alexandria, he had access to information from which he was able to compare the sun's altitude at two situations, one due south of the other. On the summer solstice the noon sun was mirrored in a deep well near Syene just below the first cataract of the Nile on the tropic of Cancer. The noon sun was therefore at the zenith. On the same day in Alexandria, 500 miles due north, the obelisk shadow showed that the sun was $7\frac{1}{2}$ degrees from the zenith. Since the sun's rays are parallel, this means that the arc, or as we now say the difference of latitude between Syene and Alexandria is approximately $7\frac{1}{2}$, i.e., $7\frac{1}{2}$ divided by 360 equals $\frac{1}{48}$ of the entire earth's circumference. Hence, the difference between Alexandria and Syene (approximately 500 miles) is $\frac{1}{48}$ of the circumference of the globe. So the earth's circumference is about 48×500 equals 24,000 miles. . . . The result agrees within 4% with modern determinations.[41]

It had normally been assumed that the sun was smaller than the earth for the simple reason that it looks smaller. Epicurus, for instance, declared that it was about two feet across, and Anaxagoras startled the court of Pericles when he suggested that it might, in fact,

be larger than Greece. Aristarchus of Samos, however, used trigono-
metrical calculations based on an eclipse of the moon and its phases
to determine its size. His figures are wrong because exact telescopic
observation was not possible but his method was sound and the thought
had been born that the sun might be larger than the earth, and was perhaps an immense distance away.

Along with knowledge of the shape and size of the earth went that
of its geographical nature. The advance here from the days of the
Greek-Aegean to Ptolemy (second century A.D.) is well summarized
by Farrington:

> It is only necessary to look at the map of the world as known to Homer,
> with the River Ocean encircling the flat disk of the world, and set beside it
> the map which can be reconstructed from the data of Ptolemy, with its
> curved parallels and curved meridians, its fulness and comparative ac-
> curacy in regions about the Inner Sea, and its immense reach from Ireland
> in the north-west corner to vague indications of China and Malaya in the
> east.[42]

Investigation into living matter was less extensive than on physical
bodies but some pioneering advances were made. Aristotle followed
the traditional view that the heart was the seat of the intelligence but
Alomaeon of Croton, in dissecting animals, discovered the optic nerve
and declared the brain to be the center of sensation and intelligence.
Eristratus of Chios came to a similar conclusion after systematically
tracing the course of the nervous system throughout the human body.
He further asserted that in the greater complexity of the convolutions
of the human brain to that of the animal lay the superiority of the
human intellect. Anatomical knowledge was much further along than
physiological (which depends upon chemistry and other sciences not
then developed). Galen's *Anatomical Exercises* in fifteen books cover
the whole range of human anatomy (with certain errors due to the fact
that the dissections were performed on apes).

In discussing these advances of Greek science we must note what
is sometimes overlooked in histories of science, namely, that they are
often connected with technological and economic needs.

Archimedes' work, like other scientific investigations, was based
on the needs of a slave-commercial civilization. He invented compound pulleys, burning mirrors, and hydraulic screws. The mirrors
and pulleys were used in war machines; the screw was used by slaves
to remove water from mines and the holds of ships. He worked out
the formulae for finding the area of a circle (πr^2) and the volume of a
sphere, a cone, and a pyramid. His famous experiments on buoyancy
and density, whether or not connected with King Hiero's crown, had

204 / Humanity and Society

a basis in practical problems (metallurgy, shipbuilding, and so on).

The knowledge of geography advanced as trade advanced; trade advanced in the competitive struggle for profits, slaves, land, and booty. As voyagers spread out from the Mediterranean to Britain (particularly in search of tin), around Africa, across the Indian Ocean, into Malaya and China, the general size and shape of the earth itself became a question of practical importance. So, too, was that of the size of the sun and moon. There was, in fact, particular interest in the moon because of its influence on tides, and, hence, on shipping. (Newton was presented with similar problems.) The more extensive the trade the more extensive the required astronomical knowledge.

Technological demands also arose from the shift from a grain-subsistence to a commercially specialized agriculture (grapes, olives, sheep), and resulted both in a new interest in plant grafting and animal breeding, and such inventions as the sheep shears, screw-press (for olives), and the rotary mill. It resulted also in advances in plant grafting and animal breeding, and so assisted that development of the biological sciences which we have just noted.

One other major factor behind the development of the biological sciences was medicine. The general motivation for medical advancement is, of course, simply the desire of people to preserve life and health. But the degree to which it can be realized in practice depends upon circumstances. Medical practice in Sumer and early Egypt was retarded, as we have seen, by the dead weight of feudal society superstition. Greek physicians, too, had to fight superstitions but in Athens and other commercial city states they were able to fight successfully and develop a medical practice (for the benefit of the upper classes). Charms and incantations were thrown out, and cleanliness, rest, and hygienic principles brought in.

In considering Greek science in general it is perhaps well to emphasize that although it clearly arose from the mercantile nature of the society—there was no scientific advance in Sparta—it was not the result of a simple give-and-take series of operations, but a complex sociocultural process. Archimedes' thinking usually concerns general matters—of mechanics, hydraulics, and so on—rather than specific problems. For this reason it is possible that Archimedes himself thought—as most thinkers do—that his mind was free in these matters to rove at will. But it was, in fact, limited, as limited as when concerned with a specific problem (say, of war machines). He could no more have propounded the differential calculus or the theory of gravity than he could have invented an automobile. The failure of Greek science to develop further than it did is not an intellectual one—Archimedes was certainly as intelligent as Newton—but a social one. A slave-commercial society could not by its very nature—especially the drive for the immense profit yielded by slave labor—advance to high commercialism or toward industrialism. Its science was similarly limited. The fact that Greek scientists made certain advances did not mean that those advances were automatically incorporated into the stream of human knowledge. Many of them, in fact, were rejected and forgotten. Some were rediscovered (by Copernicus for example). Each society rejects or accepts according to its nature and its needs. The history of knowledge is determined by the history of society.

Except for the Roman we know little of other non-Greek science in the Mediterranean area. One would expect that beginnings were made in Syria or Crete, that some science existed among such commercial peoples as the Phoenicians, Etruscans, or Carthaginians, but the main development of science in the area was doubtless the work of the Greeks.

The Romans concentrated on practical matters, producing treatises on engineering (Frontinius), architecture (Vitruvius), agriculture (Varro), and medicine (Celsus), but making relatively few technological advances and fewer contributions to science. The main reason for this difference must simply be that the Roman economy was essentially the same as the Greek, and the Greeks took it about as far as it could go; the Romans simply made it bigger and strengthened its agricultural component.

The commercial states of the Mediterranean area also made considerable contributions to social knowledge, for instance on the conduct of a commercial-banking economic system or on government and law. We know that there were major early advances in the area in the field of cultural technology, for example, the alphabet and coined money. The alphabet was apparently created about 1100 B.C. in a part of Phoenicia where there was a heavy concentration of merchants; the pressure of business demanded a simplified script instead of pictographs. Coined money also came from the eastern Mediterranean, a region not only of trade but of silver.

Considerable though the sum-total of knowledge in the Mediterranean commercial states was, development toward the social sciences was much behind that toward the natural sciences. There was no organized study of economics, sociology, or anthropology as there was of mechanics or biology. But, as we learn from Lucretius, some thinkers believed that civilization had evolved from lower social forms and attempted to give a rational explanation for it. Aristotle and Thucydides were aware of class divisions and conflicts, and made realistic speculations on social dynamics, Thucydides arguing that economic and geographic factors had shaped the early form of Greek society. But there was no grasp of the fact that society was still evolving or responding to the same kinds of forces as had shaped it in the past. Greek and Roman historical writing was largely confined to a description of events, the motive force for which was generally assumed to lie in the actions and ideas of individuals (their "ambition" and "passions").

Religion

We should not be misled by accounts of the ideas of Plato, Aristotle, Pliny, and other philosophers into thinking that the average Greek and Roman citizen shared these ideas. The ideas of most Greeks and Italians about nature were, as with other peoples, those of religion, not philosophy.

When Rome had conquered Greece, the Roman upper classes permitted themselves the luxury of absorbing Greek "culture." Roman senators sent their sons to Greek universities; Roman tourists filled excursion boats to Athens; Roman poets imitated Greek poets. As part of this process they took over the Greek gods and goddesses and identified them with their own. The impression generally conveyed is that the Greek and Roman gods were the same, that Jupiter *was* Zeus and so on. But this was not so. There was a Greek god called Zeus and a Roman god called Jupiter, both having separate histories going back into the earliest days of their respective peoples. And so, too, with the other gods and goddesses: Apollo, sun-god; Artemis (Diana), moon goddess; Demeter (Tellus), earth goddess; Hestia (Vesta), hearth goddess; Ares (Mars), war god; Poseidon (Neptune), sea god.

Before the archaeological discoveries of the present century, it was not realized that these sets of gods were simply parallels, with other names, of those of the Sumerians, Hittites, and so on. First, as we have seen, came the gods of food-gathering societies; then these were changed and agricultural deities added (the Hittite god of agriculture, as we noted, was the son of the weather-god). Other changes came with the various civilizations. The gods became State gods. In Greece, Apollo became the symbol of the aristocratic code of moderation, Hermes became the god of commerce. But, as usual, along with the State religion the old concepts and forms of worship continued.

Every [Roman] family had its tomb, where its dead went to repose, one after another, always together. This tomb was generally near the house, not far from the door. . . . Thus the ancestor remained in the midst of his relatives; invisible, but always present, he continued to make a part of the family, and to be its father.

Every family had its ceremonies, which were peculiar to itself, its particular celebrations, its formulas of prayer, its hymns. The father, sole interpreter and sole priest of his religion, alone had the right to teach it, and could teach it only to his son.[43]

These beliefs and ceremonials we have encountered before, but the most striking parallel is perhaps with China. The Greek and Roman popular religion is very largely ancestor worship, and—as in China also—with the father as the family priest. These parallels between the Greek-Roman and the Chinese (and, as Coulange points out, the Indian also), can, it would seem, best be explained as arising from the great common storehouse of food-gathering societies with their vast migrations. We saw similar beliefs and ceremonials among such surviving food-gathering societies as the Australian.

We sometimes get the impression from Christian historians that the Greeks and Romans were rather unreligious, that shrines and temples were remote and empty, that religious ceremonials were more dramatic than devout. But this is not true. Lucretius informs us—much though he must have hated to admit it—that the temples were packed "on holy days with pious multitudes."[44]

Catullus in his overwhelming grief for his dead brother performs ancient ceremonials with evident devotion:

> Dear brother, I have come these many miles, through
>   strange lands to this Eastern Continent
> to see your grave, a poor sad monument of what you
>   were, O brother.
> And I have come too late; you cannot hear me; alone
>   now I must speak
> to these few ashes that were once your body and expect
>   no answer.
> I shall perform an ancient ritual over your remains, weeping,
> (this plate of lentils for dead men to feast upon, wet
>   with my tears)
> O brother, here's my greeting: here's my hand forever
>   welcoming you
> And I forever saying: good-bye, good-bye.[45]

The plate of lentils clearly had as deep a significance for Catullus as a Christian ceremonial for a Christian.

Philosophy

PLATO

In all civilizations prior to the Athenian of the fifth century B.C. there had existed groups of intellectuals, but never before had this group been so large and so independent (separate from State officials and priests) as in Athens. Such a group of intellectuals, in fact, became from this time on a standard part of many civilized states; and in all, from Athens to New York, it has been marked by similar views and similar conflicts—conservative, liberal, and radical. Plato and Aristotle, coming as they did in the first great commercial state, developed concepts which laid intellectual frameworks for all generally similar states, and, if we know their works, we find constant echoes of them in many later-thinkers. In fact their ideas—particularly those of Aristotle—have been assimilated into a kind of credo: "extreme" views are always wrong; the "wise man" will content himself with "impartial" investigation and avoid conclusions; everything is very complicated and it is unlikely that the truth can be known about anything; reason alone will not lead to truth, for there is always "something else"; one should sympathize with the lower classes and attempt to guide their rulers into "just" rule but avoid stirring them up; one cannot accept the crudities of either popular or ruling class religious beliefs but should believe in "something"; one should not get too enthusiastic about anything; "human nature" cannot be changed; no single explanation can ever be right. As we shall see, these views were challenged in Athens and they have been even more vigorously challenged in later civilized states. But they are still very much with us.

Perhaps the best way to perceive the essence of Plato's philosophical views is to look at his famed alleogry of the Cave. As with Gautama and Confucius, it is well to sample Plato directly.

Consider men as in a subterraneous habitation resembling a cave, with its entrance opening to the light, and answering to the whole extent of the cave. Suppose them to have been in it from their childhood, with chains both on their legs and necks, so as to remain there and only be able to look before them, but by the chain incapable to turn their heads round. Suppose them to have light of a fire, burning far above and behind them, and that between the fire and the chain'd men there is a road above them, along which observe a low wall built. . . .

Observe now, along this wall, men bearing all sorts of utensils, raised above the wall, and human statues, and other animals, in wood and stone, and all sorts of furniture, and, as is likely, some of those who are carrying these are speaking, and others silent.

. . . Do you imagine that such as these see anything of themselves or of one another, but the shadows formed by the fire, falling on the opposite part of the cave?

How can they, said he, if through the whole of life they be under a necessity, at least, of having their heads unmoved?[46]

Although Plato himself discusses this allegory in a limited sense only—in regard to the "good" and the intellectual life—it has been usually recognized as symbolizing his metaphysical views. The cave represents the world, the shadows on the walls of the cave, nature, the men in the cave, humanity; the fire outside the cave (in Platonic language), the One. Hence, the general meaning of the allegory is that the things of the world are unreal, shadow-like things. They have their real existence in an invisible world beyond this world—the One. This shadow-like image people mistakenly take as reality for they know no other; they are chained so that they can only look straight ahead into the far wall of the cave and cannot see the cave's entrance or what is beyond it. What are the chains? To grasp Plato's meaning here we must first see what he means by the One—the fire creating the shadows.

The One Plato envisages as a kind of cosmic mind, a spiritual substance which is eternal, unchanging, creative, the essence of the trinity of the Good, the True, and the Beautiful. The only other substance in existence in addition to the One is matter. Matter is, in all respects, the opposite of the One. It is noneternal, changing, noncreative. As Plato defines it, matter is inferior, hence the perfect "patterns" which exist within the One are reflected in nature in imperfect forms— mere shadows on the walls of the cave.

Plato's metaphysics resolves into two parallel systems—mind and matter—each with two constituents—cosmic and human. Or to put it another way, the universe consists of matter and God (the One), Man consists of mind and body, mind being analogous to God, the body to matter. In essence, then, Plato's system is a rather simple one, and similar to one we have encountered before, namely, Hinduism, the main doctrines of which were in existence at least one and probably several centuries before Plato.

We do not read far in Plato, however, without perceiving that he is not adopting these views for their own sake, but, like the Hindu theologians before him, is leading up to the doctrine of immortality. Unlike the theologians, however, he is not content to leave the doctrine as a matter of revelation or belief but embodies it in a series of "logical" arguments. These arguments he puts into the mouth of Socrates in his (apparently completely fictitious) death scene; and they recur endlessly thereafter in European thought; for example:

> Cebes answered: I agree, Socrates, in the greater part of what you say. But in what concerns the soul [i.e., mind], men are apt to be incredulous; they fear that when she has left the body her place may be nowhere, and that on the very day of death she may perish and come to an end. . . . Surely it requires a great deal of argument and many proofs to show that when the man is dead his soul yet exists, and has any force or intelligence.

True, Cebes, said Socrates; and shall I suggest that we converse a little of the probabilities of these things? . . .

And were we not saying long ago that the soul when using the body as an instrument of perception, . . . were we not saying that the soul too is then dragged by the body into the region of the changeable, and wanders and is confused; the world spins round her, and she is like a drunkard, when she touches change?

Very true.

But when returning into herself she reflects, then she passes into the other world, the region of purity, and eternity, and immortality, and unchangeableness, which are her kindred, and with them she ever lives, when she is by herself and is not let or hindered.[47]

Like most theologians — for Plato is more theologian than philosopher — he argued the essential perfection of the soul (mind) substance and the essential evil of the body; and he added the theory (perhaps directly from Hinduism) of the transmigration of the soul. His metaphysical theory clearly has a moral puritanical base (again, as in Hinduism and other religions). The mind which remains aloof from the evil body with its evil emotions will pass through higher and higher states until it achieves immortal reunion with god (the One); the mind which allows itself to "reel" like a drunkard under the influence of the body will pass into lower and lower forms.

It has long been pointed out by the opponents of Platonism that these arguments are based on a series of untested assumptions, some of which, for instance the basic one of the absolute dichotomy between mind and body, can easily be shown to be wrong, but Plato's appeal still remains. The reason is, it seems to me, that this appeal is the same as that of religion. Scientific demonstrations have little effect on the popularity of religion because religion fulfills a need in societies faced by uncontrollable forces. And Plato's philosophy is really a religion, a religion for intellectuals. He avoids the crudities of popular religions, his logical structures, however weak their premises, are intellectually ingenious, and his language is vivid and poetic.

ARISTOTLE

It may at first appear that Aristotle disagrees only with scattered specific concepts, but, in fact, he attacks the foundations of Plato's philosophy. He begins by accusing Plato of distorting the views of Socrates. Socrates, it is true, spoke of general ideas ("universals") but he believed that such ideas arose out of reality; he arrived at them "inductively," i.e., by reasoning from the particular to the general.

But the Platonists "gave them separate existence," that is to say, they asserted that ideas have a divine origin in the One and are not dependent upon reality.

The Platonists then went further. They not only conjured up the mysterious One, of which reality was but a shadow, they argued that every aspect of reality had its "pattern" or "Form" within the One. But this, Aristotle argues, is not possible because it would result in an impossible complexity of Forms within Forms. Furthermore, there are things made by men which can have had no divine form prior to their being made. Finally, the static One could produce only static reflections. Plato cannot account for development.

Aristotle rejects the concept of an absolute, divinely established "good" (and, by implication, a "true" and a "beautiful" also) on two grounds: what is good varies in accordance with circumstances and no one "pattern" can fit all such variations; such a concept of an absolute Good not only has no practical value but would actually hinder work, research, and the acquisition of knowledge.

One might perhaps gather from these arguments that Aristotle was a materialist; but, although he opposed mysticism, he did not reject a religious viewpoint. Like some later Protestant theologians, he wanted a "sensible" religion, and in his search for it he laid the foundations for deism. "Since there must always be motion without intermission there must necessarily be something eternal, a unity or it may be plurality, that first imparts motion, and this first movement must be unmoved."[48] This "first mover," he continues, must not only be "itself unmoved" but it must also be "exempt from all change."

Here, clearly, we are back again with something akin to Plato's One or God. The difference is, however, that Aristotle admits that he does not know what the attributes of his God are; he does not know whether the primary force of the universe is one or many, a "unity" or a "plurality." In his attack on Anaxagoras he calls it simply "nature." But nature he conceives of as a kind of consciously creative force, "like an intelligent man," a force which "out of what is possible always does the best." And a similar concept is present in his comments on forms. He attacks the Platonic concept of divine Forms, but he still feels that "the Forms exist" and he implies that they are purposeful; he does not state that they are simply a manifestation of material objects and other real entities. Form is primary, and substance, or content, derivative.

Anaxagoras regarded mind as the result of "the possession of hands." But Aristotle will have none of this. It is the nature of man to be intelligent; hence, he has hands (one is reminded of the good Dr. Pangloss). But Aristotle has explained nothing. He has simply appealed to a divine creative force which made a creature called Man whose essence is intelligence. And behind all these concepts is Aristotle's famed teleology: Nature has an "end" or "goal" always in view and shapes things toward it. Such a purposeful "Nature" is, of course, simply another name for God. But it is a dynamic, immanent force and not the static, transcendental One of Plato.

In spite of this teleological outlook, however, there is an element of agnosticism in Aristotle—as his comment on the unknown nature of the First Mover shows—and it is this element which underlies most of his works. He breaks decisively with the Platonic concept of acquired knowledge as subordinate to innate ideas (which is really an argument for divine revelation): if all the basic characteristics and contents of the mind are formed in the One before birth, no important ideas can be acquired after birth—so that scientific investigation and the acquisition of knowledge could give but secondary understanding and could not touch the basic understanding, which is innate and divine. Breaking with this Platonic concept, Aristotle ranged over the various aspects of nature, society, and humanity with a systematic sweep and thoroughness not, so far as we now know, previously attempted. He believed that such knowledge was basic to understanding, and, by implication, rejected revelation and mysticism. The main divisions which he made still remain: physics, the study of inorganic matter; biology, the study of living matter; psychology, the study of mind; politics, the study of political structure and behavior; ethics, the study of individual conduct.

THE GREEK MATERIALISTS

Following the death of Aristotle, his college, the Lyceum, was taken over by his friend and former student, Theophrastus. Just as Aristotle went a step beyond Plato, so Theophrastus went a step beyond Aristotle. He challenged both of Aristotle's sacred cows, the First Mover and the teleological doctrine of ends and goals.

Aristotle had contended that motion required special explanation, on the assumption that matter was a dead, inert substance incapable of creating or sustaining motion. Some outside force must, therefore, be active in the universe. Hence, the First Mover. He ran into difficulties when he came to consider not just the beginning of motion but its continuation. Theophrastus, in considering this theory and its difficulties, raised the obvious question (later raised by the French materialists), is not motion perhaps simply one of the attributes of matter, something inherent in its very nature? Do we need to postulate any special outside force which wound up the universe and sets its "celestial system" in "rotation"? The question is obvious but it is also fundamental; for if motion is an attribute of matter then there is no need for a First Mover or a Creator.

Aristotle's teleology Theophrastus attacks as follows: "With regard to the view that all things are for the sake of an end and nothing is in vain, the assignation of ends is in general not easy, as it is usually stated to be."[49] We have to deal, first, Theophrastus argues, not with abstractions but with "real things," and when we do, it becomes difficult or impossible to state what their "goals" may be. We can speak of goals only so long as we keep the argument in the abstract and assume a Divine Cause assigning general "ends." But this is to impose an abstraction on reality instead of deriving it from reality.

LUCRETIUS

This point of view of Theophrastus is clearly the philosophical counterpart of scientific experimentalism. Its exponents, the Greek and then the Roman materialists, ranged far and wide, speculating on the nature of matter, the problem of creation, the cosmos, the mind, and came to solutions diametrically opposed to those of the reigning religions. Although many of their works have been lost (apparently destroyed by their religious opponents), fortunately one of the most important survived, Lucretius' *De Rerum Natura* (*Of the Nature of Things*). It is in Lucretius and not in Aristotle that we find a basic antithesis to Plato.

The essential philosophy of the *De Rerum Natura* (about 50 B.C.), as Lucretius acknowledges, did not originate with its author. It is an exposition in verse of the materialistic outlook of Democritus, Epicurus, and Empedocles, which was, as we have noted, related to the earlier philosophy of the Jains in India. The *De Rerum Natura*, in short, is the fullest exposition now extant of materialist philosophy prior to the development of modern science. Its anticipations of later views are sometimes extraordinary.

Lucretius begins with Democritus' concept that nothing exists but "atoms and the void." There is no "third substance,"[50] no One, no ghosts, no gods. By "atoms" he means (again with Democritus) the ultimate indivisible particles of matter. By "void" he means not only the space between objects but the space between the atoms. That there is such space between atoms he demonstrates ingeniously: water seeps through rocks, "noises pass through walls."[51]

All the states (solid, liquid, gaseous) of matter are the result of variations in these spaces between atoms. The variations of matter (what modern physics calls the "elements") are the result not of an infinity of different kinds of atoms but of the "compounding" of atoms.

We have no guide but reason, and reason is based on observation. We use reason to learn the truth about all things in our daily living. Reason reveals to us that things happen in accordance with definable, observable rational processes and we live in accordance with this premise. But reason and observation sometimes misled Lucretius, for he did not always grasp the necessity of supporting them by scientific experiment. For instance, he thought the mind was "lodged in the mid-region of the breast,"[52] and argued that the sun "cannot be either much larger or smaller than it appears to our senses."[53]

How had the universe come into being? Was there a creation? Lucretius divided the problem into two parts: the universe as such; the universe as it now is. The universe as such has always existed and was not the product of a cosmic mind: "Nothing can ever be created by divine power out of nothing."[54] It is not only infinite in space but eternal in time. The universe as it now is, however, was created, but it was created by natural causes and from the basic atoms:

> Certainly, the atoms did not post themselves purposefully in due order by an act of intelligence, nor did they stipulate what movements each should perform. But multitudinous atoms, swept along in multitudinous courses through infinite time by mutual clashes and their own weight, have come together in every possible way and realized everything that could be formed by their combinations.[55]

Out of this "fortuitous concourse of atoms" came the earth, the sun, the moon, and the stars.

Life on the earth has arisen from natural causes. Lucretius had, of course, no concept of the chemical link between inorganic and organic matter or of how the latter could arise out of the former (as in the virus). But he assumed that somehow it did arise. The earth was the great mother, giving birth to all life. First came "herbs and shrubs."[56] Then came animal life, in two stages, first birds, then mammals. Lucretius (following Empedocles) comes close to Darwinian natural selection: "In those days, again, *many species must have died out altogether* and failed to reproduce their kind. Every species that you now see drawing the breath of life has been protected and preserved from the beginning of the world either by cunning or by prowess or by speed."[57] "Living creatures," wrote Anaximander some five hundred years before Lucretius, "rose from the moist element as it was evaporated by the sun. Man was like another animal, namely a fish, in the beginning."[58] Lucretius, however, was not really thinking of an evolutionary process but of a series of "births" out of the earth in the past. The earth has now grown old and has "ceased to bear, like a woman worn out with age."

Of the nature of living matter little was known in Lucretius' time.

Some seventeen centuries were to elapse before anyone was to witness the union of an ovum and spermatazoon. Aristotle had declared that the female provided but the raw material, the male supplied the character, an anti-feminist view which has persisted into modern times. Lucretius disagreed: "In the intermingling of seed it may happen that the woman by a sudden effort overmasters the power of the man and takes control of it. Then children are conceived of the maternal seed and take after their mother. Correspondingly children may be conceived of the paternal seed and take after their father."[59] Lucretius, of course, had no knowledge of cells, chromosomes, or genes.

What, finally, of the mind? Here, again, Lucretius is at the opposite pole to Plato. The mind did not exist before birth. If it had "Why do we retain no memory of an earlier existence"? There is no dichotomy between body and mind. Mind interacts with the body through an intermediary, a "vital spirit" (what modern biologists call "nerve impulses") which gives life and movement to the limbs and veins and bones. This "vital spirit," like the body, consists of atoms.

The mind, being part of the body, grows with the body and dies with it. Death is necessary so that life may exist:[60] "The old is always thrust aside to make way for the new, and one thing must be built out of the wreck of another. There is no murky pit of Hell awaiting anyone. There is need of matter, so that later generations may arise. . . . So one thing will never cease to spring from another. To none is life given in freehold; to all on lease."

Sometimes students on first reading Lucretius, with his rational approach and brilliant insights, wonder why if all "this" was known "then," so much nonsense has been written in the meantime. The answer, of course, is that each society has its own needs in regard to ideas as it does for knowledge, and there is no simple upward spiral for either. A feudal society had no more use for the ideas of Lucretius than it had for the experimental method of Theophrastus. And in other societies the same anti-rational forces act, though sometimes in less obvious ways. We have to recognize also that Lucretius' views were intended for a narrow audience—the enlightened members of the Roman upper classes. (Cicero was one of his supporters: and Cicero was philosophically a skeptic.) The masses in Roman Italy could not read. But in later societies as education spread, the needs of rule made Lucretius' ideas seem particularly dangerous and they have been distorted or played down in various ways.

Social Philosophy

That social class plays an important part in the shaping of ideas is generally recognized by modern social scientists. Nor is the concept a new one. It was inherent in Aristotle's comments on politics, and we find it well formulated in the period of the American and French revolutions. Its single most germinal expression, however, was that in *The Communist Manifesto* in 1848: "The ruling ideas of each age have ever been the ideas of its ruling class."

As we saw in Sumer, Egypt, and the Asian feudal states, class-direction was rather obviously one of the major, formative forces for social and other ideas, but our examination indicated also that the process was a complex one. Thus, although "ruling ideas" in these states were generally those of the feudal ruling class, this was not always the case, at least not in a "pure" form. For instance, in Osaka and in some Chinese cities, there was a considerable mixture of ideas from the feudal lords, from the commercial and banking interests, from the professionals and artisans; and sometimes the capitalist views were dominant. There was a similar situation in the Mediterranean slave-commercial states. In Athens, as we saw, the ruling class at first was feudal, then capitalist, and there were bitter conflicts between the two. Yet there was a considerable area of overlap also for the two classes had common as well as conflicting interests.

The situation is further complicated, however, by the fact that, once we advance beyond practical politics and daily affairs into the realm of ideas and art, neither capitalists nor landowners were directly involved. In Athens, as we have noted, the professional class was removed to a much greater degree than in previous societies from direct State (particularly Church) control. Some of its members were more closely connected with the landowners (Socrates and Plato), some with the capitalists (Theophrastus and Aeschylus) but in all we find a blending of ideas. There was no physical barrier between the classes, their members mingled and ideas were interchanged. The professional class became a kind of intellectual crucible in which ideas from the two dominant classes mixed and mixed also to some degree with those from other classes.

It is this complexity of the ideological process which has led many thinkers to doubt the basic importance of class influence upon it. But we find a similar complexity in any actual situation, either in nature or society, if we examine it.

Aristotle and Plato

Aristotle, as we saw, feared a State dominated either by the aristocracy or the capitalists on the one hand or the small businessmen and artisans on the other, and favored one with a strong "middle class." One can hardly doubt that in this he is reflecting the views of his own class, the professional class, which occupied a middle position in society. This "middle path" concept dominates his thinking in other fields also. In his *Ethics,* for instance, he advocates the "mean" in each category. (We saw a similar obsession with the "middle way," "moderation," and so on, in Confucius.)

Although Aristotle disagrees with certain of the actions and ideas of both aristocrats and capitalists, he agrees with them on certain basic questions. He argued that social inequality was an inescapable law and slavery natural: "It is clear then, that some men are by nature free, and other slaves, and that for these latter slavery is both expedient and right."[61] But he is disturbed because this "natural" law is broken when professional men are enslaved after being captured in war.

We might note, finally, that Aristotle came from Stageira; and Stageira was a Greek colony. This fact doubtless enabled him to view Athenian society and thought with critical objectivity (such as we find later in such Irish immigrants to England as Jonathan Swift, Oscar Wilde, and Bernard Shaw).

Plato's *Republic* has for centuries been hailed as representing an "ideal" state; but in recent years it has been demonstrated that this state is far from "ideal." For instance, Plato argues that in founding a state the land must be divided equally between the citizens. This at first sounds like a Utopian communist state. The rub, however, lies in the word "citizen." Plato is not advocating equal land for every family, but only for a class of landowners; Plato's "ideal" state is a slave-serf state. Like Aristotle, he believed that inequality and slavery were "natural"; and his pathological scorn for "the many" guarantees that his "guardians" would exploit and oppress them.

If the "ruling passion" of Aristotle was the middle way, that of Plato was stability. "When each class in the state fulfills the function assigned to it, and minds its own business, this is what makes the state just—this is justice."[62] Plato's dream was to establish a settled order without political strife. When we realize that what was to be unsettled was Athenian commercialism, this becomes, in effect, a plea for a great landowning state with the commercial interests subordinated.

It is hardly surprising, then, to learn that Plato himself came from the landowning aristocracy of Athens. His father traced his lineage back to the ancient kings of Attica; his mother was related to Critias, the leader of the dictatorship of the Thirty Tyrants. Plato himself was the teacher and supporter of Dion, the wealthy would-be dictator of Syracuse, who owned a villa near Athens and was made an honorary citizen of Sparta.

As Aristotle's obsession with the "middle path" dominated his thinking on ethics and other subjects as well as his politics, so, too,

Plato's obsession with stability. His metaphysics, as we saw, was based on the concept of change as an "illusion" and the unchanging One as "reality," which sounds suspiciously like a dream of imposing the same kind of stability on nature as he envisaged for society. It is this obsession with changelessness in all spheres of reality that underlies the usual statement that Plato was concerned with "being" (whereas Aristotle concentrated on "becoming").

While the dominant culture of Greece and Rome was that of the upper classes, it was formed almost entirely by the men of those classes. A male-dominant society produced a male-dominant culture. Of all the famous writers, thinkers, historians, and sculptors of Greece and Rome only one was a woman — Sappho. And Sappho lived neither in Athens nor Rome but on the free commercial island of Lesbos a century before the rise of the Athenian empire.

This male dominance was reflected in social theory. Aristotle assumes that women — like slaves — are "naturally" inferior. Plato's scorn for women is apparent throughout his works, but nowhere so obviously as in the *Symposium*. The only worthy companions for men are other men, the only exalted love is homosexual. Women are part of the "base" emotions which drag the mind down from its pure heights. In the ideal Republic the women of the ruling class of guardians are to be "common" to all the men of the class. This concept, which has been hailed as advanced thinking, would actually result in the break-up of the family and the destruction of love between men and women by substituting brief mating episodes for a husband and wife relationship and turning women into breeders.

Lucretius

In social thought, as in philosophy, the real antithesis to Plato is Lucretius, whose views on the origin and early development of society are in some ways as close to modern social science as his views on nature are to natural science. The first people, according to Lucretius, were hunters and food-gatherers. "They hunted the woodland beasts by hurling stones and wielding ponderous clubs."[63] In this stage there was no agriculture and no marriage: "Venus coupled the bodies of lovers in the greenwood." Then came a second stage: "As time went by, men began to build huts and to use skins and fire. Male and female learnt to live together in a stable union and to watch over their joint progeny." Lucretius does not make it clear that the change from hunting to agriculture was a major step (although he perhaps implies it), and he is again unclear on time sequences, but he places emphasis on the role of fire and always seeks for a rational explanation. The next major step—civilization—however, he is somewhat clearer about, as he anticipates Rousseau's theory of the social effects of property by 1,800 years.[64] In a passage with a particularly modern ring he explains that it is economic searching ("this discontent") that has alike made for human progress and for the horrors of war.

> Skins yesterday, purple and gold to-day—such are the baubles that embitter human life with resentment and waste it with war. . . . So mankind is perpetually the victim of a pointless and futile martyrdom, fretting life away in fruitless worries through failure to realize what limit is set to acquisition and to the growth of genuine pleasure. It is this discontent that has driven life steadily onward, out to the high seas, and has stirred up from the depths the surging tumultuous tides of war.[65]

In spite of war and economic inequalities, he believes that the course of humanity has been upward and that this course has been the result of developing human reason (again anticipating eighteenth century thinkers).

How many of Lucretius' social views came from earlier thinkers whose works may have vanished it is hard to say, but there is nothing in extant earlier works that approaches them, either Greek or Asian. They seem, for instance, to be definitely in advance of the Taoist views, some of which, as we saw, ran along similar lines.

Literature

The art of these Mediterranean commercial states covers some three thousand years (from about 2700 B.C. to about 500 A.D.) and exhibits a great variety of forms, but we can again take literature as representing its essence. The first major works of literature that have survived are no earlier than about 900 B.C. and the last major works do not extend beyond the first century A.D., a span of about one thousand years. We can assume that there were literary works, now lost, produced in Crete, Carthage, Etruscan Italy, and other states. As it is, we are left with the literature of the dominant civilizations, the Greek and the Roman, the Greek falling into the two main phases of Greek-Aegean and Greek (of which Athenian was the center).

THE GREEK-AEGEAN—HOMER

For the Greek-Aegean period there are only two surviving major writers, Homer (about 850 B.C.) and Hesiod (?750 B.C.). The two make a striking contrast. The Homeric epics are sea epics. Hesiod's *Works and Days* is a farmer's poem, prescribing honesty and hard work, and warning the great landowners to treat the peasants justly. His *Theogeny* is an interesting and sometimes powerful but rather naïve account of the gods and creation (lacking Homer's sophisticated humor).

The concept of Homer as a "simple" genius singing for a "primitive" audience and living in "the dawn of literature" has become so firmly embedded in popular accounts that even those who know better sometimes find themselves affected by it. We must remind ourselves that the epic of *Gilgamesh* was composed some two thousand years before Homer, the *Rig-Vedas* about eight hundred years, and that for many thousands of years there must have been oral poems and tales, some of them perhaps of considerable length and high quality. Furthermore, the eastern Mediterranean civilization of which Homer was part had by 850 B.C. some two thousand years of history behind it; Crete — with its great ports and palaces — had risen and fallen; the heyday of the Greek-Aegean was drawing to a close, and power was soon to shift to the Greek mainland.

Homer himself gives us a vivid picture of his society in his description of the port city of Delos: "There, trailing their long cloaks, the Ionians flock with their wives and children to keep thy [Apollo's] memory with boxing matches, dances, and music — a sight so splendid that the onlooker, gazing in rapture at the throng of men, women, ships, and merchandise, might think they were free from old age and death."[66] It was such bustling port cities that produced Sappho, Thales, and Theophrastus. Homer is traditionally most closely associated with Smyrna and Chios, both major commercial centers, and it is the life and outlook of such centers which is reflected in his verse, even though he is presumably depicting an earlier period: "I am chieftain of the seafaring Taphians. As for my arrival in Ithaca, I came with my own ship and crew across the wine-dark sea. We are bound for the foreign port of Temese with a cargo of gleaming iron which we mean to trade for copper."[67] To Homer iron is beautiful — the "gleaming" iron to be exchanged for copper in ships over the "wine-dark" sea. Yet we also find: "some skipper of a merchant crew, who spends his life on a hulking tramp, worrying about his outward freight, or keeping a sharp eye on the cargo when he comes home with the profits he has snatched."[68] To express a general love for the sea, ships, and commercial adventure was acceptable but not admiration for small businessmen or those hired to trade and manufacture. The Homeric ideal — as in similar commercial civilizations (for example, the Elizabethan) was the landed aristocrat with commercial ties who fitted ships for war (the *Iliad*) or exploration (the *Odyssey*).

The main function of the poet, Homer believed, was "to enchant

. . . with tales."[69] He is not attempting—as was Virgil—to support a historical doctrine or—as were Lucretius, Dante, and Milton—to express a philosophy. He is not even attempting—as was Shakespeare —to depict real life. He is telling tales. But behind the tales, for all their romantic adventure, there is a searching vision, a vision of the intermingling stream of life-and-death (as in his picture of Delos quoted above), and a sharp, critical, skeptical intelligence. Let us look, for instance, at the tragic scene of Odysseus and the ghost of his mother:

> As my mother spoke, there came to me out of the confusion in my heart the one desire, to embrace her spirit, dead though she was. Thrice, in my eagerness to clasp her to me, I started forward with my hands outstretched. Thrice, like a shadow or a dream, she slipped through my arms and left me harrowed by an even sharper pain.
>
> "Mother," I cried in my despair, "why do you avoid me when I try to reach you, so that even in Hell we may throw our loving arms around each other's necks and draw cold comfort from our tears? Or is this a mere phantom that grim Persephone has sent to me to accentuate my grief?"
>
> "My child, my child!" came her reply. "What man on earth has more to bear than you? This is no trick played on you by Persephone, Daughter of Zeus. You are only witnessing here the law of our mortal nature, when we come to die. We no longer have sinews keeping the bones and flesh together, but once the life-force has departed from our white bones, all is consumed by the fierce heat of the blazing fire, and the soul slips away like a dream and flutters on the air."[70]

Homer is almost stark in his realism. Death is inevitable and repulsive; he has no word of comfort, no hope of a "paradise to come." Nowhere in Homer is there deep religious feeling. Above the gods is Fate, impersonal and unhearing, controlling alike the destinies of gods and people. This is not at all the attitude of Hesiod (in the *Theogony*), and it can hardly have been the accepted attitude of Homer's society. It is perhaps significant that it was in these eastern Mediterranean port cities that materialistic agnosticism later developed (in Thales and others). Apparently what commercialism, with its endless seeking for goods and markets, did was to stir up the whole sociocultural complex and affect people's thinking and feeling in ways seemingly unconnected with it. Thus while Homer might scorn lowly merchant marine captains, the aristocrats he admired and the wars he wrote about were ultimately products of the same socio-economic churning that produced the ships and the captains.

The usual explanation for Homer (and others) is "genius." But "genius" explains little or nothing. Men with potential equal to Homer were rotting daily in mines, quarries, and galleys. The real question is what combination of circumstances enabled him and a few others to fulfill this potential? It seems likely that the same kind of balanced struggle for power between commercial and landed interests which later stimulated Athenian culture prevailed also in certain port cities in Homer's time. We do know that such a situation existed on the island of Lesbos at the time of Sappho and Alcaeus.

Homer's depiction of the democratic council of the Greek chieftains was doubtless based on similar councils in his own day and these (as in Sumer) may be reflected also in his assembly of the gods (with Jupiter as a kind of chairman of the board).

Although the *Iliad* and the *Odyssey* draw upon the vast reservoirs of communal society folk-tales, they remold this material to their own ends. The leading characters are aristocratic "seafarers." Members of other classes are treated either with hostility or condescension. Eumainos, the only lower-class individual treated sympathetically, turns out to be not a swineherd after all but a prince. All women are treated as inferiors. Of Homer's two leading women characters, Helen is symbolic of the "evils" which her sex brings upon humanity and Penelope is early put in her place by her son: "So go to your quarters now and attend to your own work. . . . Talking must be the men's concern, and mine in particular; for I am master in this house."[71]

Given Homer's times and his position in society, doubtless no other attitudes were possible. But, in absolute terms, they imply a narrowing of human feeling, and Homer's adoption of them provided precedent for later writers. If the upper class hero is in conflict with a lower class person (Odysseus and the beggar) the hero always has to win: he is superior not only in intelligence and "breeding" but also in physique. The "fellow" is always "thrashed." Lower-class characters are comic and simple, their love affairs matters for ridicule, their highest sentiment a childlike devotion to the "master."

This upper-class bias not only shuts Homer off from the mass of the people, it prevents him from giving true pictures of the upper-class characters themselves. The heroes have to be super-human; if they have faults (Achilles' bullheadedness) the faults have to be on a grand scale. There is no deep depiction of character, little real dialogue, few realistic scenes. The exceptions, in which simple naturalness combines with high poetry, show us how great has been our loss; for instance, in the *Iliad,* the parting of Hector and Andromache (Hector, hurrying through Troy to return to the field of battle, meets his wife, Andromache, with their nurse carrying their baby son):

As he spoke, Hector held out his arms for his boy, but the boy shrank back into the nurse's bosom, crying, and scared at the sight of his father;

for he was afraid of the gleaming metal and the horsehair crest, when he saw that dreadful thing nodding from the top of the helmet. Father and mother laughed aloud, and Hector took off the helmet and set it down on the ground shining and flashing. Then he kissed his son and dandled him in his hands.[72]

ATHENIAN DRAMA

The surviving literature of Athens, like its philosophy, was that of its professional writers. The literature of the peasants, slaves, and others has perished (except for traces in folklore). We know from references in written literature that there were numerous work songs, and there were songs and dramatic sketches at religious festivals. Doubtless there were lullabies. Athenian literature consists, in prose, of philosophy and history (Herodotus and Thucydides), and, in poetry, of the drama (Aeschylus, Sophocles, and Euripides in tragedy, Aristophanes and Menander in comedy).

Perhaps the most marked difference between the Athenian drama and the Homeric epics is that the Athenian drama does not accept life but questions it. To Homer, fate rules and humanity cannot hope to find answers. But Aeschylus, Sophocles, and Euripides question the rule of both gods and men. They have little or no faith in the gods but considerable faith in humanity. There is, for instance, nothing in Homer like Sophocles' great hymn to the achievements of Man in *Antigone:*

> Many the forms of life,
> Wondrous and strange to see,
> But nought than man appears
> More wondrous and more strange. . . .
>
> Man, wonderful in skill.
> And by his subtle arts
> He holds in sway the beasts
> That roam the fields, or tread the mountain's height;
> And brings the binding yoke
> Upon the neck of horse with shaggy mane,
> Or bull on mountain crest,
> Untameable in strength.
>
> And speech, and thought as swift as wind,
> And tempered mood for higher life of states,
> These he has learnt. . . .

> Only from Hades still
> He fails to find escape,
> Though skill of art may teach him how to flee
> From depths of fell disease incurable.

Here, indeed, is a new note, not only in Greek literature but, quite possibly, in the literature of the world. There was, it is true, a kind of agnostic realism in Confucius, but the usual attitude in early feudal states was (as with Gautama) that of fatalistic pessimism. Sophocles not only places the main responsibility upon humanity (and not upon the "gods"), but, like Lucretius some 300 years later, rejoices in the progress of the past and looks forward to the future.

The comparatively small port cities of Homeric times had been supplanted by the great, "husky," "brawling" Athens, their merchants and manufacturers by the powerful Athenian capitalists. These men had gone on to unprecedented conquests; the whole eastern Mediterranean was at their mercy; they began to aspire toward the western Mediterranean also. The patriotic confidence, even arrogance, which inspired Pericles (as his famed funeral oration shows) also inspired Sophocles, not in a narrow, jingoistic sense but in a humanitarian one. And along with confidence went that new freedom for the professional class which we have noted.

Another new note struck in the Athenian drama is that of rebellion. There is no rebellion in Homer or in the Indian epics or plays; not that these societies did not have plenty of rebellion in them; but it was not expressed in the dominant literature. Aeschylus, however, is able to glorify the very symbol of revolt against authority in his *Prometheus Bound*.

In Hesiod, Prometheus is a sly fellow who foolishly defies Zeus to bring fire to mankind (apparently the traditional picture). But Aeschylus breaks the tradition and depicts him as the mighty Titan who gave knowledge to mankind and a "new mastery of thought." Prometheus remains defiantly certain of the ultimate end of the despotism of Zeus: "The doom that is ordained he cannot break."

We are here a long way from the devout Hesiod, even from the mocking Homer. To make the king of the gods a symbol of tyranny, specifically an anti-intellectual tyranny, and then to compound the infidelity by championing the rebel — there is nothing like this in earlier literature either in the Mediterranean area or in Asia.

Rebellion in Aristophanes has a different base. In *The Archarnians* he, in effect, pleaded the Spartan case in the war against Athens. And the antiwar satire of *Lysistrata* was dictated by the aristocratic distrust of a war led by the commercial "war hawks." Yet neither *The Archarnians* nor *Lysistrata* could have been produced if it had not been for that freedom of expression which arose ultimately out of that very commercial enterprise which Aristophanes attacked. He may have had aristocratic-inspired motives in attacking the war but in doing so he attacks all war, creates a mood of almost anarchist rebellion and in *Lysistrata* responds to the power of that feminine rebellion which apparently permeated Athenian society, for we find it as a major theme also in Aeschylus, Sophocles, and Euripides.

The powerful figure of Clytemnestra dominates Aeschylus' *Agamemnon.* When attacked by the Chorus for the murder of her husband, she attacks in turn, defiantly justifying her deed because of her husband's sacrifice of their daughter. In *Antigone,* Sophocles skilfully contrasts two types of woman, the timid, retiring Ismene, and her rebellious sister, Antigone. In Euripides we find not only the depiction of women rebels, particularly in his *Medea,* but a sophisticated anticlericalism.

Not only does the Athenian theater represent a new advance in literature, it is almost certainly also the first real drama. Although religious ceremonials and the accompanying play-sketches doubtless went back into farming society and the Athenian drama had roots there, the Athenian is the first fully developed drama of which we have any evidence. The earliest surviving Indian plays (*Shakuntala*) come almost a thousand years later than the Athenian; and the Chinese and Japanese drama (the No plays, for instance) are also later. Aeschylus appears, indeed, to have been the "father" of tragedy, and Aristophanes of comedy.

The Athenian drama reflects economic expansion, political democracy, ever-increasing knowledge. But, as we have seen, there were other aspects also to that society. The expanding economy was based on slave labor and colonial exploitation, the political democracy was limited to male citizens, the increase in knowledge was an upper-class monopoly. The Athenians might be "no man's slaves," but they enslaved others. The stench of slavery was everywhere, and everywhere there was a tight fear of the slaves and of the colonial peoples. And this fear penetrated into the culture. The dominant views on nature were, as we have seen, those of a primitive religion. Science had to fight for its existence. A section of the upper classes was obsessed with Platonic or Orphic mysticism.

These limitations manifested themselves in the drama. The very cycle of plays (the Oedipus cycle) in which Sophocles expressed his faith in humanity is dominated by an atmosphere of almost frenzied superstition. When Oedipus scorns and taunts the holy "seer" Teiresias, his doom is automatically sealed; when Creon, succeeding Oedipus, in his turn scorns Teiresias he, too, is doomed.

> And in the things that touch upon the Gods,
> 'Tis best in word or deed
> To shun unholy pride.

Here, too, we have the beginnings of a literary convention which has persisted into the present — the gods must not be defied.

As in Homer the range of character is narrow. The only seriously portrayed characters are kings, queens, princes, and aristocrats. Furthermore, the dramatists' intention is not to depict real characters but abstractions and symbols. This is made clear by Aristotle in his *Poetics*. "For Tragedy is an imitation, not of men but of an action and of life — of happiness and misery. . . ." Oedipus is not supposed to represent Oedipus (as Shakespeare's Henry V, for instance, represents Henry V), but an abstract royal personage in a certain moral situation. The "action" is not that of life but of abstract "misery" or "happiness." The reason for this must lie in a fear of the serious depiction of real life. We saw a similar shying from reality in Homer and in early Asian literatures. After a time one begins to sense that this was something "not supposed to be done." Literature must approach its subject obliquely. It must have seemed safer from a dominant class point of view to deal with abstract injustices between moral symbols than with real injustices between people or classes.

The taboos included romantic love. And the reason is doubtless in part that suggested by George Thomson in *Aeschylus and Athens:* "To the nobility love was a dangerous thing, because it implied desire, ambition, discontent."[73] We find the same phenomenon later in European feudal society with its endless homilies on the evils done to men and states by love. But there is also inherent in the attitude an element of male domination. The writers were, after all, men; and the convention was to depict women as evil or submissive, foolishly rebellious or ridiculous. One soon begins to sense a powerful repressive social force at work. Women must not be depicted as equal with men and no serious scene was permitted in which they were shown as having power over men, even personal, sexual power, unless it was tied up with evil — as in Homer or the *Agamemnon*.

In comedy somewhat more leeway was permitted (as Aristotle also indicates). Comedy was understood not to be a serious depiction of life, and, hence, required fewer restrictions. But even comedy was not supposed to become too specific, as Aristotle noted: "In Comedy . . .

the poet first constructs the plot along the lines of probability, and then assumes any names he pleases;—unlike the lampooners who write about a particular individual."

Roman Literature—Ovid

In attempting to savor something of the essence of a literature as extensive as the Roman it is necessary to concentrate. Of the great Roman poets—Lucretius, Catullus, Virgil, Ovid, Horace, and Juvenal —we have already discussed Lucretius. From the rest I shall choose Ovid as representative.

Ovid was born of a moderately wealthy landed family in the year following the assassination of Caesar. He was given the best education available, including a "grand tour" to Greece. Trained for the law he became a judge and was favorably looked upon by the Emperor Augustus, so he lived the life of an upper-class Roman in the comparative calm of the Augustan dictatorship. Turning to poetry he became famous for his short tales in verse (*The Metamorphoses*) and his love poems (especially those in *The Loves* and *The Art of Love*). As poets were not deemed fit subject for biography we know little of his personal life beyond the fact that he was married three times and was exiled by Augustus—on the pretext that he wrote "obscene" poems—to Toni (Constantia) on the Black Sea. There he wrote piteous pleas for forgiveness to the emperor and there he died ten years later, at the age of sixty (in 18 A.D.).

Let us consider as a first sample a poem on a day at the races:

> I do not sit here because I'm in love with the
>   thoroughbred horses,
>   Still, I hope that the one you like will get
>   the job done.
> Why have I come? To be talking with you, to be
>   sitting beside you,
>   Letting you know, my dear, what you are doing to me.
> You watch the races, and I watch you—what a wonderful
>   system!
>   Each of us feasting our eyes on the delights
>   that we prize.
>
> . . . .
>
> You on the right, whoever you are, don't jostle the
>   lady,

> That's no way to behave, rubbing against her
>   like that.
> You in the row behind, what has become of your
>   manners?
>
> . . . .

To say that there had never been poetry like this before would not be quite true for we find something of its lively informality in Catullus, but it is certainly a new genre. Poetry has descended from Olympus into the city streets and has become something new in the journey. It is neither "epic," nor "lyric," neither "tragedy" nor "comedy," but a medium for the direct and sophisticated depiction of life. We see the bustling, jostling life of a Roman day, and we see it through the eyes of a worldly upper-class intellectual.

These are the qualities which stand out everywhere in *The Loves* and *The Art of Love*. We are in Rome; and we are in Rome with Ovid. The bare bones of historical fact take on flesh and move as in life. He has great pride in this Rome, and in his words we sense the spirit of imperial arrogance which possessed the Roman rulers:

> Simple and rude, those days, but Rome, in our era,
>   is golden.
> Ruler of conquered tribes, holding the wealth
>   of the world.

But he shrinks from the carnage which has brought this "era" about:

> Look at what she prefers! A nouveau riche, and a
>   killer,
> Come to title and wealth, fat on the slaughter
>   of war. . . .

(A passing reference to the primitive "blue-painted Britons" brings us up sharp against the centuries.) He shows us in realistic details—the eye of the reporter as well as the poet—on what imperial grandeur is based:

> Germany now will be sending the hair of her captive
>   women
> For your adornment and grace, spoil from the
>   conquered tribes.

The same great, coiffeured ladies have castrated slaves chained to their doors: "Doorkeeper—unworthy fate!—bound to the links of hard iron . . . ," and subject to torture: "Wasn't it I, when you stood stripped and ready for flogging,/ Trembling, wasn't it I who spoke to your lady for you?" Even slaves are not without areas of power, however slight. Ovid is hopeful that the doorkeeper will help him to get into his mistress' house; serving-maid slaves can be especially useful: "You've been a good girl, Nippy, for a slave,/ Giving good service in the stealthy night. . . ."

In *The Art of Love* he writes without restraint and often with sophisticated humor:

> Oh what a thing to behold, limper than yesterday's
>   rose!
> Look at me now, erect (too late), abounding in
>   vigor,
>   Equal to any demand, ready to enter the field.
> Why do you act like that, most villainous part of
>   my body?
> . . . .
> Yet even so my girl made every effort to rouse
>   you,
>   Gently urging you on with the caress of her
>   hand.
> When she saw all her arts were wasted, a useless
>   endeavor,
>   Your indifference still sullen, unable to rise,
> "Why do you mock me?" she cried, "Are you crazy? Or
>   didn't you want to?
>   Who gave you orders to bring any such slug to
>   my bed?
> Either Circe has laid the curse of her magic upon
>   you,
>   Or you have come to me tired, worn out by some
>   other girl."
> With that, she leaped from the bed, wrapped her loose
>   garments around her,
>   Rushed, as quick as a wink, barefooted out of
>   the room,
> Yet, lest her serving-girls get the idea that no one
>   had touched her
>   (Such an unthinkable shame!), made a few spots
>   on the sheet.

Why was it that poems like this could be used as an acceptable excuse to exile the poet? The answer is presumably the same as for the lack of romance in Greek and other literatures, antifeminist church taboos. Ovid challenges the taboos and asserts the rights of the author to depict all aspects of love; and in doing so he encompasses a segment of life which had been and still is usually excluded from literature. But in Ovid we also see once more the narrow social scope of the writers of the slave-commercial states in general. "Nippy" he feels to be clever and charming, but he is still aware that she is a slave. He loves and likes women but there is an element of condescension in his attitude. He was, however, within these general limits, one of the most enlightened of the Roman poets. His women are real women, not—like Virgil's Dido—stuffed figures. He has qualms about Roman conquests; Virgil had none. He was disturbed by the suffering of the slaves; others made jokes about them. One feels, as with Byron, that both Ovid's exaltation and suffering are drawn from life. Whatever his defects he is always vigorous, earthy, and real. With him a new force entered literature.

The turning of literature into a more direct medium for the mirroring of life in Roman and in later Greek times represents, it seems to me, the major advance in these centuries (from roughly 200 B.C. to 100 A.D.). There was nothing like it in earlier Greek literature or—to judge by the translations of major works—in Asian literature either until much later. In both the Homeric and the Indian epics (about 850 and 500 B.C. respectively), the convention was to depict idealized and heroic figures and scenes. Greek tragedy looked at life obliquely and abstractly, and the comedy of Aristophanes gave a hilariously exaggerated picture of life. A new movement apparently began in the comedies of Menander (one of which was recently discovered) and was continued into those of Plautus and Terence. All three, it is true, rely on "stock characters" and standard plots, but Plautus and Terence certainly come closer than Aristophanes to *reporting* life, and, furthermore, had an influence on the structure of later European comedy (including Shakespeare) that Aristophanes did not.

We find a new element of realism also in some Roman historians. Caesar's *Commentaries,* for all their apparent objectivity actually strike a strong personal note—how strong may be seen by contrasting them with Thucydides or Herodotus; and the biographical sketches in Suetonius, for instance, are alien to the earlier Greek manner (but are in accord with the later Greek, as in Plutarch's *Lives*). We find a new realism also in fiction, in the satirical sketches of the *Satyricon* of Petronius and in Apuleius's picaresque novel, *The Golden Ass.*

In noting these various works I have been dealing only with the general characteristics of Roman literature, characteristics rooted in Roman society as such, a society which, as we have seen, did not change in its basic structure from its rise in about 300 B.C. until the disintegration of the slave system about 300 A.D., a period of some 600 years. But in a literary history so long as the Roman, there were naturally variations in different periods, for instance, between Lucretius and Virgil. Lucretius lived in the last days of the Republic, a time of bitter struggle, when Cicero, the "new man," was the rising senatorial hope of the "knights" against the entrenched aristocracy. Virgil lived in the Rome of Augustus when the battle had been won and the aristocracy was in power. Lucretius abounds with ideas, radical ideas, ideas—like Cicero's—against "superstition," ideas on the development of society, on nature, on life. Virgil virtually has no ideas. He thinks within the framework of the respectable Roman landowner, choosing for his masterpiece a literary-historical justification of Roman imperialism. His hero, Aeneas, is a model of superstitious "piety" and unthinking patriotism. Not only is the poem bereft of ideas, but even that sense of wonder and adventure that carries the Homeric narratives along at a storm-like pace has faded. We are in a sedate, moonlit world inhabited by gentlemen travellers, a world that makes Homer's look almost garish and his heroes rough-and-tumble. This atmosphere envelops not only content but style. The wild imaginative flights of Homeric imagery are replaced by the restrained and balanced simile, by austere control and measured richness—a reflection, both in content and manner—of the marbled Rome of Augustus.

I X

The Byzantine and Arab

Empires

IF A HISTORICAL OBSERVER had looked at the world in about the year 800 A.D., he would have found that as usual there was no Toynbeean profusion of diverse "civilizations." In fact the picture had been simplified by the elimination of the great historical mutation of slave-commercial states. Feudalism had come back into its own, enveloping state after state, with only minor — but significant — commercial pockets visible. In Africa, Ethiopia continued and Ghana was rising; feudal societies were developing in Europe and in Middle and South America; in Asia, there were several minor and four major civilized societies: the Iranian and the Indian in West Asia, the Chinese and Japanese in East Asia, the latter two with a strongly developing commercial component. In addition to these, our observer would have found two civilized societies on the border of Europe and Asia, the Byzantine, centered in the city of Byzantium and dominating the East Mediterranean, and the Arab, in Arabia, Mesopotamia, and North Africa. Of these two, the Byzantine was declining and the Arab was rising.

THE BYZANTINE EMPIRE

The Roman Empire, as we have seen, grew in good part by the simple expedient of engulfing already existing smaller empires, among them the Greek and the Egyptian. In order to exploit these and other states, the Romans established a secondary political center at the ancient Greek city of Byzantium on the Bosporus. With the collapse of the empire in Europe, Byzantium (renamed Constantinople) graduated from a secondary to a primary center, and then became the capital of a new empire, embracing the Balkan peninsula, Asia Minor, Armenia, Syria, Palestine, Egypt, and Libya.

From most popular accounts one would gather that the economic life of the Byzantine Empire began and ended in "trade." But in order to trade there must be goods to trade. And these goods must come from industry, manufacturing, or farming. Much, probably most, of the wealth of the Empire, it is surprising to discover, in view of this emphasis on trade, came from farming. "A class of aristocrats," writes Steven Runciman,[1] "arose, deriving vast wealth from estates that they continually sought to increase. The free small-holder tended to be bought out and either became a tenant or disappeared." How large these estates became is indicated, Barnes notes, in the fact that one noble "had no less than 60 domains, with 600 oxen, 100 plough teams, 880 horses, 18,000 sheep."[2] The estates were worked, not, as in Italy, by slave labor but by peasant labor.

The manufacturing produce of Byzantium is summarized in *The Cambridge Economic History* as follows:

> To medieval, if not to modern eyes Constantinople had the air of an industrial city. Travellers were struck by the amount of industry carried on there, not only the building or the pottery or the furniture business, or other such necessary parts of a great city's life, but especially the manufacture of luxuries. Of these the silk industry was the most remarkable. . . . In Constantinople the silk was dressed, woven and dyed, and put on the market as finished cloth. Linen was also made up at Constantinople, though in this case it seems to have arrived from Macedonia or Pontus or the other flax fields, already woven, and only received the superior dyeing and finish at the capital that distinguished it from the provincial product. . . . Cotton goods were also finished in Constantinople but apparently in much smaller quantities. The Byzantines of the capital never troubled much about fine woollen goods. Wool provided the lower classes with their garments, but the rich Byzantine preferred other materials. Consequently, though large amounts of woollen cloth must have been made to clothe the numerous poor, such cloth remained rough. Probably each family made up its own woollen wear.
>
> After the silk industry the metal industry was most renowned. This was an even more luxurious industry. Gold and silver plate were made in considerable but restricted quantities. More elaborate work . . . was in great demand; but the supply was limited owing to the expense of the materials

and the highly technical workmanship required. But the cash turnover of the industry must have been enormous. The third great industry of Constantinople was the manufacture of armaments.[3]

There was no manufacturing on this concentrated scale in Europe during these centuries (about 400 to about 800 A.D.) and probably nothing in Asia either, although there was, as we have seen, considerable total manufacturing, particularly in India and China. As usual with feudal trade, however, it consisted mainly of luxury items (silks and jewels and so on) sold by one upper class to another and these classes, although wealthy, were small in numbers. As also usual in feudal economies, the basic industrial and manufacturing labor was slave labor: "the widow Danelis, who manufactured cloth and carpets in the Peloponnese in the late ninth century employed over 3,000 slaves." And, again, industry and trade were State owned or regulated, the mines were owned by the State, and armaments were "a state monopoly." What trade the State did not actually run, it controlled by a system of duties and taxes. The rate at which money could be loaned was set by the State, the maximum of profit was set by the State, and so, too, were wages. All imports (including slaves) were subject to a 10 percent duty. In addition to customs duties there were harbor dues, market dues, tolls, and receipt stamps.

The Emperor was commander-in-chief of the army and head of the church. The realms were divided into four provinces, each with its appointed provincial governor and his bureaucracy. The Emperor could "appoint and dismiss all ministers at his will; he had complete financial control; legislation was in his hands alone."[4] He did not, however, have absolute power. He was not a hereditary monarch but an elected monarch. He was elected by three bodies: the senate, the army, and the people of Constantinople. The senate and the army were run by the great landowners. The "people" were apparently the merchants, manufacturers, and professionals in Byzantium.

What we have in Byzantine civilization is a feudal society with an unusual development of manufacturing and trade resulting from its position in the eastern Mediterranean–Black Sea area. This manufacturing and trade was either owned or controlled by the great landowners as the dominant elements in the State. The merchants and manufacturers were not, as in Athens, a ruling class, or even, as in Rome or Japan, a serious rival to the landowners, but subordinate, as in India. Their political strength, in fact, appeared to be declining. We hear that in the fifth century they became "extremely powerful"[5] and in the sixth even "threatened the State." But by 800 they seem to have been no threat at all. So long as this situation continued, the

Byzantine state, for all its wealth, was a virtually stagnant society. Whether it would have been able to develop into a commercial-manufacturing state by throwing off the stranglehold of the great landowners we do not know because, like the Athenian empire, it was overthrown by an outside force before it had run its course.

These social characteristics were reflected in the famed "Byzantine culture." The domination of the landowners, as ever, prevented any serious development of knowledge or thought. Byzantium had neither great scientists nor philosophers. Both thought and art were circumscribed by the church, preventing any serious development of literature and limiting the other arts to formalistic expression. Architecture, mosaic work, painting, sculpture, were typically feudal, placing the emphasis upon static detail, pattern, and color.

THE ARAB EMPIRE

The Arab conquests began in the seventh century and by the eighth had spread to embrace a vast territory, including Spain, North Africa, Syria, Armenia, Mesopotamia, Iran, and northern India. Most European or world histories give the impression that these conquests resulted from a kind of religious madness: a "horde" of dark-skinned anti-Christian "nomads" ("Moslems," "Moors," "Saracens," "Mohammedans") suddenly and unaccountably swarmed out of their desert fastnesses bent on the destruction of "Christendom." ("While Christendom thus with difficulty and incomplete success staved off the Moslem, another wave of nomad migration threatened on the north."[6]) Fortunately "Christendom" had its champion, Charles Martel ("The Hammer"), and "our way of life" was saved.

Arabia

In trying to untangle some of the facts in this historical melodrama, let us begin with Arabia, for, as somehow seems to be forgotten in the telling, the Arabs came from Arabia. There were but few Arabs originally in Damascus or Bagdad, which are often cited as the centers of the "Arab" domains. Two impressions seem to prevail about Arabia, that it began with Mohammed and that it was inhabited by "nomads." Arabia, however, has a long history of civilized society, much longer, in fact, than that of Europe, and it owed its basic nature not to the camel but to the ship. Arabia, as a glance at the map informs us, is a kind of extension of Mesopotamia and so it need have occasioned no surprise when it was discovered that it was a link in the sea trade between Sumer and the Indus valley civilization (as early as 2300 B.C.). The Sumerians got copper from Arabia. The Babylonians, successors to the Sumerians, were fighting Arabian kingdoms by 2000 B.C. The Kingdom of Saba (Sheba), from whence came the Queen to visit Solomon in about 950 B.C., was an Arabian kingdom. The Sabeans were not a desert people but a sea-trading people, "the Phoenicians of the southern sea," writes Philip K. Hitti in his *History of the Arabs*. In about 700 B.C. they conquered Ethiopia. Later they had trading agreements with the Romans and exercised controls over the African east coast cities. They mined copper and gold (Diodorus asserted that Arabian gold ore was so pure that no refining was necessary), raised wheat and grapes, produced innumerable spices, and were famed for their cloth manufacture:[7] "purple cloths, both fine and coarse," runs an early account, "clothing in the Arabian style with sleeves; plain, ordinary, embroidered, or interwoven with gold." In a later period this predominantly commercial aspect of the civilization continued. More extensive trade routes were opened up—with India and even with China.

The center of the early Arabian states was not the desert but the city, not the tent but the palace. Strabo (about 10 B.C.) speaks of south Arabian cities "adorned with beautiful temples and palaces." And in these cities the indication is that the merchants ruled. In the early days of the Arab empire, "the state left industry and commerce free, and aided it with a relatively stable currency."[8] "Hundreds of merchants had homes costing 10,000 to 30,000 dinars ($142,500) [in U.S. currency of the 1940's]." And these can hardly have been sudden developments.

Arabia, then, prior to Mohammed and the conquest which made the empire, consisted essentially of a series of city states run by the merchants and manufacturers. We might note also that the position of women was relatively high and that there was a considerable native culture, two aspects which we find combined in the persons of "the beautiful Suqainah" who "presided over a salon of poets, jurists and statesmen" at Medina[9]—a very different picture from that of the later harem society—and of Asma the poet, also of Medina, who was killed at the instigation of Mohammed for attacking him in her poetry.

How can we account for this predominantly commercial nature of Arabian civilization? The answer is supplied by consulting a relief map. Arabia is almost entirely wasteland, desert, steppe, or mountain. Only along the coasts are there narrow strips of fertile ground, one down the west coast (the Red Sea) culminating in a fairly large fertile section (Yemen), the other, much smaller, along the Gulf of Oman. A large and protected seacoast provided access to the Indian Ocean.

Furthermore, Arabia was relatively immune to conquest because of its terrain and geographical situation. An attempted conquest by the Romans ended in disaster.

The situation in Arabia, then, was rather similar to that which later developed in Japan. Nor was it unlike that of some sections of the Mediterranean, except for the fact that the Arabs had not the rich markets at hand which the Mediterranean provided, and their mercantile states were smaller and weaker. Nevertheless, they did develop mercantile states, and they were not, like the Mediterranean states, conquered by Rome. If it had not been for these two facts there would have been no Arab empire.

In moving out from Arabia itself to consider the vaster phenomenon of the empire, it is helpful at first simply to omit the Arab religion and the terms "Mohammedan" or "Muslim" in order to perceive the social dynamics involved.

At the beginning of the sixth century, the west coast trading town of Mecca was ruled by a group centered around a particularly rich merchant called Hashim. Hashim was succeeded by Abd al-Muttalib; Abd al-Muttalib's son, Abdullah, was the father of Mohammed. Abdullah died while on a trading expedition, and Mohammed was adopted by a rich uncle, also a merchant, who is said to have taken him on business trips. At the age of twenty-five, Mohammed married Khadijah, a wealthy merchant's widow of forty who ran her own business and for whom he worked.

The main sociopolitical events of Mohammed's life are easily summarized. He was born in Mecca (in 559 A.D.), and although he acquired a political following he was unable to win over the city authorities to his views. In 622 he was invited to Medina to settle. He soon became the political and military leader of Medina and was planning the military conquest of the other Arabian city states to form one united Arabian mercantile state. For this purpose, he formed an alliance with the Jewish merchants:[10] "The Jews who attach themselves to our commonwealth shall be protected from all insults and vexations; they shall have an equal right with our own people to our assistance and good offices; they . . . shall form with the Moslems one composite nation; they shall practice their religion as freely as the Moslems."

In 623 and 625 his still small army was defeated by forces from Mecca; in 625, he broke his agreement with the Jews, and augmented his war-chest by seizing the property of 700 Jewish merchants. Another battle in 626 ended in a draw, after which Mohammed led 3,000 men against another group of Jews who had supported his enemies, and executed 700 of them, sending the women and children into slavery. In 630, he marched with an army of 10,000 to Mecca and took the town by force, thus laying the foundations for a united Arabia. Such a state was clearly in the Arabian merchants' interests. The conflict was simply over which group was to dominate. Two years after capturing Mecca Mohammed died.

What part did religion play in these events? The religion existing before Mohammed is described by Hitti[11] as follows:

> [It] was in its essence a planetary astral system in which the cult of the moon-god prevailed. The moon, Sin, known to the Minaeans under the name Wadd (love or lover, father), to the Sabaeans as Ilmuqah (the health-giving god?) and to the Qatabanians as 'Amm (paternal uncle), stood at the head of the pantheon. He was conceived of as a musculine deity and took precedence over the sun, Shams, who was his consort. 'Athar (Venus, corresponding to the Babylonian goddess Ishtar, Phoenician 'Ashtart), their son, was the third member of the triad.

Some of the main tenets of the theology devised by Mohammed we have seen already. They were largely compounded from Judaism and Christianity, and, at least indirectly, from Zoroastrianism. They proclaimed one god (Allah) in the place of many, and emphasized immortality (with its trimmings of Heaven and Hell, the resurrection and the last judgment). The picture is familiar. A religion with roots in early farming society was supplanted by a State religion, as earlier among the Hittites, the Persians (Zoroastrianism), the Jews (Judaism), the Indians (Buddhism and Hinduism), the Chinese (Confucianism, Taoism, and Buddhism); the local tribal deities were incorporated into the State pantheon, one god declared supreme and the doctrine of immortality elevated to dominance. As we have seen, there were various social forces, feudal and commercial, which produced these results. Among the Arabians, the chief of these were clearly mercantile, for when we look at the results and forget the theological arguments, what Mohammed and his followers did was to unite Arabia under merchant-class rule. Arabia ceased to be a series of scattered city states with farming or food-gathering communistic communities in the hinterlands — "who inhabit the desert and know neither high nor low official"[12] (quoting Sargon II of Assyria) — and became a single national state. This was the first step.

The Empire

The second step was empire. Once united, Arabian merchants began to look hungrily across their borders at the lands of the "fertile crescent," their motives the same as those which caused the wars of the Greeks, Romans, Chinese, Indians, Huns, and so on, namely, a desire for wealth, land, slaves, booty, tribute, and profits. That such was indeed the main drive behind the conquest has been documented by Hitti and other scholars, but old ideas die hard, and the concept of the sweep of "Mohammedanism" still dominates the popular accounts. Actually, the religious element was, as with the later "Crusades," a secondary and derivative factor.

Once the war moved out of Arabia, a new social element entered the picture. It seems hardly to be recognized at all that the initial campaigns of the conquest, far from being retrogressive horrors threatening "civilization," were, in fact, wars of territorial liberation. The first country attacked was Syria. Syria was an "easy conquest,"[13] for, in the words of a group of native sub-rulers to the Arabs, "We like your rule and justice far better than the state of oppression and tyranny under which we have been living." What was the "oppression?" It was that of Byzantium. Syria was part of the Byzantine Empire and had been part of the Roman Empire before it. The same was true also of Egypt. When the Arabs won the Egyptians welcomed them. This liberationist aspect of the conquest is shown in other characteristics also. The Arabs were comparatively poor, and their soldiers were closer to the peasants than those of the wealthy Byzantines. They had no expensive engineering devices for breaking into walled cities. They advocated the freeing of slaves. The Byzantine ruler of Alexandria was shocked to find that the Arab delegation sent to negotiate the peace treaty was headed by a Negro.

This liberationist aspect, furthermore, enabled the conquest to gather power from new energy sources picked up on the way. The base for the movement shifted north from Arabia to Mesopotamia as the Arabs were joined by the native forces of the states that they liberated. Mecca was supplanted as the generative center, first by Damascus and then by Bagdad. The movement was actually a union of various related peoples in which the Arabs formed an initiating dynamic core. Arabia alone of these states unconquered by Rome or Byzantium set the whole charged social mass into motion. That it would have happened sooner or later is true; Byzantium could not have held on long as a feudal-dominated state; new economic and political centers were growing up just as they had within the Roman Empire in the west. But the fact that the movement did originate in Arabia has placed a special cultural stamp upon that section of Asia and north Africa today known as "the Arab World."

Powerful though the liberationist element was in the beginning, it did not last long. Arabia had been an essentially commercial society. But the Arab Empire was mainly feudal, for the territory taken over consisted mostly of landholding states ruled by feudal lords with whom the Arabs made deals. Arabia itself also apparently began to change under the total impact. We soon hear of great estates near Mecca with 10,000 slaves. And the rulers of the empire in Bagdad and Damascus lived in the luxurious palaces of which we read in *The Arabian Nights,* whereas the lot of the great majority of its inhabitants was poverty, misery, and oppression. The empire was shaken by peasant revolts and wars.

The most famous of these "servile wars" of the East was organized by Ali, an Arab who claimed descent from the Prophet's son-in-law. Near Basra [in Iraq] many Negro slaves were employed in digging saltpeter. Ali represented to them how badly they were treated, urged them to follow him in revolt and promised them freedom, wealth—and slaves. They agreed, seized food and supplies, defeated the troops sent against them, and built themselves independent villages with palaces for their leaders, prisons for their captives, and mosques for their prayers (869). . . . Ali led his men against other towns, took many of them, and captured control of southern Iran and Iraq to the gates of Bagdad. Commerce halted, and the capital began to starve. In 871 the Negro general Mohallabi, with a large army of rebels, seized Basra. . . . For ten years the rebellion continued; great armies were sent to suppress it; amnesty and rewards were offered to deserters; many of his men left Ali and joined the government's forces. . . . Finally, a government army under the vizier Mowaffaq made its way into the rebel city, overcame resistance, killed Ali, and brought his head to the victor. Mowaffaq and his officers knelt and thanked Allah for His mercies (883). The rebellion had lasted fourteen years, and had threatened the whole economic and political structure of Eastern Islam.[14]

In spite of the overall domination of the landowners, the influence of the merchants and manufacturers still remained sufficiently strong in places to give the empire more of a commercial cast than that of India or Iran during the same centuries. The following succinct account by Will Durant gives the commercial picture:[15]

Gold, silver, iron, lead, mercury, antimony, sulphur, asbestos, marble, and precious stones were mined or quarried from the earth. Divers fished for pearls in the Persian Gulf. . . . Cities and towns swelled and hummed with transport, barter, and sale; peddlers cried their wares to latticed windows; shops dangled their stock and resounded with haggling; fairs, markets, and bazaars gathered merchandise, merchants, buyers, and poets; caravans bound China and India to Persia, Syria, and Egypt; and ports like Bagdad, Basra, Aden, Cairo, and Alexandria sent Arab merchantmen out to sea. Moslem commerce dominated the Mediterranean till the Crusades.

The Culture

This unusual commercial activity resulted for a time in some development in science, particularly in astronomy and pre-chemistry (alchemy), the former because of the added needs of a wider navigation, the latter because of advances in textiles, pottery, dyeing, and other industries. There were developments also in mathematics — required for astronomy — and in medicine. There has been, however, as we have previously noted, a tendency to overestimate the "Arab" contribution in these fields of science and technology because of ignorance of the Greek, Persian, and Indian roots of much of this knowledge. Because the Arabs and the peoples associated with them introduced these mathematical and scientific discoveries into European culture, it was assumed that they had themselves discovered them. But "Arabic" numerals originated in India, much of Arab medicine in Greece, much of Arab science in India. We have to recognize also that Arab science was fragmented, that the scientific method was nowhere the only method and seldom the dominant method. In time it reached a dead-end, cut off as in Asia by the domination of the great landowners and their church.

Although the dominant ideas on nature and humanity were those of this church, there was an advance in thinking, as well as in science, over the Byzantine Empire. For one thing, the Arab Empire was larger, less subject to central landowner control and spotted with commercial centers of a certain degree of independence, in some of which we find an almost liberal cultural atmosphere. Some of the Arab theologians displayed a Voltairian wit, very different from the prevailing stuffiness of their European "medieval" counterparts:

> So great is the multitude of Christians that God alone can number them, and they can boast of sagacious princes and illustrious philosophers. Nevertheless they believe that one is three and three are one; that one of the three is the Father, the other the Son, and the third the Spirit; that the Father is the Son and is not the Son; that a man is God and not God; that the Messiah has existed from all eternity, and yet was created.[16]

Art, too, made advances over the Byzantine, not so much in the graphic and plastic arts as in literature, for instance, in the verses of Omar Khayyam (himself a mathematician) and the tales of the *Arabian Nights*. Omar's poetry reminds us also that in art as well as in science what is often called "Arab" is not Arab; Omar was a Persian. And the *"Arabian" Nights* had many roots, some of them Indian. Nevertheless, both works were products of the Arab Empire.

MARTEL'S HAMMER

Before moving on to Europe in these centuries, let us pause on a speculative question. Say Charles Martel (and others) had failed and Europe had become part of the Arab Empire? Would this have been the universal disaster which it is assumed by European and American historians it would have been? There seems no reason to suppose that it would or even that the subsequent course of sociocultural evolution would have been materially changed. Far from retarding the development (essentially mercantile) which made modern Europe what it is, it seems probable that the Arabs would have speeded it up, and that the European pattern which we are about to trace would have taken place much as it did but under mixed Arab and European auspices. The Arabs certainly do not seem to have retarded commercial development in Spain, which by the sixteenth century was one of the leading commercial nations in Europe. And the fact that Spain did not continue in this direction was not the result of Arab influences but of the power of native Spanish feudalism. The European church would, it is true, have been Mohammedan rather than Christian, but the two theologies, as we have seen, are similar and one could expect that a Mohammedan Church in Europe would have been molded by commercialism just as was the Christian (with the Mohammedan equivalents of Luther and Calvin). The content of the culture would have differed somewhat but the cultural level would have been about the same. So large a conquest would doubtless have caused a social dislocation extensive enough so that most of the present inhabitants of Europe and America would not be alive; but there would be others in our places. From the viewpoint of historical evolution, it matters little whether Charles Martel's hammer hit or missed.

X

European Commercial–Feudal

Civilization

I: SOCIETY

IN THE THREE CENTURIES BETWEEN 1600 AND 1900, history proceeded at an unusually uneven pace. European civilized society not only advanced beyond the Asiatic and African but exploited a large part of the world including most of Asia and Africa. European and not Asiatic states conquered the American continent and established there their own form of society, part of which, the United States, itself turned to exploitation—from the West Indies to the Philippines. This disparity has led Europeans and North Americans to think of their ascendency as a kind of natural dispensation which will never cease, but how temporary it actually is is indicated by the rise of capitalist Japan and Communist China and other events in Asia and elsewhere.

Nevertheless, the fact remains that Europe has in recent centuries acted as a catalyst to much of the world, a catalyst of blood and fire it is true, but a catalyst nevertheless. The examination of this European civilized society is, for this and other reasons, a matter of particular historical importance. This society, the unusual nature of which was first clearly demonstrated by such phenomena as the British conquest of India and the rise of a commercial civilization in North America, has roots that go back for a thousand or more years. As we examine these roots and their growth it becomes apparent that up to the threshold of the present the society has passed through three stages:

feudal, commercial-feudal, commercial-capitalist. Commercial elements began to emerge about 1200 and about 1600 rose to dominance. There were, of course, no absolute lines of demarcation, but the transitions, nevertheless, took place. To take England as an example, we can say that the England of King John (1200), with its baronial wars, was feudal, the England of Chaucer (1400), with its great, flourishing port of London was commercial-feudal, and the England of Cromwell and Milton (1650) was in its essence commercial-capitalist.

European Farming Societies

The history textbook view of European beginnings runs somewhat as follows: civilization began in Sumer and Egypt; but this was an inferior, an "Oriental" civilization; it was "transmitted" *via* Crete to Europe, where it was turned into a higher civilization by the "Western genius" of the Greeks and the Romans. The fact is, however, as we are beginning to learn, that Europe is a basic area of social development, like West Asia or East Asia, in which various feudal societies— Greek, Roman, Frank, German, British, Russian—grew at various times out of farming society. The fact that two of these turned into slave-commercial states and remained so for some centuries does not change the basic picture. As these various societies developed there were influences back and forth and between Europe, Asia, and Africa, but we must, as always, distinguish between different kinds of influence at different stages of development and consider the whole in terms of general sociological process.

Food-gathering societies, as we have seen, were well established 15,000 and more years ago with river trade routes and a developing culture on all continents—including Europe. During the long food-gathering millennia, the indication is that of mutual influence between Europe and West Asia but of certain native developments in each area (as in East Asia also). When we come to farming society times, however, the indication from radiocarbon dating is that the earliest European farming communities were later than the earliest West Asian ones. The earliest farming community so far discovered in Europe is of about 7000 B.C. and is located in Yugoslavia. The next site—in Greece —is of about 5700 B.C. Generally speaking (as may be seen in an interesting map in Grahame Clark's *World Prehistory*[1]) as the sites move further away from the southeast area into central and western Europe the dates become more recent (roughly from 5000 to 3000 B.C.). As some European crops, animals, tools, and pots seem to be Asian in origin the indication is that early European farming society was influenced by the West Asian. It could, nevertheless, have begun independently. Certainly once it began it developed mainly in its own style and reached sufficiently high levels to lead to the independent formation of city states and other civilized societies. We have to note also that while it is true that the earliest European farming communities are not so old as the earliest West Asian ones they are still very early — two thousand years earlier, for instance, than the earliest Egyptian ones so far discovered.

THE DANUBE VALLEY

One early European farming society originated and developed, as we might expect, in the valley of the Danube, and it is informative to note its development as given by V. Gordon Childe in his pioneering little book *Social Evolution*. In what he calls Period I, wheat and barley were grown and there were cattle and sheep. Neither the plow nor crop rotation nor fertilization were known. The population lived in settlements of some 13 houses each. The archaeological evidence indicates that the social organization, as usual in such economies (in Iran, for instance), was communal. "No building stands out as a chieftain's residence, nor do grave furnitures point to difference in rank." Some of the houses seem to have been common dwellings for more than one family. There are no temples (and presumably no priests, as there were not among the Huns or the early Germans).

By Period II both the human and the animal population have increased considerably and plow cultivation seems to have begun. Specialization of labor is indicated by the discovery of "axe-factories where rocks of superior quality cropped out"; copper smelting may have begun also. Trade has increased markedly (mainly along the rivers); one group — known as the "Beaker-folk" — seems to have lived on trading. There are still no temples or chieftain's residences.

By Period VI we see that the society is moving toward civilization. Plow agriculture has become standard; fallowing has been introduced; wheeled carts and war chariots are being built; there are "salt mines and copper mines with roasters and smelters"; granaries and stables on individual farms show the development of "private property in livestock and in the produce of fields"; the coexistence of a settlement of "thirty-eight small huts" and "a group of nine large farmhouses" plus "a few somewhat richer graves" shows that inequalities in property had arisen.

Into this story as told by the archaeological evidence we have to try to fit that told by linguistics and anthropology. Who were the early farming peoples of Europe? What languages did they speak? How long had they been in Europe? Were they the descendants of the people who, fifteen thousand and more years before them, had made the cave drawings in France and Spain? Was there a continuity of European peoples going far back into hunting society?

THE INDO-EUROPEANS

A special problem is presented by the early peoples who spoke Indo-European languages (the ancestral languages of German, English, French, Greek, Italian, Russian, Celtic, Hittite, Persian, Bengali, Urdu, etc.). The parent language of all these languages is presumed to have been spoken by a people living in the general area between the Danube and the Caspian Sea. As some or all of these languages had split off by at least 2000 B.C., the original language (and people) must have been in existence several thousand years before this time. There is indication of a considerable movement among these Indo-European peoples about 2000 B.C.: the Hittites into Anatolia, the Greeks into the Greek peninsula, the Indian peoples into northern India, storming the cities of the Indus valley, the Iranians into Iran, and apparently in the same centuries Celts, Slavs, and Germans penetrated western and northern Europe.

What caused these migrations? The key is presumably to be found in the fact that these peoples were farmers. The transition to farming was everywhere accompanied by a great increase in population; as this farming was normally of a "slash and burn" type, fields were early exhausted, and new pastures were always in demand for increasing herds. The archaeological evidence suggests for early farming society in Europe a similar evolutionary process to that in West Asia, namely, a slow, difficult accumulation of methods and tools, stage by stage, from hoe to plow, from stone to copper, from "slash and burn" to crop rotation, from communal property to private property, from equality to inequality. There was clearly no simple or wholesale importation of farming techniques from outside even though certain early impulses (7000–5000 B.C.) apparently came from West Asia, and perhaps later ones also, for the linguistic and anthropological evidence indicates considerable migration and conquest. What apparently happened is that the Indo-European speaking peoples—and perhaps others before them—came in conquering waves to subjugate already established farming communities. Although, then, some present-day European peoples may be to one or another degree descendents of European food-gathering society peoples of 15,000 or more years ago or of the earliest farming society peoples of 8,000 to 5,000 years ago, they appear in the main to be the descendants of the Indo-European peoples who invaded the area between 2000 and 1500 B.C. The indication is also that all these peoples, perhaps from food-gathering times on, were Caucasoid.

THE GERMANS

The nature of the early European farming societies (to try to fill in the archaeological bare bones still further) was doubtless about the same as that of the Germans when Caesar observed them. A somewhat later form was observed by Tacitus:[2]

> Slaves in general are not allotted, as we allot them, to special duties in the establishment. Each has control of his own house and home. The master imposes a fixed charge of grain, cattle or clothing, as he would on a tenant. . . . Freedmen rank little higher than slaves; they have seldom any serious influence in the household, never in the State, excepting only in nations under the rule of kings. There they mount high above free men and nobles. With the rest the inferiority of freedmen is the hallmark of liberty.

The rulers of the society hold power not so much because of economic superiority—they have no feudal private armies—as for their social capacities, and have limited power:

> They choose their kings for their noble birth, their leaders for their valour. The power even of the kings is not absolute or arbitrary. As for the leaders, it is their example rather than their authority that wins them special admiration. . . . Capital punishment, imprisonment and even flogging are allowed to none but the priests.[3]

The elements of tribal democracy still remain: "On matters of minor importance only the chiefs debate, on major affairs the whole community."[4]

The society described by Tacitus is a typical latter stage farming society in which some feudal elements are beginning to appear, one rather similar to those of the Canary Islands or New Zealand. It was, furthermore, the kind of society which the ancestors of the Romans had lived in not too many centuries before. It was also the type of society which must have existed throughout most of Europe and provided the roots from which feudal society grew.

European Feudalism

Although most historians seem to regard European feudal society as a unique phenomenon, it is basically the same as feudalism everywhere, from Egypt to India to China, and its specific form—that of private property feudalism—had long existed in China and was arising in Japan in the same centuries as it was arising in northern Europe. Nor did European feudalism begin in the "Dark Ages" or "Middle Ages." There was feudalism in Sparta and Macedon, and in both Attica and Italy before and after slave-commercial society. Furthermore, most of the states within the Roman Empire were feudal and this feudalism continued on into the Byzantine and Arab empires.

In the light of these facts it is clear that the apparently endless disputes on the origin and nature of "medieval" European feudalism are of but limited value unless they consider other feudal societies also. Yet in no discussion of European feudalism in the standard texts I have consulted have I found any indication that this has been done, nor any realization that the problem of "origins" might be part of the larger problem of feudal society in general. What the basic generative forces were which pulled feudal out of farming society we have already discussed (the growth of State land, inequalities in property, and so on). This does not, of course, relieve us of the necessity of examining the specific factors which lay behind any particular feudal system, but it does serve to place the problem in its proper perspective.

In the reign of William the Conqueror all the land in England was nominally owned by the king but actually it was owned (as in China or Japan) by a group of large landowners, including the Church. *The Cambridge Medieval History*,[5] in noting the profits from landownership (i.e., from peasant labor), gives a succinct picture of the situation:

The king and the king's family	£17,650
The king's sergeants	£ 1,800
	£19,450
Ecclesiastical tenants-in-chief, bishops, abbots, etc. (100)	£19,200
Earls and lay barons (170)	£30,350
English landowners (about 12)	£ 4,000
	£53,550

The peasant labor force of England, William the Conqueror divided[6] between the "freemen," 12 percent; "villeins," 38 percent; and "cottars," 32 percent; although the distinctions between them were slight. The "freeman" held somewhat more land than the others but neither he nor the others actually owned any land. The concept of the sturdy, independent English yeoman (in implied contrast to the "Asiatic" peasant) with his plot of land is baseless. The land was owned by the lord; he could take it back at will. As Clough and Cole note,[7] it is impossible to draw a clear line between serf and freeman, for the two classes graded insensibly into each other. They were, in fact, all peasants, some with larger and some smaller holdings. The essence of the system was that the lord let the peasant have enough land to keep himself and his family from starvation, so that the lord did not need to keep them, and for the rest, 3 to 4 days a week on the average, the lord got free labor on his estates.

In addition to peasant labor there was 9 percent slave labor. As in Egypt and Asia there was also forced labor ("boon work" or "corvées"). The peasant had to assist in the general upkeep of the estate, building, woodcutting, draining marshes, digging canals, raising dykes, and so on. And, as in Asian feudalisms, he was subject to a multitude of taxes, to his lord, to the king, to the church. He paid a head tax to the government through the baron, rent to the baron, a tenth of his crops to the baron, a tax to the baron on all produce he sold, a fine if he sent his son to school or into the church, a tax if his daughter married off the estate (for the lord then lost the labor of her children). He had to grind his corn at the baron's mill and bake his bread in the baron's oven, for which privileges he had to pay taxes. He paid a tax for pasturing his animals on the baron's land or for hunting or fishing on that land. When he died, the church seized what farm animals or other possessions he had. As he was riveted to the land, he and his children could be sold with it. His progeny were not called *familia* in legal documents, but *sequela* — "brood" or "litter." The serf, like the slave in Roman law, was regarded as an animal who worked the land. He differed from the slave in that he had a "brood" which represented actual or potential labor.

In addition to labor on the land there was manufacturing and industrial labor. As in Asia again, or in Egypt, each estate had its own workshops manned by its own "hands": weavers, blacksmiths, bakers, and so on. But as time passed this labor was performed more and more in the villages on the lord's estate. Mines, quarries, and forests on the estate were owned either by the lord or the State. Mines were rented out to entrepreneurs (as in India or Athens), with the landowner receiving a percentage of the profits.

In spite of these general parallels, however, there clearly existed potential for commercial growth in European feudalism which did not exist in any area of similar size in Asia, as is shown by the fact that European feudal society developed earlier into commercial-feudal and then commercial-capitalist society than did Asian. What was this potential? What were its roots in feudal society? In seeking answers we would do well to discuss southern and northern Europe separately because the patterns differed somewhat in each region.

250 / HUMANITY AND SOCIETY

South Europe—Economy

Roman slave society, as we have seen, grew out of feudal society and then collapsed back into it. Although this doubtless seemed to the Roman slave-owners to be a backward step, the fact is that feudal society contains possibilities for progress which slave society does not—as we saw in Japan and parts of China with their rich commercial development. So, too, in Europe. As early as the eighth century Venetian ships were transporting to Constantinople[8] "wheat and wine from Italy, wood from Dalmatia, salt from the lagoons" and slaves captured from the Slavic peoples of the Adriatic (from whence the word "slave itself"). By the eleventh century Venice had control of the Adriatic. In the early thirteenth century, when Constantinople was captured by the Crusaders, Venice grabbed a large part of the Byzantine markets, taking over control of the Bosporus and seizing "strategic islands, ports, market centers, and stepping stones" to become "the greatest trader in Europe."[9] By about 1400 the Venetian merchant fleet is said to have consisted of 300 "large ships," 3,000 ships of less than 100 tons, and 45 galleys, manned, in all, by some 28,000 men; the Venetian shipyards employed 6,000 carpenters and other workers.[10] And so, too, with other Italian cities. By the eleventh century the fleets of Genoa and Pisa were sufficiently powerful to defeat the navies of the Arab Empire. By the thirteenth century the merchant ships of Genoa were trading with Spain, France, and north Africa. "By 1200," according to Heaton, "the Mediterranean seaways were probably busier than they had ever been before"; the sea trade of the Roman Empire had been surpassed. And the forward march continued.

In these bustling Italian cities the situation of Constantinople or Bagdad or Damascus was not repeated. There were no great landowning overlords to whom the merchants and manufacturers were subordinate, for after long and bloody struggles against the landowners the merchants and manufacturers had gained control of the cities. "Non-noble merchants," we learn from the *Cambridge Economic History*,[11] "formed the rank and file of the private associations which set up the communes (city governments)—in some places before the end of the eleventh century, in others in the twelfth or the thirteenth. Soon they ruled the cities almost as if the cities had been their own property, making communal policy an expression of their own mercantile interests." It was almost as though "another Athens" had indeed arisen—with one major exception: there was little or no slave labor. The workers were paid workers, some of them prospering workers (the wages of the masons in northern Italy seem to have doubled between 1194 and 1228). The merchants seized power in

Venice as early as 976 and in the succeeding centuries in Florence, Genoa, Pavia, Milan, and Bologna.

How can we account for these developments? In the first place, as Pirenne and other scholars have shown, manufacturing and trade in Italy did not collapse with the decline of the Roman Empire. Mediterranean commerce[12] "continued to be active and well sustained, in marked contrast with the growing apathy that characterized the inland provinces." Many of the same cities continued: Rome, Naples, Florence, Milan, Genoa. In the second place, the Germanic and other invasions of Italy did not do away with the great estates. They simply changed ownership and boundary lines. Perhaps as in India the peasants continued to work while the wars raged around them. With the partial ceasing of invasions, the exploitation of peasant labor began to produce a surplus of goods and provide a base to aid the growth of commerce. "Behind the flexible structure of the maritime towns," the *Cambridge Economic History*[13] notes, "lay the solid organization of the kingdom, which sheltered the Lombard and Tuscan *negotiatores* as they accumulated their capital and elaborated their business methods." Finally there was the stimulus from the rich Byzantine Empire. (Byzantium had a million population at a time when few European cities had more than 20,000.) Venice early had extensive trade with this empire, and received special concessions from it. Genoa, too, was at first largely dependent on it. Other areas of southern Europe, for instance, Greece and, for a time, Spain and southern Italy, were actually part of it. (The effects of the Arab Empire seem to have been less well investigated. Some trade routes were shut off to the Italians by the Arabs, especially with the conquest of Sicily and Sardinia; but others appear to have been opened up.)

Behind these specific factors there were, of course, also the general factors which had long made southern Europe a commercial area: (a) most of it, particularly Italy, had a large coast line and harborage with a comparatively small but fertile land area; (b) in the Mediterranean the wealth of Europe, Africa, and Asia met, and met at a vast inland sea with a favorable climate which allowed for cheap, safe, and continuous trading. Not even the China seas or the Sea of Japan had so rich a potential to offer, and, once again as in the days of the Greek and Roman slave-commercial empires, the economy of the Mediterranean began to pull ahead of that in Asian areas.

Northern–Western Europe

MANUFACTURING AND TRADE

Even in the so-called "Dark Ages" manufacturing and trade in northern-western Europe did not die out. For instance, cloth manufacturing in Flanders seems to have had a continuous history from Roman times on, when Flemish weavers had supplied uniforms for the Roman army and Flemish merchants exported woolen cloth to Italy. By the ninth century commercial activity has been noted in the north of Gaul. By the tenth century Flanders could not raise enough sheep for its woolen industry and imported wool from England.

Within a few centuries, northern Europe was catching up with the south. The cloth industry in particular rose to new heights. By the middle of the second half of the thirteenth century England alone was exporting 7 million pounds of wool. In one section of Flanders "almost every town great and small was busy with the manufacture of woolens"; and in the south, in French Flanders, there were the "five great clothing towns," Arras, St. Omer, Douai, Lille, Tournai. Northward in Flemish Flanders were other manufacturing centers — Ypres, Ghent, Bruges.[14] Chaucer wrote proudly of his Wife of Bath that "Of cloothmaking she hadde swiche [such] an haunt [skill],/ She passed hem of Ypres and of Gaunt." The mining, smelting, and working of metals grew with the general growth of the economy. Iron centers[15] were opened up in Westphalia, Sweden, and the Pyrenees. "Crude iron was more needed than before for ploughshares and other farm implements, for tools, axles, cauldrons, and other accessories in the expanding industries, for anchors, keels, and nails in shipbuilding, for armour, spears, swords, and daggers to be used when the need arose in war. Iron-making prospered all over Europe. An international traffic in iron developed." Lead, copper, tin, silver, and gold were also mined. The rise, once it began, was rapid. The tin output of Cornwall doubled between 1301 and 1339. In addition to metals, quarrying and lumbering became major industries as building spread on an unprecedented scale. The products of all these industries were exchanged, as were also those of the growing coal, salt, and potash industries, particularly salt, which was widely used as a preservative. And to these were added the products of glass, leather, and pottery manufacturing. These products of industry and manufacturing were but one side of the medal, the other was the products of agriculture, cattle and sheep raising, hunting and fishing. Grain, butter, cheese, wool, furs, and fish were widely traded. Trade flowed from Bergen to Bruges, from Newcastle to Danzig, from London to Venice, from Riga to Lubeck, trade of a quantity and a variety that had never previously existed, trade directed by great combinations of merchants, such as the Hanseatic League, which by 1300 had connections in some sixty towns.

Michael Poston, writing in *The Cambridge Economic History of Europe*,[16] notes a significant difference between this trade and that of the Mediterranean:

The main currents of trade across Northern Europe and between Northern Europe and other countries flowed with products of the northern hemisphere, cruder, bulkier and altogether more indispensable than the luxuries and fineries of the text-book convention. This convention is not altogether true even of the South, for foodstuffs or raw materials also entered into the trade of the Mediterranean region. Nevertheless, what gave the southern trade its peculiar character was not the trade in bulky essentials, but those luxury trades which we associate with it. By contrast, the trade of Northern Europe was almost exclusively devoted to the necessities of life.

This was perhaps the first time in history that a major trade area had dealt "almost exclusively" with "bulky essentials"—grain, wool, iron, lumber, fish, cloth, stone, leather, salt, etc. Such trade must mean that certain socioeconomic changes were taking place in this area which had not taken place elsewhere and had brought about a greater downward spreading of wealth. This is the impression one also receives from historical and literary sources. The land was still, it is true, mainly owned by great landowners and worked by landless peasants, but there appear to be more middling farmers, smaller manufacturers and traders, professional men and paid workers than in Asia or North Africa.

Under the impact of commercial developments changes began to take place in farming. An English abbey which had previously grown grain began about the year 1300 to "devote its central farm to rearing cattle and sheep. In 1309–1310 the abbot sold over 9,000 fleeces of wool to Italian, Flemish, and German merchants, along with much livestock and cheese."[17] The example is typical. The subsistence agriculture of the great estates of early feudalism began to give way to specialized agriculture (just as many centuries before had happened in Athens). The cloth and leather trades turned the grain fields of much of northern Europe into pasture. And the wine trade turned others into vineyards.

These economic developments both led to and were assisted by inventions and new productive processes (many of them deriving from the more advanced commercial centers of Asia, particularly in China). As shipping moved out into the North Sea and beyond, larger and sturdier ships were needed, as the Gauls had discovered earlier. But larger and sturdier ships could not be propelled by Roman flat sails or steered by a Roman steering oar—operated somewhat in the manner of a gondola by a man on the stern. At a certain point in ship design and size, the fixed, sternpost rudder, fore and aft rigging, and the bowsprit were needed; being needed and being within the range of the existing social and technological potential, they were invented. Other navigational aids had already been discovered elsewhere. Asians had invented the magnetic compass, and European traders imported it, perhaps from the Arabs. The water wheel came into extensive use; windmills similarly spread; horse-power supplemented ox-power. The power of the horse was, in fact, increased three to four times by the iron horse shoe, the horse collar, and harnessing in file. The Romans and others had collared and harnessed the horse on the analogy of the ox, placing the strain upon its neck instead of upon its chest, so that the horse almost strangled itself with heavy loads. The new horse collar corrected this, and the horse became a new source of power for trader and farmer alike.

As cloth manufacturing was the main industry, new technological inventions were especially prolific there. In addition to the use of water power for fulling, the spinning wheel was invented and the loom improved. From China came the silk worm and silk manufacturing as well as the development of paper manufacturing. Although the cloth industry was the most important, metal production was on the rise. With the development of the valved bellows, casting became possible and the production of iron was greatly accelerated. But iron and steel were still not used as they are today. Machinery was still mainly made of wood with iron used only for strengthening at certain key places.

ECONOMIC ORIGINS

Once more, we have to ask, as we did for southern Europe, what were the root causes for these changes? History textbooks content themselves with a simple description of various events and processes — the conquests of the Franks, the rise of the Papacy, Charles Martel and the defeat of the "Moslems," and so on — as though narration in itself somehow embodies explanation. Only the more advanced works offer interpretations — and these usually begin with "the Germans." The Germans, we learn from *The Shorter Cambridge Medieval History*, "were a stalwart, blond, fighting race, both prolific and adventurous." Their "losses in war . . . were easily made up by their fecundity." "Their passion for war was so strong that for centuries they had been expanding from their original lands."[18]

Obviously, the Roman Empire stood little chance against a limitless supply of adventurous blonds with a "passion for war." Obviously, too, such a people, "stalwart" and fecund, would lay a fine foundation for a new European civilization. It was, however, a foundation only. "The history of the Middle Ages begins with . . . the transfer of the imperial capital to Byzantium . . . and the adoption of Christianity as the dominant religion of Europe." "These two decisions of one man" (Constantine) laid down "conditions without which medieval and modern Europe could hardly have been shaped and grown."[19] In other words, if the Emperor Constantine had not made his two "decisions," there would be no modern Europe. What the adventurous blonds started, Constantine finished.

Let us sample two more medieval historians, one English and one French. G. G. Coulton writes of the Norman invasion of England: "The spirit of adventure was fresher in them than in those Anglo-Saxons who were so many generations removed from their conquering days."[20] Henri Pirenne writes of the "Norsemen": "Their overflowing energy had driven them forth, towards Western Europe and Russia simultaneously, upon adventures of pillage and conquest."[21] Even if, for the sake of argument, we accept these various free-floating "spirits" and "energies," we are no better off. We have still (in Byron's words) to "explain the explanation"; – what caused them to flare up?

In seeking the origins of these early developments in northern Europe, let us begin with the geographical and topographical characteristics of the area. Almost all the commercial-manufacturing development which I have summarized above took place in the territories now covered by France, Germany, the Low Countries, and England. It took place, that is to say, in an area of mainly fertile land with a large sea-coast, an inland or partly inland sea area (the Baltic and North Sea), its land threaded with rivers which both added to its harborage and broke it into agricultural areas. The normal tendency, therefore, was, as in Iran, China, or Japan, for farming society to develop into private property feudalism, and the comparative smallness of the land mass kept the feudal class within limits. On the other hand the extent of the sea coast, rivers, and harbors encouraged trade (always easier and cheaper by water) and made possible the development of a trading class of considerable size. The fertility of the land, under feudal exploitation, made for a surplus of wealth, which stimulated both manufacturing and trading.

To see the importance of these physical generative factors we have only to compare them with those of the eastern area of northern Europe, where the great plains fan out through Russia to the Urals. In this vast land area a feudal class, once it arose, would clearly be of great size and power, and whatever traders came into being would be subordinate to them. And this, too, is what happened. Although important trading centers developed at Kiev, Novgorod, and other places — just as they did in parts of inner China — these were always eventually brought under the dominance of the feudal landowners.

At the other extreme, it was in England and the Low Countries—both areas with a high proportion of sea coast and harborage to land mass—that the new commercialism developed most rapidly. France—with its larger inland area—developed more slowly.

To these factors two others have to be added. First north European feudalism, developing comparatively late, received an initial commercial impetus from the rich Mediterranean slave civilizations, particularly the Roman; second, Gaul had long had a thriving economy of its own. Furthermore, agriculture developed in Germany and trade flowed along the numerous German rivers. "Thanks to these advantages," writes F. W. Walbank in the *Cambridge Economic History of Europe,* "Roman Germany became rich, and rapidly outgrew its early character as a colonial area."

Gaul in Roman times was quite highly developed and apparently had been for many centuries:

> Textiles flourished especially in the North, with its abundance of wool. . . . There was also an increased exploitation of the mines; and the building of towns was directly responsible for the opening up of quarries. . . . The tin plating of bronze was a Gallic discovery. . . . In the production of glassware too, Gaul soon became a rival to Italy.[22]

How extensive some of this Gallic industry must have been is inadvertently revealed by Caesar himself. In one passage he describes a naval battle with the Gauls. The Gauls' ships, he notes with surprise, were larger than the Roman: "Exceptionally high bows and sterns fitted them for use in heavy seas and violent gales, and the hulls were made entirely of oak, to enable them to stand any amount of shocks and rough usage. The cross-timbers, which consisted of beams a foot wide, were fastened with iron bolts as thick as a man's thumb. The anchors were secured with iron chains instead of ropes."[23] There must have been a considerable lumbering, metal, and shipbuilding industry in Gaul to build a fleet of such ships. Moreover, it was an industry centered around trade in northern Europe and not the Roman Empire. The probability is that it existed long before the Roman penetration of Gaul and that it continued to exist after the Empire collapsed. The France of Charlemagne (about 800 A.D.) must have had its roots in the Gaul observed by Caesar. Once it started northern-western European feudal society grew as did that in the south, namely by economic competition (such as that which led to and was continued by the Hanseatic League) and social conflict (the wars of Charlemagne, the Wars of the Roses, the Crusades).

THE DEMISE OF SLAVERY

One other socioeconomic characteristic of feudal Europe must also have had roots in its early formative period, namely, the paucity of slave labor (9 percent in England). Why this lack of slave labor? One obvious factor is that the native rulers of the Gauls and Germans had not the wealth to enslave other peoples, and, as we have seen, a feudal society can only enslave its own males on a very limited scale. But the fact that slavery failed to develop even when wealth increased may indicate that there was another factor at work also, and this was perhaps simply the hatred of the Gauls, Germans, British, and others for slavery. In fact an active struggle against slavery must have been deep-rooted among these peoples for they had seen their young men and women dragged off for generations by the Roman conquerors.

As feudal society developed into feudal-commercial society, slavery disappeared entirely. And this was the tendency also as such societies developed in Japan and parts of China (and perhaps in Indonesia also). There was clearly a strong antislavery force active in feudal-commerical societies. What was it? That it did not come—to look ahead somewhat—from the commercial capitalists themselves is indicated by the fact that wherever they could establish slavery they did (in the West Indies, for example). It must have come from the new city working class itself, for there was no other major social pressure group with antislavery motives in the society. For this class the struggle against slave labor was a matter of life or death. And the same must have been true in Asian feudal-commercial societies. The Greek and Roman paid workers must, of course, also have had something of an anti-slavery interest. Why, then, did the working class in feudal and commercial-feudal societies succeed while that of Greek and Roman slave-commercial society failed? The answer is that the Greek and Roman working class grew up in a predominantly slave society and became enmeshed in it—the craftsmen had their slaves to work for them—whereas that in later western Europe grew up in a society without any major slavery and with antislavery traditions. It must have been more difficult also to abolish slave labor in the major Asian feudal societies, for they, too, developed in a period when slave labor was common; and once a custom becomes set in a society it is difficult to reverse it.

Social and Political Life

By about 1300 the same commercial-feudal economy existed in most of western Europe. The south was more advanced because of its Mediterranean connections, but the north, especially Flanders, was catching up.

Throughout the period of this commercial-feudal society from about 1200 to about 1600, it is surprising to note the dominance of the farming economy. Even in fourteenth century England, which was commercially more developed than most of northern Europe, more than 90 percent of the population lived on the land and less than 10 percent in towns. The farming economy was the basic economy; manufacturing and commerce made a poor second, even though it was there that the future lay. In considering the social life of these centuries, then, we are dealing with a predominantly farming population. "Well over" 90 percent of the rural population were peasants,[24] and although by 1600 serfdom had been mitigated or abolished in some sections, the fundamental exploitation of the peasantry remained. The social structure and social life in the country did not, in fact, much differ during these centuries from that of feudalism anywhere.

CAPITALISTS AND WORKERS

In the cities there came into being with manufacturing and trade a new business class — manufacturers, traders, bankers — similar to those of Athens and Rome, but employing paid labor and faced with less powerful landowner opposition. Most of the merchants were men of "middling substance," frequently small manufacturers as well as traders. But some of them, for instance, Richard Whittington of London, Gerard von Wesel of Cologne, William de la Pole of Hull, were extremely wealthy and spread out to financial speculation and banking.

The class of wage workers that came into existence with the rise of manufacturing and industry — mining, lumbering, quarrying — was large, concentrated, and aware of its social identity. "Thus great clothing towns such as Douai, Ypres or Brussels were in effect like one vast factory. In the early morning many thousands of workers might be seen flocking to the workshops of the entrepreneurs or of the weavers, fullers, dyers or shearmen, and the streets would empty as the bell rang out and they 'clocked in' to their labours."[25] And a similar picture must have been presented in numerous other manufacturing towns and sections of towns. By the end of the thirteenth century no less than 282 trades were recorded in Paris. There had never previously been a class of paid workers of this size or power. The working class of Rome was, it is true, large and varied, and so were those in some Asian cities, but this new working class was not held back either by the competition of slave labor or indirect domination by great landowners—for the capitalists ruled the cities.

The power of the class was demonstrated in its actions. One hears much of the idyllic towns of the "Middle Ages" with their humble yet cheerful "artisans" working like bees to fabricate golden goblets or colorful tapestries. The reality was quite different. Conditions in the great factory towns were sordid and exploitive. The weavers had "to work without stopping from dawn to dusk, taking with them their bread for the day, and 'if they wished for soup their wives must bring it to the looms where they worked so that they should in no way be interrupted in their work.'"[26] The majority of the workers appear to have been unorganized, the guilds consisting largely of the master craftsmen who "worked in most cases on their own premises and owned capital equipment of some value, such as the weaver's loom, the fuller's troughs and tenters, the dyer's vats . . . men of property . . . and . . . employers of labour." Strikes were forbidden and yet they took place, probably much more frequently than we know, as is indicated by the continual necessity of passing laws to forbid them. And there must have been many secret unions, or "combinations" as they were called, again judging by the numerous statutes outlawing them.

The situation in Flanders is vividly described by Pirenne:[27]

> Against these wage-earners and proletarians, the capitalists of the great commerce, brokers or exporters, combined with the small independent *entrepreneurs* of local industry. In order to satisfy everybody they tried to establish municipal governments in which a share was reserved for each of the large groups into which the population was divided: the *poorterie* (*haute bourgeoisie*), the mass of small crafts and the cloth workers. But the equilibrium which it was hoped to attain in this way could not be, and never was, anything but an unstable one. In the eyes of the weavers and fullers, it was nothing but a fraud, since it in effect condemned them to being always in a minority in relation to the other members of the town. To gain their demands, they could only count on force, and they did not fail to use it. Throughout the fourteenth century, we see them constantly rising, seizing power and refusing to give it up except when, starved out by a blockade or decimated by a massacre, they were compelled to yield to the coalition of their adversaries.

So, too, throughout Europe:

> At Dinant, the copper-workers exercised an influence as supreme as that of the weavers and fullers at Ghent or Ypres. Florence, which was at once a city of bankers and of drapers, also saw the mass of the workers seize power by main force from the capitalist class. . . . It would be no

exaggeration to say that on the banks of the Scheldt, as on those of the Arno, the revolutionaries sought to impose the dictatorship of the proletariat upon their adversaries.[28]

Although the paid workers of Athens and other slave-civilization states attempted, in combination with the small traders and businessmen, to get some power within the city government, and in some places led armed revolts, there seems to have been nothing previously, either in Europe, Asia, or Africa, among a city working class to compare to these revolutionary movements in feudal-commercial Europe. They had a new scope and power.

PEASANT REVOLTS

The peasant revolts in the countryside did not differ from those of other feudalisms (in Iran, China, or the Arab Empire), but their size, number and degree of organization are generally not realized. Trevelyan writes of the English Peasants' Revolt of 1381:

> There is no reason to find, as some have found, cause for wonder in the simultaneous revolt of so many districts. The rising was not, in fact, everywhere simultaneous; but, on the other hand, it had been planned long before. . . . Messengers were sent all over these districts in the summer of 1381 to prepare the country for the event. They were men of various counties, and they did not always visit the localities of which they were respectively natives. Such agitators had long been at work in the villages and towns of England, but they came bearing, not general exhortations, but a particular command from the "great Society" as they called the union of the lower classes which they were attempting to form.[29]

A program of demands was worked out: "commutation of all servile dues throughout the land for a rent of fourpence an acre . . . , the disendowment of the church, free use of forests, abolition of the game laws. . . ."[30] When the time seemed most favorable, the final preparations were made, the organizers made a final tour, and the peasants downed tools and began to march on London. They were welcomed by the wage workers, took over the city, and held it for three days. The peasants were, they proclaimed, "seekers of truth and justice, not thieves and robbers,"[31] and plunderers were executed. But the pent-up hatred of generations of oppression was not to be denied. The Chief Commissioner for the poll-tax was executed, as was the Archbishop; and the palace of the greatest of the barons, John of Gaunt, was burned. The peasants held England in their hands, but, holding it, they did not know what to do with it (any more than did the Chinese or

Iranian revolutionary peasants). Scattered, untrained in rule, incapable of setting up their own economy, they could gain concessions within the old system but they could not establish a new one.

CAPITALISTS AND LANDOWNERS

In addition to these struggles of a mass character there were, as in all feudal states, those between the commercial and landowning interests. The feudal class as ever and everywhere — from Byzantium to Japan — attempted to extract part of the capitalists' profits by a network of taxes and tolls. All manufacturing and commercial enterprises were taxed. The merchant, in fact, could hardly make a move without encountering a tax. If he sent his goods down the Rhine (at the end of the fourteenth century) he had to pay almost 50 separate river tolls, more than 100 on the Loire, 35 on the Elbe. Sometimes the barons simply seized his goods. Edward I of England financed a war by seizing 8,000 sacks of wool and selling them abroad.

The capitalists fought back in various ways: by getting financial controls over baronial estates, banding together in leagues and companies, gaining political power in the towns, making use of rivalries between baronial groups (those supporting or those opposing a particular royal house), encouraging middle-farmer opposition to the barons. The great capitalist, William de la Pole, and his associates loaned the English king £100,000 — an immense sum for the time — on the security of the wool customs in order to finance the seige of Calais and the Battle of Crécy. As in Japan, capitalists held mortgages on baronial and church estates. By the thirteenth century there had emerged in London "a small but powerful class which was fast acquiring the character of a hereditary caste, dominating the civil councils of London, active in every important branch of English trade, and holding large investments in landed property and mortgages."[32]

If some capitalists made investments in land some landowners made investments in trade. And there began to emerge a group with interests on both sides. In some of the Italian city states, indeed, such groups became unusually powerful and formed a ruling class, jointly exploiting both peasantry and wage workers. And in others the capitalists arose to actual domination. The Medici family of Florence, for instance, were not primarily landowners but bankers, owning mines and factories and trading extensively in Europe, Asia, and Africa; their bank was for some fifty years in the fifteenth century "by far the greatest financial organization of Europe."[33] In international affairs the great Hanseatic League was sometimes powerful enough to enforce its will upon the baronial power.

In the slave-commercial empires the capitalists had actual power only in Athens (and perhaps in Carthage). In Rome they formed a strong pressure group but the great landholders kept them well in check. In Asia before the eighteenth century they apparently gained political power only in Osaka, and, as we have seen, they were often influential in Chinese feudal states, in Indonesia, and in parts of the Arab empire, but this rise to power within a dozen or more cities in a comparatively small area is a new historical phenomenon. In fact, nowhere up to this time had there existed the capitalist political power represented by Venice, Naples, Palermo, Rome, Genoa, Marseilles, Barcelona, Cadiz, Bordeaux, London, Bruges, Ypres, Antwerp, Lubeck, and Danzig. Under the impact of these events in the cities the national political structure began to change.

We often find the State in European feudal-commercial civilization depicted as a monolithic unit—the State of the feudal lords. In reality, the situation was more complicated. As in China each great landowner had, in effect, his own State. But they also had common interests and formed combinations for their own protection and advancement. The Magna Carta, for instance, represented an amalgamation of the great landowners against the king and the smaller landowners. As the economy became more unified with the advance of trade and specialization of manufacturing, such agreements became more frequent and we find baronial amalgamations acting as a ruling class committee over various territories. The power of these amalgamations over the cities, however, was limited, for there, as we have seen, the capitalists often ruled (sometimes in uneasy union with the small tradesmen and paid workers). Nonetheless, over most of Europe by about 1300, the great feudal lords had basic control of increasingly unifying national States, with occasional pooling of their armed forces (as in the Crusades), a developing overall legal system, and a church. There was to be no national breakthrough by the capitalists for more than 300 years (in the Netherlands and England).

The Status of Women

Legal discriminations against women in European commercial-feudal civilization are similar to those in feudal (and slave) societies in general, but there are also indications of some new developments. An upper class woman might have considerable power within a household, but the law of marriage gave her husband full authority over whatever property she owned at marriage. The Wife of Bath might slap her husband, but she could be legally punished for it, whereas he could beat her and not be punished—for wife-beating was legal both in civil law and church law. If a woman plotted against her husband's life she was guilty not of a personal crime but of "petty treason" and could be executed by burning. If a woman wished to prosecute at law her word was not accepted as evidence. Although women "were the natural herbalists and charm doctors among the common folk"[34] they could be imprisoned if they attempted legally to practice medicine. Women could not sit in parliament. In short, women were legally subordinate to men and shut off from political power. On the other hand, the unusual developments in manufacturing and commerce in these centuries brought certain gains for women. As the new trades opened up and old ones expanded, women joined them. The Wife of Bath was a weaver, apparently with her own workshop, and it was perhaps this economic independence which enabled her to stand up so vigorously to her various husbands (five in number, not counting "other company in youth"). The English crafts guilds often had as many women as men members; in Paris by the end of the thirteenth century there were fifteen guilds consisting only of women. (On the other hand some crafts excluded women because they feared that their competition would undercut men, and women's wages for the same work were lower than men's.) A larger number of women seem to have been employed at paid work—some at home, some in workshops —than in previous societies. Many middle class town and city women were owners of small businesses (presumably mainly widows), and this continued on into the industrial revolution. London commercial directories, even into the nineteenth century, show a surprisingly large number of women owners. This kind of advance plus the mass employment of women in industry was obviously more important for the advancement of women as a whole than the improvement in the status of aristocratic women—which is so often taken as the criterion. Likewise, the employment of women as teachers and minor clergy (nuns and abbesses) by the church was certainly an advance over the "priestess" temple prostitute.

There do not appear to have been political organizations of women or even clubs of the kind that existed in Roman Italy. But there seems to have been a growing sense of power among women and a growing alarm among men. This may be indicated in the profusion of antifeminist literature. There was, of course, such literature in Roman times, and, doubtless, in all other civilizations, but it now had a defensive ring. Why the reiteration of woman's subjection and its sanctifications in church law unless that subjection was being challenged? Such a challenge, indeed, is indicated in the persecution of "witches." The extent of this persecution does not usually seem to be realized. For instance, one bishop (of Geneva) burned 500 "witches" within three months, another bishop, 600, another, 900. A historian of the Inquisition recorded that the Holy Office body had burned 30,000 "witches" in the 150 years proceding 1404. If this is not mass terroristic intimidation of women, what is it? Why are not men being burned in the same proportion? For one Savonarola, there are thousands of women.

In 1344 the British House of Commons complained that "prelates . . . allow serfs and women to make wills, which is against reason," and requested the king to outlaw such practices. The king replied cautiously, "The King wills that law and reason be kept in this matter."[35] What power-pressures the serfs exercised is clear from the peasant revolts. But what power did women exercise to protect their rights and how was it exercised? That there was such power is obvious from the king's reply; and although women apparently were not organized in special societies there must have been some kind of common, united feeling that gave the king (and his advisors) pause. The indications are that the revolt of women which burst out into the open in the early days of the industrial revolution had its beginnings in commercial-feudal society.

II: The Church and Christianity

The "Medieval" European church requires emphasis not only because it pervaded so much of the life of feudal and then of feudal-commercial civilization in Europe, but because its religion, Christianity, spread with the spread of European power to America and other places.

Origins of Christianity

Rome and Palestine

Christianity originated in Palestine; and Palestine was an unusual country in various ways. It was too small to support a great land-owning class, and, as it had no sea coast (the Phoenicians had seized the coastal areas), it had few great merchants (such as Solomon). Yet it was situated in a major trading area. The result was that it became a country of small or middling farmers and merchants, with some slave and some peasant labor. It was also in an area dominated by great feudal powers and had frequently to fight for its existence. It was attacked, in turn, by Egypt, Assyria, and Persia. And yet each time Palestine survived. The reason may be that the usual practice of invading and simply changing masters would not work in a country of small farmers and traders, and the great powers could conquer it only by physically removing a large section of the population to their own territories. But each time the Palestinians succeeded in escaping and returning.

When the next great imperial power, Rome, appeared on the scene, the story was repeated. Palestine, tiny though it was, seems to have given the Romans more of a fight than any other single territory within the Empire. Repeatedly the Jews revolted; they were sold into slavery or killed, and yet the Jews would rise again and new revolts would break out. In 70 A.D. the Roman army descended in full force, the Temple at Jerusalem was destroyed, and Palestine obliterated as a Jewish state. Between 600,000 and 1 million Jews were killed; 97,000 were sold into slavery; another million were dispersed — mostly around the Mediterranean area.

But even after the "dispersion," the Jews would not give up. In 115–116 the Jews in Cyrene, Egypt, Cyprus, and Mesopotamia arose against the Roman power and more than 400,000 lost their lives. The last great revolt took place in 132; and again the Jews were slaughtered in the hundreds of thousands. But in spite of these massacres there were by the second century perhaps 7 million Jews in the Roman empire, living mainly in the cities around the Mediterranean, where some of them formed colonies of small businessmen.

Sadducees, Pharisees, and Essenes

The history of Palestine, then, was for some sixty years before the birth of Jesus (about 4 B.C.) until a hundred years after his death (in about 30 A.D.) an anti-imperialist struggle, as continuous, heroic, savage, and unyielding as any in history. This struggle must have dominated the lives and thinking of the Jews. As usual with oppressed peoples without effective political outlet (for instance, in modern times, the Irish), religion became a focal point of resistance. In its early stages, the religion of the Jews was akin to that of other communal farming peoples and sounds like an offshoot of the Sumerian-Babylonian (the Sky-god, the creation myth, the flood). As it developed into a State religion, it took over the characteristics of Zoroastrianism: immortality, Heaven and Hell, the Last Judgment, and so on. By the time of Jesus there were two leading sects, the Sadducees and the Pharisees. The Sadducees apparently represented more of the older, pre-Zoroastrian view (they did not, for instance, believe in immortality). The Pharisees had begun as a revolutionary sect (with the Maccabees) and gradually become more conservative. The Jewish national governing body was known as the Great Council of the Elders of Israel and was controlled by these two sects. Following the great rebellion of 66, the Pharisees attempted to institute a policy of compromise with the Roman government. One of their leaders, Josephus, deserted and became a Roman propagandist historian. But the people rebelled, the government of the Pharisees was overthrown and the struggle against Rome continued, hopeless though the odds appeared to be.

In addition to the Sadducees and the Pharisees there was one other religious sect, or perhaps, more accurately, group of sects, called the Essenes. The Essenes appear to have fallen into two groups, the fanatical devotees, who lived in monasteries, and ordinary church members. They pooled their possessions and ran their centers on a communal basis. They were, we learn from Josephus, among the most unyielding foes of the Romans, resisting all persecution with a fanatical courage.[36]

The Essenes hoped for salvation from the Romans not primarily by earthly means but through divine deliverance by a "Messiah." This Messiah they identified with one of their founders, the "Teacher of Righteousness," who had been persecuted by a "wicked priest" and who would return from the dead to lead Israel into the "light." The Sons of Light would triumph over the Sons of Darkness. The "Teacher" may have been known as Christ (Greek for the Hebrew word "Messiah").

JESUS OF NAZARETH

The connection between these Essenic beliefs and those of Jesus cannot be coincidental — one derives from the other. And as the Essenic groups had been in existence for 150 years before the birth of Jesus and their Teacher of Righteousness persecuted at least 60 years before, the derivation must be from the Essenic to the Christian. The idea of a divine deliverance from Roman oppression and other evils had long been in the air. Jesus of Nazareth was only one of at least two claimants to Messiahship, and of the two he was the second. Nevertheless it was he and not his predecessor who began the Christian religion. His life is probably most accurately reflected in *Mark*, the earliest and the least imaginatively embellished of the gospels.* Mark begins not with Jesus but with John the Baptist. John the Baptist, Josephus tells us, was a religious leader executed by King Herod

---

*Jesus is also referred to in the *Talmud*, and, it has been recently argued, almost certainly by Josephus.

"without trial in order to prevent a revolt since the people 'seemed ready to do anything' on John's advice."[37] John preached a gospel of moral living and the early coming of the "Kingdom of God" (on earth), which, stripped of its religious overtones, meant the overthrow of Herod and Roman rule. It was, in fact, like the Essenic message of the triumph of the Sons of Light over the Sons of Darkness (the Romans). And John had another point in common with the Essenes, namely baptism, which originally appears to have signified "purification from the pollution of Roman rule."[38] Large numbers of people gathered together for such ceremonies were clearly dangerous.

"John the Baptizer," writes Mark, "appeared in the wilderness proclaiming, for the forgiveness of sins, a baptism of repentance. All Judea went out to him, and all the people of Jerusalem. . . . After John had been arrested, Jesus went into Galilee proclaiming the good news from God. 'The time has come,' he said 'and the Kingdom of God is near. Repent and put your trust in the Good News.'"[39] Jesus, then, was the successor to John the Baptist. When John was executed Jesus continued his apocalyptic message — the "Kingdom of God is near" — and perhaps added to it a threat of violence: "I have come not to bring peace but a sword;" "Nation will arise against nation, and kingdom against kingdom."[40] (The words "Thy Kingdom come" in the Lord's Prayer is, in effect a call for the downfall of the Roman Empire.) Jesus was recognized as the successor to an executed anti-Roman religious agitator, and took pride in the role. In time, however, his followers began to feel that he had transcended his role as a successor to John, that he was, in fact, the promised divine deliverer:

"'Who do people say I am?'

"'John the Baptist,' they told him; 'others, Elijah; others again, one of the Prophets.'

"'But you?' he asked. 'Who do you say I am?'

"It was Peter who answered him. 'You are the Christ,' he said. And Jesus admonished them to tell no one about himself."[41] As the Christ (Messiah) was to overthrow the Romans and their Jewish collaborators, it is no wonder that Jesus admonished Peter to "tell no one."

John was in the south of Palestine (Judea); Jesus came from the north (the region around the Sea of Galilee). After his baptism by John, he returned to the north. There he established his headquarters in the town of Capernaum, a Roman administrative center, customs station, and garrison, and preached in the synagogue. At Capernaum Jesus obtained three followers, Matthew, who was a Roman customs collector there, Peter and Andrew, who were owners of fishing boats in the nearby Sea of Galilee.

It was at Capernaum that Jesus first ran into opposition: "But the

Pharisees, when they left the synagogue, began at once to plot against him with the partisans of Herod, considering how they might destroy him. And Jesus, accompanied by his disciples, withdrew towards the sea."[42] This does not take much interpretation. The "partisans of Herod" were the collaborators with the Romans, those whom the "dagger men" later swore to assassinate; the Pharisees were the party of compromise. Both groups considered Jesus a menace to their power. In order to escape them he left town and went into the hills around the lake. And this "hiding out" became habitual.

Once we perceive that the struggle against Rome dominated the life of Palestine many things become clear. Jesus's attacks on the Sadducees and Pharisees were really attacks on the Jewish governmental body, for in Palestine the established church and the national Jewish government (the Great Council) were identical, and the attacks implied that this body was yielding to Roman interests. The famed remark about giving to Caesar what was due him and to God what was God's due might on the surface sound innocuous, but actually it was subversive for it held the implication of resistance by nonpayment of taxes; and it was so taken by the authorities. When Jesus was arrested two charges were preferred against him: "We caught this man teaching our people sedition, telling them not to pay taxes to Caesar, and saying that he was the Christ, that is, a King."[43] Coming through all four gospels is the picture of a man obsessed by oppression and treachery. "You serpents! You brood of snakes! How can you escape being sentenced to the pit?"

As with the Essenes Jesus's disciples had to "abandon" their possessions[44] and share alike. He attacked the "rich"; as with John the Baptist his followers were "the people." "He is stirring up the people, teaching everywhere in Judea. He started in Galilee and now he has come here."[45] "This unlettered rabble is bewitched."[46] His followers, however, were not "rabble" — slaves or poor peasants. Jesus did not oppose slavery but took it for granted: "A servant [slave] is not greater than his master."[47] The common soldiers he advised to "be content with your pay."[48] He and his immediate followers belonged to the middle class — small businessmen (fishermen) and craftsmen, minor administrators, and so on. Two groups among his followers receive special mention in the gospels: women and tax gatherers. "A number of women," we learn, "travelled up with him to Jerusalem."[49] And some of his tours seem to have been financed by women. "Joanna wife of Chuza, Herod's steward; Susanna; and a number of others, who were in a position to minister to his wants out of their own resources."[50] His attitude to women was a refreshing contrast to the contemporary hardened antifeminism. He refused to condemn the woman "taken in adultery," and when he talked with the woman by the well his disciples were astonished that he would talk to a woman about serious matters.

So long as Jesus remained in the comparatively remote north (the Galilee district) the Pharisees and Herodians were disturbed but held their hand, but when he moved down into Judea and then into Jerusalem itself, they had to act: "If we just let him be the whole people will believe in him and the Romans will come and uproot our worship and our race itself."[51] One senses panic as well as anger: "He started in Galilee and now he has come here." The nature of his reception in Jerusalem was especially alarming: "On the following day a great crowd who had come in for the Festival, hearing that Jesus was on his way into Jerusalem, plucked branches off the palms and went out to meet him. They were shouting, '*Hosanna! Blessed be he that cometh in the name of the Lord! Blessed be the King of Israel!*"[52] Jesus, then, was hailed as a potential national ruler; and the Pharisees and Sadducees could not arrest him until popular feeling had subsided: "Now the Passover and the Feast of Unleavened Bread were two days off, and the Chief Priests and Doctors of the Law were eager to get him into their power by a stratagem and so put him to death. For they said: 'We must not do this during the Festival, or the people will riot.'"[53]

A few days later Jesus was arrested by the Temple police and taken first before the Jewish authorities of the Great Council and then the Roman governor, Pontius Pilate (governor from 26 to 36 A.D.). According to the gospels the Jewish authorities were more anxious for Jesus's execution than was Pilate. But the charge was sedition, and Pilate had to act. "Are you the King of the Jews?" he asked, doubtless sardonically, and when Jesus implied that he was, his death warrant was signed. "It was the third hour when they crucified him. The charge against him was set forth in writing on a placard, which read *The King of the Jews*." Mark does not describe the crucifixion, for crucifixion was only too familiar to his readers. The usual implication that Jesus was nailed to the cross, however, is without basis. He was probably tied by ropes around the hands and feet, for such was the usual procedure.

As we have seen, the doctrine of immortality became central to State religions some five centuries before the time of Jesus. In the early days of Christianity it assumed a direct and personal form that gave it a special appeal. The Kingdom of Heaven on earth not only included the overthrow of Rome but conferred personal immortality. The gospel narratives grow confused and contradictory on the events concerning and following Jesus' "resurrection," and they lack the details which give the feeling of authenticity to much of the earlier narrative. Nevertheless, it seems probable that something unusual did take place. Paul, for instance, stated some twenty years later that more than 500 people had seen Jesus after his execution, and the apostles seem to have firmly believed that he arose from the tomb. What actually happened we shall probably never know, but it seems most likely that Jesus was not dead when removed from the cross but died later from the toxic effects of the scourging that preceded a Roman crucifixion. When Joseph of Arimathaea—a man of some influence, we might note—went to request the body, Mark records that "Pilate wondered whether he could have died so soon."[54] And well he might, for usually it took two or more days for a man tied to a cross to die and Jesus had been on the cross for only six hours.

Jesus was no theologian, no Plato or Thomas Aquinas. He never attempted to "prove" the doctrine of immortality or the existence of God. His answer to all problems was "faith." "Everything is possible for one who has faith."[55] Along with "faith" went the doctrine of the Good God, the God of Love (in contrast to the traditional Hebrew God of vengeance). In its application this doctrine placed the emphasis upon "inner" religious and moral qualities, just as that of Gautama had some 500 years before, and, like Gautama's, it tended to undermine the organized church. Unlike most theologies it had a simple and direct appeal. It could be comprehended by ordinary middle class people.

The religious and the social doctrines had common roots. To a desperate, oppressed people not only were the existing social conditions intolerable; so, too, was the thought that this life was all there would ever be. Religious and social views intermingled, and the two sets of doctrines were unified and centered in the person of Jesus himself. He was the Messiah, the Christ, who at once would confer immortality and bring about a new order. Faith was not general; it became specifically faith in him. His death became at once a martyrdom that stirred the hearts of those suffering under the same tyranny and a source of hope. On these things and on the "resurrection" and the other "miracles" the disciples seem to have placed the stress rather than on the general religious "doctrine" of Jesus.

The Early Church

The spread of Christianity is, it sometimes seems to be implied, so extraordinary a phenomenon that it is only explainable by divine intervention. But although that spread was certainly rapid—by 300 A.D. about one-third of the population of the Roman Empire in the eastern Mediterranean was nominally Christian, and other competing religions were easily outdistanced — it was not únique. It was more than matched in the spread of Buddhism across Asia, from India to China to Japan, and that of Mohammedanism later — some of it in Christian territory.

"A Jewish Heresy"

Christianity, it is sometimes. forgotten, began as a branch of Judaism ("a Jewish heresy," said Heine) and this gave it a social base at the beginning. Even by the time of Jesus there were groups of Jewish businessmen and craftsmen with their families in almost all Mediterranean cities. With the "dispersion" of 70 A.D. a million more Jews were scattered into the area. When Paul and the other organizers of the new sect began, then, they had bases from which to work: Damascus, Antioch, Alexandria, Corinth, Rome, and so on. In its early days it was almost exclusively a city religion. Only later did it penetrate into the country districts — and when it did it changed its character.

If we ask ourselves why this particular form of Judaism took such hold the answer is that it continued as it had begun with Jesus, namely, as an anti-Roman religion. Although hatred of the Roman power was shared by all the oppressed peoples of the Empire, the Jewish opposition continued to have a special intensity. As late as 132 A.D., some sixty years after they had been driven from Palestine, the Jews led armed mass rebellions against the Roman power. And this opposition became particularly identified in certain places with the Christian sects. One of the earliest Christian tracts, the *Revelations* of John of Patmos, was largely a prophecy of the overthrow of the Empire. The Romans had no doubt about the political implications of the new religion and the Christians themselves did not disguise it.

As the Empire weakened, Christianity spread; as it spread the retribution became the more terrible. And then, as often happens, the retribution increased the spread, and a gathering, interacting spiral began. In the year 249, when the Empire was threatened by invasion, the Christians fought against military service, scorned the Roman religion, and prophesied the collapse of the Empire. (Clearly as Bernard Shaw pointed out in *Androcles and the Lion* they were dangerous people to have in a threatened State.) A half century later, when the Empire was rapidly losing ground, the anti-Roman activities of the Christians produced the most sweeping attack of all, and 1500 were executed. Around these martyrs many thousands gathered. The Christian church became a rallying point for revolutionists throughout the decaying Empire until the Emperor Constantine had so many of them in his army that victory became possible only by hoisting a banner bearing the Christian symbol of the cross to replace the Roman standard.

The communistic practices and anti-rich doctrines of Jesus continued into the early church: "Come, now, you rich people, weep aloud and howl over the miseries that shall overtake you! . . . The wages you have withheld from the laborers who have reaped your harvests cry aloud." So, the later Epistle of James.[56] As with Jesus himself, however, there was no opposition to slavery. "Servants [i.e. slaves]," enjoined Peter "be submissive to your masters."[57] Paul returned a runaway slave to his master. The early Christian church was not, as one would sometimes gather, a toiling-class revolutionary movement. It gained such a reputation in part from the stigma which an aristocrat-dominated culture attached to tradesmen and craftsmen — "the rabble."

A MEDITERRANEAN RELIGION

The Greek or Roman religions, it is often not realized, were national religions. Only a Greek or a Roman citizen could belong to them, and at first it appeared as though the new Jewish sect was about to make the same mistake. For most of the first century it was practiced almost entirely in synagogues and used the traditional Jewish ceremonial forms. But Paul, the first great organizer of Christianity, had early urged the spreading of the gospel beyond the Jews and in time this point of view triumphed. By the third century, the movement had developed to such a point that control had passed into the hands of the Greeks, Italians, and other Mediterranean peoples. The Jews, acting as a catalyst, helped to move the anti-Roman feelings and actions of the other Mediterranean and Near Eastern peoples into socio-religious channels of opposition.

One other factor aided the early spread of Christianity (as it did other religions also), namely the parallels in beliefs and ceremonials between Christian and other churches. For instance, the concept of a trinity is found alike in the Vishnu-Brahma-Siva triad of Hinduism and in Plato's triune Creator. The myth of the virgin birth had existed for five hundred years before "the Christ" in relation to "the Buddha." The worship of a mother goddess, the worship of Mother and Child, angels and devils, a hierarchy of saints (simply a new form of the ancient polytheism), all were common to one or more earlier religions. The emphasis on the ascetic life of the clergy was part of Buddhism and other earlier religions; the myths of Osiris, Attis, and Dionysus contain the concept of deities having suffered death that others might have immortality (it was believed that magic embodiments of them could be eaten at sacred banquets); the Jewish Seder was the "Last Supper."

Simply to state these facts, however, does not give the proper notion of how close all these religions were, in mood, attitude, and feeling. Let us take, for instance, a Greek hymn written some 250 years before Jesus:

> O God most glorious, called by many a name,
> Nature's great King, through endless years the same. . . .
> Vehicle of the universal Word, that flows
> Through all, and in the light celestial glows
> Of stars both great and small. O King of Kings
> Through countless ages, God! whose purpose brings
> To birth whate'er on land or in the sea
> Is wrought, or in high heaven's immensity.[58]

One could never tell from the reading that the hymn is to Zeus. It could as easily be to the Christian God. And so, too, with certain passages in Virgil and other Roman writers.

As Christianity moved beyond the cities it moved into landowning circles; and as the rulers of the later Roman Empire (such as Constantine) began to take it over—on the principle that if they couldn't beat it they should join it—it naturally fell under the control of the landowners of the great Roman feudal estates (for the later Roman Empire, as we have seen, was primarily a peasant and not a slave society). By about 300, the Christian church had become "the richest religious organization in the Empire." Its bishops "held lucrative offices of state," and "lent money at usurious interest."[59] In short, the church was becoming a feudal church, and a feudal church it remained.

The early Christian church, then, went through two stages, that in which it grew by fighting imperialist and great landowner oppression, and that in which it reversed the process and became the instrument of feudalism—a fate similar to that of Buddhism.

The European Feudal Church

An Amalgamation of Farms

As a social institution, the European feudal church was primarily an amalgamation of farms. The pope "held nearly 2,000 square miles of Italian wheat, forest, olive or iron lands; some French bishops in the ninth century held over 100,000 acres, while in Saxony a nunnery held 11,000 farms and a monastery had 15,000."[60] These lands were worked, in the early centuries, by mixed slave and peasant labor, later by peasant labor. The great Abbot Alcuin of Tours, for instance, was "lord of 20,000 serfs."[61] The surplus produce of this peasant labor — grain, wool, lumber — "entered the stream of commerce."[62] The church was a business as well as a farming enterprise, making commercial profits.

In addition to these revenues, the church — as in Egypt or India — obtained other funds from the general taxation of the peasantry. The tithe took one-tenth of peasants' crops; fees were paid for marriage services, masses, and law suits (in the extensive church courts); special taxes were extorted for grinding corn at the church mill or selling in the local market. As the manorial system declined with the rise of trade these taxes assumed greater importance. A veritable army of priests, monks, nuns, abbots, and bishops — ten times the ratio of clergy to the population as nowadays — lived off the peasantry.[63]

How did the church acquire its land? The question is often left unanswered, but three main sources appear even from a simple general investigation: from previous churches; from the economic engulfment of smaller landowners; from grants and bequests.

How much land initially came from the previous (Greek, Roman, Druidical) churches is not clear, but Pope Gregory writing to the Venerable Bede in the year 601 seems to regard it as important. "He is to destroy the idols, but the temples themselves are to be aspersed with holy water, altars set up, and relics enclosed in them."[64] Kings converted to Christianity customarily granted land to the new church; and these were most probably the lands of the previous church. Sometimes, in fact, the "pagan" clergy seem to have gone along with the lands.

If we ask why governments thus granted land to the Christian church in Europe, the answer is for the same reasons that they did elsewhere. It was not a phenomenon restricted to the Christian church nor to Europe. As the church grew in the first civilizations its lands grew with it. In early Egypt it apparently held about one-third of the land, and the Sumerian temples had large estates. So, too, in India, China, Hawaii, Greece. These lands grew with the church essentially because the church was needed for rule and also — the other side of the same medal — because an exploited and oppressed working mass needed the tranquilizing services of the church.

Once established, the church grew as any great landowning institution did. Unlike other landowning institutions, however, it grew also by bequests. Marion Gibbs comments, "Behind the grants of both peasants and gentry, in more cases than we know, there perhaps lay a tale of some debt which the religious house undertook to pay in return for rights over a particular tenement or of some other conditions, the details of which have been lost."[65] Many, as Pirenne points out, were death-bed bequests[66] and most of them may have been motivated by the fear of death even though willed earlier. This fear was of basic concern with every church. The natural fears arising from death and other uncontrollable elements in human life, social and biological, were systematically blown up to monstrous proportions in a nightmare of irrational terrors. "Hell is wide without measure and deep and bottomless; full of incomparable fire. . . . The Darkness therein is so thick that one may grasp it . . . ; in that same darkness they see black things as devils . . . and tailed drakes, horrible as devils that devour them whole and spew them out afterwards before and behind."[67]

Important though the church was in European feudal and commercial-feudal civilizations, we must not exaggerate it. It did sometimes, it is true, exert influence on specific historical events, but it did not determine or even greatly influence the main course of socio-historical evolution. In fact, if there had not been a Christian church but a Buddhist church in medieval Europe or if there had (hypothetically) been no church at all but simply local religious groups, modern Europe would exist essentially as it is today. So, too, with the church in Asian and other societies; Indian history was not determined by the Buddhist church nor Greek history by the Greek church. In commercial-feudal Europe, as I have attempted to demonstrate, the main course of historical evolution was determined by commercial developments resulting from both economic and social competitions and with these the church had little connection. It was mainly a landholding entity, and even as a landholding entity it did not have the preponderant power. As the great social tides of history moved the feudal church was swept along with them. Later, as we shall see, it began to take a more active part in political events (the so-called Reformation) but even then it did not, and could not, exert a decisive influence.

THE THEOLOGY—THOMAS AQUINAS AND ROGER BACON

The ideas (theology) of the Christian church came, as we have noted, from various sources. In the year 325 these ideas were put in succinct form by a general church council at Nicaea (near Constantinople). This "Nicene Creed" (rewritten in 362), which has formed the basis of Christian theology, established the following doctrine:

(1) The universe and all it contains was created by a spiritual substance called God.
(2) This God is of a triune nature (Father, Son, and Holy Ghost) and
has been such always (eternally).
(3) By divine intervention in the processes of nature one of the aspects
of this "Trinity" entered the uterus of a specific woman in Palestine
about 4 B.C.
(4) This aspect, receiving bodily form as Jesus, elected to be executed
in order that those who believed in his divine nature might receive
immortality.

To this framework—much of which is shared with other religions—
Thomas Aquinas and other theologians added various concepts, some
of them from Plato and Aristotle. Aquinas rejected—at least by implication—"faith" as sufficient basis for belief and attempted to use
reason also, for instance, in his "proof" of the existence of God: "The
first and more manifest way is the argument from motion. It is certain,
and evident to our senses, that in the world some things are in motion.
Now whatever is in motion is put in motion by another, for nothing
can be in motion except it is in potentiality to that towards which it
is in motion . . . ,"[68] and so on. If this has a familiar ring, it is because
it is essentially Aristotle's argument on the First Mover. In addition to
knowledge obtained by logic, Aquinas posited also "revelation" as a
source of "truth," in fact, as the supreme source. It was presumably
this revelatory method which permitted him to speculate on the nature
of angels and to be charged with heresy for denying that they have
corporeal bodies. This is naturally a difficult matter to confirm or deny,
but on other matters both pure logic and revelation demonstrably fail:
"But celestial bodies [stars, planets, etc.] are perfected without any
contrariety in their natures, for they are neither light nor heavy,
neither hot nor cold."[69]

Although views and method of thought similar to those of Aquinas
dominated church thinking, they were not the only ones. At least one
leading church thinker stood at the opposite pole, namely Roger Bacon,
who argued that experience and experimentations took precedence
over logic or revelation:

For there are two modes of acquiring knowledge, namely, by reasoning
and experience. Reasoning draws a conclusion and makes us grant the conclusion, but does not make the conclusion certain, nor does it remove
doubt so that the mind may rest on the intuition of truth, unless the mind
discovers it by the method of experience. . . . And, if we turn our attention
to the experiences that are particular and complete and certified or wholly
in their own discipline, it is necessary to go by way of the principles of this
science which is called experiments.[70]

When we consider the implications of this view of Roger Bacon's for theology it comes as little surprise to learn that his books were condemned and he was imprisoned for fourteen years (whereas Aquinas, scion of a great landowning family, received accumulated honors).

Bacon's views must stem, at least indirectly, from manufacturing and commercial circles because these are always, as we have seen in feudal or slave societies, the ones interested in science. Something of the democratic and defiant attitudes of such circles (as evidenced later also in Chaucer) is, indeed, apparent in his comment: "I have learned more important truths from men of humble station than from all the famous doctors."[71]

When we look over the general field of European church theology, it is apparent that it advanced little if at all beyond the Indian or Persian and that it is mostly a dead-end thought. The speculations of Aquinas, for all their ingenuity of logic, add not one single fact to human knowledge. Nor are his ideas — to take him as representative — of the kind that lead to knowledge. What, for instance can one do with the assertion that angels have no bodies? (Or that they have?) And although such typical concepts as "the being of eternity is entirely simultaneous"[72] are imaginative and poetic, they were said as well in the *Bhagavad-Gita* some 1700 years before.

III: Culture

Knowledge and Ideas

In European feudal society there were not, nor could there have been, any major advances in knowledge, for that society essentially duplicated those which had long existed in Asia and Africa. There had been, however, some advances earlier in European farming society induced by the special nature of the soil, topography, climate, and so on. For instance, the Germanic peoples early used a heavy-wheeled plow which was particularly suited to the deep topsoil of Europe, without which the development of agriculture in northern Europe would apparently not have been possible. The Germanic peoples, who seem originally to have lived in a farming society like that of the Huns, also early introduced butter, barrels, hops, the stirrup, and trousers into Europe. A Germanic people developed the long-prowed, swift, and seaworthy ships with which the Norsemen raided and traded from Sweden to the Mediterranean; and the Franks apparently made advances in ship-building also.

It used to be thought that the technological and other advances in commercial-feudal Europe were nearly all natively European, but, as we have seen, many of them had previously existed in China and other Asian countries.

The technological advances which we have noted—in shipping, in milling and cloth manufacturing, in metallurgy—some new, some borrowed, led to further advances in knowledge. Increasing trade demands led to new explorations (for instance, the travels of Marco Polo). As usual in feudal societies, the great landowners and their church, whose special realm was that of ideas, opposed scientific advance. The church view was early and pithily stated by St. Augustine: "Whatever knowledge man has outside Holy Writ, if it be harmful is there condemned; if it be wholesome it is there contained."[73] Anatomy was forbidden by church law, and surgery was discouraged on the grounds that "men vowed to religion should not touch those things which cannot honourably be mentioned in speech." It is not surprising that medical science and technology stagnated. And so, too, with other related fields. The situation in regard to philosophy and theology we have already seen. In the realm of social ideas, as we have noted, the church attempted absolute domination. In regard to the writing of history the official church view was well expressed by the French theologian, Jacques Bénigne Bossuet: "Remember, your Highness, that this long chain of particular causes, which make and unmake empires, depends upon the secret orders of God's Providence."[74] Thus the object of the historian became not the examination of historical facts but the revelation of supernatural purposes. Fortunately many historians and chroniclers ignored this directive and continued to record historical facts. Indeed, there was more intellectual strife in feudal and feudal-commercial Europe than is usually recognized. Sometimes, as we have seen, an opposing philosophy such as Roger Bacon's broke through and acquired a following. Nor were commercial centers the only ones breeding anti-establishment views. Opposition to the social and other doctrines of the church— such as that by John Wycliffe—had doubtless long existed among the peasantry and found reflection in the lower clergy. Apparently only in times of social upheaval, such as the Peasants' Revolt in England or the Peasants' Wars in Germany, were the peasants' views recorded, for instance, in Froissart's contemporary account of a speech by John Ball, Wycliffite priest and leader of the Peasants' Revolt:

> "Good people," cried the preacher, "things will never go well in England so long as goods be not in common, and so long as there be villeins and not gentlemen. By what right are they whom we call lords greater folk than we? On what grounds have they deserved it? Why do they hold us in serfage? If we all came of the same father and mother, of Adam and

Eve, how can they say or prove that they are better than we, if it be not that they make us gain for them by our toil what they spend in their profit? They are clothed in velvet, and warm in their furs and their ermines, while we are covered in rags. They have wine and spices and fair bread; and we eat cake and straw, and water to drink. They have leisure and fine houses; we have pain and labour, the rain and the wind in the fields. And yet it is of us and of our toil that these men hold their state."[75]

Simple though these ideas may seem, they nevertheless represent a social philosophy diametrically opposed to that of the dominant views of the time (as is indeed clear from Ball's history: imprisoned by the Archbishop of Canterbury, he was released by the rebellious peasants; with the failure of the revolt, he was disembowelled, castrated and beheaded in the presence of the king). If John Ball had such views, so, too, did many thousands of others.

Both centers of opposition to the feudal outlook, in the cities and among the peasantry, are usually neglected in "medieval" studies, which present a picture of absolute homogeneity. Even in so comparatively advanced a study as Arnold Hauser's *The Social History of Art,* for instance, we come across the phrase, "the mind of the Middle Ages."[76] And we are always hearing about "the Medieval man." John Ball, however, also had a "mind" and an "opinion." A priest, he was as much a "Medieval man" as Thomas Aquinas or Albertus Magnus; in fact, he doubtless had a much larger following in his day than either.

Art

THE FEUDAL IMPRINT

Except for literature the dominant art of commercial-feudal Europe was feudal and church controlled. Its illuminated manuscripts are similar to those of Persia or India, and, colorfully beautiful though they are, they represent the same kind of static and stylized endeavor. Its great cathedrals are, it is true, in a different style of architecture from the Indian (or Indo-Chinese) temples, but the genre is the same. Both represent massive power plus minute detail, works of great expenditure of labor for the overawing of the people by feudal church grandeur. As European feudalism grew it was a powerful force, reinforced, as we have seen, by commercial ties to a greater degree than the Asian, and solidly based upon political amalgamations. It did not hesitate to flaunt its wealth and power, particularly that of its church. Armor and armorial bearings, silver and gold plate, religious and other tapestries, and so on, were also feudal forms of art, and, again, had long existed in Asia.

Nevertheless advances were made. The European feudal arts had their own stamp. European castles, armor, or tapestries were not copies of the Asian or the earlier European (Greek, Roman). Tapestry weaving (especially with the use of wool) became almost a new art. In painting, a major technical advance was made in the development of perspective, and in the works of Giotto and others, painting began to depict individual human emotion and give a sense of movement. In architecture, the Romanesque style, with its solid walls and rounded domes, began to give way to the Gothic; and the Gothic was a genuinely new form, not previously seen in Europe or Asia, which combined soaring height with grace and power. With the coming of this style, another art was born, namely, that of stained glass, for, with the use of high sweeping walls with tall windows, stained glass was needed to bring in only the subdued light held necessary for church atmosphere. In music these centuries saw the coming of the staff or representational method of musical notation and the development of polyphonic music. The latter has been termed "the most significant innovation in the entire history of music," for it marked the differentiation between modern European music and previous musics.

Beowulf

Feudalism in northern west Europe emerged from a farming society with considerable sea trading. Feeling for the land is not prominent in its early literature; the real love of its writers, as with the Homeric poems, is the sea. The *Beowulf* poet (about 750) rises to his heights in the description of ships on the waves (chanted aloud with emphasis on the alliterative words the Ur-English is detectable):

> Gewat tha ofer waeg-holm winde gefysed
> flota fami-heals, fugle gelicost.
>
> (Went then over the wave-sea by the wind driven
> The foam-necked floater likest a bird.)

The warriors have a sense of comradeship each to each, and the chiefs decide in council and not individually, but the feudal loyalties are developing, and nothing is worse than to be excluded from the "court" by exile, as the "Wanderer" found. Here is a new poetry arising, one with its own style and manner. But to read the poetry alone is deceptive, for in it the old tribal ideals linger—as they did in Homer also—and we get an impression of a more primitive order than actually existed. It is somewhat startling to note, for instance, that at the same time that the *Beowulf* poet was hailing the *comitatus* warriors with their ships and combats, the "Venerable" Bede was living among flourishing towns and writing his elegant *Ecclesiastical History*.

The art of early feudal Europe, to judge from the English literature of the time (and later echoes in the Icelandic sagas), was a mixture of communal, feudal, and sea-trading elements. In all these respects it exhibits parallels to the Homeric poems. If we ask ourselves why *Beowulf* did not rise to the sustained heights of the Homeric epics, the answer is that the two societies were on very different levels. Both had communal, feudal, and sea-trading elements but there was nothing in eighth century England or the North Sea area to compare to the rich sea trade of the early Mediterranean.

Sir Gawain AND *Piers Plowman*

As the usual process of land concentration continued and the great estates began to dominate, the communal element declined and the feudal strengthened. Nor was there, later, a simple decline of the feudal and rise of the commercial. Both developed but the commercial developed more rapidly.

It was from these components that the three main types of art in European feudal-commercial civilization arose. Peasant art is generally recognized as a separate form—as "folk" art, "folk" songs and stories (for instance the Robin Hood ballads), "folk" music and dances and weaving, and so on. So, too, is feudal art, especially that of the church. But the art which stems from commercial city life is usually lost under the general catchall "medieval." To see what it is we have only to turn our gaze from the baronial castles to the sophisticated vitality of Boccaccio's *Decameron*. There were, of course, areas of overlap. Indeed, from a quite early period on we can perceive a commercial influence in European feudal art.

In English literature (which I shall take as representative) we find all three influences. The radical, peasantlike atmosphere of *The Vision of Piers the Ploughman* is apparent from its beginning, its survey of society in the vision of the "fair field full of folk." Langland uses the traditional folk alliterative verse (which the worldly wise Chaucer laughed at as "rum, ram, ruff"). I give a literal rendering as best able to catch the spirit of the verse.

> A fair field full of folk / found I there between,
> Of all manner of men / the poor and the rich,
> Working and wandering / as the world requires
> Some put them to the plow / played very seldom,
> At planting and sowing / toiled full hard,
> And earned what wasters / with gluttony destroy.

Langland angrily condemns holy "pilgrims and palmers" who visit "saints in Rome" and then have "leave to lie all their life after." His political views come out in his picture of the king: "Then come there a king / the barons led him. / The might of the Commons / made him to reign." The power of the king, that is to say, rests upon the House of Commons, not on "divine right" or baronial influence.

Little is known of the author of the poem. He was not a peasant, for peasants were nonliterate, and he was no revolutionary but stood for the *status quo* without excessive abuses. The peasant influence, however, is dominant. His hero is a peasant who leads the people, commoners and nobles alike, to Truth. He places his faith in parliament rather than in royalty. The first version of the poem was written nineteen and the second four years before the Peasants' Revolt, and we can sense in it the social pressures of this growing rebellion, exerting themselves in various, often indirect, ways. He gives the impression of being, like Wycliffe, an intensely religious man sympathetic towards the peasant cause, perhaps a poor member of the lower clergy.

In *Sir Gawain and the Green Knight* we are in a different world, the world of great castles and gracious ladies, of knightly honor and religious ceremony. The setting is one of aristocratic magnificence:

> To his steward the lord turned, and strictly commanded
> To send men to Gawain to give him good service;
> And prompt at his bidding were people in plenty.
> To a bright room they brought him, the bed nobly decked
> With hangings of pure silk with clear golden hems
> And curious coverings with comely panels,
> Embroidered with bright fur above at the edges. . . .

There is no talk here of peasants or poverty, of parliaments guiding kings or dishonest bishops deceiving the people. The author toys with the picturesque and the artificial, the well-turned "conceit," the resonant phrase; his very language, in fact, although northern in dialect, is contrived, a speech no one spoke, or, indeed, wrote. Within this framework he achieves some extraordinary beauties of scene and image, as had Kalidasa in *Shakuntala* a thousand years before — as colorfully woven and as motionless.

CHAUCER

Turning to Chaucer we are in a third world. His father and grandfather were London wine merchants. Chaucer himself was successively customs official, Member of Parliament (elected from Kent); Clerk of the King's Works at Westminster. Records of his house leases (still extant) show that he lived most of his life in London. His political views seem to have been akin to those of John of Gaunt (with whom he had connections) but his social views are primarily those of the London professional and mercantile classes. No matter what Chaucer's connection with Gaunt or the royal court, he would never have been treated by them as an equal but as a civil servant who had come from a family "in trade." It is hardly surprising then that at the beginning of the *Canterbury Tales* Chaucer enters a sardonic disclaimer of the aristocratic code of rank:

> Also, I pray that you'll forgive it me
> If I have not set folk, in their degree
> Here in this tale, by rank as they should stand.
> My wits are not the best, you'll understand.

Of the 35 persons on the pilgrimage there is no representative of the aristocracy or the church hierarchy. The only people of high rank are the knight (a professional soldier under a "liege-lord"), the monk, and the prioress. The rest are the knight's son, the knight's servant (a forester), three priests and a nun, a friar, a merchant, a poor student, a lawyer, a small property owner (franklin), five guild members (a haberdasher, a carpenter, a weaver, a dyer, a carpet maker), a cook, the captain of a trading ship, a doctor, a woman weaver who owned property (the Wife of Bath), a village priest, a tenant farmer (plowman), a miller, a food buyer for a law college, an estate manager (reeve), a court summoner, a seller of church pardons, an innkeeper, a minor church official (canon) and his servant. Within a short time Chaucer tells us he had himself "spoken with them everyone" and had been accepted into their "fellowship." When we realize that most of these people would have been considered "riff-raff" by the aristocracy, the degree of Chaucer's break with feudal customs becomes apparent. It is manifested also in his continuous and biting attacks on corruption in the church hierarchy—in contrast to the lowly village priest, who seems to have been a follower of Wycliffe (a "Lollard").

On the other hand, Chaucer's range, which at first seems so large, begins to shrink if we consider the total society. He only touches on the vast world of the peasantry or of the city workers. His attitude towards the Peasants' Revolt varies from condemnation—"The murmur, the churls' rebelling"—to wry humor: ". . . Jack Straw and his army / Never made shouts half so shrill, / When they would any Fleming kill, / As that day was made upon the fox."

He sometimes depicts lower middle class people with condescension—the carpenter in *The Miller's Tale*, the miller and his wife and daughter in *The Reeve's Tale*. The "swiving" of the miller's wife and daughter by the university students is regarded as comic but a reverse situation in which a miller "swived" the wife and daughter of an aristocrat would not be tolerated. Chaucer is clearly fond of the Wife of Bath, but he makes fun of her in a way he would not dream of doing were she a lady of rank. To all this—as to the peasant world—he is oblivious. It is the "normal" way for "people" to think.

The literary future, however, at least in the immediately succeeding centuries, lay with Chaucer and not with Langland. The peasants had no place to go. The capitalists and city professionals did. Shakespeare and Milton, Defoe and Fielding were in various ways the heirs of Chaucer. Langland was forgotten. Chaucer's attitude of combined ridicule and affection, indeed, is very similar to that of another port-city writer, Ihara Saikaku, with his barrel makers and bawds some 300 years later in Osaka. Chaucer is, in fact, much closer to Saikaku than to the author of *Sir Gawain and the Green Knight*.

There was, as we have seen, a convention in Greek and Roman (and most other) literatures that women had to be depicted either unsympathetically or superficially. In tragedy they were often powerfully depicted—Medea, Clytemnestra, Antigone—but serious treatment also meant that they had to be shown as bringing about evil. In comedy they are generally ridiculed. In the epic they are treated superficially. Penelope is little more than a symbol of patience, Nausicaa is charming but without depth, Dido is a puppet of stock "female" emotions. Ovid liked women but did not depict them seriously. When we come to Chaucer's Cressida (in *Troilus and Cressida*) we are in a different world:

> Among the small, this lady seemed not small,
> She had a figure of proportioned kind,
> Yet not the slightest mannish or too tall,
> For nature had her frame so well designed,
> And all her motions showed so well her mind,
> That men could tell, in such there would reside
> Honor and dignity and woman's pride.

Cressida can hold her own in intellectual repartee with men; she is shown as reading a book of history; she sees through the most complex plots of Pandarus with quick insight; her love with Troilus is depicted as passionate and beautiful (a far cry from the bawdy-wench scenes of Petronius or Apuleius).

Cressida is, it is true, an upper class woman, and, it is true also that it is only upper class women that Chaucer treats seriously. But he can write appreciatively of the women of the lower classes, as in his picture of Alison, the carpenter's young wife in *The Miller's Tale:*

> Her fillet was of wide silk worn full high:
> And certainly she had a lickerish [flirting] eye.
> She'd thinned out carefully her eyebrows two,
> And they were arched and black as any sloe.
> She was a far more pleasant thing to see
> Than is the newly budded young pear-tree.

Chaucer's depiction of women (and his attitude on other matters) again shows that we should not make blanket deductions about the influence of the church and its ascetic ideals (with their usual antifeminism). The church was influential, it is true, but its influence was limited, and people did not by any means live in rigid accordance with its prescriptions. Chaucer's views also show that in commercial-feudal society a certain personal and intellectual equality between men and women existed, at least in the professional class.

"In Chaucer's greatest work," writes John Livingstone Lowes, "we have to do with timeless creations on a time-determined stage." Both statements are incorrect; and yet both have a seed of truth. Chaucer's characters are not "timeless"—illustrative of the "permanent" characteristics of "human nature." And his "stage" was determined not by "time" but by a specific society, a society, however, which shared certain characteristics with others. His aloofness from the peasant mass and his shunning of political conflict is typical of many intellectuals in civilized societies, but it did not exist in food-gathering or early farming societies.

Attitudes or ideas obviously cannot come into being unless the social processes which they reflect exist. Some of the *general* modes of thought and behavior Chaucer depicts have been typical of all societies, for instance, on the relations of lovers (with their mutual confessions), the relations of mother and child, family life, humorous byplay (as that between Cressida and Pandar), and so on. The difference between Chaucer's actions or feelings on these matters and those of the Australian natives or the food-gathering peoples of 20,000 years ago is one not of kind but of degree. All societies, as we have seen, have had elements in common and there can be a community of feeling in regard to these elements. The spirit of buffoonery in Chaucer or Aristophanes is in essence the same as that in food-gathering societies. Yet the specific differences between the two are considerable.

DANTE

In Chaucer we have one representative figure of the commercial-city art of European feudal-commercial society. Let us turn to southern Europe for another—a very different one.

The political situation in Dante's Italy (about 1300) differed greatly from that in Chaucer's England (about 1400). Although both were commercial-feudal societies with the feudal interests predominant in the country and the commercial in the cities, the struggle between commerce and feudalism was rather passive in England at the time, whereas in Italy, particularly in Florence, a bloody power struggle was occurring. Business interests, led by the guilds, established a kind of guild State, with guild-controlled councils, assemblies, and magistrates, and a political party called "the Whites." The ruling political body was a council consisting of six "priors" elected from the guilds. The landed interest, in opposition, united in "the Blacks." In May 1300 the Blacks, led by the great Donati family, conspired with the Pope to take power. The Pope, in turn, called upon Charles of Valois, brother of the King of France, and Charles in 1301 invaded Florence and crushed the Whites with the assistance of the Blacks.

Dante was intimately associated with these events. He came from a family which had feudal origins but which for three generations had been "burghers." In 1300 he was elected a "prior." Although as a guild member he was naturally a White, he acquiesced in a ruling of the priors to exile the heads of both Whites and Blacks (perhaps in a vain effort to avert civil war). When that civil war broke out and the Blacks triumphed, Dante himself was, in turn, exiled and forbidden to return to Florence on pain of being burned to death. For the rest of his life he roamed through various Italian states, a bitter and shaken man, forlornly placing his hope in the unification of Italy by an "emperor." He refused an offer to return to Florence on terms he disapproved. He was buried at Ravenna. His great work *The Comedy* (later called *The Divine Comedy*) was a product of the commercial democracy of Florence and its antifeudal struggles. Without the freedoms gained by the guilds a mind of such depth and scope as Dante's could not have developed, no matter what his potential; without the political struggle he would not have achieved that acid intensity, humanitarian feeling, and intellectual scope which suffuse his poetry. Defeat and exile forced him to that reexamination of "times past" which created *The Comedy*.*
It is at once a political poem (especially *The Inferno*) reviewing the

---

*Comedy, that is to say, in the earlier sense of the word, to designate any work which ends happily (in heaven).

struggles in Florence, a personal poem turning deep into the author's life and mind, and a philosophical poem of "man's fate" viewed in terms of religious affirmation.

All three elements are apparent in the famous opening canto (in John Ciardi's translation):

> Midway in our life's journey, I went astray
> from the straight road and woke to find myself
> alone in a dark wood. How shall I say
>
> what wood that was! I never saw so drear,
> so rank, so arduous a wilderness!
> Its very memory gives a shape to fear. . . .
>
> And there I lay to rest from my heart's race
> till calm and breath returned to me. Then rose
> and pushed up that dead slope at such a pace
>
> each footfall rose above the last. And lo!
> almost at the beginning of the rise
> I faced a spotted Leopard, all tremor and flow
>
> and gaudy pelt. And it would not pass, but stood
> so blocking my every turn that time and again
> I was on the verge of turning back to the wood.
>
> This fell at the first widening of the dawn
> as the sun was climbing Aries with those stars
> that rode with him to light the new creation.
>
> Thus the holy hour and the sweet season
> of commemoration did much to arm my fear
> of that bright murderous beast with their good omen.
>
> Yet not so much but what I shook with dread
> at sight of a great Lion that broke upon me
> raging with hunger, its enormous head
>
> held high as if to strike a mortal terror
> into the very air. And down his track,
> a She-Wolf drove upon me, a starved horror
>
> ravening and wasted beyond all belief
> She seemed a rack for avarice, gaunt and craving.
> Oh many the souls she has brought to endless grief!

The political symbolism is not difficult to interpret. Dante, "in the middle of the journey" of his life entered the "dark wood" of Florentine politics. Ascending the hill of life he faces three beasts, the Leopard of Florence, the Lion of France, and the She-Wolf of the Papacy—the three forces which defeated him and the Whites. Driven back down the hill of life (his exile), bewildered and frightened, he meets the spirit of the last great Italian national poet, Virgil, and asks him for help. The answer Virgil gives him is that the Papacy—"that mad beast"—will persecute and kill until a new national Italian state is reestablished under an emperor (the Greyhound). Dante must seek "another road." He will not find the way to understanding by personal brooding over the past but only by looking at it through the vaster perspectives of life and death (Hell, Purgatory, and Paradise).

We are aware, at once, of being in an atmosphere very different from that of *The Canterbury Tales,* an atmosphere of intense personal suffering, bitter social conflict, and deep philosophical searching. And this continues throughout the *Inferno;* for instance, in the scene of Dante's confrontation with Farinata degli Uberti, who was one of the leaders of the feudal army that invaded Florence and conquered its guild democracy: "dyed the Arbia red."

The bitterness of the words shows us how savage was this strife, as two representatives of the contending factions face each other, Dante taunting Farinata with the defeat of the feudal forces and charging that the subsequent strife arose because of his bloody attack on the Florentine democracy; Farinata, the haughty and unyielding aristocrat, "predicting" the defeat and exile of his foe.

In the *Purgatory* a quieter and more contemplative mood begins, which in the *Paradise* rises to one of religious visioning: "A light there is up yonder which maketh the Creator visible unto the creature, who only in beholding him hath its own peace."[77]

Dante's great poem reflects both the particular and the general, in social, biological, and psychological life. His sufferings and exaltations, his brooding on death, his feeling about people, all follow, in their essence, a general pattern, but their particular forms are specific. Dante's hatreds arise out of the political strife of a particular city at a particular time, his manner of brooding about death is that of the Church of his time—even though he fought that Church as a political body—his concept of nature is that of the limited knowledge of his time.

In spite of certain general similarities of outlook, Chaucer and Dante were very different poets—Dante a vigorous participant in a bitter civil war, spiritually scarred, lashing back at his foes from the dark cave of his exile, Chaucer, a prosperous government administrator whose worst experience was to lose his job in the customs office when the Lord Appellants took over. Chaucer could afford the luxury of easy humor and an easy style; Dante could not. Dante has a compact and savage power that Chaucer never approaches. On the other hand, Chaucer's intellectual skepticism is a refreshing contrast to Dante's naïve religious visioning. Both were "medieval men," but neither fits the stereotype.

XI

The Capitalist Revolution

in Europe

I: SOCIETY

THAT SOMETHING NEW in the history of humanity was taking place in the centuries immediately following the development of commercial-feudal states in Europe—say from 1500 to 1850—is apparent from the course of its social and cultural events. At first it might seem that these events are unrelated, but certain group relationships are generally recognized, as is shown by the various "movements" into which historians have divided them. Leonardo, Galileo, and Shakespeare, for instance, are regarded as part of "The Renaissance," Luther of "The Reformation," Rousseau and Voltaire of the "Age of Enlightenment," Watt's steam engine and the first iron bridge of the "Industrial Revolution," Byron and Shelley of the "Romantic" movement. That there was also a fundamental development of which these "movements" were part is indicated by the fact that at one end of the period we find commercial-feudal society, and at the other end capitalist society. The capitalist differs from other societies in various major respects: industry, not agriculture, predominates; the main economy is integrated, mechanized, and concentrated (into factories, etc.); the basic labor is paid labor; the ruling class is the capitalist class. This fundamental development I shall call the "capitalist revolution." I use the word "capitalist" to include the production of industrial raw materials, the manufacturing of both industrial and agricultural raw materials into finished products, the transportation and sale of all goods, and banking and other financial transactions—all privately owned and operated for profit. I use the word "revolution" in its broadest sense to encompass economic, social, political, and cultural changes. Political revolutions, such as the French Revolution, I consider part of the general capitalist revolution; so, too, the "Industrial Revolution."

The capitalist revolution was not limited to Europe. We find similar changes in America and Asia and, somewhat later, in Africa and Oceania. In America commercial-feudal and commercial-slave societies developed into capitalist societies, and there were revolutions and wars for national independence. In Asia, as we have seen, Japan and parts of China were well along on the same path, and some areas in West Asia were beginning to move in this direction also.

Although I have given as the "period" of the capitalist revolution the centuries from 1500 to 1850, the real question, as always, is not that of period but process. We are dealing not with a mechanism but sociocultural growth. And all we can say is that the main functioning of the process took place within a certain period. By about 1500 the commercial economy in the main European states had begun the long journey to overtake the feudal-agricultural economy and to change it more and more from self-sufficiency to dependence on trade. The capitalists dominated in politics in the major cities and in some countries were gaining national influence.

By 1850 capitalism was the dominant economic form in Europe and North America and the capitalist class either was or was becoming the central economic, social, political, and cultural force in the major European countries. As in any extensive sociocultural process, however, these various components did not march along one line. The capitalists had great economic power and social influence, yet after they became politically dominant, the social and cultural influence of the great landowners persisted in various ways. In some respects the capitalist revolution continued beyond 1850, and is still continuing today. Following the mid-nineteenth century there came a great rise in industrialization in Europe and America, which brought various political, social, and cultural changes with it. And in Asia, Africa, Latin America, and Oceania, the capitalist revolution is occurring in some form in many areas. But if we look at the phenomenon in terms of the broader perspectives of world history, we can see that in Europe and America the basic forms of capitalist civilization had been established by the mid-nineteenth century; and in other areas the manifestations of the capitalist revolution have become repetitions with decreasing significance as the present century is being dominated, directly or indirectly, by the new phenomenon of the socialist revolution (in its various phases).

The Economic Revolution

The power-sources of water, wind, and horse which arose in com-mercial-feudal society spread in the succeeding centuries. So, too, did the old tools and implements—the iron plow, the blacksmith's bellows, and so on. But more important were the new economic productive forces, forces which humanity had not previously possessed.

To the old sources of power was added one more, namely steam (in conjunction with coal), and the place of tools as the basic productive instrument was taken by the machine (the spinning jenny, the steam hammer, the rolling mill, the power loom). It is obvious that these things would, in themselves, bring about an unprecedented increase in goods of all kinds (including many never seen before), but this is only part of the story. As production increased the population increased: in 1650 the population of Europe was 100 million, in 1850 it was 266 million. This increase in population, representing, as it did, also an increase in the labor force, produced further increases in production. Furthermore, the labor force was becoming more concentrated in cities and machine-operating factories, and, hence, more efficient.

All these new socioeconomic forces added to those still continu-ing from the past made possible an increase of goods on a scale and at a rate previously unknown and unimagined. For the early years of our period, before accurate statistics were kept on such matters, it is not easy to give an exact picture, but certain figures exist and they suffice to show that the new high rate of increase was under way in the sixteenth century. For instance, the English company of the Merchant Adven-turers exported 22,000 pieces of cloth in 1500, in 1600 70,000; the cloth production for Leyden was 27,000 pieces in 1584, 110,000 pieces in 1619, in 1560 the English merchant fleet totalled 7,600 tons, in 1691, 500,000 tons.

For the later years of the period there are—especially for England, where many of these developments first took place—more complete figures. For instance, the English export of cotton cloth from 1710 to 1831 has been estimated as follows (in thousands of pounds sterling):

1710	5	1790	1,662
1751	45	1800	5,406
1780	355	1831	17,200

Alongside the old commodities came new ones, and these soon became more important than the old ones. Chief among these were coal and iron. Wood had been the staple fuel for all civilized societies (and in food-gathering and farming societies also). Coal, as we have seen, had been used in China for many centuries but it had been used for domestic purposes only; it is mentioned as a curiosity by Theophrastus in 271 B.C.; it had been used sporadically in Europe since feudal times, but even about 1550 the total coal production of England amounted only to "a few hundred tons a year."[1] The smelting of iron had been done by charcoal (made from wood); and, as we have seen, it had been "wrought" laboriously by hand (not "cast") at small blacksmith-type forges. Iron, too, was of comparatively little importance. In the 1530's the total output of the forges of Styria (in Austria), one of the leading iron centers of Europe, was only 8,000 tons. But when it was learned how to use coal for iron production (creating higher temperatures), the casting of iron supplanted hand manufacturing. This development — plus the invention of pumps which made possible the mining of coal at great depths — converted the production of both coal and iron into major new industries.

Coal production in tons (Great Britain)

1700..................	3,000,000	1841..................	35,000,000
1800..................	10,000,000		

(France in 1800 produced 1 million tons, 3 million in 1841; Germany and Luxembourg together 1 million in 1800, 3 million in 1841.)

Iron production in tons (Great Britain)

1740..................	20,000	1860..................	3,800,000
1800..................	150,000		

Great strides were also made in farming. Machines such as the sowing drill and the cotton gin (from the United States) in time began to take over; the old practice of allowing land to lie fallow was abandoned for the system of crop rotation (thus increasing considerably the total land under cultivation at any given time); new crops were introduced (notably the potato and the beet); new methods of fertilizing and tilling the soil were discovered; the size of meat animals was greatly increased by selective breeding (the average weight of sheep at Smithfield market in 1710 was 28 pounds, of beef cattle, 370 pounds; in 1795 sheep averaged 80 pounds, beef cattle, 800 pounds); new land was put under cultivation (between 1700 and 1844 in England, 1.7 million acres of waste land were so cultivated); large tracts of common lands were legally stolen (4.2 million acres in England between 1700 and 1844) and put under more effective cultivation; the comparatively inefficient peasant labor was more and more supplanted by paid farm labor; rural workers acquired new agricultural skills.

These economic changes in industry and farming produced others. For instance, the new bulk of goods necessitated new forms of transportation. They could not be handled by wagons on land or small wooden ships at sea; railways and metal ships were needed, and, having been made possible by a series of other inventions – the steam engine, rails, and flanged wheels – were themselves invented. Metal ships and locomotives could not be produced by wooden machinery; metal machinery became necessary; and little by little the old wooden machinery which had been standard since the days of Egypt was supplanted by iron and steel machinery. And all these new machines, ships, and trains further stimulated the iron and coal industries and all began to climb in interlocking spirals.

Production and distribution on this new scale could not be handled by the old economic structure. For instance, although there were, as we have seen, factories in many towns, most manufacturing was handled by the "putting-out" system. In this system the main relations of production and distribution were those of the merchant, the merchant's agent, and the craftsman. The merchant bought the raw material – wool or flax – from the farmer; the merchant's agent took the raw material to the craftsman; the craftsman (sometimes also a small farmer and usually working in his home assisted by his family) carded, combed, and dyed the raw material and wove it into cloth; the agent then collected the finished product, paid the craftsman, and returned the finished product to the merchant, who put it on the market. Even as late as 1779 the total equipment required by a craftsman cost less than £10. But development of steam power and the power loom spelled the end of the putting-out system. Only a capitalist could afford a power loom; and power looms were most economically operated several at a time and, hence, in one place. Their increase was astronomical; the power loom was invented in 1785; in 1835 there were 122,801 in operation in Great Britain. The factory system, already long established in some localities, became the dominant system. And so, too, in the metal trades. The production of small quantities of "wrought" iron could be handled in individual forges. But with the coming of the cylindrical bellows, the blast furnace, the extensive casting of iron and other metals, the days of the individual forge were over and the great metalworks began to rise. So, too, with coal mining. The situation of the individual landowner working his "outcroppings" was ended by the demands of industry and the steam engine pump.

These changes in production, transportation, and economic organization necessitated changes in the financial structure. Banks had greatly to expand their activities; credit had to be extended in a wider circle; the stock market, with its accompanying financial ramifications, was born to meet the new scale of stock and bond transactions. Great insurance companies (including Lloyds of London) sprang up.

Colonization

It is obvious that economic developments of this nature would result in social and political upheavals. The rise of the commercial economy produced more and wealthier capitalists. From what we know of previous European history, we could safely predict that these capitalists would challenge the political power of the landed aristocracy. We could predict also that there would be commercial wars, similar to those in the Italian city states but on a larger scale, and that the tempo of both exploration and colonization would be stepped up. We could predict, that is to say, the general course of events in Europe from 1500 to 1850 if we were given no more than these economic facts and the history of the previous three or four centuries. We could not, of course, predict the actual events themselves; but the socio-evolutionary pattern could not have been otherwise. When the actual events did take place, the people participating in them of course had no knowledge of the existence of this underlying pattern — which produced a society that nobody planned and everybody had to live in. They saw only the events themselves and the immediate motives for them, kingly ambition, religious rivalry, national pride, and so on.

In surveying these events we have first — as in Asia — to separate those which were truly developmental from those which were mainly motion. Redivisions of territory between great landowning powers, for instance, no matter how intricate the diplomatic maneuverings or how long the wars which brought them about, were of little consequence, whereas the Dutch war for independence or the French Revolution were socially evolutionary.

The first obvious indication that something really new was stirring in society came in the voyages of exploration and the following colonization. Europeans since the days of the Roman Empire and before had traded with India and China either by a completely overland route or partly by land and partly by water (ship across the Mediterranean; overland transport to the Red Sea; ship to India), both very expensive. In the late fifteenth century voyages were undertaken to find a sea route all the way.

In considering colonization the first fact that emerges is that certain European countries were colonizing powers in this period and others were not. Spain, Portugal, Britain, France, and the Netherlands were; Italy, Germany, Russia, and Austria were not. One would think that this cleavage required some explanation, but one seldom finds it, at least in the general European or American histories. The implication is left hanging that some countries were "natural" colonizing powers, others were not. But although all the reasons for the cleavage may not be apparent, some certainly are. Britain and the Netherlands were commercial powers fronting the Atlantic, and although France, Spain, and Portugal were predominantly feudal, all three had large port cities which were at least semi-independent of the national landowning power. Furthermore, many of their landowners were tied in with commercial interests. Of the three, France and Portugal fronted the Atlantic and did considerable Atlantic-shore trading; the Portuguese, in fact, had moved out to the Azores by the middle of the fifteenth century. Spain had long had Atlantic interests (as the Spanish Armada and the struggle with the Netherlands show), and was being pressed in the Mediterranean by Italy. In seeking new markets, all these powers moved out further into the Atlantic and beyond into the Indian and Pacific Oceans. On the other hand, Russia, the Austrian dominions, and Germany were predominantly feudal — Germany being split into a group of feudal kingdoms — and their foreign trade was internal, European, or Asian, not Mediterranean or oceanic. Italy was, it is true, commercial, but Italy was split into a series of city states; and city states although suitable for Mediterranean commerce — largely in luxury items — were not individually able to create the economic, political, or military power required to seize and rule overseas colonies.

The colonizing powers moved ahead at a rapid pace. By the end of the sixteenth century the Spanish upper classes had seized vast tracts of North and South America, part of the West Indies and all of the Philippines, the Dutch had seized the East Indies and part of South Africa, the British and French, parts of North America, the Portuguese, a large section of South America and parts of Africa; Portuguese, British, French, and Dutch trading posts had been established in India. "The [Dutch East India] Company was soon following a policy of restricting production and paying low prices. When the natives refused to grow a crop for the prices the company was willing to pay, they were reduced to virtual slavery and forced to continue."[2] The profits — up to 5000 percent — of the Dutch East India Company, in brief, came from the seizure of the land and resources of the people of the East Indies and the virtual enslavement of the working population by those stolid Dutch burghers who stare out in florid benignity from the portraits of Hals and Vermeer.

In the seventeenth and eighteenth centuries the British and French further extended their conquests, partly at the expense of the Spanish and Portuguese. How extensively — and profitably — is shown by the fact that British colonial trade rose from £1.6 million in 1698 to £9.5 million in 1775!

The colonization of America in effect expanded the North Sea out into the Atlantic. New sources of raw material (minerals, lumber) and of agricultural produce (sugar, tobacco, maize, rubber) worked by serf and slave labor (the Indians and imported Africans) brought about a production of wealth on a new scale. And as America was colonized and ruling class outposts established it became a market for European goods.

There has never been colonization of quite this type before. The great feudal empires (Assyrian, Persian, Mongol) were mostly an amalgamation of predominantly agricultural territories usually adjoining each other. The slave-commercial empires, particularly the Roman, were, of course, similar in certain respects to this later European colonization—they were, for instance, more commercially than agriculturally motivated and had a similar political-administrative set-up—but they had not the economic resources to cross oceans and hold far-flung territories (and, hence, were limited in space), they were more dependent on booty and less on trading profits, they needed conquered peoples for domestic (slave) labor, and were unable to build manufacturing-commercial colonies like those in British North America.

What motivated the capitalist class in these various enterprises? Obviously the same thing that had always motivated it (in Greece, Rome, Carthage, China, or Japan)—the search for profits. Profits are to a capitalist class what land is to a landowning class. Capitalists make profits or die. They make them not primarily because of individual greed, which is pretty much a constant, but because they are part of a competitive structure. They built up a great network of factories, banks, trade routes, not because they intended to but because they had to in order to survive and develop. Each capitalist who built a factory built it to make money, not to establish a cog in a planned total system. But the sum total of these factories, banks, and trade routes nevertheless made up an economic system (with social and political ramifications) and the capitalists themselves became little by little a part of the system they had built.

If we consider the main economic facts we shall, as usual, have a clue to the social structure. This structure at the beginning of the period was essentially the same as that of commercial-feudal society: great landowners and peasants in the country, capitalists, professionals, small businessmen-craftsmen and paid workers in the cities. By the middle of the eighteenth century this structure had in most of western Europe changed in several major respects. As manufacturing and commerce spread there were more capitalists; as manufacturing moved to larger units the class of businessmen-craftsmen, which was as old as civilization, split into two: small businessmen and hired workers. By the middle of the nineteenth century a group of industrial capitalists, owners of the new industries, became the core of the class, and a group of industrial workers—particularly in the new mining and metal industries—similarly formed a new core for the working class.

The conflicts between and within these classes did not differ greatly in their general form from those of feudal or slave societies and early in the period were very much the same as those of commercial-feudal society. As the period wore on, socioeconomic developments changed the character of the conflicts. That between the capitalists and the great landowners became no longer one for the control of city councils but of nations. That between the capitalists and the mass of paid workers and small businessmen-craftsmen became more and more one between capitalists and workers, although it did not shape the main course of events. That shaping was done by the upper level conflict between capitalists and great landowners.

Two Centuries of War

Alongside these interclass conflicts there went, as ever, international ones (between the ruling classes of separate countries). As commercialism increased and feudalism declined, war was motivated more by a drive for profits (exploiting industrial labor) and less by a drive for land (exploiting peasant labor). In general the wars of the period resulted from conflict between national capitalists and the revolutions from conflict between the capitalists and the landowners.*

*The main wars of the period were as follows:

1588	England vs. Spain
1618–1648	The Thirty Years' War— Sweden and France vs. German states
1652–1657	Great Britain vs. Holland
1655–1658	Great Britain vs. Spain
1665–1667	Holland vs. Great Britain
1672–1676	Poland vs. Turkey
1672–1678	France and Great Britain vs. Holland
1689–1697	Great Britain, Spain, Portugal, German states, and Holland vs. France
1700–1721	Russia, Poland, and Denmark vs. Sweden
1701–1713	Great Britain, Holland, and Austria vs. France and Spain
1736–1739	Russia and Austria vs. Turkey
1743–1748	Great Britain, Holland, and Austria vs. France, Prussia, and Bavaria
1756–1763	Great Britain and Prussia vs. France, Russia, Sweden, Spain, and Austria
1780–1783	Great Britain vs. Holland
1792–1815	Great Britain, Austria, Prussia, and Russia vs. France

As we examine the wars, it becomes evident that the capitalists were increasingly the main beneficiaries from war in the seventeenth and eighteenth centuries. They were also the main instigators of some of them from at least the late sixteenth century on. In the war between England and Spain in 1588, which resulted in the defeat of the Spanish Armada, the English merchants not only outfitted but actually owned the fleet. The governing "Crown and Council" (controlled by the great landowners) had little heart for the fight. Even when the governments at war were controlled by the landowners and the landowners made some gains from them, the relative positions of the two classes changed in favor of the capitalists. As the centuries advanced this process became more and more evident, especially when colonial trade and territories were involved. For instance, by 1683 twenty French refineries were processing 18 million pounds of sugar obtained from the French West Indian colonies. These refineries were not owned by the French landowners but by French capitalists; and the trade was conducted in ships owned by other French capitalists. The landowners' revenue from their peasants remained relatively stable while the capitalists' revenues mounted.

Sometimes, in fact, the wars were really struggles between rival capitalist groups, for instance, those between Great Britain and Holland. In some of them international conflicts mingled with conflicts between classes. In the Thirty Years' War the continental landowners strove to overthrow the capitalist government of Holland, and similar motives instigated the wars against the young French republic. Others were fought for commercial and landowning advantage in Europe, for example, that between Russia and Sweden, 1700 to 1721, which gave Russian landowners more land and Russian merchants access to the Baltic. Others were primarily wars for land, for instance, that of Poland against Turkey. We might note also the shifting alliances. Sometimes England fought against Holland, sometimes England allied with Holland; sometimes France fought against Russia, sometimes as an ally of Russia, and so on. Catholics fought Protestants or other Catholics, and Protestants fought each other—depending on how the economic cards were stacked. And as usual the weaker powers diminished and the more powerful grew even more powerful. Thus the basically feudal powers of Spain and Portugal and the smaller commercial power of Holland were driven back by the advance of Great Britain and France; and the more industrialized Great Britain moved further and faster than France.

In most historical accounts of these wars, not only are these various economic and social factors glossed over but it is only by using our imaginations that we realize that they were wars, not sports events.

Casualties are seldom mentioned. In order to redress the balance let us look at the human losses of two of these wars, the so-called Seven Years' War between Great Britain, Prussia, France, and Spain from 1756 to 1763, and the wars against France from 1792 to 1815. I summarize from *Losses of Life Caused by War*, published by The Carnegie Endowment for International Peace.

In the Seven Years' War the Austrian losses alone have been computed as follows:

Killed	32,000
Died of wounds or disease	93,400
Missing	19,600
Prisoners	78,400
Deserters	62,200
Invalids	17,400
Total	303,000

In the war against the French Republic from 1791 to 1800 the French army dead, wounded, and missing had been calculated at 1.4 million. The total military losses of all countries in the war between France and the other European powers from 1801 to 1815 have been calculated as follows:

French War of Santo Domingo	160,000
British War (Egypt, 1802)	692
War with Great Britain, 1802–1814 (losses on both sides)	200,000
War with Great Britain, 1815 (both sides)	150,000
Calabria Revolution, 1805–1807	100,000
War in the North, 1806–1807	300,000
Spanish War, 1806–1807	2,400,000
War of Italy and Germany, 1809	300,000
Walcheren Expedition, 1809	4,392
Russian Campaign, 1812	800,000
German and French civil inhabitants	1,000,000
Wars of 1813 and 1814 (both sides)	450,000
Wars of 1815 (both sides)	60,000
Total	5,925,084

If we add these to the 1.4 million French losses from 1793 to 1800, the military losses in wars from 1793 to 1815 reached nearly 8 million. Although the majority of these losses were caused by disease and not by battle they were still losses in war, for without the war the people would not have died. In respect to disease there was a difference between land and sea warfare. As the authors of *Losses of Life Caused by War* note: "When an army has remained in one region for a considerable length of time and has engaged in several battles in that region, the ground naturally becomes full of organic detritus in which disease germs multiply with prodigious rapidity. In the case of the navy the sea is always there to swallow up everything."

One other statistic should be mentioned. In the British army between 1793 and 1815 the British upper classes, which made the major gains from the war, lost only 5,000 of their members; 80,000 sons of the lower classes were sacrificed for gains in trade and territory and some 3 to 4 million of the sons of lower classes in allied countries.

Although it is clear enough now from the record that the basic motive for these wars was economic aggrandizement, such was not the motive given at the time. Each war had its own particular slogan (as Candide discovered), each side was assured of Divine approval.

Just as it seems "understood" that slaughter in modern war "does not count" so, too, with past wars; and not only death in war but the whole mass of human suffering, a "martyrdom of man" monstrous beyond conception. The hard brutal realities are seldom faced, almost, it would seem, by mutual, if unspoken, agreement. The kingly "hand" (of Dylan Thomas' poem) might sign "the paper," but it was not the kingly hand that "felled" the "city." The city was felled by bodies and blood; each man of these millions that died was an individual. Nor does the fact that these men have long turned to dust or the cries of grief for them long faded diminish their reality.

The Reformation—Luther, Muenzer, Calvin

Blended with these economic, social, and political developments in their earlier stages was The Reformation. The term like others in the writing of history has grown out of hand. Properly used it refers to the "reform" of the church in Europe whereby it was split in the sixteenth century into a "Catholic" and a "Protestant" ("protest-ant") section, but it has come to be used incorrectly to represent virtually the whole of the social and cultural changes of the fifteenth and sixteenth centuries.

One of the practices which had grown up within the European Christian Church was that of selling an "indulgence" or pardon for sins. In the year 1517, the Pope, requiring funds for the repair of St. Peter's Church in Rome, had his agents peddle a large number of indulgences throughout Europe, with national sovereigns and others pushing them to get a "cut" from the total. Henry VIII of England, for instance, was to get 25 percent of the English "take." The indulgence (issued in the duchy of Brandenburg in Germany) which touched off the reformation of the church in Germany read as follows:

May our Lord Jesus Christ have mercy on thee, and absolve thee by the merits of His most holy Passion. And I, by His authority, that of his blessed Apostles Peter and Paul, and of the most holy Pope, granted and committed to me in these parts, do absolve thee, first from all ecclesiastical censures, in whatever manner they may have been incurred, and then from all thy sins, transgressions, and excesses, how enormous soever they may be, even from such as are reserved for the cognizance of the Holy See; and as far as the keys of the Holy Church extend, I remit to you all punishment which you deserve in purgatory on their account, and I restore you to the holy sacraments of the Church . . . and to that innocence and purity which you possessed at baptism; so that when you die the gates of punishment shall be shut, and the gates of the paradise of delight shall be opened; and if you shall not die at present, this grace shall remain in full force when you are at the point of death. In the name of the Father, and of the Son, and of the Holy Ghost.

This was, indeed, as Will Durant remarks, a "splendid bargain," for it not only absolved one from all past sins but future sins as well and carried with it an unconditional guarantee of immortal bliss. The problem was that it was a little too splendid. When word of it came to Martin Luther, a priest at the University of Wittenburg in adjoining Saxony, he pointed out in 95 "theses" nailed to a Wittenburg church door that such activities undermined the faith of the people in the church and its rulers:

This unbridled preaching of pardons makes it no easy matter, even for learned men, to rescue the reverence due the pope from . . . the shrewd questionings of the laity, to wit: "Why does not the pope empty purgatory for the sake of holy love and of the dire need of the souls that are there, if he redeems a . . . number of souls for the sake of miserable money with which to build a church?"

Luther argued also that the "word of God" lay not in the doctrine of the church but in the Bible—thus undermining church authority. Church courts and law should be done away with. "Salvation" can come not by "works" (giving money to the church, going to confession, etc.) but by "faith" in the divinity of Christ. In spite of these views the actual theological points at issue were trivial. Both Luther and the Pope agreed on all the basic beliefs of Christian theology as put forth in the Nicene Creed. And this remained so even after the Protestant churches split away from the Catholic.

At about the same time similar views were arising in Switzerland. John Calvin agreed with Luther—with one notable exception. "Salvation" came no more by "faith" than by "works," but was "predestined," decided by God for each individual before birth: "In conformity, therefore, to the clear doctrine of Scripture, we assert that by an eternal and immutable counsel God has once for all determined both whom He would admit to salvation, and whom He would condemn to destruction."

In England most of the ideas which Luther put forward in the sixteenth century had been put forward by John Wycliffe in the fourteenth. Wycliffe denounced the Pope as "this alien proudest priest of all," denied the (virtual) divinity of the priesthood, advocated withholding money from Rome, and based his theology on the Bible, which he translated into the vernacular. Like Luther's movement, Wycliffe's was associated with a peasant's revolt, that of 1381. Wycliffe was sympathetic toward the revolt, and the rebel leader, John Ball, himself a priest, claimed to have learned his communistic doctrine from him. It was perhaps because of this sympathy that Wycliffe's movement was suppressed. The next attack on "Rome" came with Henry VIII. Whatever the weaknesses of the religious reform movement under Henry, obscurity of motive was not one of them. When his government seized the lands of the monasteries and proclaimed Henry head of the church in England, it was a simple act of power politics. Why should he take a 25 percent cut when he could have it all? There was no question of a doctrinal clash. Church services and doctrine were left untouched. Henry and his advisors not only remained Catholics, but burned at the stake those who they suspected were not. Doctrinal controversy developed only later in the century.

Luther, too, had an economic motive: "Some have estimated that every year more than 300,000 gulden find their way from Germany to Italy. . . . *We here come to the heart of the matter.* . . . How comes it that we Germans must put up with such robbery and such extortion of our property at the hands of the pope?"[3]

Before the days of Luther, the German states had begun something of a commercial transformation (later and less extensive than in Britain). More landowners depended upon trade; capitalists bought their way into the aristocracy; landowners received income from mining and other rights; the capitalists gained political control in the cities. In the country, peasant revolts took place in 1431, 1476, 1491, 1502, 1512, and 1517, that of 1517 involving 90,000 peasants. In 1525 the Peasants' War began. But the State power everywhere remained firmly in the hands of the great landowners, who had managed to dam both the peasant and capitalist revolt until the mid-fifteenth century but did not have the centralized power necessary to break with Rome. Thus, whereas in England things happened by stages—peasants' revolt, a break with Rome, doctrinal change—in Germany, they happened all

304 / H u m a n i t y   a n d   S o c i e t y

at once. The Peasants' Revolution combined with the landowners' antipapal moves and the rise of the commercial classes in the cities. Luther's support came from large and middle landowners, who wanted both to break with Rome and suppress peasant revolt. His main patron was the Elector of Saxony, who derived much of his wealth by leasing out mining rights.

The movement for church reform in Germany, however, spread far beyond Luther; the peasants had a powerful religious movement of their own. In 1476, more than forty years before Luther wrote his theses, a peasant leader, Hans Boeheim, had preached to crowds of 40,000, demanding a communistic society and church. He raised a peasant army of 34,000, but it was defeated and he was burned alive. On the eve of the Peasant War, a delegated body, representing 30,000 peasants, met and drew up a credo of "Twelve Articles." The peasants were not interested in a mere change in church management, with the power centered in German instead of Italian great landowners, but a church over which they themselves had control. And they had their own religious leaders, the most influential of whom was Thomas Muenzer, a priest and Doctor of Divinity. Muenzer organized a great "union of the People" and became "the centre of the entire revolutionary movement of southwest Franconia and Suabia up to Alsace and the Swiss frontier." The power of his movement and the terror which it inspired in the landowners may be seen in its bloody ending:

> Muenzer stood with his people on the mountain which is still called Mount Battle (Schlachtberg), entrenched behind a barricade of wagons. . . . After a brief resistance, the line of the wagons was broken, the peasants' cannon captured, the peasants dispersed. They fled in wild disorder, and fell into the hands of the enveloping columns and the cavalry, who perpetrated an appalling massacre among them. The city was taken . . . Muenzer was put on the rack in the presence of the princes, and then decapitated.[4]

Luther at first supported the peasants, but when the revolt came, his tune changed: ". . . nothing can be more poisonous, hurtful, or devilish than a rebel. It is just when one must kill a mad dog; if you do not strike him he will strike you, and a whole land with you." Muenzer and other priests—as had John Ball in England—marched with the peasants and died with them. But not Luther. His outlook is that of the professional man attached to the landowning classes. He is mildly indignant about the oppression of the peasants by the aristocracy but rabid at the prospect of peasant oppression of the aristocracy. If the peasants wished to "be instructed," that was one thing; if they themselves decided to do the instructing, that was another.

The situation in Switzerland—which had considerable commerce and no peasant mass—was somewhat simpler than in Germany. In addition to predestination, Calvin preached another doctrine: "What reason is there why the income from business should not be larger than that from landowning? Whence do the merchant's profits come, except from his own diligence and industry?"[5] He advocated interest rates of 10 percent and state loans to finance industry. A far cry, indeed, from St. Jerome's dictum: "A merchant does not easily enter heaven."

Calvin's doctrinal views were, like Luther's, designed to change the existing church structure. The theory of predestination, for instance, meant that only the "elect" will be "saved"; and if the "elect" are chosen from eternity by God, the church has no control over such matters. Furthermore, if God chooses the "elect," he is just as likely to choose a businessman as an aristocrat, and, indeed, the "elect" were everywhere business or professional people.

The Political Revolution

The main political result of the events of the capitalist revolution in Europe was that the capitalist class became the ruling class, even though for some time after it took power it had to make compromises with the great landowners. It also had to face pressures from the small business, professional, and working people who had done the fighting that had put it in power. In feudal society the ruling class was well defined and its methods of rule were direct. In commercial-feudal society the situation was complicated by the fact that the landowners had to make concessions to the capitalists and other city classes. As capitalist society developed, the capitalist class itself split into more gradations, it had to rule indirectly (via parliaments), and it had to make adjustments with other classes. Nevertheless it was the ruling class.

What we witness in these centuries was neither, as some historians put it, an "advance" of the "middle classes"—which obscures the central role of the capitalists—nor a direct march of a single class to absolute power. Nor are we dealing with plots or executive decisions or individual ambitions or kingly quirks. As always, it was a sociological process in which, out of many crisscrossing currents, those emanating from the capitalist class emerge as dominant. For instance, the swift rise of industry and the comparatively slow development of agriculture made it inevitable that revolution would, like war, favor the commercially based classes over the agricultural, and, within these classes, especially favor the capitalists. So, too, with nonrevolutionary political advance. The kind of penetration the Fuggers made into the State in the sixteenth century increased all over Europe, and this kind of day-by-day undermining placed the class in a position both to instigate revolutions and to take full advantage of them whether they instigated them or not.

In discussing the capitalist advance I shall concentrate on Great Britain and France, for in them we can see different specific patterns and a general pattern in which both shared. Both, furthermore, stand at the beginning of a larger historical movement of similar revolutions which today may be witnessed on all continents. The techniques they display, particularly those of using lower classes for the achievement of power and later sloughing them off, have become standard procedure. For all, the British Revolution provides the original and classic pattern.

THE BRITISH REVOLUTION

The British capitalist class (English and Scottish) achieved power in two waves, the first in the seventeenth century, the second in the nineteenth, the first a revolution, the second a political "reform" movement. On both we have facts and figures in an abundance not previously available.

What is alternately called the English Civil War or the Puritan Revolution was primarily neither. There was, it is true, a civil war, and there was a revolution. But the civil war was not simply that and nothing more, and the revolution was not a "Puritan" one. Both were parts of a general social revolution which I call the British Revolution (on the analogy of the French Revolution), in which British commercial interests defeated the great landowners. This social revolution began with a civil war between classes and blended with a political revolution that concluded in the reforms of a commercially based government. The fact that the revolutionary leaders belonged to the Presbyterian and other dissenting churches loosely known as Puritan does not make the revolution a "Puritan" one. (Once more, as with the "Moslems," a historical event is titled by secondary characteristics, which obscures its real character.)

The British Revolution, although it had been gathering for some fifty years, grew immediately out of a conflict between the Lords and the Commons, with the king, Charles I, on the side of the Lords. In 1625 Parliament granted the king the privilege of receiving customs duties ("tonnage and poundage") for one year only but he continued to collect them beyond the expiration date and seized the goods of businessmen who refused to pay. In 1629 Parliament declared all who paid enemies of the realm. For the next eleven years the king governed without calling Parliament. Finally, desperate for funds, he had to do so. Parliament promptly struck back, abolished the repressive Star Chamber Court and passed a bill to raise an army. The king ordered the arrest of five leaders of the House of Commons. The Commons established a "committee of public safety" and put an army of 24,000 men into the field. The king moved to Nottingham in the north midlands, and the battle was joined. By 1645 the Royalist armies were defeated. In 1649 the king was executed, the House of Lords was abolished and a Commonwealth declared, its chief of state an elected official, Oliver Cromwell. Political power went to the House of Commons with its 460 members.

Even in this skeleton outline the general social character of the conflict is apparent. The king and the House of Lords were great landowners, church and secular, the Commons members were mainly city business and professional men and farmers of middle wealth. The conflict between the two groups was a continuation of that between business and agricultural interests which we saw in earlier commercial-feudal England, and, indeed in all feudal societies. But it was a continuation on a larger scale, and it ended, as no such previous conflict anywhere had, with the *national* triumph of the commercial forces. The reason was that these forces had a greater power relative to that of the landed interests than had ever previously existed. (And the same was true at the same time in Holland.) From a contemporary observer who had access to tax records and from an accounting of the estates of the Duke of Newcastle we derive the following rough figures on the per capita income of the landowning classes:[6]

Class	Number in class	Annual income
Great landowners	60	£22,000–3,000
Middle landowners	16,500	£2,000– 500
Small landowners	80,000	£500– 300

Comparable figures for the city classes do not seem to be available but general estimates can be made. In 1611 the East India Company made 211 percent profit, in 1612, 220 percent. "It is well known," reported a contemporary observer, "that at this time there are in London some merchants worth £100,000 and he is not accounted rich that cannot reach £50,000 or near it."[7] That rise of the commercial capitalists which we noted in earlier European commercial-feudal society as unprecedented had been surpassed. Their power was, in fact, even greater than the figures indicate, for their wealth was growing at a much faster rate than that of the aristocracy and was the concentrated wealth of a concentrated (city) class. Furthermore, the penetration of commercialism into the farming economy was continuing. Other landowners were beginning to exploit coal reserves and some entered manufacturing. The Sidneys, whose most distinguished member was Sir Philip, set up a cannon foundry on their estates and traded its products widely in Europe. Other landowners bought shares in commercial enterprises, such as the East India Company. As a result the unity of the great landowning class was undermined. When the civil war broke out some of the leading aristocratic families supported the Parliament.

The general line-up of forces was noted by a contemporary observer:

> A great part of the Lords forsook the Parliament. . . . A very great part of the knights and gentlemen of England in the several counties . . . adhered to the King. . . . And most of the tenants of these gentlemen, and also most of the poorest of the people, whom the other call the rabble, did follow the gentry and were for the King. On the Parliament's side were . . . the smaller part (as some thought) of the gentry in most of the counties, and the greatest part of the tradesmen and freeholders and the middle sort of men, especially in those corporations and counties which depend on clothing and such manufactures.[8]

The main power of the Parliament lay in the cities, particularly, of course, London. But on the whole the revolution did not go very deep either in town or country. It was not a mass revolution like the Peasants' Revolt of 1381. There were never more than 150,000 men under arms and they were mostly conscripted. Desertion was common. The great mass of the peasants, rural laborers, and city workers were not actively involved. On the one side were the great landowners and most of the middle landowners with their "tenants," and on the other a coalition of business and professional men, middle landowners, plus a few commercially oriented aristocrats.

The difference in the wealth and influence within the so-called middle classes must have been obvious from the beginning (although, as usual in such situations, it was considered impolitic to stress it). Everyone must have known that the East India Company capitalists would have more say in the revolutionary government than a similar sized group of smaller businessmen or lawyers. And so it turned out. In 1652 Cromwell took up the company's claims against the Dutch and after defeating the Dutch in war forced them to pay the company £85,000 indemnity. The most important economic measure passed by Parliament was the Navigation Act of 1651 whereby "No goods produced in Asia, Africa, or America were to be imported into England or its colonies save in English or colonial vessels." That this Act would assist British commerce in general was true, and in doing so it would spread some wealth among smaller businessmen, professionals, and paid workers, but it clearly helped the capitalists (shipbuilders, ship-owners, merchants, bankers) to a much greater degree than it did any other class. The Act began: "For the increase of the shipping and the encouragement of the navigation of this nation . . .," but the "nation" did not own a single ship or have investment in a single voyage. The capitalists owned the ships and made the profits. They also controlled the government.

They gained governmental control by ousting from power the groups which had supported them in the war, and had, in fact, done most of the fighting. In October 1647 the General Council of the Army met to debate the form which the new State would take (the old having by then been broken). The records of this debate have, fortunately, been preserved, for they begin a pattern which in the succeeding centuries has been repeated endlessly. On the one side were Cromwell and his Commissioner-General, Ireton, on the other representatives of the small propertied classes of town and country (especially the "Levellers").

Mr. Petty: We judge that all inhabitants that have not lost their birthright should have an equal voice in elections. . . .

Commissary-General Ireton: I think that no person has a right to an interest or share in the disposing of the affairs of the kingdom, and in determining or choosing those that shall determine what laws we shall be ruled by here—no person hath a right to this, that hath not a permanent fixed interest in this kingdom. . . . Those that choose the representatives for the making of laws by which this state and kingdom are to be governed are the persons who, taken together, do comprehend the local interest of this kingdom; that is, the persons in whom all land lies, and those in corporations in whom all trading lies. . . .

Sexby (Agitator): We have engaged in this kingdom and ventured our lives, and it was all for this: to recover our birthrights and privileges as Englishmen; and by the arguments urged there is none. There are many thousands of us soldiers that have ventured our lives; we have had little property in the kingdom as to our estates, yet we have had a birthright. But it seems now, except a man has a fixed estate in this kingdom, he has no right in this kingdom. I wonder we were so much deceived.[9]

Nor was the argument carried on by discussion only. The government imprisoned John Lilburne, the Leveller leader; his release was secured by a petition of 10,000; various regiments sympathetic to the Levellers revolted, and were defeated only after several pitched battles. Following this "victory" a banquet was given for Cromwell by the London merchants.

So much for those who had "little property." What, however, of those who had no property? Even the Levellers had no sympathy for them. The Levellers' program (1648), "Agreement of the People," in fact, specifically excluded "those receiving wages" from the vote.[10]

The predominantly commercial nature of the new government was shown in its foreign policy. As early as 1641 London financiers were speculatively buying up "rebel" estates in Ireland at as low as £100 per 1,000 acres. In 1649 Cromwell invaded Ireland, defeated the Irish armies in bloody battles and incorporated the country once more firmly within the Empire. Great tracts of land were handed out to the wealthy speculators and the rest was parcelled out to army officers in Caesarian fashion. Three years later, in 1652, Parliament declared war on Holland, the main commercial rival of the British merchants, and, in a series of naval battles, won control of the seas. (The reversal of events here is interesting. Under Queen Elizabeth England had assisted the Netherlands — Sir Philip Sidney died there — in its rebellion against Spain but when Holland itself became a commercial rival it became an "enemy.")

In spite of all these advances, however, the British capitalists did not have the absolute control of a feudal ruling class. Only the Commons could levy taxes and grant supplies. And the Commons represented a continuation of the coalition which had won the war. True, the small landowners had been sloughed off. But the middle ones and the professional men could exert pressures of various kinds in their own interests. So, too, with the city working class (with its power to strike). Furthermore, as Commissioner-General Ireton had stated, political power was to rest in the "persons in whom all land lies" — primarily the great landowners — as well as in those "in corporations in whom all trading lies" — the capitalists. Clearly also, the capitalists needed the great landowners as a source for raw materials. Although some great estates were sold to big capitalists, most of them remained in the hands of their original owners, who were soon collecting their rents as before. The result was that the great landowners made another bid for power and succeeded in making considerable inroads into the State: the monarchy was restored, the House of Lords came back and the Bishops with it. But the Commons still retained control of the national purse strings and the commercial interests did not give up the economic rights they had won. For the next 170 years Great Britain was ruled by a coalition of landowners and capitalists in which the mercantile interests (part of them aristocratic) predominated. Toward the end of the century, however, the coalition began to break and a new period of political turmoil began, which reached a climax with the Reform Bill of 1832.

POWER BY "REFORM"

This new turmoil arose with the Industrial Revolution, which had profound social and economic effects, as can be seen in a few representative figures. For instance the amount of cotton employed in manufacturing rose from £30 million in 1790 to £123 million in 1820. Increased manufacturing meant increased trade; the financial needs of the new industry and trade fostered the rise of banks and insurance companies.

As usual, economic increase produced a population increase; and, as this economic increase was mainly centered in the cities, we find a particular rise in city population. Not only did the population of London rise from 864,000 in 1801 to over a million in 1811, but that of the new industrial cities of the north and midlands rose also:

	1801	1821
Manchester	109,000	155,000
Glasgow	84,000	150,000
Liverpool	77,000	118,000
Birmingham	73,000	106,000

Not only, however, were these city classes increasing numerically, some of them were also changing in their nature. To the great trading capitalists were being added the new industrial capitalists as well as the new financial capitalists.

Changes were also going on in the country. As the result of inventions and improved agricultural methods farming efficiency increased greatly. One farmer, using these new methods, increased his annual profits from £2,000 to £20,000. These developments naturally helped the great landowners more than the small farmer because the big farmer had the money to experiment with and the small farmer did not. The balance was tipped still further by the "enclosure" of common lands (their seizure by the great landowners). Between 1700 and 1845 one-quarter of the arable land of England—14 million acres—was thus "enclosed." As a result the small landowners were largely driven out, the great landowners became dominant, and estates were being run more by hired labor and less by tenants.

One result of these events in the countryside was that political power shifted in the eighteenth and early nineteenth centuries to the great landowners. They controlled the House of Lords and always had for the simple reason that only important landowners (either lay or clerical) were members. And they now gained control of the Commons, which had consisted mainly of businessmen, professionals and smaller landowners, in part because the engulfing of a large section of the smaller landowners had enabled the great landowners simply to buy their parliamentary seats. Thus of 555 seats in the Commons, 300 in 1820 were owned by 144 members of the House of Lords, and "the government and 123 persons together nominated 187 more" — the famous "pocket" and "rotten" borough system.[11] The word "borough," moreover, although it included settlements of a dozen or less people on a Lord's estate, did not include the new industrial towns. Manchester with its population of 155,000, for instance, did not elect a single member to Parliament.

The capitalists were not the only ones interested in parliamentary "reform." The small businessmen and professional men of London had been urging such reform since the 1760's. Middle and small farmers had similarly been agitating, putting pressure on the Whigs (the mercantile interest party). And the workers, especially in the new towns, became vocal in the shattering economic crisis which followed the Napoleonic Wars (1815). The reform movement was not started by the capitalists. They mostly joined it in the 1820's and when they did they took control of it.

The dual nature of the movement showed up early in the division over the degree of extension of the franchise. The businessmen and professionals (for instance, Leigh Hunt and *The Examiner*) advocated the vote for property owners only ("moderate" reform). The smaller farmers and city craftsmen and workers (led by William Cobbett and "Orator" Hunt) advocated the vote for all adult males regardless of property ("radical" reform). The moderates believed in quiet, behind-the-scenes manipulations; Cobbett and the "radicals" led enormous demonstrations of 50,000 to 100,000 people. To cut a long story short the Whigs took over the "moderates" movement, used the radical demonstrations to frighten the Tories, and, finally, threatened to create sufficient new peers to control the Lords. The result was the passage of the Reform Bill of 1832, which, although it only increased the electorate from 400,000 to 600,000 in a population of 14 million, broke the hold of the Lords over the Commons because it wiped out the rotten and pocket boroughs and granted parliamentary seats to 22 cities.

The passage of the Reform Bill did not mean that the capitalist class had overnight become the ruling class. The great landed interests still had considerable power in the Lords and even in the Commons. Middle class agitation continued. The industrial workers, furious at their failure to receive the vote, turned to Chartism and became a social pressure bloc. But the capitalists had advanced to the threshold of power and were not to be stopped. There was not to be this time any intertwining rise of landed and business interests but an unprecedented and overwhelming increase in industry and the commerce connected with it. By 1860 free trade was in the saddle. And this was all part of the general advance of capitalist policies. "Trade concessions were granted by Persia in 1836, 1841, and 1857, and by Japan in 1858. By the Opium War with China (1840–1842) trade with that country was forced open; and the Crimean War against Russia preserved British commerce in the Danubian provinces and the Black Sea Area. Thus Britain pursued the dualistic scheme of allowing goods to come into its home markets because they offered little competition and of forcing weaker powers to take its export commodities."[12]

The political pattern of the commercial revolution in England, then, was that of (a) revolution and civil war, (b) compromise between landed and commercial interests, and (c) parliamentary reform. At the end of it all the landowners were out of power and the capitalists in.

THE FRENCH REVOLUTION

The British Revolution occurred earlier than the French because British commercial development came earlier; a second revolution was not necessary in the nineteenth century because, although the capitalists let some of their political power slip, they remained entrenched in the economic and social structures. In France all had been suppressed for so long that when it burst it burst all at once.

At the outbreak of the revolution in France, of a total population of about 26 million, about 24 million lived in the country and 2 million in cities and towns. Of the 24 million who lived in the country, 23.6 million were peasants, 400,000 were "nobles." The 400,000 "nobles" included both large and middle landowners. The large landowners lived in their magnificent "chateaux." The middle owners were the "provincial" gentry, corresponding to the English country squires. Perhaps 10 percent of the 400,000 were really "nobles." Although, as usual, the legalities of land ownership were complex and we hear the usual tales about peasant "ownership," the essence of the situation was that the nobles, church, and rich merchants owned about two-thirds of the land outright—worked by peasant labor—and the peasants rented the remaining third. The agriculture, it should be noted, was basically grain agriculture supplying an internal market and, hence, not dependent on commerce (as was the English sheep-raising). The French, in short, still had a basically feudal, self-sufficient agriculture.

Commerce on the other hand was expanding. Foreign trade is said to have trebled between 1716 and 1770, largely because of colonial conquest. "Marseilles, Bordeaux, Nantes, Rouen and smaller ports were quickened by receiving, processing, and distributing the rising influx of colonial or oriental produce and by the production or collection of goods needed for the slave trade, the islands, the fur traders, and India. . . . West Indian cotton fed a virtually new textile industry in Normandy. . . ."[13] On the eve of the Revolution Paris had a population of 500,000, Lyons (a major manufacturing center) 160,000, Marseilles and Bordeaux about 100,000 each.

The capitalist class had its own internal hierarchy. The top group were—in contrast to mercantile England—those who serviced the aristocracy and its government. Aristocrats—as in India or Greece—leased out mine concessions and water and timber rights. "Financiers were grand personages allied by marriage with the aristocracy. . . . In addition, toward the end of the Old Regime Paris saw a great increase in the number of bankers. . . . For all of them the making of government loans was their main business, but on the eve of the Revolution the first stock companies were founded, the Paris water company by Perier, life and fire insurance companies by Clavière."[14] Next in the social hierarchy came the merchants. "For merchants the chief source of wealth continued to be sea-borne commerce. . . . Industry remained socially and economically subordinate. It was in general an auxiliary to commerce."

Connected with these increasing commercial operations was a growing number of small businessmen and professionals. Some professionals were still tied up with the landholding (especially church) interests but more and more were gaining their living from commercial sources.

The largest of the city classes, that of the industrial workers, made up at least half the population of Paris. In some towns factories were arising (notably at Reims, Sedan, and Louviers for the cloth workers), and we hear of one coal company with 4,000 employees, but generally there were few factories. Most workers still worked at home, receiving the raw material from the capitalist. The rest of the working class was employed mainly either in small manufacturing or trading shops owned by small businessmen or in transportation (ship or wagon).

The political regime which grew out of and supported this socio-economic structure was exactly what one would expect. The old feudal political body of the "Estates General" had not met since 1614, a period of 175 years. In the meantime the kings had governed, advised by their "ministers." When we hear that "with the exception of Necker [a banker] all of Louix XVI's ministers were nobles,"[15] it becomes clear that this was simply a variety of the usual Asian and European feudal ruling council of top landowners.

In addition to this national government, however, we find also city governing bodies run by coalitions of the commercially based classes. The most elaborate of these was in Paris, which was divided into 48 wards, in each of which the so-called active citizens (men with property) met regularly and elected representatives to the city council.

The national State, however, was firmly in aristocratic hands, and the aristocrats, as usual, used this power for the twin oppression of capitalists and peasants, the capitalists being their economic rivals and the peasantry the class on whose labor they lived. "To give effect to government control of industry a continual stream of orders poured out, regulating such matters as the quality of raw materials, method of manufacture, and the standard of the finished articles. All these regulations required another horde of officials to enforce them and the imposition of fees to pay for the process of inspection. They prevented, and were intended to prevent, the development of new methods of manufacture."[16] It is not surprising, then, to learn that "weaving, carding and fulling were not mechanized to any extent until after 1850."[17] In 1789 only one French firm had a steam engine.

The peasant was hit by both national and local taxes, the usual feudal produce tax and various indirect taxes. The proceeds from these taxes went to the State. Next came the inevitable church tax on grains and produce, then the various ancient "rights" of the local landowner in the form of rents and tolls. And finally came the inevitable forced labor including the "corvée des routes," or work on the roads.

As a consequence of these various factors the revolution, when it did break out, took the dual form of a capitalist political revolution and a peasants' revolt.

The political revolution was triggered by the king's summoning the Estates-General to meet at Versailles in June 1789. The three "estates" were the nobles, the clergy, and the commons—the "third estate." Although popularly interpreted as the inevitable "middle classes," the third estate actually comprised some 96 percent of the population and ranged from capitalist to peasant. The real leading force within this amorphous mass is indicated in the voting system by which its delegates to Versailles were chosen: (a) the vote was restricted to guild members (businessmen) or those who paid certain minimum taxes (businessmen, landowners, professionals); (b) delegates were chosen by stages (for instance, each town elected delegates, then the delegates from the towns in a district elected district delegates); (c) in the lower stages voting was by word of mouth and not by secret ballot. As a result the capitalists and professionals (particularly lawyers) were in control.

The peasants' revolt followed the pattern of all such revolts from the early Chinese to the German. The peasants seized land, burned castles, destroyed manorial tax records, took back the "common" land, broke down walls and fences. As a result all feudal dues, taxes, and tithes were abolished along with the feudal courts. It was this massive revolt in the countryside and not the orators at Versailles that undermined the power of the French aristocracy. Without it the revolution would have taken—as it had in England—the form of a civil war. Once the aristocracy was weakened, however, the nature of the revolution was shaped not by the peasants but by the capitalists. The peasants had gone as far as they could. They seemed unable to take the next step and actually divide up the great estates to form the basis for a government. If they had, they would have faced capitalist opposition —the Rights of Man declared property "an inviolable and sacred right"—for, although the capitalists were happy enough to sit back and watch feudal tolls, tithes, dues, and courts disappear, they did not want to see large property holdings disappear also, partly because they owned or had interest in some of them and partly because a general revolt against property might spread to the cities.

The revolution in the cities was not, in its form, much different from the usual city revolts against aristocratic power, and like them found its political base of operations in the already existing city governments. It was led by the same coalition of capitalists, professionals, and small business people that dominated the third estate. Most of the "conquerors of the Bastille," as modern research has shown, were not wild-eyed "rabble" but "tradespeople from the Faubourg Saint-Antoine and the Marais Quarter."[18] It was, of course, in the joint interest of both capitalists and small business people to get rid of aristocratic taxes, dues, and tolls. But once this was accomplished splits within the coalition began to appear. Small and middle businessmen asserted their own interests and formed their own political group. Of these the most important were the Jacobin clubs, led by Robespierre (himself a lawyer): "Although the membership of the Jacobin Clubs was broadened later, it has been shown that even under the Terror they remained largely middle-class in composition: the tax assessments of the Jacobins were well above the average. They were opposed both to the rich and to the propertyless."[19] The complex and seesawing struggles of the revolution in Paris and other cities essentially reflected a jockeying for power between large and small business interests (a struggle hidden by the umbrella word "bourgeois"). The capitalists were strengthened by the fact that, as in the British Revolution, a number of aristocrats—Lafayette, Condorcet—joined the revolutionary forces and aligned themselves against the middle and lower classes.

As the revolution wore on some groups of city workers began to act independently of the small business people, and not just gather behind them as they had earlier. This action, although sometimes massive, had, like that of the peasants, really no place to go. The class was broken into small and scattered units and had neither the size nor the concentrated power of the present-day industrial working class. For all this, however, it is obvious that any stirrings in a class that formed half the population of Paris would help to crystalize upper class coalitions, and hence indirectly shape the direction of the revolution. In the spring of 1795 they "swarmed into the hall of the [revolutionary] Convention, crying for bread, attempting to make speeches at the bar of the assembly" and were driven out by military force.[20] They also had some independent or partly independent political movements. The Hébertists in the Paris city government ("commune") were certainly subject to pressures beyond those of the small business interests and such pressures are evident also in François Babeuf's "Conspiracy of the Equals."

One other social phenomenon which winds its way through these events was the revolt of women, which reached its most dramatic point in the march of the women of Paris on Versailles in 1789:

> On Monday October 6 groups of women from the Faubourg Saint-Antoine and the public markets gathered. . . .
> These women demanded bread. Bailly and La Fayette being absent, they lost no time in deciding to go to Versailles. . . . On the way many more women joined the first, willingly or by force. In the rain, to the number of six or seven thousand, if we can believe Maillard, they set forth by way of Sèvres, where the shops were plundered.[21]

After the women arrived at the royal palace a delegation of 35 was received by the king, who promised them extra bread supplies for Paris.

In certain basic respects the French Revolution was the same as the British of 150 years earlier; in others it differed. In France as in Great Britain, the commercially based classes arose against the great landowners; within this class coalition the capitalists formed the most influential group; some great landowners joined the capitalists; the working class did not play a leading part; the revolution was largely centered in the cities and the cities had previously had governments of their own. On the other hand, the British Revolution took the form primarily of a civil war whereas the French Revolution took that of a revolution plus a peasant's revolt, and the aristocratic State in France fell with comparative ease. One reason that it did so was, as we have seen, because the peasants' revolt undermined the aristocratic power (in England such a revolt had taken place long before the revolution); another was that the French commercial classes of the 1790's were more powerful than the English of the 1640's even though on the surface they may not have seemed so because of the parade of aristocratic pomp. Because of this greater strength of the commercial classes the smaller businessmen were able to make a bid for power which gave the revolution a seesaw character, as, to paraphrase a young English observer, William Wordsworth, the ship of state tossed at anchor. For the same reason the working class was more influential than it had been in Britain and posed a future threat that the British had not. Finally, the French Revolution had wider international repercussions than had the British, because by the 1790's European commercial development had arrived at a point at which potentially serious opposition to the great landowners was gathering everywhere, whereas in the seventeenth century outside of England and the Netherlands it had not. This threat was compounded by a "voice from over the sea"—the American revolution.

In spite of these differences, the French Revolution ended very much as had the British, namely in a balance of power between capitalists and great landowners with the small businessmen and most of the professionals pushed out to the peripheries of power. As in the British revolution the great landowners' howls about losing their land were greatly exaggerated. The land that was sold was—as in Britain—largely bought up by the capitalists, with some middle farmers getting "title to scattered strips."[22] In the main the peasants went back to work on the big estates. That neither they nor the industrial workers would have much political say was ensured by limiting the right to vote. The national legislature was elected not directly but by "assemblies" and assembly membership was restricted to men who owned land with an annual value of 100 to 200 days' labor (the great and middle landowners, the capitalists and wealthier small businessmen and professionals).

Of the two ruling classes the capitalists fared better on the whole than the great landowners. The taxation system favoring the aristocracy was, as we have seen, abolished, and with it went the river and other tolls. A Navigation Act similar to the English was passed: "No foreign commodities, products or merchandise may be imported into France, or into the colonies or possessions, except directly by French vessels . . . ," and so on. Strong protective tariffs were adopted for the protection of French industry, and, to some degree, for farm products also. Trade unions were declared illegal; but the legality of the slave trade, upheld alike by merchants and colonial plantation owners, was reconciled with the Rights of Man. Nor was this situation materially changed by Napoleon. The basically commercial direction of the Napoleonic Wars is obvious in the Continental System, which was designed to break English trade on the continent of Europe and substitute French for it.

Following the defeat of Napoleon the European great landowners and British capitalists combined to assist the French great landowners to hold the capitalists back. Thus, in the 1820's, the nobles whose land had been seized were granted an indemnity of $200 million which was to be paid by the government bond-holders, who were mainly capitalists. But commercial development had gone too far to allow the clock to be turned back. In 1830 and 1831 the workers of Paris, Lyons, and other cities revolted against the government; the capitalists and upper class professionals (who essentially formed one class) rushed in and established a new government, which, parallelling the situation in England of the Reform Bill of 1832, shut out the workers: out of a population of 30 million only 250,000 had the vote. Following this, as in England also, the workers began to take an independent road. In 1848 the events of 1830 were repeated on a larger scale (and can most significantly be discussed as a part of working class history). As a result of these various developments the French capitalists became the ruling class. This did not happen in any one year or any one decade, but by the time of the Franco-Prussian war, in which two great capitalist, industrial nations for the first time made war upon each other, it had been consummated. This consummation is revealed also in the difference between the bumbling, half-hearted colonial policies of France in the eighteenth century and the ruthless French imperialism (in Africa and Indo-China) of the late nineteenth century.

As we look over the total movements in Britain and in France, then, it is apparent that they are the same in their general pattern and different in their specific patterns. The similarity in general pattern raises a question which those who portray historical development as resulting from conflicting motives, personalities, and ideas fail to face. If history does result from these factors, how are we to explain these similarities? Nor is the difference in pattern usually noted, or, if noted, an explanation attempted. The result is that the reader is left with a feeling that "it just happened," but it could have just as well happened some other way.

Holland, Italy, Germany

When we turn to the rest of Europe we find the same phenomenon: the same general pattern and end-result with different specific patterns in different countries. Each specific pattern has its reasons. In two countries, for instance, Holland and Italy, the political revolution was connected with wars for national freedom.

The Netherlands (of which Holland was one state) came under Spanish control in 1548. As Spanish oppression (stemming from great landowning interests) increased, Dutch capitalists and landowners united against them. After a bloody war national independence was gained in 1648. Even as independence was being achieved the usual internal conflict between landowning and commercial interests broke out. In 1650 the royal army attacked Amsterdam but failed to capture it. The following year a Grand Council of all Netherland states was convened and each state was given considerable autonomy. States with large commercial centers, such as Holland, were ruled by a combination of commercial and landed interests, a situation similar to that in Britain but on a smaller scale. In 1848 revolutionary pressures shifted the balance of power between landed and commercial interests further toward the commercial. A new constitution was adopted whereby the Upper Chamber, formerly appointed by the king, was to be elected by the Provincial Estates and the Lower Chamber was to be elected by men paying a certain amount in taxes (the usual exclusion of the lower classes and women).

The Italian city states, as we have noted, although satisfactory for Mediterranean trading, had not the strength for colonial conquests. Italy could only have shared in the new wealth by becoming a united nation but whatever possibilities for this may have existed were obliterated by the conquest of the city states by nations, such as France, Spain, and Austria. By the early eighteenth century Italy had become very largely an Austrian possession, and, hence, was under great landowning political control, although Italy, too, shared in the general advance of the European economy. New manufacturing and trading centers developed in the northern cities of Milan and Turin, shifting the balance of capitalist power northward from the old commercial areas of Venice, Naples, Florence, and Genoa.

In 1848 revolution broke out in Milan and the local Austrian forces were defeated; the adjoining state of Piedmont (which included Turin) declared war on Austria but was defeated. In the 1850's the Piedmont government abolished the church courts, revised the tariff structure in the direction of free trade, and encouraged railroad building. In 1859 Piedmont again fought Austria, and, in addition, led armies into the central Italian feudal stronghold of the Papal States. In 1861 the independent Kingdom of Italy was proclaimed, and for the first time since the days of the Roman Empire most of Italy was under one government. The new Kingdom adopted the Piedmont constitution, which meant, in effect, joint control by commercial and landowning interests, with the commercial dominant.

Thus in Italy the revolution assumed the triple form of a war for national liberation, a struggle for national unification, and a conflict of capitalists and landowners. It was not in the interests of those Italian great landowners who were not tied up with commercial enterprise to achieve either liberation or unification. Austrian support helped them to keep down both capitalist and peasant opposition; and they could function just as well in a small state as in a large one. But to the capitalists both liberation and unification were vital. Without them they could not compete successfully in the world market or develop their industries. As it was they came too late upon the imperialist scene.

Germany, like Italy, was divided into states and faced the same urgency. In Germany, however, one State, Prussia, was large enough to dominate the rest and to hold its own as a European power. As a result of capitalist pressure the landowning local tolls on trade had been abolished by 1844 and a single tariff system favoring commercial interests was established. In 1830 and 1848, revolutions similar to those in France took place, and, as in France, both advanced the interests of the capitalist class. The Prussian constitution embodied the usual upper house dominated by great landowning interests and lower house elected by a tax-restricted voting system.

In other European countries the great landowning power was too strongly entrenched to be overthrown. The Austrian nobility not only survived 1848 but suppressed revolts in Vienna, Prague, and Hungary as well as in Italy. The Russian nobility continued in power until 1917, the Spanish and Portuguese are still largely dominant.

II: KNOWLEDGE AND IDEAS

As new means of economic production were developed, trade routes explored, colonies seized, wars fought, governments and churches overthrown, there could not but have been a considerable increase in human knowledge. Nor could a society be thus churned up without releasing a flood of ideas and inspiring artistic creation.

Science

Knowledge made greater strides during the capitalist revolution than it had since the transition from farming society to civilization — as science developed to a new level. As we have seen, there had been embryonic science in the commercial centers of feudal India and China and elsewhere, accompanied — especially in China — by considerable technical knowledge. Further elements of science developed in Greek slave-commercial society, and continued on into Roman Italy but there had hard going under the suspicious eye of the great landowners. Arab empire commerce had some need for this ur-science and developed its alchemical and other aspects, but, as we might expect, Byzantium and feudal Europe had little use for it. Even in commercial-feudal Europe no important advances were made in science. Although technology expanded, the areas of ignorance far transcended those of knowledge. The concept of the earth as a globe was gaining limited acceptance but it was believed to be located at the center of "creation" with the sun, moon, and planets revolving around it in perfect circles; beyond the "spheres" of the sun and planets was the "sphere" of the "fixed stars"—in which they were stuck like so many jewels in a crown —and beyond that, a final sphere, which, under the direct guidance of God, wound up the other spheres like a clock and kept them in motion although itself remaining stationary (derived from Aristotle's "first mover"). Matter consisted of the four "elements" of earth, air, fire, and water, as well as various "spirits" which produced such phenomena as sound or light. The human body consisted of four "humors" corresponding to the four elements, the humors of blood, black bile, red bile, and phlegm; "health" consisted in keeping these humors in balance. If they were off balance, it might mean that the stars were "unfavorable," and the physician could help to bring them into balance by stamping a favorable horoscope in wax and hanging it around the patient's neck.

It was not known that the heart pumped the blood, or that air was necessary to life. Ignorance shrouded elementary facts of biological reproduction. There was no knowledge even of the existence of ova or spermatozoa. A man was supposed to plant seed in a woman as one planted seed in a field; and it was generally assumed that the woman's part in producing life was that of acting like soil to the male seed—which alone contained the inheritable characteristics (a concept embodied in law). There was no conception of the function of the brain or nerves (Greek advances in these matters had long been forgotten). All motion—both in Man and in nature—was presumed to be due to "force." Without "force" all would be static, and "force" emanated from God.

The development of the natural sciences came about largely from the problems presented by navigation, shipbuilding, and canal construction. In European feudal society, navigation had been restricted to inland seas or coast hugging, but with the development of ocean travel—the Azores were discovered in 1419—new techniques were needed. There were no charts of the Atlantic; the captain had to find his position by the aid of the compass, the astrolabe, and the ship's log. Prizes were offered by the British and French governments for the solution of navigational problems, particularly that of determining longitude. Latitude reckoning was solved by the invention of the quadrant and the sextant, which gave more accurate star-moon-sun determinations than the astrolabe. As the new map-making also depended on a knowledge of the stars, astronomy received particular attention. Whether the earth was flat or round, whether it moved or was still, whether the moon was a perfect sphere or a small world, was of little consequence to the rulers of Egypt or Babylon or feudal Europe. But to the businessmen of Antwerp or London whose ships were being wrecked and profits lost, it was a different matter.

COPERNICUS, KEPLER, GALILEO

The significant beginning came with the publication of Copernicus' *De Revolutionibus Orbium Coelestrium* (*On the Revolutions of the Heavenly Bodies*) in 1543 with its simple but graphic words:

> Fourth in order, an annual cycle takes place, in which . . . is contained the earth, with the lunar orbit as an epicycle. In the fifth place Venus is carried round in nine months. Then Mercury holds the sixth place, circulating in the space of eighty days. In the middle of all dwells the sun.

The theory of the earth's orbiting around the sun, as we have seen, was not new. Both Indian and Greek astronomers had held it in the past; and Copernicus pays tribute to Aristarchus. But whereas in the past there had been no economic or social motive for preserving or developing the theory, now there was—even though Copernicus himself was not aware of it:

> Nothing urged me to think out some other way of calculating the motions of the spheres of the world but the fact that, as I knew, mathematicians did not agree among themselves in these researches. For in the first place they are so far uncertain of the motion of the Sun and Moon that they cannot observe and demonstrate the constant magnitude of the tropical year.

But why were the mathematicians so eager to find solutions? The problems had existed for many centuries, and no one in Europe had been disturbed by them since the time of the Greeks. Among those who were also being "urged" to "think" about them was one of Copernicus's own professors, Domenico de Novara, at Bologna, a commercial center, and so more directly concerned with such matters than Copernicus's native Poland. If Copernicus had not formulated the theory, someone else would have done so. It might perhaps have had to wait for another few decades, but sooner or later, it would have come to birth, for it was needed.

Following Copernicus came Kepler. And, again, let us quote; for in all these men we are dealing with great creative moments in human knowledge, and the words of the creator have a special fire. Kepler tackled the problem of the orbits of the planets. The way to this had been cleared by Copernicus, but Copernicus had believed that the orbits were circular. This at first misled Kepler: "My first error was to take the planet's path as a perfect circle, and this mistake robbed me of the more time, as it was taught on the authority of all philosophers, and consistent in itself with Metaphysics."[23] "Metaphysics" had "taught" that the paths of the planets must be circles for no other reason than that circular motion was the most "perfect" of all motion. But Kepler's calculations revealed that the orbit of Mars was not circular, and, so armed with fact, he dealt short shrift to "the authority of all philosophers" from Aristotle to Aquinas. "Thus it is clear, the orbit of the planet is not a circle, but passes within the circle at the sides, and increases its amplitude again to that of the circle at perigee. The shape of a path of this kind is called an oval."

Another great moment in the mind of humanity came when Galileo turned the first astronomical telescope upon the moon (1610):

> From observations of these spots repeated many times I have been led to the opinion and conviction that the surface of the moon is not smooth, uniform, and precisely spherical as a great number of philosophers believe it (and the other heavenly bodies) to be, but is uneven, rough, and full of cavities and prominences, being not unlike the face of the earth, relieved by chains of mountains and deep valleys. . . . Let us note, however, that the said small spots always agree in having their blackened parts directed toward the sun, while on the side opposite the sun they are crowned with bright contours, like shining summits. . . . these spots on the moon lose their blackness as the illuminated region grows larger and larger.[24]

No further speculation or "revelation" was needed. The moon was not a small, perfect silver circle, but a world like the earth, something which no one had previously known.

Galileo next turned to the planets and stars:

> Deserving of notice also is the difference between the appearances of the planets and of the fixed stars. The planets show their globes perfectly round and definitely bounded, looking like little moons, spherical and flooded all over with light; the fixed stars are never seen to be bounded by a circular periphery, but have rather the aspect of blazes whose rays vibrate about them and scintillate a great deal. Viewed with a telescope they appear of a shape similar to that which they present to the naked eye. . . .[25]

The planets, too, might be worlds like our earth; and beyond the planets lay an immensity of stars such as no one had dreamed of. But although Galileo had come this far, he could go no further. He had no knowledge of the law of gravity (Newton, *Principia,* 1687) or the size of the universe. The size of the solar system was not determined until 1672 (by Giovanni Cassini). Only slowly did scientists begin to grasp the immensity of space. Among the first to do so was Immanuel Kant who argued as early as 1755 that a "nebula is not a unique and solitary sun, but a system of numerous suns . . . in a word to be Milky Ways."[26] Herschel with his new large telescope counted some 5,000 nebulae. "Man," wrote Laplace, "now appears, upon his small planet almost imperceptible in the vast extent of the solar system, itself only an insensible point in the immensity of space."[27] How "insensible," however, even Laplace did not know, for the distance from the earth to a star was not determined until 1838 (by triangulation, using the earth's orbit as a base).

PHYSICS AND CHEMISTRY

In these astronomical matters, the capitalist revolution, although the ultimate directing force, was for Kepler and Galileo, as it had been for Copernicus, general and indirect in its actions. But in other advances of science it was direct and specific. For ocean voyages, stronger and more manageable ships were needed. To make such ships one had not only to understand naval architecture but to delve into the general problems of the actions of solids floating in liquids, which led to those of the nature of liquids and of solids themselves, then into water pressure and wind pressure. Better instruments of navigation were needed. Perhaps the compass could be improved and other devices made by the study of magnetism (William Gilbert, *De Magnete*, 1600), and magnetism led to electricity (Faraday, Galvani, Volta). More accurate clocks were needed for nautical and other purposes, and clocks led to the problem of the pendulum (Galileo, Huygens). The telescope was no sooner developed than it was put into immediate use by navigators and admirals; and the telescope led further into the science of optics (Newton). For the first time — following Newton's classic experiment with prisms and Römer's demonstration in 1676 of the velocity of light — some people began to have an understanding of the nature of light and color.

When canal travel was added to sea travel the problems of water pressure and water efflux in the construction of locks led to the science of hydrostatics. Castelli published a treatise in 1642 on the movement of water in canals: Torricilli worked on theories of the efflux and pressure of liquids; Stevinus showed that the pressure of a liquid was dependent only on the "head" of liquid and hence that one pound of water could be made to exert 100,000 pounds of pressure — the principle used later in the hydraulic brake. The more intensive mining of coal and metals, requiring mining in depth, brought with it special problems of pumping. Ordinary pumps, it had long been known, would not pump water higher than about 30 feet, but it had not been known why. Torricilli reasoned that perhaps the atmosphere itself had weight, weight equal to some 30 feet of water, or, he calculated, 29 inches of mercury. So he filled a long glass tube — such as Italian glass makers could make — with mercury, and placed the open end in a bowl of mercury. The liquid fell to 29 inches, and, at one stroke, the weight of the atmosphere was established and the first vacuum created (which, according to the schoolmen, was something which could not exist because "nature abhors a vacuum"). With the establishment of this principle, the way was open to the invention of Newcomen's atmospheric steam engine, which itself led the way to the first true steam engine (both used immediately for mine pumping). And the steam engine brought with it a new set of problems, both mechanical and theoretical (on the condensation of liquids, on heat, on gas pressure).

Mining also created mechanical problems on trucking, mathematical problems on the directing of shafts and corridors, geological problems of rock formation, problems of air currents and ventilation, problems of explosive gas — for which Davy invented his safety lamp in 1815, itself based on the new knowledge of gases arising from the work of Priestley and Scheele. The smelting of metals also presented new problems, and the cylindrical bellows, the blast furnace, the rolling mill each brought a host of difficulties, particularly those connected with heat. What was heat? No one knew, until Rumford bored a piece of metal under water with a blunt drill and raised $2\frac{1}{2}$ gallons of water to the boiling point in $2\frac{1}{2}$ hours, and concluded (correctly) that heat was "a vibratory motion of the constituent parts of heated bodies," in short, not an inherent "spirit" but a motion of atoms.

Other developing industries were also presenting problems of a special nature, for instance textiles, those of bleaches and dyes; distilling and brewing, those of heat, chemical analysis, and gases. Priestley first bottled carbon dioxide gas from the fermenting vats of a brewery; Scheele discovered chlorine in 1774, and it was put to use as a bleach in textile manufacturing (which also used sulphuric acid, alum and soda). Priestley and Scheele went on to the discovery of oxygen. A new science, chemistry, dealing with the molecular and atomic units of matter was born, in part from the old alchemy.

Gunpowder and cannon had brought with them special problems of falling bodies and trajectories. Stevinus made a beginning by dropping two bodies of different weights and finding that they hit the ground at the same time. Galileo repeated the experiment and ingeniously devised others with rolling balls on an inclined plane, which enabled him to determine the speed and rate of increase of falling bodies. He determined also that the path of a projectile was a parabola, and praised the great arsenal at Florence as an experimental station in his *Mathematical Demonstrations*. His first telescope he donated for war purposes: "Perceiving of what great utility such an instrument would prove in naval and military operations, and seeing that his Serenity the Doge, desired to possess it, I resolved on the 24th inst. to go to the palace and present it as a free gift."[28]

BIOLOGY, GEOLOGY, MATHEMATICS

Soil chemistry, plant crossing, and animal breeding (Bakewell) blended with the demands of medicine to produce the new sciences of biology and physiology. In the sixteenth century, Vesalius was dissecting human bodies and coming to bold and seminal conclusions: "As regards the structure of the brain, the monkey, dog, horse, cat and all quadrupeds which I have hitherto examined . . . resemble man in almost every particular."[29] Harvey, going beyond anatomy into physiology, analyzed the heart as a pump (just at the time that pumps — for canals, dikes and mines — were much in discussion) and discovered the circulation of the blood. In the seventeenth century, with the invention of the microscope, spermatozoa and bacteria were seen for the first time, and the stamen of plants was recognized as the male sex organ. In the eighteenth century, Albrecht von Haller, in his nine-volume *Elementa Physiologiae,* argued that the nerves are the instruments of sensation and the cause of animal motion by their action on the muscles; as the nerves are gathered up in the central parts of the brain, the brain, too, must feel and present to the mind the impression transmitted by the nerves. But there could be no real basis for physiology or neurology until chemistry developed. A landmark came in 1828 when Wöhler made urea by chemical means.

One other science developed also, that of the earth itself (in response to the needs of mining, agriculture, and so on). Leonardo da Vinci's theory that fossils had been laid down under long-vanished seas was not only shown to be correct but it was demonstrated that similar processes were still in action; and it was shown — by Perrault in 1674 — that rainfall alone would account for rivers and springs. There were no "waters under the earth." The direction of mathematics (abstract though it may seem) was shaped by the advance of astronomy and physics:

Nearly all the great mathematicians of the sixteenth and seventeenth centuries, from Tartaglia and Stevin to Cavalieri, Descartes, Newton and Leibniz, were at least partly interested in the physical sciences. . . . A

328 / Humanity and Society

number of their advances in method were first denoted by the solution of some problem in mechanics, which offered from about 1650 onwards a most rewarding opportunity for the display of mathematical inventiveness, formerly more commonly devoted to the improvement of the mathematical procedures in astronomy.[30]

Compared to these advances even Greek science seems a pale and flickering flame. Some aspects of the movement, however, should be stressed. For instance, a listing of names and discoveries inevitably places too much emphasis on the individual. That each of these discoveries would have come from some other investigator is apparent from the fact that some of the most famous of them (on which historical research has been done) were being investigated independently. Servetus and others were working on the problem of the circulation of the blood and had, indeed, partially solved the problem. The differential calculus was invented independently by Newton and Leibnitz. Furthermore, the work of scientists was more closely allied with that of craftsmen than is usually realized. The telescope was the invention of a craftsman (as Galileo acknowledges); the laboratory air pump was derived from the ordinary well pump. Discoveries which at first may seem solely the product of individual and undirected genius turn out on investigation to be the result of common efforts, efforts themselves built upon a long chain of past work by other scientists and craftsmen. Furthermore, the whole is seen to be primarily a response to the economic drive of the capitalist sector of the society and to be limited by the general socioeconomic level. Newton, no more than Archimedes, could have produced an atomic pile.

Science was needed, but it was not needed by all. The great landowners and their church soon perceived that it would aid their capitalist opponents and perhaps weaken popular "faith." Luther's attack on Copernicus was typical: "People give ear to an upstart astrologer who strove to show that the earth revolves, not the heavens or the firmament, the sun and the moon. . . . This fool wishes to reverse the entire scheme of astronomy; but sacred Scripture tells us that Joshua commanded the sun to stand still, not the earth."[31] Such attacks had their effect. Copernicus withheld publication for thirteen years, fearing the persecution of the church. Vesalius was sent by the church on a penitential pilgrimage to Jerusalem and died in shipwreck as a consequence. Giordiano Bruno—who doubted that the "fixed stars" were really fixed—was burned at the stake; so, too, was Servetus. Galileo, haled before the Inquisition, was forced to recant publicly in penitential garb.

Social Thought

LOCKE

The first major theorist of the capitalist revolution was John Locke. Locke came first because the British revolution came first. Moreover, by the time he wrote, the fighting was over and the capitalists had made their compromise with the landowners, so that his views represented not the extreme of, say, Milton's *The Ready and Easy Way to Establish a Free Commonwealth* with its projected anti-aristocratic "soviets" but the sober second thoughts of the class, second thoughts which seemed to others to present a workable "middle way."

Locke's father was a lawyer (if he had been an aristocrat, Locke's works would probably never have been written) who joined the Commonwealth troops, and became a cavalry captain. Locke was on the liberal side in politics. With the overthrow of James II, he returned to England from Holland, where he had fled during the reign of Charles II, and began the publication of a series of works which established him as the leading European champion of capitalist economic and social views: *Consequences of the Lowering of Interest and Raising the Value of Money; Two Treatises on Government* (advocating parliamentary government); *Essays on* [Religious] *Toleration*. As a result of his Whig politics and his interest in economics, he became a commissioner of the Board of Trade. The essence of his views on government can be given in a few sentences. "The end of government is the good of mankind. And which is best for mankind, that the people should be always exposed to the boundless will of tyranny, or that the rulers should be sometimes liable to be opposed, when they grow exorbitant in the use of their power and employ it for the destruction, and not the preservation, of the properties of their people?" When we remember that almost all of Europe in Locke's day was under the absolute rule of great landowning monarchies, the revolutionary nature of this doctrine becomes evident. But its limitations are evident also. The emphasis on property was not incidental: "The great and chief end therefore of men's uniting into commonwealths and putting themselves under government is the preservation of their property." Clearly, although Locke speaks of "mankind" and "men," he means only those who own property. Nor is he thinking only of landed property, but, as his economic writings show, of all property, including property in factories, shops, ships, banks, and so on.

Locke, then, is a radical in regard to feudal property but, like Cromwell before him, a conservative in regard to the mass of the working people, whom he regards as a threat to "property" and to be restrained by "government." (This use by Locke of "men" and "mankind" for the business and professional classes has continued in political and other writings ever since.)

The same ambivalence underlies Locke's *Essays on Toleration.* The absolutist, feudal church is to be replaced by a "tolerant" one. "The toleration of those that differ from others in matters of religion is so agreeable to the gospel of Jesus Christ, and to the genuine reason of mankind, that it seems monstrous for men to be so blind, as not to perceive the necessity and advantage of it in so clear a light." This apparently universal toleration, however, is quickly narrowed down. The English Catholic Church is excluded; so, too, are atheists. "Lastly, those are not at all to be tolerated who deny the being of God. Promises, covenants, and oaths, which are the bonds of human society, can have no hold upon an atheist. The taking away of God, though but even in thought, dissolves all." Locke's views, then, both on government and the church, are a theoretical justification of commercial enterprise, upper and middle class parliamentary government, and the Protestant Church.

ROUSSEAU

Following Locke came Rousseau—and the first influential attack upon the sacred cow of property:

> The first man who, having enclosed a piece of ground, bethought himself of saying "This is mine," and found people simple enough to believe him, was the real founder of civil society. From how many crimes, wars, and murders, from how many horrors and misfortunes might not any one have saved mankind, by pulling up the stakes, or filling up the ditch, and crying to his fellows: "Beware of listening to this impostor; you are undone if you once forget that the fruits of the earth belong to us all, and the earth itself to nobody."[32]

Property was not only responsible for war and social evils but it had corrupted and psychologically distorted humanity: "It now became the interest of men to appear what they really were not. To be and to seem became two totally different things; and from this distinction sprang insolent pomp and cheating trickery, with all the numerous vices that go in their train."[33] To perceive the significance of Rousseau's views let us compare the *Discourse* (1750) with *Paradise Lost* (1667). Although in some respects Milton was a more advanced social thinker than Rousseau, nevertheless in his general theory, he traced the origin of evil to "Mans First Disobedience, and the Fruit Of that Forbidden

Tree," without seeming to realize that in doing so he was, in effect, condemning mankind to impotence, for if evil was the result of a flaw in human nature, alleviation could come about only by divine intervention. But if evil came from a flaw in the structure of society it could be overcome by changing that structure. Specifically, if "man" was made what he was by a society with property and inequality, then he could be remade by a society without property and based on equality. The germs of modern sociological thinking are clearly present in Rousseau. Rousseau, however, had little concept of how or why a new order of society might come about.

CONDORCET AND GODWIN

The theory that history had laws and processes just as nature did was developed simultaneously in France and in England. Condorcet in 1793 in his *Esquisse d'un tableau historique des progrès de l'esprit humain* argued that one could predict future development by these laws:

> If man can predict, almost with certainty, those appearances of which he understands the laws; if, even when the laws are unknown to him, experience of the past enables him to foresee, with considerable probability, future appearances; why should we suppose it a chimerical undertaking to delineate with some degree of truth, the picture of the future destiny of mankind from the results of its history?[34]

In William Godwin's *Enquiry Concerning Political Justice* also published in 1793, natural and social laws are viewed as alike subject to an iron necessity beyond human control: "This view of things presents us with an idea of the universe as connected and cemented in all its parts, nothing in the boundless progress of things being capable of happening otherwise than it has actually happened."[35] Behind the movements and events ("appearances") of history lie the working of deeper "laws." These laws not only govern history, they have been operating in a progressive direction. Throughout all the apparent ups-and-downs of the past, there has been a dominant upward trend: "First, there is a degree of improvement real and visible in the world. This is particularly manifest, in the history of the civilised part of mankind, during the three last centuries."[36] This upward march of history will continue: "And, as improvements have long continued to be incessant, so there is no chance but they will go on. The most penetrating philosophy cannot prescribe limits to them, nor the most ardent imagination adequately fill up the prospect." So, too, in Condorcet there is "an eternal chain of human destiny" which leads to a future in which humanity will be in control of its own destinies: "released from the dominion of chance."

In reading Rousseau, Condorcet, and other professional men of the eighteenth century in France, we should neither exaggerate their meaning nor underplay their significance. When the French Revolution actually broke out, Condorcet was a "moderate" who opposed the Girondists and voted against the execution of the king; he was consequently imprisoned by the revolutionary government (and died in prison). The ultimate state which both he and Rousseau looked forward to was to have as its economic foundation equality of private property. They were not socialists, and had no concept of a society with a centralized, integrated economy. On the other hand, their language anticipates in some way that of the early socialists and the fire of their vision transcends their practical politics. The reason for this fire—which makes so noticeable a difference between them and Locke—is doubtless to be found in the feudal oppression under which the professionals in France were laboring (in contrast to England). They had only to look across the channel or across their northern border into Holland to see their fellow writers, lawyers, and so on, enjoying comparative freedom, both political and cultural. They themselves not only had no parliamentary representation, but lived under the constant threat of prison and exile. They had certain legal rights on paper, but few in reality. When Voltaire annoyed the Duke of Rohan, he was beaten like a dog in the streets by the duke's lackeys and had no legal recourse.

Behind the aristocracy loomed the gray mass of the peasants. Hence the French professionsals were ambivalent. They needed the threat of this mass force in order to secure their aims, but they feared it as much as they needed it. It is this dualism which pervades the social theories of Rousseau and Condorcet and the rest. Their own desperation and their realization that they could not win out alone sharpened their language and broadened their vision; but their fear of the peasants and their dependence upon the capitalists kept the base of their views narrow.

We might note also that, although Condorcet and Godwin had a concept of society moving in accordance with historical "laws" independently of human conscious intervention, and in this we have the seeds of later socialist thought, they really had no concept of objective social processes. For instance, when Godwin tried to explain why society had been moving forward his answer was that it was the nature of the human mind to develop, and as it developed it pulled society along with it. There was, of course, no evidence, neurological or otherwise, to show that such was the "nature" of mind, nor could he have explained why if such was the case, the progress of humanity had not been constant. But like Copernicus' view that the planets moved in circles, the concept although specifically false was, nevertheless, in its general implication, germinal.

THE ECONOMISTS

In economic thought, English writers were, as we should expect, busily engaged in the seventeenth and eighteenth centuries in providing theories which would both explain and increase commercial profits. Thomas Mun (1571–1642) argued in his *England's Treasure by Foreign Trade,* that national prosperity, like that of a store, depended on selling and buying. (The leading French economists, on the other hand, living in a feudal-dominated state, argued that the basic source of wealth lay in the land and that trade was essentially unproductive.) Adam Smith argued that national wealth consisted of "the sum total of all material objects having value in exchange" — the embodiment in general theory of the viewpoint of the capitalist trader.

MARY WOLLSTONECRAFT

One other aspect of social thought, namely that on the social status of women, made a great advance in the late eighteenth century. We have noted, as we have gone along, various views held on this subject in different civilizations. But one thing has been lacking, namely, a book on the subject by a woman (a lack noted by the Wife of Bath). There were no such books because in most of the world's civilized states there were few educated women and the pressure to prevent those who were educated from writing down their views must have been considerable. Educated women, however, in many states, from the India of Maurya and the Rome of Lucretius to the Japan of Lady Murasaki and the Italy of Castiglione, must have discussed these questions, and doubtless sometimes wrote about them. But it was not until the eighteenth century in Europe that any full length treatise on the subject was published, Mary Wollstonecraft's *A Vindication of the Rights of Woman.* (That the subject was in the air at the time is shown by the fact that the *Vindication* had been preceded by briefer works by other women, for instance, Catherine Macaulay and Madame de Staël.)

To appreciate the importance of Mary Wollstonecraft's work, we have to realize that some of the most advanced men thinkers of the period were hostile toward the social and cultural aspirations of women. They generally simply omitted women from their views of society or history, and when they did write of women, they often wrote with condescension; for instance, Rousseau: "To please, to be useful to us, to make us love and esteem them, to educate us when young, and take care of us when grown up, to advise, to console us, to render our lives easy and agreeable: these are the duties of women at all times, and what they should be taught in their infancy."[37] If Rousseau's view was an advance over Luther's—"Take women away from their housewifery, and they are good for nothing"[38]—it is not much of an advance.

Mary Wollstonecraft hit these concepts head on. Women were oppressed. As a result of this oppression "a state of warfare . . . subsists between the sexes." Women should be admitted into some professions and should receive the same education as men.[39] She wrote—something unheard of at the time—sympathetically of the prostitute: "I cannot avoid feeling the most lively compassion for those unfortunate females who are broken off from society, and by one error torn from all those affections and relationships that improve the heart and mind. It does not frequently even deserve the name of error. . . ."[40] She issued some blunt warnings to men: "Marriage will never be held sacred till women, by being brought up with men, are prepared to be their companions rather than their mistresses."

So far as one knows, society had never witnessed writing like this by a woman before. The *Vindication* heaves up to the surface the suppressed indignation and aspirations of women through the ages. Yet, broad though it is in one sense, in another, the work is narrow. Although Mary Wollstonecraft speaks of women, she means primarily women of the upper classes, particularly the wives and daughters of the men of the business and professional world. Not that she was speaking in the same narrow terms that Locke was, in his use of "men," for she has a fellow-feeling for all women because all women and not only upper class women were oppresed, but she is not really thinking of the great mass of working women. Furthermore, even within these limits, her book suffers from vagueness of practical program. She does not advocate votes for women, or the right of women to sit in parliament, or to become doctors or lawyers, and so on. But when we read the vilification that was poured down upon her in press and pamphlet—"For Mary verily would wear the breeches. / God help poor silly men from such usurping bitches"—it is apparent that she was striking a serious blow at the Establishment.

The oppression of women, as we have seen, had been a characteristic of all civilized states. There must, therefore, have been some special factor which called forth protest at this time. That rise of the women of the business and professional classes which we noted in

European feudal-commercial society had been continuing. With the capitalist revolution there were more and more women of these classes; they were living in cities, and not isolated on great estates as were women of the landowning classes. In the cities, the men of these classes were achieving a more democratic structure, and the women of the classes began to push forward their own rights as women. They began first to achieve a place in the artistic professions—as actresses, dramatists, novelists—because there were no legal barriers to entering them; publishers or theater owners were as willing to make profits from women as from men. And women began to push at the doors of other professions, particularly the teaching profession, in which they already had a traditional place.

We might note, finally—because the point is sometimes missed—that Mary Wollstonecraft was not primarily a feminist but a radical humanitarian. As her works show, she regarded the cause of women as part of the cause of humanity. She stood, in fact, in the forefront of the advanced thought of her age, sometimes anticipating future socialist concepts more nearly than did her husband, William Godwin: "From the respect paid to property flow, as from a poisoned fountain, most of the evils and vices which render this world such a dreary scene. . . . One class presses on another. . . ."[41]

If we consider this whole development of ideas from Locke to Mary Wollstonecraft, it becomes evident that it represented a new stage in social thought. Not, of course, that it was entirely new. Thucydides and Lucretius had concepts of social evolution; Aristotle had examined the class nature of politics and had laid a basis for democratic political theory. The dependence of both Locke and the French thinkers upon Lucretius seems to be heavy. Possibly Locke's and certainly Rousseau's concepts of the "state of nature" of primitive society derive from him (and may ultimately, as we have speculated, stem from the Taoists). And both Rousseau's and Condorcet's theories of the evolution of human society from a "savage state" to civilization are present also in Lucretius. But Lucretius, as we noted, had no hope for future development and mixed biological and social matters in a curious and morbid medley of the aging earth and declining society.

The New Philosophy

FRANCIS BACON

The capitalist revolution, with its science and its attacks upon various feudal bastions also produced, as we might expect, new concepts of nature and of humanity's relationship to it, biological and physical. These in toto amounted to a "new philosophy," which, John Donne lamented, "calls all in doubt." The first major exponent of the philosophy was Donne's contemporary, Sir Francis Bacon (1561–1626). Bacon is said to have died as a result of an experiment in freezing a chicken for preservation. Whether the story is true or not, it certainly serves to point out the essence of his philosophical innovations, namely his conceptualizing of scientific method.

Born into the England of the "reformation," Bacon carried the attack beyond theology to metaphysics, striking out particularly at that ultimate philosophical pillar of the church, Aristotle, but taking a few blows at Plato also: "We have as yet no natural philosophy that is pure; all is tainted and corrupted; in Aristotle's school by logic; in Plato's by natural theology." Plato based philosophy upon theology, Aristotle subordinated facts to "logic." Bacon's own method was the opposite, "inductive" instead of "deductive"—first find the facts and then form generalizations: "The induction which is to be available for the discovery and demonstration of sciences and arts must analyze nature by proper rejections and exclusions. . . ." The elements upon which this method is to be used are those of nature itself (not of "logic"): "Matter rather than forms should be the object of our attention, its configurations and changes of configuration, and simple action, and law of action or motion; for forms are figments of the human mind unless you will call those laws of action forms."

Nature is not either a reflection of ideal (Platonic) forms or abstract (Aristotelian) ones; nor is it an infinite series of disconnected facts. It has a certain limited number of basic characteristics and general processes ("laws of action") out of which, in their combinations, arise the phenomena of nature. To find these "laws" one must act, change, and experiment. One cannot, however, change nature either at random or absolutely but must understand the laws of nature and work within them: "Man is the helper and interpreter of Nature. He can only act and understand in so far as by working upon her or observing her he has come to perceive her order. Beyond this he has neither knowledge nor power." "To be ignorant of causes is to be frustrated in action." The same "practical" method should be followed in the social as in the natural sciences. "It may be asked whether I speak only of Natural Philosophy, or whether the other sciences, logic, ethics, politics, should be carried on by this method. I certainly mean what I have said to be understood of them all." The object of the sciences, both natural and social, was not simply the accumulation of knowledge but "to improve human well-being."

It is well to observe the force and effect and consequences of discoveries. These are to be seen nowhere more conspicuously than in those three which were unknown to the ancients, and of which the origin, though recent, is obscure; namely, printing, gunpowder, and the magnet. For these three have changed the whole face and state of things throughout the world; the first in literature, the second in warfare, the third in navigation; whence have followed innumerable changes.

Bacon in spite of his title did not come from a great landed family. Like Sir Walter Raleigh (who was warden of the tin mines) he was attached not to the land but to the Court of London, a Court responsive to the ever growing streams of commerce and interested in science and invention. It was this commercialized Court outlook that inspired both Bacon's natural and social philosophy. The kind of England he wanted was one—as he anticipated Locke—"whose wealth resteth in the hands of merchants, burghers, tradesmen [i.e., manufacturers], freeholders, farmers in the country, and the like."

That Bacon had great limitations was inevitable. Science was still in its infancy; Newton was not born until 25 years after Bacon's death. The biological and geological sciences had hardly begun to form. Evolutionary theories were more than 200 years off, and the origin of humanity was an apparently insoluble mystery. But, taking Bacon all in all, his philosophy was in some respects the most advanced that humanity had yet created. In certain fundamentals he surpassed the Greeks. Neither Theophrastus nor Strabo, in spite of their emphasis on experimentations, proposed "practice" as a general criterion for truth, both in regard to nature and society. Nor did they (or Lucretius) have either Bacon's massive, if somewhat hazy, vision of advancing humanity, or his confidence in the capacity of humanity to master nature.

DESCARTES

Following Bacon came Descartes (1596–1650). Descartes' father was also a lawyer with money invested in land (which gave Descartes a fixed income); and his philosophy represents the situation in France just as Bacon's represents that in England. France was dominated by great landowning interests (including the church) against which the commercial-manufacturing segment of the economy was fighting an uphill battle, and Descartes, in order to find freedom to express his ideas, had to reside for many years in Holland. It is hardly surprising in view of the scope of the feudal power (Descartes himself went to a Jesuit school) to find that these ideas show more of a balance between the feudal and the capitalist than do Bacon's. To Descartes, although nature appeared as much a large machine as it did to Bacon, it was *essentially* a machine run by "God"; although Man had mechanistic aspects, the "soul" was fundamental.

Biological and psychological concepts lay at the base of Descartes' philosophical dualism. "Brutes" work "by springs like a clock"; they cannot have a mind because if they did "they would have an immortal soul as well as we, which is unlikely. . . ." In humans the mind and the body, although essentially different and separate entities, are conjoined by the "pineal gland" in the brain. The concept of the dichotomy of mind and body, with the emotions as part of the body, was an integral part of Plato's philosophy. The concept of bodily spirits was also standard among Greek and Roman philosophers; we noted it, for instance, in Lucretius, but, whereas Lucretius felt that thought was simply the result of still more subtle "particles" of matter, Descartes—like Plato—held it to be a different substance, linked not with matter but with God. Unlike Bacon, Descartes placed almost no emphasis upon experimentation but believed (with Aristotle) that truth can come from logic and reason alone. For instance, he has no concept of conducting experiments to determine the function of the pineal gland but simply states that he has "examined the matter with care."

This emphasis upon reason is both Descartes' strength and his weakness. In a feudal atmosphere still dominated by dogma and revelation, an assertion of the rights of reason was an advance, but with the progress of science—Galileo was Descartes' contemporary—it was becoming outmoded even as he was enunciating it. His criticism of Galileo, in fact, is particularly revealing: "he has merely sought reasons for certain particular effects, without having considered the first causes of nature." But how were these "first causes" to be ascertained if not (as Bacon argued) by accumulating "particular effects"? Descartes is here back with Aristotle and the supremacy of "logic."

On the other hand Descartes advanced in some ways beyond Bacon. Bacon had little interest in epistemology (the problem of how the mind knows); Descartes made it a major division of philosophy, and he inadvertently provided a basis for skepticism in his famous motto, "Cogito ergo sum." In addition to his contributions in philosophy, he made others in mathematics: the famed "Cartesian" curves and coordinates.

LOCKE

Following Descartes, we find ourselves in England once more, and once more also, with John Locke. The problems with which Locke was concerned in his famous *Essay Concerning Human Understanding* were how knowledge comes into the mind and to what degree the mind can grasp reality. The usual assumption of philosophers (as we saw in Plato) was that ideas existed in the mind before birth (having come from God) and that all learning was simply an unfolding of these ideas. Although many thinkers must have concluded that this was false—Aristotle, certainly, did—there had generally been much confusion on the point. Locke was the first major philosopher to state unequivocally that the mind at birth was "a blank tablet," containing capacities and instincts but no ideas, and that the raw material for all ideas was taken in by the senses during life and could have no other possible source. The human mind is neither divinely furnished with ideas nor capable of creating them out of nothing. The idea of a centaur, which at first sounds like a creation, is simply a combination of two things observed in nature: a horse's body, joined to a head of human shape. The most "complex ideas" are simply "compounded" from "simple ideas"; and the "simple ideas which we receive from sensation and reflection are the boundaries of our thought." Locke does not, it is true, offer experimental proof of his theory—nor could he; that had to come later with the development of experimental psychology—but he does throw the burden of proof upon those putting forward an opposite view, for his own view is in accordance with observation and the opposite is not.

On the second problem, namely the extent of the grasp of reality by the human mind, Locke contended that there were two kinds of ideas, those of primary qualities and those of secondary qualities, both based on different phenomena in nature. By primary qualities he meant "solidity, extension, figure and mobility." These exist in nature just as we perceive them. Physical bodies are solid, of a certain size, a certain number, and either move or are at rest. Secondary qualities are such things as "colours, sounds, tastes"; these are "in truth nothing in the objects themselves but powers to produce various sensations in us by their primary qualities; i.e., by the bulk, figure, texture, and motion of their insensible parts" (constituent parts not perceivable by the senses).

If Locke's philosophy at first seems remote from science, a little thought shows a direct connection; the concept of primary and secondary qualities is clearly a reflection of the scientific investigations of Newton, Boyle, and others into the nature of matter. Bodies in motion (as in Galileo's experiments) were pretty much as they seemed to be. But what of light? Newton had advanced the theory that light was due to the action of infinitely small particles; and light could be broken down by a prism to its primary colors. Colors, in short, were not what they seemed; invisible particles in matter stimulated the senses to the perception of color. There was, then, properly speaking, no color in bodies themselves, but only a "power" to produce color.

Those social changes which we saw reflected in Locke's economic and political views were reflected also in his philosophy, for instance his theory of knowledge arising from experience alone. For what is this but a frontal attack—in contrast to Descartes' limited skirmishing—upon dogma and revelation, those two theoretical props of the feudal church, and an assertion of the English business or professional man's need for freedom from feudal domination for his thinking as well as his business? As Locke himself put it: "I can no more know anything by another man's understanding than I can see by another man's eyes."

BERKELEY, HUME, KANT

The antifeudal (and antitheological) implications of Locke's philosophy were as obvious to his contemporaries as those of his political views and came under just as vigorous attack, notably by Bishop Berkeley. Berkeley, as the "Bishop" denotes, was not, properly speaking, a philosopher, but a theologian, and what he did, in effect, was to extend theological concepts into the theory of knowledge. He attacked Locke's theory of knowledge from two directions. "Matter" could not impress anything upon "mind" because such totally different entities could not make contact; hence, Locke's view that ideas have a base in material phenomena must be false. The mind has and can have knowledge of nothing but ideas; hence, what Locke calls primary and secondary qualities are alike simply ideas. Reality, therefore, consists of nothing but ideas. These ideas are of two kinds, those in the human mind and those of all the phenomena of the so-called external world, which are, in fact, simply ideas produced by the mind of God.

> When in Broad daylight I open my eyes, it is not in my power to choose whether I shall see or not, or to determine what particular objects shall present themselves to my view: and so likewise as to the hearing and other senses; the ideas imprinted on them are not creatures of *my* will. There is therefore some other Will or Spirit that produces them.

These concepts, also, are not particularly new. The concept of matter and "spirit" as antithetical was asserted by philosophers from Plato to Descartes and had roots in Indian philosophy. Plato never solved the problem he posed, for he presumed that matter did somehow affect the mind. Descartes tried to solve it by his "pineal gland" theory. Berkeley simply declares, in effect, that there is no matter—

all is mind, even that which looks like matter. This drastic solution was not so much a development of Plato as a retreat to a pre-Platonic position, for it stems from the same concept we find in the *Bhagavad-Gita* or some of the Taoists of reality as a dream.

After Berkeley came David Hume. Hume pointed out that Berkeley did not posit the existence of ideas only but of two other entities as well, namely "myself" and "some . . . Spirit." But if we know nothing but ideas, then what is "myself" but an "idea" and what is the "Spirit" (God) but another idea? If all is reduced to a succession of ideas, then we cannot know or show that the self or God or nature exists.

Hume widened his attack to take in the theoretical bases of idealism and theology in general: "If the material world rests upon a similar ideal world, this ideal world must rest upon some other; and so on, without end. It were better, therefore, never to look beyond the present material world."

Connected with this "infinite regress" theory—which sardonically pictured an endless succession of Gods—is Hume's attack upon "cause": "The first time a man saw the communication of motion by impulse, as by the shock of two billiard balls, he could not pronounce that the one event was *connected:* but only that it was *conjoined* with the other. After he has observed several instances of this nature, he then pronounces them to be *connected.* What alteration has happened to give rise to this new idea of *connexion?* Nothing but that he now *feels* these events to be *connected* in his imagination. . . ." There is, then, nothing in reality but succession; the idea that one event actually *causes* the other is supplied by the mind. Hence, one cannot argue—as did Aristotle, followed by the Christian theologians—from causes back to a "first cause," namely, to God. As we have seen, skepticism is a very old trend in philosophy; but there had not previously been a skepticism so thorough-going as Hume's. It is, in essence, the all-questioning outlook and systematic method of the new science applied to philosophy.

Hume, however, has thrown out the baby with the bath water. In demolishing Berkeley and the theologians, he reduces reality to a simple succession of images with no mind to perceive them and no way to distinguish dream from reality. Locke may have been thinking of just such pitfalls of ultra-subjectivism when he penned the following wry warning: "He that will not eat, till he has demonstration that it will nourish him; he that will not stir, till he infallibly knows the business he goes about will succeed; will have little else to do, but to sit still and perish." What Locke is apparently saying is that disembodied reason (which Hume uses as his radial point) is a nonexistent abstraction. In

342 / HUMANITY AND SOCIETY

reality, we have an indissoluble complex in which thought, feeling, action, and matter are intertwined.

How great was the disaster which Hume had wrought upon the old "pure logic" philosophy was shown in the reconstruction efforts of Immanuel Kant in his *Critique of Pure Reason* (1781) and other works. The essence of Kant's position is inherent in the famous comment in the conclusion of the *Critique:* "Two things fill the mind with ever new and increasing wonder and awe—the starry heaven above me and the moral law within me." In considering this statement, it is only fair to note that although Kant was remarkably abreast of the science of the day—he was, as we saw, the first to grasp the infinity of the universe with its galaxies beyond galaxies—he had no knowledge either of the neuropsychological nature of the mind or of its evolution, for such knowledge was not available, but regarded it as a set entity with its own inherent laws, one of which was the "moral law." In these "laws" ("forms of intuition," "categories") lies the essence of his answer to Hume and to Locke. The mind is not a blank tablet at birth but possesses frameworks into which it places the knowledge which it acquires. Among these are time, space, and causality. Time and space have no objective existence but are simply ways in which the mind digests what the senses reveal to it. There is causality, but it is an internal, not an external, phenomenon. Kant's salvage method is, in effect, to build a series of scaffoldings around "mind." For all this, his approach is essentially dualistic. There is mind ("moral law") and matter ("the starry heavens") and the former did not emerge from the latter. They are simply different phenomena. It is surprising, also, in view of Kant's unusual sense for cosmic evolution and movement, to see how static this concept is. Mind and matter are not only different; they are frozen into abstract categories.

VOLTAIRE, HOLBACH, DIDEROT

Following Locke and Hume, the main new development in philosophy, as in social thought, came in France. And for the same reasons, namely, that the large professional and business classes growing up there—a hundred years after Descartes—were more confident and sweeping in their attacks on the feudal State—and its church. A bitter anticlericalism developed that is the philosophical counterpart of French revolutionary social views. Locke could deliver his broadsides against the feudal church with a certain logical detachment because that church had already had its fangs pulled in England. But the French professionals, faced by an entrenched and arrogant foe, struck hard and sharp, some from deistic, others from atheistic points of view.

The deists, of whom Voltaire was the best known, argued that, although the specific theologies of Christian and other religions were false, nevertheless, a creative God existed but his attributes were unknowable (the religions had created him in their own image), and he had perhaps withdrawn from the actual workings of the universe. Voltaire in spite of all his barbed and brilliant scoffing at the Christian church came in the end to philosophical compromise: "all nations pray to God; wise men resign themselves and obey Him. Let us pray with the people and resign ourselves with the wise men."

All that the French capitalists and professional men really wanted of course, was a church of their own. But sentiment against the Catholic hierarchy had arisen to such heights after centuries of persecution and blind intransigence that the conflict could not be contained within these bounds (as it had been in England). The old church could be broken only by a full, frontal attack, and once the controversy began, a flood of anticlerical, even antitheological, ideas was let loose.

In reading some accounts of the French materialists, we get the impression that materialism was their invention, but materialist concepts, as we have seen, had existed in many civilized societies, from the Jains and Theophrastus on. And these are simply the visible tenth of the iceberg. Exhortations to "faith" by all churches indicated the continuous presence of a large body of nonbelievers whose influence was feared. Only occasionally, however, did materialistic views receive public form. The last renowned materialist writer in Europe had been Lucretius. But there must, in the succeeding centuries, have been many thousands who thought like him, for, after all, the idea that the universe was made and is run by an invisible Spirit who can be persuaded to change his mind by prayer or sacrifice runs counter to every-day observation. And the opposite idea, namely that the universe has always existed and operates out of its own materials would normally occur to some educated people in civilized societies even though they might have hesitated to express it.

When materialism came anew to the surface, it did not take quite the same form as in the Greeks or Lucretius. The main postulates were, of course, the same, because there are no others, but their formulation had broadened and deepened with the development of science. Its leaders were the Baron d'Holbach and Denis Diderot. Of the two, although Diderot is the more famous, Holbach is the more consistent, his *System of Nature* being by far the most complete expression of materialism written to this time. Holbach begins by attacking religion, not only as an intellectual absurdity but as a social evil: "Religion is the art of intoxicating people with religious fervor, to prevent them being cognizant of their troubles, heaped upon them by those who governed."

He then advances his own (atheistic) philosophy. He puts forward four main premises:

(a) "Man is the work of nature: he is submitted to her laws; he can not deliver himself from them; nor can he step beyond them even in thought"; (b) "The moral man is nothing more than this physical being considered under a certain point of view"; (c) "The only test of truth is experience"; (d) "The universe, that vast assemblage of everything that exists presents only matter and motion."

The deists, following Aristotle, had argued that motion was something separate from matter, and required a cause (a "Prime Mover"). Holbach replied, as had the Greek materialists before him, that, on the contrary, motion was inherent in matter. "The essence of matter is to act." The only general active force in the universe—if one could call it that—is "necessity"; and necessity is not a supernatural "fate" but an inherent part of nature.

This irresistible power, this universal necessity, this general energy, is then only a consequence of the nature of things, by virtue of which everything acts, without intermission of constant and immutable laws.... Nature is an active living whole, whose parts necessarily concur, and that without their own knowledge, to maintain activity, life and existence.

Biological matter came from physical matter: "In short, experiment proves beyond a doubt that matter, which is as inert and dead, assumes sensible action, intelligence and life, when it is combined of particular modes." Mind, too—as Lucretius had argued—is a form of matter. Holbach, influenced by the chemical and other discoveries of his age, compared its action to that of fermentation. Fermentation must be the result of particles of matter in motion; yet these particles and their actions are alike invisible; only their results can be perceived. Thought, too, must somehow result from the motion of invisible particles. "Mind" or "moral man"—in contrast to Descartes or Kant—interacts with "physical man."

The mind dies with its body. To say that mind or soul continues to live after is "to pretend that a clock shivered into a thousand pieces, will continue to strike the hour." People must face the fact of death frankly, but not allow it to become an obsession which makes their lives miserable.

The French materialists have been charged with being "mechanical" and failing to take flux and development into account. As Holbach's crude parallel of mind with fermentation shows, they were, indeed, sometimes mechanical, but they were not static. "Everything changes and everything passes away," writes Diderot, "only the whole endures. The world is for ever beginning and ending; each instant is its first and its last; it never has had, it never will have, other beginning or end. In this vast ocean of matter, not one molecule is like another, no molecule is for one moment like itself." Diderot, in fact, began to develop concepts of evolution: "The vegetable kingdom might well be and have been the first source of the animal kingdom, and have had its own source in the mineral kingdom; and the latter have originated from universal heterogeneous matter." He even had a glimpse of a selective process in evolution: ". . . that monsters annihilated one another in succession; that all the defective combinations of matter have disappeared, and that there have only survived those in which the organization did not involve any important contradiction, and which could subsist by themselves and perpetuate themselves."

Brilliant though all this was, Diderot had not and could not have a true theory of evolution. In view of the condition of biology and geology at the time, his ideas were necessarily fragmentary, and embraced such wild theories as that of the sudden appearance and disappearance of animal forms. "The elephant, that huge organized mass, a sudden product of fermentation! Why not?" Or Holbach's on Man: "There have been perhaps men upon the earth from eternity."

The idea of Man being eternal like the universe itself is clearly a rather desperate attempt to find a solution to the problem which the theologians kept posing—if Man was not created by God, whence had he come? And it shows, furthermore, that Holbach had little concept of geological time spans, for he mixes them up with the centuries of history in a general "catastrophe" series theory of a kind later developed by Cuvier. It was not realized either that there were different basic units for inorganic matter and living matter, and for living matter in its biological and psychological aspects. Holbach and Diderot did not in this respect advance beyond Lucretius.

As we have seen with Copernicus and others, knowledge does not come in gleaming nuggets of pure truth, but in a crude ore mixed with ignorance and half-truths. So, too, with ideas. Diderot's views on evolution, for instance, far off the mark though some of them were, nevertheless laid foundations from which others could build toward Darwin, whereas Berkeley's universal mind or Kant's "categories" were, like Plato's "divine pattern," dead-end concepts.

PRE-DARWIN

In the decades following Diderot and Holbach, ideas on evolution began to take further shape. As a result of geological investigation, the concept of geological time-sequences began to emerge. "The formation of the exterior part of the globe and the creation of its various inhabitants," wrote James Parkinson in his *Organic Remains of a Former World* in 1811, "must have been the work of a vast length of time, and must have been effected at several distant periods." "All vegetables and animals now existing," wrote Erasmus Darwin, grandfather of Charles Darwin, in *The Temple of Nature* (1803), "were originally derived from the smallest microscopic ones, formed by spontaneous vitality," and these by "innumerable reproductions, during innumerable centuries of time, gradually acquired the size, strength and excellence of form and faculties, which they now possess."[42] Lord Monboddo speculated that the orangoutan was an earlier form of Man, Erasmus Darwin, following Buffon and Helvetius, that "mankind arose from one family of monkeys on the banks of the Mediterranean." The path was being cleared both to *The Origin of Species* and *The Descent of Man*.

III: LITERATURE

During the centuries of the capitalist revolution in Europe the advances in art begun in commercial-feudal times rose to unprecedented heights. In painting, these centuries saw the rise of great Italian art (Leonardo da Vinci, Michelangelo, Tintoretto), German (Dürer and Holbein), Dutch and Flemish (Vermeer, Rembrandt, Breughel), Spanish (El Greco, Velázquez, Goya), British (Hogarth, Blake, Turner); in music, the great German movement of the eighteenth century (Bach, Handel, Mozart, Beethoven); in literature, the English Elizabethan (Shakespeare, Jonson, Spenser, Marlowe), seventeenth century (Milton), eighteenth century (Swift, Fielding), and early nineteenth (Blake, Wordsworth, Coleridge, Byron, Shelley, Keats, Jane Austen); the French sixteenth century (Rabelais, Montaigne), seventeenth (Molière, Racine), eighteenth (Voltaire, Rousseau), early nineteenth (Balzac, Hugo, George Sand); the German eighteenth and early nineteenth (Goethe, Schiller); the Russian early nineteenth century (Pushkin, Gogol).

Among the advances represented in the work of these writers, artists, and musicians, we find new uses of color, perspective, light, and shading in painting, plus a greater range of subject matter, moving well beyond the religious theme; in music the creation of harmony, which laid a base for new musical forms such as the opera and the symphony; the development of new forms both in the novel (Fielding and Jane Austen) and the drama (Shakespeare and Molière), developments which went beyond the Greek, Roman, or Asian and gave both

drama and novel greater scope and realism. In addition, the older
forms continued: the epic (Ariosto, Milton), the satire (Voltaire, Swift),
the lyric, the narrative poem, and so on, all of them with changes
and improvements (for instance, the addition of humor to the epic in
Ariosto, of humanitarian scope to satire in Swift).

Some of the connections of these developments with the society
are immediately apparent—the printing press, the discovery of the
technique of oil painting, the invention of new musical instruments
(for instance, the piano). The painting of the great Italians of the sixteenth century clearly reflects in its colorful magnificence the similar
magnificence in the living of the great merchant princes of the Italian
city states. The Dutch and Flemish paintings (Breughel's *Wedding
Dance*) reflect the views of the Dutch burghers. In the Metropolitan
Museum of Art in New York, there is in the entrance room a large
altarpiece of the Madonna by Raphael (seated on a lavish throne and
crowned with a gold halo) and in the next room Tintoretto's immense
and colorful panorama of the miracle of the loaves and fishes. A few
rooms over one finds Rembrandt's "Old Woman Cutting Her Nails"
and then Vermeer's "Young Girl with a Water Jug." Imagine Michelangelo painting an old woman cutting her nails! Rembrandt, however,
not only paints her but paints her with such understanding and sympathy that one can see the whole of a tragic life etched in her dim
lighted features.

As we look over these movements in the various arts, we note two
European peaks: the sixteenth century into the seventeenth, the late
eighteenth and early nineteenth, the peaks of the so-called "Renaissance" and "Romanticism." Nor are these peaks in the arts only. In
the first, along with Leonardo and Shakespeare went Galileo and
Bacon, in the second along with Goethe, Beethoven, and Goya went
Kant, Herschel, and Lavoisier. Furthermore, although within each
movement there was divergence between nations both in quality and
specifics (for instance, Holland was producing great painting while
England was producing little painting but great literature), nevertheless, there are clearly present in both periods the broad outlines of a
general European cultural movement. This becomes even more apparent if we compare the total movement with others. If we compare
it, for instance, with that of the European slave-commercial civilizations, we can see that we are in a new world of art. If we attempt to
break through the complexities of this world and ask ourselves what
is its essence, the answer, it seems to me, is that it is a sense of humanity's power to advance, the same sense that pervades the science
and thought of these centuries. There is little of this sense in slave-
commercial culture. Even in the highest artistic development of that

culture—the Athenian drama—there is little of it. There is, it is true, a sense of social revolt in Aeschylus, but there is no real feeling of advance. In the end of *Prometheus Bound,* Prometheus, for all his heroic defiance of Zeus, is defeated. The spirit of humanity—once it had succeeded in partially freeing itself from the oppression of the landed oligarchy—burst forth in a cry of mingled pain, indignation, rebellion, and restless questioning. Man can struggle but Man is always in the end destined to suffer defeat, socially as well as biologically.

Nor even in commercial-feudal times is there much advance in these respects. Petrarch's "Triumphs" end not in triumph but in defeat. Dante's hope for man lies not in this world but in the "next." Even Chaucer, for all his vitality, has no hope for a better future. To "strive" against power is to "fall." The base of art broadened. People in society, not the abstract Man of Aristotle became its subject, but there was no feeling that humanity could advance.

With Leonardo and Shakespeare a new outlook begins. Henry V is no tortured Oedipus or doomed Agamemnon, no Troilus laughing ironically in death at the world's vanities. The paths Henry treads are not those of Hell nor Paradise but earth. And he treads the earth—like Marlowe's Tamburlaine—that he may conquer. He has his eyes on Empire and he feels that he can achieve it. Man can conquer, and not territory only but—like Faustus—the world of nature. In the second "peak," with the releasing of the new powers of the industrial revolution, this sense of conquest rose—with Beethoven and Shelley, Blake and Goethe and Schiller, Byron and Hugo—and acquired a sense of direction. Prometheus now triumphs; humanity surges forward with irresistible power to a future of freedom and happiness, controlling both nature and its own destiny.

Shakespeare and His Age

The greatest writer in the first part of the movement, in the peak of the Renaissance, was William Shakespeare. Shakespeare is not, as one would sometimes gather, unique. Some of his plays are poor, some mediocre, some good, and some half dozen are great, but these half dozen are not on a higher general level than the best in other great writers (Homer, Aeschylus, Dante, Goethe, Shelley, Whitman, Joyce) and in some respects are inferior. We do not need to appeal to special forces to "explain" Shakespeare. He was not a divine Spirit standing above his age or mankind, but was part of that age and part of mankind. Specifically he was a product of the Elizabethan theater.

Plays had been acted on regular circuits for several centuries before the birth of Shakespeare. These were (as in Greece or India) mainly religious plays, but in time professional actors and professional play-wrights took over and the drama acquired a center in London. Their theaters, as is not usually recognized, were very small, about 80 feet by 80 feet on the outside, 55 feet by 55 feet on the inside—with the stage occupying about half of this; even with its balconies the Globe could hardly have held more than a hundred people. They were "little theaters" whose outstretched stage with spectators on three sides made for intimacy between playwright and spectators.

Before Shakespeare's arrival in London, stage managers had assembled a group of talented dramatists: Thomas Kyd (son of a scrivener), Christopher Marlowe (son of a shoemaker), Robert Greene (son of a saddler), George Peele (son of a charity school clerk), Thomas Lodge (son of a grocer), Thomas Nashe (son of a curate). And these were soon joined by Ben Jonson, ex-bricklayer. The Elizabethan was not so much an English theater as a London theater and a London theater of the middle class—a product of that mercantile hurly-burly and growing radicalism of London life which within fifty years burst out into revolution. It had little connection with the semifeudal countryside. At times it came into conflict with the aristocratic national State—for instance in the fight over *The Isle of Dogs* (1597), a play (now lost) by Thomas Nashe and Ben Jonson. The play was declared in the Privy Council to contain "seditious and scandalous matter." A number of the players and Jonson—"a maker of parte of the said Plaie"—were arrested for their "mutynous behavior" and Nashe's lodgings were raided. (Nashe had the good sense to leave town.) On the other hand the theater received support from some of the great court aristocrats such as Leicester, Essex, and Southampton. As a result, the new drama had both a realistic component (middle class city life), and a heroic grandeur emanating from the *de facto* union of merchant capitalists (who owned the fleet that beat the Armada) and aristocrats with mercantile connections against the great landowning interests. It is this Armada spirit that dominates the plays of Marlowe, the travel literature of the age, and much of the poetry, including Spenser's patriotic epic, *The Faerie Queene*.

Middle class realism pervades much of the literature of the age, including the earthy pamphlets of Nashe, Greene, and Dekker and the working class stories of Deloney (for instance *Jack of Newberry*—on shoe factory workers). In the drama we find it in the "domestic" tragedies (the anonymous *Arden of Feversham* and Thomas Heywood's *A Woman Killed with Kindness*), and in the "low life" comedy scenes in Greene, Jonson and others. There are no kings or palaces in these plays, but ordinary people of moderate means whose "tragedies" are taken seriously and told in homely style (completely remote from either the Athenian theater or the plays of Sakuntala). We can imagine how the great lords and ladies in the countryside would have turned up their noses at this shopkeeper drama. But the shopkeepers were on the march and were not to be stopped.

It is often stated that we know little about the life of Shakespeare (and completely unbased theories have grown up that Bacon or others wrote his plays). The fact is, however, that, considering his times and social status, we know a good deal. Official records and references to him by his contemporaries show that he was well known in London. He was for fifteen years the chief dramatist for the leading dramatic company, known as The King's Men. His plays were performed at court as well as in the theater. In an age of magazines and popular biographies as much would have survived for posterity as has for, say, Bernard Shaw. (We would have had motion pictures of Shakespeare as we do of Shaw.) But in an age still under the spell of feudal social values, biographies were written only of kings, aristocrats, or churchmen. (Izaak Walton wrote the life of John Donne not because he was a poet but because he was the Dean of St. Paul's.)

Shakespeare came from a commercial background. His father was a well-to-do merchant who rose to become mayor (chief councillor) of the town of Stratford and was granted a coat of arms. The first time we hear of William Shakespeare he is already in London, 28 years of age, serving his apprenticeship as a playwright, and under attack by a fellow playwright for plagiarism — "an upstart Crow, beautified with our feathers." The following year he dedicated his first book of poetry to the Earl of Southampton; his second book (a sonnet sequence), shows an intimate personal acquaintance with the earl. Within six years of the attack upon him as an "upstart" he was hailed as the leading dramatist of the age in the preface to an anthology containing specimens from 150 authors: "As Plautus and Seneca are accounted the best for Comedy and Tragedy among the Latins: so Shakespeare among the English is the most excellent in both kinds for the stage." Twenty-five years later the verdict was reaffirmed by Ben Jonson: "The applause! delight! the wonder of our Stage!" Jonson tells us that Shakespeare's plays in their production at the royal court were applauded alike by Queen Elizabeth and King James. His greatest success was traditionally achieved with *Henry IV,* whose Falstaff became a universal favorite. In time he became rather better off than most playwrights — a leading shareholder in the Globe Theatre and the owner of the town mansion at Stratford — but he remained part of the playwriting group and, as Ben Jonson's comments show, he was popular with his fellows: "honest and of an open, and free nature"; "I loved the man and do honour his memory (on this side idolatry)."

The general social forces acting upon him, then, were the same as for the dramatic group as a whole, namely those from the mercantile aristocracy—for national unity and expansion—and those from the London business and professional circles—for representation of their lives and values. The first of these influences can be seen biographically in Shakespeare's relationship to the Earl of Southampton and the Earl of Essex (father of the earl who commanded the first parliamentary army in the British Revolution). When the Earl of Essex, young, handsome, patron of the drama and an unyielding advocate of national expansion, was sent to Ireland by Queen Elizabeth to suppress a national revolt there, his departure was a matter for imperial exaltation. Shakespeare exalted with the rest, inserting a special tribute to Essex in the final Prologue of *Henry V*. But after Essex' return from Ireland he lost favor with the Queen and was punished by having his national wine monopoly taken away. Supported by Southampton, he gathered together several hundred armed men to stage a demonstration in London. Representatives of the rebels approached Shakespeare's dramatic company and requested that Shakespeare's *Richard II*, which depicted the dethroning and execution of a monarch, be played the day before the rebellion—an indirect, treasonous threat to the Queen. And so it took place. A group of Essex' and Southampton's supporters appeared at the performance and noisily applauded it. The rebellion failed; Essex was beheaded, Southampton imprisoned for life.

Whether or not Shakespeare agreed with this use of his play we do not know; but there can be no doubt of his admiration for both Essex and Southampton. And it is in this admiration for the imperial-minded aristocracy that we have the key to the spirit which pervades *Henry V* and other historical plays. In fact, Henry V himself, filled with patriotic fervor—

> Once more unto the breach, dear friends, once more;
> Or close the wall up with our English dead—

and yet "democratic" with his subordinates is a type of Essex.

Nor does this spirit motivate the historical plays only. As in Marlowe it finds general expression in the themes and characters of human greatness in all forms, in Brutus, the "noblest Roman," motivated—as Shakespeare doubtless believed Essex was—by "general honest thought and common good to all," in Othello and Antony and Macbeth, with their drives to power, drives, which, like that of Essex, failed. But the spirit which emanates from this section of what we might call the capitalist aristocracy, is, it seems to me, much more pervasive even than this; and not only in Shakespeare, not even only in England. It gives, as similar elements did in Homeric and other cultures, a kind of heroic magnificence to the art of the time—in Leonardo, Michelangelo, Raphael, Tintoretto, Spenser, Sidney, Marlowe. It added to capitalist-generated aspirations the cultural forms of aristocratic art and created that "grand style" in literature, shared in its general characteristics by Shakespeare, Spenser, Marlowe, and Sidney.

The grand style, however, is not Shakespeare's only style. We have, for example, the rollicking tavern scene in *Henry IV, Part One*, in which Prince Hal (later Henry V) abuses Falstaff:

> Why dost thou converse with that trunk of humours, that bolting-hutch of beastliness, that swollen parcel of dropsies, that huge bombard of sack, that stuffed cloak-bag of guts, that roasted Manning-tree ox with the pudding in his belly, that reverend vice, that grey iniquity, that father ruffian, that vanity in years? Wherein is he good, but to taste sack and drink it? wherein cunning, but in craft? wherein crafty, but in villany? wherein villanous, but in all things? wherein worthy, but in nothing?

Here is the very language of the tavern, the earthy realism of Delaney, of the criminal underworld pamphlets of Robert Greene, of Jonson's comedies, of the paintings of Breughel, which arose from the demand by the prospering city classes for an art of their own, an art they could understand. Shakespeare, in fact, in this very scene makes fun of the grand manner, the manner of so many of his own plays (for instance, in Falstaff's clowning parody of the kingly speech—directed at the laughing hostess of the tavern as "queen.") Furthermore, the scene reflects the ambivalence of the city classes toward the aristocracy. They supported the aristocracy as the national ruling class, which, in protecting all property, protected theirs, but, at the same time, they resented it. Something of this resentment comes out in the scene in Falstaff's parodying of royalty and its ways, yet, typically, the scene is soon pulled back into a framework of respect and loyalty. (Falstaff is later "banished.") In such scenes Shakespeare is writing realistically, in others—in the great tragedies—he writes impressionistically:

> I am dying, Egypt, dying; only
> I here importune death awhile, until
> Of many thousand kisses the poor last
> I lay upon thy lips.

No one ever actually spoke on his death bed as does Antony here. And Shakespeare is aware of this. He is trying to distill in poetry the essence of a great love affair and its tragic end, the essence of mood and character—as Leonardo did in the *Mona Lisa* or Michelangelo in the tomb of the Medici.

No writer before Shakespeare had his scope, variety, or depth. If we think, for instance, only of his range of characters and style, it is at once apparent that none of the great writers of the past can match him; nor do they have the depth of insight into character and human motive that he does. But in other respects they surpass him. Homer at his best has a sustained and swelling beauty beyond Shakespeare. Shakespeare falls far behind Sophocles or Marlowe in philosophic depth. He nowhere approaches the dark intensity or exalted visioning of Dante. Great though his comedy is he has not the sophisticated comic touch of Chaucer. Shakespeare stood, like Leonardo, on the topmost peak of a cultural movement greater than those of feudal-commercialism—which produced Dante or Chaucer (or Lady Murasaki)—or slave-commercialism—which produced Homer and Sophocles. As the movement rose higher than those of the past so did its best writers and artists; but it was a movement with many limitations; and if we wish to view Shakespeare in even wider perspective—and, in view of the virtually religious cult that has grown up around him, it is perhaps well to do so—it is apparent that, for all his sensitivity and insight, his concept of human life is in some ways very narrow. Although he makes an advance over the past in treating some middle class characters in depth, he bears the marks of his age. He emphasizes the upper classes—kings, queens, princes—and lower class characters he generally ridicules. He exalts in Essex' triumphs in Ireland but exhibits no feeling for the oppressed Irish. He knew nothing of the new science that gives Goethe's *Faust* a sophisticated depth and scope beyond even the best Renaissance thinking, or of the social philosophy that brought to Shelley, Zola, and Shaw alike the perspectives of historical evolution. He was trapped within a set dramatic structure of temporal progression through five acts and a stylistic tradition that fell to bombast when inspiration failed. Given these limitations, however, one can only wonder at the degree to which he triumphed over them, the depth of character that he *was* able to achieve, the great range of his verse, his compassionate insights into human situations and motives, his healthy scorn for affectation, his unerring sense for dramatic projection and compactness, his earthy, often sardonic philosophy:

> Men must endure
> Their going hence, even as their coming hither:
> Ripeness is all.

Revolution and Compromise

Following the Elizabethan age came the British Revolution—and its poet, John Milton, who was Latin secretary to Oliver Cromwell and the leading publicist for the revolutionary government. Students in classrooms read his great sonnet to Cromwell — "our chief of men" — without realizing that it was the equivalent of, say, a sonnet to Lenin in the 1920's. His *Tenure of Kings and Magistrates* and *Eikonklastes* justified the execution of the king: "It is not, neither ought to be, the glory of a protestant state, never to have put their king to death; it is the glory of a protestant king never to have deserved death." His *Doctrine and Discipline of Divorce* was a pioneer work, his *Areopagitica* one of the first clarion calls for freedom of speech.

It is this spirit also that animates *Paradise Lost*. Satan, the rebel leader, cries out to his defeated armies in Hell — "Awake, arise, or be for ever fallen" — as Milton's identification with the revolution overcomes his religious scruples, and Satan in the first two books becomes a heroic rebel. When he wrote *Paradise Lost,* however, the revolutionary government had collapsed, and, having narrowly escaped execution, Milton was living in virtual exile in the country, "blind, old, and lonely," hurling treasonous thunderbolts at the government. And the revolt in *Paradise Lost* is not one that triumphed but one that failed. Milton catches fire when he portrays that revolution in its ascendancy, and he depicts its rallying after defeat with power and dignity. But the poem contains many passages of personal struggling with despair arising from his isolated situation, and the sense of approaching death runs through the whole. True, it is essentially a revolutionary epic — without the British Revolution it would not have taken the shape it did — but it is also a Puritan revolutionary epic, with all that that implies of emphasis upon religious and moral questions.

That Milton did not produce the body of great work that Shakespeare did (although the best of *Paradise Lost* and *Samson Agonistes* are on a level with the best of Shakespeare) was also due to Puritanism, not so much Milton's personal Puritanism as that of the age. The capitalists, as they advanced to power, became more conservative and one form of this conservatism was moral. They not only suppressed painting and music, as connected with the feudal church, but they attacked the stage and literature in general for they feared all emotional and aesthetic freedom as potentially dangerous. Consequently Milton had no fellowship of the theater or the Mermaid Tavern, no "great audience," but wrote his poetry in isolation and for a small readership.

The dominant note of the literature of the long period of political compromise (1660–1785) which followed the revolution was struck by John Dryden when he said that the task of the writer was now to "retrench the superfluities of expression" and curb the "lawless imagination." The comments form an interesting example of how social situations create an intellectual atmosphere which embraces not only content but style. What did Dryden mean by the "lawless imagination"? He meant Shakespeare and Milton, Marlow and Spenser. Not that he disapproved of all of Shakespeare and Milton, nor that he was himself lacking in power, but he felt that his predecessors had sometimes dangerously outrun the bounds of "good taste." "Order" and "system" were needed in literature.

Following Dryden came Pope:

> True Wit is Nature to advantage dress'd,
> What oft was thought, but ne'er so well express'd.

Not to find new paths in thought, but to put into smooth couplets what everyone (in the ruling classes) agreed upon, the polished elegance of the style reflecting a mind unruffled by "lawless" views, a repudiation, in short, of the wild magnificence of Lear or the revolutionary exhortations of Satan.

The main upper class direction of Dryden and Pope, however, was not the only one. There were also Defoe, Richardson, Fielding, creators of the new novel. The century was not as unchanging as it appeared, and the difference between the two groups reflected a difference in class audience. *Robinson Crusoe* (1719) became a popular story; so, too, did the realistic *Moll Flanders*. By the middle of the century this new audience had risen to unprecedented proportions. (England was by then well ahead of its continental rivals in manufacturing, trade, and colonization.) When Clarissa, the heroine of Richardson's serialized novel *Clarissa Harlowe* (1747–48), died, bells tolled all over England. Past literary history had nothing to show on this scale; even the audience of the Athenian drama was limited in comparison, for Athens had no such large middle strata of the population; Shakespeare did not have one-tenth of this audience, Milton (for his poetry) not one-hundreth. At the very time, then, that Pope's tripping couplets were entertaining the upper classes, the middle classes were becoming a major reading public and turning to the novel, which depicted them and their world (as in *Tom Jones*).

In addition, a new strain, one of a different nature, began to enter English literature in this century — as it had in Athens — an outside influence from a subject nation, namely Ireland; and this influence, once begun, was to continue. Swift, Goldsmith, and Sheridan were the forerunners of Wilde, Yeats, Shaw, Joyce, and O'Casey. The Irish writer in England naturally viewed the "master race" from his own angle. In Swift, this produced a scope of satire that went beyond its apparently limited purpose of attacking Whigs and Tories into an ironic condemnation of ruling class politics: "That if his Majesty, in consideration of your [Gulliver's] services, and pursuant to his own merciful disposition, would please to spare your life, and only give order to put out both your eyes, he humbly conceived that by this expedient justice might in some measure be satisfied, and all the world would applaud the lenity of the Emperor, as well as the fair and generous proceedings of those who have the honour to be his counsellors." We see also a new, direct simplicity of style here, which was, in effect, a rejection of the aristocratic (Latinized) grand manner in prose.

THE CONTINENT

While literature was thus developing in Britain, art in the continental countries was following various paths. The Renaissance died in an Italy which remained divided into a series of purely Mediterranean-oriented states, while the Atlantic opened to put commerce on a new basis for other countries. The opening of the Atlantic spread the "Renaissance" to Spain (Cervantes and El Greco) but Spain was so fundamentally feudal that it had but sandy soil in which to grow. Cervantes' brilliant attack on feudal values in *Don Quixote* was not followed up by a school of writers (comparable, say, to the Elizabethans). In France, Rabelais' boisterous satires *Gargantua* and *Pantagruel* are primarily antifeudal in content and manner, although they also contain feudal values. The same is true of the great drama of the next century (the seventeenth), the tragedies of Corneille and Racine and the comedies of Molière. Molière, himself the son of a merchant, attacks "bourgeois" attitudes yet does so with a typically capitalist-society verve and aims some barbs at aristocratic values also. The plays of Corneille and Racine have a typically feudal stylized beauty—like a Byzantine mosaic or a minuet—depicting life in indirect constructs of scene and character, a narrow framework but one which Racine sometimes infused with passion and intellectual humor. Even in the eighteenth century we find feudal formalism in the tragedies of Voltaire at the same time as he has broken loose in his prose and is bombarding the feudal State with a savage satiric wit (*Candide, A Philosophical Dictionary*). Like Voltaire, Rousseau and Diderot are fundamentally revolutionary, not only as social critics but as writers. Rousseau's assertion in his novels and autobiography of the importance of the individual and of the emotional life is a repudiation of the feudal creed of subjugated regimentation and the "danger" of emotional freedom. In these centuries the German states produced no great writer between Luther and Lessing but made unprecedented strides in music as Handel and Bach created a harmonic music on a new level (although still tied to church values).

The history of cultural development—as one would not suspect from textbook surveys—is filled with unsolved problems. Why, for instance, did literature and not music develop in England in these centuries and music and not literature in Germany? Whatever the explanation it cannot be the usual cliché (which I quote from Alfred Einstein's *Short History of Music*): "Music is not the natural means of expression for the Englishman to the same extent as it is for the Italian."[43] Earlier Einstein had informed us that England "had given a new impulse to the whole of European music, and she still [in the sixteenth century] retained her rightful position beside the other nations."[44] Music can hardly have been the "natural" expression of Englishmen in the sixteenth century but not in the eighteenth. Let us turn our regard from British "nature" to British society. The dominant English painting and music had been traditionally connected with the aristocracy and its church. In attacking the church's capitalism, Puritan revolutionaries crippled painting and music, and crippled them in an important formative period. If it be asked why literature survived, the answer is that literature had been more closely connected with the city business classes than were painting or music, but, as we have noted, literature also suffered somewhat as the attack, like all such, developed its own momentum and swept beyond its specific objectives.

Literature did not advance notably beyond the feudal-commercial stage in Germany because Germany had no powerful capitalist city center comparable to London or Paris but remained divided into a series of feudal states, each dominated by the great landowning interests and each with its court poets and musicians. Nevertheless, there was an antifeudal groundswell (which in 1848 finally broke out into revolution). Perhaps it was because it was denied expression in literature—a more dangerous medium—that it came out in music, as it did later among the enslaved American Negroes.

AN AGE OF REVOLUTION

In the late eighteenth century the tide began to quicken; by the early nineteenth it was in full flood. A movement in literature and the other arts of greater depth and scope than the "Renaissance" came into being, a movement among whose giants were Mozart, Beethoven, Goya, Goethe, Schiller, Blake, Byron, Shelley, Balzac, and Hugo. With Mozart and Beethoven music burst beyond the clerical bounds of

Bach and Handel, and, with Beethoven, became a sophisticated medium for the expression of social revolution. Music, of all the major arts, was historically the latest to develop into one that could depict life in depth. With Goya the art of painting similarly rose to a new level. When we look through his realistic *Disasters of War*, we realize how limited in content had been even the best graphic art of the past. How many wars had been fought in Europe and Asia and the sufferings of the people — murder, rape, mutilation, executions, imprisonment, disease, famine — left unrecorded while the artists were painting Holy Families or Buddhas or princes or burghers? How many workers had toiled at how many forges but had had no artist to depict their power and grace until Goya's "The Forge" (now in the Frick Collection in New York)?

The movement first flowered in Great Britain, which was also the first to feel the new economic and social forces. British coal production more than tripled from 1700 to 1800 and cotton exports went from 5,000 in 1710 to £5 million in 1800. These figures may seem to have little to do with literature, but let us consider their implications. They mean, in the first place, that a major social change was taking place. If there were more mines to produce coal and more mills to produce cotton there were more capitalists to own them and more workers to work in them. There were more small businessmen and more professional men to handle the affairs of the capitalists and businessmen. And as agricultural production was not rising at the same rate, this meant a relative gain for the capitalist, small business, and professional classes. It meant a still further shift in the balance between city and country in favor of the city. But the city had but a limited voice in the affairs of state for the aristocracy controlled the House of Lords and virtually controlled the House of Commons by the aid of property restrictions on voting rights, "rotten boroughs," and other devices. Of a population of 11 million about 11,000 had the vote. The result was that England became a scene of social and political turmoil as the politically dispossessed but ever-growing classes demanded parliamentary reform. International was added to internal conflict: the American Revolutionary War, the French Revolution, the wars against the French republic, and the Napoleonic Wars. The struggle for parliamentary reform and allied causes went through two phases, the first from about 1785 to 1800, the second from about 1810 to 1832. In the first the movement was narrow but radical, its intellectual leaders, Paine and Godwin; it was broken by the repressive measures of the Pitt Government. The revival began about ten years later, at first led by "left" Whigs and broadening out to move the Whig party and win a partial victory in the Reform Act of 1832. The literature of the period rose and fell with these two waves. The outstanding writers in the first were Blake and Wordsworth, in the second, Byron and Shelley.

BLAKE AND WORDSWORTH

In order to see the nature of the changes brought about in English poetry by Blake and Wordsworth let us look at what it was that they were changing. The best of the preceding poetic tradition, the dominant tradition of the eighteenth century, was Pope, and among the best of Pope was *The Rape of the Lock,* a mock heroic poem on a quarrel that ensued between two aristocratic families when the son of one family snipped a lock of hair from the head of the daughter of the other. Pope imagines "Belinda's" lock as guarded by numerous invisible "sprites"; as she bends over her cup at a tea party the hero (or villain) approaches with the extended scissors:

> The Peer now spreads the glitt'ring Forfex wide,
> T'inclose the Lock; now joins it, to divide.
> Even then, before the fatal engine closed,
> A wretched Sylph too fondly interposed;
> Fate urged the shears, and cut the Sylph in twain,
> (But airy substance soon unites again)
> The meeting points the sacred hair dissever
> From the fair head, for ever, and for ever!
> Then flashed the living lightning from her eyes,
> And screams of horror rend th' affrighted skies.

All is elegant, clever, and trivial, the atmosphere of the aristocratic drawingroom, with its boredoms, polish, and wit.

When we go from this to Blake we are in a different world — a world of chimney sweeps:

> A little black thing among the snow,
> Crying "weep! weep!" in notes of woe!

There were chimney sweeps in Pope's day, but he did not write about them. In the intervening half century, industry had spread, the workers were forming "combinations" (which were declared illegal), agitation on child labor was beginning, revolution was astir in France and America, and Blake projects it all with a crescendo of power not seen in English verse since Milton, and, at times, surpassing Milton:

What is the price of Experience? do men buy it for a song?
Or wisdom for a dance in the street? No, it is bought with the price

Of all that a man hath, his house, his wife, his children.
Wisdom is sold in the desolate market where none come to buy,
And in the wither'd field where the farmer plows for bread in vain.
. . . .

Then the groan & the dolor are quite forgotten, & the slave grinding at the mill,
And the captive in chains, & the poor in the prison, & the soldier in the field
When the shatter'd bone hath laid him groaning among the happier dead.
It is an easy thing to rejoice in the tents of prosperity:
Thus could I sing & thus rejoice: but it is not so with me.

English literature, indeed, literature in general, had never seen anything
like this before. Such passages reveal how limited were Homer and
Dante and Shakespeare in their feelings for humanity, how little they
reflected the sufferings of the oppressed mass of the population, how
little concept they had of any kind of social solution of the ills of
humanity.

Blake, by trade an engraver, was of the London lower middle class.
His economic position kept his hatred of the ruling class and his feeling
for all the·oppressed at a white heat, but the position of his class was
such that it had not—any more than had the peasantry in the fourteenth century—a viable alternative to the existing order. It was an
angry, isolated, intellectually muddled class (mixing Methodism with
"reform"), alternating hostility and servility, lacking the confidence
either of the aristocracy or the capitalists. Blake both reflected it and
transcended it. He reflected its intellectual muddle—but on a more
sophisticated plane—and he transcended it in his humanitarian scope
and revolutionary visions. He attacked the government, church marriage, economic exploitation, war, Puritanism, and not in poetry alone
but in a new art form combining poetry and graphic art. As he went
along the attack became less direct as he devised a complex set of
symbols which kept him free from prosecution and both obscured and
enhanced his meaning. His *Four Zoas* (which I quote above) is both
the most difficult to follow and the greatest revolutionary poem written
until that time.

For his longer poems Blake devised a new kind of "grand style"—
a mixture of the Bible and "Ossian"—and for his shorter ones a simple,
direct style—with roots in folk ballads and hymns, both repudiations
of the aristocratic manner and assertions of middle class values. These
innovations in style were also independently created by William
Wordsworth. Change was "in the air." Wordsworth examined the
change and produced a critical theory based upon it (as Blake did not):

The Reader will find that personifications of abstract ideas rarely occur in
these volumes; and are utterly rejected, as an ordinary device to elevate the

style, and raise it above prose. My purpose was to imitate, and, as far as possible, to adopt the very language of men; and assuredly such personifications do not make any natural or regular part of that language. . . [as in a sonnet by Gray]:

> "In vain to me the smiling mornings shine,
> And reddening Phoebus lifts his golden fire:
> The birds in vain their amorous descant join,
> Or cheerful fields resume their green attire. . . ."

What is Wordsworth objecting to? Such phrases as "reddening Phoebus" for the sun, "golden fire" for sunshine, "amorous descant" for song, and so on. Such language represented to Wordsworth aristocratic values as clearly as did the gold-painted carriage or the silks and satins of the great noble. He was advocating in poetry the equivalent of the plain business suit in social life, a change which also began about this time. Simplicity and power combine in his great sonnet on Toussaint L'Ouverture, the Haitian revolutionary:

> Though fallen thyself, never to rise again,
> Live, and take comfort. Thou has left behind
> Powers that will work for thee; air, earth, and skies;
> There's not a breathing of the common wind
> That will forget thee; thou has great allies;
> Thy friends are exultations, agonies,
> And love, and man's unconquerable mind.

Nor did Wordsworth restrict himself to the simple style. He also developed a new kind of "grand style" and sometimes, as did Blake, used it to express revolutionary views, and to express them with power and beauty, for instance, his excitement in the early days of the French Revolution:

> But Europe at that time was thrilled with joy.
> France standing on the top of golden hours,
> And human nature seeming born again.

Passion and imagination have come back into English poetry and have molded a style of their own, grand, but at the same time, direct, supple, and unaffected.

Such was the young Wordsworth. This Wordsworth had first been a revolutionary and then a humanitarian liberal. As a revolutionary he advocated breaking up the great estates, abolishing of the House of Lords, establishing a revolutionary dictatorship by violence, if necessary, as "indispensable from a state of war between the oppressors and the oppressed." As a humanitarian liberal who had repudiated his former views and colleagues, he faced a deep moral crisis of guilt (the tortured product of which was *The Prelude*), for he did not wish to face the distasteful fact of his having knuckled under to the threats of power (as had a whole section of the upper and middle classes). Within a few years he gave up the struggle (helped by patronly handouts and a government sinecure as a revenue stamp collector), urging support for the great landowners—"the stability and might of a great estate, with proportional influence in the House of Commons"—and calling for a special cavalry to ride down the striking workers.

BYRON AND SHELLEY

As Wordsworth collapsed Byron and Shelley arose. They rose with the new movement for parliamentary reform. Byron's maiden speech in the House of Lords, a passionate attack on the proposal to use capital punishment against the Luddite strikers, expresses the temper of this new movement:

> Is there not blood enough upon your penal code, that more must be poured forth to ascend to Heaven and testify against you? How will you carry the Bill into effect? Can you commit a whole county to their own prisons? Will you erect a gibbet in every field, and hang up men like scarecrows? . . .

In his second speech in the House of Lords, Byron attacked British policy on Ireland, stigmatizing the Act of Union between England and Ireland as "the union of the shark with his prey." His third and final speech was in defense of the radical parliamentary reformer, Major Cartwright, who had been arrested.

All this, we should note, was a new kind of activity for writers. They had not in the past (in feudal, slave-commercial, or commercial-feudal societies) supported "causes" or "cases." To have done so would have been to have courted imprisonment, torture, or execution. Shakespeare did not use his pen to help Essex; no writers came to the defense of Raleigh. The first important European writer to take up such matters was Voltaire, and with Voltaire the emphasis was on the individual victim of local or church injustice.

Shelley engaged in actions similar to those of Byron. He went to Ireland and spoke at a public meeting on the same platform as Daniel O'Connell, the Irish nationalist leader, and printed two pamphlets and a broadside in support of Irish independence and Catholic Emancipation. When a radical publisher, Daniel Isaac Eaton, was imprisoned, he wrote an impassioned and revolutionary pamphlet attacking the judge who had sentenced him (*A Letter to Lord Ellenborough*). He similarly defended another publisher, Richard Carlile, editor of *The Republican,* and subscribed to the defense funds of two others. As a result he was put under surveillance by government spies. When three workers were executed (in 1817) after being framed by a government labor spy known as Oliver, he tried to arouse a national protest.

In spite of the fact that it was so different in style from his own works, Shelley hailed Byron's *Don Juan* as a new genre, the epic form for their times. *Don Juan* covers the whole scope of the age, but, unlike the Homeric, Virgilian or Miltonic epics, deals with it directly and in a wide variety of styles and moods. Byron rejects the traditional epic convention of the impersonal poet standing above his subject and throws himself into the midst of the life he is describing. He has been accused of not having deep or sincere feelings. But this is to misread his pose of satiric indifference. Behind the pose lies humanitarian concern and passionate hatreds, as in his turbulent scorning of Lord Castlereagh (who stamped out the Irish rebellion of 1798, led the war against the French republic, and presided at the Congress of Vienna):

> Cold-blooded, smooth-faced, placid miscreant:
> > Dabbling its sleek young hands in Erin's gore,
> And thus for wider carnage taught to pant,
> > Transferred to gorge upon a sister shore;
> The vulgarest tool that tyranny could want,
> > With just enough of talent and no more
> To lengthen fetters by another fix'd,
> And offer poison long already mixed.

The solution was to lie with the people ("it") and revolution:

> At first it grumbles, then it swears, and then,
> > Like David, flings smooth pebbles 'gainst a giant;
> At last it takes to weapons such as men
> > Snatch when despair makes human hearts less pliant.
> Then comes the "tug of war"; — 'twill come again,
> > I rather doubt; and I would fain say "fie on't,"
> If I had not perceived that revolution
> Alone can save the earth from hell's pollution.

Once again with Byron as with Blake we are aware of a new force in the literature of the world. Byron combines Ovid's intimate jauntiness with surging, epic energy, a panoramic sweep of society and a revolutionary philosophy. Unlike Blake — who was virtually unknown and unread — he became the greatest literary force in his age, perhaps, indeed, the greatest literary force of any age up to that time.

Shelley, although lacking Byron's earthy power, sophistication, and sustained brilliance, had greater depth of understanding and of psychological and aesthetic sensitivity. Of all the poets of the age he saw the furthest and the deepest and had the greatest range of subject and style. Byron, a member of the House of Lords, moved in aristocratic circles. Shelley came from a nouveau riche county family and was early and sharply flung out of the orbit of his class (expelled from Oxford and alienated from his family). Like Byron he supported nationalist, antifeudal revolutions, and supported them with passion and power (as in the following, on the Greek revolution):

> Let the tyrants rule the desert they have made;
>   Let the free possess the paradise they claim;
> Be the fortune of our fierce oppressors weighed
>   With our ruin, our resistance, and our name!
>
> Our dead shall be the seed of their decay,
>   Our survivors be the shadow of their pride,
> Our adversity a dream to pass away—
>   Their dishonour a remembrance to abide!

Like Blake (and unlike Byron) he envisaged a social revolution which included the working class—

> Rise like Lions after slumber
> In unvanquishable number—
> Shake your chains to earth like dew
> Which in sleep had fallen on you—
> Ye are many—they are few—

and uncovered the economic roots of exploitation:

> The seed ye sow, another reaps;
> The wealth ye find, another keeps;
> The robes ye weave, another wears;
> The arms ye forge, another bears.
>
> Sow seed,—but let no tyrant reap;
> Find wealth,—let no impostor heap;
> Weave robes,—let not the idle wear;
> Forge arms,—in your defence to bear.

Byron, for all his revolutionary fervor, really had no concept of a future society beyond that of a republican democracy. Shelley, although lacking the elementary revolutionary surge of Blake, had a deeper insight than did Blake both into the forces producing change and the kind of new order which these forces might bring about. Social change was arising inevitably from social forces not under direct human control, and the new order, based on economic equality, would bring psychological and moral transformation:

> The loathesome mask has fallen, the Man remains,
> Sceptreless, free, uncircumscribed, but Man;
> Equal, unclassed, tribeless and nationless,
> Exempt from awe, worship, degree, the King
> Over himself, just, gentle, wise, but Man.

In this future communistic society there will be neither classes nor nations nor churches; at some point in the future the power of humanity would extend beyond our planet.

Shelley's revolutionary vision permeated the whole of his life and poetry, even in ways that seem at first sight remote from their source; for instance in the liquid and flowing beauty of "To a Skylark":

> Higher still and higher
>   From the earth thou springest,
> Like a cloud of fire;
>   The blue deep thou wingest,
> And singing still dost soar, and soaring ever singest.

There is certainly nothing directly social here, yet such a stanza could no more have been written in the years between 1660 and 1780 than the electric light could then have been invented. Both the sentiment and the language would have been rejected by the "Augustans" as "imagination run wild." And both, just as certainly, would have struck a responsive note in the breasts of the liberal intellectuals of the age of the French Revolution and parliamentary reform. So, too, would Keats' *Hyperion* (which reflects humanity's advance from the lower beauty of Hyperion to the higher beauty of Apollo) and the wild and misted sea-scapes of Turner. The revolution penetrated every corner of art.

None of these changes, of course, need have happened exactly at this time. The works of Shelley and Byron, as we have seen, were the product of the new wave of social "reform" that began about 1810, but if certain economic and other forces had developed more slowly it could well not have begun until 1820. If so it would have come too late to influence these poets. Nor, to take a broader scope, need the American and French revolutions or the English reform movement as a whole have arisen when they did. That they would have arisen was inevitable, and whenever they did would have inspired poets and painters. But Byron and Shelley would not have been among them. If they had turned to literature at all they would have written works of competence but not of greatness, on the level of Pope before them or Arnold after them.

To what degree did the writers of the time have an understanding of these matters? The mere posing of the question reminds us that in previous ages they had virtually none. The beginnings of social sciences in the late eighteenth century in Europe, however, gave new insights; how deep these went in the best minds of the time is revealed in Shelley:

> The peculiar style of intense and comprehensive imagery which distinguishes the modern literature of England, has not been, as a general power, the product of the imitation of any particular writer. The mass of capabilities remains at every period materially the same; the circumstances which awaken it to action perpetually change. If England were divided into forty republics, each equal in population and extent to Athens, there is no reason to suppose but that, under institutions not more perfect than those of Athens, each would produce philosophers and poets equal to those who (if we except Shakespeare) have never been surpassed. We owe the great writers of the golden age of our literature to that fervid awakening of the public mind which shook to dust the oldest and most oppressive form of the Christian religion. . . . The great writers of our own age are, we have reason to suppose, the companions and forerunners of some unimagined change in our social condition or the opinions which cement it. The cloud of mind is discharging its collected lightning, and the equilibrium between institutions and opinions is now restoring, or is about to be restored.

Shelley did not know what the deeper relationship of economic and social forces to each other or to literature were, but he perceived that they existed, whereas no writer in the past had perceived them at all. He perceived, too, the basic truth that the question is not one of "genius" or "mind" but of social forces developing "capabilities" which for every age are potentially the same.

JANE AUSTEN

One other English writer of these decades must be mentioned even in so general a study as this, namely, Jane Austen. All the great writers that we have so far mentioned — and not writers only but painters and musicians also — were men. Jane Austen was the first major woman writer in English literature, representing in literature what Mary Wollstonecraft did in social thought. Nor did she come alone. Her way was prepared by such women intellectuals and writers as Lady Mary Wortley Montague, Catherine Macaulay, Fanny Burney, Elizabeth Inchbald, Mary Hays, Mary Robinson; and she was succeeded by a group of talented women writers, Mary Shelley, Elizabeth Barrett Browning, Charlotte Brontë, Emily Brontë, Christina Rossetti, George Eliot. And in the same decades women writers and painters began to arise in France (Madame de Staël, George Sand, Rosa Bonheur). This movement was apparently unprecedented not only in European art but in art anywhere. Sappho and Lady Murasaki seem to have written alone or almost alone. But now, as we have seen, the wives of the capitalists and professional men took advantage of the general advance of the classes to put forward their interests as women. Economic and social developments — the rise of a large middle class reading public, the lack of legal restrictions — made possible the rise of a group of women writers.

Jane Austen broke away from the heavy, operatic romances of Scott with their cardboard characters and unreal plots to produce direct and searching pictures of the society that she knew, and although that society was not wide in range — she was a small town minister's daughter — she depicted it truly and in a supple, clever style that made other novelists look clumsy in comparison. She was no social reformer, but we are in no doubt that her novels are written by a woman. In *Pride and Prejudice* she very skilfully brings in a protest against the disinheritance of daughters by the "entail" system. Her leading women characters are intelligent and witty, well able to hold their own with the men. It would not escape the notice of her women readers that, in the scene in which the stuffy, snobbish clergyman William Collins proposes to the brilliant, high-spirited Elizabeth Bennet, a woman writer was painting a devastating caricature of a man:

The idea of Mr. Collins, with all his solemn composure, being run away with by his feelings, made Elizabeth so near laughing, that she could not use the short pause he allowed in any attempt to stop him farther, and he continued: —

"My reasons for marrying are, first, that I think it a right thing for every clergyman in easy circumstances (like myself) to set the example of matrimony in his parish; secondly, that I am convinced it will add very greatly to my happiness; and thirdly — which perhaps I ought to have mentioned earlier, that it is the particular advice and recommendation of the very noble lady whom I have the honor of calling patroness.

XII

America and the Capitalist

Revolution

I: The Societies of the American Indians

If we turn a globe of the world we see that our planet contains four great land masses, one immense one, one large one, and two smaller ones. The immense one is Eurasia-Africa, the large one is America, the two smaller ones are Australia and Antarctica. If we look more closely we can see that the Atlantic coasts of America and Eurasia-Africa seem as though they had once been fitted together, and that if we do so fit them, Australia and Antarctica will fit in roughly at the bottom. According to some recent geological evidence this was, in fact, the original state of the continental mass; there were not four continents, but one, which for some reason broke into four sections, each sliding — like ice-floes — away from each other. Some early evolution apparently took place while they were joined, but later evolution took place in two main centers, which, although separate, were not insulated each from each.

There is in the American Museum of Natural History an illuminated map of America and Asia which shows by means of moving lights the migrations of animals from one continent to the other. For instance, we see the ancestors of the moose, the sheep, and the bear all evolved in Asia, passing across the Bering Straits (then a land bridge) into America. Other lights show animals which evolved in America emigrating to Asia, for instance, the ancestors of the horse and the camel.

In the period of human society, this fact of continental division has also meant three developmental centers. The effect of this on Australia, as we have already noted, was to hold back society there at the food-gathering stage. America, being larger, more varied in terrain, and in some contact with Asia, was able to advance further. Farming society had developed to the early stages of civilization in Middle and South America when it was cut down by European invasion.

Food-Gathering and Farming

As Clark Wissler points out in his *Indians of the United States,* the present day popular concept of the American Indian is still that established by Buffalo Bill and his Wild West Show. And the Indians that Buffalo Bill featured were the Dakotas, with their elaborate eagle-feather headdress. "We expect all Indians to wear the Dakota costume, so that no matter what the tribe, all modern Indians appear in it. . . ." The caricature—for such it has become—obscures the variety and scope of Indian life and culture. At the time of the European invasion there were about one million Indians in North America; in America as a whole there were some 15 million (today there are about 25 million), including the Aztecs, Mayas, and Incas, living in many and diverse societies.

Let us make a brief survey of American society as it was at the time of the European invasion, beginning in the north and working our way south.

The Eskimos and Athapaskans at the time of the European invasion both were still in the food-gathering stage and exhibited the usual ingenuity of food-gathering peoples. The Athapaskans invented the snowshoe and the toboggan. The Eskimo igloo, kayak, and harpoon (with floats for whale-hunting) are little masterpieces of construction. Their art—in bone, leather, and fur—is varied and beautiful.

From the Pacific Northwest the Kwakiutl and Tlingit exhibit in the American Museum of Natural History includes an immense war canoe some sixty feet long, with warriors in most "un-Indian" (un-Dakotan) dress standing on its ample deck, a boat completely at variance with one's concept of the Indian canoe which is derived from the small birch bark river canoes of the eastern forest Indians. Then come the great and magnificently carved totem pole supports and cedar beams for the houses, and one realizes that these Indians did not live in "tepees" but in large and sturdy wooden houses—and had so lived for many centuries.

In the South Pacific Coast we move out of the food-gathering belt proper and find a people in a pre-farming state, who gathered and stored acorns, from which they made bread.

The Southwest Indians, of whom the Hopi are modern representatives, were a farming people raising corn (maize) and cotton. They were skilled in pottery and basketwork, and their great one-village houses (some dating from 900 A.D.) were often several stories high and could have accommodated 300 families.

Along the lower Mississippi and its delta was another farming people, the Natchez. They raised corn, millet, tobacco, and melons and had orchards of peach and fig trees. They had wooden houses plastered with mud and whitewashed. And they had temples with sacred fires.

The area from the Atlantic coast inland to the St. Lawrence, the Great Lakes and the Mississippi system, now the eastern United States (including the "south") and eastern Canada, was populated by various semi-food-gathering, semi-farming peoples (Algonquin, Iroquois, Cherokee, Seminoles) whose general pattern of life was the usual one of such peoples everywhere, namely that of the men hunting and fishing and the women raising crops (maize, beans, squashes) and food-gathering (acorns, maple sap, nuts, strawberries). As elsewhere also we find a good deal of fighting between the tribes over hunting territories. About the year 1500 an Iroquois leader, Hiawatha, united the original five tribes of the Iroquois in a confederation which at the time of the European invasion was making steady progress into Algonquin territory.

In the vast area now known as the West were the "plains Indians," mainly the Sioux and their related tribes. Some of them lived off the buffalo as the Huns had lived off the horse or the desert Arabs off the camel: "his flesh was used for food, his bones for tools, ornaments and arrow points, his horns for spoons and small containers, his dewclaws and hoofs for rattles, his hair was twisted into ropes for horses [after the European invasion], tendons for thread, skins for robes, tepees, moccasins, etc."[1]

Middle America (from what is now Mexico to Panama) was dominated by Indian peoples in civilized societies (Toltecs, Aztecs, Mayas, and others).

The Pacific coast of South America was also dominated by civilized peoples, the latest of whom were the Incas. Below the Inca empire, in what is now Chile, were the Araucanians, a semi-food-gathering, semi-farming people, who had developed the art of weaving to a high degree. They used the guanaco, a member of the llama family, much as the plains Indians did the buffalo, eating its meat and using its hide for clothing and rugs. About 100,000 Araucanians live in Chile today.

At the extreme tip of South America were the Ona and other Indians who, as we have seen, were living in about the same kind of food-gathering society as the Australian natives. Up the eastern side of South America were various peoples, living at various stages of development, mainly mixed food-gathering and farming, the Charruas, in what is now Argentina, the Guaranis, the Tupis, the Arawaks, the Mantañas in what is now Brazil, and further north, spreading out into the islands of the Caribbean, the Caribs. The Mantaña and other tribes of the Amazon basin had a fairly well developed agriculture (as may be seen in the Mantaña exhibit at the American Museum of Natural History). Clearing the steaming jungles, they grew maize, cotton, and manioc (a tuber which is the source for tapioca) and were skilled in weaving and pottery.

In looking over the record we may note, once more, the various ways in which early economic systems are conditioned by geography and topography. The Eskimos and Athapaskans were necessarily hunting and fishing peoples because farming was impossible in the far north; the unusual wealth of the Tlingit hunting society is explained by the abundance of the fish and game of the Pacific northwest, an abundance which discouraged adventures into farming; the similar abundance of acorns in the south Pacific area likewise hampered agricultural experiment. On the other hand conditions in New Mexico and the Mississippi Delta were both favorable to farming, although farming of a different character in each; the forests of the East created a semi-food-gathering, semi-farming society as did the jungle in South America. We may also note that, as elsewhere, the general nature of each society was determined by its economy. In the food-gathering and semi-farming societies, although there were the usual chiefs and shamans, there were no classes and the government was run by the older men of each tribe, sometimes, as among the Iroquois, with considerable influence from the older women. Among the farming peoples, however, we can see the beginnings of classes. The Natchez had wealthier and poorer farmers, the wealthier forming a small class of "nobles," the poorer a large class of "commoners"; and we find the chief—sometimes a woman—carried in a kind of sedan chair. We might note, too, that the old sex division of labor—the women farming and the men hunting—was beginning to break down among the farming peoples. The Pueblo men, for instance, did the weaving and spinning. The craft division which robbed women of their previous economic roles was beginning.

The culture of these societies was, as always, determined by their socioeconomic character (plus some specific elements from different natural environments). Their level of knowledge was that of their economic life (the technical knowledge of hunting, planting, weaving) and social life (knowledge of family relationships, tribal government). This they shared with other such peoples. But they made a unique contribution in raising crops unknown to Europe, Africa, and Asia,[2] among them potatoes, artichokes, cultivated strawberries, dried beans, chocolate, tabacco. Their general framework of thought was largely dominated by the concept of the visible and invisible worlds, "biased in favor of a kind of brotherhood of men, animals and birds, all guarded by the same supernatural power."[3] Of the great variety and richness of the art which grew out of these societies we can get some impression from museums and illustrations and what written records have been made of Indian folk literature.

In short, there was on the American continent at the time of the European invasions a rich and varied society stretching from the Eskimo in the north to the Ona in the south. How had this come about?

American Origins

So far there has been no firm evidence presented of human inhabitation of the American continent earlier than 12,000 years ago, and, although the possibility is still open that this date will have to be pushed back by many thousands of years, it seems certain that no human (or ape) evolution took place in America and that it was never inhabited by sub-people. As the earliest societies seem to have been those of big game hunters living a life similar to the people of the great Siberian plains, and as the later Indians have racial affinities with these peoples, it is most probable that the first people in America came from these plains or the regions adjacent to them and were the ancestors of the Indians. It is also suggested that they crossed over at a time when the glaciers had soaked up the sea-water and what is now the Bering Sea was dry land. If so this would mean that no land immigration took place between about 27,000 and 13,000 years ago because the glaciers blocked the route south during that period. It does not, however, mean immigration could not have taken place by land before 27,000 years ago or by water either before or between these dates. After all the Australians got to Australia by at least 19,000 years ago and the route they followed must have been partly by water. In the period between 13,000 years ago and, say, 5,000 years ago, there may have existed boats on the Asian shores large enough to get to America by hugging the coast—similar to the great dugout canoes of the Maoris or the Pacific coast North American Indians (60 feet long)—and, somewhat later, boats like those of the Polynesians capable of extensive ocean travel. The probability is that there were many and not just a few crossings, some by sea and some by land, without the immigrants, of course, realizing that they had gone from one continent to another. The Bering Straits and the Pacific Ocean were by no means absolute barriers; they were, nevertheless, barriers. Although there is later indication of some continuing intercourse between Asia and America, it was not the same kind of intercourse as existed between East Asia and West Asia. Otherwise we might have had an invasion of America by, say, the Huns, and Attila's capital set up in Mexico City, instead of Budapest. The indication in fact is that after the first waves of settlers, migrations were comparatively sparse. For instance, it has not proved possible to establish a relationship of any of the 200 or so Indian languages with those of Asia or to reconstruct ur-languages as can be done for the Indo-European group. And, although languages can change comparatively rapidly, so complete an isolation probably means that the original linguistic break was made quite early. Furthermore, the general picture seems to be one of primarily native sociocultural development, with but secondary and catalystic external influence. The evidence points to a native development of farming. As we have seen, we find all stages in Indian life between simple food-gathering and farming; some peoples (the California Indians) have begun to store and process the fruits of their food-gathering; others (the Algonquins and Iroquois) have begun to supplement hunting with farming; others (the Hopi) have moved into farming. The main North American crop, Indian corn (maize), is a native American plant, successive domesticated stages of which can be traced from a wild form which existed before people came to America. The main Eurasian cereals, wheat, millet and rice, were unknown in America; so, too, were the yams of southeast Asia, which were specially adapted to the Brazilian jungles (whose Indians raised manioc, unknown in Asia). Indian farmers had no pigs, sheep, cattle, or horses; and no plow. There is evidence of farming 7,000 years ago (in New Mexico), and still earlier dates may yet be established.

On the other hand, the indication of some forms of influence is strong and is becoming stronger as investigations proceed. In food-gathering society, we might note the following: the bow and arrow; the blow-gun and head-hunting common to both the Brazilian jungles and southeast Asia; the mounds of the American and Asian mound builders. And in farming society: cotton, beans, squashes, gourds, the coconut, and the sweet potato, pottery, weaving. Moreover, the evidence indicates that the main, if not the only, direction of influence in these matters was from Asia to America. It indicates, for instance, that the sweet potato came to America from Asia, via Polynesia. Cotton was grown both in the Indus Valley and Peru by about 2500 B.C., but the biological evidence indicates that the American was a blend of that from India with wild cotton. Thus, although Africa was probably the originating point for cotton, it seems to have come across the Pacific (via Asia) rather than the Atlantic. Direct African influence on America, however, is not to be ruled out. Pottery and weaving may have been developed independently in America after they had already been developed in Asia. Both could have arisen out of the basket weaving of food-gathering society; and there is a native Indian tradition of pots coming from lining baskets with clay. But it seems more likely that such complex processes were copied rather than reinvented. That such was indeed the case is indicated by the fact that although there is evidence of farming by 5000 B.C. there is no evidence of an actual farming society with pottery and weaving until 1500 B.C.—some 4,500 years later than the rise of such societies in West Asia. On the other hand, assimilations of such techniques cannot take place unless a society has already natively advanced to a point at which it needs them and can use them.

Civilized Societies—Aztec, Maya, Inca

Although it is general knowledge that there were three main centers of American Indian civilization, the Aztec and Maya in Middle America and the Inca in South America, the level and extent of these states are not generally understood. Let us look at an eyewitness account by one of the Spanish invaders of the imperial capital of the Aztecs at Tenochtitlán (Mexico City), Bernal Diaz del Castillo. He, Cortes, and others ascended to the top of a great temple ("Cue") towering up over the city where the Aztec king, Montezuma, awaited them.[4]

So we stood looking about us, for that huge and cursed [i.e., non-Christian] temple stood so high that from it one could see over everything very well, and we saw the three causeways which led into Mexico, that is the causeway of Iztapalapa by which we had entered four days before, and that of Tacuba, and that of Tepeaquilla, and we saw the fresh water that comes from Chapultepec which supplies the city, and we saw the bridges on the three causeways which were built at certain distances apart through which the water of the lake flowed in and out from one side to the other, and we beheld on that great lake a great multitude of canoes, some coming with supplies of food and others returning loaded with cargoes of merchandise. . . .

After having examined and considered all that we had seen we turned to look at the great market place and the crowds of people that were in it, some buying and others selling, so that the murmur and hum of their voices and words that they used could be heard more than a league off.

Reading Diaz we sense a feudal magnificence approaching that of early Babylon or Egyptian Thebes. And we begin to grasp the horror of the destruction wrought by the Spaniards. Tenochtitlán had a population of 300,000 (at a time when London had 60,000). And Cuzco, the Inca capital, had 100,000. Such were the capital cities of the American Indians.

At the time of the Spanish invasion the Aztec civilization was centered in what is now Mexico, the Mayan to the south in Guatemala and Honduras, the Inca in Peru but stretching north and south along almost the whole Pacific Coast of South America. The tendency of archaeologists and historians is to emphasize the differences between the three, and, although there are, indeed, many differences, this emphasis has tended to hide the fact that they are basically similar.

THE ECONOMY

As with other early-stage civilizations the economy was primarily based on irrigated agriculture. The Inca irrigation system with its immense water reservoirs in the mountains, its great canals, its miles of underground stone pipes was apparently as fine as anything in Sumer. And the Aztec technique of gridding marshland with canals also reminds us of Sumer. But, advanced though it was, it was still an agriculture without wheat, cattle, pigs, sheep, horses, carts, or plows. The main crop was corn (maize) and this was planted laboriously one seed at a time with digging sticks and hoes.

In communal farming society, as we have seen in Asia and Europe, manufacturing is almost entirely home manufacturing. With the development of civilization we get the royal workshops in the Palace (Ur, Thebes, Crete, the Great City Shang) and some royal factories. We find a similar pattern in America:

> Let us go on and speak of the skilled workmen Montezuma employed in every craft that was practised among them. We will begin with lapidaries and workers in gold and silver and all the hollow work, which even the great goldsmiths in Spain were forced to admire. . . . Let us go on to the great craftsmen in feather work, and painters and sculptors who were most refined; then to the Indian women who did the weaving and the washing, who made such an immense quantity of fine fabrics with wonderful feather work designs.[5]

As with other early-type feudal civilizations, the main products of manufacturing were textiles, pottery and metal work (in copper, gold and silver). Mining and metallurgical techniques were similar to those developed some 4,000 years previously in West Asia and 2,500 years previously in East Asia: "Gold was collected in nugget form or panned as dust; copper also was mined as nodules or nuggets. . . . The melting furnaces were heated with charcoal and their draught forced by a man blowing on the embers through a tube"[6] as in Egypt. "Copper was cast into bells and ornaments, and the process, used also for gold, was the cire-perdue, or lost-wax, method" used in Sumer and elsewhere. In Peru there were many mines worked by thousands of workers. How extensive the metalwork was is indicated by the fact that the Inca king offered a room filled with gold ornaments to his Spanish captors as ransom.

There was both sea and land transportation. There were no ships comparable to those of the early Mediterranean, but the Mayas had large dugout canoes capable of holding forty men. The Inca rafts, like the modern Kon-Tiki, were large, capable of accommodating fifty men, and equipped with sails. As Thor Heyerdahl has demonstrated, such rafts were capable of crossing the Pacific. In the Inca empire there were 10,000 miles of roads:

> The Andean "Royal road" was 3,250 miles in length (making it longer than the longest Roman Road—from Hadrian's Wall in Scotland to Jerusalem); the coastal road was 2,520 miles in length.
>
> In addition to these arterial roads, there were numerous laterals, careening down the sides of the V-shaped valleys and connecting the mountain roads with the coastal one. . . . Roads also pervaded the jungle. They were built at the highest altitudes ever used by man in constant travel; the highest Inca road recorded is the one behind Mount Salcantay, 17,160 feet. The standard width of the Inca coastal road was 24 feet.[7]

Rivers were bridged and the roads supplied at regular intervals with post-houses and store-houses. One is reminded of the great road system of Maurya in India, but we have to remember also that along this vast highway system there travelled not a single wagon, chariot or horse. They were primarily military roads (sometimes 50,000 warriors marched along them) rather than trading roads. Goods were carried either by people or llamas, sometimes in great llama "pack trains" similar to the camel caravans of the Arabian desert.

Something of the extent of trade and manufacturing can be gathered from Diaz' description of the great market of Mexico City:

> Each kind of merchandise was kept by itself and had its fixed place marked out. Let us begin with the dealers in gold, silver, and precious stones, feathers, mantles, and embroidered goods. . . . Next there were other traders who sold great pieces of cloth and cotton, and articles of twisted thread, and there were *cacahuateros* who sold cacao. . . . Then

those who sold honey and honey paste and other dainties like nut paste, and those who sold lumber, boards, cradles, beams, blocks and benches. . . . Paper, which in this country is called *amal,* and reeds scented with *liquidambar,* and full of tobacco, and hollow ointments and things of that sort are sold by themselves, and much cochineal is sold under the arcades which are in that great market place, and there are many vendors of herbs and other sorts of trades. There are also buildings where three magistrates sit in judgment, and there are executive officers like *Alguacils* who inspect the merchandise. . . . I could wish that I had finished telling of all the things which are sold there, but they are so numerous and of such different quality and the great market place with its surrounding arcades was so crowded with people, that one would not have been able to see and inquire about it all in two days.[8]

When we realize that there were similar markets throughout the territories of the Aztecs, Mayas, and Incas, we begin to see the extent and variety of the trade and manufacturing of these Indian states; but we have also to recognize their limitations. The merchandise on sale, as Diaz describes it, was mainly either agricultural or the product of home manufacturing. There was no money; exchange was mostly on a barter basis and was between communities each with its special form of handicraft manufacture or farming.

Trade, however, was not limited to small territorial units: "Shells from the Caribbean have been traded from hand to hand as far as the central United States; pottery vases from Salvador were carried to distant Tepic in Mexico; gold ornaments from Panama appeared as votive offerings in the Sacred Well of Chichen Itza in Yucatan."[9] How much of this trade was by sea does not appear to be known. But on the basis of recent discoveries in Asia, we might guess that it was more than has been realized, both up and down the Pacific coast and around the Gulf of Mexico. According to early Spanish observers, Maya sea-borne trade was very important.

The general picture of the productive and exchange aspects of these economies, then, is that of primarily agricultural production, with home manufacturing the standard method, some factory-type manufacturing and mining, royal and aristocratic workshop handicrafting, transportation by llama, people, or raft, trade by barter in extensive markets. The economic level was somewhat lower than that of the first West Asian or Mediterranean states. There was nothing comparable to the mining and metallurgy which supplied the Egyptian armies with their chariots, the ship building industry of Crete, the bulk trade between Sumer and the Indus valley civilizations, the banking houses of early Babylonia (with their Mediterranean branches).

In spite of this technical backwardness the general economic structure, for instance, in ownership and labor, was similar to that of the early Asian and Mediterranean states. The key question in regard to ownership in a predominantly farming economy is, of course, who owns the land? And here we have a familiar picture: the land, according to Von Hagen, "belonged to the community." Mason writes as follows: "All arable land was divided into three categories, though not into three equal parts, although fields of the three classes were necessarily close together. The produce of those of one class was for the government, of the second for the gods and religion and of the third for the people."[10] Land was "awarded" to the "nobility." Individual nobles, however, could not sell it—it was legally still the property of the "group" of the nobles—but they could will it. And as with the land, so, too, with the great herds of llamas (the source of wool). The "communal" land—less than one third of the whole—was allotted on a family basis each year by "the local official" of the government. No peasant actually owned any land; he only had the "use" of it. The "local official," however, was subject to popular pressure from tribes and families. Among the Aztecs the communal land was redivided each year by the tribal council. The Inca tribes had an elected leader who was "guided by a council of old men."[11] The mines and all metals (gold, silver, and copper) were owned by the "state"—the king and the nobles. The king also owned the royal workshops and their products. Commerce was "'a government monopoly.'"[12] There was no "private business."[13] Labor—as one could guess—was mainly peasant labor and forced labor. The forced labor took two forms: work on the government and church lands, which had to be done before the peasant could touch his "own" land, and work in the mines and on construction projects, roads, forts, canals, palaces. The great Inca fortress of Sacsahuaman was built by the forced labor of 30,000 peasants over a period of seventy years.

SOCIAL LIFE

All this is familiar. The American Indian civilizations were clearly State feudal societies in which the means of economic production were owned by, and the labor force exploited by, a small group of great landowners, of whom the king was the leader. Each member of the group had his private estate, but, as in Egypt or India, his main source of income was from the joint ownership of the State land.

Among the Aztecs the peasants lived in "huts with thatched roofs resting on walls of wattles smeared with mud."[14] The aristocracy lived in large houses on raised platforms "faced with stone."[15] "Rooms for social purposes, sleeping, cooking, storage and quartering slaves were arranged in a rectangular plan about a central court." Everywhere the aristocracy wore fine clothes and jewels and were carried in litters; the poor wore plain clothes, had no jewels, and walked. The sons of the aristocracy were educated; the sons of the peasants were not.

The Mayas and the Aztecs had slaves, but apparently the Incas did not. Diaz describes them in the marketplace:

> Then there were other wares consisting of Indian slaves both men and women; and I say that they bring as many of them to that great market for sale as the Portuguese bring negroes from Guinea; and they brought them along tied to long poles, with collars round their necks so that they could not escape, and others they left free.[16]

But although the total number of slaves may have been large, they must have formed — as in all peasant labor economies — but a minor part of the whole labor force. They seem to have been mainly household servants, workers on private plantations, and, perhaps, assistants to the skilled craftsmen.

> Craftsmen and other skilled labourers . . . were government servants, supported at public expense. Actually they were court artificers, as their handiwork was for the emperor, who distributed it as favours to the nobility. Goldsmiths, potters, woodcarvers, sculptors, and similar artisans fell into this class, as well as the *quipucamayoc* who kept accounts. These positions were generally hereditary, since the father trained his sons in his craft [as in Egypt or India].[17]

The professional class, as in similar civilizations everywhere, was mainly State employees: priests, army officers, governmental administrators. There was no class of private manufacturers, but, among the Aztecs at least, there was a growing class of merchants.[18]

The social status of women was about the same as in Sumer or Egypt. The great mass of the women were peasants; as Mason elegantly puts it, they "participated in their husbands' agricultural activities as well as having their own domestic ones."[19] There seems to have been special economic exploitation of women: "A celebrated Mochica ceramic exhibits a row of women (all with backstrap looms) weaving industriously, while a male supervisor sits under a sunshade and directs them."[20]

We find also the usual pattern of one wife (or none) for the peasant man and harems for the aristocracy. The only professions open to women — again, as in Asia or the Mediterranean area — were the

Church or prostitution, and the two—as usual—were connected. Among the Aztecs, however, aristocratic women could "hold property, enter into contracts and go to courts to obtain justice."[21]

POLITICAL LIFE

The political structure—using the word in its broadest sense—was also similar to that of Egypt or India. The State consisted of a government, church, army, police, and legal system. The governmental core was formed by a top committee of the aristocrats, of whom the king was the most powerful, and below it was a vast administrative pyramid. The Aztecs had a "supreme council" consisting of a member from each clan and an executive committee of four council members, two of whom were concerned with the legal system, one of whom was the chief executioner, and one an intermediary between the government and the military. Among the Incas there were 1331 officials for each 10,000 persons.

At the base of the pyramid was the *puric,* an able-bodied male worker. The workers were controlled by a straw boss (*Conka kama-yoq*): ten straw bosses had a foreman (*Pacaka-Koraka*); ten foremen had a supervisor, ideally the head of the village. The hierarchy continued in this fashion to the chief of a tribe, reportedly composed of ten thousand workers (*Hono Koraka*), to the governor of a province, to the ruler of one of the four quarters of the Inca empire, and finally to the emperor, the Sapa Inca, at the apex of the pyramid.[22]

Again as in Egypt and India, behind this administrative network was military force and a class-oriented legal system. The legal code prescribed death and beatings for the peasants and reprimands or fines for the ruling class for the same offenses. The crimes of the peasantry, such as theft or robbery, were usually punished among both Incas and Aztecs with death.

The Inca government had a standing army of 10,000, which in times of war rose to 100,000. Sometimes for one offense "against the royal majesty" a whole village would be "levelled with the ground,"[23] and sometimes "the entire population [was] put to death." As what written material existed was mainly destroyed by the Spaniards, we do not have written records of peasant revolts, but the archaeological evidence suggests that the Mayan civilization was once torn apart by such a revolt. After about 900 A.D. the cities were deserted but life went on in the countryside.

As in all feudal societies, the church was a powerful organization with an enormous priesthood; and—as in Babylonia or early China—

the Aztec and Mayan church made use of human sacrifice as a ter-roristic means of rule. The Mayan clergy was divided into ranks (corresponding to bishops and priests) and confession was practiced. Colossal and magnificent temples—many of the ruins of which are still extant—dominated the towns.

The army was divided, as everywhere, into an officer caste and the mass of soldiers; and within the officer caste itself was a secondary "pyramidal ranking." The peasants were forced into military service and discipline was maintained when necessary by mass execution. In times of war the functions of the church and army blended: "In addi-tion to ceremonies, sacrifices, fasts, and other rites to increase the sympathy and favour of their gods, an incantation was performed be-fore the opening of hostilities to weaken the power of the enemy gods and supernatural spirits."[24]

War, as in Europe, Africa, or Asia seems to have been almost continuous. Out of it the Incas gained an empire along the Pacific Coast of South America as large as the whole eastern United States. They built it up by systematic conquest reminiscent of the Romans: "When they went to war it was a true military operation and no raid: conquests were planned, sieges laid, roads were built and kept in condition, communications were maintained by runners, forts . . . were built. . . ."[25] This conquest was by no means easy. The farming, food-gathering society Indians fought through tangled jungles and on mountain fastnesses. Some, such as the Araucanians of Chile, were never conquered. Those who were conquered became subject peoples, their function to provide "tribute" for the Inca ruling class. Their rebellions were met with mass executions and barbaric tortures. Al-though the territories of the Mayas and the Aztecs also held subject peoples there was no tight-knit empire in either because no one tribe succeeded in gaining supremacy. The issue was being fought out among the Aztecs when the Spaniards arrived, and this divisive struggle eased the way for Spanish conquest.

Culture

Two factors make it difficult to assess the culture of the American Indian states, their lack of an adequate writing and recording system, and Spanish feudal vandalism. The Spanish invaders destroyed almost everything they could lay their hands on. They tore up manuscript (pictographic) books as "un-Christian"; they melted down the gold ornaments, vases, and statues. The Maya calculation of the length of the year (365.2420 days) was closer to the truth (365.2422) than was the corrected Gregorian calendar (365.2425). Such calculations cannot be isolated phenomena but must indicate the existence of a cultured professional group which, if it had had an adequate script, could have developed a body of literature, social thought and philosophy. We find also a considerable body of technical knowledge. The Incas, for instance, performed surgical operations, including the trepanning of the skull, apparently with some form of anesthetic. But, as in all feudal societies, we find in medicine and other fields a mixture of fact and superstition. As with the Australian natives or the Romans we find the exorcising of disease-causing demons and divination by examining the inner organs of birds and beasts.

In religion there was the usual early feudal pattern of the Creator God (Viracocha of the Incas, Tonacatecuhtli of the Aztecs, Hunanku of the Mayas) who goes back into food-gathering society and has faded into a kind of elder statesman, plus the executive gods of farm life, the sun god, the rain god, the wind god, the mother-earth god, the spring god, and so on. We even have the bad gods or Satans (the Aztec god of death) who struggle against the good gods. Among the Mayas there was (as with the Persians) an "unending struggle between the benevolent gods of life . . . and the malevolent powers of darkness."[26] We find, also (as among the Hittites), that the common people tend to stick with the old gods while the State attempts to organize a central religion corresponding to the central church. "The worship of Viracocha was apparently, mainly, if not exclusively, a function of the upper classes."[27] The Aztecs' ruling class had its own special heaven. Among the Incas all the nobility, good or bad, went to heaven. Religion, nevertheless, was a deep spiritual force. The spirit of worship and wonder of the following Inca hymn to Viracocha is similar to that of the Vedas or the Psalms:

> Creator of the world, Creator of man,
> great among my ancestors,
> before Thee my eyes fail me,
> though I long to see Thee;
> for, seeing Thee, knowing Thee,
> learning from Thee, understanding Thee,
> I shall be seen by Thee, and Thou wilt know me.
> The Sun—the Moon; the Day—the Night;
>   Summer—Winter,
> not in vain, in orderly succession,
> do they march to their destined place, to their goal.
> They arrive wherever Thy royal staff Thou Bearest.
> Oh! Harken to me, listen to me,

let it not befall that I grow weary
and die.

The art of the American Indian civilized societies falls into the usual divisions of upper class art and the art of the people. The latter is essentially the same as that of the American Indian food-gathering and farming societies, namely, folk crafts and tales, music, dance, song. Something of its variety and beauty (pottery, weaving, feather work) can be seen in book reproductions or a visit to such exhibits as that of the South and Central American Indians in the American Museum of Natural History.

The upper class art — mostly resulting from the ruling class' harnessing of the creative powers of the people — is largely church dominated. As among the feudal Egyptians, Babylonians, and Europeans, the emphasis is upon vast magnificence, designed to give a sense of power and inspire fear. The great temple from whose top Montezuma allowed Cortes to survey the city was — to judge from its reconstructed picture — as grand as anything in Thebes or Babylon. Along with the vast went the intricate; for instance, the sculpture on the Mayan temples and gateways (which seems equal to that of its early Asian counterparts). So, too, with metalwork, pottery, painting, and mosaics. The dictation of form and the recurrence of theme are no more excessive than in Egypt or Byzantium, and the beauty achieved within these narrow frameworks is almost as fine as theirs. The gold work of the Incas seems to compare favorably with Shang or Benin bronzes. Durer, viewing in 1520 some Inca gold work brought to Europe, was ecstatic: "I have never seen in all my days what so rejoiced my heart, as these things. For I saw among them amazing artistic objects, and I marvelled over the subtle ingenuity of the men in these distant lands."[28]

Native Growth and Asian Influence

Let us in conclusion look at some fundamental problems. Why did civilization in America develop later than in Asia? Why did it fail to reach the same level as in Asia and Europe? Why did it develop in Middle and South America but not in North America? To what extent was its development influenced from Asia?

As we have noted, although there is evidence of some farming by 5000 B.C., there was apparently no real farming society until about 1500 B.C. The earliest civilized societies may have arisen as late as 300 B.C. The reasons for these lags must lie initially in natural factors; for instance, the comparative lack of river valleys of the type of the

Nile or the Tigris and Euphrates in America, deficiencies in animal and plant life, and less favorable juxtaposition of topographical regions. The MacKenzie or St. Lawrence river valleys were both unsuitable for a beginning agriculture; even the Mississippi river land — except for the delta — required considerable working; the Amazon, although in a tropical climate, was overgrown with jungle. What was needed was clear, sandy soil with natural irrigation. And this either existed only in two places or at least only in two places close to the original agricultural centers, namely the valley of Mexico and the South American Pacific coast river valleys. On the Peruvian coast, there are more than forty rivers which each year bring down from the highlands "a renewal of fertile silt."[29] In both places, then, we have somewhat similar conditions to those under which agriculture developed in West Asia (and later in China). And in both we find a repetition of the Asian pattern of extending natural irrigation by manmade irrigation. But in America there was no wheat, millet, or rice, no draught or transportation animals. The main American crops were either corn or tubers (potatoes, sweet potatoes, manioc), with corn the main crop of the areas in which civilized societies developed. Both crops require little more than the digging stick, the universal implement of food-gathering society, for both the corn seed and the tuber section naturally need only a series of individual holes in the ground. Neither calls for broadcast sowing. Hence, neither requires the plow, the development of which was further hindered by the lack of draft animals, particularly oxen and horses.

The failure to develop the plow and the lack of such crops as wheat or rice meant that agriculture was unable to produce the surplus of wealth that it did in Asia (and later in Europe); and this surplus — small though it may seem now — was nevertheless the thing that made the whole difference, because the degree of the surplus determined the rate of development, both toward civilized society and then within it. It was out of this surplus that commerce and manufacturing grew to the level that they achieved in Egypt and Sumer, and once trade and manufacturing reached a certain level they pulled the rest of the society along with them.

The lack of draft and transportation animals was probably responsible for the failure to develop the wheel for vehicular and machine purposes. The American Indians did, in fact, have the wheel (in the American Museum of Natural History we can see within a case of children's toys one which is on wheels), but they did not develop it because there was not a strong enough incentive to do so. True, if they had been a mobile people with easy access to, say, China, they might simply have adapted it (as the Chinese and Europeans doubtless did from West Asia). But they had no such easy access and had to depend upon the inner forces of their own society.

The backwardness of American Indian society should not, however, be exaggerated. (It is symptomatic of a tendency in this direction that whereas the Egyptian, Sumerian, early Greek, and so on, relics are in the Metropolitan Museum, those of the Mayas, Aztecs, and Incas are in the Museum of Natural History—among the "primitive" peoples.) We have to recognize that the American Indians did reach, in spite of great natural limitations, the first stage of civilized society; namely State feudal society, and that their backwardness was not that of a different order but was within the general framework of this society.

That they were, indeed, within this framework is clear from the parallels already noted with West Asian and other feudal societies; to take a few at random: the land was owned by a class of great landowners; trade was a State monopoly; the armies were class-divided and immense; the peasants were taxed; there was one set of legal punishments for the upper classes and another for the lower; there was a State religion and a popular religion. Some, looking at such parallels, might conclude that the American Indian states were simply copies of the West Asian. But if so, what of the East Asian, the European, the Niger area African, the Hawaiian, all of them later than the West Asian? Were they all somehow "imported" from West Asia? As we have seen, the evidence everywhere points to primarily native sociological development from farming society into feudal society. Once the fight for land begins, the rest follows. So, too, in America. How the land was divided and how the great landowning class arose among the Aztecs we have already seen. It arose in the same way among the Incas and Mayas (and Greeks).

Within this general native sociological process, however, there was certainly influence from Asia on developing civilized society in America just as there had been on food-gathering and farming societies. It is not easy to say when or how such influences came about, but the parallels compiled from a few general, popular works shows that they must have existed: the similarity between the Sumerian-Babylonian and the Toltec and Aztec temples; "the series of likenesses in temple art motifs between the Hindus and the Mexican-Mayan area";[30] the "lost wax" method of casting copper and other metals used in Asia generally and by the Aztecs; the emphasis upon jade ornaments and work in jade among the Aztecs as among the Chinese—and the Maoris; divination by consulting the inner organs of animals among the Incas as among many peoples of Asia and Europe (including the Romans); the wearing of sandals, and, by the men, robes and tunics but not trousers—the West Asian but not the Central Asian pattern (boots and trousers); human sacrifice, particularly the killing and burying of slaves along with the great nobles and king as in Sumer and China; similar methods of quarrying; blowing air on the fire through a tube in metallurgical processes; the mixing of tin with copper to make bronze; litters for the carrying of nobles, kings and great churchmen; pictographic writing; parallels between Japanese and Ecuadorian pottery; the use of "tie-dyeing" in Peru and Indonesia.

Once again, as with the parallels in food-gathering and farming society patterns, the impression grows that while some of these could have been independently arrived at, not all of them could.

As we have seen, the evidence has been steadily growing of contacts for many thousands of years between West Asia, East Asia, Europe, Africa, and Oceania. Ancient land routes continued into civilized society and were added to and improved: across the Sahara, and from the Niger to Ethiopia, between India and China, between China and Byzantium, and so on. Even more extensive were the sea-routes: from Africa (Carthage) to the Azores; across the Indian Ocean; from Madagascar to India to Borneo; up and down the China seas from Borneo to Japan; from East Asia out to Polynesia, and, within Polynesia, from Tahiti to Hawaii and New Zealand, from the Marquesas to Easter Island. When we remember that the Polynesians constructed craft from two canoes 6 feet wide and 60 to 100 feet long with a deck and sails in between, that in these craft they made voyages of 2,000 and more miles in the Pacific, that they made exploratory voyages in search of land, that they reached Easter Island (1,500 miles from the nearest other Polynesian Island), it seems most likely that they at least touched the American shores. Polynesian stone tools have been found in South America and one of them (an adze) is referred to by a word akin to the Polynesian. One cannot look at a great Maori dugout canoe or totem pole and then look at a Pacific coast American Indian dugout canoe or totem pole without feeling that both societies were somehow connected, however remotely or however indirectly.

There may also have been direct contacts between American civilized societies and those of Asia. If such direct contact seems hard to believe, we have to remember that a thousand years before Columbus, ships were crossing from Ceylon to Java with 200 passengers, that by the time of Augustus, ships of 75 tons (the Nina was 60 tons) were crossing the Indian Ocean, that the Chinese had ships of 500 to 800 tons by 700 A.D., and that these and other vessels of the great China Seas trade could certainly have reached the American shores at least by way of the northern Japanese Islands, the almost contiguous Aleutians and the Gulf of Alaska (as a globe of the world will show). Furthermore, to consider the reverse side of the picture, Thor Heyerdahl, mistaken though he was in his general theory of the American origins of Polynesia, did demonstrate that Inca-type rafts could get to Polynesia and perhaps even to Asia.

One final question inevitably occurs, namely, what would have happened to the American Indian civilized states if they had not been overthrown by the European invasion? Clearly, only a hypothetical answer can be given, but the indication is that they could not have followed the Asian pattern unless they had acquired at least the ox, the horse, the plow, the wheel, and grain agriculture other than corn. The lack of these not only made impossible the accumulation of the wealth necessary for commercial development but prevented the spread of civilized societies on the continent. If these plants, animals, and inventions had been acquired or developed, the Gulf of Mexico might have become another Mediterranean or Sea of Japan, and individual feudal society (with its commercial potential) developed. America would then have repeated the pattern of clashing feudal empires and developing mercantilism. But before such development could have long progressed, American civilization would doubtless have been overwhelmed by invasion either from Europe or East Asia. In terms of the actualities of world history the American Indian civilized states were doomed to be dead-end societies.

II: MIDDLE AND SOUTH AMERICA

The explorations of Columbus which began to reveal the American continent to Europeans in the late fifteenth century were certainly notable historically but hardly a discovery. There had clearly been contacts with Asia both by land and sea for thousands of years. The Vikings had colonies in Greenland for some three centuries (1000–1300) and from there had set up fishing and hunting bases in America. If we wonder why these Viking contacts left no records with the North American Indians the answer is that this is a usual phenomenon among nonliterate peoples. All traces of certain events later recorded as important by white explorers were completely lost among the Indians within a few decades.

The "discovery" of America led to the *invasion* of America; and the invasion to the *migration*. It was, in fact, the last of the great invasion-migrations in history, greater even than those of the Huns or the Arabs. Invasions and migrations do not, of course, in themselves materially raise or lower the general level of human society, but they can lead to movements which can either retard or accelerate that development. The Huns' invasion of Russia retarded Russian social development. The Arab invasions of West Asia and Africa escalated the commercial component of feudal societies. But no invasion or migration in history had so catalytic an effect as that of America by Europe. This was due to the fact that at the time the capitalist revolution was taking place in Europe. When the invasion began these changes in Europe were in an early stage. The invasion and subsequent colonization speeded them up, and this, in turn, reacted back upon America.

The "Discovery"

At 2:00 A.M., October 12, Rodrigo de Triana, lookout on *Pinta*, sees something like a white cliff shining in the moonlight, and sings out, *Tierra! tierra!* "Land! land!" Captain Pinzon verifies the landfall, fires a gun as agreed, and shortens sail to allow the flagship to catch up. As *Santa Maria* approaches, the Captain General shouts across the rushing waters, "Senor Martin Alonso, you *did* find land! Five thousand maravedis for you as a bonus!" . . . At dawn they made full sail, passed the southern point of the island [San Salvador] and sought an opening on the west coast, through the barrier reef. Before noon they found it, sailed into the shallow bay now called Long or Fernandez, and anchored in the lee of the land, in five fathoms.[31]

Just when or by what participants this event would have taken place no one could have predicted, but that it would have taken place sooner or later was inevitable once the commercial component of European commercial-feudal society developed to a certain point. If it had come later the participants would most likely have been British or Dutch or French. But in the late fifteenth century the main drive to Atlantic exploration came from the situations in Spain and Portugal. Italian commerce dominated the Mediterranean and was capturing a good part of the Asian market (via Turkey — where it was heavily taxed), a trade mostly in luxury goods purchased by gold. Spain and Portugal, driven out of these markets by the Italian commercial states, had to turn elsewhere. If they could find a new and cheaper route to Asia (and perhaps gold also) they could get a jump on the Italians. The Atlantic would perhaps afford such a route. At first it seems strange that such exploration was undertaken by a primarily feudal power but it was precisely a feudal power with a commercial component that would have undertaken it. Of the other possibly Atlantic-directed powers Britain was not primarily interested in luxury trade (British trade was largely in woolen cloth and similar "necessities" in the North Sea area), France felt no particular pressures to find new markets, and the Netherlands were still under Spanish control. The result was that Spain and Portugal got almost a hundred years' head start. By the time the other powers seriously moved in, Middle and South America were almost entirely taken.

When Columbus landed he was astonished at the friendliness of the people. "Then all came, men and women, as soon as they had confidence in us, so that not one, big or little, remained behind, and all brought something to eat and drink, which they gave with marvelous love."[32] The reason for this friendliness was not that these people were a special "race" but that they lived in a communal society — primarily hunting and fishing with some farming. "I have been unable to learn whether they hold private property, but it appeared true to me that all took a share in anything that one had, especially in victuals." Their behavior filled Columbus with joy, not, however, the joy of friendship:

> For almost a year the Columbus brothers were occupied with subjugating and organizing Hispaniola in order to obtain as much gold as possible. Several forts were built in the interior, and armed men were sent to force the natives to deliver a tribute of gold, the alternative to being killed. . . . As Las Casas wrote, the system was irrational, abominable and intolerable. . . . Indians took to the mountains, where the Spaniards hunted them with hounds; many who escaped their torturers died of starvation; others took cassava poison to end their miseries. . . . By 1508 a census showed 60,000 of the estimated 1492 population of 250,000 still alive, although the Bahamas and Cuba had been raided to obtain more slaves. Fifty years later, not 500 remained. The cruel policy initiated by Columbus and pursued by his successors resulted in complete genocide.[33]

There were, thus, two aspects to Columbus — although only one is usually mentioned — Columbus the mariner and Columbus the killer. The imperialist pattern which he established in the West Indies was followed in all Middle and South America.

The Invasion

The events designated by their historians as "the conquest of Mexico" and "the conquest of Peru" were, more exactly, the destruction of the Indian civilized states by European invaders. It was, in a way, as though a European power of the sixteenth century had returned through time to ancient Egypt or Sumer and destroyed them.

Let us glance at some of the highlights of the destruction of the Aztec civilization as told by one of its destroyers, Bernal Diaz del Castillo, whose vivid accounts of the Mexico City of Montezuma we have already seen. Diaz had little understanding of the historical significance of what was going on, but he gives us the facts without which such understanding would be difficult.

Cortes — with 550 soldiers, including cavalry and artillery — landed on the coast to the south of Mexico City on March 12, 1519, 27 years after Columbus first sighted land. Unlike Columbus he did not find a friendly population. On the contrary, the shore was lined with 12,000 warriors ready to fight. And soon after the landing the first battle took place.[34] At the end of the battle,

> we went to look at the dead lying on the plain and there were more than eight hundred of them, the greater number killed by thrusts, the others by the cannon, muskets and crossbows, and many were stretched on the ground half dead. Where the horsemen had passed, numbers of them lay dead or groaning from their wounds. The battle lasted over an hour, and the Indians fought all the time like brave warriors, until the horsemen came up.

In order to prevent more slaughter the Indian rulers made a truce and presented their conquerors with gold treasure and twenty girls as slaves. The girls were distributed by Cortes among his officers with the injunction that they should not be raped until they had been baptized. The Aztecs were informed that they had been butchered in the name of the true God, hitherto unknown to them, whose faith they should now embrace.[35]

> One other thing Cortes asked of the chiefs and that was to give up their idols and sacrifices, and this they said they would do, and, through Aguilar, Cortes told them as well as he was able about matters concerning our holy faith, how we were Christians and worshipped one true and only God, and he showed them an image of Our Lady with her precious Son in her arms and explained to them that we paid the greatest reverence to it as it was the image of the Mother of our Lord God who was in heaven.

Following this battle Cortes moved into the territory of the Totonac Indians; and here he received unexpected assistance. As we have seen, the Aztecs were in the process of forming an empire — similar to that of the Incas — and had already subjugated many tribes, who were forced to pay them tribute. Among these were the Totonacs, who "welcomed the invaders as the spearhead for an open revolt."[36] As he proceeded, Cortes received the support of other oppressed tribes, and of the Tlaxcalans, who were independent rivals of the Aztecs. The "conquest" turned into a civil war, with the Spaniards heading up the anti-Aztec forces including 6,000 Tlaxcalans. Cortes then moved to the systematic destruction of Mexico City and its 300,000 inhabitants.

Hunger and thirst, plagues and wounds, had so weakened the Aztecs that they could not resist. The horrors of the last stand made by these desperate people are too awful to describe. "For long after, the memory of the tragedy lingered about the place, a sort of exhalation of spiritual uncleanliness like that of a haunted house or the scene of a crime.[37]

The "conquest" of Peru was essentially a repetition of that of Mexico. Pizarro landed just as the Inca Empire was in the throes of civil war, lined up with one side against the other, and conquered, using terror as a main weapon (for example, the mass rape of 500 Inca nuns, known as the Virgins of the Sun, in the town square of Caxas). The climax was reached in a massacre in the city of Caxamalca. The Inca emperor was condemned to be burned alive but was given the choice of garroting if he accepted Christianity. (He accepted.)

It is clear from Diaz' account that there was nothing mysterious about the rapid military overthrow of the Aztec power. It was not due — contrary to Vaillant's view[38] — to a "sense of paralysis" being "in the air." The essence of the situation was that a poorly developed feudal society was overthrown by a highly developed one. Events would have taken the same form had the invasion come from Italy, France, England, Japan, China, or Russia. It did not, in fact, differ materially from the British imperialist conquests in India.

The proceeds from the Spanish conquest were, for the time, immense. The Spanish ruling class got more than $5 million in gold and silver immediately and directly from the conquest; Cortes' share of the loot enabled him to establish a feudal estate with several hundred serfs. The Spanish imperialists secured a labor mass of some 15 million in Middle and South America to exploit, along with land, mines, and forests. Whatever was necessary to subdue and harness this labor mass they did, and they did it in the same way it had always been done, namely by wholesale butchery, terrorism, church domination, and political dictatorship.

The Colonies

Out of the Spanish and Portuguese invasions came most of the present nations of Middle and South America, the three largest being Mexico, with a population of 47 million, Brazil, 88 million, and Argentina, 23 million. The area of Brazil is but slightly smaller than that of the United States. Brazil began as a Portuguese colony, the others as

Spanish colonies, but their population, social life, languages and cultures are still very largely Indian. And so, also, in Peru and other nations. It is estimated that there is today an Indian population in Central and South America of some 25 to 30 million, with a total 69 to 80 million having some "Indian blood." In the country districts, Indian languages still predominate — Uto-Aztekan in Mexico, Tupi-Guarani in Brazil, Araucanian in Chile and the Kechuan family of languages from Colombia to southern Peru. The story, that is to say, is the old one of a foreign ruling class bringing with it a dominant language and culture (as with the Arabs in Persia or the Saxons in England). During the first two centuries of colonization there were two Spanish "viceroyalties," New Spain (including Central America and a large section of the present United States' southwest and west) and Peru (including all Spanish holdings in South America) and one Portuguese viceroyalty — Brazil. In the eighteenth century the South American holdings were broken into three viceroyalties: Peru (mainly modern Peru and Chile), New Granada (mainly Colombia and Venezuela), La Plata (mainly Argentina).

The nature of the colonies that Spain established was partly determined by the fact that political changes were taking place in Spain: "Towns had sprung up in the early Middle Ages and had won charters, elected councils, and enjoyed much local self-government. . . . In the middle centuries the towns had united under *juntas* to protect themselves against nobles, Moslems, and even the kings. They had formed *hermandades,* or brotherhoods, armies for self-defense."[39] The pattern is a familiar one and is, in fact, rather similar to that of Japan in about the same period. Semi-independent, capitalist-run cities grew up and united their forces, but central political control — the national army, government, legal system, church — remained in the hands of the great landowners, many of whom had commercial interests. The situation in Portugal was similar, except that Portugal was smaller (about one million population to about six for Spain) and, hence, was unable to invade on the same scale.

SERFDOM AND SLAVERY

The essence of the social order in the colonies is succinctly described by John A. Crow in *The Epic of South America:*

The division of colonial society into the two extremes of landlords and day laborers was now becoming clearer with each passing year. One group had property, the other did not. One group worked, the other did not. One group enjoyed economic and social privileges, the other did not. The old curse of Spain's own agricultural economy, the latifundia, or huge estate, had been transported to the New World with a vengeance. Once started on its path of concentration of landownership in a few favored hands, it moved with a startling rapidity. . . . [Moreover] such land could not be sold, for it represented the very heart of family name and privilege.[40]

Specifically, it has been estimated there were in Spanish America some 4,000 Spanish families owning great estates and 5 million Indians working for them or for the "crown." This did not include the church estates (euphemistically known as "missions"). In the "Jesuit Empire" alone it was calculated in 1767 that 2,260 priests had 717,000 Indian serfs working these estates, which contained 719,761 head of cattle, 44,183 oxen, 27,204 horses and 138,827 sheep.

In addition to peasant labor there were also forced labor, paid labor, and slave labor, the peasant and forced labor being Indian, the paid labor (mainly skilled) Spanish and Portuguese, the slave labor Negro. There has been a good deal of talk about the Indians not making good material for slave labor because of their "native pride" and feebler frames (whereas the Negroes were a "lower race" with less pride but stronger frames). The Indians were, indeed, difficult to enslave—although some were—but not for psychological or genetic reasons. Those who lived in the most populous areas, Mexico and the Inca territories, were already peasants and the transition to a new feudalism was mainly a change of masters. To establish slavery in the countryside would have meant a major social disruption which the colonists had not the economic or military resources to accomplish. It proved easier to leave them as peasants (the debt peonage system). The Indians living in food-gathering and farming societies were difficult to enslave, for they had not endured oppression and they fought to the death against slavery—as in Haiti, where they died by the hundreds of thousands. Those in large territories could, if captured, often escape back to their native communities. On the other hand, the Negro had no such protection to escape back to, and, for a long time, no social base for struggle. He was alone in a strange land. Imported (slave) labor was not, of course, needed everywhere, but only where there were not enough Indians. Some regions were, from natural causes (the Amazon jungles), sparsely inhabited; in other regions (the West Indies) the Indian population had been slaughtered. Hence large numbers of slaves were imported into Brazil and the West Indies but very few into Mexico or Peru. By 1580 there were, it was estimated, some 13,000 Negroes in Brazil; by 1800 there were 1,500,000.

The basic worker in the Spanish colonies was the Indian, working either at peasant labor or forced labor:

There were several kinds of labor which the Indians were forced to perform: tilling the soil, mining, and work in the *obrajes,* or cloth factories, or the mountains. Farming was the least evil of the three, for the work at least was done in the open fields.

The workshops also employed a certain allotment of workers doing forced labor, and in them the poor Indian carried out his task tied to the lathe, while his body slowly lost its vigor in the exhausting and interminable operation assigned to him. . . .

The priests, for their part, received or extorted by a thousand means the little that was left to the Indian, the principal means being collections for saints, masses for the dead, domestic and parochial work on certain set days, forced gifts, and so forth. The tithe collectors also appeared at the moment of harvest to collect the portion which was due them.[41]

One-seventh of the adult males were continuously employed in forced labor, largely in the mines. The mines were, as usual in feudal or slave societies, legally owned by the king, but—also as usual—capitalists moved in and the king ended up with getting only his one-fifth. Working conditions were savagely exploitive. Observers reported that sometimes of 7,000 workers leaving their villages for six months labor in the mines, only 2,000 returned. A labor force of 65,000 Indians and 6,000 Negroes was used in the Potosi mines. Out of their toil there arose a glittering *nouveau riche* ruling class:[42]

Social living and dress were in keeping with the wild fortunes of these newly rich. The ladies of Potosi had jewels and dresses for each fiesta which were worth from twelve to fourteen thousand dollars; one lady spent five hundred dollars merely for pearls to adorn her overshoes. The mestizas wore sandals and belts of silk and gold, with pearls and rubies, skirts and jackets of fine cloth, and other rich jewels. The town boasted fourteen big dancing schools, thirty-six gambling houses, and a single theater to which the price of admission ranged from forty to fifty dollars.

COMMERCE AND CLASSES

In addition to farm produce and mining there was manufacturing, apparently mainly of cloth. The silk and woolen factories of Mexico and the woolen factories of Peru early became famous for their fine work. There was also some manufacturing of wine, sugar, leather, vanilla, indigo, flour, furniture, and ships. Indian home manufacturing continued but was kept to a minimum by the government.

Trade was mainly conducted at great fairs (the tradition of both Indian and European feudal societies here blending), at which the merchants from Spain and Portugal sold mainly manufactured articles—

hardware, machinery, tools and implements, clothing, shoes, lace, and furniture — and the colonists sold farm produce, raw materials, and home handicraft articles — cotton, coffee, tobacco, wool, hides, salt, copper, tin, pearls.

The main classes in such a society were naturally the great landowners and the peasants (many of them enserfed), or, in Brazil and the West Indies, landowners and slaves. The capitalist class was comparatively small. There were few paid workers, and the professional class consisted largely of those connected with the State (government, church, army, legal system). As usual in feudal societies the number of clergy was enormous. More than one million persons were employed by the church in the Spanish colonies alone. The various governmental agencies employed more than 400,000. Pay below the very top level was poor. The Viceroy of Peru received the equivalent of $65,000 per year (in 1946 dollars), the captains in his army, $600, and the soldiers, $300.

WOMEN

As in any feudal society established by conquest we find mass sexual exploitation of the native women. The Indian women were simply taken wholesale by the Spanish and Portuguese "master race." Some great landowners kept veritable harems; even common soldiers were sometimes granted three women apiece; and in some regions almost all the landowners "lived with Indian women." The extent of this sexual exploitation may be seen from the fact that in Spanish-Indian America today there are at least 30 million "mestizos" (the offspring of Indian and Spanish mixture). In Brazil and the West Indies, Negro women slaves were similarly appropriated. One quarter of the population of Brazil today are offspring of Negro women and Portuguese men.

Nor was the lot of the Spanish or Portuguese lady of the feudal ruling class exactly enviable: "Upper-class women were narrowly limited in their social contacts. An exceedingly close chaperonage was insisted upon. No career was open to them. The one goal that was sought by or sought for every young woman was marriage; and even here she was relieved from all worry, because the parents arranged for a husband."[43]

POLITICAL AND SOCIAL CONFLICT

In the political sphere we also have the feudal pattern with colonial variations, one of which, namely the oppression of both great landowners and capitalists by the "home" government, was of major importance. The State in the colonies was based on the Spanish or Portuguese States. Over each of the five viceroyalties ruled the viceroy ("vice-king") who, like the feudal king at home, was also commander-in-chief of the army and chief justice. The viceroyalties were set up as minor feudal kingdoms. The "vice-kings" ruled—as in the Babylonian or Assyrian empires—with the aid of an appointed council with both judicial and political powers. There was no elected central governmental body. In addition to the viceroyalties there were vassalages known as "captaincy-generals," of which there were four: Cuba, Venezuela, Guatemala, and Chile. It was from these that the present day nations with these names arose.

Along with the governmental power went that of the church. The Spanish government (and not the Papacy or the Spanish church) furnished the money to found the church estates ("missions") and, hence, had direct control over them. The church had its own armed forces—satirized by Voltaire in *Candide*—and, as in Spain, used the Inquisition as a terrorist political weapon. "The first auto-da-fe, burning of a victim of the Inquisition, was celebrated in Lima in 1573, the second in Mexico in 1574, in each case within two years of the founding of the respective tribunals." Lima burned 59 persons alive, Mexico "a few less."[44] In all the colonies together the Inquisition tried six to seven thousand cases.

The authority of the government and the church, however, was not so absolute as it at first appears. There were, as we have noted, town councils in Spain, and similar councils sprang up in America also. At first these councils were appointed, but, as the towns grew stronger, they were elected; and in time they began to amalgamate and form what were, in effect, provincial assemblies. The Spanish great landowners soon perceived the dangers inherent in such assemblies and hastened to exert controls over them.

Manufacturing in the colonies was suppressed. When Mexican factories began to produce excellent silks, satins, and velvets in the seventeenth century, they were simply shut down by a royal decree. Similar attempts were made to stop woolen weaving in Peru. All trade had to be handled exclusively by Spanish ships and to go through Spanish ports. Then there was taxation: (a) an import tax on goods coming to the colonies from Spain, (b) an export duty on goods leaving Spain, to be paid by the colonists, (c) a duty on goods landing at colonial ports, (d) a duty on goods passing from one port to another in the colonies, (e) a sales tax on all goods sold.

Although these measures were aimed particularly at the capitalists, they adversely affected the colonial great landowners, who also traded. Furthermore, there were direct attempts to stifle farming which produced major trading surpluses. In 1595, a law was passed forbidding the replanting of Peruvian vineyards, and tobacco growing was permitted in the colonies only if the surplus was sent directly to Spain.

As with all autocratic systems, however, the Spanish and the Portuguese functioned better on paper than in reality. The answer of the colonial merchants to these restrictive measures was massive smuggling and contraband trade. It has been estimated that half the goods brought in on Spanish ships were smuggled through the customs and escaped all duties.

The contraband trade was mainly with Britain, much of it in slaves. The British government was granted by the Treaty of Utrecht in 1713 the right to transport 4,800 Negro slaves a year for thirty years to the Spanish colonies—they transported 38,000 a year to their own colonies —and also to send in one shipload a year of other merchandise. The British took advantage of the Treaty by sending a whole fleetload of goods along with the one permitted ship, and then set up permanent slave-business headquarters. After the conclusion of the Treaty of Utrecht agreement, the British kept up this trade by illegal means.

Because of its harassment by the "home" government, the capitalist class which grew up in the colonies was not only small but was mainly a trading and banking and not a manufacturing class. Moreover, it was largely dependent upon the great landowners, for much of its trading produce was agricultural. It had neither the independence, the strength, nor the social stability of a capitalist class with a solid core of manufacturers.

One overall result of these various forces was that the main historical struggle in Middle and South America was not, as in European commercial-feudal society, that between the capitalists and great landowners, but that of the capitalists and great landowners of the colonies against the great landowners of the colonizing powers, who, on this question, were supported by their own capitalists. A secondary struggle, which today is becoming primary, was that of the working mass of town and country against their exploiters. In time both struggles took revolutionary form.

The Revolutions

SLAVE AND PEASANT REVOLTS

In the 1690's the first slave revolt broke out, in Brazil. One of the problems faced by the Negro slaves was that they had no social base and no community refuge in the interior as did the Indians. But in Brazil so many of them escaped that they were able to establish a farming and trading community of some 20,000 in the jungle, and organized "an independent republic with administrative officers, judges, and appropriate laws."[45] After many unsuccessful expeditions the Brazilian army finally succeeded in penetrating their defenses and physically exterminated the whole community—men, women and children.

A hundred years later came the massive Haitian revolution. The Caribbean Islands had been seized not only by Spanish imperialists but by British, French, and Dutch as well. Following the decimation of the Indians, the main labor was slave labor and conditions were similar to those of slave labor everywhere. The size of this slave labor force, however, is not generally known. For instance, between 1680 and 1786, more than 2 million African slaves were imported into the British Antilles alone. The Spanish island possessions had a constant slave labor force of 2.4 million. In the Barbados and Bermuda a master could not be punished (even by fine) for killing a slave. Slaves were regularly punished by being whipped, castrated, or having their ears or noses cut off. Women slaves were sexually exploited. J. B. Moreton in his *West Indies* (London, 1793) gives a vivid picture of the British Jamaican planters and their women slaves that may serve as representative of all such activity:

> In the evening the manager is obliged to procure some of the finest young wenches for the gentlemen; about sunset they are ordered from the field to wait upon their master and his friends. These poor wretches wash themselves in some river or pond, brace up their breasts, and meet at the great house, where they exercise themselves with great dexterity, by dancing in all the varied wriggles peculiar to their sex; the gentlemen sit in the piazza with their feet extended against the posts, to keep them from cramp; against bedtime, they are thus properly drilled, and hastened to the different chambers; their black husbands, or poor *bockra* partners, being neglected, silently pass those nights in disagreeable slumbers, wracked with jealousy and torture.

In Haiti there were half a million Negro slaves, 30,000 "free" Negroes, 35,000 white "masters." In 1791, the Negroes, slave and nonslave, led by Toussaint L'Ouverture, a former slave, arose in revolt, took possession of the country and established an independent republic. In 1794 they defeated a Spanish army, in 1798 a British army (15,000 men under General Maitland), in 1801 a French army (of 29,000). The republic survived, in time developed its own ruling class, and has continued until the present day.

The greatest of the peasant revolts took place in Peru in the 1780's. It was led by an Inca who took the name of Tupac Amaru II and announced that he was reestablishing the Inca Empire:

Indians deserted their work in mines, fields, and shops, and joined his banner. At the head of six thousand men he advanced against Cuzco, the old Inca capital. Only three hundred of his soldiers had rifles; the rest were armed with lances, Indian slings, spears, daggers, and various other implements. In the vicinity of Cuzco he was met by a well-organized force and defeated, but he escaped into the hills and a few weeks later appeared again, this time at the head of an army of twenty thousand men. The viceroys both at Lima and Buenos Aires became alarmed, and each of them assembled forces which advanced on Tupac Amaru from several directions. The Indians were defeated. . . .[46]

Tupac Amaru was captured. His family were executed before his eyes and he was then torn apart by four horses tied to his arms and legs. The result of this terrorism was not what the Spanish rulers had expected. "The Indians of the mountain country rose in spontaneous masses and continued the war. . . . It was not until 1783, two years after the death of Tupac Amaru, that order was finally restored. The civil war had cost approximately eighty thousand lives, and the country was devastated." This massive revolt reveals, as do all such revolts, the reality beneath the façade: the great northwest of South America was not basically Spanish but Indian; the Inca empire might be dead but Inca society and its traditions were a living force 250 years later; the Indian was bitterly aware of his exploitation and oppression, both class and racial, and willing to fight if an opportunity arose. The Indian peasants, that is to say, did not differ from Chinese, German, or English peasants.

Because there was so little manufacturing, there was but a small city working class, and no working class revolts of any consequence. What revolts there were in the cities were led by the merchants and directed against the domination of both the native great landowners and the "home" governments.

NATIONAL INDEPENDENCE

When the revolutions and wars for national independence from Spain and Portugal began in 1808 to 1810, there was a powerful, native class of great landowners, mass classes of peasants and slaves, and comparatively weak capitalist, professional, and working classes. The great landowners resented the economic and political restrictions imposed upon them by their "home" governments and wished to be independent; but at the same time, being themselves an exploiting class ruling a rebellious mass of peasants and slaves, they feared the potential influence of nationalistic movements on this mass, for the peasants and slaves were willing to join in any rebellion which might give them an opportunity to trim the claws of the native landowners. The capitalists, although comparatively weak, were more interested in national independence than the landowners, for the main burden of colonial economic restrictions fell upon them. But they, too, were ambivalent—they needed the landowners to secure national independence, but they also feared them. Similarly they feared the peasant masses, yet in their desperation they were sometimes prepared to use them, within the limits of their own leadership, to secure their aims. The pattern of social forces, that is to say, was the general one of such situations—similar to that in Germany at the time of Luther, for instance—but modified by colonial conditions.

The revolutions began in 1808-10 because in 1808 the King of Spain was deposed by Napoleon and a French puppet (Napoleon's own brother) put on the throne. The Spanish people, in rebellion, formed city and provincial committees of protest, and large scale guerrilla warfare broke out. The colonies were left, almost overnight, without a "home" government. The landowners and city upper classes, already combined in provincial assemblies, formed regional governing bodies. The merchants and professional men took advantage of the situation to form city governments. In the majority of cases the previous pattern of provincial meetings controlled by the landowners—with city participation—prevailed.

The actual revolutionary movement extended over several decades and, as we would expect from the complex class patterns that prevailed, took various forms. It differed somewhat in the five viceroyalties, but the end results in all were similar.

In Mexico the national independence movement was at first overshadowed by a peasant revolt. In 1810 an army of 100,000 Indian peasants followed a group of lower paid professional men (including two priests, Hidalgo and Morelos) in a struggle against both the government and the great landowners. It took three years to defeat the peasant armies and another eight years for the great landowners and merchants to stage a "safe" revolution from the top and declare their independence from Spain (1821).

In New Granada and Peru, on the other hand, the pattern was that of a movement beginning in the cities reaching out to embrace the landowners but with very little peasant participation. The reason for this was perhaps the heavy defeats suffered by the previous peasant revolts (as well as that in Peru there was one in Colombia involving a peasant army of 20,000). The revolutionary leader in both viceroyalties was Símon Bolívar, a wealthy landowner and member of the Caracas town council. Bolívar fought heroically against the entrenched might of Spain, beginning with capitalist support and gradually winning the landowners to his cause. That his base was narrow (and consequently his objectives limited) is shown by the small size of his armies, usually only a few thousand and sometimes as low as five hundred. It was an upper class movement ultimately aimed at securing the right to the exploitation of the peasants and city workers without outside interference.

The leader in the southern part of South America corresponding to Bolívar in the north was San Martín, an Argentinian. In 1817 he invaded Chile with an army of five thousand and marched north to meet Bolívar in Ecuador in a combined pincers movement against the Spanish power. The center of activities in the south was at Buenos Aires, the landowners — as one would gather from subsequent events — taking little part in it.

The independence movement in Brazil was also precipitated by European events. When the French armies invaded Portugal the Portuguese king was transferred under an escort of British warships to Brazil. In 1820 the great landowners, merchants, and professionals in Portugal overthrew the government and two years later fought off a new Portuguese attempt at domination. An independent Brazilian monarchy was established under great landowner control.

Although this national independence movement in Latin-Indian America was mainly instigated by the city merchants and professional men, they were too weak to follow the example of their European counterparts and assume national power. The great landowners engulfed the cities almost from the beginning. So far as the peasants and slaves were concerned, their status remained unchanged. They still toiled on the great estates, ranches, plantations (largely sugar cane and coffee), and mines. Voting rights were restricted to Spanish or Portuguese males who owned property. Although opposition to the church developed in the cities there was no real separation of church and State, and the church became one of the main instruments for great landowner rule. The great estates, it goes without saying, remained. There was no division of land, no major class of small or middle farmers arose.

On the other hand certain minor gains were made which, as the years passed, assumed more significance. The great landowners, for instance, were unable to establish a monarchy. The revolutions strengthened the city governments and within some cities liberal political and cultural centers were able to develop, centers in which the church did not have the kind of power that it had in the provinces. The breaking of the ties with the Spanish and Portuguese governments gave manufacturing a chance to develop, and this was further assisted by the virtual independence of some of the cities. All these gains, however, took place within the framework of great landowner national control. Nevertheless the capitalists might in time have taken national power in some states if a new factor had not entered the situation.

The British and other European governments early took an interest in these various nationalistic movements, sometimes even sending armed forces to assist the rebels, hoping to forward their own imperialist interests as the Spanish and Portuguese power was broken. In this they were soon joined by the United States (which in 1845–46 seized Texas, California, New Mexico, Arizona, Nevada, and Utah from Mexico). And although the nations of South and Middle America were by then too fully developed to permit either the European powers or the United States to turn them into actual colonies, both – especially the latter – succeeded in making considerable economic inroads. And in this they were assisted by the great landowners. The combination of the native great landowners and foreign imperialists, in short, was able to hold back native capitalist economic development everywhere. And the apparently tangled web of South and Central American politics is explained by this simple fact. Both the capitalist class and the industrial working class remained comparatively weak and this resulted in a series of see-sawing conflicts with shifting coalitions among great landowning and parasitic capitalist interests. Only in the present century have other classes begun to share power (as for a time, in Mexico) or actually to take power (as in Cuba).

III: North America

In the sixteenth and seventeenth centuries colonies were set up in North America by four European nations: Spain, France, Holland, and Great Britain. The other major European countries – the Italian and German states, Austria, Russia – were hampered by the same factors which held them back in South and Middle America. The only one of them which later secured a foothold on the continent was Russia, whose colony of Alaska was bought by the United States in 1869. Spain held Florida and sections of what is now the southwest of the United States with settlements at San Diego, Los Angeles, Monterey, and San Francisco on the Pacific coast and Santa Fe inland. Great Britain held the Atlantic seaboard, and France a wide corridor between the Spanish and British possessions extending from the St. Lawrence River, along the Great Lakes and down the Mississippi to the Gulf of Mexico. The Dutch held a comparatively small colony along the Hudson River with a port (New Amsterdam) on Manhattan Island.

At the present time the territory occupied by these colonies is occupied by two nations, the United States and Canada, and the resulting nationalisms obscure certain basic North American unities of terrain and history—shared in part also by one Middle American nation, Mexico.

In the North American struggle, the British and then the British colonies won out and today dominate the whole territory above the Mexican border. The Dutch strain has virtually vanished; the French is powerful in the Province of Quebec but elsewhere exists only in sociocultural pockets (New Orleans); Spanish social and cultural influence—continuously renewed from Mexico—remains strong in the southwestern United States but has no political power.

During the period of colonization, two of the colonizing nations, Spain and France, were predominantly feudal, the other two, Great Britain and Holland, were largely commercial and, as we have seen, went through political revolutions in the early colonizing period. The Spanish and French colonies were, like their "mother" countries, predominantly feudal and the British and Dutch predominantly commercial but with secondary feudal elements. The Dutch colony at New Amsterdam (New York), for instance, was a trading colony, but there were large feudal estates inland.

North Atlantic Seaboard Colonies

The difference between the first British northern colonies and the Spanish and Portuguese was demonstrated in their origins. The Spanish and Portuguese colonies were established under the direct control of the government, the British were set up by private capitalists. The Plymouth settlement of 1620 was financed by a joint stock company arrangement whereby seventy London merchants advanced £7,000 to be sold in £10 shares. This was possible because the English capitalists were by 1620 virtually running their own State in London, a situation with roots going back in the great causal chain of history into the twelfth or thirteenth centuries (and, ultimately, to the geographical fact that Great Britain, as an island, had a large seacoast relative to its land area). If it had not been for this prior development, the British colonies would have taken the same feudal form as the Spanish and Portuguese.

Following the Plymouth settlement came the much larger Boston settlement. The Plymouth settlement cost £7,000, the Boston settlement £200,000; the Plymouth settlement had 102 people, Boston 840 and within ten years had swollen to 15,000; the Plymouth settlers (apparently largely craftsmen) were financed by London merchants, the Boston settlement contained a wealthy minority who had considerable interest in the founding company (the Massachusetts Bay Company). The Boston settlement was, in fact, for the time, a large capitalistic enterprise and contained the germs of a little capitalist State within it. Although other morthern colonies began with royal grants to proprietors, they, too, were essentially commercial. Pennsylvania, for instance, was "granted" to William Penn, but Penn was no feudal Lord. The constitution that he drew up for his domains was a commercial-farmer document (rule by an assembly of property owners; trial by jury; no State church). New York was "granted" to the king's brother, but it was, as the king himself pointed out, "a place of great importance to trade."[47] and had already been set up on a commercial basis by the Dutch.

THE ECONOMY

By the middle of the eighteenth century, manufacturing in the northern British colonies was following the same pattern as in England. It was mainly commercial and not home handicrafting. Less diversified than in England, it centered around wood products. Forests abounded, and the British upper classes soon saw in them a source of supply for naval and other uses. The extent of this manufacturing is surprising in view of the usual picture of simple "Puritan" life. As early as the first quarter of the eighteenth century, one small river alone had more than 70 sawmills on its banks turning out 6 million feet of planks and other wood products a year. A great shipbuilding industry sprang up. "By 1775, 30 percent of England's merchant marine were of American construction and 75 percent of the commerce of the colonies were served by colonial ships."[48] One third of the British merchant marine meant more than 200,000 tons of shipping, a total of perhaps 20,000 ships. In addition to this there were 2,000 native American ships manned by 33,000 seamen. Along with shipbuilding there went, as usual, a large number of subsidiary industries. "Ships Stores" became a major industry, producing tar, pitch, resin, turpentine, canvas, hemp for ropes, not to mention the clothing, tools, and dishes of the seamen.

In addition to the lumbering-shipbuilding-fishing complex there were several other areas of industry: mining and metallurgy, leather, papermaking, hat manufacturing. It is difficult to obtain figures on these industries, partly because the alarm of British capitalists at the competition they provided caused colonists to hide their extent, and partly because statistics were not normally kept. But that the total output was large is clear from a report by the Lords Commissioners of Trade and Plantations to the House of Commons in 1731. "They have in

New England six furnaces and nineteen forges for making iron; and that in this province many ships are built for the French and Spaniards. . . . Great quantities of hats are made in New England. . . ."

Another large and profitable industry was distilling, which was linked to the slave trade. The British sugar plantations in the West Indies produced molasses as a by-product of sugar. This surplus molasses American capitalists purchased for a mere two to three shillings a hogshead, transported it home, and distilled it into rum. In 1769 almost 4 million gallons of molasses were imported from the West Indies, and another 3 million from elsewhere. Some of the rum was consumed in the colonies but most of it was traded and much of it was traded for slaves. On the Gold Coast of Africa a Negro man or woman could be purchased for 100 gallons of rum (valued at $50) and sold as a slave in the colonies for from $100 to $250. One slave captain reported that on a typical trip his expenses ran about $39,000 and his profits about $41,000 (more than 100 percent), and this in spite of the fact that 8 to 10 percent of the slaves died on the voyage. Much of the wealth of Boston, Newport — which had 22 distilleries — and other New England cities came from rum and slaves.

In addition to international trade there was a large volume of inter-colonial trade, some of it along the Atlantic Coast, some on the rivers. (The cost of land transportation was, as usual, excessive.) In 1770 more than 100 ships traded along the Hudson River between New York and Albany.

This vigorous commercial capitalism was naturally centered in the cities; and although the cities formed but a small part of the whole — in the 1760's out of a total northern population of some 820,000, the three largest cities, Boston, Philadelphia and New York had populations, respectively, of but 16,000, 13,000, and 11,000 — it was, nevertheless, the cities that determined the essential nature of the economy. For instance, between 1763 and 1766 Pennsylvania and New York exported 600,000 barrels of flour and biscuits. But the flour was ground in mills owned by millers, the biscuits were baked not on the farm but in bakeshops, the shipping was done by shipping firms; more than half the total money value of all Pennsylvania and New York exports came from flour and biscuits. As in England, the cities were beginning to pull the country along; farming was mostly com-mercial, not subsistence or manorial.

The primary form of labor was the same as in other commercial economies, say, England or Holland, namely paid labor working in small units. There were few factories and most production came either from shops (the small businessman-craftsman and his helpers) or the putting-out system (whereby work was done at home by a weaver, or other worker, and his family). But unlike England or Holland there was also slave labor and the unpaid labor of the so-called indentured servants, who were generally not servants at all but craftsmen who worked without pay in small shops for seven years to pay off their passage to the colonies. After the seven years they became paid workers. In 1754 the white population of the northern colonies was 778,000, the Negro population 42,000, most of whom were slaves (largely unpaid household servants). The smaller farms were run by the farmer and his family with some "hired help" and the larger ones by paid laborers.

SOCIAL LIFE

The denial of the existence of classes in present-day United States has in some circles become an obsession, usually taking the form of an implied framework concept of a population of 80 percent "middle" orders, 10 percent "uppers" and 10 percent "lowers" in a democratic, upwardly mobile society. So, too, in the past—the idyllic picture of undifferentiated pilgrims or Puritans working industriously side by side: "In general the life in the colonies was simple and often rude, with few extremes of poverty or wealth, little in the way of luxuries, but an assured subsistence as the reward of industry."[49] The colonial planters and capitalists were themselves assiduous in propagating this image, for, after all, what would be the point of setting up a "new" society if it were the same as the old one? Charles Pinckney of South Carolina at the Philadelphia Convention of 1787, which drew up the Constitution of the United States, put the matter thus: "Where are the riches and wealth whose representation and protection is the peculiar province of this present body? . . . They are in the general body of the people, among whom there are no men of wealth, and very few of real poverty."

That the picture cannot really be true is clear even from the above sketchy notes on the economic structure. There were obviously wealthy merchants who owned shipping firms, wealthy manufacturers in fishing, shipbuilding, shipping, distilling, milling, and other forms of enterprise, and there were bankers who financed them. In the 1730's Peter Faneuil held £15,000 in Bank of England stock alone; Willing and Gerrard were mainly tobacco merchants but they were said in 1775 to be expecting £10,000 profits from gunpower contracts; William Duer received $30,000 for a single army contract in 1776; John Lowell was director of the Massachusetts Bank and helped to finance the insurance company set up by John Hurd and nineteen other merchants in Boston in 1783.

The economic structure also dictated that there were large numbers of workers in shipbuilding and other industries. By 1720 there were fourteen shipbuilding yards in Boston alone. And shipbuilding required a large number of other trades.

The contrast between the living conditions of these workers and the wealthy merchants was extreme. On the one hand we have John Hancock: "dining from imported china, drinking the choicest of European wines, and clothed, according to contemporary description," elegantly. On the other hand the craftsman:

> Sand sprinkled on the floor did duty as a carpet. . . . What a stove was he did not know, coal he had never seen, matches he had never heard of. . . . He rarely tasted fresh meat as often as once in a week. . . . A pair of yellow buckskin or leathern breeches, a checked shirt, a red flannel jacket, a rusty felt hat cocked up at the corners, shoes of neat's-skin set off with huge buckles of brass, and a leathern apron, comprised his scanty wardrobe.[50]

Furthermore, the same kind of class division existed in the country between the large proprietors and farm laborers or small dirt farmers. Thus although this is not, as in the Spanish or Portuguese colonies, a feudal society, it is, nevertheless, a class-divided society, rather similar to that in Great Britain: capitalists (merchants, manufacturers, bankers), small businessmen-craftsmen, and paid workers in the cities, great landowners, middle farmers, small farmers and farm laborers in the country—plus slaves and indentured servants. On the other hand, although there were great estates, there was no hereditary aristocracy and no peasantry, for the people who came to the northern colonies were mainly from commercial and antifeudal backgrounds. The result was that by the middle of the eighteenth century northern American colonial society was in essence more deeply commercial than was the British, even though it was not absolutely so powerful.

There was some difference also between the two societies in the status of women of the propertied classes. As more men than women emigrated, colonial women were in an advantageous position. Wives were entitled by law to one-third to one-half of their husbands' estates if there was no will. New England laws protected wives against physical punishment by their husbands; desertion and cruelty were made grounds for divorce as well as adultery. The rights thus begun were widened during the industrial revolution, so that American women were among the first to secure rights to education, some access to careers in the professions, and the vote. There were during colonial times a goodly number of prominent women leaders in social and cultural life, for instance, Anne Hutchinson, mother of fourteen—"voluble of tongue, more bold than a man," lamented Governor Winthrop—

who led a revolt against the Puritan hierarchy of Boston and, banished from Massachusetts, founded Portsmouth (in 1638). Or Anna Maulin Zenger, who took over her husband's newspaper, the New York *Weekly Journal,* after his death. The picture is, again, very different from the feudal oppression of women in the Spanish colonies. But when we note also that only a comparative handful of women were able to play any important role in the shaping of society, we are once again aware that although the society was not feudal, it was class divided.

Political Life

The political relationship of the colonies to Great Britain was stated in the Declaratory Act of 1766, which asserted that the British Parliament "had, hath and of a right ought to have full power and authority to make laws and statutes of sufficient force and validity to bind the colonies and people of *America,* subjects to the crown of Great Britain, in all cases whatsoever." This power was to be exercised in each colony by a governor who was, like the Spanish viceroys, head not only of the government but of the armed forces and the legal system. In actual fact his power was limited, for most governors were early beset by colonial legislatures. And these legislatures, unlike the provincial assemblies in the Spanish colonies, had actual legislative powers and usually managed to get control of the budget. Who ran the legislatures? According to some historians "the people" did; but only 16 percent of the "people" of Massachusetts had the vote and only two percent exercised it. The right to vote was restricted to males with certain minimum property holdings. And so, too, in the other colonies —the mass of the people had no vote; women, even if they possessed property, had no vote. In Philadelphia only one-tenth of the male population had enough property to meet the voting qualification. What we have, then, is a governor representing the British ruling classes and colonial legislatures representing the wealthier farmers, capitalists, and upper professionals. There was a regular army subject to the command of the British government; but there was also a militia manned by the colonists. The basic laws were British and were enforced by the governor; but the colonial legislatures also passed their own laws, and the local judges and lawyers were American. The church was generally under upper class colonial control. In Massachusetts, New Hampshire, and Connecticut the Congregational Church was declared a State church, and everywhere the religious hierarchies of the main sects dominated the religious and often the cultural life of the people. In some colonies they were able to make "heresy" a crime punishable by death. They controlled the system of higher education and often of all education. Harvard, Yale, Princeton, Dartmouth, and Columbia were founded as religious colleges. A kind of dual State thus arose, partly British, partly American. The British section was unified — going back ultimately to the British government; the colonial section was split. Each colonial legislature or militia was an independent body within its colony.

As in the Spanish colonies and Brazil, the upper class colonists fought both the "home" government and the lower class colonists, and sometimes made alliances with one against the other. In the later seventeenth century, for instance, the Leisler rebellion in New York opposed enforcement of the law whereby all foreign trade had to pass through Manhattan, enabling the wealthy New York shippers to set the freight rates. The rebels overthrew the royal regime, jailed those who opposed their regime, and forced contributions from wealthy merchants. In time, however, these merchants, the clergy, the great landowners, and the British government united their forces. The revolutionary government was overthrown and Leisler was hanged for treason in May 1691.

South Atlantic Seaboard Colonies

Although only about one-sixth of New England production was agricultural and the rest commercial-manufacturing, about nine-tenths of Virginia and Maryland production was agricultural and one-tenth commercial-manufacturing; and southern agriculture was almost entirely a one-crop (tobacco) agriculture. Furthermore, three-fourths of the trade of the southern colonies was with Great Britain, whereas that of the northern colonies was distributed between Great Britain, Europe, and the West Indies; southern imports and exports to Great Britain were about evenly balanced, but the northern colonies imported about twice as much from Great Britain as they exported. Not only was the South mainly agricultural but it was dependent for its very existence on the British market.

To these figures let us add some on landholding. Although there were many small farms, the best land was occupied by large estates. The Robert Carter estate in Virginia had 70,000 acres (the average New England farm was 150 acres, of which usually only 10 to 15 acres were cleared); the Byrd estate in Virginia had 100,000 acres; in North Carolina, the Moores, Moseleys, and other families had title to 500,000 acres. In time, it is true, these vast holdings were subdivided but even when subdivided they remained enormous and the subdividing served to push the small farmer out, for the holdings still remained with the great families. To complete the picture let us add two more facts: (a) in 1770 there was but one town in the whole South that had a population of more than 8,000, namely Charleston, South Carolina; (b) in 1754 the Caucasoid population of New England was 425,000, the Negroid, 14,400; in the same year the Caucasoid population of the southern colonies was 387,000 and the Negroid 222,000. The Negroid supplied slave labor for the large estates.

These southern British colonies were clearly closer in nature to the Spanish or Portuguese than to the British northern colonies. If we ask ourselves how this came about the germ of the answer may be found in a statement of Charles I in 1625, only a few weeks after he came to the British throne: "To the end there may be one uniforme course of Government in and through our whole Monarchie, That the Government of the Colonie of Virginia shall immediately depend upon Our Selfe, and not be committed to any Company or Corporation. . . ." In short, British commercial interests were sufficiently powerful to establish the northern colonies but not to dominate the whole Atlantic seaboard; and the feudal interests were powerful enough to set up their general kind of society in the southern section (aided by the fact that the terrain and climate were particularly favorable to the establishment of large estates). But why slave labor and not peasant labor? For the same reasons as in the West Indies or Brazil—there was not enough native (Indian) labor to make up a plantation serf labor force, and slave labor was for such work the most profitable. It found no roots in the northern British colonies in North America because the forms of labor in those colonies were dictated by the (commercial) nature of the society to be those of small-unit farmer, paid worker, and small businessman-craftsman. The subsistence farmers could not afford slaves and the paid workers would not allow the competition of slave labor.

The largest number of slaves—before the rise of cotton—were in the tobacco plantations. In 1700 tobacco exports totalled 28 million pounds and the slave population was about 50,000; in 1775 tobacco exports had grown to 85 million pounds; in the first census, in 1790, the number of slaves was 697,000. Altogether some 7 million Negro slaves were brought to the Americas in the eighteenth century.

The social conditions of the North American slaves were about the same as in Brazil, the conditions, that is to say, of the extreme of human exploitation and oppression: unpaid labor, subsistence living, long hours, the auction block, the lash, the chain. As in Brazil, it meant also for women slaves sexual exploitation. The constitutions of the planters, a contemporary observer complained, "are frequently destroyed before they arrive at Manhood. . . . This flows from their early connections with the Negroe Wenches."[51]

The form of the political structure in the southern colonies was similar to that in the north, but the content was somewhat different. Four states (Georgia, South Carolina, North Carolina, and Virginia) had royal governors, two (Delaware and Maryland) had governors appointed by their proprietors. As in the north there were colonial legislatures elected by property owners. In South Carolina the vote was restricted to those who owned 500 acres and ten slaves or £1,000 worth of other property. The legislatures were dominated not by commercial but agricultural interests. In five of the southern colonies the Anglican or Episcopalian Church, which in England had been associated with the aristocracy (in contrast to the dissenting sect churches in the north), became the established church.

The great planters controlled everything, but not without opposition. In 1676, one of the smaller farmers, Nathaniel Bacon of Virginia, led an armed rebellion with followers "of the basest sort of people; they were said to have included slaves." The rebels, four hundred strong, captured the colonial capital, Jamestown, and forced legislation giving "all freemen" the vote through the legislature (which they surrounded with cocked muskets). They defeated a troop of mercenaries raised by the governor, burned Jamestown and captured a twenty-gun warship. The rebellion collapsed shortly afterward with Bacon's premature death from malaria. Twenty-three of the leaders were hanged.

The struggle of the slaves began on the slave ships. "They are fed twice a day," one slave captain recounted, "at ten in the morning and four in the evening, which is the time they are aptest to mutiny, being all upon deck; therefore, all that time, what of our men are not employed in distributing their victuals to them, and settling them, stand to their arms; and some with lighted matches at the great guns that yawn upon them, loaded with partridge [shot], till they have done and gone down to their kennels between decks."[52] Conditions on the plantations made large scale revolts difficult. The largest was that in South Carolina in 1739. Led by a slave named Cato, it finally ended in a pitched battle in which 21 Whites and 44 Negroes were killed. Many thousands of slaves took advantage of the revolutionary war to escape, most of them to the north but a few into Indian communities. In one year alone (1778), according to Thomas Jefferson, 30,000 slaves fled from Virginia; and it has been estimated that the southern colonies lost by flight one fifth of their slaves. The slaves were apparently not entranced by life "on the old plantation."

The picture in the British South Atlantic seaboard colonies, then, does not differ in essentials from that of the Spanish or Portuguese colonies. In fact, if the southern colonies had existed alone, without a growing commercial society to their north, their history would have followed about the same path as that of Brazil. They would have expanded little and, although they would have eventually secured their independence, it would have been an independence ruled by native great landowners under external imperialist influence.

The French Colonies

The French colonies began, like some of the British, under the auspices of a private company and were later taken over by the crown. In 1627 the Company of New France, a corporation of French businessmen with a capital of 300,000 livres, was granted a monopoly over all trade in the colonies for fifteen years plus considerable governmental authority. French businessmen's interest in the colonies may be reduced to one word — fur. And the word tells us much. The enterprise was mainly a luxury trade venture, and would not lead either to stable colonization or further capitalistic development. It was, in fact, in the interest of the fur trader to keep the wilderness a wilderness. Fur trading posts were set up in a long funnel of territory whose main settlements were Quebec, Montreal, Detroit, St. Louis, Fort Prudhomme (Memphis), Mobile, New Orleans.

Along with fur trading went farming — mostly along the St. Lawrence River valley between Quebec and Montreal. Wheat was the main crop, and was grown in sufficient surplus for export, but tobacco, flax, and hemp were also raised. As in the Spanish colonies and the southern British colonies the land was granted to royal vassals — seigneurs — in holdings that ranged from one to 1,000 square miles. Between 1623 and the middle of the eighteenth century 375 such seigniories were granted and were "subdivided among feudal tenants, or habitants" in holdings of about 100 to 400 acres.[53] The seigneur was entitled to exact a variety of payments and tributes[54]; in other words, French feudalism was simply exported to the colonies.

So far as manufacturing and trade was concerned the story was the same as in the Spanish and Portuguese colonies (or in any feudal society). Manufacturing "made little progress . . . ; every craft was minutely regulated . . . ; trade was rigidly supervised, and was so hampered by taxes and monopolies that to the end of the French regime exports remained small and consisted almost entirely of raw materials."[55] The government comprised a governor and an appointed council; the members of the first council set up in 1647 were the governor himself, the Superior of the Jesuits, and the Commander of the troops at Montreal. There was no elected legislature and no local government.

If we survey the picture of America in the mid-eighteenth century, it is clear that it was predominantly feudal, from Quebec to Buenos Aires. Only on a narrow strip along the North Atlantic seaboard was there a comparatively small island of commercialism. The British colonies dominated North America both economically and in population. In 1750 the population of the French colonies was about 65,000; that of the British colonies was about 1,400,000, of whom about 800,000 lived in the northern colonies. If we ask ourselves why the difference between the northern British and French colonies, the answer may be found in the fact that the British Revolution occurred in 1642, the French not until 1789.

The Indians

The region of the French and British settlements, as we have seen, was inhabited by peoples in semi-food-gathering, semi-agricultural societies, the Indians of the eastern forests and shores. These people were at a lower economic and social level than the Natchez or the Pueblos, who were farming peoples, but they did have a stable social order and a culture that embodied considerable knowledge and art. The region was inhabited by two major groups, the Algonquins and the Iroquois. The Iroquois at the time of the European invasion had effected a tribal confederation and had steadily been moving into Algonquin territory.

The Indians—as in the West Indies—received the first settlers kindly, and it seems doubtful that the Plymouth settlement would have survived without their help. But the colonists, hungry for land and profits, soon began a terroristic war against them. "The settlers cut off the heads and hands of Indians they killed and set them up on poles in the towns to enrage the Indians, who in turn scalped and tortured such whites as fell in their way. In a short time all the colonies were offering bounties for Indian heads and scalps. An infant's scalp brought just as much as that of a man or woman."[56] One of the early raids against the Indians was that on the Pequot tribe in 1637. "Mason . . . with his replenished forces . . . rushed the wigwams and kindled them with torches. As the Pequots fled through the burning wigwams they were riddled with musket fire. 'God is over us,' Captain Mason shouted, 'He laughs His enemies to scorn, making them as a fiery oven.' Dr. Cotton Mather furnished a written account of the massacre: 'It was supposed that no less than six hundred Pequot souls were brought down to hell that day.'"[57] Miles Standish (Longfellow's hero) once had four friendly Indian chiefs lured into a room, hacked to pieces by swords, and the head of their leader carried back in triumph to Plymouth. Something of the extent of the fighting may be gathered from the records of the Indian reprisals. (Every time the Indians won an encounter it was called a "massacre.") In two years alone, 1675 to 1677, the Indians burned twenty-five towns, including Springfield and Providence, and 900 Indians and 800 colonists were said to have been killed.

The story in the French and Spanish colonies was similar. Don Hernando de Soto, in Georgia and Florida, "burned the Indian villages, laid waste the cornfields, dragged Indians with him from place to place in chains as carriers, and applied tortures to exact information."[58] The settlers made use of the Indians in their own conflicts. The French colonists supported the Algonquins against the Iroquois; the English supported the Iroquois, gave them firearms and sent them against the tribes who were selling furs to the French. The French armed the Indians, sent them against the English settlements and paid bounties for White scalps and captives.

Wars Between the Colonies

Before the American Revolutionary War the main intracolonial wars were between the British and French colonies, wars for land and profits. Between 1689 and 1754 there were four such wars (although fighting of some kind was practically continuous). Of these the most important was the last, the French and Indian war of 1754 to 1763. As a result of General Wolfe's victory at Quebec in 1759 the French colonies passed into British control. An even more important result was the increase in American economic and military power. American industry grew rapidly during the war, strengthening the capitalist class, and American military men (including Washington) gained valuable experience in the field.

The Revolutionary War

The American Revolutionary War and the American Revolution are often confused. They were, however, distinct, although connected, phenomena. The war lasted from 1776 to 1783 and resulted in the political independence of the colonies; the revolution began in the 1770's, lasted into the first decade of the nineteenth century (the administration of Jefferson), and resulted in the establishment of a balance of power between the great landowners and capitalists. The succeeding decades saw this balance tip steadily toward the capitalists until the Civil War decided the issue of power decisively in their favor.

In introducing the economic and other restrictions which the British parliament imposed upon its American colonies, the Beards comment: "In giving effect to mercantilism and British ideology in general, the Parliament in London enacted many laws pertaining to American economic enterprise and political affairs."[59] If so, "British ideology" was curiously similar to Spanish ideology, for the restrictions were essentially the same as those in South and Middle America. The blunt-spoken governor of Massachusetts, Sir Francis Bernard, placed the emphasis elsewhere: "The two great objects of Great Britain in regard to the American trade must be: 1. to oblige her American subjects to take from Great Britain only, all . . . she can supply them with; 2. to regulate the foreign trade of the Americans so that the profits thereof may finally center in Great Britain. . . ."

The Spanish restrictions, as we noted, fell into four categories: (a) those channeling all colonial trade into Spain; (b) those channeling all foreign trade with the colonies into Spain; (c) those designed to stifle manufacturing; (d) taxes and duties. The British restrictions fell into the same categories but were less rigid, for Britain being less agriculturally self-sufficient and more highly commercialized than Spain required greater colonial economic activity. Her colonies were also more difficult to restrain. In fact, from about the middle of the eighteenth century on, Britain faced a young rival capitalism whose growth it was unable to hold back.

The basic act designed to channel colonial trade into Great Britain was the Navigation Act of 1660. By this act certain specified commodities could not be traded except to or through Britain. In time these included tobacco, rice, lumber, naval stores (tar, pitch, etc.), bar and pig iron, copper ore, and furs and hides. The act affected both northern industry and southern agriculture; they were alike cut off from all European markets except British. Nor could they buy from Europe. The Staples Act of 1633 "prohibited the importation into the colonies of the growth, production, or manufacture of Europe, unless from English ports and in British-built and manned shipping."

The British capitalists, regarding the colonies as sources of raw materials for their own manufacturing profits, suppressed or discouraged colonial industry; in 1699 the exporting of woolen cloth, even from one colony to another, was prohibited; in 1732 the export of hats was prohibited; in 1750 iron manufacturing was virtually outlawed, although the mining of iron ore and the production of pig iron (to be exported only to Great Britain) were still allowed.

Taxes and duties were imposed in a series of acts. The Molasses

Act of 1733 put prohibitive duties upon the importation of sugar, molasses, and rum. (Fortunately for the rum and slave traders, the act was not strictly enforced.) Next came the Sugar Act and the Stamp Act, taxing newspapers and documents, designed to get money from the colonists for the British military establishment. Finally came the Townshend Acts of 1767, which imposed duties on glass, lead, paper, and tea.

In addition to these direct economic restrictions the British government attempted to restrain the growth of its now powerful colonies by physically limiting their size. French territory, as we have noted, extended from Quebec in a wide swathe down the Mississippi to the Gulf of Mexico. As a result of the French defeat in 1759 this vast territory passed from the French to the British empire. Hardly was the war over than the wealthy colonists began to form land companies, designed then, as later, to acquire vast tracts for planters, merchants, and bankers and sell parcels at a high profit to small farmers. But the British government announced in effect that it was reserving this territory for the Hudson's Bay Company and that the existing colonies should be restricted to the eastern seaboard. In 1774 the Quebec Act granted all territory north of the Ohio River and west of the Appalachian Mountains to Canada.

The colonial capitalists fought back. As in the Spanish colonies they resorted to large-scale smuggling. Even as early as 1700, it was estimated, one-third of the trade of Boston and New York was illegal (entering without duty or being with forbidden countries). They resorted to the boycott in reaction to the Stamp Act and the Townshend Act. American merchants agreed to cease all importing from Britain, and refused to remit British debts. While successful in the North, the boycott was completely ineffective in the South. Southern trade, as we have seen, was basically in one product, tobacco, and almost entirely with Britain, while northern trade was varied and with a number of countries, so that a boycott which would mean only a decrease in profits for the northern merchants would have spelt ruin to the southern planters.

The usual picture of the growing conflict is that of an "oppressed people" rising against "injustice." But it was clearly in its roots a struggle between Britain and American capitalists. The "injustice" consisted of acts designed to favor the interests of British capitalists and directed against American capitalists. And when the American capitalists retaliated they aimed at the purses of their British counterparts. In these actions they were supported by the middle classes of town and country who were threatened with higher prices by the British restrictions. These classes were influenced also by the fact that they lived in a structured society in which the capitalists (and planters) were strategically placed to exert influence by their control of colonial legislatures and town councils, newspapers, the church, and the educational system. They supported a large section of the professional class (lawyers, architects, notaries, and so on), gave employment to many thousands of paid workers and small businessmen, and marketed the produce of the farmers. The social mechanism involved, that is to say, was essentially the same as in the British Revolution or the French Revolution. As in the British Revolution its influence did not go beyond these classes. That the war was no more a mass social movement—comparable to the German peasant wars—than was the British Revolution is clear from the comparatively small numbers in the American army. Out of a total of 500,000 men of military age only 30,000 to 40,000 were under arms. Washington never at one time had more than 16,000 troops; in the summer of 1776 he had but 5,000. And these came mostly from the middle classes. "All the tailors and all the apothecaries," a French observer remarked, "must have responded to the call, one recognised them by their round wigs, nearly all miserably mounted, wearing game-bags and shoulder-belts."[60] This does not mean, however, as some historians seem to feel, that the war was, in essence, a "middle class" war. The tailors, shopkeepers, and farmers did not have at their disposal the economic, political or military apparatus either to arouse a population or conduct a war. Control over this apparatus lay where the money lay. The (surface) confusion came only during the war when there was an amalgamation of class interests. It was the capitalists who conducted the boycotts and formed the core of the anti-British opposition. The "Boston tea party," for instance, was the work of John Hancock, who was once sued by the British authorities for £100,000 for smuggling—which gives us some concept of the size of his fortune. And when the war was over it was not middle classes that took power, but the capitalists and planters.

Although no basic difference in the general social mechanism involved in the British and French revolutions and the American Revolutionary War existed, there were important specific differences. Whereas in England and France the struggle was one of capitalist versus feudal interests (plus, in France, a peasant revolt), in America both capitalist and feudal interests were allied against foreign capitalist and feudal interests.

As a result of these various factors, the war, when it came, was a complex of social forces: (a) a war for national independence; (b) a civil war between British and American supporters in the colonies; (c) a war between nations (in which France and Spain joined the colonists). And the whole was permeated by a political struggle for power in the emerging new State: the American revolution.

In reading the works of Thomas Jefferson and others in these years, one has the impression of men feeling their way cautiously. The actual interest of capitalists and planters alike lay in national independence, an end to British interference with their profits and growth. But the intertwining of British and American economic interests was strong and, as a consequence, pro-British sentiment rife. They were fighting only—as loyal Englishmen—to remove abuses within the English system. "We have not raised armies," declared Jefferson and Hancock as late as July 1775, "with ambitious designs of separating from Great Britain and establishing independent states." The first important call for independence came in Thomas Paine's *Common Sense* in January 1776, when Washington's armies were already in the field. As sentiment for independence spread, the would-be ruling classes began to sense that in its propagation lay the key to arousing the incipient nation; and the war became officially a war for independence.

The degree to which the war was a civil war is shown by the fact that 30,000 to 50,000 Americans fought in the British armies—as many as fought on the revolutionary side.

The French and Spanish motive in assisting the American colonists was not, of course, sympathy for colonial independence, but the hope of gaining colonies or, at least, trade by weakening the British ties. Nonetheless, without French help the American colonists would have faced a longer and bloodier struggle, if not actual defeat. The French loans totalled $6,300,000 in gold, and nine-tenths of the munitions at the battle of Saratoga came from France. When Cornwallis surrendered at Yorktown he had the French fleet at his back.

Assistance to the American cause rendered by anti-Establishment forces in England should also be noted. To the English parliamentary reformers (and to Burns and Blake), Washington was a hero and George III a tyrant; the Whig party split on the war issue. It became difficult to gather an army, and German mercenaries were consequently used.

Yet, even if the colonists had been defeated in this particular war, they would eventually have won. Native commercialism by the 1770's had taken too deep a hold to be driven back; it would have continued to develop in spite of all efforts at restriction; it would have evolved into industrial capitalism despite British opposition and then no power on earth could have kept it in subjection. The national independence of the colonies was, at least from the middle of the eighteenth century on, simply a matter of time.

THE REVOLUTION

Like all revolutions the American was a struggle for political power, a struggle that involved the destruction of the British State apparatus in America and of pro-British landholdings and other forms of property (as distinct from the defeat of the British armies). As the attack upon British power was extended by the middle classes to include American planters and capitalists, the two struggles converged as they had in the Spanish colonies.

Conflicting class interests, as we have seen, had a long history in the colonies and manifested themselves in a variety of ways: property restrictions on the right to vote; the domination of colonial legislatures by the planters or capitalists; rebellion of small farmers; strikes and political action by the city workers and small businessmen. In the aldermanic campaign in New York in 1734 the Court Party, representing the mercantile interests, was opposed by the Popular Party, which distributed handbills urging the workingmen of New York to vote for "poor honest men" and not "rich knaves." "If her [New York's] *merchants* offer to sell us [to the British]," wrote Dr. Joseph Warren at the time, "her *mechanics* will forbid the auction."

With the war came the confiscation of great estates: "All the way from New Hampshire, where Sir John Wentworth lost his domain, to Georgia, where Sir James Wright suffered the same fate, small farmers jubilantly moved on to rich lands that would once have taken them only as tenants."[61]

The directly political struggle centered around the colonial (provincial) legislatures and town and county councils. In some legislatures the pro-British forces were so solidly entrenched that new legislative bodies had to be set up. But apparently almost everywhere the county and town governmental bodies were already in pro-American hands when the war broke out. And it was largely out of these local bodies that the new American State found its resources. It was from them that delegates were elected to the revolutionary colonial legislatures and then to the national Congress.

Through these anti-British political struggles some internal class conflicts also threaded their way. Agitation was begun by small farmers and city artisans to eliminate property restrictions on voting rights. In Pennsylvania, as the result of "a tremendous demand," the vote was extended to all male taxpayers. In Delaware, North Carolina, Georgia, and Vermont property restrictions on the ballot were removed, so that "'any taxpaying biped of the forest,' as one disgusted conservative put it, might vote."[62] In the southern colonies the Anglican (State) Church was everywhere—except in Virginia, where it outlasted the war—supplanted by dissenting churches, Baptist and Presbyterian, as in the north.

Strong though this internal class conflict was, it was tempered, as we have seen, by common interests prevailing during the war. Once the war was over, the struggle for power began in earnest, and it assumed a new scope and intensity. With the economy completely in the hands of American interests and British restraints removed there came a great increase in production. The rate of this increase was greater in manufacturing than in agriculture. Between 1799 and 1819 income from farming rose from $264 million to $294 million, income from manufacturing rose from $32 million to $64 million. Thus, although farming was still the main national economic activity, it had increased by but a small percentage while manufacturing had doubled. In 1799 American sawmills produced 300 million feet of lumber; by 1819 this had risen to 550 million feet. In 1789 American shipyards produced 202,000 tons of shipping, by 1810 they were producing 1,425,000 tons. In 1800 there were eight cotton mills in New England; in 1810 there were 269. The "putting out system" was declining and the factory system rising. The greatest agricultural increase was in cotton, and came largely from the invention of the cotton gin, which increased the amount of cotton that one slave could clean in a day from one pound to 150 pounds. The increase was spectacular. In 1790, 3,000 bales were produced; in 1810, 178,000; in 1820, 335,000. With these increases in production came an increase in trade: in 1789 the total number of ships entering American ports was 234 (124,000 tons), in 1810 it was 989 (981,000 tons).

These economic developments naturally brought about social change. The rise in manufacturing increased the working force and the factory system began to change its character from one scattered in small shops or at home into one concentrated in larger units and, hence, better able to strike. The increase in manufacture and trade brought about an increase in the number of small merchants and professionals. The old class of small businessmen-craftsmen began to divide into businessmen and craftsmen. The increase in farming brought about an increase in the number of both small farmers and slaves. Because of the victory in war the previously withheld territory of the eastern interior opened, and was followed by a wave of farm migration. As much of this land, being mountainous, was not adapted to big plantations, a greater proportion of small and middle farmers arose in the southern section of the new territories. But the area of plantations increased absolutely and there was a great increase in the number of slaves. The census of 1790 showed 698,000 slaves; in 1820 there were

1.5 million. Economic increase produced an increase in population: 3.9 million in 1790; 7.2 million in 1810; 9.6 million in 1820.

These economic and social developments combined with the close of the war to produce political turmoil. In 1786–89 came Shays' Rebellion. This rebellion started in Massachusetts, where the concentration of commercial capital had resulted in the assumption of power by a mercantile oligarchy which proceeded to throw the burden of State maintenance upon the farmers and other middle class people. In August 1786 delegates from fifty towns met to discuss their grievances. They decided to take action, and 1,500 armed farmers took possession of the courthouse at Northampton, and other courthouses were also seized. Let by a veteran of the war, Daniel Shays, the farmers assembled to march on Boston. As the regular militia was sympathetic to the farmers, the Boston capitalists raised $200,000 in twenty-four hours to equip a militia of their own. Shays' forces were defeated. They regrouped and marched upon the provincial arsenal at Springfield and were again defeated.

Alarm at Shays' rebellion and similar anti-Establishment actions elsewhere motivated the convening in the year following of a representative gathering of great landowners and capitalists at Philadelphia to draft a constitution for the new nation. Of the 55 men present, 45 held public securities, 15 were slaveowners, 11 were capitalists, 24 were bankers or moneylenders, 14 were great landowners.[63] They included James Madison, plantation owner and lawyer, Edmund Randolph of Virginia, owner of 5,000 acres and 200 slaves, Robert Morris, the Philadelphia banker, Gouverneur Morris, land speculator of New York and Philadelphia. Jefferson, Paine, Sam Adams, Patrick Henry, and the "radicals" in general were not present. The desideratum in the framing of the Constitution was the "augmentation of property and wealth." The implied objective was to restrict the rights and power of the propertyless majority. There was no reference to civil rights or liberties in the Constitution and slavery was tacitly legalized:

> No person held to service or labor in one State, under the laws thereof, escaping into another, shall, in consequence of any law or regulation therein, be discharged from such service or labor, but shall be delivered up on claim of the party to whom such service or labor may be due.

In order to regulate the conflict of interests between capitalists and landowners a series of checks and balances between judiciary, congressional, and executive powers were introduced as well as different methods of representation for the Senate and the House of Representatives. As in England some aristocrats allied themselves with the popular forces against the capitalist expansion and its dangerous directness of political oppression. "A bill of rights," Jefferson argued in a letter to Madison, "is what the people are entitled to against every government on earth." After five years of political agitation such a Bill was passed by Congress in the form of ten amendments to the Constitution, the first of which indicates the flavor—and the value—of the whole:

> Congress shall make no law respecting an establishment of religion, or prohibiting the free exercise thereof; or abridging the freedom of speech, or of the press; or the right of the people peaceably to assemble, and to petition the government for a redress of grievances.

As in England, each of the two ruling classes formed a political party, the Federalists representing the mercantile interests and the Republicans the landowning interests. It soon became apparent that the mercantile interests were forging ahead of the landed interests, as shown by the selection of Alexander Hamilton as Secretary of the Treasury. Hamilton proposed the establishment of a "national" bank (to be two-thirds controlled by private bankers) which would give the big capitalists power over both small business and landed interests; high tariffs for the protection of native manufacturing; major taxation of the working mass of the population ("excise taxes"). Manufacturing, he felt, might be helped by child labor and woman labor.

> Women and children are rendered more useful, and the latter more early useful, by manufacturing establishments, than they would otherwise be. Of the number of persons employed in the cotton manufactories of Great Britain, it is computed that four sevenths, nearly, are women and children and many of them at a tender age.[64]

The taxation problem was complicated by the war bonds issue. In order to pay for the war, bonds had been issued and had been bought by a large number of persons; but when the price of these bonds fell (as low as ten cents on the dollar) they were widely sold, and at that point were bought by comparatively few wealthy merchants and property owners. Hamilton decided that these bonds should be paid off at their original (high) prices, and for that purpose he proposed a tax upon the distillation of whisky. As whisky was widely distilled by farmers and others, this meant, in effect, a tax on the mass of the population to pay off the wealthy bond speculators. The farmers, as in Shays' Rebellion, took to arms. Revenue officers were tarred and feathered, red flags waved from town poles, the governor refused to call out the local militia. Washington sent a force of 15,000 men into the field, with Hamilton himself at their head. Faced by a force of this size—larger than the army at Yorktown—the so-called Whisky Rebellion faded, but, as a precaution, troops were left in the area. A new centralized, basically capitalist, government had shown its teeth and won. It moved to consolidate its victory by the Alien and Sedition Laws (1798), the first of which gave the president powers to deport aliens considered dangerous to the State; the second made it a crime to issue a statement about the president or Congress that could bring them into "contempt or disrepute" – a wide territory indeed. Something of a reign of terror – including 25 arrests – against Jeffersonian editors and politicians began.

But, again, the ruling oligarchy had gone too far. The farmers and city middle class rallied, and in 1800 Jefferson was elected president. The Alien and Sedition Laws were repealed, the jailed editors were freed, the whisky tax was abolished and the Bill of Rights enforced. "Every day proves to me," wrote Hamilton in the bitterness of defeat, "that this American world was not made for me." Hamilton, however, need not have despaired. The new capitalist rulers had not been thrown from power. They were simply being made to share power with the great landowners, and were, along with them, subject to certain popular pressures. The new note was struck by Jefferson in his inaugural address: "encouragement of agriculture, and of commerce *as its hand-maiden.*"

The United States' political revolution, then, came to a different conclusion from those in the Spanish or Portuguese colonies. Whereas they ended up with a dictatorship of great landowners opposed by city-oases of business and professional men, that in the United States ended – as in the main European states – with a balance of power between capitalists and landowners, a balance of power whose center moved steadily in the succeeding decades toward the capitalists, until the same kind of State existed in the United States and most of Europe. The same general sociological processes – of the capitalist revolution – everywhere produced the same results.

To balance matters with a different point of view let us look at a popular history book account (Nevins and Commager):[65] "The keynote of Hamilton's public career was his love of efficiency, order, and organization. . . . When we turn to Jefferson, we turn from a man of action to a man of thought. As Hamilton's talents were executive, Jefferson's were meditative and philosophical." This certainly simplifies matters, but it raises questions. What made Hamilton "efficient" and Jefferson "meditative"? What were they efficient and meditative about? Had Hamilton been meditative and Jefferson efficient would the course of United States history have been changed?

The Spread of the Nation

The national formative development which we have discussed so far was limited to the eastern seaboard. But the nation, so to speak, not only developed upward, it also spread outward. As a result of the war with Great Britain, the former colonies gained a stretch of territory much larger than themselves, namely, all the land from the Adirondack Mountains west to the Mississippi River, the great funnel of land that the French government had claimed and the British had seized in 1759. Following this came further moves west; in 1803 a large tract beyond the Mississippi was bought from the French government; in 1819 Florida was taken from Spain, in 1836 Texas from Mexico; and so on until the whole territory to the Pacific was occupied by United States armed forces and settlers.

As with the previous Spanish, British, and French advances this new advance was made through the blood of the Indians. Let us take Florida as an example. De Soto conquered Florida by force of arms, slaughtering and torturing the Indians and burning their cornfields. When a more powerful nation sprang up to the north it, in turn, took over. In 1810 West Florida was seized by the United States government; in 1814 General Andrew Jackson (later president) pursued some Indians into East Florida and occupied it; five years later the territory was formally ceded to the United States for $5 million. But let us look beyond the bare facts and consider the Indians Jackson had pursued. Why was he pursuing them? The answer is that they (the Seminoles) were giving sanctuary to Negro slaves. Two years after Jackson's foray, the United States army attacked a Seminole village and killed 300 men, women, and children. When the territory was finally ceded to the United States, a systematic attempt to annihilate the Seminoles began, an operation on a much greater scale than anything the "barbaric" Spanish conquistadores had attempted. The Seminoles, like the Araucanians of South America, remained undefeated. Other tribes, however, had been uprooted from their farms and driven west, and still others were slaughtered where they stood.

One expansionist effort failed, namely, the attempt to conquer Canada, for this, as was recognized at the time, was the main objective of the War of 1812. "The conquest of Canada is in your hands," declared Henry Clay, southern slave and plantation owner, in the House of Representatives. But the French Canadians suspiciously refused the lure of a new mastership, and the entrenched British armies proved too powerful for the still comparatively unindustrialized nation to conquer. The motive for this expansionism came, not as one would expect, primarily from commercial interests (Massachusetts opposed the War of 1812) but from the landowners. The American landowners simply wanted more land and labor and were prepared to fight to get them. They also joined with their capitalist brothers in the new national game of "land speculation."

In this game there were differences between the northern and southern patterns. In the new northern territory of Ohio, for example, the land was put up for sale in blocks of 640 acres at $1.00 an acre with considerable reductions for larger purchases. In the latter part of the same year some 18,000 settlers arrived; by 1800 the population of the Ohio territory was 55,000. The land companies resold the land at a high profit to the growing numbers of settlers. In the south, as Alabama, Mississippi, and Missouri opened up, the great planters purchased the best land, moved slaves in, and set up new plantations. There were thus—as is not always made clear in the covered wagon picture of Americans forging westward—two distinct streams of migration, one from the northern states and one from the southern. In both the new north and south the vote was restricted to male property owners, but in the north, there were more property owners and no mass of voteless slaves.

Thus, although the nation spread, its basic character did not change. The same two kinds of society simply moved west. When the far west opened, however, the split did not continue, for far western society did not assume solid form until the era of industrial capitalism, and by that time the plantation economy had been far outdistanced by northern capitalism and, as a result of the Civil War, had had its slave labor converted into peasant labor and been politically weakened. The Far West took over the capitalist economy of the Northeast both in manufacturing and in farming. Furthermore, the Northeast continued to dominate national economic affairs.

Canada

With the defeat of France in 1759 Canada passed from French to British control, but British social and cultural influence did not really begin until after the American Revolutionary War. As we have seen, that war was, in one of its aspects, a civil war, with a large section of the population supporting the British. At the conclusion of the war some 30,000 of these "loyalists" left the United States for Canada, where they settled in Ontario (Upper Canada) and Nova Scotia. Although there had been some early British settlers, Canada as an English-speaking nation was born of the American Revolutionary War. As these new settlers came almost exclusively from the northern colonies they set about establishing a primarily commercial society— in contrast to the great landowning (French) society in Quebec (Lower Canada). Thus Canadian society was split much as American society had been, into basically commercial and great landowning sections.

In the year 1790 the British parliament recognized this situation by setting up two separate provincial governments, Upper Canada and

Lower Canada, along similar lines: (a) a governor appointed by the king; (b) a legislative council appointed by the governor; (c) an assembly elected by property owners. Control over navigation, commerce, and customs was retained by the British parliament, and, in practice, local power was in the hands of the governor and his hand-picked council. Both provinces were blessed with a state church, Catholic in Lower Canada and Church of England in Upper Canada. But with the development of native manufacturing and commerce opposition to these colonial and semifeudal patterns began to rise in both Upper and Lower Canada.

In Upper Canada the leader of the opposition was a Toronto editor named William Lyon MacKenzie, who with his followers formed a majority in the provincial legislature. They put forward a kind of bill of rights, the heart of which was the transference of power over both economic and political matters from the governor and his council to the assembly. In 1836 the British authorities met the crisis by simply dissolving the assembly.

In the meantime a similar movement had been gathering in Lower Canada. Under the leadership of Louis Joseph Papineau the Lower Canada Provincial Legislature adopted a set of demands similar to those in Upper Canada and incorporating a petition signed by 87,000 citizens. The French Canadian demands were more anti-British and pro-national than the British Canadian ones, which were aimed only at reforms "under the Crown." A Quebec mass meeting in 1837 passed a resolution reminiscent of the American colonial revolt: "We deny the right of the Parliament of England to legislate for the internal affairs of this colony, against our consent and without our participation."[66] Papineau, however, was no peasant leader, his movement no mass movement. "I am a great reformer in regard to the necessary political changes," he informed the legislature, "but I am a great conservative in regard to the sacred right of property."[67] And MacKenzie could have subscribed to the statement also.

In 1837 both movements took to arms. Papineau's followers fought a number of engagements with government troops in the region around Montreal but were defeated. MacKenzie and his followers—apparently about 800 in number—marched on Toronto but were also defeated. Although the rebellions were put down, their demands were ultimately gained, some of them, indeed, within three years (in the Union Act of 1840). In 1856 the appointed council was abolished.

In spite of the MacKenzie and Papineau movements, however, clearly there was no revolutionary ferment in Canada comparable to that in the British American colonies. And it is instructive to look at some of the reasons for the difference. For instance, there was virtually no manufacturing-commercial development in Canada during the seventeenth and eighteenth centuries. When commercial capitalism did begin to develop, its leaders, particularly in Upper Canada, hesitated to arouse nationalistic fervor because separation from Britain would have left Canada at the mercy of the United States (whose intentions were made clear in the War of 1812). And, finally, British capitalism developed so much more rapidly than Canadian in the nineteenth century that separation became impossible, for not only was the Canadian economy penetrated by British interests but the British military potential was immensely greater than the Canadian. There was never, that is to say, a situation in Canada parallel to that in the American colonies in which a certain equality of forces between the colony and the "mother" country existed.

Yet, although the capitalist revolution in Canada was muted by the ever present influence of two greater powers, it did take place. The system which grew to dominance was not feudalism but capitalism; in time even the Quebec rural economy was changed to commercial farming, and today a French Canadian capitalism is demanding an independent state.

IV: CULTURE

The advances in knowledge, ideas, and art in the Americas during the colonial and revolutionary periods were slight compared to those in Europe (from Galileo to Beethoven). Nor could it have been otherwise. Not only was the European capitalist revolution on a much larger scale than the American but American development was retarded both by colonialism itself and by its own feudal and slave-holding societies. Feudal cultural dominance was, as usual, largely in the hands of the church; and in the commercially oriented colonies, the Puritan church acted as a special cultural deterrent. Nevertheless there was some advance, especially in knowledge (technology in particular) and, for a time, in social (revolutionary) ideas.

Technology

Most of the knowledge of nature needed for the operation of a commercial capitalist society had already been made in Europe before American economic development reached the European level. There was no need to repeat the work of Copernicus, Kepler, Galileo, Newton, Lavoisier, Laplace, Herschel, Priestley, or Cavendish. But there were still many areas that needed to be explored, and little by little groups of American men of science were formed (almost exclusively, as we would expect, in the commercial colonies in North America). One of the most spectacular and important of their discoveries was Benjamin Franklin's, that lightning was an electrical phenomenon. His kite experiment, like so many other great experiments, was simple and decisive. In Franklin we saw also the beginnings of the practical, rather than theoretical, turn of American science. He went on, not into further explorations of electricity as such, but to the invention of the lightning rod; and he also invented a more efficient heating stove (through the study of air currents and heat), a battery, bifocal spectacles, and a street light.

Ever since the first cultivation of cotton in ancient Egypt, the seeds had been separated by hand, a necessary process for spinning, but exceedingly laborious; one man could thus "gin" — as it was called — but one pound of cotton a day. In 1792, Eli Whitney — a northerner on vacation in the South — constructed a machine which consisted essentially of a saw-toothed cylinder that pulled the raw cotton through wires and left the seeds behind. With this machine 150 pounds of cotton could be ginned in a day. Also, since the days of ancient Egypt, ships had been propelled by either oars or sails. Following James Watt's invention of the steam engine in the 1760's, various men had considered its possibilities for ship propulsion, but the first successful steamboat was Robert Fulton's *Clermont,* which in August 1807 sailed by steam-powered paddle wheels from New York to Albany. These inventions were the harbingers of many others: the steel plow, the McCormick reaper, the mechanical thresher, the clipper ship, the magnetic telegraph, the sewing machine, the cylindrical printing press, the steam hammer, all coming from the northern section of the United States. No such inventions, nor even scientific work of consequence, originated in Middle America, South America, Canada, or the southern states.

Theology and Revolution —
Edwards to Madison

It is surprising to note how early such basic cultural tools as universities and printing presses were established in South and Middle America: universities in Mexico City and Lima in 1551; a printing press in Mexico City in 1535. The first book was published in America by 1539. By the end of the eighteenth century, almost every large town in South and Middle America had its university or college and printing press. Similar North American development generally came later but moved ahead more rapidly. Harvard was established in 1636,

Yale in 1701, Princeton in 1747. By the 1780's, there were more than 40 newspapers in the United States; by 1810, there were 350. Unfortunately the educational system in Middle and South America was controlled by a great landowning church, and the press was under government censorship. The British North American universities were, as we have seen, also under church control, the landowner's church in the South and a capitalist church in the North; in neither was the development of ideas encouraged. Philosophy made no advance and scientific theorizing was held to a minimum. Theology reigned supreme—as witness Jonathan Edwards:

> So that thus it is, that natural men are held in the hand of God over the pit of hell; they have deserved the fiery pit, and are already sentenced to it; and God provoked, his anger is as great towards them as to those that are actually suffering . . . his wrath in hell. . . . In short they have no refuge, nothing to take hold of; all that preserves them every moment is the mere arbitrary will, and uncovenanted, unobliged forbearance of an incensed God.

Edwards' sermon is the cultural counterpart of the dungeons of the Inquisition in Mexico or the hanging of women ("witches") in New England. How deeply the outlook it represented penetrated the society is, as usual, difficult to ascertain, for it was the "official" view and opposing views were perforce "underground." But the strong anti-clericalism that later developed in some Middle and South American cities cannot have been an overnight growth, nor can the deism of such leading North American thinkers as Franklin, Paine, or Jefferson. In a letter to James Fishback, September 17, 1809, Jefferson wrote: "Reading, reflection, and time have convinced me that the interests of society require the observation of those moral precepts only in which all religions agree (for all forbid us to murder, steal, plunder, or bear false witness), and that we should not intermeddle with the particular dogmas in which all religions differ, and which are totally unconnected with morality." Advanced though it was in a colonial atmosphere, Jefferson's deism did not go beyond that of the earlier English or French deists. The colonists produced no Diderot or D'Holbach; in Paine, however, they came close to a Voltaire (in *The Age of Reason*):

> The Christian Mythologists, after having confined Satan in a pit, were obliged to let him out again to bring on the sequel of the fable. He is then introduced into the Garden of Eden, in the shape of a snake or a serpent, and in that shape he enters into familiar conversation with Eve. . . . He persuades her to eat an apple, and the eating of that apple damns all mankind.

After giving Satan his triumph over the whole creation, one would have supposed that the Church Mythologists would have been kind enough to send him back again to the pit; or [otherwise] . . . prevent his getting again among the women and doing more mischief. But instead of this they leave him at large, without even obliging him to give his parole — the secret of which is that they could not do without him; and after being at the trouble of making him, they bribed him to stay. They promised him ALL the Jews, ALL the Turks by anticipation, nine-tenths of the world beside and Mahomet into the bargain. After this, who can doubt the bountifulness of the Christian Mythology?

In social thinking, the American revolutionaries surpassed their French and English predecessors, and, for a time, stood at the forefront of world social thought. This has not been generally recognized, in part because of a formalistic history-of-ideas approach to those predecessors, particularly John Locke. "Locke and the thinkers who stood with him were profoundly admired by all educated Americans interested in politics. The Americans in fact inherited their political philosophy at the very time that the British diverged from it. . . . When trouble with the mother country began in 1765, Americans found that they had a political philosophy full-fashioned to their needs."[68] But Locke was the philosopher of the English capitalist and professional classes not at the time of the British Revolution but in the calmer succeeding period in which they worked out an arrangement for coexistence with the aristocrats. Locke had no desire to have power shared with the farm laborers or working class and placed the emphasis upon property rights. Hence he had a considerable appeal to a certain section of the American capitalists, aristocrats, and professionals, but this was mostly before and after the revolutionary war, and it was the ideas forged in the heat of the struggle which were distinctive and vital. There was no "full-fashioned" political philosophy waiting on the English docks to be exported.

When Jefferson was accused of copying Locke and James Otis (an American radical) in the Declaration of Independence, he replied: "Otis' pamphlet I never saw, and whether I gathered my ideas from reading or reflection I do not know. I only know that I turned to neither book nor pamphlet while writing it." The central question was not one of the academic transmission of ideas, but of a revolutionary situation demanding ideas, some of which had arisen in similar situations before, some of which had not. True, we can find similar concepts in Locke, Montesquieu and others, but the essence is new. In the revolutionary fervor of the struggle, property is forgotten and the rights discussed are (in contrast to the later French *Rights*) the rights of "all men." Certainly Jefferson and his colleagues did not mean that all men should have equal economic power or should share equally in the government, but they certainly intended a greater scope for political action than did Locke.

If we widen our view and see the Declaration of Independence not only in the perspective of its immediate English or French predecessors but in that of previous social thought in general, it becomes apparent that it was the most advanced document of its kind produced at that time. No dominant social thinkers in Asian feudal society or Mediterranean slave society or European commercialism, not Aristotle or Bacon or Milton or Voltaire had ever asserted the "rights" of "all men" to "liberty" and "happiness." And even though these rights were but very partially realized, the fact that they could be demanded showed that new historical forces were astir.

Some further advances in social insight took place in the revolutionary struggle for power that succeeded the war. During the war, there was little talk of class; even so radical a document as Paine's *Common Sense* gives the impression of society consisting simply of "people." But in the later struggle, sociological concepts of class began to unfold as class divisions reasserted themselves—for instance, in the following by James Madison in the tenth number of *The Federalist:*

> But the most common and durable source of factions has been the various and unequal distribution of property. Those who hold and those who are without property have ever formed distinct interests in society. . . . A landed interest, a manufacturing interest, a mercantile interest, a moneyed interest, with many lesser interests, grow up of necessity in civilized nations, and divide them into different classes, actuated by different sentiments and views. The regulation of these various and interfering interests forms the principal task of modern legislation, and involves the spirit of party and faction in the necessary and ordinary operations of the government.

These concepts of the political and economic aspects of social class are well in advance of Locke, and they must have been shared by such contemporaries of Madison as Jefferson or Hamilton. When Jefferson opposed Hamilton's "financial system" he must have been aware that he was opposing a project of the manufacturing-commercial interests. And Hamilton knew whose interests he represented in his *Report on Manufactures.*

Neither Madison nor Jefferson nor Hamilton, however, were consistently sociological in outlook. For instance, in the sentences prior to the passage from Madison just quoted we find that the "latent causes of faction are thus sown in the nature of man." The "nature of man" then, is not really seen as an entity molded by social forces but as a special phenomenon. Man is "naturally" contentious; hence — in any society — there would be social conflicts and war. Nor does Madison have the concept — soon to be developed by Godwin and Condorcet — of historical "Necessity," a sociorevolutionary process independent of the will of man.

The revolutions in Middle and South America produced similar thinking — in Bolívar, Francisco de Miranda, and others. So, too, in the Papineau and MacKenzie rebellions in Canada. This thinking arose essentially out of the particular situation in each country or related group of countries, but there was considerable influence from the country of the first American revolution. Washington and Jefferson became heroes throughout Middle and South America.

Literature — Freneau

In art, the North, Middle, and South American colonies were much below the level of their "mother" countries. In literature, as Pedro Henriquez-Urena points out, the colonies were "only inferior rivals of their European capitals";[69] and so, too, in "painting and sculpture." North America produced no group of creative writers comparable to those in social thought, science, and technology. Part of the reason for this artistic inferiority doubtless lies in the domination of colonial culture by the church. The Catholic and Anglican churches as churches of the great landowners had no sympathy for nonclerical art (including literature), for such art was likely to represent the views of the aspiring city classes. The novel, a city product, was banned in Middle and South America — where there was a lively theater but no dramatists. In the colonies, however, there was no London — no single powerful, commercial center — and the churches opposed not only secular music and painting but creative literature also. All forms of art were, in fact, frowned upon as "sinful." Nevertheless a limited form of art was, as in Europe and Asia, possible within the church framework: church architecture, church music, church painting, and so on. Furthermore, peasant art flourished as everywhere. And in Middle and South America, Indian art penetrated the general culture and influenced colonial architecture, painting, literature, and drama.

As the commercial segment of the society developed, its special art expressions developed with it, and, although this art was not really great, it was, nevertheless, often of high quality and original. In the United States, a group of painters portrayed the new "democratic" spirit of the forming American society. In Gilbert Stuart's best known portrait of George Washington, for instance, only the head appears and there are no robes of state and no presidential mansion in the background. Stuart, as James Thomas Flexner comments, is translating "the Bill of Rights into portraiture." And similar concepts appear in the paintings of John Singleton Copley, Benjamin West, and Charles Wilson Peale. West, for instance, in his picture *The Death of General Wolfe,* depicted the soldiers in their actual uniforms and boots — to the horror of Sir Joshua Reynolds, who argued that such realism was fit only for popular prints. On the other hand, United States art, although often depicting everyday scenes, had no realist like Hogarth, no revolutionary like Blake; its cultural temper was that of a "democratic" blending of upper class interests. There was no really powerful and resurgent city middle class.

Of all the arts literature was the most advanced, if we take literature to include political, historical, theological, and other writing. At the very time that a writer in the English *Monthly Magazine* (1800) was complaining that there was "not one author" to be found in the United States, Jefferson, Paine, Madison, Hamilton, and Burr were still alive, and Franklin had been dead but one decade. If the Declaration of Independence, *The Crisis,* the *Federalist* papers, and the letters and journals of Burr are not literature, what are they? And not only the *Autobiography,* but many of Franklin's shorter pieces are written in a direct clear prose, the opposite of all feudal elaboration (as Franklin, at least by implication, anticipates Wordsworth): "The words used should be the most expressive that the language affords, provided that they are the most generally understood. Nothing should be expressed in two words that can be as well expressed in one. . . . Summarily it should be smooth, clear, and short, for the contrary qualities are displeasing." In Middle and South America, too, there was powerful prose writing, most of it political, but some historical, for instance, the *Royal Commentaries* (1609–1617) of the Inca, Garcilaso de la Vega, which tells the story of the Inca empire and its conquest.

Once we move, however, into the realm of *belles lettres,* the writing lacks originality and fire. The essays and other "literary" writings of Franklin and Washington Irving have charm and grace but are largely derivative from such earlier English writers as Addison or Goldsmith, and, like them, deal in pleasant trivia and safe ideas.

The earliest of the colonial poets was apparently Alonso de Ercilla (1535–1594), whose epic *Araucana* depicts the struggles of the heroic Araucanian Indians of Chile against their would-be conquerors. In the British North American colonies, the best-known poet was a woman, Anne Bradstreet, daughter of Thomas Dudley, governor of Massachusetts, who wrote simple moralistic verse in English seventeenth century style.

The revolution, too, produced its poets: José Joaquin de Olmedo of

Ecuador (with his ode to Bolívar, "The Victory of Junín"), Juan Cruz Varela of Argentina, and Phillis Wheatley, a slave, and Philip Freneau in the United States:

> . . . Roused by the REASON of his manly page,
> Once more shall PAINE a listening world engage:
> From Reason's source, a bold reform he brings,
> In raising up mankind, he pulls down kings,
> Who, source of discord, patrons of all wrong,
> On blood and murder have been fed too long:
> Hid from the world, and tutored to be base,
> The curse, the scourge, the ruin of our race,
> Their's was the task, a dull designing few,
> To shackle beings that they scarcely knew,
> Who made this globe the residence of slaves.
> And built their thrones on systems formed by knaves.

Here certainly is power and originality in content but the style is that of the English verse of fifty years before (Phillis Wheatley was even more derivative). Freneau was not able—as was Blake or Shelley—to forge a new style for the new content and give it its full expression, and he recognized this lack. Political independence and literary independence he considered to be very different; the first took but seven years, "the latter will not be completely effected perhaps for as many centuries." The pessimism of his estimate shows how stifling the hand of colonial oppression was, its psychological and cultural effects long outlasting the political regime.

FROM SUMER TO THE INDUSTRIAL REVOLUTION

As we look back over the centuries from the first civilizations to the threshold of the present, it becomes apparent that the central socio-evolutionary pattern is from feudal to capitalist society. The slave-commercial societies of the Mediterranean were, as we have seen, an aberration around which this central pattern flowed. That they were not necessary to the pattern is apparent from the fact that capitalism developed in Japan, where there had been no slave society, and that it developed in northern west Europe where the Roman influence was minimal. As with the development from food-gathering to farming society and that from farming society to civilization, the development of feudal into capitalist society would seem to have been inevitable, for there were, once more, a comparatively small number of factors involved. As commerce develops more rapidly than agriculture, it was simply a matter of time until in certain states the capitalists would move ahead of the landowners. As this happened other things followed: the State changed over from feudal to capitalist rule; wars between capitalist states broke out; less highly developed countries were conquered and exploited by the capitalist states. As with food-gathering and farming societies also, these basic patterns were not under conscious human control but emerged from the socioeconomic struggle for existence. (The struggle produced structure, the structure further struggle.) The British no more "decided" to introduce a capitalist society than had the Egyptians some 4,500 years before to introduce a feudal one, and they had as limited a control over it once it was established. They did not control its expansion in the last century nor can they control its decline in the present one.

Seen thus, the story of civilized society is at once simpler and more complex than it appears in most histories. It is more complex because it is neither a matter of naïve biological parallels—"the civilization of China was already old and weary in the days of Ming Huang"—nor "race"—". . . the most energetic and civilized races"—nor supernatural intervention—"this long chain of particular causes, which make and unmake empires, depends upon the secret orders of God's providence"—nor free-floating ideas—"the political consequences of this vast release and expansion of European ideas in the fourteenth and fifteenth centuries"—nor of individual conflicts motivated by "ambition" or "greed." These literalist concepts must be discarded along with the view that the earth is flat because it looks flat. The sociocultural processes of historical evolution are, as we have seen, complex, interactive and not subject to a mechanical cause-and-effect analysis. They are at first difficult to perceive because they run, as it were, below the surface of society. But once they are perceived the apparently meaningless maze of history becomes intelligible.

The movement from food-gathering to the first civilized societies was, as we have seen, progressive. So too with this later movement— in spite of its trail of blood and fire. Commercial-feudal society was a higher form of society than either feudal or slave-commercial societies. And commercial capitalist society was a still higher form. Economically there was, in these five thousand years, great expansion, slow and uneven at first, but later powerful and swift. Socially the period witnessed the end of slavery, forced labor, and serfdom, and the rise of paid labor. Through revolution more people achieved political influence than in past societies. True, these various forms of progress primarily affected only a small percent of the population but this was a larger percent than had been affected by previous advances. To perceive that there was progress we need simply take a long enough perspective, to compare the serf to the farmer, the slave to the worker, the feudal State to parliamentary government.

Although social and cultural patterns are interactive, it is apparent from our survey that the social patterns are primary. (Confucius was the product of a feudal society, Newton of a capitalist one.) Being interactive, they have advanced together. Knowledge, especially that coming from science and technology, obviously made great strides. The ideas connected with knowledge — of nature, society, and people — advanced also, but, because of the exigencies of rule in class-divided societies not to the same extent as knowledge itself. Art, as we have seen, developed in scope and depth — from Homer to Shakespeare, from Giotto to Goya. But culture could not at any time develop beyond the limits of its society. Even at the crest of the capitalist revolution there was little comprehension of the size or nature of the universe, almost nothing was known of the components of the atom or of living matter (the gene or the virus). The great fossil finds of early humans and prehumans were yet to come, as were the excavations of Sumer and Egypt. Evolutionary processes in life and society were just beginning to be uncovered. (*The Communist Manifesto* was published in 1848, *The Origin of Species* in 1859.) Modern writers and others have probed psychological depths and depicted aspects of society that reveal limitations in even the best art of the past — but reveal also that a truly humanity-oriented art is yet to come. When we speak of advance in the capitalist revolution, either social or cultural, we are, we must recognize, speaking relatively and not in terms of the full human potential.

Although this study stops at the threshold of the present it is apparent that the same general sociocultural processes are active today as have been active in the past. What seems (as always) to be on the surface a senseless welter of brutalities is, in fact, an evolutionary pattern. The situation today, it is true, differs from any in the past in that war and possibly industry — with its pollution of water and air — can eliminate life from the planet, but this is counterbalanced by the fact that some sections of humanity have now achieved a measure of societal control. The probability is that humanity will master these threats to its existence. If so, what we have witnessed so far is but the unfinished Preface to a very long work — of several, perhaps many, million years.

Bibliography

Chapter I

Asimov, Isaac. *The Wellsprings of Life*. New York, 1960.
Berrill, Norman J. *Sex and the Nature of Things*. New York, 1953.
Clark, Grahame. *From Savagery to Civilization*. New York, 1953.
Clark, Grahame. *World Prehistory*. Cambridge, 1969.
Fox, H. Munro. *The Personality of Animals*. London, 1952.
Howells, William. *Back of History*. New York, 1954.
Köhler, Wolfgang. *The Mentality of Apes*. New York, 1959.
Montagu, Ashley. *Man: His First Million Years*. New York, 1958.
Schaller, George B. *The Year of the Gorilla*. Chicago, 1964.
Sherrington, Sir Charles. *Man on His Nature*. New York, 1953.
Simpson, George G. *The Meaning of Evolution*. New Haven, 1952.
Watson, James D. *The Double Helix*. New York, 1969.

Chapter II

Bandi, Hans-Georg. *The Art of the Stone Age*. New York, 1961.
Beals, Ralph L., and Harry Hoijer. *An Introduction to Anthropology*. New York, 1953.
Beauvoir, Simone de. *The Second Sex*. New York, 1961.
Berndt, Ronald M., and Catherine H. Berndt. *The First Australians*. New York, 1954.
Berrill, Norman J. *Man's Emerging Mind*. New York, 1962.
Braidwood, Robert J. *Prehistoric Men*. Chicago, 1951.
Brockington, Fraser. *World Health*. Penguin Books, 1958.
Childe, V. Gordon. *Man Makes Himself*. New York, 1955.
Childe, V. Gordon. *Social Evolution*. New York, 1951.
Clark, Grahame. *From Savagery to Civilization*. New York, 1953.
Clark, Grahame. *World Prehistory*. Cambridge, 1969.
Coon, Carleton S. *The Story of Man*. New York, 1955.
Dunn, L. C., and Th. Dobzhansky. *Heredity, Race and Society*. New York, 1958.

Hawkes, Jacquetta. *Prehistory*. New York, 1965.

Herskovits, Melville J. *Economic Anthropology*. New York, 1952.

Howells, William. *Back of History*. New York, 1954.

Jacobs, Melville, and Bernhard J. Stern. *General Anthropology*. New York, 1955.

Lathrop, Samuel K. *The Indians of Tierra del Fuego*. New York, 1928.

Lowie, Robert H. *An Introduction to Cultural Anthropology*. New York, 1955.

Malinowski, Bronislaw. *The Sexual Life of Savages in North-Western Malanesia*. New York, 1941.

Mongait, A. L. *Archaeology in the U.S.S.R.* Penguin Books, 1961.

Montagu, Ashley. *Man: His First Million Years*. New York, 1958.

Montagu, Ashley. *The Natural Superiority of Women*. New York, n.d.

Powell, T. G. E. *Prehistoric Art*. New York, 1966.

Thomas, N. W. *Natives of Australia*. London, 1906.

Thompson, J. Eric S. *The Civilization of the Mayas*. Chicago, 1954.

Thomson, George D. *Studies in Ancient Greek Society: The Prehistoric Aegean*. New York, 1949.

CHAPTER III

Beals, Ralph L., and Harry Hoijer. *An Introduction to Anthropology*. New York, 1953.

Boas, Frank (Ed.). *General Anthropology*. New York, 1938.

Braidwood, Robert J. *Prehistoric Men*. Chicago, 1951.

Caesar, Julius. *The Conquest of Gaul*. Penguin Books, 1953.

Childe, V. Gordon. *Man Makes Himself*. London, 1956.

Childe, V. Gordon. *The Prehistory of European Society*. Penguin Books, 1958.

Clark, Grahame. *World Prehistory*. Cambridge, 1969.

Coon, Carleton S. *The Story of Man*. New York, 1955.

Frankfort, Henri. *The Birth of Civilization in the Near East*. New York, 1956.

Ghirshman, R. *Iran: from the Earliest Times to the Islamic Conquest*. Penguin Books, 1954.

Herskovits, Melville J. *Economic Anthropology*. New York, 1952.

Howells, William. *Back of History*. New York, 1954.

Linton, Ralph. *The Tree of Culture*. New York, 1955.

Lowie, Robert H. *An Introduction to Cultural Anthropology*. New York, 1955.

NcNeill, William H. *The Rise of the West*. Chicago, 1963.

Montagu, Ashley. *Man: His First Million Years*. New York, 1958.

Petrie, W. M. Flinders. *Social Life in Ancient Egypt*. London, 1924.

Tacitus. *Tacitus On Britain and Germany*. Penguin Books, 1954.

Thomson, George. *Studies in Ancient Greek Society: The Prehistoric Aegean.* New York, 1949.

Vaillant, George C. *The Aztecs of Mexico.* Penguin Books, 1951.

CHAPTER IV

Allchin, Bridget and Raymond. *The Birth of Indian Civilization.* Penguin Books, 1968.

Aldred, Cyril. *The Egyptians.* New York, 1966.

Atkinson, Donald T. *Magic, Myth and Medicine.* New York, 1958.

Breasted, James Henry. *The Conquest of Civilization.* New York, 1938.

Calder, Ritchie. *Medicine and Man; The Story of the Art and Science of Healing.* New York, 1958.

Capart, Jean. *Primitive Art in Egypt.* London, 1905.

Childe, V. Gordon. *Man Makes Himself.* New York, 1955.

Childe, V. Gordon. *New Light on the Most Ancient Near East.* New York, n.d.

Childe, V. Gordon. *The Prehistory of European Society.* Penguin Books, 1958.

Childe, V. Gordon. *What Happened in History.* Penguin Books, 1948.

Clark, Grahame. *World Prehistory.* Cambridge, 1969.

Coon, Carleton S. *The Story of Man.* New York, 1955.

Delaporte, L. *Mesopotamia.* New York, 1925.

Durant, Will. *The Story of Civilization. Our Oriental Heritage.* New York, 1954.

Emery, W. B. *Archaic Egypt.* Penguin Books, 1964.

Fairservis, Walter A., Jr. *The Ancient Kingdoms of the Nile.* New York, 1962.

Frankfort, Henri. *Ancient Egyptian Religion.* New York, 1948.

Frankfort, Henri. *The Birth of Civilization in the Near East.* New York, 1956.

Frankfort, Henri, H. A. Frankfort, John A. Wilson, and Thorkild Jacobsen. *Before Philosophy: The Intellectual Adventure of Ancient Man.* Penguin Books, 1949.

Gardiner, Sir Alan. *Egypt of the Pharaohs.* Oxford, 1964.

Gilgamesh. Trans., William Ellery Leonard. New York, 1934.

Howells, William. *Back of History.* New York, 1954.

Jacobs, Melville, and Bernhard J. Stern. *General Anthropology.* New York, 1955.

Kramer, Stanley. *History Begins at Sumer.* New York, 1959.

Lloyd, Seton. *The Art of the Ancient Near East.* New York, 1963.

McNeill, William H. *The Rise of the West.* Chicago, 1963.

Mendelsohn, Isaac. *Slavery in the Ancient Near East.* New York, 1949.

Mertz, Barbara. *Red Land, Black Land: The World of the Ancient Egyptians.* New York, 1966.

Murdock, George Peter. *Africa, Its People and Their Culture History*. New York, Toronto, London, 1959.

Murray, Margaret A. *The Splendour That Was Egypt*. London, 1949.

Petrie, W. M. Flinders. *Social Life in Ancient Egypt*. London, 1924.

Piggott, Stuart. *Prehistoric India*. Penguin Books, 1952.

Rostovtzeff, Michael. *A Large Estate in Egypt in the Third Century B.C.* Madison, Wisconsin, 1922.

Thomson, George D. *The First Philosophers*. London, 1955.

Thomson, George D. *Studies in Ancient Greek Society. The Prehistoric Aegean*. New York, 1949.

Vaillant, George C. *The Aztecs of Mexico*. Penguin Books, 1951.

Wheeler, Sir Mortimer. *The Indus Civilization*. Cambridge, 1968.

Chapter V

Allchin, Bridget and Raymond Allchin. *The Birth of Indian Civilization*. Penguin Books, 1968.

Atkinson, D. T. *Magic, Myth and Medicine*. New York, 1958.

Ballou, Robert O. *World Bible*. New York, 1956.

Basham, A. L. *The Wonder That Was India*. New York, 1954.

Berry, Gerald L. *Religions of the World*. New York, 1956.

Bouquet, A. C. (Ed.). *Sacred Books of the World*. Penguin Books, 1955.

Cambridge History of India. Cambridge, 1922.

Cheney, Sheldon. *A World History of Art*. New York, 1939.

Childe, V. Gordon. *Man Makes Himself*. New York, 1955.

Childe, V. Gordon. *New Light on the Most Ancient Near East*. New York, n.d.

Chin P'ing Mei. *The Adventurous History of Hsi Men and His Six Wives*. New York, 1947.

Creel, Herrlee Glessner. *The Birth of China*. New York, 1961.

Dampier, Sir William Cecil. *A Shorter History of Science*. New York, 1945.

Dilts, Marion Mary. *The Pageant of Japanese History*. New York, 1949.

Durant, Will. *The Story of Civilization. Our Oriental Heritage*. New York, 1954.

Eberhard, Wolfram. *A History of China*. London, 1950.

Fairservis, Walter A., Jr. *The Origins of Oriental Civilization*. New York, 1959.

Fisher, Charles A. *South-East Asia*. London, New York, 1964.

Frankfort, Henri, H. A. Frankfort, John A. Wilson, and Thorkild Jacobsen. *Before Philosophy, the Intellectual Adventure of Ancient Man*. Penguin Books, 1949.

Frye, Richard N. *The Heritage of Persia*. New York, 1963.

Ghirshman, R. *Iran*. Penguin Books, 1954.

Giles, Herbert A. *A History of Chinese Literature*. New York, n.d.

Goodrich, L. Carrington. *A Short History of the Chinese People*. New York, 1951.

Granet, Marcel. *Chinese Civilization*. New York, 1958.

Grilli, Elise. *Katsushika Hokusai*. Rutland, Vt., and Tokyo, 1958.

Grousset, René. *The Rise and Splendour of the Chinese Empire*. Berkeley and Los Angeles, 1958.

Gurney, O. R. *The Hittites*. Penguin Books, 1954.

Hall, D. G. E. *A History of South East Asia*. New York, 1955.

Huart, Clement. *Ancient Persian and Iranian Civilization*. London and New York, 1927.

Janson, H. W. *History of Art*. New York, 1965.

Kennedy, Malcolm. *A Short History of Japan*. New York, 1964.

Lin Yutang (Ed.). *The Wisdom of China and India*. New York, 1942.

Liu Wu-chi. *An Introduction to Chinese Literature*. Bloomington, Ind., and London, 1966.

Lloyd, Seton. *Ancient Highland Peoples of Anatolia*. New York, 1967.

McGovern, William M. *The Early Empires of Central Asia*. Chapel Hill, N.C., 1939.

McGrindle, G. W. *Ancient India as Described by Megasthenes and Arrian*. London, Bombay, Calcutta, 1877.

Murasaki, Lady Shikibu. *The Tale of Gengi*. Trans., Arthur Waley. New York, 1935.

Needham, Joseph. *Science and Civilization in China*. Cambridge, 1954.

Nehru, Jawaharlal. *Autobiography*. London, 1936.

Piggott, Stuart. *Prehistoric India*. Penguin Books, 1952.

Polo, Marco. *The Travels of Marco Polo*. New York, 1926.

Pym, Christopher. *The Ancient Civilization of Ankor*. New York, 1968.

Reischauer, Edwin O. *Japan, Past and Present*. New York, 1953.

Reischauer, Edwin O., and John K. Fairbank. *East Asia, The Great Tradition*. Boston, 1960.

Saggs, H. N. F. *The Greatness That Was Babylon*. New York, 1962.

Saikaku, Ihara. *Five Women Who Loved Love*. Rutland, Vt., and Tokyo, 1957.

Sédillot, René. *The History of the World*. New York, 1953.

Sharp, Andrew. *Ancient Voyagers in the Pacific*. Penguin Books, 1957.

Smith, Vincent A. *The Oxford History of India*. Oxford, 1928.

Suggs, Robert C. *The Island Civilizations of Polynesia*. New York, 1960.

Thapar, Romila. *A History of India*. Vol. I, Penguin Books, 1966.

Thomson, George D. *The First Philosophers*. New York, 1955.

Wheeler, Sir Mortimer. *The Indus Civilization*. Cambridge, 1968.

Wheeler, Sir Mortimer. *Rome Beyond the Imperial Frontiers*. Penguin Books, 1955.

Willetts, William. *Chinese Art*. Penguin Books, 1958.

CHAPTER VI

Beals, Ralph L., and Harry Hoijer. *An Introduction to Anthropology*. New York, 1955.

Coon, Carleton S. *The Story of Man*. New York, 1955.

Day, A. Grove. *Hawaii and Its People*. New York, 1955.

Heyerdahl, Thor. *Aku-Aku*. New York, 1959.

Heyerdahl, Thor. *Kon-Tiki*. New York, 1956.

Howells, William. *Back of History*. New York, 1954.

Jacobs, Melville, and Bernhard J. Stern. *General Anthropology*. New York, 1955.

Kuykendall, Ralph S. *The Hawaiian Kingdom*. Honolulu, 1947.

Linton, Ralph. *The Tree of Culture*. New York, 1955.

Mead, Margaret. *The Maoris and Their Arts*. The American Museum of Natural History, New York, 1945.

Metraux, A. *Easter Island: A Stone Age Civilization in the Pacific*. New York, 1957.

Sharp, Andrew. *Ancient Voyagers in the Pacific*. Penguin Books, 1957.

Sinclair, Keith. *A History of New Zealand*. Penguin Books, 1959.

Suggs, Robert C. *The Island Civilizations of Polynesia*. New York, 1960.

Te Rangi Hiroa (Sir Peter Buck). *The Coming of the Maori*. Wellington, New Zealand, 1949.

Vayda, Andrew P. (Ed.). *Peoples and Cultures of the Pacific*. New York, 1968.

Chapter VII

Bohannan, Paul. *Africa and Africans,* New York, 1964.

Bovill, E. W. *The Golden Trade of the Moors*. London, New York, Toronto, 1958.

Breasted, James Henry. *The Conquest of Civilization*. New York, 1938.

Clark, Grahame. *World Prehistory*. Cambridge, 1969.

Clark, J. Desmond. *The Prehistory of Southern Africa*. Penguin Books, 1959.

Davidson, Basil. *A History of East and Central Africa*. New York, 1969.

Davidson, Basil. *The Lost Cities of Africa*. Boston, Toronto, 1959.

Frankfort, Henri. *The Birth of Civilization in the Near East*. New York, 1956.

Fage, J. D. *A History of West Africa*. Cambridge, 1968.

Gibbs, James L., Jr. (Ed.). *Peoples of Africa*. New York, 1966.

Gobel, Creighton, and Norman R. Bennett (Eds.). *Reconstructing African Culture History*. Boston, 1967.

Murdock, George Peter. *Africa, its People and their Culture History*. New York, Toronto, London, 1959.

Oliver, Roland, and J. D. Fage. *A Short History of Africa*. Penguin Books, 1962.

Ranger, T. O. (Ed.). *Aspects of Central African History*. Evanston, Ill., 1968.

Stearns, Marshall W. *The Story of Jazz*. New York, 1956.

Warmington, B. H. *Carthage*. Penguin Books, 1968.
Wheeler, Sir Mortimer. *Rome Beyond the Imperial Frontiers*. Penguin Books, 1955.
Wiedner, Donald L. *A History of Africa South of the Sahara*. New York, 1962.

CHAPTER VIII

Aeschylus. *Prometheus Bound*. Trans., Gilbert Murray. New York, 1931.
Apuleius. *The Golden Ass*. Trans., Robert Graves. New York, 1951.
Aristophanes. *Lysistrata*. Trans., Charles T. Murphy. *Greek Literature in Translation*. New York, 1944.
Aristotle. *Aristotle Selections*. Ed. W. D. Ross. New York, Chicago, Boston, 1927.
Auden, W. H. (Ed.). *The Portable Greek Reader*. New York, 1955.
Boardman, John. *Greek Art*. New York, 1965.
Boren, Henry C. *The Roman Republic*. Princeton, New Jersey, 1965.
Botsford, George Willis, and Charles Alexander Robinson, Jr. *Hellenic History*. New York, 1956.
Breasted, James Henry. *The Conquest of Civilization*. New York, 1938.
Caesar, Julius. *The Conquest of Gaul*. Penguin Books, 1958.
Cambridge Economic History of Europe. Cambridge, 1952.
Cambridge Medieval History. Cambridge, 1966–67.
Catullus. *The Poems of Catullus*. Trans., Horace Gregory. New York, 1956.
Childe, V. Gordon. *What Happened in History*. Penguin Books, 1948.
Cicero. *Select Letters*. New York, 1891.
Clark, Grahame. *Prehistoric Europe: The Economic Basis*. London, 1952.
Coleman-Norton, P. R. (Ed.). *Studies in Roman Economic and Social History in Honor of Allan Chester Johnson*. Princeton, 1951.
Coon, Carleton S. *The Story of Man*. New York, 1955.
Couch, Herbert Newell, and Russell M. Geer. *Classical Civilization: Rome*. New York, 1950.
Coulange, Duma Denis Fustel de. *The Ancient City*. New York, 1956.
Cowell, F. R. *Cicero and the Roman Republic*. Penguin Books, 1956.
Dampier, Sir William. *History of Science*. Cambridge, 1949.
Derry, T. K., and T. I. Williams. *A Short History of Technology*. Oxford, 1960.
Durant, Will. *The Story of Civilization. Caesar and Christ*. New York, 1944.
Durant, Will. *The Story of Civilization. The Life of Greece*. New York, 1939.
Farrington, Benjamin. *Greek Science. Its Meaning for Us*. Penguin Books, 1953.
Ferguson, William Scott. *Greek Imperialism*. Boston and New York, 1913.
Forrest, W. G. *The Emergence of Greek Democracy, 800–400 B.C.* New York, 1966.

Forsdyke, John. *Greece Before Homer.* New York, 1964.
Frankfort, Henri, H. A. Frankfort, John A. Wilson, and Thorkild Jacobsen. *Before Philosophy.* Penguin Books, 1949.
Glotz, Gustave. *The Aegean Civilization.* London, 1925.
Glotz, Gustave. *Ancient Greece at Work.* New York, 1926.
Glotz, Gustave. *The Greek City and Its Institutions.* New York, 1930.
Grant, Michael. *Roman Readings.* Penguin Books, 1958.
Gurney, O. R. *The Hittites.* Penguin Books, 1954.
Harden, Donald. *The Phoenicians.* New York, 1962.
Harrison, Jane. *Prolegomena to the Study of Greek Religion.* New York, 1957.
Hencken, Hugh. *Tarquinia and Etruscan Origins.* New York, 1968.
Hogben, Lancelot. *Science for the Citizen.* New York, 1938.
Homer. *The Iliad.* Trans., W. H. D. Rouse. New York, 1950.
Homer. *The Odyssey.* Trans., E. V. Rieu. New York, 1946.
Homo, Leon. *Roman Political Institutions.* London and New York, 1929.
Hutchinson, R. N. *Prehistoric Crete.* Penguin Books, 1968.
Lewis, Naphtali, and Meyer Reinhold (Eds.). *Roman Civilization, Sourcebook II, The Empire.* New York, 1966.
Lucretius. *On the Nature of the Universe.* Trans., Ronald Latham. Penguin Books, 1951.
MacKendrick, Paul. *The Mute Stones Speak: The Story of Archaeology in Italy.* New York, 1966.
Mason, Stephen F. *Main Currents of Scientific Thought.* New York, 1953.
McDonald, William A. *Progress into the Past: The Rediscovery of Mycenaen Civilization.* Bloomington, Indiana, and London, 1969.
Menander. "The Dyskolos," Trans., Gilbert Highet. *Horizon* I (July, 1959), 78–88.
Nilsson, Martin P. *A History of Greek Religion.* New York, 1964.
Ovid. *The Art of Love.* Trans., Rolfe Humphries. Bloomington, Indiana, 1957.
Paul-Louis. *Ancient Rome at Work.* New York, 1927.
Plato. *The Republic of Plato.* Trans., H. Spens. London and Toronto, 1927.
Plato. *The Works of Plato.* Ed. Irwin Edman. Trans., Benjamin Jowett. New York, 1928.
Pliny. "Letters." Trans., Selatie E. Stout. *Our Heritage of World Literature.* Ed., Stith Thompson. New York, 1938.
Rostovtzeff, Michael. *The Economic and Social History of the Hellenistic World.* Oxford, 1941.
Rostovtzeff, Michael. *The Social and Economic History of the Roman Empire.* Oxford, 1926.
Seltman, Charles. *Women in Antiquity.* London, 1956.
Seyffert, Oskar. *A Dictionary of Classical Antiquities.* New York, 1956.
Tacitus. *Tacitus on Britain and Germany.* Penguin Books, 1954.
Theocritus. *The Syracusan Ladies.* Trans., Andrew Lang. New York, 1928.
Thomson, George D. *Aeschylus and Athens.* New York, 1950.
Thomson, George D. *The First Philosophers.* London, 1955.

Thomson, George D. *Studies in Ancient Greek Society. The Prehistoric Aegean.* New York, 1949.
Thompson, Stith (Ed.). *Our Heritage of World Literature.* New York, 1938.
Toutain, Jules. *The Economic Life of the Ancient World.* London, 1930.
Toynbee, Arnold J. (Ed., trans.). *Greek Civilization and Character.* Boston, 1950.
Usher, Abbott Payson. *A History of Mechanical Inventions.* Cambridge, Mass., 1954.
Vaillant, George C. *The Aztecs of Mexico.* Penguin Books, 1951.
Virgil. *The Aeneid.* Trans., C. Day-Lewis. New York, 1953.
Wheeler, Sir Mortimer. *Roman Art and Architecture.* New York, 1964.
Wheeler, Sir Mortimer. *Rome Beyond the Imperial Frontiers.* Penguin Books, 1955.
Winspear, Alban Dewes. *The Genesis of Plato's Thought.* New York, 1940.
Winspear, Alban Dewes. *Lucretius and Scientific Thought.* Montreal, 1963.
Woolley, Sir Leonard. *A Forgotten Kingdom.* Penguin Books, 1953.

CHAPTER IX

Barnes, Harry Elmer. *A Survey of Western Civilization.* New York, 1947.
Bouquet, A. C. (Ed.). *Sacred Books of the World.* Penguin Books, 1955.
Cambridge Economic History of Europe. Cambridge, 1952.
Dampier, Sir William. *The History of Science.* Cambridge, 1949.
Diehl, Charles. *Byzantium, Greatness and Decline.* Brunswick, New Jersey, 1957.
Durant, Will. *The Story of Civilization. The Age of Faith.* New York, 1950.
Ghirshman, R. *Iran.* Penguin Books, 1954.
Guillaume, Alfred. *Islam.* Penguin Books, 1954.
Hitti, Philip K. *History of the Arabs.* New York, 1953.
Levy, Reuben. *The Social Structure of Islam.* Cambridge, 1957.
McNeill, William H. *The Rise of the West.* Chicago, 1963.
Piggott, Stuart. *Prehistoric India.* Penguin Books, 1952.
Runciman, Steven. *Byzantine Civilization.* New York, 1956.

CHAPTER X

Age of Belief, The. The Medieval Philosophers. Ed., Anne Fremantle. New York, 1957.
Allegro, J. M. *The Dead Sea Scrolls.* Penguin Books, 1956.
Anglo-Saxon Poetry. Trans., R. K. Gordon. London, Toronto, New York, 1930.

Aquinas, Thomas. *On the Truth of the Catholic Faith (Summa Contra Gentiles). Book Three: Providence. Part I.* New York, 1956.

Barnes, Harry Elmer. *A Survey of Western Civilization.* New York, 1947.

Bede. *A History of the English Church.* Penguin Books, 1955.

Bouquet, A. C. (Ed.). *Sacred Books of the World.* Penguin Books, 1955.

Breasted, James Henry. *The Conquest of Civilization.* New York, 1938.

Caesar, Julius. *The Conquest of Gaul.* Penguin Books, 1958.

Cambridge Economic History of Europe. Cambridge, 1952.

Chaucer, Geoffrey. *The Canterbury Tales.* Trans., J. U. Nicholson. New York, 1934.

Chaucer, Geoffrey. *Troilus and Cressida.* Trans., George Philip Krapp. New York, 1932.

Childe, V. Gordon. *Social Evolution.* New York, 1951.

Childe, V. Gordon. *What Happened in History.* Penguin Books, 1948.

Clark, Grahame. *World Prehistory.* Cambridge, 1969.

Clough, Shepard Bancroft, and Charles Woolsey Cole. *Economic History of Europe.* Boston, 1952.

Coulton, G. G. *Medieval Panorama.* New York, 1957.

Dampier, Sir William. *The History of Science.* Cambridge, 1949.

Dante. *The Divine Comedy.* Trans., Carlyle-Wickstead. New York, 1944.

Dante. *The Inferno.* Trans., John Ciardi. Rutgers University Press, 1954.

Davies, A. Powell. *The Meaning of the Dead Sea Scrolls.* New York, 1956.

Durant, Will. *The Story of Civilization. The Age of Faith.* New York, 1950.

Durant, Will. *The Story of Civilization. Caesar and Christ.* New York, 1944.

Fichtenau, Heinrich. *The Carolingian Empire.* New York, 1964.

Gibbs, Marion. *Feudal Order, a Study of the Origins and Development of English Feudal Society.* New York, 1953.

Green, John Richard. *A Short History of the English People.* New York, Cincinnati, Chicago, 1916.

Hauser, Arnold. *The Social History of Art.* New York, 1957.

Heaton, Herbert. *Economic History of Europe.* New York, 1948.

Hollister, C. Warren. *Medieval Europe, A Short History.* New York, 1964.

Holmes, George. *The Florentine Enlightenment, 1400–1450.* New York, 1969.

Mason, Stephen F. *Main Currents of Scientific Thought.* New York, 1953.

McNeill, William H. *The Rise of the West.* Chicago, 1963.

Nostrand, John J. Van, and Paul Schaeffer. *Western Civilization, a Political, Social and Cultural History.* New York, London, Toronto, 1949.

Ogg, Frederick Austin. (Ed.). *A Source Book of Medieval History.* New York, 1935.

Piggott, Stuart. *Prehistoric India.* Penguin Books, 1952.

Pirenne, Henri. *Economic and Social History of Medieval Europe.* New York, n.d.

Pirenne, Henri. *Medieval Cities.* New York, 1956.

Previté-Orton, C. W. *The Shorter Cambridge Medieval History.* Cambridge, 1952.

Rieu, E. V. (Trans.). *The Four Gospels.* Penguin Books, 1953.

Robertson, Archibald. *The Origins of Christianity*. New York, 1954.
Runciman, Steven. *Byzantine Civilization*. New York, 1956.
Muller, Herbert J. *The Uses of the Past*. New York, 1954.
Sir Gawain and the Green Knight. Trans., Theodore Banks, *in Our Heritage of World Literature*. Ed. Stith Thompson, New York, 1938.
Studies in Roman Economic and Social History in Honor of Allen Chester Johnson. Ed. P. R. Coleman Norton. Princeton, 1951.
Tacitus. *Tacitus on Britain and Germany*. Penguin Books, 1954.
Thompson, Stith (Ed.). *Our Heritage of World Literature*. New York, 1938.
Trevelyan, George Macaulay. *England in the Age of Wycliffe*. London, 1925.
Trevelyan, George Macaulay. *History of England*. London, 1929.
Virgil. *The Aeneid*. Trans., C. Day Lewis. New York, 1953.

CHAPTER XI

Ashton, Thomas S. *An Economic History of England: The Eighteenth Century*. New York, 1955.
Barnes, Harry Elmer. *The History of Western Civilization*. New York, 1935.
Brinton, Crane. *A Decade of Revolution, 1789–1799*. New York, London, 1963.
Cambridge Economic History of Europe. Cambridge, 1952.
Carr-Saunders, A. M. *World Population, Past Growth and Present Trends*. London, 1964.
Cipolla, Carlo. *Economic History of World Population*. Penguin Books, 1962.
Clough, Shepard Bancroft, and Charles Woolsey Cole. *Economic History of Europe*. New York, 1952.
Cobban, Alfred. *A History of Modern France*. Penguin Books, 1957.
Cole, G. D. H., and Raymond Postgate. *The British Common People, 1746–1938*. New York, 1939.
Condorcet, Marie Jean, Antoine Nicolas de Cardat. *Outlines of a Historical View of the Progress of the Human Mind*. London, 1795.
Darwin, Erasmus. *The Temple of Nature*. London, 1803.
Davies, Mansel. *An Outline of the Development of Science*. London, 1948.
Dawson, Philip (Ed.). *The French Revolution*. New York, 1967.
Diderot, Denis. *Diderot, Interpreter of Nature: Selected Writings*. Trans., Jean Stewart and Jonathan Kemp; ed., Jonathan Kemp. New York, 1943.
Duby, George, and Robert Mondrau. *A History of French Civilization*. New York, 1966.
Dumas, Samuel, and K. O. Vedel-Petersen. *Losses of Life Caused by War*. Oxford, 1923.
Durant, Will. *The Story of Civilization. The Reformation*. New York, 1957.
Einstein, Alfred. *A Short History of Music*. New York, 1955.
Engels, Frederick. *The Peasant War in Germany*. New York, 1934.

Erickson, Arvel, and Martin G. Havran. *England: Prehistory to the Present.* New York, 1968.

Farrington, Benjamin. *Francis Bacon, Philosopher of Industrial Science.* London, 1951.

Foster, William. *The East India House, Its History and Associations.* London, 1924.

Galileo. *Discoveries and Opinions of Galileo.* Ed., trans., Stillman Drake. New York, 1957.

Godwin, William. *Enquiry Concerning Political Justice.* Ed., F. C. L. Priestley. Toronto, 1946.

Halevy, Elie. *A History of the English People. Book II: Economic Life.* Penguin Books, 1947.

Hall, A. R. *The Scientific Revolution.* Boston, 1956.

Hammond, J. L., and Barbara Hammond. *The Bleak Age.* Penguin Books, 1947.

Harrison, G. B. *Introducing Shakespeare.* New York, 1947.

Heaton, Herbert. *Economic History of Europe.* New York, 1948.

Henderson, W. O. *The Industrial Revolution in Europe: Germany, France, Russia, 1814–1914.* New York, 1968.

Hessen, B. "The Social and Economic Roots of Newton's *Principia.*" *Science at the Cross Roads.* London, 1931.

Hill, Christopher, and Edmund Bell. *The Good Old Cause, Extracts from Contemporary Sources.* London. 1949.

Holbach, Paul Henri Tiry, Baron d'. *Common Sense, or Natural Ideas Opposed to Supernatural.* New York, 1795.

Holbach, Paul Henri Tiry, Baron d'. *D'Holbach's Moral Philosophy.* Ed. Virgil W. Trapazio. Geneva, 1956.

Holbach, Paul Henri Tiry, Baron d'. *The System of Nature.* Trans., H. D. Robinson. Boston, 1889.

Jeans, Sir James. *The Growth of Physical Science.* New York, 1948.

Jones, R. Ben. *The French Revolution.* New York, 1968.

Jonson, Ben. *Ben Jonson.* Eds., C. H. Herford and Percy Simpson. Oxford, 1925.

Laplace, Pierre Simon, Marquis de. *The System of the World.* Trans., Henry H. Harte. Dublin, 1830.

Lefebvre, George. *The French Revolution.* New York, 1964.

Mantoux, Paul. *The Industrial Revolution in the Eighteenth Century.* New York, 1965,

Morton, A. L. *A People's History of England.* London, 1938.

Parkinson, James. *Organic Remains of a Former World.* London, 1811.

Pledge, H. T. *Science Since 1500.* New York, 1959.

Prall, Stuart E., ed., *The Puritan Revolution, a Documentary History.* New York, 1968.

Rousseau, Jean Jacques. *The Social Contract and Discourses.* Trans., G. D. H. Cole. New York and London, 1950.

Stewart, John Hall. *A Documentary Survey of the French Revolution.* New York, 1951.

Tawney, R. H. *Religion and the Rise of Capitalism.* New York, 1947.
Thomson, David. *England in the Nineteenth Century.* Penguin Books, 1950.
Turberville, A. S. *The House of Lords in the Age of Reform. 1784–1837.* London, 1958.
Wardle, Ralph M. *Mary Wollstonecraft, A Critical Biography.* Lawrence, Kansas, 1951.
Willey, Basil. *The Seventeenth Century Background.* New York, 1953.
Wollstonecraft, Mary. *A Vindication of the Rights of Women.* London, 1891.

CHAPTER XII

Alden, John Richard. *The American Revolution, 1775–1783.* New York, 1951.
Aptheker, Herbert. *The Negro in the American Revolution.* New York, 1940.
Beals, Ralph L., and Harry Hoijer. *An Introduction to Anthropology.* New York, 1953.
Beard, Charles A., and Mary R. Beard. *A Basic History of the United States.* New York, 1944.
Bogart, Ernest L., and Donald L. Kemmerer. *Economic History of the American People.* New York, London, Toronto, 1955.
Bouquet, A. C. (Ed.). *Sacred Books of the World.* Penguin Books, 1955.
Bushnell, G. H. S. *Peru.* New York, 1966.
Clark, Grahame. *World Prehistory.* Cambridge, 1969.
Collier, John. *Indians of the Americas.* New York, 1954.
Coon, Carleton S. *The Story of Man.* New York, 1955.
Crow, John A. *The Epic of Latin America.* New York, 1946.
Diaz del Castillo, Bernal. *The Discovery and Conquest of Mexico.* New York, 1956.
Donnan, Elizabeth. *Documents Illustrative of the History of the Slave Trade in America.* Washington, D.C., 1931.
Elliot, J. H. *Imperial Spain, 1469–1716.* New York, 1963.
Faulkner, Harold Underwood. *American Economic History.* New York, 1960.
Faulkner, Harold Underwood. *American Political and Social History.* New York, 1941.
Fite, Gilbert C., and Jim E. Reese. *An Economic History of the United States.* Boston, 1965.
Flexner, James Thomas. *The Pocket History of American Painting.* New York, 1950.
Foner, Philip F. *History of the Labor Movement in the United States.* New York, 1947.
Gallenkamp, C. *Maya: The Riddle and Rediscovery of a Lost Civilization.* London, 1960.
Gibson, Lawrence Henry. *The Coming of the Revolution, 1763–1775.* New York, 1962.

Hacker, Louis M. *American Capitalism, its Promise and Accomplishment.* Princeton, New York, Toronto, London, 1957.

Haring, C. H. *The Spanish Empire in America.* New York, 1963.

Henriquez-Urena, Pedro. *Literary Currents in Hispanic America.* Cambridge, Mass., 1949.

Herring, Hubert. *A History of Latin America.* New York, 1955.

Heyerdahl, Thor. *Kon-Tiki.* New York, 1956.

Historical Statistics of the United States, 1789–1945. Bureau of the Census, Washington, D.C., 1949.

Howells, William. *Back of History.* New York, 1954.

Josephy, Alvin M., Jr. *The Indian Heritage of America.* New York, 1968.

Mason, J. Alden. *The Ancient Civilizations of Peru.* Penguin Books, 1957.

Mead, Margaret. *The Maoris and Their Art.* American Museum of Natural History. New York, 1945.

Moore, David R. *A History of Latin America.* New York, 1942.

Morais, Herbert M. *The Struggle for American Freedom.* New York, 1944.

Morison, Samuel Eliot. *Christopher Columbus, Mariner.* New York, 1956.

Morison, Samuel Eliot. *The Oxford History of the American People.* New York, 1965.

Nevins, Allan, and Henry Steele Commager. *The Pocket History of the United States.* New York, 1943.

Nye, R. B., and J. E. Morpurgo. *A History of the United States. Volume One. The Birth of the United States.* Penguin Books, 1955.

Pendle, George. *A History of Latin America.* Penguin Books, 1967.

Rochester, Anna. *American Capitalism, 1670–1800.* New York, 1949.

Ryerson, Stanley. *French Canada, a Study in Canadian Democracy.* New York, 1944.

Spears, John R. *The American Slave Trade.* New York, 1960.

Thompson, J. Eric S. *The Civilization of the Mayas.* Chicago, 1954.

Vaillant, George C. *The Aztecs of Mexico.* Penguin Books, 1951.

Von Hagen, Victor W. *Realm of the Incas.* New York, 1957.

Walett, Francis G. *Economic History of the United States.* New York, 1957.

Wissler, Clark. *Indians of the United States, Four Centuries of their History and Culture.* New York, 1956.

Wittke, Carl. *A History of Canada.* New York, 1941.

Wright, Louis B. *The Cultural Life of the American Colonies, 1607–1763.* New York, 1963.

Notes

CHAPTER I

1. Simpson, p. 135.
2. Clark, *Savagery,* pp. 33–34.
3. Howells, p. 40.
4. Ibid., p. 49.
5. Ibid., pp. 39–40.

CHAPTER II

1. Childe, *Man Makes Himself,* p. 53.
2. Berndt and Berndt, pp. 49–50.
3. Beals and Hoijer, p. 486.
4. Ibid., p. 498.
5. Berndt and Berndt, p. 61.
6. Thompson, p. 7.
7. Malinowski, pp. 329–30.
8. Lowie, p. 334.
9. Ibid., p. 335.
10. Ibid., p. 327.
11. Berndt and Berndt, pp. 129–30.
12. Ibid., p. 115.

CHAPTER III

1. Childe, *Man Makes Himself,* pp. 84–85.
2. Tacitus, pp. 109–110.
3. Beals and Hoijer, pp. 454–55.
4. Coon, pp. 175–76.
5. Frankfort, pp. 46–47.
6. Ghirshman, pp. 35–36.

CHAPTER IV

1. Petrie, p. 15.
2. Frankfort, *The Birth of Civilization,* p. 103.
3. Ibid., p. 41.
4. Petrie, p. 15.
5. Thomson, *Studies,* p. 328.
6. Vaillant, pp. 128–29.
7. Murray, p. 117.
8. Petrie, pp. 24, 194.
9. Murray, p. 76.

10. Durant, p. 164.
11. Ibid., pp. 164–65.
12. Childe, *Man Makes Himself,* p. 183.
13. Durant, p. 25.
14. Frankfort, *Birth of Civilization,* pp. 104–105.
15. Murray, p. 77.
16. Kramer, p. 48.
17. Petrie, p. 17.
18. Murray, p. 14.
19. Frankfort et al., p. 139.
20. Frankfort, *Birth of Civilization,* p. 58.
21. Kramer, p. 3.
22. Ibid., p. 82.
23. Frankfort et al., p. 184.
24. Kramer, pp. 131, 134, 125, 121 122.
25. Frankfort et al., p. 155.

Chapter V

1. *Cambridge History of India,* vol. IV, p. 450.
2. Basham, p. 145.
3. Ibid., p. 152.
4. Ibid., pp. 85–86.
5. Durant, p. 444.
6. Ibid., p. 493.
7. Ibid., p. 401.
8. Basham, pp. 221–22.
9. Smith, p. 85.
10. Basham, p. 200.
11. Nehru, p. 531.
12. Sedillot, p. 30.
13. Gurney, p. 103.
14. Ibid., p. 70.
15. Ibid., p. 100.
16. Ibid., pp. 66–67.
17. Ibid., pp. 102–103.
18. Ghirshman, pp. 84–85.
19. Ibid., p. 285.
20. Ibid., p. 310.
21. Ibid., p. 303.
22. Creel, p. 310.
23. Ibid., p. 316.
24. Granet, p. 143.
25. Goodrich, p. 42.
26. Creel, p. 316.
27. Ibid., p. 285.
28. Granet, p. 154.
29. Polo, p. 175.
30. Ibid., pp. 156–57.
31. Atkinson, pp. 51–52.
32. Creel, p. 350.
33. Grousset, pp. 66–67.
34. Granet, p. 128.
35. Ibid., p. 283.
36. Eberhard, p. 292.
37. Reischauer, p. 12.
38. Dilts, p. 6.
39. Reischauer, pp. 39–40.
40. Dilts, p. 55.
41. Reischauer, pp. 41–42.
42. McGovern, pp. 387, 368.
43. Ibid., p. 405.
44. Durant, pp. 780–81.
45. Ibid., pp. 526–32.
46. Piggott, p. 260.
47. Durant, p. 420.
48. Ibid., p. 431.
49. Bouquet, p. 503.
50. Ballou, p. 547.
51. Ibid., pp. 558–59.
52. Needham, vol. II, p. 102.
53. Ibid., p. 58.
54. Ibid., p. 34.
55. Gurney, pp. 132–33.
56. Frankfort, p. 67.
57. Durant, pp. 715–16.

Chapter VI

1. Sinclair, p. 19.
2. Te Ranji Hiroa, p. 375.
3. Ibid., p. 380.
4. Sinclair, pp. 20–21, 24.

5. Ibid., p. 21.
6. Linton, p. 54.
7. Suggs, p. 203.
8. Ibid., pp. 162–63.
9. Kuykendall, p. 11.
10. Suggs, p. 161.
11. Ibid., pp. 166–67.
12. Ibid., p. 105.

13. Day, p. 290.
14. Suggs, p. 162.
15. Kuykendall, p. 9.
16. Linton, p. 55.
17. Suggs, p. 166.
18. Linton, p. 56.
19. Kuykendall, p. 10.

CHAPTER VII

1. Murdock, pp. 64–65.
2. Ibid., p. 125.
3. Davidson, *Cities,* p. 58.
4. Wheeler, p. 121.
5. Murdock, p. 150.
6. Ibid., p. 127.
7. Davidson, *Cities,* p. 85.
8. Murdock, p. 129.
9. Ibid., pp. 73–74.
10. Bovill, p. 127.
11. Ibid.
12. Davidson, *Cities,* p. 135.
13. Murdock, pp. 249–50.
14. Davidson, *Cities,* p. 93.
15. Stearns, pp. 269–70.
16. Murdock, p. 120.
17. Breasted, pp. 491–92.
18. Murdock, pp. 150–51.
19. Davidson, *Cities,* p. 44.
20. Ibid., pp. 36–37.

21. Murdock, p. 181.
22. Breasted, p. 96.
23. Wheeler, p. 142.
24. Ibid., p. 157.
25. Murdock, p. 205.
26. Davidson, *Cities,* pp. 153–55.
27. Ibid., p. 180.
28. G. Clark, p. 203.
29. Davidson, *Cities,* pp. 164–65.
30. Murdock, p. 207.
31. Davidson, *Cities,* p. 209.
32. Ibid., pp. 228–29.
33. J. D. Clark, pp. 289–90; Davidson, *Cities,* pp. 246–48.
34. J. D. Clark, p. 294.
35. Murdock, p. 211.
36. Davidson, *Cities,* p. 243.
37. Murdock, p. 286.
38. Davidson, *Cities,* pp. 291–92.

CHAPTER VIII

1. Coon, pp. 340–41.
2. Botsford and Robinson, p. 80.
3. Glotz, *Ancient Greece,* p. 225.
4. Ibid., p. 273.
5. Ibid., pp. 292, 295.
6. Ibid., pp. 193–201.
7. Thomson, *Aeschylus and Athens,* pp. 160–61.
8. Ibid., p. 366.
9. Glotz, *Greek City,* p. 256.
10. Ibid., p. 104.
11. Auden, p. 543.

12. Toynbee, pp. 145–47.
13. Ibid., p. 151.
14. Glotz, *Aegean Civilization,* p. 184.
15. Ibid., p. 177.
16. Ibid., p. 174.
17. Couch and Geer, p. 3.
18. *Cambridge Medieval History,* vol. I, p. 54.
19. Apuleius, pp. 178–79.
20. Pliny, p. 400.
21. Paul-Louis, p. 142.

22. Thompson, p. 400.
23. Apuleius, p. 183.
24. Durant, *Caesar*, p. 334.
25. Ibid., p. 370.
26. Ibid., p. 89.
27. Cowell, p. 227.
28. Cicero, p. 16.
29. Childe, p. 225.
30. Homo, p. 88.
31. Cowell, p. 70.
32. Rostovtzeff, *Hellenistic World*, vol. II, p. 757.
33. Toynbee, pp. 76–79.
34. Tacitus, pp. 79–80.
35. Durant, *Caesar*, p. 140.
36. Tacitus, p. 63.
37: Rostovtzeff, *Roman Empire*, p. 305, Childe, p. 275.
38. Dampier, p. 52.
39. Mason, p. 14.
40. Farrington, pp. 173–74.
41. Hogben, pp. 70–71.
42. Farrington, p. 293.
43. Coulange, p. 36.
44. Lucretius, p. 206.
45. Catullus, p. 169.
46. *Republic*, pp. 220–21.
47. *Works*, pp. 125, 133, 139.
48. Aristotle, pp. 100–101. See also pp. 45, 48–49, 222, 224, and Farrington, pp. 129–30.
49. Farrington, p. 162.
50. Lucretius, p. 50.
51. Ibid., p. 37.
52. Ibid., p. 100.
53. Ibid., p. 188.
54. Ibid., p. 131.
55. Ibid., pp. 183–84.
56. Ibid., p. 195.
57. Ibid., p. 197.
58. Mason, p. 15.
59. Lucretius, p. 168.
60. Ibid., p. 125.
61. Aristotle, p. 293.
62. Auden, p. 290.
63. Lucretius, p. 200.
64. Ibid., p. 205.
65. Ibid., p. 215.
66. Thomson, *Aegean*, p. 551.
67. Homer, *Odyssey*, p. 23.
68. Ibid., p. 106.
69. Ibid., p. 26.
70. Ibid., pp. 149–50.
71. Ibid., p. 27.
72. Homer, *Iliad*, p. 82.
73. Thomson, *Aeschylus and Athens*, p. 156.

CHAPTER IX

1. Runciman, p. 83.
2. Barnes, p. 253.
3. *Cambridge Economic History of Europe*, pp. 103–104.
4. Runciman, p. 51.
5. Ibid., p. 59.
6. McNeill, p. 442.
7. Hitti, p. 49.
8. Durant, p. 208.
9. Ibid., p. 228.
10. Ibid., pp. 167–68.
11. Hitti, pp. 60–61.
12. Ibid., p. 37.
13. Ibid., p. 153.
14. Durant, p. 210.
15. Ibid., pp. 207–208.
16. Ibid., p. 305.

CHAPTER X

1. Clark, p. 121.
2. Tacitus, p. 121.
3. Ibid., p. 106.
4. Ibid., p. 109.

5. Quoted in Gibbs, p. 57.
6. Heaton, p. 90.
7. Clough and Cole, p. 16.
8. Pirenne, *Cities*, p. 81.
9. Heaton, p. 153.
10. Clough and Cole, p. 61.
11. *Cambridge Economic History*, p. 295.
12. Pirenne, *Cities*, p. 2.
13. *Cambridge Economic History*, p. 280.
14. Ibid., p. 372.
15. Ibid., p. 439.
16. Ibid., pp. 119–20.
17. Heaton, p. 118.
18. Previté-Orton, vol. I, p. 37.
19. Ibid., p. 1.
20. Coulton, p. 61.
21. Pirenne, *Cities*, p. 67.
22. *Cambridge Economic History*, p. 40.
23. Caesar, p. 98.
24. Gibbs, p. 57.
25. *Cambridge Economic History*, p. 386.
26. Ibid.
27. Pirenne, *Economic and Social History*, p. 202.
28. Ibid., p. 204.
29. Trevelyan, *Wycliffe*, pp. 202–203.
30. Trevelyan, *England*, p. 240.
31. Green, p. 252.
32. *Cambridge Economic History*, p. 240.
33. Ibid., p. 351.
34. Coulton, p. 618.
35. Ibid.
36. Davies, appendix.
37. Robertson, p. 78.
38. Ibid., p. 79.
39. Rieu, p. 2.
40. Ibid., pp. 6–7, 35.
41. Ibid., p. 21.
42. Ibid., p. 6.
43. Ibid., p. 185.
44. Ibid., p. 102.
45. Ibid., p. 185.
46. Ibid., p. 214.
47. Ibid., p. 231.
48. Ibid., p. 126.
49. Ibid., p. 44.
50. Ibid., p. 140.
51. Ibid., p. 226.
52. Ibid., pp. 227–28.
53. Ibid., p. 37.
54. Ibid., p. 44.
55. Ibid., p. 24.
56. Durant, *Caesar and Christ*, p. 597, quoting James.
57. Ibid., p. 578.
58. Bouquet, p. 217.
59. Durant, *Caesar and Christ*, p. 657.
60. Heaton, p. 83.
61. Durant, *Age of Faith*, p. 564. See also Robertson, p. 182.
62. Heaton, p. 83.
63. Coulton, p. 123.
64. Bede, p. 86.
65. Gibbs, p. 89.
66. Pirenne, *Cities*, p. 88.
67. Barnes, p. 88.
68. *Age of Belief*, p. 152.
69. Aquinas, p. 275.
70. *Age of Belief*, p. 138.
71. Durant, *Age of Faith*, p. 1007.
72. Aquinas, p. 200.
73. Coulton, p. 442.
74. Ibid., p. 706.
75. Green, p. 250.
76. Hauser, vol. 1, p. 127.
77. Dante, Carlyle-Wickstead trans.

Chapter XI

1. Clough and Cole, p. 184. See also Heaton and *Cambridge Economic History*.
2. Ibid., p. 318.
3. Durant, p. 353.
4. Engels, pp. 139–40.
5. Tawney, p. 93.
6. Hill and Bell, pp. 36–38, 62–63, 417–18.
7. Ibid., p. 55.

8. Ibid., p. 240.
9. Ibid., pp. 355-57.
10. Morton, p. 246.
11. Cole and Postgate, p. 87.
12. Clough and Cole, p. 476.
13. Heaton, p. 303.
14. Lefebvre, pp. 36-37.
15. Ibid., p. 15.
16. Cobban, p. 42.
17. Clough and Cole, p. 408.
18. Lefebvre, p. 86.
19. Cobban, p. 174.
20. Brinton, pp. 204-205.
21. Lefebvre, p. 169.
22. Clough and Cole, p. 435.
23. Hall, p. 124.
24. Galileo, pp. 31-32.
25. Ibid., p. 47.
26. Jeans, p. 218.
27. Laplace, vol. II, p. 342.

28. Davies, p. 62.
29. Dampier, p. 54.
30. Hall, pp. 227-28.
31. Durant, p. 858.
32. Rousseau (*Discourse on the Origin of Inequality*), pp. 234-35.
33. Ibid., pp. 247-48.
34. Condorcet, p. 4.
35. Godwin, vol. I, p. 384.
36. Ibid., p. 450.
37. Wardle, p. 148.
38. Durant, p. 416.
39. Wollstonecraft, p. 56.
40. Ibid., p. 250.
41. Ibid., p. 212.
42. Darwin, p. 45.
43. Einstein, p. 81.
44. Ibid., p. 58.

CHAPTER XII

1. Wissler, p. 159.
2. Collier, p. 19.
3. Wissler, p. 60.
4. Diaz del Castillo, p. 218.
5. Ibid., pp. 213-14.
6. Vaillant, p. 150.
7. Von Hagen, pp. 179-80.
8. Diaz del Castillo, pp. 215-17.
9. Vaillant, p. 131.
10. Mason, p. 176; von Hagen, p. 53.
11. Von Hagen, p. 53.
12. Ibid., p. 93.
13. Mason, p. 168.
14. Thompson, p. 72.
15. Vaillant, p. 136.
16. Diaz del Castillo, pp. 215-16.
17. Mason, pp. 179-80.
18. Vaillant, p. 122.
19. Mason, p. 181.
20. Von Hagen, p. 85.
21. Vaillant, p. 118.
22. Von Hagen, pp. 53-54.
23. Mason, p. 185, quoting Garcilaso de la Vega.

24. Ibid., p. 195.
25. Howells, p. 302.
26. Thompson, p. 32.
27. Mason, p. 203.
28. Collier, p. 59.
29. Von Hagen, p. 20.
30. Howells, p. 314.
31. Morison, *Columbus*, p. 42.
32. Ibid., p. 152.
33. Ibid., p. 99.
34. Diaz del Castillo, p. 58.
35. Ibid., p. 63.
36. Vaillant, p. 233.
37. Ibid., p. 254.
38. Vaillant, p. 230.
39. Moore, pp. 7-8.
40. Crow, p. 163.
41. Ibid., p. 404.
42. Ibid., p. 219.
43. Moore, p. 164.
44. Ibid., p. 145.
45. Ibid., p. 274.
46. Crow, p. 407.
47. Nye and Morpurgo, p. 78.
48. Rochester, p. 435, quoting

Curtis P. Nettels, *The Roots of American Civilization*, New York, 1940.
49. Bogart and Kemmerer, p. 97.
50. Faulkner, *Social History*, p. 211, quoting J. B. McMaster.
51. Nye and Morpurgo, p. 143.
52. Donnan, vol. I, p. 406.
53. Wittke, p. 21.
54. Ryerson, p. 112.
55. Wittke, p. 23.
56. Wissler, p. 57.
57. Collier, p. 115.
58. Ibid., p. 113.

59. Beard and Beard, p. 91.
60. Nye and Morpurgo, p. 232.
61. Nevins and Commager, p. 112.
62. Ibid., p. 110.
63. Morais, p. 249, citing Charles A. Beard.
64. Rochester, p. 96.
65. Nevins and Commager, pp. 145–46.
66. Ryerson, p. 38.
67. Ibid., p. 46.
68. Nevins and Commager, pp. 81, 82.
69. Henriquez-Urena, p. 90.

Index

acquired characteristics: inheritance of, 4-5

Aegean civilization, 181-183

Aeschylus, 223, 224, 225, 348

Agamemnon, by Aeschylus, 225, 226

agnosticism: of Aristotle, 211-212; of Confucius, 224

agriculture: origins, 36-38; significance of, 51, 110, 384; and irrigation, 52; in China, 98-99; Maori, 139; in Africa, 146, 157, 159; in India, 161; in Athens, 170-171; specialized, 171, 185, 253; in Roman Empire, 185-186; in Byzantine Empire, 233; in Great Britain, 253, 311; in Germany, 256; in France, 313; during the economic revolution, 293; American Indian, 373-374, 375

Ainu, 106

Akbar, emperor, 90

Algonquin Indians, 370, 413

Alien and Sedition Laws, 423

Alomaeon of Croton, 203

alphabet: developed, 205

America: discovery of, 387

American Indians. *See* Indians, American

American Museum of Natural History, 21, 35, 152, 383, 385

American Revolution, 414, 419-423

American Revolutionary War, 414, 417-418

Ammianus Marcellinus: quoted, 109

Anaxagoras, 202, 211

Anaximander: quoted, 214

ancestor worship, 32, 122, 207

Anglican Church, 303, 411

anti-feminism, 118, 230, 333-334, 363-364

Antigone, by Sophocles: quoted, 223-224

Apache Indians, 25, 30

Apuleius, Lucius, 189, 230

Aquinas, Thomas. *See* Thomas Aquinas

Arab Empire: beginnings, 235-238; conquests, 238-239, 242; feudal society in, 239-240; slave revolt in, 240

Arab influence: 241-242

Arab religion, 238

Arab science, 241

Arabia, 236-238

Arabian Nights, 128, 241

Araucanian Indians, 370-433

Archimedes, 203, 204

architecture: of India, China, and Japan, 127; Romanesque and Gothic, 280

Aristarchus of Samos, 203, 323

aristocracy. *See* landowning class

Aristophanes, 224-225

Aristotle: 205, 339; ideas compared to Taoism, 120; and the "golden mean," 125, 207, 216-217; and Plato, 210-212; on slavery, 217; and Thomas Aquinas, 276; and Bacon, 336; and Descartes, 339

army: controls land, 55, 61, 64; in Egypt, 55, 64, 66; in India, 88, 90; Roman, 195; British, 301; Inca, 380, 381

arrow wounds: treatment of, 103

art: of food-gathering society, 20, 21, 32-33; and sociocultural process, 68; Egyptian and Sumerian, 74; Chinese, Indian, and Japanese, 126; Maori, 141; Hawaiian, 143-144; European, 279, 347; Aztec, Maya, and Inca, 383

Art of Love, by Ovid: 227-228; quoted, 229

Aryabhata, 113

Asian and European civilizations compared, 167-169

Asian influence on American Indians, 373-374, 385-386

Asma, 236

Assyria, 92

astronomy: Egyptian, 70; Hindu, 113; Arab, 24; European, 322-324

Athapaskan Indians, 369, 371

atheism, 343-344

Athenian drama, 223-226

Athenian Empire: 170; economy of, 170-173; social life of, 173-175; power structure of, 175-178; expansion and collapse, 178-180

Athens, 170

Attila, 109, 110

Aucassin and Nicolette, 130

Augustine, Saint: quoted, 278

Austen, Jane: 366-367; quoted, 367

Australian natives, 8, 25-26, 28, 30, 31, 34